BOCCACCIO

A Biography

Marco Santagata

Translated by Emlyn Eisenach

The University of Chicago Press

Chicago and London

The University of Chicago Press, Chicago 60637
The University of Chicago Press, Ltd., London
Published 2025
Printed in the United States of America

34 33 32 31 30 29 28 27 26 25   1 2 3 4 5

ISBN-13: 978-0-226-82094-1 (cloth)
ISBN-13: 978-0-226-84255-4 (e-book)
DOI: https://doi.org/10.7208/chicago/9780226842554.001.0001

Originally published in Italian as *Boccaccio: Fragilità di un genio* © 2019
Mondadori Libri S.p.A., Milano.

This book has been translated thanks to a contribution from the Italian Ministry
of Foreign Affairs and International Cooperation. Questo libro è stato tradotto
grazie a un contributo del Ministero degli Affari Esteri e della Cooperazione
Internazionale italiano.

The translation of this work has been funded by SEPS
Segretariato Europeo per le Pubblicazioni Scientifiche

Via Val d'Aposa 7 — 40123 Bologna — Italy
seps@seps.it   -   www.seps.it

Library of Congress Cataloging-in-Publication Data

Names: Santagata, Marco, author. | Eisenach, Emlyn, 1967– translator.
Title: Boccaccio : a biography / Marco Santagata ; translated by Emlyn Eisenach.
Other titles: Boccaccio. English
Description: Chicago : The University of Chicago Press, 2025. | "Originally
   published in Italian as Boccaccio: Fragilità di un genio (c) Mondadori 2019."—
   Title page verso. | Includes bibliographical references and index.
Identifiers: LCCN 2024037628 | ISBN 9780226820941 (cloth) | ISBN 9780226842554
   (ebook)
Subjects: LCSH: Boccaccio, Giovanni, 1313–1375. | Authors, Italian—To 1500—
   Biography. | LCGFT: Biographies.
Classification: LCC PQ4277 .S2613 2025 | DDC 853/.1 [B] —dc23/eng/20240916
LC record available at https://lccn.loc.gov/2024037628

♾ This paper meets the requirements of ANSI/NISO Z39.48-1992
(Permanence of Paper).

CONTENTS

PART I. Youth (1313–1340)

1. A Boy in Florence   *3*

2. Naples, a New World   *18*

3. Canonist and Scholar: A Life Plan   *36*

4. The Birth of the Author   *47*

PART II. Maturity (1341–1360)

5. In His Father's House   *75*

6. In Search of an Alternative   *122*

7. Years of Service   *136*

8. The Dignity of the Vernacular   *154*

9. Highs and Lows   *190*

PART III. Old Age (1361–1375)

10. Disgrace   *213*

11. Return to the Florentine Stage   *247*

12. Twilight   *264*

Primary Sources   287
Notes   293
Index   435

PART I

Youth
(1313–1340)

1

A Boy in Florence

A wineskin full of lead

I was a man, and am a wineskin full,
oh, not of wind, but of most grievous lead,
so grievous I can hardly walk at all

Ei m'ha d'huom facto un otre divenire,
non pien di vento, ma di piombo grave
tanto, ch'appena mi posso mutare

Rime, VII (CXXII).9–11[1]

Like a wineskin full of lead: this is how Giovanni Boccaccio felt during the final period of his life—he would die within two years, on December 21, 1375—unable to move, like the dropsical Maestro Adamo, the forger from Dante's *Inferno* with a belly swollen like a drum.[2]

It could be, indeed, that while writing these lines Boccaccio was thinking of just this character. On October 23, 1373, in the Church of Santo Stefano in Badia, he had begun "reading," that is, commenting on, the *Commedia*. There was criticism, to say the least. In particular, an unknown humanist accused him of prostituting the Muses. This was not a novel charge. While Dante was composing the last cantos of *Paradiso*, a grammarian from the Studio di Bologna (forerunner of the University of Bologna) named Giovanni del Virgilio sent a Latin poem exhorting him to stop writing poetry for the common people, casting pearls before swine, to abandon the vulgar tongue of the marketplace.[3] Sure of the value of his work, Dante did not bother to defend himself against the accusation of using a language that shamed the Muses. But Boccaccio, who had adored Dante since boyhood, and who had worked harder than anyone else to spread Dante's works and exalt their greatness, yielded. Internalizing the criticism directed at him, he declared himself guilty as charged. And—as Boccaccio writes in the sonnet addressed to the unknown accuser from which the verses above are taken—it is as punishment for this sin that Apollo reduced him to his painful condition, transformed from man into wineskin.

Boccaccio, now old, was weary, body and soul. Over the years, his problematic character traits had hardened, and his physical ailments worsened. Always a large man, he grew fat, then obese; in his final decade, heaviness degenerated into illness (perhaps edema). Even without his letters, in which Boccaccio repeatedly refers to a heavy body that makes moving difficult and travel painful, we would still have the testimonies of those who knew him. "He was rather fat, but tall with a round face, his nose a little flattened above the nostrils, his lips somewhat fleshy, but pleasantly shaped"[4] is how Filippo Villani, who was present at Boccaccio's Dante readings, described him. And this portrayal corresponds to the image sketched by Boccaccio himself at the end of a codex containing Dante's works, an exceptional image that appears to be the first and only known self-portrait by a medieval author. Some have suggested that his closest friends might have joked about his size. But while Boccaccio alluded to his own stoutness in jest at least once, it is unlikely he would have accepted the mockery of others with good grace. Indeed, the plump, rounded face of his portraits, including the one he drew himself, and the sense of the *Decameron*'s readers that they are dealing with an individual who observed the world with tranquility and a smiling detachment, would lead us to think of Boccaccio as a calm, peaceable man, open and affable, wisely indulgent toward himself and his friends. In short, the opposite of how we regard the personality of Francesco Petrarca (Petrarch), which is to say, doubtful, tormented, and prone to depression. But Boccaccio too had a difficult character: he was introverted, full of anxieties, suspicious, and, it seems, exceedingly touchy.[5]

One day, a friend accused him of being a "man of glass," that is, fragile, capricious, unable to tolerate inconveniences, and quick to be offended by trifles. True to character, Boccaccio responded with a letter meticulously refuting the accusation. Another friend—one with whom Boccaccio had a quite difficult relationship—gave him the nickname *Giovanni delle Tranquilità*, or "Giovanni of Tranquility." Boccaccio was offended, all the more because when calling him this, the friend laughed nastily, failing to conceal his mockery.[6] Now, the mocker, Niccolò Acciaiuoli, may well have had personal reasons for calling Boccaccio a fair-weather friend, for Boccaccio had turned his back on Niccolò at a time when he faced great danger. Still, from multiple incidents, a picture emerges of Boccaccio as a man who craved quiet and shunned risk. Rather than lazy, though, he appears to have been insecure, a man for whom the imaginary world of literature, parallel to but connected with the real one, offered not only a means to make a name for himself, but also a way, through fantasy, to fulfill his deepest wishes and soothe unhealed wounds. And yet, in the realm of scholarship and literature, too (which Boccaccio called "poetry"), some of his confessions of inadequacy, more sincere and tormented than normal declarations of modesty, allow glimpses of his doubts about his ability to achieve his aspirations. We read the resigned sadness with which Boccaccio laments the many failures that marked his life: "I have no doubts that if my father had accepted it with a favorable mind when my age was more suited for it, I might have found my place among the famous poets. Instead, forced as I was to at first to attend to a lucrative trade and then to a lucrative practice, it happened that I became neither a merchant nor a canon lawyer and missed, at the same time, the opportunity to become an illustrious poet" (*GDG*, XV.10, 8).[7] And how he candidly admits that he has pursued poetry "with more fervor of spirit than with heights of genius" ("con più fervore d'animo che con altezza d'ingegno," *Corbaccio*, 191).[8]

Boccaccio, however, was also curious. He was curious as a man of letters, always in search of the new, and he was curious as a careful observer of the social environments he inhabited. Over the course of his life, he was attracted by vastly different areas of knowledge, and, as a writer, he experimented with a great number of literary genres; he was a man of court, a merchant, and an administrator of the Comune, as the Florentine municipal (communal) government was known; he worked to spread literature written in the vernacular, and he played an active role in elite humanist circles. His great open-mindedness was accompanied by an extraordinary capacity to receive, absorb, and introject. Thanks to this innate disposition, Boccaccio became the most versatile and experimental writer of his age.

And yet, even his tendency to embrace what was around him betrays a psychological fragility. Boccaccio welcomed, but he also adapted; he modeled himself on the environments around him, redrawing his intellectual profile to conform to their expectations, or at least what he believed them to be. He wrote for courtiers when at court, for his fellow citizens when engaged in municipal life, for humanists when he joined their circles. Something similar could be said about Boccaccio's behavior as a person: his desire to assimilate seems to have been a way to temper his fear of not being accepted. Even his tireless experimentation with genres and literary typologies manifests the desire to be seen, to have his name inscribed in the annals of the great writers. This is why his curiosity about others, whether written texts or living people, which was such a strength, could also at times limit both Boccaccio the man and Boccaccio the intellectual. In fact, it was the combined pressures of the increasingly combative exponents of humanism that pushed Giovanni Boccaccio—who had spent his whole life preaching the Dantean gospel, who had tried to convert even the reluctant Petrarch to the cult of Alighieri—to make the astonishing claim that he had been punished by Apollo for commenting on the *Commedia* in public.

Certaldo or Florence?

Giovanni was born in either Certaldo (a small Tuscan town between Florence and Siena) or Florence itself on an unspecified day
in June or July 1313, almost nine years before Dante's death and
nine years after Petrarch's birth. He was the illegitimate son of an
unmarried merchant and a young woman about whom nothing is
known except that she, too, was unmarried.[9] We are unable to establish whether he was born in Certaldo or Florence because while
his father, while keeping property in his town of origin, moved permanently to the city around the year of his son's birth, though we do
not know whether this was before, during, or after 1313. Even if he
was born in Certaldo, then, Giovanni must have been taken to Florence as an infant. As a boy, however, as evidenced by the few childhood memories scattered through his works, he must have lived
for stretches of time in Certaldo, perhaps during the summers.[10]

In that summer of 1313, the exile Dante Alighieri, perhaps in
Pisa, was following with trepidation the preparations for the military expedition that the new emperor Henry VII of Luxembourg
was about to undertake against the king of Naples, Robert of Anjou. Henry would depart with his army on the first of August, the
same day the troops of his ally Frederick III of Aragon, the king
of Sicily, landed in Calabria. But Henry's unexpected death on
August 24 would prevent the imperial forces from achieving an
almost certain victory, and Dante saw his dreams of returning to
Florence dashed in just a few hours, a return that had seemed all
but guaranteed. In Carpentras, in Provence, Francesco Petrarca
was just beginning the first stage of his education at the school of
Convenevole da Prato, a "White" Guelph who had been banished
from Florence in 1302 following the coup carried out by the Black
Guelphs. Petrarca was, in a sense, also an exile: his father, the notary Ser Petracco, had also been banished from the city as a White.
Ironically, Francesco had been born in Arezzo the night before the
day (July 20, 1304) on which the Guelph exiles, badly losing the
battle of La Lastra fought right into the center of Florence, had
thrown away their last chance to return home armed.[11]

Boccaccio's family had not been involved in the Florentine

civil war. At that time, although they had owned property in Florence since the end of the thirteenth century, the Boccacci did not yet enjoy citizenship. Nonetheless, even if Boccaccio cannot be included in the great diaspora that deprived Florence of its best minds, his biography bears a curious similarity to those of Dante and Petrarch. Dante was exiled from the city at the age of thirty-six, never to return; and while Petrarch was fond of signing himself "florentinus" ("Florentine") and recalling his origins "on the banks of the Arno" ("in su la riva d'Arno," *Rvf*, 366, 82), he was a *florentinus* who set foot in Florence a total of twice, for only a few days, and who spent more than half his life far from Italy. Boccaccio's life was also divided into two parts: a long and crucial period of cultural and literary development in Naples that was followed—but only when he was nearing thirty—by a mostly settled residence in Florence. In short, all three Florentine authors who revolutionized Italian literature with resounding repercussions throughout Europe (they were once commonly called "the three crowns"), due to historical upheavals or family choices, either wrote their masterpieces far from Florence (in the case of Dante) did not know Florence (Petrarch) or, in Boccaccio's case, developed his literary vocation elsewhere entirely.

A Motherless Child

At the time of Boccaccio's birth, Florence was a mercantile, manufacturing, and, above all, financial power. The overwhelming economic development of the city, whose population by about 1280 was already between forty and fifty thousand, had begun many decades earlier, and was ratified in 1252 by the minting of the florin, a twenty-four-carat gold coin that quickly established itself as the principal currency of international trade, a sort of dollar of the age. The dynamism of the economy and the growth of the regional power had produced—and was still producing when Boccaccio was born—a tremendous process of urbanization, fed primarily by the immigration of laborers from the countryside, but also by the settlement in the city of rural landowners and holders of feudal rights, as well as artisans and professionals (judges, lawyers, and notaries) from other urban centers.

For Dante, all of this had disfigured the face of Florence. In his view, nascent capitalism perverted society: the florin was a "cursed flower" ("maladetto fiore," *Para.*, IX.130)[12] blossoming from corruption. The great size, confusion, and bustle of a city in which everyone, noble or common, was engaged in some form of economic activity made Dante long for the small city of a century earlier, which, "within the ancient circle" ("dentro da la cerchia antica," *Para.*, XV.97)[13] of its walls had lived soberly with peace and modesty. At the time, the Florentines were a close-knit community, respectful of immutable social hierarchies, and ignorant of the upheavals caused by the arrival of outsiders from the countryside ("la gente nuova" ["the new people"]) and the rapid enrichment of families with no past ("i subiti guadagni" ["the rapid gains"]).[14] If it had been up to him, Dante would not have allowed Boccaccio's family to move from Certaldo to Florence.

The two brothers, Boccaccino (Giovanni's father) and Vanni (short for Giovanni), the sons of Chelino or Ghelino (Michelino), not only owned buildings and land in Certaldo, but also engaged in trade and money changing.[15] It was therefore natural that Boccaccino and Vanni would decide to move their activities from the outskirts to the nearby capital. Although their presence in the city is documented (at least in Vanni's case), and they appear in partnerships with Florentine merchants at the end of the thirteenth century and the first decade of the fourteenth, the brothers requested and obtained citizenship only in 1320. But even before this date they must have enjoyed a certain social status, as attested by their network of business relationships and the fact that, from 1314 or a little earlier, they were living in the *sestiere* (district) of Porta San Piero. In this district there resided both magnate families—nobles or ones who had been dignified by knighthood—and common folk, some quite wealthy albeit of humble origin: in short, today we would call this a "good" neighborhood. Dante had once lived in this *sestiere* and the family of his beloved inspiration Beatrice, the Portinari, still did.

Within a few years of becoming a full-fledged Florentine citizen, Boccaccino had acquired a prominent role in the life of the city, not only in the economic realm (he was twice, in 1322 and 1325, consul of the Arte del Cambio, the bankers' guild) but also in the political arena, so much so that he was elected prior, one of the Comune's highest offices, for the term ranging from December 1322 to February 1323. In contrast, we know very little about the life of his brother, Vanni, who almost certainly did not hold office in Florence's municipal administration or even in the guilds. His activity is documented in both Florence and Certaldo, so we can presume that he practiced the profession of merchant alongside his brother, probably in partnership with him. After settling in Florence, the sons of Chelino did not cut ties with Certaldo, where they maintained friendships and continued to invest in real estate.

Florentine merchants and bankers were active across a geographical area encompassing the Mediterranean coasts and the whole of Europe. French, and especially Parisian, squares were the most well trodden. Boccaccino and Vanni had not waited for citizenship to expand their business dealings beyond Italy: we know that the first three months of 1313 found them in Paris (which they may have visited on earlier occasions) practicing the trade of money changing.

It will be recalled that, in *Paradiso*, Dante's ancestor Cacciaguida tells the poet with nostalgia that in his own time, the twelfth century, unlike that of Dante, no woman in Florence would lie alone in her marital bed because her husband had gone off to haggle in France.[16] Well, in 1313, no wife complained about Boccaccino's absence, who would remain unmarried for several more years. Nonetheless, a son would soon be born to this bachelor. The concurrence of his father's stay in Paris and his own birth did not escape Giovanni. Indeed, when he began writing romances in his twenties, Giovanni would look back at this curious fact and, disguising himself as a character named Idalogo, entertain the fantasy of his own birth in Paris, to a daughter of the king of France no less. This literary fantasy would blossom and take shape at a particular moment in Giovanni's life, when he frequented circles close to the Neapolitan court and, above all, sought in literary fancy a form of revenge against the worldly successes of his friend Niccolò Acciaiuoli; but it had sprouted from the depths of an illegitimate child's psyche.

Boccaccio never knew his mother. Indeed, he probably never even knew her name. In the *Filocolo*, the youthful romance in which he recounts the Parisian adventures of his father (here called Eucomos), the seduced princess had the name Gannai, an anagram of Gianna (Giovanna). If this is the case, Boccaccio would have been imagining that he had been named not after his uncle Vanni, but rather after his mother. In the writings of an author who often speaks of himself, directly or through an intermediary, the absence of the mother, the real one, stands out. It is true that medieval writers do not give voice to family affections, but even Dante was not exempt from alluding to his mother, blessed for having brought forth such a son: "blessed be she who was pregnant with you!"[17] exclaims Virgil, admiring her moral rectitude. And Petrarch commemorated the death of his mother, Eletta, with a Latin poem that may be, if not his very first, then one of his first poetic compositions.[18] Boccaccio had no mother to lament, or even remember. To compensate, he populated his works of fiction with imaginary mothers, seduced and abandoned by men who were unworthy (and, strangely enough, all French).[19]

In other words, the only parental figure watching over Boccaccio's childhood was his father. There is little to shed light on the tenor of their relationship. However, with the exception of the acrimonious verses written after his forced return from Naples, Boccaccio's works are full of affection and esteem for Boccaccino, and this despite the profound gap between a merchant's view of life and that of a man of letters. The words of the *Amoroso visione* have a sincere tone: "he himself who, / freely and happily, had so kindly / nourished me like a son; and I had called him / and still call him my parent" ("colui che me stesso / libero e lieto avea benignamente / nudrito come figlio, ed io chiamato / aveva lui e chiamo mio parente," *AV*, XIV.42–45).[20] It therefore seems that Giovanni had a happy childhood, at least until his father's marriage.

Shortly before 1320, Boccaccino finally took a wife, marrying Margherita, daughter of Giandonato dei Mardoli and Lippa Portinari. In either 1320 or 1321 they had a son, Francesco.[21]

There is no definite information about disagreements or misunderstandings between young Giovanni, who would have been about seven, and his stepmother, nor about those with Lippa, who, as a widow, had settled in her son-in-law's house. Indeed, the only (indirect) hint with respect to Lippa seems to suggest that she and

Giovanni conversed with each other. In the commentary on the *Commedia* based on his public lecture of 1373, Boccaccio wrote that Beatrice was the daughter of Folco Portinari ("according to a trustworthy source, who knew this lady and who was a very close blood relative of hers"; "secondo relazione di fededegna persona, la quale la conobbe e fu per consaguinità strettissima a lei," *ECD*, II [I].83):[22] since Lippa "was the daughter of a cousin of Folco Portinari, a thus a second cousin of Bice and her same age . . . and lived with her daughter and son-in-law," it is very likely that she was the one who spoke to him about her celebrated kinsman.[23] Boccaccio would leave Florence for Naples in the autumn of 1327 and return only in 1340, after Lippa had died. It would not have been unlikely that, at the age of thirteen or fourteen, Giovanni already knew the *Commedia* or at least was curious about the life of his famous fellow citizen. It should also be remembered that the Mardoli house was located next to that of the Alighieri.

We would have no reason to suspect that Boccaccino's marriage disturbed his relationship with Giovanni or created a difficult climate in the new family were it not that the autobiographical Idalogo, immediately after telling of the betrayal of his mother by his "treacherous father" ("ingannatore padre") and the father's marriage to Garemirta (an anagram of Margherita), goes on to say that one day, upon entering his father's house, he found himself before "two ferocious bears . . . with their eyes flaming and desiring my death" ("due orsi ferocissimi . . . con gli occhi ardenti, disiderosi della mia morte," *Filoc.*, V.8, 15).[24] From that moment, he had always felt afraid when entering that house, and so decided to leave it. Were the two ferocious bears Giovanni's stepmother and her mother? We cannot say for certain, but this is quite likely. In addition to the crudeness of the image, what is striking is that a narrator usually quite expansive and, in his juvenile efforts such as the *Filocolo*, downright verbose, dispatches in so few words an episode of such importance in his character's life.[25] It is as though Giovanni had touched a raw nerve. He wanted to speak, but at the same time not reveal too much—perhaps even to himself. In short, it is hard to shake the impression that this child may have felt cheated of his father's affection, which, up until that point, had been completely his own. It is as if he had experienced his father's marriage as a betrayal similar to the one already perpetrated against his mother, and as a result, this wound, never completely healed, found a way to come out into the open under the protective shield of literature.

School

At the age of five or six, Giovanni began his formal education. In the school—what we would today call an elementary school—of master Giovanni di Domenico Mazzuoli da Strada, he would learn to read and write, and, toward the end of his time there, would also learn some rudimentary Latin. On these same school benches also sat two boys with whom he would have relationships for almost his entire life and of whom we will speak again: certainly Zanobi da Strada, *maestro* Giovanni's son, who was only a year older than Boccaccio; and probably Niccolò Acciaiuoli, scion of one of the city's most powerful merchant dynasties, who was three years older.

Around the age of ten, having finished primary school, the boys of the medieval Italian commune cities had two options open to them: a course of Latin grammar study with the aim of learning the language (knowledge of which was indispensable to entering university and the notariate), or a school that led to specific professions. In these *abbaco* (abacus) or *algorismo* schools, future merchants, independent artisans, and bank employees studied (in the vernacular) basic mathematical-scientific concepts as well as subjects roughly corresponding to commercial mathematics, product analysis, and monetary economics, in addition to the practice of writing business letters. In a city like Florence, this second path was much more crowded than the first, and it is easy to understand why, given that commerce and finance offered more skilled jobs and solid earnings prospects than any other sector.[26]

Giovanni had no choice. His father wanted him to be a merchant and settled on the abacus school. And Giovanni could not have expected any other decision. It was around 1322–23, and during the period from December 15, 1322, to February 15, 1323, Boccaccino had crowned his social ascent by being elected as prior. It was beyond question that his elder son would follow the same career path. A recurrent accusation in Boccaccio's writing is that his father, forcing him to direct his talents toward lucrative activities, trampled his scholarly and literary ambitions. On several pages of the *Genealogia deorum gentilium*, which dates to roughly the mid-1360s, while retracing the steps of his development, Boccaccio accuses his father of dissuading him by every means available from the kinds of "poetic meditations" ("poeticas meditationes") to which he had been so inclined "from my mother's womb" ("ex utero matris") that as a child of not even seven, by natural disposition he practiced "composing" ("fingendi") a few little things; and then, "almost at a mature age, when I was my own master, without anyone prodding me, without a teacher and, indeed, acting against the will of my father," he had begun to read the books of the poets and, although he did not even "know the proper kinds and number of feet in a verse . . . I was given by almost all the persons who knew me the title of poet" (*GDG*, XV.10, 6–8).[27] But are we sure that this ten-year-old child experienced his father's decision to guide him into trade as coercion? There is no doubt that Boccaccio had a natural predisposition for literature, and it is also likely that he became conscious quite early on of "having been born for" poetic meditations ("in hoc natus sum," *GDG*, XV. 10, 6); but it is doubtful that, at age ten, he had the mature awareness that he would attribute to himself looking back at the age of fifty.

Whatever the case, whether attended willingly or unwillingly, that practical-scientific school left its mark on Boccaccio's eclectic humanism. In his first youthful writings, love of historical-mythological erudition, aspiration to eloquence, and pursuit of literature and poetry in the vernacular coexist with strong scientific interests, astronomy, above all. However, it should also be said that failure to have followed a regular course of Latin weighed against his mastery of the language. And even Boccaccio was aware that not even the best natural inclinations could completely make up for a lack of systematic study. At the end of the 1330s, he still showed such uncertainty in writing Latin that, as one scholar wrote, "Boccaccio was in the same condition as the Christian writers of the late Empire, who stumbled into gross grammatical errors every few steps while at the same time making a great display of rhetorical color, like an elegantly dressed gentleman walking barefoot."[28] Once he had mastered the grammar, it would still be some time before he was capable of making an acceptably elegant literary use of Latin. This is why a great humanist such as Leonardo Bruni could write (with a generous dose of exaggeration, it must be said): Boccaccio "learned Latin [*grammatica*] as an adult, and for this reason he never had a great command [*balìa*] of the language."[29]

A Duke Arrives

For decades, Guelph (that is, pro-papal) Florence had been locked in bitter struggle with the pro-imperial Ghibellines. In more recent times, following the disappearance of the threat of Henry VII of Luxembourg, the city had taken up arms against Uguccione della Faggiola, the lord of Pisa who had become the leader of the Ghibelline coalition, and then, once Uguccione's star had set, against Castruccio Castracani, the de facto lord of Lucca and reference point for Tuscan Ghibellineism. The war unleashed by Castruccio's occupation of Pistoia reached a dramatic climax in September 1325 at Altopascio, where the troops of Castruccio and those of Azzone Visconti, son of the lord of Milan, inflicted a disastrous defeat on the Florentines.

At this juncture, Florence turned to the aid of the king of Naples, Robert of Anjou, and gave his son Charles, Duke of Calabria, *signoria*, or lordship, of the city for ten years. The decision to temporarily entrust power to the king of Naples or his close relative was not new: Florence had already done this in 1267 during the final phase of the war with the Swabians, granting the office of *podestà*, the commune's highest magistracy, to the then-sovereign Charles I. It did so again almost fifty years later when, in 1313, in order to resist the Pisans of Uguccione, the power to appoint the *podestà* was entrusted to King Robert himself, who had kept it for more than eight years (as we will see, Florence would do this for a third time in 1342, entrusting *signoria* to Robert's nephew by marriage). Florence and the Kingdom of Naples were tightly bound: if Naples was the military arm of the Guelph coalition, Florence was its financial lung.

Charles of Anjou made his entry into Florence in July 1326 but remained for less than six months: in December, with the threat looming of Louis the Bavarian's descent into Italy to assert his right to the imperial crown, Charles departed for Naples.

Thirteen-year-old Giovanni Boccaccio could not have known that the Duke of Calabria's sojourn in his city would shortly lead to a turning point in his own life, one that would influence his path both as a person and as a man of letters for ever after.

The enterprising Boccaccino must have at that time already established a close working relationship with the Bardi merchant banking house, "the most important merchants of Italy," a firm that, along with the Peruzzi and the Acciaiuoli, played a dominant role in the economic life of the Kingdom of Naples and the management of royal finances.[30] It is almost certain that the heir to the throne of Naples discussed business with representatives of those companies; it is likely that Boccaccino was one of those representatives. Just a few months before the duke's arrival, Boccaccino had been elected as one of the five councillors of the Ufficio della Mercanzia (Office of Trade), representing the Arte del Cambio, the guild of the money changers, an office that he held during the January–March quarter. The Mercanzia was an important magistracy: it combined judicial functions in the commercial arena (bankruptcies, disputes between companies) with regulatory duties and monitoring international trade. Therefore, both as an official of the Mercanzia as well as a connection of the Bardi bank, Boccaccino was one of the Florentines most suited to negotiate with Charles of Anjou regarding the financial and business relations between the city, the merchant companies, and the Angevine court.

It is almost certain that the two men developed a relationship of trust. Evidence of this is that at the end of February 1327 — a time when Charles was no longer in Florence even though he still held the powers that had been vested in him — he named Boccaccino adjunct councillor to the Mercanzia for three months. From the documentation, one cannot tell definitively whether Boccaccino actually exercised the role of councillor for this second time, but it is certain that he had been appointed (not elected) at Charles's behest. It was likely due to the favor Boccaccino had gained from the heir to the throne that, the same year, the Bardi decided to send him to Naples, first assigning him alongside their agent

Bentivegna di Buonsostegno supervising that important branch, then, less than a year later, entrusting its entire management to Boccaccino. He would hold this prestigious, highly responsible (thus well compensated) post for eleven years.[31]

Boccaccino left for Naples between October and November of 1327. Of his family he took with him only Giovanni.[32] Having sold the Florentine house in Porta San Piero, he moved his wife, mother-in-law, and son Francesco to Certaldo, where they would remain until about 1333, when they again settled in Florence, in a house in Oltrarno in the *popolo* (parish) of Santa Felicita.[33] The choices to house his family in the village, where they could be helped by relatives and friends, and to spare them the journey to Naples are both understandable. Boccaccino surely did not plan to remain there permanently: Florence was the center of his economic interests, and, in any case, his service to the Bardi would have brought him back home often in addition to traveling elsewhere (he was in Paris in 1332 and in Venice in 1334 on the Bardi's behalf).[34] As for Giovanni, his father's wish to have him along could be a further sign that relations in the household had broken down after the marriage and Francesco's birth. And it is perhaps also significant that, during the twelve or thirteen years that Boccaccio spent in Naples, there is nothing to suggest that he ever returned to Florence, not even for occasional visits.[35]

We do not know whether Giovanni journeyed to Naples along with his father; in any case, even if they traveled separately, he would have joined him not much later.

2

Naples, a New World

Apprentice to the Bardi

Once they had finished abacus school, young men who intended to take up the merchant's profession served an apprenticeship at a bank or merchant company. Under these arrangements, which lasted for varying periods of time, the apprentices, called *fanciulli* or *garzoni*, having familiarized themselves with basic accounting techniques, then learned true banking methods. An apprenticeship generally began when a boy was about fourteen years old. Giovanni Boccaccio was no exception. "When I had not yet entered adolescence, having been instructed in arithmetic, [my father] gave me to a great merchant as an apprentice, where for six years I did nothing but waste time that can never be recovered" (*GDG*, XV.10, 7).[1] This is how Boccaccio would recall his passage from school to workplace when recounting the stages of his youthful development. So, at around the age of fourteen, between the summers of 1327 and 1328, Boccaccio began an apprenticeship at a merchant company that would last six years.[2]

The "great merchant" to whom Giovanni's father bound him could only have been the Naples branch of the Bardi company. In his writing, Boccaccio displays a knowledge of this environment that seems to come not just from his father but from his own experience, for example, in the famous passage in the *Decameron* describing the Palermo warehouse or customhouse (*dogana*):

> In all the maritime cities that have ports, it used to be the custom—and perhaps it still is today—for any merchant arriving there with his goods to unload them and have them all transported to a warehouse, which in many places is called the customshouse and is maintained either by the commune or by the local ruler. There, once those in charge have been presented with a bill of lading describing the entire cargo and its value, they assign the merchant a storeroom where it is kept under lock and key. The men, who are called customs officers, then record all the goods belonging to the merchant in their register, after which they make him pay a duty on what he retrieves from the customshouse, whether he takes all or just a portion of his goods at a time. It is by using the register that brokers, more often than not, obtain information about the amount and value of the goods that are being stored there, together with the names of the merchants involved, with whom they later make arrangements to exchange, barter, sell, and otherwise dispose of the merchandise when a suitable opportunity presents itself.[3] (*Dec.*, VIII.10, 4–6)

Boccaccio had never been to Palermo, but he knew the warehouse described here well, for it was in reality the one in Gaeta, where the Bardi had held the contract since 1302.[4]

Boccaccio would certainly have preferred to do something else, but he could not oppose his father's wishes. Toward the end of the 1330s, to practice his Latin he would write a fictitious epistle to an equally fictitious friend who was in many respects a projection of his own self. In this letter, "To the beloved man of holy and angelic fame" ("Sacre famis et angelice viro dilecto forti"), when retracing the stages of his imaginary interlocutor's life, he actually describes his own. Thus, this friend had been born for poetry, but, Boccaccio wrote, "your family's ardent love of profit, against your will, made you pass from the pious bosom of Rachel [the contemplative life] to the lap of Lia [the active life]" (*Ep.*, IV.5).[5] In other words, it made him a merchant.

Still, over six years, Boccaccio must have gained some competence in commercial practices. His works, particularly the *Decameron*, demonstrate substantial knowledge of this world. Although
for us, Boccaccio is a humanist man of letters, his fellow citizens
would have also considered him a man who could manage accounts and knew his way around a tax code. During the 1350s, the
citizens of Florence granted him a number of public offices, but,
not by chance, almost all were of a fiscal or administrative nature
and therefore politically unimportant. This is a signal that, while
they did not hold his political ability in great esteem, they nonetheless appreciated his honesty and the accounting skills he had
developed during his youth.

There is no question that Boccaccio disliked the merchant's
profession; but it is unlikely that at such a young age he took moral
or ideological exception to the world that he was in training to join.
At that time, he was still far from seeing an opposition between
profit, wealth, and power, on one side, and scholarship, literature,
and poetry, on the other. Also still to come was his criticism of avarice, which he would describe as "a deficiency in giving where it
is necessary and an inordinate desire for what is not necessary"
("difetto di dare ove si conviene e soperchio volere quello che non
si conviene," *ECD*, VII [II].56), which would resound across the *Decameron*. He would also dedicate a small treatise to this topic in his
commentary on Dante's *Commedia*, making specific reference to
the "wretched vice" ("miserabile vizio") of merchants, who "think
it is the easiest thing in the world to cross the Alps and mountains
and rivers and go by ship to foreign nations, for they are inflamed
by an enormous desire to become rich" ("in tanto disiderio s'ac-
cendono di divenir ricchi, che il trapassar l'Alpi e le montagne o'
fiumi, e navicando divenire alle nazioni strane, tirati dalla speranza e sospinti dal disiderio, par loro leggierissima cosa," *ECD*, VII
[II].58).[6] It is implausible that an inexperienced youth would have
already developed an ethical view of business. Instead, it is more
likely that Boccaccio's own temperament, as much as the contrast
between commerce and the life of the mind, contributed to making the profession unappealing. Just as Boccaccio seemed averse
to risk as an adult, we can safely assume that he preferred the quiet
life even as a young man. As an apprentice he saw on a daily basis

how full of worries merchants' lives were, and it is possible that it made him anxious to observe, as he would write in his old age, the life led by "those who are entirely given to the acquisition of worldly goods" ("coloro li quali all'acquisto delle cose temporali son tutti dati," *ECD*, III [II].25), exemplified by merchants:

> Every trivial event that takes place now in England, now in Flanders, now in Spain, now in Cyprus, now in one place, now in another, drives these men who are impatient, mindful, and scheming to write not only letters, but great tomes, to their associates. And even before they read the letters they are suspicious of the reports. Every gust of wind keeps them onboard ships. At the tiniest rumor of war, they are immediately fearful for the merchandise they have shipped. Every middleman who speaks with them causes them to change their minds and plans.[7] (*ECD*, III [II].26–27)[8]

A Merchant Scholar

Someone who felt he had been born for poetry would not easily resign himself to a life amid account ledgers, inventories, and business correspondence, and Boccaccio indeed did not. In the fictitious letter referred to above, after writing that his friend—to repeat, a stand-in for Boccaccio himself—had been forced by his father to become a merchant, he continues, saying that since natural predispositions cannot be stifled, his friend, although "dressed in the garb of a merchant, [was] enclosed in sacred studies, and in secret [*furtive*] eagerly savored the waters of the Heliconian fountain, sweeter to [his] palate than if tasted openly" (*Ep.*, IV.7).[9] Saying that he studied in secret is literary license. At the time of this epistolary exercise (1339), Boccaccio had already presented himself publicly as a writer, and the word "furtive" alludes to the fact that during his early youth literature was for him a private activity.[10]

Naples was a grand capital, home to one of the most prestigious European courts, and thus it offered a much richer cultural life than Florence, which, despite being a financial power, had become cultural backwater following the exile of the Whites. Although the many learned men of Naples operated in multiple sectors, overall these were organized along two major axes. One axis was guided by the university and the associated large library that Robert of Anjou had collected in Castel Capuano. It included the exponents of what could be called official culture, approved and supported by the sovereign: a high culture, obviously in Latin, that was concerned with ethics, philosophy, law, historical scholarship, and, above all, medicine and scientific topics, most prominently astronomy. These scholars followed time-tested paths far from the ferment of modernity and certainly untouched by the innovations of incipient humanism. They showed little interest in works of classical antiquity (which were largely absent from the library) and, even more, disregarded philology used for the restoration of ancient texts, were immune to the charms of poetry, and wrote in old-fashioned Latin rife with "rare words, convoluted phrasing, baroque contortions."[11] The second cultural axis was oriented to the court and its milieu, the nobility and the highest levels of the mercantile and financial elite. These circles consumed literature in the vernacular that we would today call pleasure reading, particularly romances. Overall, reading works in French and, to a lesser degree, Provençal prevailed over those written in the Tuscan language.[12]

Thanks to his father, who by virtue of his role as the Bardi's plenipotentiary had access at court, the young Giovanni was able to frequent both of these cultural milieus. He not only had contact with court scholars, but directly professed himself a disciple of some. The geographer, physician, and astronomer Andalò del Negro, Boccaccio wrote, had "once [been] my teacher on the motions of the stars" ("Olim in motibus astrorum doctorem meum," *GDG*, XV.6, 4), and in another work called him "my venerable teacher" ("venerabile precettore," *ECD*, V [I].162).[13] From the mathematician and astronomer Paolo da Pergia, "who was long director and keeper of King Robert's library," Boccaccio said as a "young boy" he "learned many things," which, however, he had not been capable of fully understanding at the time (*GDG*, XV.6, 8).[14] On the other hand, several passages in Boccaccio's works testify to the close relationships he also maintained with Neapolitan aristocrats. Just one example is the passage from a 1363 letter in which Boccaccio boasts to the recipient about his past associations: "If you don't know, my friend, I lived, from childhood until I was fully grown, in Naples and among young nobles of a similar age to me, who, even though they were noble, were not ashamed to come to my house and visit me" ("Se tu nol sai, amico mio, io sono vivuto, dalla mia puerizia infino in intera età nutricato, a Napoli ed intra nobili giovani meco in età convenienti, i quali, quantunque nobili, d'entrare in casa mia né di me visitare si vergognavano," *Ep.*, XIII.37).

In Boccaccio's literary works, one of his most original innovations would be to bring together high culture and pleasure reading, writing narrative works of a sort never seen before, in which the goal of entertainment—not coincidentally, women would be his typical audience—is united with themes and texts from the scholarly realm. The boy who arrived in Naples from a faded Florence, however, had no such project in mind, and a world whose existence he had likely never even suspected lay open before him. Bombarded from all sides by cultural ferment and enticements of every sort, he allowed himself to be seduced. Embracing this environment that surrounded him, sharing its interests and even its lifestyle were essential aspects of his character. Perhaps he was driven by the desire to be accepted, to assimilate; either way, he was certainly also animated by an extraordinary curiosity and an equally extraordinary capacity to learn.

By absorbing the disparate cultural influences Neapolitan culture had to offer, the young Boccaccio, the product of a technical-professional school, began to develop into an intellectual. He benefited in part from some formal instruction—though it is unknown precisely from whom or when—but by and large he proceeded on his own, self-taught. He was already, as he would continue to be, an omnivorous reader. This education, however, was disorganized and varied, drawing indiscriminately from fields that could appear disparate: historical and geographical encyclopedism of the medieval Latin tradition sat alongside scientific and mathematical-astrological texts, Provençal lyric works in the *langue d'oc*, and romance in the *langue d'oïl*. Boccaccio must have already gained some familiarity with Tuscan authors, particularly Dante, when he lived in Florence. Overall, though, what is striking about his reading habits during these first Neapolitan years is the lack of emphasis on works of classical antiquity (though he was at the time working to increase his knowledge of Latin) and, more generally, the predominance of his scientific interests over more literary ones: the abacus school, it seems, had left its mark.

The great majority of texts he read during this period were stored in his mental library, and we get an idea of just how varied and numerous they were only from their reemergence in his writings. A smaller part, however, we can actually read because Boccaccio transcribed them in his own hand. Acting as a scribe, in the sense of literally copying texts, was one of his favored activities. Probably even before becoming an apprentice he had begun copying documents of various sorts both ancient and modern into a parchment codex, or notebook, that he had prepared with the aim of assembling a personal collection, which is today known as the "Zibaldone Laurenziano." Between 1327 and 1334—the years he worked for the Naples office—he transcribed a typically heterogeneous series of works to which he added two treatises on astronomy by Andalò del Negro accompanied by drawings.[15]

Boccaccio would remain a tireless copyist of both his own and others' works for his entire life. In his time, no one came close for quantity of texts transcribed. He would recopy Dante's *Commedia* in full three times; even in old age he would copy in his own hand the *Decameron* and his compilation of biographies of illustrious women, *De mulieribus claris*. Boccaccio never had the material resources that allowed Petrarch to acquire books and hire professional copyists, and yet, in his indefatigable activity there is also something compulsive, a voracity that is well suited to an author characterized by excess: the modern complete edition of his works in eleven volumes has more than eleven thousand pages; even if one were to remove introductions, translations, notes, and indexes, an imposing tome would remain. For Boccaccio writing seems to have been a necessity, almost an addiction. His most intimate friends probably made fun of this obsession, and he knew it: in a comical letter written in Neapolitan dialect for his closest friends he confesses, under the mask of "Abbot Ja' Boccaccio," to do nothing other than write day and night, and this "for wanting to learn" ("pe' voler addiscere," *Lett.*, I.13–14).

It is possible that if the young apprentice did not know Giotto di Bondone, he would have at least caught sight of him. The artist worked in Naples between 1329 and 1333, painting among other things the fresco cycle *Uomini illustri* in Castelnuovo, and it is also possible that it was then, when he had the chance to see some of Giotto's paintings, that Boccaccio's admiration for his art was born, one that he would express many times in his writing. A famous page in the *Decameron* exalts the realistic, almost illusionistic, power of his painting: "Giotto possessed a genius so lofty that there was nothing from nature that he could not represent with lead stylus, his pen, or his paintbrush. . . . He was able to imitate it, or rather, to make his work resemble the thing itself so closely that he often deceived men's eyes, making them think that what he painted was real" (*Dec.*, VI.5, 5).[16]

According to Boccaccio, Giotto took the imitation of nature typical of figurative art to its highest level. The special attention he devoted to Giotto, which was shared by Dante and Petrarch, should be located within his wider interest in all the figurative arts — consider the notable presence of painters in the *Decameron* — an interest also supported by his own innate predisposition for drawing, as shown by the rich array of sketches in his autograph codices.[17]

High Society

Naples, home to one of the most important courts of Europe, had an especially vibrant social scene. Feasts, balls, hunts, knightly tournaments in which the king himself participated, parties, boat rides and outings followed one another other with hardly a break in between. The young apprentice was fascinated. Once he became a writer, he would enthusiastically describe the delights of that society over and over again, delights he would continue to recall with great nostalgia even after he had left Naples.

Many pages testify to how deeply this fascination with the Neapolitan social world was engraved in Boccaccio's mind and imagination. In a chapter of the *Elegia di Madonna Fiammetta*, written in Florence when he had been away from Naples for some years, he recalls the pleasures and sweetness of that beautiful world through Fiammetta's voice. The result is a picture painted with great detail and precision. Much space is reserved for Baia, "high

above the seashore, than which no site under the sun is more beautiful or more pleasant" ("sopra i marini liti, del sito delle quali più
bello né più piacevole ne cuopre alcuno il cielo," *EMF*, V.16, 2),[18] and
the countless amusements it offers:

> There, for the most part, time is spent in idleness, and when it *is*
> spent more actively, women, either alone or in the company of
> young men, speak of love; there people consume nothing but del-
> icacies, and the finest old vintage wines strong enough not only to
> excite the sleeping Venus but also, if she were dead, to bring her
> back to life in every man, and those who have tried the power of
> the baths know to what extent their beneficial effects also contrib-
> ute to this. There the beaches, the lovely gardens, and every other
> place always resound with festivities, novel games, most grace-
> ful dances, music, and love songs composed, sung, and played
> by young men and young women as well. Therefore, in this place
> those who can should be on guard against Cupid, who, insofar as
> I know, in that very place, which seems to be his choice domain,
> exercises his powers with little effort.[19] (*EMF*, V.17, 4–6)

These were delights in which the pleasure of the company,
singing, and dancing were mixed with thrills of sensuality:

> In many places around there one would see the whitest of tables
> spread so beautifully and so preciously decorated that the mere
> sight of them could arouse appetite even in the most indifferent
> person, and elsewhere people could be seen having their morning
> meal, since it was already that time, and we or anyone else pass-
> ing by were cheerfully invited to join their pleasure. When like the
> rest we too had finished our festive meals, the tables were cleared,
> and as usual we whirled around in joyful dancing; then we boarded
> our boats and swiftly sailed around. In some places an extremely
> desirable sight appeared before the young men's eyes: beautiful
> women covered by sheer, silky tunics, barefooted, and with bare
> arms, walking in the water, picking seashells from the hard rock,
> and as they bent in their task they revealed the hidden delights
> of their ripe bosoms. Elsewhere more resourceful people, some

with nets and some with other novel devices, were seen luring the hidden fish.²⁰ (*EMF*, V.26, 5–9)

Boccaccio is much more explicit in verse, where the theme of Baia as a place of license and corruption appears several times.²¹ For example:

> There, the people are keen on having fun,
> on music and song, on snaring with empty
> words the minds of the undiscerning,
> and on boasting of their amorous triumphs.
> There, Venus displays such license
> that a woman who has arrived as honest
> as Lucretia, might go home a Cleopatra.

> Quivi s'attende solo a festeggiare
> con suoni et canti et con parole vane
> ad inveschiar le menti non ben sane,
> o d'amor le victorie a ragionare;
> et havvi Venere sì piena licenza,
> che spess'advien che tal Lucrezia vienvi
> che torna Cleopatrà allo suo hostello.

> *Rime*, LXXI (LXXV).5–11²²

Especially noteworthy is the joyful enthusiasm with which Fiammetta-Boccaccio describes the celebration by the people and nobility animating the entire city on the occasion of a spring knightly tournament:

> Among other things, [Naples] appears especially splendid during its frequent jousting tourneys. So when the rainy winter days are over and spring has restored its lost beauty to the world with flowers and green grass, it is an ancient tradition on the most important holidays to gather together the noble ladies at the knights' quarters, where they all come wearing their most precious jewels, because youthful minds are excited by the character of the season

and more than ever ready to express their desires.... Here among such a large and noble company, one does not sit or keep silent or whisper for long; rather, as the older men look on, the bright young men take the ladies by their delicate hands and sing aloud of their feelings of love as they dance, and in this manner and in as many joyful ways as can be imagined, they spend the hot part of the day. When the sun's rays begin to grow cool, one can see the honorable princes of our Ausonian kingdom arrive, clad as magnificently as their rank requires, and after having admired the charms of the ladies as well as their dances, they leave with nearly all their young men, knights as well as pages, and return shortly thereafter with a very large following, wearing costumes entirely different from what they had worn before.... I will then say that our princes arrive on horses which run not only faster than any other animal but so fast that in running they would leave behind even those very winds believed to be the fastest; and the princes' youth, their remarkable beauty, and their notable excellence makes them exceedingly pretty to those who look at them. They appear on caparisoned horses, dressed in crimson or in garments woven by native hands with designs of different colors and interwoven threads of gold and also garnished with pearls and precious stones; their long blond hair falling onto their extremely white shoulders is tied onto their head with a gold ringlet or held by a small garland of fresh branches. Furthermore, their left hand is armed with a very light shield and their right one with a lance, and at the sound of the summoning trumpets, one after the other and followed by many others all wearing the same costume, they begin their jousting before the ladies, who praise most the one who in such a game gallops on his horse, keeping the tip of his lance closest to the ground and holding himself most tightly under his shield without any awkward movements.... After having paraded at a slow canter two or three times in front of the surrounding crowd, the cheerful company began their competition; straight in their stirrups, tightly protected by their shields, but still with the points of their light lances nearly touching the ground, they ride their horses faster than the fastest winds; the atmosphere resounding with the cheering voices of the surrounding crowd, with the ringing of bells, with the sounds of all kinds of instruments, and with the flapping of mantles that covered horses and men, encourages them to ride better and more vigorously.[23] (*EMF*, V.27, 2; 29, 1–2)

Notably, in describing these martial games, Boccaccio devotes little space to the tournament itself while expanding on the beauty of the spectacle: the rich parade, the showy display of the women's clothing and ornaments, the presence of the princes of the court and nobility of the city, the festive atmosphere shared by both the elite and the cheering populace. A description at once realistic and idealized, it encapsulates the nostalgic state of mind with which Boccaccio remembered the city of his youth after returning to Florence. It is the same state of mind with which the narrator in the *Comedia delle ninfe fiorentine*, the first work written in Florence after his return, bids farewell to the place of delight where the story of the shepherd Ameto took place and from which he is about to depart:

> In that place are beauty, gentility, and worth, charming words, examples of virtue, and supreme pleasures along with love; there is desire that moves man to salvation; there is as much good and gaiety as man can know; there the worldly delights are fulfilled, and there sweetness is to be contemplated and enjoyed.

> Quivi biltà, gentilezza e valore,
> leggiadri motti, essemplo di virtute,
> somma piacevolezza è con amore;
> quivi disio movente omo a salute,
> quivi tanto di bene e d'allegrezza
> quant'om ci pote aver, quivi compiute
> le delizie mondane, e lor dolcezza
> si vedeva e sentiva

CNF, XLIX.67–74[24]

Clearly, the enchanted evocation of what the narrator saw and heard refers also to the happy Naples that the author had recently left. That his description of the tournament gives almost no space to the armed confrontation can be seen as a sign of his deliberately rosy vision of those years. And even more telling is the fact that Boccaccio passes over in complete silence the bloody games, true gladiatorial combats, which took place in the same area of Carbonara that hosted the jousts, and which the court and Neapolitan nobility also attended. Petrarch, taken unsuspecting to see one of these combats during his sojourn in Naples in 1343, described with horror the killing of a handsome young man, stabbed right at his feet to the applause of the spectators.[25]

It is conceivable that during his time as a young clerk in the Bardi firm Boccaccio had been little more than a spectator to this social whirl, but everything suggests that once he was older he actually participated in Neapolitan high society. Just as he would boast that Neapolitan nobles visited his house, in old age he would let slip with marked nonchalance that as a young man he had access to King Robert's "hall" ("aula," *CVI*, IX, 26, 1).[26] Moreover, many doors, including perhaps those of Robert's court, were open to him thanks to the position of his father, who was not a simple merchant banker but as the Bardi's plenipotentiary had influence on many matters of state. In 1328, within just a few months of Boccaccino's arrival in Naples, the king had already awarded him the titles of councillor and chamberlain; though they were honorifics with no real content, they were coveted by merchants because they increased their prestige at home, but were nonetheless also signs of distinction in the world of the court. Boccaccio, however, did not want to be accepted just because he was his father's son; he wanted to be recognized and welcomed for his own merits. This is where literature came in.

Literary Debut

It says a great deal about the young Boccaccio's anxiety for social advancement and his naively instrumental vision of literature that the first work he published was a short poem in Dantean terza rima entitled *Caccia di Diana* (*Diana's Hunt*) that celebrates the Neapolitan aristocracy. There is no solid evidence for its date, but 1334–35 is thought to be plausible.[27]

Its plot is thin:

A narrator relates that one fine spring morning the goddess
Diana gathered together sixty Neapolitan noblewomen—
all named except one, the most beautiful and valiant of
them all—divided them into groups and instructed them
to go hunting. At midday, at the end of a morning during
which the huntresses had killed (sometimes quite blood-
ily) a very large number of animals—both those actually
hunted during the Middle Ages as well as more exotic
beasts that certainly did not live in Neapolitan forests,
and others, like bulls, that were not considered hunting
quarry or that inhabited only bestiaries, as well as land
and water snakes, swans, beavers, and a large quantity of
birds—Diana called them back to restore themselves. The
huntresses brought with them the slain animals, heaping
them in a big pile. Diana then ordered them to sacrifice the
catch by fire to Jupiter, but the unnamed beauty opposed
her, arguing vehemently that a passion other than that for
the hunt now warmed her and her companions' hearts. Offended, Diana returned to the heavens, and, on the suggestion of the unnamed beauty, the women decided to sacrifice
their victims to Venus. As soon as they set fire to the pile,
the goddess, whom they had all invoked, descended naked
from the sky and, turning toward the pyre, transformed the
burning animals into young men. After the men had joyfully
immersed themselves in a stream and dressed in vermilion
cloaks, Venus commanded them to love the women who
had captured them and to woo the women until they con-
quered them. Even the narrator, who had witnessed Diana's
retreat, the lighting of the bonfire, Venus's descent, and
the miraculous metamorphoses she enacted, found himself transformed from the stag he had been into a rational,
human creature. And thus his account ends with a paean
to the angelic beauty of the unnamed woman to whom he
owed the miracle of having been transformed into a man.

In fact, the plot is not just thin; it's also a bit rough. The revelation that the narrator was actually "changed from a stag . . . into a

human being and a rational creature" ("cervio mutato in creatura /
umana e razionale," *CD*, XVIII.11–12)[28] arrives completely unexpectedly only at the end of the poem. Nothing foreshadows the
fact that the speaker had experienced as a "brute beast" ("brutta
belva," *CD*, XVIII.24)[29] the same events that he then recounts as a
man. Moreover, since he was able to witness the fire that engulfed
the kill and the metamorphoses, it is clear that the narrator had
not *himself* been hunted and slain. In what way and where did his
miraculous transformation take place?

In short, toward the end of his tale Boccaccio abandoned the
literal along with narrative coherence in order to ascend, without
having prepared the reader, to the heights of symbol and allegory.
It is true that allegory was an irresistible temptation for the young
Boccaccio, and that in this first work he already shows allegorizing
ambitions. However, here the allegory unfolds intermittently, in
isolated scenes, and does not succeed in constructing a unified,
homogeneous edifice. The victory of Venus, that is, of love, over the
active life symbolized by the hunt—a victory recounted through
the overturning of traditional myths about men transformed into
beasts—should be understood in a moral sense: without love, man
is an animal. However, on the nature of a love that transforms animals into men Boccaccio proves to be rather imprecise: just as the
unknown beauty invokes Venus to "banish base thoughts from our
breasts" and "make excellent our spirits and generous and noble
our hearts" ("Caccia de' petti nostri i pensier vili"; "fa eccellenti / gli
animi nostri, e' cor larghi e gentili," *CD*, XVII.22–24), the narrator-
made-man also affirms that love "ennobles every base mind"
("ingentilisce ciascuna vil mente," *CD*, XVIII.39).[30] In short, there
is nothing more about the now assumed opposition between the
noble and the base. The transformation of the brutes into rational
creatures has weighty significance to be sure, but the fact remains
that when Boccaccio needs to give substance to the miraculous
workings of love, he only repeats popular, courtly themed motifs
of spiritual elevation.[31]

This confirms that the heart of the poem is gallant homage.
The *dame*, that is, the married women, and the *pulcelle/donzelle*
Diana gathers, the unmarried women who are nonetheless already
promised in marriage, are all Neapolitans. Each woman is identi-

fied by both her first name as well as that of her family of origin, all except one, precisely the most beautiful and virtuous one who transforms the narrator into a man with her love.[32] The poem's encomiastic approach requires that the huntresses be fully identifiable, but the autobiographical narrator is not only unable to name his beloved, he cannot even allude to her in any recognizable way. This is either because, as was very likely, the young Boccaccio did not have a real object of desire or because, as is certain, the most basic rules of social behavior would have kept him from placing himself among the ranks of their noble partners, ones who were further elevated by their actual or at least potential connections with the listed noblewomen. In effect, the long female catalog functions as a kind of grand courtly synecdoche: the celebration of the noblewomen cannot help but reflect on the gentlemen who are, or are soon to be, joined to them in marriage. More even than a gallant homage, then, this is a courtly homage.

This does not mean that the court was the work's intended recipient. Obviously, the families to which the women-huntresses belonged, families that represented the poem's first-line audience, gravitated around the court, but the court in its essential core is completely absent: no lady of the royal house of Naples, married or unmarried, appears among the fifty-nine huntresses. Less than ten years later, in Florence, Boccaccio would compile another catalog of women, but there, along with Florentine ladies, the women belonging the house of Anjou by birth or marriage stand out for their number and their assigned importance.[33] At this earlier time, however, he did not dare claim familiarity with the court's highest levels.

Viewed as a whole, this collection of names depicts a rich and varied urban elite, from the feudal nobility, both native and imported, to that of the city, both the ennobled and the bureaucratic elite, and even includes non-nobles, that is, particular individuals, not clans or families. Yet, the catalog never refers to the world of the aristocracy of money, to the high finance sphere of the Bardi, the Peruzzi, the Acciaiuoli, whose leaders frequented court circles and with whom some of the families cited in the poem must have had business relationships.[34] In this first work, there is no trace of this sphere, the one that the son of the Bardi's *fattore* actually inhabited, albeit in a marginal position. In other words, Boccaccio in this case exhibited at least two forms of omission: he declined to address members of the royal family, on the one hand, and, on the other, he ignored the elite sector of the society to which he himself belonged.

His goal was to become known, but in some other way than as the factor's son, to carve out an autonomous space; but he had not yet acquired the ease and self-confidence that he would show not too far in the future. He was timid before the elite, too extreme in repressing the details of his own milieu. But perhaps it was precisely something from this environment that pushed him to put himself forward.

Niccolò Acciaiuoli had arrived to work in the Naples branch of his family's business in 1331. It may be that Boccaccio, as we have said, was his classmate in Giovanni da Strada's school; Niccolò's father, Acciaiuolo, certainly worked in close contact with Boccaccino. It was therefore natural that Giovanni and the slightly older Niccolò would become friends. This friendship would last for a long time, albeit with ups and downs; already in these early days, though, there were already plenty of reasons for tension. While Giovanni remained an apprentice clerk, Niccolò's career took off and, within the space of a few years, lifted him into the heights of Neapolitan society, so much so that he became the administrator of assets as well as tutor for Louis of Taranto, son of Catherine of Valois-Courtenay, the widow of King Robert's brother Philip. For Boccaccio, the extraordinary ascension of this young man of roughly his own age, like him the son of a merchant who had arrived in Naples, as he would maliciously point out years later, "content with only one servant" ("d'un fante solamente contento," *Ep.*, XIII.37, 116), must have created several psychological problems. Admiration was not necessarily free of envy; literature was the only way to compete with this unlettered man. In all likelihood, this was one of the forces that drove Boccaccio to present himself in society in the garb of a poet.

As noted, the *Caccia di Diana* is in some ways lacking; however, in this first work some of the fundamental characteristics of Boccaccio's writing were already established and would remain virtually unchanged for many years. First, his choice of the vernacular:

aside from a few minor exceptions, it would be another ten years before Boccaccio would devote himself to literary texts in Latin. Clearly, Dante had not lived in vain. His *Commedia* had not only given a powerful boost to the diffusion of vernacular literature but had also contributed significantly to reversing the power balance between short lyrical works and longer narrative texts. Further, in the *Caccia* Boccaccio already appears as the narrator, a position he would occupy for his entire writing career in both prose and verse, despite a sporadic production of lyric poetry.

This trait by itself made him the most modern writer of his day, but it also did so because of its connection to another of his characteristic tendencies: experimentation, the search for variety and the new. Literary critics have compiled a great number of references to disparate genres in the *Caccia*, but in truth this text cannot be directly related to any of the preexisting literary genres because Boccaccio created a new one.[35] Already in his first work there emerges what would become another of his distinctive characteristics: the ability to create the new out of the known. Finally, it should be emphasized that from the very beginning Boccaccio identified his preferred audience as female. This choice, which would continue throughout his literary production up to and including the *Decameron*, had a number of consequences, not least the predominance of love as a theme. It is with Boccaccio that writing about love in the Italian context, previously confined almost exclusively to lyric poetry, moved into the main channel of narrative literature.

3

Canonist and Scholar:
A Life Plan

Law Student

It is not surprising that the composition of the *Caccia* took place in 1334–35: these years marked a turning point for the young Boccaccio. He was at last able to leave his position with the Bardi company and, thanks to this newfound freedom, devote himself to scholarship and literature.

It had taken a few years for Boccaccino to accept that his son was not cut out to be a merchant. Boccaccio would later complain that he had wasted six years of his life on this profession: since it is unlikely that he misremembered or forgot the length of time spent on such highly disagreeable work, and since it almost certainly began shortly after his arrival in Naples, we can surmise that his farewell to commerce likely occurred in 1334, perhaps in the latter part of the year. However liberating this farewell may have been, it nonetheless raised the problem of what alternative path to take. Boccaccino had likely understood quite early on that his son would not follow in his footsteps, but it must have been difficult to identify another career that would not completely disappoint paternal hopes. Giovanni's bent for letters seemed obvious, but in Naples, where there were no professorships of rhetoric and poetics, such an inclination could not be satisfied. And then, this successful merchant did not have the open-mindedness, or perhaps even the desire, to indulge propensities with so little financial promise. In short, if university it had to be, then the Faculty of Law appeared to be the only choice that could satisfy the son's inclinations while at the same time ensuring good economic prospects. His father, as Boccaccio would write in the *Genealogia*, "ordered that I should study for holy orders, as a good way to get rich" (*GDG*, XV.10, 6).[1] In tracing the story of the long struggle to realize his literary vocation, Boccaccio presented his father's decision as an imposition, but it is more likely that father and son agreed on the choice. It was, after all, a reasonable compromise: Boccaccino set his son on a path to a lucrative career, and, for his own part, Giovanni could finally replace little-loved accounting ledgers, if not with coveted books of poetry, at least with others closer to his taste.

There was another problem, however, and it was that Boccaccio was what we might call an "unconventional" student. He had not attended a school of Latin grammar, as was normal for university graduates, and it does not seem that he took the preliminary course in grammar and logic offered in Naples by the Faculty of Arts. Since it was necessary to have good knowledge of Latin to be admitted to university study, Boccaccio had to first acquire a sufficient command of the language. He must have continued to study it independently, as he had been doing for some time, and he may have had private tutoring as well. In any case, Boccaccio was a "lettered" merchant by the time he came knocking on the door of the University of Naples, a most unusual event. For this reason, among others, he likely did not enroll in 1334 but somewhat later.

But how much later?[2] Despite a lack of documentation, a few clues point to a plausible date. The most substantial is a rental contract that Boccaccino entered into in Florence at the beginning of 1337 with a certain Scarpa, the prior of the Florentine church of Santo Stefano al Ponte. For a term of five years beginning on November 1, 1337, Boccaccino rented, in his name and that of his son Giovanni, the property, rights, and income of the church of San Lorenzo alla Croce in Capua, of which Scarpa was the rector. The rent was initially twenty-six gold florins, which would have been rather high—bear in mind that as the Bardi's agent Boccaccino received an annual salary of one hundred florins—a sign that to guarantee an appreciable profit margin the income of the church

must have been quite substantial.³ Why did Boccaccino, in Florence, rent property in Capua? Why sign a five-year contract?

It seems clear that the real beneficiary of the operation was
Giovanni. Lacking any income of his own, he was economically
entirely dependent on his father. So the problem arose of how to
provide for his needs, given that Boccaccino, after many years of
stable residence in Naples, had begun traveling again on behalf of
the company and, at least starting in 1336, was once again living in
Florence more or less permanently. His commitments in Naples
must have lessened right around 1336–37, prior to his giving up his
position as factor at the beginning of October 1338. (Renunciation,
and not dismissal or removal, since Boccaccino's relationship with
the Bardi would remain close in the following years.) In short, with
this financial arrangement, the father provided a stable income for
his distant son who was otherwise without support. That the contract was for five years from the beginning of November 1337 likely
means that this is how many years of study remained before the
conferral of Giovanni's law degree. In Florence, the duration of this
type of contract was generally left up to the parties, and so to have
entered into it for five years was Boccaccino's choice or, if it was a
condition imposed by the owner, it was one that Boccaccino accepted. Now, since the course of study at the University of Naples
lasted six years, we can reasonably suppose that Giovanni enrolled
the year before the contract, that is, in the academic year 1335–36.

A second clue fits with this theory. Boccaccio's first demanding
literary work, the one to which, released from the warehouse, he
affixed his own name as author, is an imposing prose romance entitled *Filocolo*. The most commonly accepted hypothesis, to which
we will return, dates the start of its composition to 1336, more
precisely after March 30, 1336, the day on which the "compiler"
("componitore"—that is, the author) states that he first met the
book's dedicatee. Now, at the end of the work's first chapter, which
serves as its introduction, the "compiler," invoking Christ to support his "weak hand in this task," ("non forte mano alla presente
opera") qualifies as a student of canon law: "I . . . who now spend
my time in studying the holy laws of your successors on earth [the
popes]" ("ora nelle sante leggi de' tuoi successori spendo il tempo
mio," *Filoc.*, I.1, 30).⁴ Considering that the academic year began on

October 5 and ended on June 5 of the following year, we can posit that Boccaccio was admitted as a student either after June 1336 or after June 1335. In short, everything points to the likelihood that he began to attend university lectures during the period 1335–36.[5]

Of course, this calculation is an approximation; if we wanted to move the date earlier, however, we certainly could not push it back as far as 1331–32. This allows us to clear up the oft-repeated claim that the young Boccaccio was a student of Cino da Pistoia — direct contact with whom would have given Boccaccio an entrée to Tuscan poetry along with knowledge of rare texts by Dante and Petrarch, strengthening his vocation for poetry.[6] However, Boccaccio could not have taken Cino's classes because while there is no question the scholar taught civil law at Naples during the academic year 1330–31 and perhaps also the following year, he then left the city (in 1332–33 he was in Perugia), hurling in his wake a disdainful and bitter diatribe against at it and especially its jurists entitled, "Deh, quando rivedrò 'l dolce paese" ("Ah, when will I see this sweet land again").[7]

We have no evidence, however, to either exclude or confirm that, before Boccaccio became a student, he developed a relationship with Cino in some sphere of Neapolitan elite society to which his father's connections gave him access. Still, it seems unlikely that they were personally acquainted. Boccaccio was always generous in acknowledging those he considered his teachers: regarding the Neapolitan years, we have already spoken of Andalò del Negro, but Dionigi da Borgo Sansepolcro was also mentioned affectionately as both "father and . . . master" ("padre e . . . maestro," *Ep.*, V.7). Although not explicitly calling them teachers, Boccaccio did name individuals among the intellectuals gravitating around the court to whom he felt himself indebted in some way, such as Paolo da Perugia[8] and the Minorite friar Paolo or Paolino da Venezia, "a tremendous investigator of history" ("hystoriarum investigator permaximus," *GDG*, XIV.8, 3).[9] Cino, by contrast, was never mentioned in such terms.[10]

Just as he had regarding his apprenticeship, Boccaccio blamed his father's venality for the time he had had to spend in university lecture halls: Boccaccino had ordered his son to "become rich." And toward his studies Boccaccio showed, if not his earlier impatience, then boredom and listlessness: "My teacher was famous, but I wasted under him almost as much time as before," almost six years, but, he adds, "I so disliked these lessons that neither my teacher's admonitions, nor my father's authority, who kept torturing me with ever renewed orders, nor the pleas and importunities of my friends, could make me yield, so great was my one passion for poetry."[11] The image of the father who urges his son to apply himself and the friends who partly scold and partly plead with him would indeed seem to be based on lived experience were it not that Boccaccio wrote these phrases many years after the events described, at a time when he was constructing an image of himself as a person who had struggled to realize his poetic ambitions, and they thus cannot be wholly accepted as credible autobiographical evidence. It is true that, when he was still a student, he referred to the vexations of studying the canon law—in the fictitious letter he asked the fictitious merchant-turned-scholar friend for the loan of a book, Statius's *Thebaid*, so he could mitigate his reading of the papal decretals with stories about the woes caused by love (Venus), Fortuna (Ramnusia), and financial straits (Juno).[12] But it is equally true that assertions of this sort were also influenced by the traditional contrast between study of the liberal arts and study directed toward a profession, and thus has the flavor of a cliché.

To the contrary, the autobiographical note placed at the beginning of the *Filocolo*, far from showing annoyance with legal study, instead gives the impression that Boccaccio was showing off his new status as a student of law. There was no need for him to identify himself in this way; he evidently not only felt it was a better fit for his inclinations, but must also have been convinced that it was a more dignified status in the eyes of Neapolitan society than that of merchant-in-training. In short, attending university classes seemed to him a sign of distinction.

Boccaccio never exercised the profession of lawyer and also never embarked on the ecclesiastical career that the study of canon law would have enabled. On the contrary, just as he railed against merchants' greed, he was also unsparing in his criticism of the greed of jurists and canon lawyers.[13] However, just as six years of apprenticeship had endowed him with a great deal of knowledge of the world and techniques of merchants, his years of university study gave him more than just a veneer of legal culture. His considerable expertise in marital, criminal, and procedural law is apparent in certain episodes of his life and especially in his writings (including the *Esposizioni sopra la Comedia di Dante* [*Expositions on Dante's Comedy*] and, above all, some of the stories of the *Decameron*).[14]

The Cleric

Boccaccio enrolled to study canon law. His father must have had an influence on this choice of field. It is possible that the profession of canon lawyer, which among other things opened the way to an ecclesiastical career with its associated benefices, struck Boccaccino as more economically attractive than that of a civil lawyer. But it is even more likely that the practical-minded father was looking to the immediate present before any future prospects. It was common practice, in fact, for students of canon law to take at least minor orders while still at university; by doing so, they could immediately take advantage of benefices with which they could support themselves, as if they were scholarships, during their studies.[15]

Did Boccaccio follow this path as a student? The answer is rather complicated.

Boccaccio was definitely a cleric in 1360 and had been for some time. On November 2 of that year, a bull from Pope Innocent VI confirmed the dispensations that had earlier been granted to the Florentine cleric Giovanni Boccaccio, which enabled him to receive ecclesiastical benefices although he was illegitimate (a dispensation "super defectu natalium"). It also expanded the permission to allow him to hold offices, including canonries, and to enjoy benefices and prebends in even cathedral churches.[16] Obviously, to become a canon Boccaccio would have to have been elected to a position. We can imagine that such a post was vacant or was about to be established in Santa Maria del Fiore, the cathedral church of Florence, and that Boccaccio, afflicted as always by economic hardship, sought this income. Yet he never held a canonry.

As mentioned, the issue of Boccaccio's clerical status is complicated. Not only did he never obtain the canonry in anticipation

of which he had requested the dispensation, but (and this is especially odd) he also never received the tax exemptions in Florence
allowed to the religious: "for the taxman Boccaccio was always a
layman,"[17] at least until a few months before his death. It could be,
however, that the disappearance of his name from the communal
tax rolls after March 1375 (he would die in December) can be attributed to his late acquisition of ecclesiastical status. Other than
Innocent VI's bull, the only circumstance in which Boccaccio was
designated "cleric" in a document dates, in fact, to March 18, 1374,
when the bishop of Florence, Angelo Ricasoli, "having the utmost
confidence in the ability to evaluate and in the purity of faith of the
prudent signor Giovanni di Boccaccio da Certaldo, Florentine citizen and cleric," appointed him to oversee the faithful execution of
the testamentary wishes of a certain Lipaccio di Cesco da Castelfiorentino, at the time of his will a resident of Certaldo.[18] Boccaccio's acquisition of clerical status could perhaps be corroborated
by the bequests of vestments and other liturgical objects listed in
his August 1374 will, were it not so unlikely that he ever used these
items for their true purpose. In short, Boccaccio certainly received
minor orders, but it is almost equally certain that he was never
ordained and never held benefices or ecclesiastical office.[19]

Had he already taken clerical status when he was a student of
canon law in Naples? It is true, after all, that Boccaccio never married, a decision he could have made in his youth and then never
again questioned, (at least) five illegitimate children notwithstanding. But this is pure speculation.

That he was already a cleric in the 1340s might be supported by
biographical information drawn from the *Amorosa visione*. This
poem in tercets, written in Florence presumably between 1342 and
1343, is preceded by three sonnets—the first and second caudate,
the third caudate and *rinterzato*—which together contain one of
the most complicated acrostics in world literature: the 1,502 letters
that constitute them correspond exactly to, and are in the same order as, the initial letters of each of the 1,502 tercets and single final
lines of the fifty chapters of the longer poem. As if this were not
enough, it seems that a second, higher-order acrostic can also be
identified: at the beginning of the first sonnet, the initial letters of
the odd lines read from top to bottom spell out the name "Maria"

(that is, the Maria/Fiammetta to whom the book is dedicated); conversely, mirroring this, the odd lines of the expanded sirma of the last sonnet, if read from bottom to top, spell the word "prete" ("priest").[20] This is not hard proof, but it would be very strange if this double arrangement of letters with such meaning were completely coincidental. And perhaps we can look further at the basis for the comical letter in Neapolitan dialect written in 1339 in which, as a joke, Boccaccio calls himself "Abbot Ja' Boccaccio" (*Lett.*, I.13). Indeed, it is possible that, ironically and hyperbolically, he transformed his clerical status, known to the friends to whom he wrote, into a lofty ecclesiastical office.[21] In short, some substantial clues could indicate, as one scholar has written, "the attraction of a habit and profession from a fairly early date":[22] that this early date was the one of his entry to the university seems quite likely. This would have been an immediate way to ensure economic support and, looking ahead, to provide a respectable and tranquil life, free of work obligations and distracting worries: a bit like the motivation that Boccaccio attributed to Petrarca, who, in Boccaccio's telling, "assumed clerical life and status so that he might better avoid the troubles of worldly affairs" (*VP*, 19).[23] And yet, taking orders did not gain Boccaccio, either then or later, the prebends to which he aspired. Perhaps he leased the church in Capua precisely because the hoped-for benefices were late to arrive.

From Science to Literature

The turning point of 1334–35 not only meant a great change in Boccaccio's life: it also marked the start of the process that, over the course of five years or so, would make him into a writer in the vernacular.

The death of Andalò del Negro shortly before June 1334 was a symbolic watershed. In that year Boccaccio was transcribing into his notebook an astronomical treatise by Andalò, the *Tractatus theorice planetarum*, which, however, he left uncompleted, perhaps because of the author's death.[24] With the passing of Andalò, the young Boccaccio's main cultural reference point disappeared. This, his "venerable teacher" ("venerabile precettore," *ECD*, V [I].162) and "teacher on the movements of the stars" ("in motibus astrorum doctorem," *GDG*, XV.6, 4) had been the torchbearer of scientific-astronomical knowledge: "When I was still a youth in Naples, I studied with Andalò del Negro from Genoa—a famous and respected master who taught us about the movements of the heavens and of the stars" ("A Napoli, da giovane, sotto la guida di un uomo insigne e venerabile, il genovese Andalò del Negro, imparavo i movimenti dei cieli e delle stelle," *CVI*, III 1.1).[25] Equally symbolic in 1334 was the arrival in Naples from Bologna (where he had been the longtime chancellor of the commune and from which he had been exiled) of the notary Graziolo Bambaglioli, the author a decade earlier of a Latin commentary (later translated into the vernacular) on Dante's *Inferno*. It is not known whether he and Boccaccio formed a friendship, but it is not unlikely. In any case, Boccaccio certainly did not have to wait to meet Bambaglioli to develop a passion for Dante's work. However, contact with this commentator (who had also probably known Dante's correspondent Giovanni del Virgilio personally) would have helped Boccaccio read the beloved poet from a perspective different from the predominant Florentine-centric point of view.[26]

In effect, between 1334 and 1335 Boccaccio began a process of evolution (evidenced also by the *Caccia di Diana*) characterized by a shift from a scholarly scientific approach to a more literary and rhetorical focus. The arrival of the Augustinian Dionigi da Borgo Sansepolcro in Naples between 1337 and 1338 would contribute substantially to this evolution. After Andalò's death and before Petrarca came to be the leading model for Boccaccio, Dionigi was his most influential mentor. Dionigi had come from Avignon, where he had befriended Petrarca, and although a "teacher of theology" ("magister theologie," *VP*, 10), "he was essentially a fervent teacher of rhetoric, poetics, and classical history."[27] Before this time, Boccaccio had read some of Petrarca's poetry, but it was discussion with Dionigi that led him to write, as one of the epistolary exercises to which law students devoted themselves, a fictitious letter to this most learned and virtuous resident of Avignon[28] of whose works he still had a very partial knowledge even after hearing about them from Dionigi.[29] Thanks to this Augustinian, Boccaccio got his first glimpse of the new humanistic culture; his intellectual voracity began to focus on the classics and proceed in a more selec-

tive fashion. Thus, Dionigi's influence must have encouraged Boccaccio in the process of reorientation that was already underway.[30]

We can retrace Boccaccio's cultural itinerary in the second half
of the 1330s thanks in part to the great number of texts he transcribed into his notebook,[31] and even more thanks to the abundance of allusions, echoes, and references spread through his creative works of this period. But in truth Boccaccio himself provided
the best description of his own trajectory.

Let us return to the *Sacre famis*, the fictitious letter (*Ep.*, IV)
written in 1339 to a fictitious friend, referred to earlier. We have
seen that many of the biographical events attributed to this close
friend, a "brother," are based on those of the writer: like Boccaccio,
the friend had been compelled to become a merchant, but, also
like Boccaccio, the friend did not resign himself to this and had
secretly pursued "sacred studies." There is no doubt, therefore,
that Boccaccio projected his own experiences onto those of this
imaginary character (or at least up to the pivotal moment when
the friend transforms into a cruel warrior). And this supports
the idea that the account of the stages of the friend's intellectual
development mirrors in broad outline the path followed by Boccaccio himself. At a young age, before being forced to become a
merchant, the friend had studied grammar, dialectic, and rhetoric;
then, when he was older, after he had studied the fundamentals of
mathematics, he began to apply himself to music, geometry, and
finally, in depth, to astronomy (in the letter, science is given more
space than all the other disciplines combined). It is in this period
of the friend's life—the letter continues—that Giovanni had met
him, befriended him, and shared his studies, which gradually expanded from scientific subjects to literature: he had moved on to
study Virgil, sing Ovid's verses, declaim those of Lucian and Statius, read Sallust's and Livy's histories. Finally, he progressed to
the next and final stage with the study of philosophy and sacred
eloquence. The axis along which his friend's cultural journey un-
folded led from scientific-astronomical study to that of rhetoric
and literature.[32]

Whether inventing the biography of a fictional character or recounting the life of a real person (as in the case of Petrarch), Boccaccio tended to talk about himself: in both cases, the characters'

basic backgrounds remain constant despite the men's many differences. Thus, we can deduce that the autobiographical glimpses are reliable. Also similar to the path followed by the imaginary friend is the one followed by Idalogo, a character in the *Filocolo*, in which, as we know, Boccaccio poured out many of his own youthful experiences. It should also be kept in mind that the depiction of Idalogo likely dates to a period shortly before that of the fictitious correspondence. Now, Idalogo, "left behind [his] father's fields" ("abbandonati i paternali campi") of Tuscany, and moved to Naples to work metaphorically in commerce: the pastoralism he had learned from his father. Here Calmeta, "most exalted of shepherds, to whom . . . the greatest part of things were known" ("pastore solennissimo, a cui . . . la maggior parte delle cose era manifesta"), reveals to him the wonders of astronomy and astrology. This shepherd can only be Andalò del Negro, particularly because the lengthy description of astral phenomena Idalogo launches into (similar to the description in the fictitious letter in its enthusiasm, its mix of science and mythology, and, not least, its verbosity) is interwoven with echoes of Andalò's tracts. Idalogo's fascination with Calmeta's stories leads him to decide to study this discipline, and he becomes "expert" ("esperto") in it. Idalogo then abandons "the pastoral life" ("la pastorale via"), that is, commerce, and "prepared to follow Pallas exclusively" ("del tutto a seguitar Pallade mi dispongo"), that is, to devote himself to poetry and literary studies (*Filoc.*, V.8).[33] The imaginary friend, Idalogo, and Boccaccio himself thus all follow the same trajectory: from the practice of commerce they move on to devote themselves to scientific disciplines and then arrive at last at literature.

4

The Birth of the Author

A Long and Winding Romance

To Petrarch, who was reluctant to recognize Dante's greatness, Boccaccio would confess that the poet had been his "first guide and the light" of his studies.[1] And indeed, the *Caccia di Diana*, the work with which Boccaccio made his debut on the literary stage, is replete with Dantean elements: its meter, the *terzina* (triplet), is that of the *Commedia*; its depiction of the beautiful unnamed woman takes many features from Dante's Beatrice;[2] and its ending is modeled on the closing section of Dante's *Vita Nova*. That earlier text ends with Dante's resolution not to compose more poetry until he is able "to write about her in a nobler way" ("più degnamente trattare di lei") and his assertion that he is striving with all his might to reach that goal, cherishing the hope that he will one day be able "to write of her that which has never been written of any other woman" ("dire di lei quello che mai fue detto d'alcuna").[3] Likewise, the *Caccia* ends with an analogous promise from Boccaccio, who intends to reserve "for a place more praiseworthy . . . my words to praise more truthfully" the beauty of the woman who had transformed him into a man ("in parte più di lode degna / serbo di dir con laude più verace," *CD*, XVIII.49–54).[4] Dante promised a work of the highest literary merit centered on Beatrice: perhaps he

was referring to a heavenly vision in Latin, perhaps he had even begun to write one but abandoned it. The readers of his "little book"
("libello"), however, interpreted these words — and some continue
to do so — as the announcement of the *Commedia*. Late in life, Boccaccio also understood them this way.[5] He saw in Dante's passage
the announcement of a work intended to be continuous with the
Vita, so one can suspect that at the end of his own first work — as
the *Vita Nova* was for Dante — Boccaccio similarly intended to
announce a future, more elevated work centered on an unnamed
beauty. If he really had conceived of a project analogous to Dante's,
and if that project was not abandoned early as in Dante's case, we
should ask ourselves which of Boccaccio's Neapolitan works could
have been conceived of as connected to the *Caccia*.

   In the first chapter of the *Filocolo*, when the "compiler" ("componitore"), Boccaccio himself, speaks of the girl maturing into the
woman with whom he will fall in love, his words openly echo those
Dante used at the beginning of the *Vita* to describe Beatrice upon
meeting her when she was nine.[6] Boccaccio continues, describing
his reaction on seeing the adult woman for the first time ("As soon
as I saw her, my heart began to tremble so strongly that the trembling seemed to echo powerfully through the most minute veins
of my body" ["la quale sì tosto com'io ebbi veduta, il cuore cominciò sì forte a tremare, che quasi quel tremore mi rispondea per
li menomi polsi del corpo smisuratamente," *Filoc.*, I.1, 8),[7] physical
effects that are identical to those produced in Dante by the first
appearance of Beatrice: "the vital spirit, the one that dwells in the
most secret chamber of the heart, began to tremble so strongly
that it appeared horribly in the most minute veins of my body" ("lo
spirito della vita, lo quale dimora nella secretissima camera del
cuore, cominciò a tremare sì fortemente, che apparia nelli menomi
polsi orribilmente," *VN*, 1, 4–5). To summarize: in the *Caccia di Diana* an unnamed woman with traits like Beatrice's is presented as
so superior to all others that she is enveloped in a royal aura (she
alone has the honor of hunting with an eagle);[8] in the *Filocolo*, the
woman to whom the work is dedicated, as we will see, is said to be
of royal blood and manners. Again: like the *Vita Nova*, the *Caccia
di Diana* closes by referring readers to a future, "more praisewor-

thy" work; the *Filocolo* opens with a meeting closely modeled on that of Dante and Beatrice. This does not mean that the unknown beauty and the dedicatee of the *Filocolo* are the same person, but it does indicate Boccaccio's wish to draw attention to the continuity between the two texts. By echoing and expanding upon some of the unknown woman's traits, he suggests that the *Filocolo* is the fulfillment of the promise he made at the end of the *Caccia*.[9]

The *Filocolo* is a rambling, overflowing romance in prose that extends for more than six hundred pages in the modern edition. Today it might seem like a difficult and tedious read, but it must have been quite striking when it first appeared. In Italy, such a literary object had not yet been seen: in the Italian Middle Ages, this book comes closest to the idea of the novel, which would only begin to develop almost three centuries later. And, above all, its most innovative aspect was its vernacular prose, which was unusually lexically rich and syntactically complex, but also flexible, even powerful. This is the ambitious work with which a very enterprising and enthusiastic university student, imbued with a good dose of the exhibitionism befitting an autodidact, aimed to impress the cultured and worldly society of Naples. This attempt to impress started right from the title, coined from the Greek, a language over which Boccaccio had only the vaguest command, as demonstrated by the false etymology by which he interpreted the name Filocolo as "labor of love" ("fatica d'amore," *Filoc.*, III.75, 5)[10]—and also a language, it must be said, that was entirely unknown to the court audience to whom the romance was directed.[11]

The plot is indirectly derived from the *Floire et Blanchefleur*, a short twelfth-century French verse romance that enjoyed great popularity and was reinvented in many subsequent versions (one in *ottava rima*, entitled *Fiorio e Biancifiore*, was circulating in Italy around the same time as the *Filocolo*). The fabulous tale is set in the sixth century CE, around the time of the empire of Justinian, but, with supreme disregard for narrative plausibility and chronological consistency, from roughly its midpoint it is filled with references to places dear to Boccaccio (in particular Naples, but also Certaldo), as well as then-living historical figures and people from the author's own life.[12]

During a pilgrimage to Santiago de Compostela, the Roman spouses Giulia and Quintus Lelius Africanus are attacked by soldiers of Felice, the king of Spain: Giulia, pregnant with Biancifiore, is saved. She dies giving birth to her daughter at the king's court on the same day that the queen gives birth to Florio. The two children grow up together and, upon reaching adolescence, fall in love. To thwart their love, Florio's parents separate the pair, sending their son far from the court and then accusing Biancifiore of plotting against the king and sentencing her to death. Florio saves her, however, and the two rejoin the court. The sovereigns then sell Biancifiore to merchants who take her to Alexandria in Egypt. Florio, who had been led to believe that his beloved was dead, discovers the truth and departs on his search, calling himself Filocolo. After traveling through Italy and stopping in Naples, he finally reaches Alexandria, where he tries to free Biancifiore from the tower where she is being held prisoner. Captured, they are condemned to burn at the stake, when the admiral in command of the city discovers that Florio is his nephew. Freed, the couple marry and shortly after they undertake the return journey, passing once again through Naples and then Certaldo and Rome, where they discover Biancifiore's noble origins and both convert to Christianity. Upon their return, the Spanish court also converts and, when King Felice dies, Florio ascends to the throne.

The plot would have been simple and straightforward had Boccaccio not stuffed it with passages on learned theories and digressions—almost a hundred pages devoted to a brigade in a Neapolitan garden debating thirteen questions about love—mixed different time frames, moving from the story's legendary age to the narrator's present, and multiplied the number of characters and even that of literary genres. The result is a hodgepodge of literary, legendary, mythological, historical, and scientific material, in other words, a sort of cultural self-portrait that the young author exhibits in an almost impudent way.

A hodgepodge then, yes, but not an accidental one. Boccaccio had a specific cultural project in mind. He explained it in the first chapter when he wrote that he had composed the book in response to the dedicatee's request that he redeem the "memory of these young lovers [Florio and Biancifiore]," which is "not exalted with a suitable memorial in the verses of some poet, but is left only to fanciful chatter of the ignorant" ("memoria degli amorosi giovani," "non essaltata da' versi d'alcun poeta, ma lasciata solamente ne' fabulosi parlari degli ignoranti," *Filoc.*, I.1, 25).[13] Boccaccio's plan, in short, was to elevate what we would today call commercial or popular fiction. It was an ambitious project, one Boccaccio would pursue for almost the entire course of his production of vernacular literature, and it represented perhaps the most innovative feature of his work. Specifically, his plan "intended to join the two 'souls' of the Angevin court: a learned, scientific 'high' culture and a worldly 'low' culture of amusement aimed particularly at a female public."[14]

Maria, Natural Daughter of Robert of Anjou

In the first chapter of the *Filocolo*, after a lengthy, grandiose panegyric of the Angevin dynasty, the author introduces the woman he loves, upon whose request he has penned the romance that he now dedicates to her. He says that before ascending the throne, Robert of Anjou had fathered her with a "a noble maiden living in the royal household" and baptized her Maria. Robert had raised her "lovingly," but "under the assumed surname of a different father," "since he wished to preserve his own honor and that of the young lady" ("una gentilissima giovane dimorante nelle reali case"; "teneramente"; "sotto nome appositivo d'altro padre"; "volendo di sé e della giovane donna servare l'onore," *Filoc.*, I.1, 14–15).[15] Thus, Maria is the illegitimate daughter of the king and a lady of the court. As she is the work's dedicatee, she must be understood as a real person, a lady who, under the name of a father not her own, may have frequented Neapolitan court circles. Is Maria her real name—indicated in the *Filocolo* only indirectly, by periphrasis—or an invented one? All we can say is that, in the 1330s, after Dante's Bice-Beatrice, Cavalcanti's Vanna-Giovanna, Lapo Gianni's Lagia-

Alagia, and Cino da Pistoia's Selvaggia, identifying a beloved by her actual given name would not have raised any eyebrows.[16]

In this same chapter, Boccaccio indicates the precise time and place of their first meeting—Holy Saturday, the sixteenth day after the sun had entered the constellation Aries, at the fourth hour in the Franciscan Church of San Lorenzo Maggiore[17]—and even names, again using periphrasis, the convent of Sant'Arcangelo in Baiano as the place of their second encounter.[18] Indeed, identifying locations is one of the *Filocolo*'s innovations. While it is true that there are some precedents in vernacular literature when it comes to lovers meeting in churches (above all, Dante in the *Vita Nova*)— not surprising given that in the Middle Ages churches were some of the places where young people could more easily meet, and for just this reason, as attested by the particular attention given them by preachers, moralists, and authors of didactic works on female behavior, some of the more dangerous ones (along with balconies, windows, and streets) for the honor of girls and women—no other literary examples of churches so precisely identified come to mind.[19] The emphasis on the specific liturgical day (Holy Saturday) should also be seen as Boccaccio's innovation, an innovation that, lacking literary precedent to suggest it, might have had its roots in an actual episode in his life.[20]

From the circumlocutions Boccaccio used to identify the day of their first meeting it is possible to reconstruct with sufficient certainty the omitted year, 1336, in which Holy Saturday fell on March 30.[21] And this year, which, as we have already seen appears to coincide with the initial period of Boccaccio's university study, can also be understood as the earliest possible date for the beginning of the romance's composition.

The first chapter alludes discreetly to the emotional relationship between the author and Maria, avoiding any mention of possible reciprocity: the passion is entirely on the author's side. In asking him to compose the work—her only direct discourse—the woman appeals to the amorous feelings that link him to her, but neither here nor anywhere else does she refer to her own love for him. In the last chapter, the author begins speaking again in the first person, asking his "little book" ("piccolo libretto") to go to the woman to whom it is dedicated and receive from her a well-earned reward: words of "welcome" and, perhaps, a few kisses from her "sweet lips" ("ben venuto"; "dolce bocca"; *Filoc.*, V.97).

Maria-Fiammetta

After Maria's entrance onto the stage in chapter 1, the book does not mention her again for many pages. She reappears suddenly more than halfway through the work when a character named Caleon introduces to Florio, who has landed in Naples during his journey to the East, "an especially revered lady, full of marvelous beauty and virtue" ("una donna più che altra da riverire, piena di maravigliosa bellezza e di virtù," *Filoc.*, IV.15, 1),[22] and tells him that she is the king's daughter and her name is Maria, although their troop of friends call her Fiammetta.[23] A daughter of the king named Maria obviously refers to the dedicatee of the book. We can see, then, that the lady or damsel of the court whom the "compiler" Boccaccio addresses sometime in the mid-1330s is duplicated as a fictional character in a story set in the sixth century CE.

In her passage from the dimension of historical reality, be it true or fictitious, to that of the imagination, Maria acquires the pseudonym (or *senhal* in Provençal) that was destined to become her calling card over the course of her many character transformations in Boccaccio's oeuvre. Fiammetta is an invented name: Boccaccio may have created it by superimposing the form of the names of the beloveds of *stil novo* poets (Fioretta, Violetta, Lisetta, Mandetta, and so on) onto that of the protagonist Flamenca ("Flemmish woman") of the fourteenth-century eponymous Occitan romance, a name that on the basis of a facile para-etymology he would have interpreted in the sense of *fiammeggiante* or "flaming, shining."[24]

The brigade of young people elects Maria-Fiammetta as their queen in a game that consists of proposing and debating a series of *questioni d'amore*, "questions of love." She is present for a sustained period in this role, but from a narrative point of view does not perform any important action. It is Caleon who introduces narrative cues.

This character, too, originates from a process of duplication parallel to Maria's. The "young man named Caleon, elegant in manner and abounding in gracious speech" ("giovane chiamato Caleon, di costumi ornatissimo e facundo di leggiadra eloquenza," *Filoc.*, IV.16, 1)[25] is, in essence, a projection of the author himself (notably, when he reaches the end of his journey of maturation, Caleon becomes the founder of Boccaccio's hometown of Certaldo, whose walls had been marked out by Florio himself).[26] Caleon is in love with Fiammetta, just as Boccaccio the author says he is in love with the work's dedicatee, Maria. But, as is already the case with Maria in the prologue, there is no indication throughout the long section of the fourth book in which Fiammetta is present that she nurtures a similar sentiment for the man who loves her. When the debates on love have ended, Fiammetta again sinks out of sight and only reappears—although indirectly, through others' words—toward the end of the work. Having stopped once more in Naples during his return voyage from the East, accompanied by the now-recovered Biancifiore, Florio asks Caleon "for news of the lovely Fiammetta, who had been their queen earlier, in the garden of love," to which Caleon, sighing, replies that the "star" by which he had navigated had "disappeared" ("che sia della Fiammetta, per adietro stata loro reina nell'amoroso giardino," "stella," "sparita," *Filoc.*, V.30, 1–2): Florio then declares that Caleon loves a "cruel lady without being loved by her in return" ("crudelissima donna sanza essere da lei amato," *Filoc.*, V.47, 2). Caleon's sad love story is not foreshadowed by any narrative signs and is told in only a few pages, after which Fiammetta is never mentioned again. It should be kept in mind that, at the end of the work, the author will not allude to any crisis in his relationship with Maria; rather, his statement to the reader that the book's task is to "convince her to be happy with a single lover" ("confermarla ad essere d'un solo amante contenta," *Filoc.*, V.97, 2, 4) suggests the opposite.[27]

Fiammetta would become something of a mythic figure in Boccaccio's fiction, a symbolic character in his love stories, a little like Laura for Petrarca, but in the *Filocolo* the myth is decidedly still in an embryonic state. At that time, not even Boccaccio suspected that Fiammetta would become one of the pivotal figures for large portion of his fiction. So much so that, after the *Filocolo*, he would forget Fiammetta, and only rediscover her once he had moved back to Florence.

Pseudo-Autobiographical Fragments

In the *Filocolo* and the other works in which the Maria-Fiammetta character reappears, the author himself and the woman who is the object of his love are both doubled, copied from the plane of reality onto that of imagination. This practice is the clearest expression of Boccaccio's penchant for autobiography, which led him to project himself onto many fictional characters, with a refractive effect that is one of the most distinctive characteristics of his vernacular fiction. In the *Filocolo*, where this autobiographical impulse is particularly strong, the phenomenon occurs multiple times.

Among the many characters who share recognizable traits with the author, Idalogo is undoubtedly the one closest to him, a true stand-in. We have already seen how in the epistolary exercise, Boccaccio's personal life (moving from Tuscany to Naples) and his development (progressing from pastoralism/commerce to scientific study and then to poetry) parallel those of his fictitious friend, which are closely modeled on events in Boccaccio's own life. Idalogo — who is ultimately transformed by Venus into a pine tree to free him from the pain of love — has a noble heart, his nobility "derived not from his shepherd father but from his royal mother" ("tratta non dal pastore padre, ma dalla reale madre," *Filoc.*, V.8, 36).[28] Indeed, Eucomos had fathered him with a daughter of the king of France, Gannai. Since Boccaccino actually had been living in Paris in 1313, the year Boccaccio was born, this became the origin of the legend of Boccaccio's Parisian birth, which would hold center stage in biographies for centuries to come. Plainly, however, it was an invention, with which Boccaccio, exploiting the obvious overlap between his own personal history and the character's and, as usual, mixing things up (Idalogo is not connected to the love story involving Maria-Fiammetta), intended to attribute a noble status to himself equal to the one he, as author, had assigned to Maria.[29] This is an invention, moreover, that is linked to elements that would substantiate its authenticity. On the one hand, Boccaccio played on the fact that at the time of his birth his father had really been in Paris; on the other, he was aware that this kind of story was part of a discursive galaxy that circulated widely in merchant circles, a sort of fabulous epos that transmuted merchants' foreign experiences, including their erotic ones, to often extravagant degrees.[30]

Indeed, Boccaccio must have liked this myth quite a bit, for he encouraged it even outside of literature.

In 1339, on December 14 if we believe the *subscriptio*,[31] Boccaccio sent his friend Francesco dei Bardi, who was living in Gaeta (where the company had its most important warehouse), a short letter in Neapolitan dialect[32] informing him that a certain Machinti (perhaps a prostitute) had given birth to a son who, according to the midwife, in every way resembled his father ("tutto s'assumiglia allu pate")—who was perhaps Francesco himself.[33] It also described the party thrown to celebrate the child's baptism, attended by a disparate crowd of prostitutes, common folk, and members of the merchant and aristocratic worlds. The letter was a joke, written to entertain the recipient and a group of friends. Indeed, it is likely that Boccaccio wrote it at the behest of those friends. At the end of the letter, Boccaccio jokingly signed himself "Jannetta di Parisse," that is, Giannetto of Paris. The fact that Boccaccino had lived in Paris was probably known to the letter's intended audience, which included merchants and sons of merchants. However, the signature "Giovanni the Parisian" would have surprised them quite a bit had they not also known the passage in the *Filocolo* where Idalogo speaks of his French birth. In short, in this epistolary joke, just as Boccaccio called himself "abbot" as a hyperbolic allusion to his study of canon law and perhaps the ecclesiastical status to which he aspired, so too, with a somewhat sophomoric braggadocio, he alluded to his royal lineage. The chumminess pervading the *Epistola napoletana* also prevailed among the young Boccaccio's friends: his royal origins must have been frequently bandied about in his closest circles if he could call himself "the Parisian" and be sure the joke would be understood.[34]

All this allows us to close the circle of the chronology of the *Filocolo*'s composition. Begun in 1336 and lasting "many years" ("più anni," *Filoc.*, V.97, 1), if the final book, at least its first chapters, was already known in 1339, then it must have been completed in 1338 or the early months of 1339 at the latest.[35]

Disguised as a fictional character, Boccaccio proclaimed himself the son of a princess royal; in the first person, in the garb of the

book's "compiler," he boasts of loving a daughter of Robert of Anjou. This was a bold, perhaps reckless, gesture, a further sign that,
in penning this romance of imposing dimensions and grand cultural ambition, the young student wanted to impress. Both inven-
tions let the gleaming outlines of private fantasies show through
the literary screen. The notion of Idalogo's birth to a French princess seems to have grown out of the daydreams of a son of an unknown mother, a son who, perhaps without being fully aware of
it, compensated for this traumatic absence with literature. And
behind his supposed romantic connection to the king's daughter
may have loomed, once again, the shadow of his conflicted relationship with Niccolò Acciaiuoli.

Among the rumors and whispers that accompanied Acciaiuoli's meteoric rise, the most insistent and widespread was that
he was the lover of his patron, Catherine of Valois-Courtenay, the
titular Empress of Constantinople and, in 1331, widow of Philip I,
Prince of Taranto. This was gossip to which Boccaccio lent credit,
at least at a certain point in his life, as shown by his eclogue (referring to events of 1355) in which Acciaiuoli, in the guise of the greedy
shepherd Midas, seduces a recently widowed nymph (Caterina)
for financial gain, and by intrigue succeeds in associating himself
with the gods, "though long before he had been scarcely known
by peaceful Arno" (*BC*, VIII.55–56).[36] The social ascent of his near
contemporary must have distressed the young Boccaccio, who was
living on the outskirts of the aristocratic heights that Acciaiuoli
had so easily scaled, and who, like all merchants and merchants'
sons, must have harbored intense anxiety over the issue of social
advancement. Literature was the only terrain on which he could
compete. The invention of a romantic attachment to a daughter of
the reigning monarch could have been imaginary compensation
when faced with a friend who boasted a *real* romantic relationship
with one of the most illustrious women of the court.

The Discovery of *Ottava Rima*

To what degree the Neapolitan audience fulfilled the expectations
that Boccaccio had placed in the *Filocolo* is not known. That his
youthful works were "immediately and fully disseminated," that

is, that they had an "immediate diffusion,"[37] and that the *Filocolo* enjoyed "local and international success"[38] is doubtful. The court audience, accustomed as they were to the pleasure reading of French romances, may have been attracted by the protagonists' love story and the plot's rich complexity, but, lacking the proper cultural background, they were perhaps less interested in the displays of erudition, array of allusions, and references to rare and ancient texts that gave the work its distinctive heft. Conversely, learned circles, while capable of appreciating Boccaccio's attempt to rescue the story from the "fanciful chatter of the ignorant," may have been repelled by a book in the vernacular so openly bent on entertaining. It is therefore plausible that this hodgepodge of a romance did not enjoy the success its author anticipated.[39]

Nevertheless, Boccaccio did not abandon his project of ennobling vernacular entertainment literature through uniting aspects of "high" tradition, taken for the most part from classical and medieval Latin literature, with elements derived from the less illustrious prose and verse romance literature. To the contrary, this intent is even more evident in the two works he composed after the *Filocolo*, the poems *Teseida* and *Filostrato*, especially because, with them, the author gave up on engaging the learned audience of the library, university, and small circle around King Robert in order to focus more doggedly on the audience of the court, which consumed almost exclusively vernacular works that were far from demanding.

In both poems, Boccaccio's plan hinged on the adoption of *ottava rima*. Beginning in the fourteenth century, this metrical form became typical of verse tales (*cantari*) treating various topics that were recited or sung in public by professionals (*cantarini*) or amateurs who took on the role occasionally to entertain mixed but chiefly popular audiences. The *cantari* were spread primarily through oral performance; although their first written documentation is from roughly the same period as Boccaccio's poems, we cannot rule out, and it indeed seems likely, that oral circulation had begun earlier. Hence, the question arises of whether Boccaccio invented the meter or was instead the first to adopt it for texts that, in contrast to the *cantari*, aspired to the status of literature. The second option seems more plausible; but whatever the case, it was definitely Boccaccio's works that established *ottava rima* as the preferred meter for Italian verse storytelling for many centuries to come, from Boiardo to Ariosto, Tasso, Marino, and beyond.[40]

Boccaccio thus used a meter with a strong popular flavor to treat subjects with illustrious pedigrees, from Statius's classical epic the *Thebaid* to the medieval narrative tradition based on the *Iliad*.

Boccaccio's *Teseida*—a Hellenized form of *Thebaid*—wants to be a classical epic poem, so much so that at its conclusion Boccaccio boasts that he is the first to introduce the epic into Italian literature: "But you, o book, are the first to make [the Muses] sing about what has never been seen before in the vernacular of Latium: the sufferings caused by Mars" ("ma tu, o libro, primo a lor cantare / di Marte fai gli affanni sostenuti, / nel volgar latio più mai non veduti," *Teseida*, XII.84).[41] Here, he is openly harking back to the passage of *De vulgari eloquentia* in which Dante writes that, while of the three "great things" ("magnalia") worthy of being treated in an exalted style, namely, "prowess in arms, the fire of love, and the right direction of the will,"[42] the latter two had been written about by Dino da Pistoia and Dante himself, but, he says, "as for arms, I do not find that any Italian has yet treated them in poetry."[43] This reference to Dante's work, implicit but perfectly clear, is, in fact, extraordinary: Boccaccio is alone, along with Giovanni Villani, in showing that he knew the *De vulgari eloquentia* before its sixteenth-century rediscovery by Gian Giorgio Trissino. Scholars are divided on where and when Boccaccio might have encountered the work: some hold that his knowledge dates from the Naples years, others that it was instead soon after his return to Florence. The facts that the only indisputable testimonies were located in Florence, came from people associated with each other, and coincide in factual errors, lead us to fix Boccaccio's encounter with Dante's work in that city after his return from Naples in the autumn of 1340.[44]

> Theseus, the duke of Athens, wages war on the Amazons, forces their surrender, and establishes an alliance by marrying their queen, Ippolita. Shortly after returning home with his wife and her sister, Emilia, he organizes a new military

expedition against Creon, the tyrant of Thebes. Having killed him in battle, Theseus returns to Athens bringing with him Arcita and Palemone, two grandsons of Cadmus, the founder of Thebes, who had been wounded in battle. From prison the two see Emilia in a garden and both fall in love with her. Arcita, who had been set free on the condition that he leave Athens, returns in order to see her again and, without being recognized, enters service to Theseus. But Palemone does recognize him, and, jealous, fearing that Arcita might win Emilia, manages to free himself, seeks out his friend and challenges him to a duel. Theseus surprises them and, having been told their story, pardons them and then orders them to compete in a tournament. During this encounter, Arcita is thrown from his horse and is killed, but before dying requests that Emilia be given in marriage to Palemone. The poem ends with the description of their wedding. And in fact, the work's full title reads: *Theseid of the Nuptials of Emilia* (*Teseida delle nozze di Emilia*).

Even from a simple plot summary we understand that the *Teseida* is a poem with two faces: "the tale of the exploits of Theseus" — the properly epic part — "actually serves as the background for the book's main story, which is a tale of loves, deaths, and marriages."[45] The caesura falls between the first two books, which are in Mars's domain, and the other ten, ruled by Love. A caesura that not only separates two different narrative tonalities, but also two types of stories (and their related sources), the first centered on Theseus and Hippolyta based on the ending of the *Thebaid*, and the second focused on the Arcita-Palemone-Emilia love triangle, events that appear to have been invented by Boccaccio.[46]

The *Filostrato*, in contrast, is a poem exclusively about love, and, while perhaps more enjoyable, is certainly less ambitious than the *Teseida*. Set at the time of the Trojan War, it was part of the rich vein in Romanic and medieval Latin literature of reworking Homeric subject matter:[47] suffused with an atmosphere of courtly romance, it recounts "in light rhyme," "with a style which would excite pity" ("in legger rima," "con stile assai pietoso"; *Filos.*, Proemio 29), that is to say, with a predominantly lyrical-elegiac tone, a story of unhappy love (to Boccaccio the Hellenizing name Filostrato meant "vanquished and laid prostrate by love" [*Filos.*, incipit; "vinto e abbattuto da amore"]).[48]

> The soothsayer Calchas abandons the city of Troy to go over to the Greek side, leaving his daughter Criseida behind. Troilo, Priam's son, is in love with her and manages to win her affection with the help of his friend Pandaro. The two live happily in love until Calchas asks for his daughter to come to him. And so Criseida is separated from Troilo, promising, however, to return in eight days. A promise that she breaks because while in the Greek camp she yields to Diomede's advances. Troilo doubts his beloved's faithfulness, frets waiting in vain, and suffers the throes of jealousy. He accidentally comes into possession of proof that Criseida has betrayed him—he sees the broach that he had given her on a cloak torn from Diomede in battle—and throws himself into the enemy troops seeking to kill his rival, but it is he who is vanquished by Achille's hand.

In the opening octaves, after noting that some poets begin their works by invoking Jove and others Apollo, the author recalls that he used to appeal to the favor of the Muses, but now, having recently fallen in love with the dedicatee, it is she whom he invokes directly as his Muse. It has been observed that the only Proem in which Boccaccio invokes the Muses is that to the *Teseida*,[49] which indicates that the *Filostrato* was likely composed later than at least the beginning of that work, and therefore that the *Filostrato* can be dated to 1339 or shortly after. Moreover, this year is also the one toward which all dating hypotheses converge, even those formulated on other bases.[50] Starting from the relationship between the two proems, some have hypothesized that the writing of the *Filostrato* was nested within that of the *Teseida*. That is, Boccaccio began the epic *Teseida*, but soon after interrupted it to dedicate himself instead to the romantic *Filostrato*, only to then turn again to the *Teseida*, which he finished and revised following his return to Florence.[51] If in fact, as seems likely, the composition of the *Filostrato* interrupted that of the *Teseida* for a time, it would strengthen the theory that the conclusion and final revision of the *Teseida* took place in Florence in the early 1340s.[52]

Silence on Fiammetta

A dedicatory letter to Fiammetta precedes the text of the *Teseida*: since the letter contains a detailed summary of the full plot, it must have been written after the text was completed, and therefore in Florence in 1341.[53] This means that during the two years that Boccaccio was in Naples after the publication of the *Filocolo*, there was not the slightest trace of the woman who had played such an important role in his first romance.[54] This is because the autobiographical tension that had pressed so strongly on the *Filocolo* was eased, or even exhausted, by the time of the *Teseida* and the *Filostrato*. These two new works do not contain characters in the body of the story who are either the author's projections or fictional manifestations of people whose reality (actual or purported) the book itself asserts; they attribute narrative life to women romantically linked to the author only in the dedications, dedications that, even if we accept that they were contemporaneous with the texts, remain independent of them.

Boccaccio dedicated the *Filostrato* with a prose letter to a Neapolitan lady named Giovanna,[55] but nicknamed Filomena, whom he loved passionately. In telling her the story of Troilo, who was first happily loved and then cruelly abandoned, he reveals to her his own suffering caused by her move from Naples to Sannio, because of which he can no longer see her. The depiction of Giovanna-Filomena is marked by extreme discretion; there are no details that might identify her (that she was a widow is the felicitous interpretation of a modern reader, but not specified by the author).[56] Boccaccio speaks to and about Giovanna-Filomena in a way that is very different from his manner with Maria-Fiammetta: in the *Filocolo*, while observing the due conventions of courtesy, he does provide readers with a few "realistic" traits of his beloved, both personal and regarding the nature of their sentimental relationship. In contrast, in the dedication to the *Filostrato*, silence on such matters is accompanied by an unusually frequent recurrence of the motif of protecting the woman's honor. For example, the author gives up the idea of going to Sannio because "*no proper reason* for seeing you could ever lead me" there; and again: "I can scarcely control [my desires], after they have overthrown every suitable *propriety* and reasonable consideration, from pulling me to where you are staying. But, still overcome by *the desire to respect your honor* more than my health, I restrain them" ("*niuna onesta cagione* a vedervi mi doveva mai potere menare"; "appena in me reggere li posso che non mi tirino, posta giù ogni debita *onestà* e ragionevole consiglio, colà dove voi dimorate; ma pur vinto *dal volere il vostro onore* più che la mia salute *guardare* gli raffreno"; *Filos.*, Proem, 10, 18–19, emphases added).[57]

It may be significant that, in the aforementioned fictitious letter to Petrarca, after describing his unexpected reversal of circumstances from all-too-brief happiness to sudden ruin, Boccaccio accuses himself of being "rustic" and "unsophisticated" ("rudis").[58] "Rusticitas" ("rusticity" or "rustic manners") can be understood as a lack of culture and experience. A writer about love—which is how Boccaccio presents himself in the letter—is "rusticus" if he has not mastered codes of proper behavior, essentially that of courtesy, which is above all, a social code. In short, through this strange form of autobiography in *dictamen*, a letter-writing exercise, Boccaccio seems to attribute his romantic failure to his own inadequacy in observing the canons that a lover-writer should follow. Both the Boccaccio who wrote the dedication for the *Filocolo* and the one who depicted himself in the fictional letter are very different from the Boccaccio who had spoken of his love affairs with youthful boldness and naivete only a short while earlier. Had he perhaps realized that he had made a mistake, namely, that a student on the margins of high society should not so rashly mix life and literature?

Naturally, this is only a supposition. And, indeed, raising questions that remain unanswered is yet another aspect of the love stories he told in his first active years, stories that are united, despite their many differences, by a common thematic thread: a happy love that turns into its opposite by his beloved's change of heart. This thread links the stories of Fiammetta and Caleon, of Criseida and Troilo, of Boccaccio the letter writer and the unknown woman and, then, of Fiammetta and the author of the dedication of the

Teseida. The woman's change of heart is felt as an injustice, is attributed to fortune, is caused by an event that, with the exception of the *Filostrato*, is never revealed. The love affairs end without a reason, or, better, for obscure reasons. "I do not know for what reason adverse fortune took away from me" "the flame" that burns in Fiammetta, confesses the author at the end of the dedication of the *Tescida* (*Teseida*, To Fiammetta; "Non so per che cagione, inimica fortuna m'ha tolta"; "la fiamma").[59] Is this not knowing merely a rhetorical gesture or does it come from the author's reluctance to reveal something potentially volatile, something that could or should not be said publicly?

Between Latin and Vernacular

The years 1339–40 were intensely productive ones. The composition of the two poems was accompanied, as always, by a great deal of reading, thanks to which Boccaccio widened his knowledge, which was already considerable at the time of the *Filocolo*, of Latin classics (for example, his familiarity with Apuleius's *Metamorphoses*, which was not widely circulated, dates from this period).[60] With reading and practice Boccaccio honed his Latin linguistic skills. The four letters written in his notebook in 1339,[61] some of which we have referred to repeatedly, were fictional, and thus never sent, composed for practice as a law student within the framework of epistolary-style exercises then in vogue in law schools.[62] His true workshop, however, the place where he perfected his Latin, was literature. While writing the *Filocolo*, imitating (or, more often, rewriting) in vernacular prose passages from Valerius Maximus, Ovid's *Heroides*, and the *Aeneid* itself, Boccaccio "kept open on the same table Latin text and vernacular version": in other words, he modeled his prose on that of translators because he was seeking "a Latinate style, but one close to the sensibilities of a semi-cultured audience, whose taste had been formed on the pages of vernacular translations"; however, with the *Teseida* he made a leap forward, omitting the middlemen and quite often serving as translator himself.[63] It is therefore not surprising that Boccaccio wrote his first poem in Latin in about 1339, the so-called *Elegia di Costanza*, on the death of a young Neapolitan bride.[64] Even if he still hesitated to venture into writing Latin verse, with this poem Boccaccio opened a new path: though more experiments would have to take place before he would feel sure he had mastered this form of expression.

His interest in contemporary literature, and in Dante in particular, did not fade—far from it. Boccaccio had long known a few of Dante's poems well, the *Vita Nova* and the *Commedia*, but he ceaselessly sought out and transcribed little-known minor works. It is due precisely to his autograph copies that we today have such Dantean texts as his letters to Cino da Pistoia, to Italian cardinals, and to his Florentine friend. Though it was not copied into the *Zibaldone Laurenziano*, Boccaccio also knew Dante's letter to Moroello Malaspina, and hewed closely to it in his own letter of praise to Francesco Petrarca, *Mavortis milex* (*Ep.*, II).[65] But, evidence that he was interested in everything concerning Dante including documents that mention him, Boccaccio also transcribed into his notebook the so-called Epistola di frate Ilaro, the letter sent by a Benedictine monk at a monastery at the mouth of the River Magra along with the gift of a copy of *Inferno*, with glosses, to Uguccione della Faggiola, the lord of Pisa, to whom Dante had supposedly dedicated the work.[66] Boccaccio also copied the correspondence in verse between Dante and Giovanni del Virgilio of 1319, the exchange where Dante revived, in a resounding sensation, after "long centuries of medieval neglect and distortion," Virgil's "ancient eclogue . . . in its original rhetorical, linguistic, and metrical forms." Boccaccio's transcription has great value, first of all, because without it we would not know these texts, which were Dante's final compositions and the only ones he wrote in Latin verse.[67] But no less important is the effect that the compositions had on Boccaccio himself: with this discovery he found himself captivated by the genre, a fascination that would spur him to develop it in Latin as well as in the vernacular even before Petrarca made Latin bucolic one of the primary forms of the new humanistic poetry.

Dionigi da Borgo Sansepolcro may have been lavish in his praise of the exceptional young man he spent time with in Avignon, but no works of significance by this young man circulated in Naples.

For Boccaccio, Petrarca was an author of poems in the vernacular, a few of which he had encountered in the early 1330s, perhaps through Florentine correspondents. In contrast, at the end of decade he read a number of Petrarca's poems, we do not know how many, and they seem to have dazzled him. He encountered the verses while in the process of composing the *Filostrato*.[68]

Troilo, suffering on account of Criseida's long absence, visits the places that had witnessed their love, and when he sees them, abandons himself to disconsolate lamentation. Here are the first two of the six octaves of his lament:

> Quivi rider la vidi lietamente,
> quivi la vidi verso me guardando,
> quivi mi salutò benignamente,
> quivi far festa e quivi star pensosa,
> quivi la vidi a' miei sospir pietosa.
>   Colà istava, quand'ella mi prese
> con gli occhi belli e vaghi con amore;
> colà istava, quand'ella m'accese
> con un sospir di maggior fuoco il core;
> colà istava, quando condiscese
> al mio piacere il donnesco valore;
> colà la vidi altera, e là umile
> mi si mostrò la mia donna gentile.

> *Filos.*, V.54–55

Here I saw her laugh joyfully, here I saw her glancing toward me, here she graciously greeted me, here I saw her rejoice and here stay thoughtful, here I saw her full of pity for my sighs.

There she was when her fair and beautiful eyes captured my love; there she was when she kindled my heart with a sigh of the greatest fire; there she was when through her womanly worth she graciously pleased me; there I saw her disdainful; and there my gentle lady showed herself submissive to me.[69]

In fact, these lines almost rewrite a sonnet Petrarca sent to his friend Sennuccio del Bene:

Sennuccio, i' vo' che sapi in qual manera
tractato sono, et qual vita è la mia:
ardomi et struggo anchor com'io solia;
l'aura mi volve, et son pur quel ch'i' m'era.

Qui tutta humile, et qui la vidi altera,
or aspra, or piana, or dispietata, or pia;
or vestirsi honestate, or leggiadria,
or mansüeta, or disdegnosa et fera.

Qui cantò dolcemente, et qui s'assise;
qui si rivolse, et qui rattenne il passo;
qui co' begli occhi mi trafisse il core;

qui disse una parola, et qui sorrise;
qui cangiò 'l viso. In questi pensier', lasso,
nocte et dì tiemmi il signor nostro Amore.

Francesco Petrarca, *Rvf*, 112

Sennuccio, I want you to know the way
I'm treated and the kind of life I lead:
I burn and suffer as I always have,
caught in the aura, I'm still just what I was.

All humble here, and there I see her haughty,
now harsh then kind, now cruel then merciful,
now clothed in virtue, then lightheartedness,
and now docile, and then fierce and disdainful.

With sweetness she sang here, and here she sat,
here she turned round, and here held back her steps,
here with her lovely eyes she pierced my heart,

here she pronounced a word and here she smiled,
and here she changed expression. In thoughts like these,
alas, our lord Love keeps me day and night.[70]

The connection is certain; the problem is determining the direction of the influence.[71] For this, one must establish which of the two texts was composed first, but the available information does not support a firm conclusion either way. Philology does not lead to any sure answers, but Boccaccio's poem itself suggests another possible path.

Waiting for Criseida's return weakens Troilo spiritually and physically. Sometimes, "tired of grieving" ("stanco di dolersi"), to lift his heart exhausted by such sadness, he begins to sing. And so, after finishing the lamentation modeled on Petrarch's words, he strikes up a song, though no less despairing, of which these are the first two octaves:

> La dolce vista e 'l bel guardo soave
> de' più begli occhi che si vider mai,
> ch'i' ho perduti, fan parer sì grave
> la vita mia, ch'io vo traendo guai;
> ed a tal punto già condotto m'have,
> che 'nvece di sospir leggiadri e gai,
> ch'aver solea, disii porto di morte
> per la partenza, sì me ne duol forte.
>
>   Oh me, Amor, perché nel primo passo
> non mi feristi sì ch'io fosse morto?
> Perché non dipartisti da me, lasso,
> lo spirito angoscioso che io porto,
> per ciò che d'alto mi veggio ora in basso?
> Non è, Amore, al mio dolor conforto
> fuor che 'l morir, trovandomi partuto
> da quei begli occhi ov'io t'ho già veduto.

Filos., V.62–63

The sweet sight and the fair gentle look of the most beautiful eyes that were ever seen, which I have lost, make my life so grievous that I go about heaving sighs. And they have led me to such a point already that, instead of the light and joyous sighs which I used to give, I bear desires for death because of your departure, so strongly does it pain me.

Alas, Love, why at the first step did you not wound me so that I might have died? Why did you not separate from wretched self the anguished spirit which I bear, because I now see myself brought from high to low? There is no comfort, Love, for my sorrow except death when I find myself parted from those beautiful eyes where I have formerly seen you.[72]

Troilo's song, which is five octaves long, in the first four octaves is a replica, a reproduction, of the first five stanzas of the song *La dolce vista e 'l bel guardo soave* by Cino da Pistoia. These are the first two stanzas of Cino's work:

> La dolce vista e 'l bel guardo soave
> de' più begli occhi che lucesser mai,
> c'ho perduto, mi fa parer sì grave
> la vita mia ch'i' vo traendo guai;
>   e 'nvece di pensier' leggiadri e gai
> solea d'Amore,
> porto disir' nel core
> che son nati di morte
> per la partenza, sì me ne duol forte.
>
> Omè, Amor, perché nel primo passo
> non l'assalisti sì ch'io fossi morto?
>   Perché non dipartisti da me, lasso,
> lo spirito angoscioso ch'ïo porto?
>   Amore, al mio dolor non è conforto,
>   anzi, com' io più guardo,
>   a sospirar più m'ardo,
>   trovandomi partuto
>   da que' begli occhi ov'io t'ho già veduto.

> Cino da Pistoia, *Rime*, I (CXI).1–18

The loveliness, the glances soft and clear
Of sweetest eyes that e'er unveiled their glow,
Lost unto me, make this my life appear
So grievous that in heaviness I go;
Instead of the gay thoughts that I used to know,
Because of love for her,
Now at my heart's core stir

Thoughts that of Death are born
By reason of this parting whence I mourn.
            In the beginning, Love, alas, alas,
Why didst not wound me so that I might die?
Why didst not part from me, O Love, alas,
The tortured spirit whereon I rely?
In this my sorrow unconsoled am I:
Indeed, the more I yearn
The more regret doth burn,
Since gone away from me
Are the sweet eyes within I mirrored thee[73]

Troilo mourns his separation from Criseida; the exiled Cino grieves his from his lover Selvaggia: from a narrative point of view the connection is weak. It is true that Boccaccio's is "the most unequivocal and resounding homage ever rendered from one poet to another in the fourteenth century (and perhaps not only the fourteenth century),"[74] but no true narrative necessity required him to pay tribute to Cino side by side with Petrarch. The pairing of these two reworkings seems to resonate with the excitement of recent discovery, as if Florentine couriers had delivered a package that revealed for the first time a treasure trove of vernacular lyric poetry. It is perhaps significant that Cino's *La dolce vista* had left no trace in Boccaccio's writing prior to this sudden appearance.[75]

Who could have conveyed these poems of Petrarch's and Cino's to Boccaccio? In the narrow window from 1339 to 1340 (or 1341 at the latest), Boccaccio came into possession of Latin texts with extremely limited circulation that were associated with the names Dante, Moroello Malaspina, and Cino da Pistoia. It is highly likely that the Florentine Sennuccio del Bene was the conduit. This "White" banker, a lyric poet in his own right, had been exiled at the time of Henry VII's invasion and moved to Avignon; recalled from exile in 1326, he returned to Florence — we do not know exactly when, but likely shortly after his banishment was rescinded — where he died in 1349. Now, Sennuccio had known Dante, was a friend of Cino's, and had connections with the Malaspina. And in Avignon he had also befriended Petrarch, whose primary verse correspondent he became. Considering that Cino's *La dolce vista* was a full-fledged member of the league of rare texts, to the point that Boccaccio's reuse is its only fourteenth-century attestation, and that the sonnet of Petrarch's that Boccaccio rewrote was in fact addressed to Sennuccio, it would not be strange if it was, in fact, he who provided them.[76]

PART II

Maturity
(1341–1360)

5

In His Father's House

"Here One Never Laughs"

Here one never laughs, or rarely; and the house, dark, mute, and exceedingly sad, receives me and keeps me against my will, where the crude and horrible sight of a cold man, rough and miserly, saddens me ever more . . .[1]

> Lì non si ride mai, se non di rado;
> la casa oscura e muta e molto trista
> me ritiene e riceve, mal mio grado; indicated
>   dove la cruda e orribile vista
> d'un vecchio freddo, ruvido e avaro
> ognora con affanno più m'atrista.

CNF, XLIX:76–81

Ameto is about to leave the delightful place where the Florentine nymphs have been telling their stories of love in order to return home. Speaking through this character, Boccaccio voiced his own desperation at finding himself again living in his father's house, and identified his father as "the one responsible for his current suffering."[2] What had happened? We left Giovanni in Naples in

1340, busy studying canon law, looking ahead to receiving a degree and completing his epic poem, and now, in 1341, we find him in Florence, anguished and bitter. A state of mind he revealed behind the veil of literature in the *Comedia della ninfe fiorentine*, but also did not hesitate to broadcast by telling his friends. In a letter of August 28, 1341, to Niccolò Acciaiuoli rejoicing in his friend's safe return to Naples from the Morea, Boccaccio wrote: "About my unwilling presence in Florence I write nothing here, because it would be better shown with tears than with ink" ("Dell'essere mio in Firenze contra piacere niente vi scrivo, però che più tosto co' lagrime che con inchiostro sarebbe da dimostrare," *Ep.*, V.6).[3] It is striking that this last phrase echoes the one he used in his earlier fictitious letter to Petrarca in speaking of his beloved's sudden change of heart: "a subject to be described not with ink but with tears" ("causa non atramento sed lacrimis describenda," *Ep.*, II.6). In the fictive epistle of 1339, he was engaged in fictional autobiography; in the real letter of 1341, he was speaking instead about his own life. One has to wonder if his return to these same words is a sign that a similar knot of pain lay behind two such different texts: as if Boccaccio, perhaps without being fully aware of it, had conflated and condensed into one wound his failure as a writer about love and the disappointment of his hopes for his life.

So what had transpired? There had been no portents of such a drastic change of location and circumstances.

Goodbye, Naples

The departure from Naples is one of the most mysterious episodes in Boccaccio's biography. Something unsaid hangs over it, a sort of self-censorship: although he recounted episodes from his life liberally, Boccaccio never spoke of this one. Something emerges only in his works of fiction. It appears that his departure from Naples was unplanned, caused by an unforeseen event and, above all, involuntary.

Nothing documents his date of departure. Scholars long maintained that Boccaccio was still in Naples in February 1341 when Petrarch arrived to be examined by Robert of Anjou prior to his coronation as poet laureate in Rome, but today it is accepted that

Boccaccio neither attended any of the celebrations at court nor met Petrarch. We can be certain of this for two reasons: first, had it happened, Boccaccio would surely have talked about it often; and second, Petrarch's own words confirm it. Reminiscing in a letter about their first meeting, which took place in Florence in 1350, Petrarch wrote that he had never seen Boccaccio before then.[4] And so, February 1341 is not only a terminus ante quem, or date by which he must have already left the city, but also a strong indication that Boccaccio was forced to go. Since Fra Dionigi was one of the organizers of the of the coronation, he would have known for months that Petrarch was coming to Naples. It is a safe bet that had circumstances beyond his control not prevented it, Boccaccio would have postponed his departure at least until the arrival of his longtime idol. At the other end, for establishing the limit for the latest possible date for his departure, there is testimony from Boccaccio himself that he was not in Florence "during the Plague of 1340" (*ECD*, VI [I].65; "nell'anno pestifero del 1340"). We know from Giovanni Villani's chronicle that in that year the plague epidemic began in March and "lasted . . . until the coming winter" ("durò . . . infino al verno vegnente"),[5] that is, until late autumn.

With these two boundaries in mind, the chronological information contained in a passage of the *Elegia di Madonna Fiammetta* acquires a particular value. In this fictional work written four or five years after Boccaccio's return to Florence, the protagonist, Fiammetta, recalls the first anniversary of the departure from Naples of Panfilo, yet another fictionalized version of the author: "Since the time of Panfilo's departure, the Sun had returned once again to that place in the sky which had been scorched when was recklessly driven by his presumptuous son [Phaeton]" ("Egli era già un'altra volta il sole tornato nella parte del cielo che si cosse allora che male li suoi carri guidò il presuntuoso figliuolo, poi che Panfilo s'era da me partito," *EMF*, VI.2, 1);[6] that is, the sun had again entered the constellation of Scorpio, where it remains between October and November. And then, more straightforward is the fact that, although Boccaccino had paid Prior Scarpa the annual rent for the church property in Capua punctually in November 1338 and 1339, he did not do so in November 1340, delaying it until January of the following year. If, as it seems, there was a dispute between

Boccaccino and Scarpa, the likely reason was that Boccaccino was trying to end the contract early (which he would succeed in doing a year later) because Giovanni had left Naples that fall. In sum, even in the absence of documentary proof, it is almost certain that Boccaccio left Naples in the autumn of 1340.[7]

The problem is understanding why.

Boccaccino's Role

For Giovanni leaving Naples was surely painful and almost certainly forced. The aforementioned *Elegia di Madonna Fiammetta* casts some light on the reasons. In his final farewell to Fiammetta, Panfilo says that he must go "where a compelling need forces me" ("dove necessità strettissima me tira per forza," *EMF*, II.3, 1) and then, asked by his lover to clarify that need, he explains: "Inexorable death, which is the ultimate end of human things, has recently left me the only survivor among my father's several sons; he is old and without a wife, and I am the only one of my brothers left to care for him; he is also without hope of having other children and is calling me back to see him since he has not seen me for several years, and to be of comfort to him" ("La inevitabile morte, ultimo fine delle cose nostre, di più figliuoli nuovamente me solo ha lasciato al padre mio, il quale, d'anni pieno e sanza sposa, solo d'alcuno fratello, sollecito a' suoi conforti, rimaso, sanza speranza alcuna di più averne, me a consolazione di lui, il quale egli già sono più anni passati non vide, richiama a rivederlo," *EMF*, II.4, 1–2).[8]

His father appealed to "the filial obedience I owe him" ("debita obedienza filiale," *EMF*, II.4, 2);[9] later, another character will reiterate to Fiammetta that "his father, who had been left with no other sons, called him back home" ("il padre, non essendogli rimaso altro figliuolo, il richiamò a casa sua," *EMF*, V.2, 6).[10] Giovanni's departure, then, was imposed by Boccaccino. Moreover, we saw above, in the lines written in the heat of the moment, when the command (in the guise of emotional blackmail) still stung, how much rancor he harbored toward Boccaccino: "the crude and horrible sight of a cold man, rough and miserly."[11]

If Boccaccio's father made this decision, the question remains why.

The picture of the family in the *Elegia* mirrors the actual situation in Boccaccino's household in 1340. Over the course of a few months, it had been ravaged by a series of losses: his wife Margherita died between October 1339 and June–August 1340; in the late spring or early summer of 1340, so did his mother-in-law, Lippa Portinari; finally, in the latter half of the year he lost his son Francesco, perhaps to the plague. Boccaccino had been left alone, and for this reason it is credible that, "left with no other sons," he had "called back home" Giovanni. Boccaccino had never had any scruples about using both his wife and Francesco as figureheads for his commercial transactions; now, having lost his designated heir, perhaps he was planning to involve Giovanni in his business affairs. Giovanni had gained a certain amount of experience in the Naples branch of the Bardi company, and now, as sole heir, it could be he who helped with his father's business dealings and then, in due course, took charge of the family business. And, indeed, it does seem that in the early days after his return Boccaccio was employed by his father in his business; however, the hypothesis that Boccaccino actually planned to make Giovanni a merchant runs up against the fact that the ample body of archival records concerning Boccaccino does not show that he made Giovanni a partner in any of his financial transactions, as he had with Francesco. Moreover, it should not be forgotten that Boccaccino could rely on the experience and assistance of his brother, Vanni.[12]

Giovanni left Naples at roughly the midpoint of his penultimate (or final, depending on the calculation) academic year. Interrupting his studies must have been a very serious decision, and would have been even if, hypothetically, he had believed it would be only a temporary hiatus. His hopes of freeing himself forever from the despised profession of merchant lay in a degree in canon law. And it is a fact that he never resumed these studies. But even for Boccaccino it must have been a difficult decision: he had a great deal invested, including economically, in his son's legal career, whether ecclesiastic, civil, or both. And then why had Boccaccio abandoned his efforts now, when he was so close to his goal? It is logical to think that he would have done so if a more appealing alternative or, at any rate, one that guaranteed good future earnings had presented itself. But this does not appear to have been the case.

The opening lines of the eclogue *Galla*, the first of the *Buccolicum carmen*, refer to the period of Giovanni's return to Florence. The shepherds Damon and Tindarus, both stand-ins for the author, following his usual practice of doubling and multiplying, are talking together. Damon asks Tindarus, "Would it not have been better to inhabit now the green fields of Vesuvius and tender leafing woods of Gaurus Mountain and draw down streams so pleasing to the flocks, than vainly roam the Arno's sterile plains?" Tindarus responds that indeed, it would have been better, but fate had prevented him, and so he is "obliged to lead Alcestus' bulls to pasture; thus pernicious greed has ordered and commands" (*BC*, I.1–4; 11–13).[13] The metaphor "to lead Alcestus' [i.e., his father's] bulls" means "to manage large amounts of capital," an allusion to "the commercial activities to which Boccaccio had to submit."[14] Alcestus/Boccaccino had ordered him to leave Naples, and had done so out of greed. What Boccaccio means here by "greed" is not entirely clear; it is clear, however, that he had been reduced to collaborating with his father, and therefore that his father had not presented Giovanni with any other alternative to the abandoned legal career.[15]

Boccaccino did not wait long to remedy his marital solitude. About five months after Giovanni's arrival, between March and May 1341, Boccaccino married Bice Bostichi and in the spring of the following year she bore him a new son, Iacopo.[16] So, after just a few months, the filial obligations that held Giovanni in Florence "unwillingly" ("contra piacere," *Ep.*, V.6) had somewhat eased; with the birth of his half brother, they must have entirely disappeared. On the other hand, it is conceivable that his discomfort increased. With this birth Giovanni was reliving the situation of his childhood, forced to live again with a stepmother and displaced for a second time from his position as only child. Old wounds from when his father had pushed him aside must have been reopened. At about the same time that little Iacopo came into the world, Giovanni wrote the *Comedia delle ninfe fiorentine*, in which he introduced a character whose name, Ibrida, alludes "to his illegitimate birth to parents of difference natures and nationalities."[17] Ibrida's grandfather, a peasant, "a plebeian of no fame and of less patrimony" ("uomo plebeio di nulla fama e di meno censo"), with "a crude nymph" ("una rozza ninfa") had had a son who was handsome but identical to his father in his "manners" ("costumi"), who, having devoted himself to commerce, moves to Paris and there seduces a young widow by secretly marrying her. Ibrida is born of their union. But the father then, breaking his vows, marries "another woman in his country" ("un'altra nelle sue parti," *CNF*, XXIII.21–39), hiding that he already has a wife. The gods punish him by condemning to death the father, his second wife, and the children of their marriage. Once the young Ibrida grows up, he devotes himself to poetry, through which he achieves fame. The myths and fantasies of the *Filocolo* had returned, welling up from the most intimate recesses of Boccaccio's heart: myths of revenge and self-gratification, but also fantasies embodying the most unspeakable desires—the death of his father, his stepmother, and his half brothers.

So it would seem that, at least in 1342, Boccaccio could have returned to Naples, resumed his interrupted studies and the friendships he had left behind. Instead, in May of that year, Boccaccino and Scarpa resolved the dispute that had been dividing them for months: Boccaccino resigned himself to paying the rent due for 1341, but in exchange obtained an early termination of the lease, saving the fifth annual payment, and quashing any hopes his son had of returning to Naples in the near future.

Another enigma in this thoroughly mysterious episode is Boccaccio's relations with Naples following his return to Florence. Naples was the city of his dreams, of culture and refined living where he hoped to make a name for himself as a poet. Nostalgia for this lost paradise permeates all the works he composed in Florence during the first half of the 1340s. He had many friends in Naples, and some of them were also quite influential; in the summer of 1341, Niccolò Acciaiuoli had returned to the city, now with even greater power, and Boccaccio was still on good terms with him; nonetheless, it does not seem that Boccaccio asked anyone to help him come back or, if he did ask, that anyone responded. Boccaccio would look for employment opportunities in Romagna but would not set foot in the Kingdom of Naples again until 1355, a good fifteen years after his departure, and even then he did not lay eyes on the capital; he would go to the city of Naples, for a few days, only in 1362, and for the last time between the autumn of 1370 and May 1371. He would never stop thinking about it, identifying it with the happy period of his youth; but for a long time he would have only indirect contact with the actual Naples. It is as if the city were forbidden to him, as if, at least in the first years after his departure, someone or something was keeping him away.

A Literary Sin?

The answers that documents do not provide may be hidden in literature. Let us return, then, to the *Filocolo*, the romance with which this bold young man aspired to conquer both the intellectuals and courtiers of Naples. So bold, not to say reckless, that he presented himself as personally in love with a young lady of high society who was not in fact the offspring of the man whose name she bore, but no less than the daughter of King Robert. Even if the romance was read by few in court circles, we can well imagine the gossip and rumor this particular notion might well have given rise to. When was the last time a book had circulated in Naples, even a work of fiction, that maintained—and not in passing but in plain sight, on the title page, so to speak—that the reigning monarch had an unrecognized and illegitimate daughter who frequented high society? Not a fictional character, but a real person who, according to this story, lived among those for whom the book was written, a young woman, in short, who was one of them. Wouldn't this have set off a race to discover who the mysterious Maria might be? Robert of Anjou, who probably did not even speak an Italian vernacular,[18] would certainly not have read the *Filocolo*, but sooner or later the rumors must have reached his ears: how would he have reacted? More: it is possible that, as the gossip spread, names were named, and that a noble family in the court's ambit was identified as the supposed one of the illegitimate daughter and, as a result, this family became the subject of speculation. In such a case, would they have suffered in silence? In addition, possibly contributing to Robert's sensitivity were, first, the circumstance that in

Naples an unrecognized and illegitimate son, Charles d'Artois, had in fact been attributed to the king, and, second, the particular imprudence of Boccaccio's choice of name for his protagonist, given that the king actually had a daughter named Maria,[19] who was, however, still a child at the time of the *Filocolo* (in 1343 she would marry her cousin Charles of Durazzo).

Giuseppe Billanovich is the only other scholar to have posed similar questions, quite a number of years ago now. He wanted to refute the many nineteenth- and twentieth-century attempts to attribute a real identity to the character Fiammetta and, more broadly, reconstruct Boccaccio's biography on the basis of his literary works. According to Billanovich, the myth of Fiammetta was entirely the product of the author's imagination; as he put it, "Fiammetta was not a creature who suffered on this earth and caused suffering." Although too radical, this was an admirable project at its time: while the many reworkings of her story should indeed be categorized as literary invention, the first Maria, the dedicatee of the *Filocolo* from whom the myth originated, does not seem to have been an entirely fictional character.[20] In order to support his thesis that the entire Fiammetta affair was a "literary fairytale" with no correspondence to reality, Billanovich pointed out precisely the fact that "a love aimed so high and, if true, with the possibility of such great uproar" had apparently not provoked any reaction from either King Robert or "Maria's powerful family": "Boccaccio's revelations of this love, and his dedications and his proems and his conclusions, were too transparent and too repeated: in works immediately and abundantly disseminated (without poison or, more openly, the dagger assailing the author, in the expected revenge)." Further, "How ... imprudent and insulting the revelation of actual secrets about the birth and the dissolute life of this noble lady would have been: for the king, for Maria's powerful family, and for her powerful husband. Indeed, any contemporary of mediocre acuity would have foreseen the risks of such boasts, if they were really applied to real living people, who were actually among the highest in the kingdom." Serious risks if, as this scholar says, they potentially involved being poisoned or stabbed. Billanovich thought that Boccaccio had "sinned out of naivete," that his actions regarding King Robert were driven by "dreamy and spontaneous gallantry" and that this was a "candid homage," but the scholar also believed that Robert and the implicated families had understood all this, and "owing to the medieval propensity toward mythological and traditional etiquette in life and literature," had "forgiven" it.[21] But if, instead of encompassing the fully developed Fiammetta myth, we limit Billanovich's arguments to the *Filocolo* alone, they do not lose their validity: it should be pointed out that while neither Maria's family nor her husband play any part in the story, this does not rule out that the contemporary public may have cast certain families in choice roles.

Can we really assume that the Neapolitan readers of the *Filocolo* and, especially, the ones Boccaccio incorporated into the story, said to themselves that this was just literature? I repeat: when had a sovereign ever found in his hands, or had recounted to him, a tale that began with a resounding panegyric to his dynasty and ended with the revelation of the intimate secrets of his bed chamber? Nonexistent secrets, to be sure, but presented as real. Were Robert and his courtiers really equipped with such literary expertise that they could distinguish between fact and fiction, and, above all, even if they were, could they have been certain that others were making the same distinction? That it would not generate rumors, notoriety?

The annoyance must have been strong and increasing, even threatening. as Boccaccino would have become aware through his contacts. Perhaps it was suggested to him that it would be prudent to remove Giovanni from Naples. In any case, he likely realized that there was no future for his son in the city; the hoped-for ecclesiastical benefice had not and would never come.

This is all speculation. But it is a hypothesis that, on the one hand, fits well with many aspects of the works Boccaccio would write in Florence in the years immediately following his departure from Naples and, particularly, with his treatment of Fiammetta in these works; on the other hand, it sheds fresh light on much Boccaccio wrote in the years just before he left, works centered on the theme of protecting a ladylove's honor and doubts over the propriety of lovers' behavior; and, above all, it explains the disappearance of Fiammetta from his literary works.

A City in Crisis

The Florence that Boccaccio found following his long absence was a city in the throes of economic, political, and institutional crisis. On top of that, in the months preceding his arrival, the city, along with most of Tuscany, had been struck by an epidemic of plague, not as disastrous as the Black Death that would rage in 1348, but still of considerable severity.

The epicenter of the upheavals that rocked Florence for some five years was finance. The Florentine banks' problems had first arisen in the early 1330s, grown worse over the course of the decade, reached a critical level in the early 1340s, and culminated in an impressive chain reaction of failures over a short period of time, which, thanks to the banks' interconnections, involved almost the entire system, from the great international companies, to mid-sized firms, all way down to a significant number of small merchant-bankers: 1344 saw the failure of the Peruzzi and Acciaiuoli companies; early 1346 the collapse of the largest and most powerful of all, the Bardi. Furthermore, in 1343, the Comune was constrained to consolidate its public debt, distributing only 5 percent interest to creditors. A disaster of this magnitude had multiple, overlapping causes: the effects of the companies' rash credit policies were amplified by international events and governmental shortsightedness. Fundamental, however, was the absence of governmental checks on the operations of the banking companies, the largest of which, in fact, had the power to influence the government, as well as the fact that these companies habitually used unsecured deposits for their financial activities and for loans, including exceptionally large ones, to European states and sovereigns. Specifically, at the end of the 1330s their exposure was enormous with regard to Edward III of England, who had begun the so-called Hundred Years' War against Philip VI of Valois in 1337.[22] It is a common misperception, created by Giovanni Villani to hide his own responsibility and that of the company of the Buonaccorsi of which he was one of the senior directors, that what set off the financial collapse was Edward III's decision not to repay his debts.[23] In fact, the Italian bankers were the only ones to whom Edward did not suspend payments, and, indeed, he served as guarantor for their debts.[24] What triggered the crisis was the spreading distrust of large depositors, including the Apostolic Camera (the papal treasury), in the face of the banks' increasing exposure both abroad and to Florentine municipal finances, and thus their ever more frequent requests to withdraw their deposits.

A part of the picture was the shortsightedness of the oligarchic government of the time, that of the so-called *popolo grasso*, or members of the major guilds, a government that excluded, on the one hand, the magnates (aristocrats) and, on the other, the *popolo minuto*, members of the minor guilds.[25] In pursuit of a policy of regional expansion, in August 1341, the Florentines, evidently not understanding the gravity of their city's situation, at the conclusion of a complex affair that had included a minor military confrontation, acquired the nearby commune of Lucca from Mastino della Scala with an agreement to pay the conspicuous sum of 250,000 florins (a "mad purchase,"[26] according to Villani).[27] The Pisans, however, besieged Lucca and occupied it while it was still under Scaliger control. War became inevitable (which would end in a great humiliation for the Florentines July 6, 1342). As they were accustomed to doing when finding themselves in a critical situation, the Florentines turned to the Angevins for aid, but King Robert hesitated for so long that in the spring of 1342 Florence appeared inclined to abandon this traditional alliance and seek Ghibelline help, Emperor Louis IV of the House of Wittelsbach. The temptation quickly passed, but the possibility that Florence would change its international position so radically was one of the factors that exacerbated the crisis of depositor confidence.

The spark that appears to have transformed the many existing individual fires of crisis into one unstoppable conflagration seems to have been the sudden flight from Naples in the early morning hours of June 17, 1342, of all the partners and factors in the Buonaccorsi company office (the company would fail in November). That company, of which the Villani brothers were important partners, was of only middling size, but the Kingdom of Naples was its most important commercial center, and there it was the equal of the Peruzzi, Bardi, and Acciaiuoli. The Buonaccorsi appear to have acted unscrupulously, attempting to salvage what they could for themselves. This set off a wave of repayment requests by nobles, ecclesiastics, and Neapolitan financiers, dramatically swelling the already headlong rush of creditors, Florentine and otherwise.

It was now clear that it would be difficult for the banks to save themselves: their only chance, especially for those operating in international markets, was to buy enough time to pursue a moratorium on debt repayments from the government and recovery of large claims against the Comune itself as well as foreign governments.

Under these conditions, the internal political situation could only have been very tense and confused. The irreconcilable demands of the companies, the aristocrats who were excluded from government, the pope, and other states supporting their subjects' requests rained down on the city's government. The government had already foiled a conspiracy on All Saints' Day 1340, which had been hatched by the Bardi and Frescobaldi with unclear aims: perhaps, more than an aristocratic conspiracy, it was one inspired by banking groups with the goal of altering the government's timid, not to say absent, credit sector policies. The most impatient appear to have been the Bardi, not surprisingly, the most exposed to the market crisis.[28]

The turning point came during the spring and early summer of 1342, when, following the restoration of the good relationship between Florence and Robert of Anjou, the king sent the Frenchman Walter of Brienne, nominally Duke of Athens and married to one of Robert's nieces, Margherita, to support the Florentine military effort in the war against Lucca.[29] A few months later, on September 8, the Florentines named Walter as *signore*, or lord, for life: an institutional revolution that was strongly supported by the great banking houses, foremost among them the Bardi and Acciaiuoli, and the magnate families, while also not disliked by the popular classes. The magnates' goal was the abrogation of the Ordinances of Justice, which forbade their participation in the government; the banking companies, many of which were, moreover, both owned and run by aristocratic families, hoped that a "strong" regime could help them, if not survive, then limit their damage. With a large number of companies already bankrupt, many others having ceased operations and on the verge of bankruptcy, and still others nearing the brink, the situation had become critical. To the banks' problem of obtaining an extension on repaying deposits and an acceleration of recovering claims was added that of selecting which creditors to repay. The great companies calculated that Walter, partly thanks to his Neapolitan connections, would be able to reassure southern creditors by offering them preferential treatment, but the other, smaller, companies who constituted the majority aimed to redirect repayments in favor of Florentines. In any case, everyone's goal was to buy time in order to shelter as much real estate as possible either through fictive sales or by conferring nominal possession on individuals (such as widows) or religious entities not subject to expropriation.[30] None of these hopes would be fulfilled.

Brienne could not satisfy the great companies' demands, and so the alliance of oligarchs and magnates that had brought him to power turned against him, the Bardi leading the way. Brienne, also weakened by the death of the king of Naples at the beginning of 1343, then relied ever more heavily on the support of the popular classes, enacting numerous measures in their favor (for example, allowing the wool workers to organize their own association, which had been strenuously denied up until then). In the space of a few months, however, helped by a few ostentatious displays of signorial power and, it seems, blatant private use of public funds, his opponents succeeded in inciting the populace to revolt (July 26, 1343). In the ensuing political and institutional chaos, the alliance of magnates and major guilds (especially the banking companies), which had first supported the duke's ascent and then plotted his fall, sought to intervene to pass anti-popular and pro-magnate provisions: a sort of provisional government was appointed, headed by Bishop Angelo Acciaiuoli, Niccolò's cousin, and charged with drafting the reforms and coming to an agreement with Brienne, who was barricaded inside the Palazzo della Signoria, the seat of government (he would be forced to leave the city at the beginning of August). But the reform proposals provoked further popular rebellion. The Ordinances of Justice were not abrogated, and, instead, a "popular" regime was installed in Florence that called for the participation in the city's government of all twenty-one guilds, not just the six major ones as in the past.

Public offices and executive positions, including the priorate (the chief magistracy), were shared with the *popolo minuto*, the "little" people: artisans, small traders, brokers, shopkeepers, secondhand dealers, new men ("novi cives"), who had never before had roles in city politics and now confronted the traditional ruling classes from within.

In the Bardi's Circle

Boccaccio was only a spectator to these dramatic events. It has been said that "Boccaccio did not have precise political ideas. He did not develop any of his own principles, but instead reflected the circumstances of his own lived experiences and, even more, his social environment."[31] We have almost no information about what he did and thought during his first five years back in Florence; it is plausible, however, that he viewed events through his father's eyes and judged them from his father's perspective. It does not appear that Boccaccino was involved in the "great conspiracy"[32] of the autumn of 1340. But this attempt to overturn the citizen government was inspired and led above all by the Bardi, and Boccaccino was connected to the Bardi, as well as to the Rossi family, also among the conspiracy's organizers. Even if he did not play an active role, he must have been a supporter. Giovanni was almost certainly not yet in Florence at the time the conspiracy took place, but when he did arrive, his political sympathies would be no different from his father's. The protagonist in the *Elegia di Madonna Fiammetta*, in trying to convince Panfilo not to leave, contrasts the political and social situation in Florence, "full of pompous talk and cowardly deeds, ruled not by a number of laws but by as many opinions as there are men, torn by strife and war within and without, and turbulent and filled with haughty, avaricious, and envious people and with innumerable troubles; and all these things are ill-suited to your spirit" ("piena di voci pompose e di pusillanimi fatti, serva non a mille leggi, ma a tanti pareri quanti v'ha uomini, e tutta in arme e in guerra così cittadina come forestiera fremisce, di superba avara e invidiosa gente fornita: cose tutte male all'animo tuo conformi"), with the situation in Naples, which she knows is "very

pleasing" ("gradita") to Panfilo: "joyful, peaceful, rich, magnifi-
cent, and under a single ruler" ("lieta, pacifica, abondevole, mag-
nifica e sotto ad uno solo re," *EMF*, II.6, 20–21).[33] The *Elegia*, whose
dating is uncertain, recounts a story that unfolds over the course
of about two years beginning with Panfilo-Boccaccio's departure
from Naples: so with Fiammetta's words the author could be referring either to the situation before the "tyranny" of the Duke of
Athens, since at that time there were no longer "as many opinions
as there are men," or projecting back in time (regardless of the
fact that even in Naples with the death of Robert at the beginning
of 1343 the steady rule of one sovereign had collapsed) the disor-
dered "democratic" situation created by the popular government
the followed the duke's ouster.[34] In any case, these are statements
that would have found approval perhaps from Boccaccino and certainly from members of the oligarchy like the Bardi, who had tenaciously set their sights on the political solution of a "strong" man.

Boccaccio was connected to the Bardi both through his father
and by his own long-standing friendship with Niccolò Acciaiuoli.
For this reason, the episode of the rise and fall of the Duke of Athens probably caused him to feel significant awkwardness: while
the Acciaiuoli family had indeed been among "the great" who supported the seizure of power, during the crisis and crash, despite
the presence of Bishop Angelo among the opposition, they had be-
haved rather deviously, seeking to steer a middle course between
the Florentine alliances and their own interest in not antagonizing
the Angevins. Niccolò's prominent role in the Kingdom of Naples
would have been put in serious jeopardy by a stance of direct confrontation with its rulers.[35] Although he had personally witnessed
the events related to the Duke of Athens, moreover from a vantage
point close to the main actors, Boccaccio would say nothing about
them for many years. It would not be until after Walter's death in
the Battle of Poitiers in September 1356, when Boccaccio added
his profile to the *De casibus virorum illustrium* (*The Downfall of
the Famous*), at the end of this gallery of famous people (men and
women) who having reached the greatest heights had fallen either
by the hand of God or of Fate.[36] It would be a hostile and disparaging portrait of Brienne, as well as highly critical of the magnates
who had conspired against the liberty of Florence and subjected

it to tyranny. But that would be another era: by then Boccaccio's friendship with Niccolò Acciaiuoli would have long soured.

In His Father's Shadow

In Florence, Boccaccio remained a private citizen for almost a decade. While Boccaccino held public offices until the day he died,[37] for the city government and professional associations, Giovanni did not exist: he was just his father's son. He had been absent from Florence since the age of fourteen and so did not have his own group of friends in the city: it is thus presumable that, at least during the first few years after his return, his social relationships remained within his father's circle.

In the Florence of the time, interpersonal relations largely depended not only on kinship, but also on proximity, common territorial origin for immigrant families, and residence within the city: the *quartiere* (quarter), the *gonfalone* (literally "banner," a subdivision of the quarter, perhaps best translated as "ward"), the parish, or *popolo*. The *vicinìa* (neighborhood), an institution recognized socially but not legally regulated, covered the territory of a *gonfalone* and had great importance in determining political, economic, matrimonial, and friendship bonds.[38]

The Boccacci lived in the quarter of Santo Spirito, the *gonfalone*, or ward, of Nicchio, and parish of Santa Felicita. Santo Spirito was the residence of magnate and high-ranking common families and clans who were primarily active in the banking sector, like the Bardi, Frescobaldi, Rossi, and Canigiani, families who made up the principal nucleus of the aristocratic movement that we have seen was involved in the plot of 1340, first supporting the Duke of Athens and then opposing the popular regime. Some families, like the Rossi, residents of Santa Felicita, were neighbors of the Boccacci. Their network of relationships with the Certaldesi, both those still living in the village and those who had emigrated to the city, was also extensive and solid. Because these were relationships between families, they were enduring, passing from one generation to the next. Giovanni shared them with his father and then, at least in part, inherited them.[39] Some of these bonds of acquaintanceship would develop over time into friendships (for example, with Pino de' Rossi), but, at least in the years immediately after his return home, for Giovanni *vicinìa* connections or those from his quarter did not become true friendships. One senses that he was a man essentially alone.

Boccaccio described as his "only friend" the dedicatee of the first literary work he wrote in Florence, the *Comedia delle ninfe fiorentine*:

> And you, my only friend, and the truest example of real friend-ship, Niccolò di Bartolo del Buono di Firenze . . . take this rose, born among the thorns of my adversities, which the Florentine beauty wrenched from the rigid thistles while I dwelled in deep-est gloom.[40]

> E tu, o solo amico, e di vera amistà veracissimo essemplo, o Niccolò di Bartolo del Buono di Firenze . . . prendi questa rosa, tra le spine della mia avversità nata, la quale a forza fuori de' rigidi pruni tirò la fiorentina bellezza, me nell'infimo stante delle tristizie. (*CNF*, L.3)

It is a pained, almost resigned, dedication that was penned shortly after the bitter portrait of his father and bleak description of his house. The dedication of a man who does not have friendly people to confide in. The dedicatee's identity is revealing. Niccolò del Buono lived in Santo Spirito, in the parish of San Jacopo, ad-jacent to the Boccaccio family's parish of Santa Felicita, but his friendship with Giovanni—and this the revealing point—had be-gun a few years earlier in Naples, where Del Buono had been a fac-tor for the Peruzzi company from 1336 to 1339.[41] In short, in 1341–42, Boccaccio's Neapolitan bonds, if not his only ones, were still the ones that mattered to him. Among these should be included his connection to Pietro, or Piero, Canigiani, his close friend in Naples, who returned to Florence around 1340.[42]

Niccolò Acciaiuoli's arrival in Florence in November 1341 must have provided temporary solace for Boccaccio, who was isolated, without employment or other autonomous activity, and fractious: only a few months earlier he had written Niccolò a letter that was cry of pain and also perhaps an implicit plea for help.[43] Niccolò came to Florence as part of an embassy sent by Robert of Anjou in response to the request for aid in the thorny situation with Lucca, but in addition to this, Niccolò was interested in resolving other problems that more directly touched his family, such as regaining Prato, which had been taken from their control after the death of the head of the family firm, Acciaiuolo Acciaiuoli, who had ruled the city with the title of vicar. Niccolò also intended to carry out his long-cherished project of founding a Carthusian monastery: a way to celebrate himself and the power of his family in the eyes of both the Florentines and Neapolitans. The act of foundation for the monastery, which would be built on Monte Acuto in the town of Galuzzo, was drafted at the beginning of February 1342.[44]

Niccolò and Giovanni met and they spoke. Relations between the two were friendly, so much so that Niccolò would make Boccaccio one of the agents responsible for conveying the assets for the future monastery to its prior. We do not know if during their meetings Boccaccio asked Acciaiuoli to help him return to Naples, perhaps by giving him a paid office: if Boccaccio did ask, however, he did not receive anything.

Readers of Dante and Friends of Petrarch

The first two works Boccaccio composed after his return home, the *Comedia delle ninfe fiorentine* and the *Amorosa visione*, are prosimetra (works composed of alternating prose and verse sections) just like the *Vita Nova* and the terza rima *Commedia*. Dante had been Boccaccio's idol since his youth, but the cultural air Boccaccio breathed in Florence increased his regard even more. Florence in the 1330s and 1340s was a hotbed of Dante studies. Dante's son Iacopo had moved back in 1325 following the official reversal of his banishment in October; between 1330 and 1331, Forese Donati, parish priest of Santo Stefano in Botena, prepared a sort of "edition" of the *Commedia*; in the mid-1330s an anonymous author produced a systematic commentary on all three books of the *Commedia*, known as the *Ottimo Commento* (*Excellent Commentary*); between 1341 and 1343, the notary Andrea Lancia also commented on the *Commedia*; sometime before 1341, the banker and chronicler Giovanni Villani, who owned a complete codex of the poem even before 1330, wrote the first ever biographical profile of Dante. Since these Dante enthusiasts were connected with each other—and some of them with Boccaccio as well—we can safely assume that they exchanged both information and books. It is thus likely that Boccaccio read Dante's *De vulgari eloquentia*—conceivably made known to him by Iacopo Alighieri—in time to echo it in the *Teseida*,[45] which he was completing in the period immediately after his arrival in Florence.[46] The linguistic treatise does not seem to have particularly impressed him, however: the only sign he had read it is the boast that with his poem he remedied the lack of vernacular epic works Dante had decried. What excited Boccaccio were not his discoveries in Florence in 1341, but the ones of a few months earlier, very likely when he was still in Naples: Dante's eclogues. Reading these bucolic poems must have dazzled him: he grasped their extraordinary originality and began to wonder how Dante had managed to write a vernacular bucolic poetry that brought back to life this genre that Virgil had made famous but that had then spent centuries in obscurity. In fact, Boccaccio's *Comedia delle ninfe fiorentine* is an "original 'pastoral tale,'" an "early effort to transpose Latin eclogue into the vernacular."[47] It is also possible that concurrently with this, and thus a few years before he would dedicate himself systematically to bucolic poetry in Latin, Boccaccio wrote what would become the first eclogue of the *Buccolicum carmen*, which begins by referring to his return to his father's house.[48]

Another member of the Neapolitan embassy to Florence in 1341 was Giovanni Barrili, a prominent court official and, more importantly, one of Boccaccio's closest friends. Boccaccio and Barrili had much to talk about, and in particular they discussed—likely along with Sennuccio—the great event of the spring in Naples and Rome that Boccaccio had missed: the crowning of Francesco Petrarca with poetic laurels on the Campidoglio on April 8, following his "examination" by Robert of Anjou in Naples in March. In Naples, Barrili had forged a friendship with Petrarch that would grow deeper over the course of the rest of his life. Barrili had not only attended the meetings between the king and candidate (along with Barbato da Sulmona, another of Boccaccio's friends and later Petrarch's), but had been delegated by Robert as the king's representative to place the laurel crown on Petrarch's head in Robert's name at the ceremony (Robert, unfortunately, failed to arrive in time, having been the victim of an ambush in the town of Anagni a few days earlier). It is likely that in Florence Barilli introduced Boccaccio to some of Petrarca's writing, particularly his address from the coronation in Rome, but more than anything else Barilli must also have rekindled Boccaccio's excitement about the poet, which Dionigi di Borgo Sansepolcro had earlier inspired.[49]

Between 1341 and 1342, therefore immediately after these encounters, Boccaccio turned to Petrarca with renewed attention: he transcribed into the *Zibaldone Laurenziano* what few of Petrarca's Latin poems he had been able to get a hold of and, most importantly, sketched out a biography, *De vita et moribus Domini Francisci Petracchi de Florentia* (*On the Life and Mores of Messer Francesco Petrarca of Florence*), to which he would return with additions and revisions over the course of the decade.[50] It is a biography not only "conspicuously devoid of concrete data"[51] and yet full of errors, but that, above all, reveals a remarkably poor knowledge of his subject's works. Nonetheless, the text is still of great interest because, in speaking about Petrarch, Boccaccio also spoke about himself. Indeed, at many points, implicitly but openly, he established parallels between events of his own life and those of his great idol's.

This is evident in Boccaccio's account of the conflict between Petrarch, determined to follow his poetic calling, and his father, intent on forcing him to study law. As Petrarch applied himself to the study of civil law in Bologna, Apollo began to beguile him with his song;

> when, however, through the reports of many, his father came to know about it . . . because he aspired more to material rewards than to eternal glory . . . he was angry with his son and called him back home; and after reprimanding him in various ways for such interests, and saying to him, "Why are you studying a useless subject? Not even the Meonides [Homer] left behind wealth," he immediately sent his son to Montpellier with strict orders to study law again. But, at the bidding of fate, which is not easy to resist, the noble chorus of the Pierides [Muses] took him in their unbreakable embrace, and, indignant that the one they had raised from infancy, and whose glittering fame they preserved, should be led

astray by the abhorrent intricacies of the law and the deafening
quarrels of the rabid court, indignantly seized the laws of the Cae-
sars and the tablets of the jurists from him.[52]

The Muses distracted Petrarch from his legal studies, "putting
before his eyes" examples of great men of the past—Homer, Terence, Virgil, Horace, Statius, Juvenal—and it was thus that "unbeknownst to his father, he gave himself over to poetry."[53]

Now, we know that things did not actually happen that way,
either for Petrarch or for Boccaccio; but we also know that prior
to this, Boccaccio, identifying himself with his imaginary friend
forced to pursue "sacred studies" in secret, had recounted his own
journey of liberation.[54] But the anger at his own father that colors Boccaccio's portrayal of this period of Petrarch's life dates to
shortly after his forced return to Florence, a time when his resentment for having been made to leave Naples exploded, almost violently, in the final pages of the *Comedia della ninfe fiorentine*, and
these feelings would not endure. Already in his next work, the *Amorosa visione*, the scene of the father who scrabbles uselessly with
his fingernails at the mountain of riches is imbued with understanding and affection. More nuanced but equally clear is another
autobiographical projection, regarding the "lust" that "harassed"
Petrarch:

> A very scrupulous Christian, to such an extent that it could
> scarcely be believed except by experience and knowledge of him.
> Only by lust was he, not to say completely conquered, but rather
> much harassed; but whenever he surrendered to it, in accord with
> the precept of the Apostle, what he could not do chastely, he at
> least did cautiously.[55] (*VP*, 26)

What surrender to lust is Boccaccio talking about? What did
he know about Petrarch's private life? Had he been told that Petrarch had fathered a son, Giovanni, born in 1337? This could well
be the case.[56] And then, accepting as authentic the well-known
saying "si non caste tamen caute" ("if not chastely at least cautiously"), which the apostle Paul had not actually said, or at least
not in those words, but had originally been a play on words (caste/

caute = chastely/cautiously) in the early Middle Ages, which had spread until it became something of a recognized tenet justifying the sinful sexual conduct of the clergy, Boccaccio here justifies the surrender of the flesh of a man who had taken holy orders: "And in order to better avoid the anxieties of worldly things, he took on the life and state of a cleric" (*VP*, 19).[57] Even if we do assume that Boccaccio knew about his subject's private life, the question would remain, what circumspection of Petrarca's had been publicly revealed? In fact, however, Boccaccio was not talking about Petrarca's sex life, but about his love poetry. The issue was how must a poet who is also a cleric treat eros? The answer: allegorically. Indeed, the passage above continues:

> And although in a great number of his splendidly written vernacular poems he declares he loved a certain Lauretta with great passion, that does not negate my statement; for, as I myself thoroughly believe, I think that this Lauretta should be understood allegorically for the laurel [*laurea*] wreath which he later received.[58] (*VP*, 26)

The autobiographical implications of this reference to Petrarca's clerical state are obvious: Boccaccio too had taken holy orders. However, although more covertly, the points regarding lyric poetry also had personal implications for him: indeed, the very fact that Boccaccio saw himself in them seems to have been the inspiration. He too was a cleric who wrote about love. During precisely this period, he either was in the process of writing or had just finished a series of tales of seduction in the *Comedia delle ninfe fiorentine*, tales narrated, what's more, by the female characters themselves, in which the sexual urges, advances, and physicality of the encounters were depicted with a realism he had never before attempted. Yet Boccaccio thought he was justified, that he was acting appropriately "cautiously" like Petrarch, precisely because, like Petrarch, he clothed his tales in moral allegory. However, he, who was already as a young man a very scrupulous Christian (and would become obsessively scrupulous as an old one), must have had some doubts, for in the final dedication to Niccolò del Buono he entrusted the judgment of his work's ethical correctness to the

"Most Holy Roman Church" (*CNF*, L.6; "Sacratissima Chiesa di Roma").[59] These autobiographical elements also fit the period of the composition of the *De vita*, not long after Petrarca's coronation as poet laureate.[60]

Neither Chaste nor Cautious

Upon his arrival back in Florence, Boccaccio was not yet thirty years old and unmarried. His clerical state prohibited taking a wife. Later, after he had gotten to know Petrarch, and in accord with the older author, he would engage in a sustained attack on marriage: the bond prevents intellectuals from dedicating themselves to study with a mind unencumbered by worry, distraction, and deviant thoughts. About a decade after writing Petrarch's biography, he would write Dante's, the so-called *Trattatello in laude di Dante* (*Little Treatise in Praise of Dante*).[61] In this, after recounting how Dante's relatives had convinced him to marry in order to recover from his dejection following Beatrice's death, Boccaccio disgorges an extensive list of the troubles, tribulations, and woes that conjugal life produces, concluding that "if the things I have said above are true . . . we can imagine the many sorrows that remain hidden inside private chambers, which, from the outside, are believed to be delights by those whose eyes are not sharp enough to pierce the walls" ("se le cose che di sopra son dette son vere . . . possiamo pensare quanti dolori nascondano le camere, li quali di fuori, da chi non ha occhi la cui perspicacità trapassi le mura, son reputati diletti," *TLD*, [I].57). His tirade also intends to decry the great difficulties that married life brought to Dante's intellectual work, but in this it seems to go too far, and leaves the impression that Boccaccio was really objecting to marriage itself.

One gets the feeling from many passages in his writing that the topic of marriage touched him personally, not only as a cleric or writer, but also more deeply, as a man. A good example is a letter from much later, 1365, in which Boccaccio wrote to one of his closest friends, Donato Albanzani, about a number of personal matters. One of these was that Boccaccio had agreed to his detested half brother Iacopo's request to take Iacopo and Iacopo's recently acquired second wife into his house. This cohabitation,

Boccaccio said, was ruining his old age, he considered it almost a form of divine punishment: the two brothers were too different. Among other things, he wrote, "I am single, he is married" (*EpA*, 64). More than anything else, this seems to be the selfish outburst of a prematurely aged fifty-year-old who has had his routine disrupted and his equilibrium threatened.[62] Yet, in Boccaccio's rancor and bitterness, one senses an undercurrent of envy for what his brother has and regret that he himself never would. His thoughts traveled to his daughter who had died as a little girl—we will speak of her shortly—and he wrote: "Alas, God took away my daughter, that I might take another's into my keeping, and while that one was to have been my joy, this one, I foresee, will be my distress" (*EpA*, 75).[63] This cleric seems to have wanted to have his own family, but fate had forced him to live with the families of others, first with Boccaccino's and then with Iacopo's. In this case, living with a young couple in a small house ("domuncula") would have also brought with it other, more serious turmoil: "Moreover, with what thoughts do you imagine one rushing toward death can watch girlish games? Listen to brazen yowling? Witness behavior steeped in wantonness?" (*EpA*, 69).[64] Such a spectacle might rouse sinful desires, "the devil's weapons." Desires a married man might gratify freely, but that a cleric-intellectual must guard against, particularly a cleric-intellectual for whom as a youth "women's kisses were sweet" (*EpA*, 39).[65]

It is indisputable that, as a young man caught up in the social whirl of Naples, Boccaccio had enjoyed women's kisses; all his literary works of that time centered on love affairs and were addressed to a female audience. And right from the start, Boccaccio was developing the theory that love alone confers true humanity. We have no information about any of his actual romantic experiences, but it is very likely that a kernel of truth lay behind some of the many tales of passion, happy and unhappy, spread across his fiction. Back in Florence, Boccaccio had by no means changed his ideas about love as essential to full human development, yet it is difficult to find details identifiable with a specific person in any of the characters in the amorous adventures that continued to be common in his works of this period. Emilia in the *Comedia delle ninfe fiorentine* might be an exception.

Like the other six nymphs in this prosimetrum, Emilia is an allegorical character, but she is depicted with "realistic" traits that seem to refer to a person who actually existed:[66] born into a family involved in the wool industry, educated in a convent, she contracted a bad marriage to a man named Giovanni, and made Ibrida—who we already know is among the most obvious of the autobiographical characters in Boccaccio's fiction—fall in love with her. Since a woman named Emilia with many of these same traits recurs in his literary works of 1341–43, and since from these various appearances emerges with certainty the portrait of a Florentine lady renowned for her beauty who was named Emilia or Emiliana Tornaquinci, wife of the spice merchant Giovanni di Nello, it has been suspected, with some foundation, that Boccaccio fell in love soon after his return home.[67]

Whether real or not, this would have been a love suitable for literary transformation. Whereas events from his life that clearly revealed surrender to lust were never permitted to enter the literature.

With one important exception, however. As has been mentioned, Boccaccio had fathered a daughter. She was named Violante and she died in the autumn of 1355, when she was about seven.[68] In his old age, Boccaccio would dedicate a moving Latin eclogue to her,[69] which is both one of the most beautiful pieces he ever wrote, and also extraordinarily innovative: this poem marks the first time that domestic affection, in violation of the prohibitions of medieval poetics, broke through into a literary creation.

> It is almost dawn, Silvius (Boccaccio), restless and sorrowful, cannot sleep, the dog Lycus is whimpering. Silvius sends a servant outside to see what is disturbing the dog, and he returns crying that the forest is on fire and the flames are threatening the house. Silvius rushes out, but realizes it is not a fire producing the glow but a luminous ghost: his daughter Olympia (Violante),[70] come from heaven to console him. The last time he had seen her she was five and a half; now, although little time has passed, she is a woman ready for marriage.[71] Olympia is not alone; with her are her brothers, Marius and Iulus, and her sisters, all dead before

her. Silvius has difficulty recognizing his sons: their cheeks are shadowed by beards. In heaven, Olympia says, she has also found Asylas (Boccaccino). Asylas deserves to be there, Silvius exclaims, "he was gentle and a bright example of ancient faith" (*BC*, XIV.228–29).[72] "But . . . did he recognize you?" he then asks. "Indeed he did," responds his daughter, "Rejoicing he threw his arms about my neck, and after glad embraces and a hundred fond kisses on my brow, . . . he said, 'You have come, our Silvius' dearest offspring!'" and then she adds that he called her "my grandchild" (*BC*, XIV.230–33).[73]

It has been said that in this eclogue Boccaccio is documenting the existence of his family.[74] Of his potential family, we might add, and in any case a family that had been completely wiped out by the time this eclogue was written.[75] Violante/Olympia, thus, was born around the end of the 1340s: she was probably conceived in Ravenna in 1347—during her father's first sojourn in Romagna— and born in 1348, when Boccaccio was in Forlì or perhaps already back in Florence. She apparently continued living in Ravenna, where the physician Guglielmo da Ravenna and Donato Albanzani knew her.[76] Less credible is the hypothesis that Boccaccio took Violante with him to Florence quite young and raised her there in his house; this hypothesis, in fact, requires that her grandfather Boccaccino, who died before April 16, 1349, had actually been able to see her.[77] And it also cannot be taken as proof of this that Boccaccio says in the eclogue that a woman named Fusca, who can be identified as his faithful housekeeper Bruna di Ciango da Montemagno, was the one who sent news of his daughter's death to him while he was en route to Naples: because Boccaccio was traveling, the people in Ravenna, not knowing where to find him, sent the sad news to his house in Florence and from there Bruna forwarded it to her master.[78] Given the detail of their beards, his sons Mario and Iulio must have been at least a few years older than Violante; her sisters are unnamed, perhaps because they died at or very soon after birth before they were given names. In short, it is almost certain that Boccaccio began to father illegitimate children around the mid-1340s. Embarking on the difficult and uncertain path of renouncing carnal pleasures would have to wait until after he met Petrarca in the early 1350s, that is, until Petrarch began "acting as Boccaccio's spiritual director in matters of love and sexuality."[79]

Between Allegory and Autobiography

During these five years of uninterrupted residence in Florence, Boccaccio did not have a defined job, did not participate in the political and administrative life of the city, had no role in the guild system, did not enjoy a social life comparable to the one he had enjoyed so much in Naples. For five years he wrote. He finished the *Teseida*, composed the *Comedia delle ninfe fiorentine*, the *Amorosa visione*, the *Elegia di Madonna Fiammetta*, and the *Ninfale fiesolano*, as well as some lyric poems in the vernacular. An outpouring of creativity that seems almost like compensation. With the exception of a few Latin works—the *Canaria*, the biography of Petrarca, maybe some initial drafts of eclogues—they were all in the vernacular and, except for the few lyric poems, all narratives. After 1345, his only vernacular works would be the *Decameron*, the *Corbaccio*, and a few more lyric poems; in other words, 80 percent of Boccaccio's vernacular narrative fiction production was concentrated in the span of a little less than a decade, with a notable clustering in precisely the period he was living in his father's house.[80] We would search in vain for any trace of contemporary events in this writing, even the dramatic events taking place in Florence at that time: "it was the private, not the social that concerned him";[81] like the Neapolitan works before them, these also focus on themes of love. It feels as if Boccaccio was looking backward: to Naples, to the experiences he had there, to the myths created then, to the creative consciousness formed at that time. But we know how strongly he was influenced by his environment, how he constantly sought to align himself with his day-to-day surroundings, and therefore also worked to tailor his writing to what he believed to be the expectations of the audience near at hand. Hence, under the influence of the female, Naples and Florence end up amalgamating into an imaginary dimension that transcends geographic distance and the nature of the author's daily experience.

This appears with particular clarity in his first two Florentine works: the *Comedia delle ninfe fiorentine* and the *Amorosa visione*. Although these are two profoundly different literary objects—the ever-experimental Boccaccio never repeated the same compositional scheme—they share an allegorical framework infused with a strong autobiographical tension. Beginning with the *Filocolo*, the narrator Boccaccio had ceased speaking about himself, or about episodes from his own life, either real or imaginary, and from then on projected himself onto one or more fictional characters. Moralizing allegory and autobiography mapped directly onto one another: that which the text presents as contingent, the characters' adventures and the author's self-representation, the allegory elevates to the level of universal discourse; and at the same time, the allegory justifies the presence of the contingent by giving it a second, higher meaning. In short, allegory provided the author with an alibi for his own more-or-less veiled intrusions into the story.

The *Comedia*, as already noted, is a prosimetrum: a text in prose that incorporates nineteen passages in terza rima verse. It tells the story of the initiatory journey of Ameto, an uncouth and boorish shepherd, not without autobiographical traits, who lives near Florence between the Arno and Mugnone rivers. The bucolic setting, the nature of the protagonist, as well as certain stylistic motifs make the *Comedia* an "allegorical-pastoral romance,"[82] and this pastoral universe is also one of the elements "that allows the reconstruction . . . of the writer's personal mythology."[83]

> Wandering through the woods, Ameto comes across a group of beautiful nymphs devoted to Venus who are on their way to bathe and listen to the song of a member of their group, Lia. Ameto is seized by a fiery passion for her. At nightfall the company disperses, but from that day forward, Ameto never stops looking for Lia. He finds her again at the feast of Venus. During the celebration Lia proposes to her six companions and Ameto that they gather around a fountain underneath a laurel tree and each nymph take a turn telling the story of her amours. Ameto is given the task of setting the rules that the storytellers must follow. Mopsa, Emilia, Adiona, Acrimonia, Agapes, and Fiammetta speak; each nymph "relates her birth and first years of life, then

tells of having married, but then finding love after and outside of marriage through relationships with young men
whom the nymphs have from time to time encouraged and
improved, raising them from their initially flawed state
to a more refined one through love."[84] The last to speak is
Lia, who reveals her love for Ameto and how this love has
changed him. Venus appears, and Ameto is purified in the
water, which enables him to see the goddess and to understand that he has been transformed from "brute animal"
("animale bruto") to "man" ("uomo"). The whole story is
told by a narrator who has been observing the action from
a hiding place off to one side, and who at the end returns
disconsolate to his father's house where he lives.

The nymphs correspond to real people (Lia was the daughter
of Angelo dei Regaletti; Mopsa is Lottiera dei Visdomini; Emilia,
as discussed above, might be Emiliana Tornaquinci; Adiona is
Alionora Gianfigliazzi; Acrimonia may be the Vanna of the *Contento quasi*; Agapes belonged to the Strozzi family) or to already existing characters from Boccaccio's fiction (Fiammetta is the same
in the *Filocolo*), and they would all reappear in the *Amorosa visione*.
Here in the *Comedia*, however, they also have symbolic value: they
represent the four cardinal and three theological virtues (Wisdom,
Justice, Fortitude, Temperance; and Hope, Faith, Charity). The
love stories and the characters' actions taken together trace the allegorical parable of a rough shepherd who, by acquiring the knowledge that love overcomes the sensual instinct, gains consciousness
of his own humanity. Although here weighted with greater moral
meaning, this message is very similar to the one conveyed by the
transformation of animals into human beings in Boccaccio's first
work, the *Caccia di Diana*, and that is communicated again in the
Amorosa visione: "Life that persists without [Love] is worth / neither more nor less than if it were / of a brute animal or deprived of
all sense" ("Vita che sanza lui dura non vale / né più né meno che se
ella fosse / cosa insensata o d'un bruto animale," *AV*, XLII.73–75).[85]
Real women and imaginary women, moral significances and gallant homages, polyphony of tones and coexistence of multiple
genres, a tendency toward exemplarity and personal confession:

the *Comedia delle ninfe fiorentine* is the closest of all Boccaccio's works to the *Filocolo*, yet still differs from it. In the *Comedia*, the conflicts are more distinct, the text's numerous structural levels and the author's too many objectives struggle to come together, to harmonize. We have already observed that the allegorical veil is insufficient to redeem the many detailed and quite risqué descriptions of seduction and lovemaking in the nymphs' stories: in the author's schema, these should be interpreted as representations of the sensual and instinctive eros that Ameto's purificatory journey will raise to spiritualized love; but, in fact, the allegorical invention seems instead to serve as a free pass for an eroticism that—although it might perhaps find some justification in the medieval Platonic philosophical tradition[86]—Boccaccio seems to have been inclined to by nature.[87]

The *Amorosa visione*, a poem in fifty cantos of Dantesque terza rima, grafts moral allegory onto a "vision" genre foundation. The dreamer and storyteller is Boccaccio himself, who for the first time "does not remain on the edges of narrative as spectator . . . or project himself onto one or more characters," but "enters directly onto the stage."[88]

A noblewoman appears to the narrator in a dream and offers herself as his guide for a journey in search of "highest felicity" ("somma felicità"). Together they reach a castle with two gates: one, small and narrow, opens onto the path to virtue; the other, larger one onto the way leading to worldly goods. The narrator chooses to walk through the easier gate. They enter a large, frescoed hall: on the four walls are depicted the Triumphs of Wisdom, Glory, Wealth, and Love. Love is accompanied by a woman as beautiful as an angel who is unknown to the narrator. They pass into the next room, decorated with frescoes illustrating the Triumph of Fortune. Exiting the palace, they find themselves in a splendid garden where they meet nineteen beautiful women: among them is Fiammetta, the same woman who had accompanied Love in the fresco and whom the narrator had not recognized. Fiammetta and the narrator are left alone and, seized by love for each other, are about to satisfy their desire, but, at the very moment when he is about to take her, he wakes up. The woman who had been his guide in the dream appears again and promises that she will accompany him once more to Fiammetta in the garden, but this time by going through the narrow gate.

Many threads link the *Amorosa visione* to the *Comedia delle ninfe fiorentine*, and others, such as the theme of progression from instinctual animality, to love and the creation of full humanity, and finally to purification and virtuous love, seem to develop premises that had originated in the *Caccia di Diana*. The tone of the *Caccia*, pitched between the encomiastic and the courtly, also resonates in the *Amorosa visione* and, more covertly, in the *Comedia*.[89] The *Amorosa visione* is clearly the more ambitious work, but perhaps also the less successful, due precisely to its excess of ambition. Boccaccio did not merely set the story in a symbolic-allegorical dimension, he loaded the narrator-protagonist's journey—which should be his personal journey to true (that is, virtuous) love—with confusing philosophical connotations, and then piled on dense layers of encyclopedic facts and courtly encomiastic ambitions, not to mention the insistent autobiographical undercurrents. Too many disparate components for everything to be able to blend together successfully into a smooth and coherent whole.

Fiammetta Arrives

From a biographical perspective, for both Boccaccio the man and Boccaccio the writer the most important phenomenon in the vernacular writing of his early years in Florence is the arrival of the character Fiammetta. Maria-Fiammetta had had a not-insignificant role in the *Filocolo*, but after that she disappeared entirely from Boccaccio's writing, or at least from his published or publishable writing. Now, in Florence, she reappeared: and not just with a previously unknown importance, but with a frequency that bordered on the obsessive. From the *Teseida* to the *Comedia*, from the prosimetrum in praise of beautiful women to the *Amorosa visione*, there was no work in which she did not have a prominent role or was not at least mentioned. In the *Elegia di Madonna*

Fiammetta, she is both narrator and main character. In short, during this period, her myth took shape. Was her reappearance related to the fact that Boccaccio's forced departure from Naples may have been the result of a series of problems originating with this character, and if so, related to what degree? Might the Florentine Fiammetta be Boccaccio's public response (even if, of course, not only this) to the rumors, ill feelings, perhaps even threats, provoked by the Fiammetta of Naples?[90]

First of all, the timing is striking. Boccaccio completed the *Teseida* in the first few months after his return. Among the parts that were added in this period, particularly the paratextual ones, the letter dedicating the work to Fiammetta stands out. In this letter, modeled on the one in the *Filostrato* addressed to Giovanna-Filomena, Boccaccio grasps at straws to identify connections between the author and dedicatee's love affair and the stories in the work itself, which refer neither to Fiammetta nor to any other beloved.[91]

The dedicatee, the letter says, had once returned the author's feelings, but had then gone from "agreeable" to "unfairly . . . scornful" (*Teseida*, To Fiammetta; "piacevole," "ingiustamente . . . sdegnosa"); the flame of love had gone out, and the writer does not know the reason for her change of heart. This is, in short, an adaptation and expansion of the unhappy love affair between Fiammetta and Caleon that was briefly mentioned in the *Filocolo*. A new trait of the character, destined for further development in subsequent works, is the hint that Fiammetta had granted the author's desire for physical possession ("the desire of aptly concealing what is not appropriate to reveal concerning the two of us" [*Teseida*, To Fiammetta; "Il volere bene coprire ciò che non è onesto manifestare da noi due infuori"]).[92]

From the *Comedia delle ninfe fiorentine* forward, Fiammetta develops to her full capacity as a character, and does so along two pathways, pathways that are apparently different and yet also typical of the way Boccaccio treated his creations. On the one hand, Fiammetta is openly a work of fiction, but, on the other, is credible as a real person.

In the *Comedia*, the author picks up the story of Maria and the "compiler" that was sketched at the beginning of the *Filocolo* and develops it in a way that is at once romance-like and (so-to-speak) realistic, while, at the same time, combines it with the *Filocolo*'s story of Fiammetta and Caleon. The result is a tale that is not only very different from its source, but in certain respects even antithetical to it.

The Fiammetta of the *Comedia* recounts for Ameto the salient facts of her life up to her love affair with Caleone,[93] who was not of royal origins (just as the Caleon of the *Filocolo* was not), but instead born in France, like the figures of Idalogo, Ibrida, who is another character in the *Comedia*, and Fiammetta's unnamed noble mother. In the *Filocolo*, Boccaccio had portrayed Maria-Fiammetta and the story of his love for her with a light hand and great caution: he was deferential toward King Robert, whom he portrayed as sensitive and generous; he was respectful toward the lady herself, whose anonymity, even though her true given name might be Maria, he safeguarded, avoiding any reference to her family; he was reticent almost to the point of narrative irrelevance in recounting the story of their relationship, which was guided by the rules of courtly love. In the *Comedia*, Boccaccio handled things quite differently. Here Fiammetta reveals that she is the daughter of Robert of Anjou, born shortly after he was crowned king, and a French noblewoman whom the sovereign had given as wife to a man with a prominent position at court. This man might even be her true father: the doubt arises from the fact that her mother, submitting to a kind of blackmail, had sexual intercourse with the king on the same day she did also with her husband. Having been entrusted "at a very young age" ("piccioletta") to the care of nuns, Fiammetta wanted to embrace the religious life herself, but was forced by the king to marry a wealthy man; after her marriage, however, she continued to visit the convent where she had hoped to be cloistered. At the time she is telling Ameto this story, she is still the wife of that man and still visits the convent. She will not say the name of her father, whether actual or putative, but does disclose that his house is that of the aristocratic Campanian d'Aquino. Her tale of falling in love is quite a romance. After she had been married for a number of years, she found herself alone because her husband had gone on a trip to Capua. One night she was dreaming of enjoying herself in her husband's arms when, awakening, she realized that she was in the actual embrace of a young stranger, Caleone; her first impulse was to call the servants, but, faced with the young man's confession that he loved and his threat to kill himself if he was rejected, she decided to listen to what he had to say and, in fact, promised to give herself to him if she found him worthy of her. Caleone then told her that he was born in France, spent his childhood in Tuscany, and, upon "coming to a more mature age" ("in più firma età"),[94] moved to Naples: here he had had various romantic and erotic adventures, which had, however, been painful, until, preceded and announced by premonitory dreams and visions, he encountered Fiammetta one Holy Saturday and Easter Sunday in the church of San Lorenzo (that is, the same place and circumstances in which the author of the *Filocolo* had encountered Maria). Suffused with love and desire, he succeeded in entering her room with the help of magic. Fiammetta, inflamed by Venus, gives herself to Caleone and the two swear eternal fidelity, fidelity that still unites them: "I still retain him as mine and will always hold him so; for he patiently serves me and my teachings" ("lui ancora tengo per mio e terrò sempre; elli me e' miei ammaestramenti seguita paziente," *CNF*, XXXV.116).[95]

Unlike in the *Filocolo*, here Boccaccio abandoned all reticence: Fiammetta is an adulteress who gives herself both to her husband ("I was therefore, and still am, the wife of the one who sought me with such eagerness" ["Fui adunque, e sono, di quello che con sollecitudine mi cercò," *CNF*, XXXV.59]) and to her lover ("I shall always be yours" ["sarò sempre tua," *CNF*, XXXV.115]).[96] Their nocturnal bedroom encounter is described in explicitly erotic terms.[97] In sharp contrast to his earlier discretion, here Boccaccio violated the courtly imperative of preserving the lady's anonymity: while Fiammetta's given name is never uttered, in exchange, that of her house of origin is explicitly identified. Likewise very different in this work is Boccaccio's treatment of Robert of Anjou. The young prince of the *Filocolo*, gallant, caring, and respectful toward both the seduced woman and the child conceived, in the *Comedia* becomes a king who entraps married ladies of his court and uses his power to seduce them, in short, an extortionist who promises to grant a husband's requests in exchange for his wife's favors: this is why Fiammetta's mother "fell into the snare laid, and against her will she submitted to the king" ("cade ne' tesi lacciuoli e, invita, diventa del re," *CNF*, XXXV.45). It should be added that Fiammetta's marriage was also the result of the king's fiat: once he, "who perhaps believed me to be his daughter" ("che forse sua figliuola la reputava"), had agreed to a suitor's request to marry her, Fiammetta could not "escape the gratification of that youth" ("di colui i piaceri fuggire," *CNF*, XXXV.57). A king, therefore, who is anything but "courteous." The heart of "courtesy" or courtly behavior was generosity: not only does the Robert of the *Comedia* not care about the honor of the ladies of his court, but "miserly and greedy of riches, he could even be called King Midas by Midas himself" ("cupido di ricchezze e avaro di quelle, meritevolmente Mida, da Mida, si può nominare," *CNF*, XXXV.32).[98]

All these features return, and even more markedly, in his next work, the *Amorosa visione*, where, in a dizzying game of mirroring and doubling, Fiammetta divides in two: a fictional character in the romance—who in turn is presented both as a painted figure in a fresco and as an actor in the story—and as a person whose actual reality is asserted, all this even though the author repeatedly declares that she is a single character. And as if this were not enough, in a scene of explicit eroticism, the imaginary Fiammetta of the fictional work almost manages carnal union with the dreaming author, namely, Boccaccio himself.[99]

Fiammetta's name not only appears at the outset of the poem and serves within the work as both pseudonym and actual name but, uniquely within all of Boccaccio's work, it is linked to the author's full name: "Thus to You, whom I hold as my lady, / and whom I always wish to serve, / I commend it, lady Maria . . . Dear Flame ["Fiamma"], through whom my heart takes heat, / he who sends You this Vision / is John of Boccaccio from Certaldo" ("Adunque a voi, cui tengho donna mia / et chui senpre disio di servire, / la raccomando, madama Maria . . . Cara Fiamma, per cui 'l core ò caldo, / que' che vi manda questa Visione / Giovanni è di Boccaccio da Certaldo," *AV*, Acrostic Sonnets, I.9–11, 15–17).[100]

The poem provides precise personal information about the real woman, almost like a birth certificate. After the poet exits the castle into a splendid garden, a band of nineteen women appears—some called by name, more identified indirectly by periphrasis—the majority of whom were undoubtedly real people: they were members of the royal family or the Angevin court, or else Florentines or in some way connected to Florence.[101] And who does this company include, but Maria d'Aquino, identified both by her own name and by that of her family (but, significantly, not by the pseudonym). She is the only woman whose personal identifying information is fictional and the only one—unlike many others with double identities, both real and literary—who lives exclusively in literature. A periphrasis at once lofty and precise identifies her as a descendant of Saint Thomas, the "Campagnin," that is, a native of Campania:

> And, as I knew, she was of the family
> of the Campanian who followed the Spaniard [Saint Dominic]
> with mantle, speech, and mind,
> making God so benevolent to him
> that, as became clear later,
> he became a worthy, broad river of knowledge,
> opening, with his clear genius,
> what lay hidden in Scripture, and then,
> given a push by Charles [I of Anjou], went to the kingdom
> of God.
> She took her name from her in whom He was
> implanted who ennobled our
> nature [Maria], and who then redeemed with His pain
> the excess of the first creature.[102]

> E come seppi, ella era della gente
> del Campagnin che lo Spagnuol seguio
> nella cappa, nel dire e con la mente,
> a sé faccendo sì benigno Iddio,
> che d'ampio fiume di scienza degno
> si fece, come poi chiar si sentio,
> faccendo aperte col suo sommo ingegno
> le scritture nascose, e quinci appresso
> da Carlo pinto gì nello dio regno;
> faccendo sé da quella, in cui compresso

stette Colui che la nostra natura
nobilitò, nomar, che poi l'eccesso
    absterse della prima creatura
con la sua pena.

AV, XLIII.46–59

Let us put ourselves in the shoes of readers in Naples or Florence: how could a lady of the house of Aquino portrayed with such
precision possibly have been imaginary to them? A lady, moreover,
who appears to have relationships with other real women who are
well known, members of their own social class and, as it happens,
linked, if only occasionally, to the Neapolitan court. For the poem's
readers, there would have been no doubt that the double-named
woman of the dedication and the company in the garden was a living contemporary of the author.

Beyond its more purely literary aims, the portrait of Fiammetta
in the *Comedia* and the *Amorosa visione* gains further meaning if
we look at it in the light of the hypothesis that Boccaccio had left
Naples because of negative reactions in and around the royal court
to what he had written in the *Filocolo* about Maria and Robert of
Anjou. Perhaps with this new portrayal Boccaccio aimed, more
than to extend, to enhance the earlier character, to give "realistic"
depth to his sketch in the first work, to divert readers, to send off
them onto a different path from the one they thought they had embarked upon in the *Filocolo*.[103]

The doubts Fiammetta expresses in the *Comedia* about whether
her mother had really been impregnated by the king and not by her
mother's legitimate husband may have been Boccaccio's attempt
to correct the claims about her birth made in the *Filocolo*. If behind
the uncertainty about the identity of Fiammetta's biological father
lay Boccaccio's desire to mitigate King Robert's responsibility and,
therefore, to defend himself from the criticisms that the *Filocolo*
may have provoked, well, the result was worse than the mistake
it was trying to fix, all the more so, because in that same work the
king is depicted in such distasteful colors. Sometimes Boccaccio
displayed a quite disconcerting naivete.

In contrast, his goal in identifying Fiammetta's family is very clear: to divert attention away from Maria's true family. A way to rectify the awkward situation he had unintentionally gotten himself into could have been to rekindle the debate about Fiammetta's parentage by clearly indicating the name of a family that was definitely prominent in Naples, but that the Neapolitan audience would also be sure was unconnected to the situation recounted in the *Filocolo*. Essentially, before putting down on paper that an Aquino was believed to be the father of a daughter not in fact his own and that, after the daughter married, she committed adultery with a young law student, Boccaccio must have made sure that no Aquino man was married to a French woman and that there was then no member of the family named Maria: not coincidentally, genealogical research confirms both these points.[104] One might also wonder if the fact that at this time Boccaccio was focusing intensely on the works of Saint Thomas Aquinas (whose commentary on Aristotle's *Nicomachean Ethics* he copied) also influenced his choice: that is, the name Aquino could have come to his mind spontaneously.[105]

Perhaps also related to this episode is the malevolent portrayal of Robert of Anjou, presented in the *Comedia* and reaffirmed in the *Amorosa visione*, of the (still living) monarch as miserly, mean, and greedy; not only "is he the only of the great men of the time mentioned in the poem,"[106] but he is explicitly contrasted with his grandfather, Charles I "il Nasuto,"[107] he "of the masculine nose / and of so much power ("ch'ebbe il maschio naso / insieme con virtù molta," *AV*, XII.20–21). At the center of the fresco of the Triumph of Wealth the dreamer sees a great mountain made of gold, silver, and precious stones. Among the crowd of people digging in it was Boccaccino, who, however, was scrabbling with his fingernails and so attained little; higher up the mountain was the very different figure of Robert, "holding a strong twin-headed axe" ("con forte biccicuto," *AV*, XIV.28), who struck great blows, each of which would have knocked down a wall, and so "took out a great quantity, and all that treasure was kept in a hidden place, and he almost had more than any of the others" ("assai levava, e quel tesoro / in parte oscura tutto si serbava, / e quasi più n'avea ch'altro di loro," *AV*, XIV.31–33). In a word, Robert of Anjou was king of the grasping and greedy.

Why, after the panegyrics of the Angevins and the depiction of Robert in the *Filocolo* as someone with respectful intentions, was Boccaccio now telling such grim stories and using such caustic tones? What had caused his opinion of the sovereign to change so radically? Many argue that the shift was due to the tense climate that developed between Florence and its traditional Angevin ally at the beginning of the 1340s, in other words, that Boccaccio was expressing negative local feeling.[108] However, that Boccaccio, who had only recently arrived in Florence, would suddenly become anti-Angevin is puzzling. It was 1341–42 and his friendship with Niccolò Acciaiuoli was still strong: at this time, Boccaccio was working with him on the arrangements for founding the Carthusian monastery, and was expecting Niccolò's help to extricate himself from his painful circumstances. And, as we have seen, the Acciaiuoli family was one of the pillars of the Florentine pro-Angevin party.

And more: at this point, the affair of the Duke of Athens was in its early stages, the Bardi still supported him, and Boccaccio was connected to the Bardi. It would have been truly strange if at this difficult juncture in his life Boccaccio had sided against his friend and patron as well as the circles closest to him. Moreover, his negative portrayal is not of the Angevin court as a whole—the court's female members, indeed, are celebrated—but only of Robert of Anjou himself. All of which leads one to believe that the accusation of greed did not arise from politics but from personal animosity: in short, that Boccaccio held the king responsible (along with his own father) for his forced departure from Naples.[109] While Boccaccio's animosity toward his father exploded violently in the *Comedia* but was tempered in the *Amorosa visione* (even if it would still peek out in some passages of the *Elegia di Madonna Fiammetta*),[110] Boccaccio's bitterness toward Robert would never fade.[111]

Mourning

For a little over two years, Fiammetta and the love story built upon her occupied Boccaccio's imagination obsessively. Around this nucleus tales multiplied, then refracted into more versions, even within the same work, each with its own protagonist with a new name and social condition, a Maria/Fiammetta whose personal details changed and changed again, tales that culminated in tragedy or euphoria. Tales marked by a high degree of rhetorical figuration, by plot complications, by layer upon layer of erudition, by the intrusion of intertextuality, and, not least, by jumbles of allegorical symbolism. What might explain why a youthful infatuation unleashed such a great rush of creative energy, and over such a long period of time; and, especially, why this infatuation maintained such a persistent and tenacious centrality? The desire to remedy an error, to dispel the doubts and ill will provoked by the lady's first appearance as a character, is not by itself a sufficient explanation. Deeper in, behind this practical aim, hidden causes, more private motivations must have been at work. Perhaps a traumatic complex coalesced around Fiammetta and gained a means of expression, a knot in which Giovanni's frustrations about his sudden reversal of fortune, his dashed hopes for worldly and literary success, his exclusion from a world that now from a distance appeared a paradise swirled together and then fused. A wound that the exiled Boccaccio struggled to heal, a loss he was unable to grieve; a tumult of rage, resentment, nostalgia, and desire that powerfully disturbed him, but then, at last, subsided. And subsided in a literary ritual that was also a process of mourning: this was the composition of the *Elegia di Madonna Fiammetta*, the most openly autobiographical of all the works dedicated to this character (which indeed has been cited many times as a possible source of information), but, not coincidentally, also devoid of symbolism and allegorical veiling.

The *Elegia* is a prose work, written, as the title says, in the form of an elegy and inspired in particular by Ovid's *Heroides*, epistolary love poems purportedly written by famous women of antiquity abandoned by their lovers or husbands, but which Boccaccio rendered in vernacular prose, following Florentine Filippo Ceffi's example of a few decades earlier.[112] This work is commonly dated between 1343 and 1345, but the terminus post quem at least is based on unsupported assumptions.[113] In any case, although it accurately recounts events in Boccaccio's life and the city of Florence that can be dated between the late autumn of 1340 and the end of 1342, we can be almost certain that the story was not composed at the time of the events it describes. The simple tale is told in the first person by Fiammetta herself in a linear fashion without overly intrusive insertions or digressions.

> Fiammetta is a beautiful Neapolitan noblewoman married to a kindhearted man of the same rank. In church during one Easter celebration, she is watched intently by a young man, Panfilo, and she instantly falls in love with him. United by their mutual passion, the two enjoy a period of great happiness until one autumn night after making love, Panfilo tells her that his father has asked him to return to his city of birth (Florence) and that he cannot refuse this request. Despite Fiammetta's attempts to dissuade him, Panfilo leaves, swearing to her, however, that he will remain faithful and that he will return to Naples within four months. Fiammetta's wait becomes agonizing, especially after the date by which Panfilo had said he would return comes and goes. One day a merchant who has arrived from Florence speaks to her about Panfilo and she learns that her lover has married. This news sends her into such deep despair that her husband, in the hope of distracting her, takes her to Baia, but instead of reviving her, the parties, pageants, and entertainments deepen her depression: Fiammetta becomes sad and ugly. A year passes, and a household servant returns from Florence with the news that it was Panfilo's father who had married, not Panfilo himself, but also that Panfilo is in love with a woman in his hometown. So—Fiammetta thinks—her beloved has forgotten her, and as a result, instead of consoling herself, she sinks deeper into despair. Meanwhile, more than sixteen months have passed. One day she learns that Panfilo is about to return, but it is a misunderstanding and her joy is short-lived: the Panfilo expected in Naples is not hers. At this point, Fiammetta becomes so desperate that she attempts suicide. She does not die, but is, however, condemned to live without hope.

Here Boccaccio collected the various and contradictory narrative threads dispersed throughout his earlier works, and wove them into a single coherent story that has at its center Panfilo's departure from Naples. A taboo was broken: for the first time Boccaccio recounted the repressed event in one of his literary works; and, not coincidentally, this was Fiammetta's final reincarnation as a protagonist of one of his stories (the Fiammetta of the *Decameron* retains only the name, she does not chafe at the author's life). Here, too, as always, Boccaccio plays on ambiguity, on slippages and overlappings between planes. To a reader of the *Elegia* who is familiar with the *Filocolo*, the dedications of the *Teseida* and the *Comedia*, or even with just one of these works, it indeed seems clear that Fiammetta is also Boccaccio, and that Panfilo displays characteristics of Fiammetta as well as of Boccaccio: in these co-existences, the roles of victim and betrayer are interchangeable. Unambiguous, however, is the reversal of the story as compared to how it had been told previously: now it is Panfilo who abandons and then betrays Fiammetta. It is not a punishment inflicted on Fiammetta—the idea of punishment assumes a biographical reality that is not present here—but a sort of score settling against fate, almost a revolt. The reversal of the narrative roles has in it something of a liberation; from the author's point of view, it is at once a way of freeing himself and a gesture of self-affirmation. It is as if he, who until that moment had seen himself in betrayed and abandoned victims, now affirmed: I have abandoned and betrayed Fiammetta, and she must spend the rest of her life in mourning for *me*. In short, something in Boccaccio the man had released: the painful clot that had solidified in his imagination around the myth of Fiammetta.[114]

In the *Elegia*, autobiography dispensed with allegorical veils; the very next work, the *Ninfale fiesolano* (*Nymphs of Fiesole*), dispensed with autobiography, as well as with the city of Naples, and Florence took its place.

The *Ninfale* is an etiological poem in octaves that recounts the mythic origins of Fiesole and Florence in the form of a pastoral fable. There is no evidence for its date: the assumption is that it was written between 1344 and 1346, "after the composition of the *Comedia delle ninfe fiorentine* and the *Elegia di Madonna Fiammetta* and just a step away from the *Decameron*, if not quite touching the piecemeal drafting of the first novellas."[115]

The young shepherd Africo, who lives with his parents on the hills of Fiesole, while secretly observing a group of nymphs, catches sight of Mensola, a follower of Diana and thus bound to chastity, and falls madly in love with her. Heedless of the warnings of his father, who fears the goddess's revenge, Africo sets out in search of her and, with the help of Venus who advises him to disguise himself as a woman, manages to be accepted into the group of nymphs. One day, however, having to undress to bathe, he reveals to the nymphs that he is a man: frightened, they flee, and, left alone with Mensola, Africo takes her by force. The violated young woman threatens to kill herself, but Africo dissuades her and she falls in love with him, gives herself to him, and promises to see him again. But then, seized by feelings of guilt, Mensola decides never to meet Africo again; he, who waits for her in vain, kills himself in despair with an arrow; dead, he falls into the river below which takes its name from him. Mensola discovers that she is pregnant, hides in a cave and gives birth to a son, Pruneo. Diana, however, finds her and in revenge transforms her into the river that will bear her name. Pruneo, raised by his paternal grandparents, as an adult enters the service of Atalante, the founder of Fiesole, who gives him the territory between the Mensola and the Mugnone rivers; Pruneo marries and has ten children, whose descendants will later move to Florence, and its history of destruction and reconstruction will follow.

It has been said that this is "the only of Boccaccio's works completely devoid of any autobiographical intention."[116] Which is true if we are referring to the absence of allusions to events and situations from his life. There is, however, hidden autobiography, of which the author himself may not even have been aware. The story's fundamental pattern—Mensola reciprocates Africo's love and yields to his desire, but then flees and is found no more—is practically Boccaccio's signature on every love story he ever wrote. After a brief period of happiness the beloved woman spurns the man, sometimes goes far away, often betrays: consider Fiammetta and Caleon, Criseida and Troilo, the Giovanna/Filomena of the dedication of the *Filostrato*, the Fiammetta of the dedication of the *Teseida*. The few variations only underscore the steadfastness of the pattern: Mensola promises to return and breaks her word, like Panfilo; Africo kills himself in despair, just as Fiammetta when abandoned attempted suicide. It is as if the imagination of Boccaccio the narrator was imprisoned within a few constant situations, even for love stories other than Fiammetta's. The idea of refusal is central: one of the two parties (almost always the woman) refuses or else does not reciprocate the other's love (the widow of the *Corbaccio* will do the same); their encounter, when it happens, is brief; the solitude of one or both is enduring. Here one can ask if this pattern does not have some connection with the one, also repeated multiple times, of the child who was deprived of his mother and felt rejected by his father.

Following the *Elegia*, Fiammetta as a character disappeared from Boccaccio's writing, but the echo of the love story of which she had been the protagonist for so long continued to resonate in his writing, albeit faintly. In the preface to the *Decameron*, Boccaccio would turn to the commonplace, though enriched with new ethical implications by Petrarca's influence, of youthful amorous passion that is tempered in maturity, writing that "from my earliest youth up to the present," that is, until the age of forty, "I have been enflamed beyond measure by a most exalted, noble love, which, were I to describe it, might seem greater than what is suitable for one in my low condition," that is, he had loved a woman of a much higher social status, but that by "those discerning individuals," that is, those with capacity to understand, "I was praised and held in high regard for that love"; the love, however, had made him suffer because it was so excessive that it "could not be altered or extinguished by the force of reason or counsel or public shame or the harm it might cause" (*Dec.*, Preface, 3, 5).[117] Commonplaces to be sure, and yet these references to the effects of social striving, as well as to shame and harm, tally too closely with the young Boccaccio's social and emotional situation to think that they were completely devoid of autobiographical implications, if only literary autobiography.[118] Nor did the character Fiammetta vanish from his poetic imagination. In his verses he would lament the death of a beloved woman named Fiammetta, whom he placed in the heaven of Venus;[119] toward the end of his life, contemplating the recently deceased Petrarca,[120] he would appoint her the symbol of his entire body of love-themed work, as Laura was for his mourned master's:

> Now you are there, where often your desire
> to gaze on your Lauretta bade you rise —
> there where my lovely Fiammetta lies
> beside her in God's marvelous empire[121]

> Or sè colà, dove spesso il desio
> ti tirò già per veder Laüretta;
> or sei dove la mia bella Fiammetta
> siede con lei nel conspecto di Dio

Rime, XCIX (CXXVI).5–8

Just as she did not disappear from the imagination of the man Boccaccio. Moreover, this mythic figure had ramified in his writing to such an extent that it would have been strange if her specter had not continued to visit him. Take the autograph of the *Teseida*. Not only did he copy this manuscript a decade after its composition, but in this poem, as we know, Fiammetta is absent. Well, "in the upper part" of one of the cross-reference marks decorated with branches that Boccaccio penned throughout the codex "there is a crown [and a little below it perhaps the letter *c*]; at the center of the lower part, framed by the coil of branches, the letter 'F' [the first letter of Fiammetta's name?]." This is not to say that the crown per se is a reference to the myth of royal birth, but the mysterious *c* could be that of Caleon/Caleone, Fiammetta's lover par excellence; in that case, the crown would be the sign that while sketching Boccaccio had that tale in mind: "with these sketches," it has been said, Boccaccio "indulged" "his imagination and his heart with a sweet tale repeated silently to himself."[122] Nor is it certain that Boccaccio repeated the tale only to himself; he could have indulged the innocent vanity of a lonely old man in a provincial village. At the end of the seventeenth century, the prior of the church of San Iacopo in Certaldo, Andrea Arrighi, nicknamed "Capranica," wrote that in 1366 Boccaccio had given the church two panels on which his likeness had been painted along with some saints. On one panel, the writer was depicted with Saint Catherine, "who, it was said by the oldest people of the village, who had heard it from those older than them, who had learned it from their own fathers, that she was a portrait from life of that Queen Maria of Naples so beloved by him."[123] It makes you wonder just what old Boccaccio might have told his neighbors about that ancient tale.

6

In Search of an Alternative

Ravenna

We do not know precisely when he arrived, but in 1345–46 Boccaccio was living in Ravenna. It is not hard to understand why he would have decided to leave Florence. He must have been tired of living in his father's shadow, with no financial autonomy, no public role in the city, and in a family that, once his half brother Iacopo got older, more and more resembled the one he had left, or been sent away from, almost twenty years earlier.

It is possible that before settling on Ravenna he had looked for a situation in Naples, and may even have planned a return to the city of his youth. Even if he did in fact conceive of such a journey, however, he must have been forced to give it up.[1] Naples at this time was not the best place for Boccaccio to find employment, given that it had fallen prey to the dynastic upheavals of the Anjou, which, among other things, had considerably weakened Niccolò Acciaiuoli.

On his death on January 20, 1343, Robert of Anjou had designated as heir to the throne his granddaughter Joanna, daughter of his long-deceased son Charles, Duke of Calabria, and, because of her youth, placed her under the guardianship of a regency council. That same January saw the celebration of Joanna's wedding to Andrew of Hungary, son of Charles Robert, king of Hungary, a member of the Charles Martel branch of the house of Anjou: the two had been bound by a nuptial contract ten years earlier, when she was only eight and Andrew six. This succession satisfied the interests of the Anjou of Hungary, but it also aroused the discontent of the heirs of King Robert's brothers, the sons of Philip of Taranto and of John, Duke of Durazzo, who all aspired to the throne. For two years, via intrigues and matrimonial alliances, a covert war was fought—one that also involved the papacy, of which the Kingdom of Naples was a fief—that was driven primarily by two widows: Agnes of Périgord, mother of Charles, Duke of Durazzo, and Catherine of Valois-Courtenay, the mother of Robert and Louis of Taranto and in whose service Niccolò Acciaiuoli was. The night of September 18–19, 1345, saw a dramatic turn of events when Joanna's husband, Andrew, was strangled. The assassins were never identified, but the Taranto brothers (as well as Acciaiuoli) were the suspected masterminds: now, with Andrew eliminated, the brothers could seek to marry Joanna (their cousin Charles, Duke of Durazzo, could not, having in the meantime married Joanna's younger sister, Maria). The victim's brother, Louis I, king of Hungary, sought justice from the pope and threatened armed intervention. This was the prelude to the war that would rock the kingdom in the years that followed.[2]

While it is easy to understand Boccaccio's reasons for leaving Florence, it is difficult to comprehend what expectations sent him to Ravenna.[3] Who recommended it? Who invited him? What promises lured him? We do not know. Boccaccio definitely moved in the highest levels of Ravenna society and was in contact with the lord of the city, Ostasio da Polenta. Evidence of the latter comes from Boccaccio's, if it really is Boccaccio's, vernacular translation of the Fourth Decade of Livy's *History of Rome*, in the prologue to which he calls Ostasio, "my most excellent lord, at whose request I set myself to this great work" ("spetialissimo mio signore, ad istantia del quale ad opera così grande io mi dispuosi").[4]

Dante had spent his final years in Ravenna, where something of a circle had formed around him. Some of these friends and disciples Dante had included as characters, in pastoral disguise, in the eclogues he exchanged with Giovanni del Virgilio. It is not likely (though it is believed by many) that Boccaccio moved to Ravenna because of his interest in Dante alone; we do know, however, that he met and established some friendships with the members of Dante's circle, from whom he obtained valuable information about the poet's life. Among his informants were the Florentine notary Dino Perini (the Melibeoeus of Dante's first eclogue), who had acted as messenger between Ravenna and Bologna carrying the verse letters Dante and del Virgilio exchanged, and another notary, Pietro Giardini, of Ravenna, absent from the eclogues but very close to Dante. The strongest bond (a true, lasting friendship) was one Boccaccio formed with yet another notary, Menghino Mezzani, who, at the end of the fourteenth century in a letter to Nicolò da Tuderano, chancellor of Ravenna's Da Polenta lords, the humanist Coluccio Salutati would call "a close friend and follower of our Dante."[5] Menghino enjoyed composing poetry in Latin (including an epitaph of Dante in hexameters) and, especially, in vernacular, in which he also wrote verse summaries of part of *Inferno* and the entire *Purgatorio*. He was particularly valued by Ostasio, who entrusted him with important political and administrative positions.[6] It is also possible that while in Ravenna during Ostasio's rule, Boccaccio first made the acquaintance of Donato Albanzani, who would become one of his closest and most trusted friends.[7]

Ostasio died in November 1346. His son Bernardino's succession met opposition: he would gain full control over Ravenna and Cervia only in September 1347, after imprisoning, and then having killed, his brothers Pandolfo and Lamberto. Once he consolidated power, Bernardino began a ferocious repression of his opponents, imposing exile and death sentences and expelling those who had held prior political and administrative positions under Ostasio. Among them was Menghino Mezzani, who was not only pushed aside but imprisoned, perhaps for as long as a decade. Boccaccio would lament his friend's sad fate and spoke out harshly against Bernardino. How did this lord treat Boccaccio? From a few (obscure) lines in the tenth eclogue, it appears that Boccaccio was forced to leave Ravenna, but the grammarian Giovanni Conversini—who had been sent as a young child to a monastery in Ravenna, where he began his studies at Donato Albanzani's school in about 1348 and associated with Boccaccio in 1353—wrote, "Bernardinus Ravenne dominator Bocacii studia magnifice instruxit," that is, that Bernardino supported Boccaccio generously in his studies.[8]

Voluntary or not, Boccaccio's departure from Ravenna must have taken place in the autumn of 1347, following Bernardino's definitive seizure of power in September. Boccaccio moved to Forlì, where its ruler, Francesco Ordelaffi, grandson of the Scarpetta with whom Dante had collaborated in the first years of his exile, had offered him a job.

Forlì

It was Boccaccio's fate that Naples was to play a fundamental role in his life even when he found himself far away from it and his interests lay elsewhere. It was, in fact, developments in the Angevin dynastic crisis that took him to Forlì and to a position that would have very negative repercussions for his relationships with his Neapolitan patrons.

Following Andrew's assassination, as his brother King Louis of Hungary was seeking justice and threatening armed intervention, the problem arose of who would marry the widowed Queen Joanna. Between the two candidates for the role of prince consort, the princes of Taranto, Robert and Louis, after long and intricate negotiations, Louis prevailed, and celebrated his marriage to Joanna in August 1347. It was a triumph for Catherine of Valois-Courtenay and also for Niccolò Acciaiuoli, of whom Louis of Taranto was the protégé. Except that at this point King Louis, seeing that Hungarian interests had been compromised, stopped delaying: at the beginning of November he descended into Italy in person at the head of a powerful army, in short order occupied Abruzzo, and headed toward Naples. Toward the end of January 1348, Joanna fled the city and took refuge in Avignon (the Anjou were counts of Provence). In March she was joined by Niccolò Acciaiuoli and Louis of Taranto, whom Florence had refused to shelter during their journey.

In December 1347, Louis of Hungary passed through Forlì. Francesco Ordelaffi, who had long pursued an expansionist policy against the church's secular domains in Romagna, took this opportunity to weaken the pope and was organizing a military expedition in support of the Hungarian. An expedition in which Boccaccio would have to participate. He says this himself in a letter sent to his friend Zanobi da Strada in Florence. After speaking about copyists who had to be paid for an address ("sermo")[9] of Zanobi's that he had had copied, Boccaccio wrote that he had still not received the book by Varro that he was waiting for and that he would surely have it in hand within a short time were it not that he was "about to join the illustrious King of Hungary in the furthest reaches of the Abruzzi and Campania, where he is located," because "his glorious lordship [Ordelaffi] was preparing along with many noblemen of the Flaminia [the area between the Adriatic and the Apennines] to follow the king's most just weapons," and Boccaccio himself, "by order of his lordship was about to leave, not in as a sword-bearer, but—so to speak—as an arbiter."[10] We have no other information about this projected expedition; however, if indeed one took place, something that is far from certain,[11] Ordelaffi must have had to return to Forlì almost immediately. And it is also unclear what Boccaccio meant by "arbiter": judge? historian? But we are confident that Ordelaffi had entrusted him with a post: indeed, that may have been the reason that Boccaccio moved there from Ravenna. It remains unclear, however, on the basis of what references the lord of Forlì, a Ghibelline, had taken into his service a person known neither as a man of letters nor as a government official, and who lived in the orbit of the Guelph court of Ravenna. In Forlì, however, Boccaccio was connected to Ordelaffi's secretary and chancellor, the notary Checco (Francesco) di Meletto Rossi, and accordingly we can surmise that before Boccaccio's move Checco had received information from notarial circles in Ravenna about his legal education and his familiarity with the Neapolitan context.

Whether there was an expedition or not, whether Boccaccio did or did not take part, the fact remains that he had made a complete volte-face regarding the Anjou of Naples and his friend and patron Niccolò Acciaiuoli. This is a perfect example of the way he adapted to whatever surroundings he found himself in, as well as, perhaps, the first manifestation of a simmering grudge against Acciaiuoli. In any case, the choice to side with Niccolò's enemies signaled a fracture in their relationship. Additionally, because Boccaccio had not simply accepted the position from Ordelaffi, but had also made his support for the Anjou of Hungary public in an eclogue, *Faunus*[12]—written "in the heat of the moment, while the drama was in full swing"[13]—which he sent to Ordelaffi's secretary, deploring Andrew's murderer (Alexis) and praising the vengeance of the Hungarian king (Tityrus). In November of the following year, after the political storm had passed, Acciaiuoli would name as secretary to the king of Naples Zanobi da Strada—a cultured man and expert in Latin, but who until that moment had exclusively been involved in running, along with his brother Eurenio, the school in Florence inherited from their father—without taking Boccaccio's candidacy into consideration: an omission that must have been influenced by the fact that Boccaccio had sided against him at his time of greatest peril. Boccaccio was wounded: in all likelihood this appointment caused the first crack in his friendship with Zanobi, which from then on would grow colder and colder amid misunderstandings and recriminations.[14]

The situation in the Kingdom of Naples, however, shifted quickly. After seizing Naples, Louis of Hungary proved to be a bloodthirsty occupier (among other things, he had Charles of Durazzo beheaded), thereby alienating the majority of the nobility; Joanna and Acciaiuoli in Provence were very skilled at contriving alliances and exploiting discontent in the kingdom from a distance. In May, Louis returned to Hungary, leaving behind deputies and an army of occupation; Joanna refilled her coffers by selling Avignon to the pope, appointed Acciaiuoli Grand Seneschal of the Kingdom, and in August landed in Naples with her husband. At the beginning of January 1349, she liberated the city from the Hungarian forces and began the reconquest. There was one more act to follow, for in 1350, Louis of Hungary would mount a second expedition, but this would fail. In May 1352, Joanna and Louis of Taranto would be crowned rulers of Naples.

Boccaccio adjusted his aim—we might even say he executed a second out-and-out about-face. Over the course of 1348, he composed three eclogues depicting the Neapolitan affair. In the first poem, Louis of Taranto (Dorus) recounts the killing of the disgraced Andrew of Hungary (Alexis), "who headed too sternly, irksome to the woods" (*BC*, IV.54),[15] his own marriage to Joanna (Liquoris), thanks to the "gift" of Acciaiuoli (Phytias),[16] his flight because of King Louis's (Poliphemus) anger, and the Florentines' refusal to shelter him, thus betraying their "ancient faith" (*BC*, IV.24).[17] The second eclogue portrays the desolation into which Naples falls after Joanna's (Liquoris) flight.[18] And the third recounts Naples' joy upon the return of Louis of Taranto (Alcestus) after the departure of the "savage" ("trux") Louis of Hungary (Poliphemus).[19]

Boccaccio not only transformed from a supporter of Hungary into a panegyrist of the victorious royal couple; he was also not stingy with praise for Acciaiuoli, for whom "a great posterity's prepared."[20] The fact that the hero of these eclogues is Louis of Taranto, Acciaiuoli's patron, rather than Queen Joanna, shows that Boccaccio was following political developments at the Neapolitan court closely. At the court, the rift between Joanna and Louis was "such that it dictated the existence of two separate courts: Joanna's, of which the Provençals were the main focal point . . . and Louis's, where an important role was played by Florentines close to Niccolò Acciaiuoli, who, at the time of the kingdom's reorganization, had not hesitated to push systematically for the appointments of his relatives, former associates, and friends to leading positions."[21] Giovanni, therefore, was trying to heal his rift with Niccolò, but, even if on the surface they would overcome their differences, he would never fully regain Niccolò's trust.

Faunus formed part of an exchange of eclogues between Boccaccio and Checco di Meletto.[22] Boccaccio had been in Ravenna, where he would surely have discussed the verse correspondence between Dante and Giovanni del Virgilio on many occasions. He had long been familiar with Dante's eclogues, which had resurrected the genre, had been influenced by them, and frequently introduced a bucolic atmosphere and pastoral settings into his vernacular works. The conversations in Ravenna must have revived his interest and inspired him to experiment with Latin bucolic poetry himself. Dantes' poems were eclogue-epistles, alternatives to more traditional letters in verse; while in Forlì, Boccaccio likewise engaged in a dialogue conducted via letters in the form of eclogues with Checco, Boccaccio taking the lead. In the end, the pair produced two works each, for a total of four, which together were the origin of what would become one of the principal genres of poetry for the whole of the age of Renaissance humanism, first in Latin and then in the vernacular.[23] His book of eclogues, the *Buccolicum carmen*, would be dedicated, at his request ("which he asked me to dedicate to himself"), to Donato Albanzani, "a poor but honorable man, and a great friend of mine":[24] it is thus quite possible that Donato, who must have associated with the same friends in Ravenna with whom Boccaccio had earlier discussed Dante's eclogues, was also a party in the discussions during this experimental phase of the genre, if not with both correspondents, at least with Boccaccio.[25]

The Plague

From his letter written in Forlì to Zanobi, it appears that Boccaccio had expected to continue in Ordelaffi's service after the successful conclusion of the military expedition, but instead, in 1348, he returned to Florence. He was definitely in the city before September 10, the first day of his fourth-month term as *Signore delle gabelle*, superintendent of indirect taxation for the municipality. This was his first public office: at a time when the plague epidemic had surely opened many gaps in the ranks of citizens qualified to carry out administrative duties, even someone like Boccaccio, until then a stranger to public life but possessing a certain legal competence, was useful to the city government.[26]

Had he returned to Florence because his hopes had once again been dashed (as would also happen several more times in the future), or because some event had compelled him?[27] It has been suggested that the reason was his father's death, but Boccaccino's demise seems to have taken place not in the summer of 1348 but rather toward the end of the year or the beginning of 1349,[28] while Giovanni was already in Florence at least in August 1348 and perhaps earlier, if we believe his claims in the *Decameron* that he witnessed the plague's massacre.[29]

Florence was devastated by the epidemic. The contagion had begun with an outbreak in the East, which then circulated by sea through port cities, before flooding all of Europe. In Italy, the wave of illness swept from the port of Messina up through the south;

from Genoa it came ashore at Marseille, whence it overran all of Provence and France; from Venice it spread through the Veneto, Emilia, and Tuscany. Over the course of five years, from 1347 to 1352, the pandemic, one of the largest and most devastating in history, extended over the entire continent, from the Mediterranean to Scandinavia to the Balkans, killing, it is estimated, one-third of Europe's population. In Florence, the outbreak began to be felt strongly in the early spring of 1348 and raged continuously until autumn. Here, too, the population was ravaged.

At the beginning of the *Decameron*, Boccaccio paints a portrait of rare power of the social, economic, and ethical turmoil caused by the inundation. Here is how he describes its origins and the first useless attempts to stem it:

> Let me say, then, that one thousand, three hundred, and forty-eight years had passed since the fruitful Incarnation of the Son of God when the deadly plague arrived in the noble city of Florence, the most beautiful of any in Italy. Whether it descended on us mortals through the influence of the heavenly bodies [planets] or was sent down by God in His righteous anger to chastise us because of our wickedness, it had begun some years before in the East, where it deprived countless beings of their lives before it headed to the West, spreading ever-greater misery as it moved relentlessly from place to place. Against it all human wisdom and foresight were useless. Vast quantities of refuse were removed from the city by officials charged with this function, the sick were not allowed inside the walls, and numerous instructions were disseminated for the preservation of health—but all to no avail. Nor were the humble supplications made to God by the pious, not just once but many times, whether in organized processions or in other ways, any more effective. For practically from the start of spring in the year were mentioned above, the plague began producing its sad effects in a terrifying and extraordinary manner.[30] (*Dec.*, I, Introd., 8–9)

Survivors interpreted this scourge as a punishment from God, who was angered by moral corruption; an "end of the world" feeling was widespread and accompanied by insistent calls for repentance. Boccaccio too pointed to God's "righteous anger," but located it on the same level as astral influences without favoring one or the other: in short, in this regard and in his attention to "human wisdom and foresight," we see on his part a "rational" analysis of the phenomenon that differentiates him from the prevailing apocalyptic attitudes.[31]

The plague shattered communities, tore apart networks of friends, destroyed families. "Time, as they say, has slipped through our fingers: our former hopes are buried with our friends. The year of 1348 left us alone and helpless": this was Petrarch's desolate summation.[32]

Boccaccio was left literally alone. He not only lost many friends (Sennuccio del Bene, Giovanni Villani, and Iacopo Alighieri, to name just a few), but almost all of his family: between 1348 and 1349, his stepmother, Bice dei Bostichi; his uncle Vanni; and Boccaccino all died.[33] Boccaccio, along with little seven- or eight-year-old Iacopo, remained. His feelings might well have been expressed by Pampinea's words in the *Decameron* when she exhorts her companions in Santa Maria Novella to abandon the devastated city:

> And when we return home, I do not know whether you have the same experience that I do, but since, out of a large household, there is no one left except my maid, I get so frightened that I feel as if all the hairs on my head were standing on end. And what terrifies me even more is that wherever I go in the house, wherever I pause for a moment, I see the shades of those who have passed away, and their faces are not the ones I was used to, but they have strange, horrible expressions on them that come from who knows where.[34] (*Dec.*, I, Introd., 59)

Head of the Family

Boccaccio, who up until then had been a son, suddenly found himself the head of the family and his life radically changed. Now it was up to him to manage the assets (held in common with his half brother until 1359–60) inherited from his father and, perhaps, his uncle Vanni.

The inheritance was of decent size: in addition to real estate in Florence (the residence and a few low-value properties) and Cert- aldo (the family dwelling, a couple of farms, and a few small pieces of land), his assets included a credit for a loan of approximately eighty florins to which Boccaccino had a claim from the Comune, placing him in the middle rank of the taxpayers in Santo Spirito. In brief, at the beginning of the 1350s, one would not have called Boc- caccio especially rich, but he was certainly comfortable.[35] While the management of houses and farms did not pose special prob- lems, however, that of movable assets demanded a certain entre- preneurial spirit.

In December 1343, the Comune had consolidated the public debt by creating the *Monte* (literally, "mountain"), the funded debt, and then, the following year, made *Monte* shares, which yielded a perpetual income of 5 percent, negotiable (these are what Boccaccio had inherited from his father); shortly after this, in order to deal with growing deficits, the government had insti- tuted the system of *prestanze*, that is, forced loans, loans that were technically extraordinary but in fact exacted with ever-greater fre- quency, and which taxpayers resident in the city subscribed to, al- most always forcibly, on the basis of their incomes. Along with the gabelles, that is, indirect customs duties and consumption taxes, the forced loans became the Comune's most important source of income. Although the subscription was, with rare exceptions, obligatory, these were in reality government bonds: repayable at maturity, providing a rather high interest rate, ranging from 5 to 15 percent, and tradable.[36]

The buying and selling of *prestanze* generated a thriving and highly speculative market.[37] A citizen subject to a forced loan could respond to this obligation in different ways: 1) he could pay the re- quested sum and at maturity collect the face value of the security plus the accrued interest, which was the most common and wide- spread practice; 2) he could subscribe *ad perdendum*, that is, re- nouncing interest payments in exchange for a significant discount; this was the practice followed by the less well-off, for whom, in- deed, the loan was thus transformed into a tax; 3) he could reassign the loan obligation and its associated interest to another person by paying a sum much lower than the obligation: this is what people without liquidity did. Needless to say, this tax system produced great inequality of treatment: it penalized the middle and lower classes and enriched speculators and middlemen. And this is why successfully navigating the market in *prestanze* required a certain spirit of enterprise.

A few months after his father's death, Boccaccio ceded the shares he had inherited: it is estimated that he received 25 percent of their face value, or roughly the not-insubstantial sum of twenty florins. Given that the full capital could not be redeemed and the return was low, it could have been a gambit to free up liquidity for investment. But that would have Boccaccino's style of maneuver, and Giovanni was not his father; in character he was the opposite. It seems, in fact, that Boccaccio's anxiety drove his decision to get rid of the shares. After he had received his first interest payment, the Comune temporarily suspended *Monte* payments in July–August 1349. Boccaccio, therefore, appears to have feared the fund's insolvency. To someone like him, unwilling to take risks, selling the shares might have seemed the most reassuring solution—as we know, the desire for tranquility was one of his signature characteristics.

We do not know, however, if and how he invested those twenty florins. He certainly fulfilled his tax obligations punctually, but he also almost certainly—although no documentation survives for the period 1351–55—stayed away from the market in government securities. Still, thanks to his earnings from the Comune, until 1355 he enjoyed considerable prosperity: tax assessments of 1352 and 1355 estimate his taxable wealth exceeded 1,000 florins. That around the middle of the 1350s he was in excellent economic circumstances is also supported by the fact that in April 1355 he was able to give Petrarch, then living in Milan, a beautiful codex of enormous size (and therefore very expensive) containing the entire series of Saint Augustine's *Enarrationes in Psalmos* (*Expositions on the Psalms*).[38]

In Romagna Once Again

Following the plague and his father's death, we lack information about Boccaccio's life for about two years. He remained in Florence, but he did not hold any public office or advisory position. We can imagine that legal and financial matters associated with his inheritance and new family configuration occupied him for some months: between April and May 1349, as mentioned above, he received as heir the "wages" ("paghe"), that is the accrued interest, for the *Monte* shares owned by Boccaccino; at the beginning of 1350 he assumed guardianship of Iacopo (but as soon as May he asked for and obtained the appointment of two procurators to assist him).[39] It is likely that he went to Certaldo several times, if only to check on the work of his tenant farmers.[40] And in Certaldo, he also had to tend to neighborly relations with the heirs of Boccaccino's great friend Biagio Pizzini, who would be immortalized in the novella of Frate Cipolla.[41] The Pizzini house and Boccaccio's shared a courtyard, which the Pizzini family could only reach by a corridor that crossed Boccaccio's house. After Giovanni's death, a protracted dispute would arise between Iacopo and Biagio's daughter, Banca Botticini, which would, however, ultimately be resolved amicably.[42] A few minor matters of the family business in Florence also needed to be dealt with: for example, the leasing of two properties in Santo Spirito.[43] In short, Boccaccio must have been busy, and yet, the silence that weighs on this period of his life leads one to suspect that something had broken in his relationship with the city. With so many of his friends dead, did he feel alone, or pushed aside by the Florence that counted? In 1348, as we saw, he had been *Signore delle gabelle*, and after that, nothing. Boccaccio was prickly and sensitive, easily offended. Leaving aside its possible motivations, Boccaccio's divestment in January 1350, shortly after becoming his brother's guardian, of all the holdings in the *Monte* inherited from his father,[44] could be significant. This gesture, too, has an almost symbolic quality, seeming to denote a detaching from the city.

And, in reality, Romagna called to him. He had left dear friends there, and it was also where he had deepened his knowledge of Dante and made breakthroughs in Latin poetry. Above all, in Ravenna lived a daughter whom he had perhaps never seen, or seen only fleetingly. He wanted to feel like a father, to act as one, a desire that must have been sharpened by the involuntary paternity his cohabitation with Iacopo had forced upon him.

In the second half of September 1350, he was in Ravenna. This was the second of what would become many stays in the city, so many that Petrarch would refer to him as a person "of Ravenna."[45] He saw little Violante, perhaps for the first time, who was taking her first steps.

This was a personal trip, or rather, as we will see shortly, semi-personal: in any case, he was not on a mission for the Comune. In fact, we now know that he carried out the diplomatic mission "ad partes Romandiole et Lombardie" not on this occasion—as biographers and other scholars thought until very recently—but in the following year, 1351.[46]

The reason the trip was only semi-personal was that on September 11, the leaders (*capitani*) of the Confraternity of Orsanmichele[47] had entrusted Boccaccio with the task, which he must have found particularly pleasing, of delivering ten gold florins to Sister Beatrice, a nun in the convent of Santo Stefano degli Ulivi. Beatrice was the religious name taken by Dante's daughter, Antonia, probably in homage to her father: it is therefore conceivable that this gift was a sort of compensation for the damages Florence had inflicted on the Alighieri family. It is unclear if there is a connection, and if so what kind, between this gift and the fact that more than twenty years later, in September 1371, Donato Albanzani would present, on behalf of an unspecified friend, three gold ducats to this same convent of Santo Stefano as heir to Sister Beatrice.[48] Indeed, the friend could have been Boccaccio himself, were it not that in 1371 three ducats would have been a nontrivial sum for him given his particularly unhappy financial situation: at that date he had not yet received the appointment to publicly comment on the *Commedia* with the considerable remuneration of one hundred florins.

At the beginning of October 1350, Boccaccio was once again in Florence, where he would have one of the most decisive encounters of his life, his first meeting with Francesco Petrarca.

7

Years of Service

Petrarch in Florence

On a cold day in early October 1350, approximately the sixth of the month, Boccaccio hurried through the uncertain twilight to meet Francesco Petrarca, who was drawing near Florence. This would be their first meeting in person; for Petrarch, en route from Parma to Rome, where he was headed for the jubilee, it was also the first time he would enter the city of Florence.[1] It might seem strange that this man, who signed himself "florentinus" ("Florentine") and by this date had already traveled through half of Europe, been to a large number of the cities in northern Italy, lived in Bologna, Imola, Parma, Verona, and Mantua, visited Naples twice and Rome four times, had yet never once set foot in his parents' city. And after stopping there a second time for a few days on his return from Rome, he would not do so again. Petrarch never turned down the opportunity to live in places of true power, even if in their more obscure corners, particularly when their cultural life was rich. Avignon was an international metropolis, which, in the space of a few years, had become the most important political and cultural crossroads of the age, the signorial courts of the Po Valley promoted cultural activity through central organization; midcentury Florence, in contrast, had been a dispirited backwater for decades. It was thus not attractive to the new type of intellectual that Petrarch was in the process of bringing into being: a modern intellectual who ignored traditional school and university channels in favor of learning from personal exchanges and a direct engagement with texts.

Petrarch's decision to stop in Florence during his pilgrimage to Rome was not because his route happened to pass by, or because of a sudden desire to at last see "his" city. The reason was that, thanks to the efforts of Sennuccio del Bene, for some years now a group of his admirers had been gathered here: Bruno Casini, a teacher of rhetoric who died in his thirties during the plague of 1348; Francesco Nelli, a cleric and notary linked to the bishop's curia and, from early 1350, prior of the church of Santi Apostoli; Zanobi da Strada, a scholar very close to Niccolò Acciaiuoli (whom Petrarch had known in Naples in 1343 and with whom he always maintained excellent relations); and, of course, Boccaccio himself. Casini and Zanobi had written to Petrarch even before the plague broke out, probably in March 1348. They lamented that he had settled in northern Italy when he had long been awaited in Florence, and they further declared they found incomprehensible that he had put another city ahead of the one where his family had originated.

In one of his replies, Petrarch responded that while many cities insistently invite him, his "fellow citizens had cast him out into exile and barred the door even if he had wanted to enter," which, he said, is not surprising: "Who does not know about the harm perpetrated by a few, encouraged by the tolerance of a heedless populace, or about the house taken by force, and my ancestral fields devastated, about the unheard prayers and vain laments?"[2] In 1349, the attempts to attract Petrarch to the city coalesced into a plan: a university had been founded in Florence (including a faculty of theology), and since his coronation as poet laureate had conferred on him the degree of "magister," he thus had the right to teach at a *Studium*. Giving him a professorship might be the way to convince him to come, especially if at the same time the Comune rescinded his father Ser Petracco's banishment and restored the family's confiscated assets. Discussions must have intensified during the summer of 1350, preceding Petrarch's October arrival, and it is not known if Boccaccio was one of the proponents of the project or had any leading role in it. The first letter (in verse) he sent to Petrarch (recall that his much earlier letter written in 1339 was fictitious and never sent) dates to the end of that summer, and, as far as we can tell—it has not survived—Boccaccio complained in it that he had been slighted by Petrarch, that he was the only one to whom Petrarch had never sent any of his work. And perhaps he was not completely wrong, since Petrarch replied to him only months later, after they had met in person, offering as an excuse (also communicated in person when they met) that he had lost the verse response he had jotted down in a rush immediately upon receiving the letter-poem from Boccaccio.³

These, then, were the real reasons that Petrarch stopped in Florence. His stay, however, would be brief: by October 16, he was in the town of Bolsena.⁴ The meetings with Florentine leaders about the restitution of the confiscated assets were put off until his next visit to the city upon his return journey. During this October stay, Petrarch met in person the friends he had made by letter: Nelli, whom Petrarch nicknamed Simonide, and whom he would never see again but who would remain his most loyal and prolific correspondent until Petrarch's death in 1363; and Lapo da Castiglionchio; not, however, as is commonly claimed, Zanobi da Strada, who had been in Naples since August.⁵ The friends gathered to listen to Petrarch read his poems; they surely discussed books:⁶ Lapo possessed a rich library containing classical texts still unknown to Petrarch, including Quintilian's *Institutiones oratoriae* and a handful of Cicero's orations. Lapo gave him the Quintilian on the spot and a few months later, at Petrarch's request, sent him the orations so he could have copies made.⁷

Because of a serious knee injury sustained during his journey, Petrarch remained in Rome longer than planned. After two weeks confined to bed, he returned to Florence in early December. Almost certainly on this occasion he spoke with representatives of the Comune about the restitution of his family's assets. In early January, he was back in Parma. One would not say that the visits to his ancestral city had affected him emotionally: aside from his (so-to-speak) economic interests, his interests lay in books and people, and he does not seem to have paid any attention to the city itself with its history and memories. In the letter of thanks written to Boccaccio from his bed in Rome, Petrarch had devoted not one word to Florence, instead complaining about how his forced immobility kept him from satisfying his "insatiable desire to see the queen of cities; for the more I see her, the more I marvel at her, and the more I am led to believe whatever we have read about her."[8]

Following Petrarch's departure for Parma, negotiations regarding his university appointment began in earnest, and this time Boccaccio, who in the meantime had been elected to an important public office, played a leading role, so much so that he was put in charge of conveying the Comune's decision to Petrarch. Toward the end of March 1351, he traveled as "legatus," that is, envoy, to Padua, where Petrarch had held a cathedral canonry for the past year. He bore an official letter from the Comune's chief magistrates, the *priori delle arti* ("priors of the guilds") and the *gonfaloniere di giustizia* ("standard-bearer of justice"), but almost certainly written by Boccaccio himself, informing Petrarch of the decision to restore the lands and houses confiscated from his father (through an extraordinary procedure, "bought back at the expense of the public treasury" [*Ep.*, VII.3]),[9] as well as offering him a professorship at the university, for which he could freely choose the discipline "best suited to his honor and studies" (*Ep.*, VII.15).[10] This was the first time Boccaccio was officially assigned a mission for the Florentine government: it has almost symbolic significance that his first two appearances as a public actor, this and the earlier one in Ravenna on behalf of the Confraternity of Orsanmichele, were connected to the two guiding lights of his scholarly and literary endeavors.

Boccaccio stayed at Petrarch's house for about a week, during which time their bond grew stronger. Walking through the city, Petrarch showed Boccaccio Livy's purported gravestone, which at the urging of Giacomo da Carrara had been restored and placed at the door of Santa Giustina. During the day, Petrarch devoted himself to his studies and Boccaccio to copying various of his friend's writings ("compositiones"): eclogues as well as Latin letters in both verse and prose. Toward evening they retired to the garden for conversation; they discussed politics: Emperor Charles IV who ignored Italy, and the tyranny of the Milanese archbishop Giovanni Visconti, who profited from Charles's inattention. And, naturally, they discussed literature: Petrarch would have described his plan to collect into a book his scattered letters, both prose and verse, along with his vernacular poetry; Boccaccio would have told him a bit about the things he had written up until then and rhapsodized about Dante.[11]

Boccaccio left Padua on April 5 or 6; in May, Petrarch would depart for Avignon. Upon their farewell, he entrusted Boccaccio with a warm letter of thanks addressed to the Florentine government,[12] but also told him to personally convey his refusal of the professorship. While it is true that Pope Clement wanted Petrarch in Avignon, it is equally true that being a university professor would never have suited him, given his entire career as an independent intellectual. Learning of his refusal, the Florentine leaders were offended and, in retaliation, decided to revoke the offer to restore his assets. Boccaccio, who felt like a party in the dispute, harshly condemned the decision: it was "appalling" (*Ep.*, V.24) and sullied those who had made it.[13] The trip had been a failure for his mission; from a personal standpoint, though, it could not have been more successful.

Boccaccio and Petrarch would not meet again for another eight years. However, in Padua the firmest of friendships had been born; over time the two would become so close that in Petrarch's household Boccaccio would be considered a member of the family.[14] Although they would have no lack of personal contact, their relationship would be nurtured more by their uninterrupted exchange of letters, surely more numerous than those that have survived, most of them, moreover, sent by Petrarch. Unlike Petrarch, who considered his letters monuments bequeathing his intellectual portrait to posterity, Boccaccio, who filled both his fictional and scholarly works with autobiographical references, would never bother to gather together his own letters, but instead collected those of his friend and organized them into a volume.[15]

Their relationship would face only one crisis, although a serious one, in the summer of 1353, and it would be because of politics. Petrarch, who had decided to leave Provence permanently for Italy, accepted Giovanni Visconti's invitation to move to Milan, where he lived, the guest of Florence's worst enemy. Boccaccio reacted with such fury that their communication ceased for months. We do not know who took the initiative to reestablish contact, but in the spring of 1354, Boccaccio sent Petrarch Augustine's commentary on *Psalms* (the book reached him on April 10) and their correspondence resumed in connection with this gift.

Public Man

With his father's death, it was as if a door was thrown open wide. The Boccaccio who had been essentially a stranger to the public life of the city (with the sole exception of the four months in 1348–49 overseeing the office of indirect taxation) was now actively involved in its administration. For roughly five years, he alternated, practically without interruption, between political-administrative posts and governmental missions.

He received his first office in January 1351, shortly after Petrarch's visit to Florence, and it was an important one: *Camerlengo* of the *Camera*, that is, municipal treasurer. From this we can surmise that, whatever Boccaccio himself thought, his work in the office of the gabelles had been positively perceived. On February 23, in his role as treasurer, he was one of the five witnesses to the ratification of the agreement between Florence and Naples for Florence's acquisition of Prato. Treated as a gift from the Angevins, it was in reality a sale. On the Neapolitan side, the negotiations were directed behind the scenes by Niccolò Acciaiuoli, who had been named that city's administrator for precisely this purpose: the Angevins needed financial resources to ransom Robert of Taranto from Louis of Hungary's prison; for its part, Florence wanted to strengthen its bulwark along the Pre-Apennine Hills against possible military offensives by the Visconti, who had just established themselves in Bologna. The negotiations took place in a climate of tension both between the Neapolitans and the Florentine government, and between Niccolò Acciaiuoli and his fellow citizens: in the end, Acciaiuoli had to let Prato go for a very modest sum, a failure that must not have displeased Boccaccio, who was embittered about being passed over for the position of royal secretary in favor of Zanobi da Strada.[16]

It is easy to predict that a man who entered public life with a post of such great responsibility as municipal treasurer would have a rapid and honorable political career ahead of him. And indeed, apart from an early hiccup at the end of his term as *camer-*

lengo in February 1351, when he did not receive enough votes to be "imborsato" (that is, to have his name included in the "pouch" [*borsa*] from which officeholders were selected by lot) for an un-known post, Boccaccio chalked up a series of positions in various governmental offices: from November 1351 to April 1352, he was *Difensore del contado* (defender of the countryside); from August 1352 to February 1353, *Ufficiale della gabella del pane* (official of the bread tax); from January to April 1354, *Ufficiale di torre* (tower of-ficial). But note what kind of positions these were: without excep-tion in tax offices. The *gabella del pane* was a tax on bread baked and sold in the countryside; the *Ufficiali di torre* were responsible for recovering and managing assets that individuals had usurped from the state; the *Difensori del contado* did indeed keep watch over the security of the realm, though not by exercising policing duties, but by checking for illegal extortion of gabelles (indirect taxes). Boccaccio, therefore, was entrusted with technical respon-sibilities, and not even ones that were very important. None of the offices he was elected to carried true political weight. Nor in the decades that followed, when his prestige in the city had consid-erably increased, would he ever be a candidate for or selected for positions of true leadership: unlike his father, he would never be elected as one of the priors and only once, in 1364, would he be in-cluded among those eligible for the so-called Tre maggiori, the three major offices (the *Signoria*, and their two councils of advis-ers, the *Gonfalonieri* ["Standard-bearers"], and *Dodici buonuomini* ["Twelve Good Men"]). "To put it succinctly, messer Giovanni was not a member of the political elite."[17] Evidently, his fellow citizens appreciated his honesty and the skills he had acquired during his years as an apprentice merchant, but either he did not have a wide network of connections in the city or else did not enjoy the esteem necessary to be entrusted with true governing responsibilities.

His political career, in fact, ended in April 1354, when he stood as a candidate to become one of the "captains" or leaders of Or-sanmichele, a wealthy and powerful lay confraternity devoted to providing poor relief that was closely aligned with (some might say effectively an arm of) the Florentine communal government. This was the first time since his term as treasurer that Boccaccio aspired to a position of power and prestige, and he was resoundingly rejected: he was excluded from the draw, having received only twenty of the forty votes necessary. Over the rest of his life, he would hold, sporadically, a few other public offices, but they would be positions of little importance, and not commensurate with the prestige he by then enjoyed in the city as a man of letters.[18]

Whatever the reasons for his failure, the thin-skinned Boccaccio must have been injured by the Orsanmichele rejection. When he felt he had been wronged, he generally reacted by loosening or cutting ties with the milieu that had injured him. This defeat, therefore, may have influenced his decision the following year to attempt a new life in Naples.

Travels and Embassies

His fellow Florentines did not recognize great political talents in Boccaccio, yet they often turned to him for even delicate missions abroad. There is a striking contrast between the overall modesty of the governing offices entrusted to him and the importance of at least some of his many foreign assignments. One might think that his intellectual profile—knowledge of languages, especially Latin, eloquence honed by reading and writing, a rich trove of historical and geographical knowledge—would have made him an ideal candidate for diplomatic missions that required a representative with more prestige than experience and skill in diplomatic maneuvering. And instead, leaving aside the missions to the pope, in the embassies Boccaccio was entrusted with, the confidential seems to have prevailed over the public and official. It was not by chance that his destinations were lords, like the Polentani and the Ordelaffi, with whom he had personal relationships. To be sure, they were missions arranged and funded by the Comune, yet they give the impression of being at a lower level than that of communications between states proper, a level that involved the Florentine government only indirectly, without burdening it with responsibility. In other words, these were not so much embassies in the true sense of the word as confidential missions.

The background to Boccaccio's diplomatic activities was the conflict of 1350 to 1353 between Florence and Giovanni Visconti, archbishop and lord of Milan.

Taking advantage of King Louis of Hungary's descent toward Naples, the small lordships of Romagna had effectively freed themselves from papal power. In 1349, in an attempt to regain control of the region, Pope Clement VI (who was in Avignon) had sent his nephew Astorgio di Durfort (Hector de Durfort) into Italy with the title of Count of Romagna and a substantial military force. The expedition was not only a failure, but threw open the doors to Visconti encroachment. Having acquired Bologna from Giovanni and Giacomo Pepoli in October 1350, Archbishop Visconti made it his bridgehead from which to directly threaten nearby Florence. Supported both politically and militarily by almost all the lords of Romagna, in July 1351, the archbishop sent his troops under the command of Giovanni Visconti d'Oleggio into the Mugello, just the other side of the Apennine ridge, bringing them to within a few miles of Florence itself. Working with him were Francesco Ordelaffi and, primarily with guerrilla actions, Ubaldini. In this truly critical situation, Florence responded with a broad diplomatic offensive aimed at cracking the great alliance of lords and Ghibelline cities that had coalesced around the Visconti, and forming their own coalition of friendly cities (in December 1351, Florence succeeded in launching a league of the Tuscan Guelph communes). Military operations ceased in the spring of 1353, after the Milanese forces twice sought and failed to occupy the strategic site of Scarperia: thus, on April 1, 1353, a peace treaty was agreed upon at Sarzana, which was supposed to establish spheres of influence. It was clear, however, that the Peace of Sarzana established only a truce and that the confrontation between Florence and Milan would continue (indeed, Milan would violate the terms of the agreement as soon as October by taking Genoa).[19]

Boccaccio's first political embassy occurred a few months after his meeting with Petrarch in Padua, during the period he was official of the bread tax. Starting August 25, 1351, he was assigned an unspecified mission as "ambassador to the regions of Romagna and Lombardy"; the mission was scheduled (and funded) for thirty-three days, but Boccaccio was actually back in Florence on September 19. We do not know either his purpose or whom he met with and where. Biographers generally pass over the mention of Lombardy and focus almost exclusively on his destinations in

Romagna, and therefore assume that Boccaccio made contact with Francesco Ordelaffi of Forlì and Bernardino da Polenta of Ravenna. Indeed, he was presumably chosen precisely because of his recent visits to their courts. Toward the end of July, the Milanese under Giovanni Visconti d'Oleggio had invaded the Mugello, and during August and September Florence mounted its diplomatic counteroffensive, sending embassies to a large number of cities, with particular attention to Romagna and "Lombardia": Rimini, Imola, Faenza, and Forlì, but also Verona, Ferrara, and Padua. Perhaps Boccaccio's assigned task, rather than evaluating the intentions of Ordelaffi and da Polenta, who openly sided with Visconti, was gathering intelligence and studying their possible moves. It remains unclear what the Florentine officials had meant by "Lombardia": perhaps the northern Italian cities that were not in Romagna. Since Boccaccio by his own admission was definitely in Verona prior to 1353, this city might have been another destination of his embassy in 1351. It could even be hypothesized that the reason his mission was completed sooner than expected was because on September 22 another ambassador was sent to Verona, or that Boccaccio was in Verona not on that occasion but in the course of his mission to the region around Trent several months later, between late 1351 and early 1352.[20]

Whether or not he met with Bernardino da Polenta, it is certain that upon finding himself in Romagna, Boccaccio would not have let the opportunity slip by to go to Ravenna to embrace his daughter Violante again after not seeing her for a year.

Toward the end of 1351 (December 12), Boccaccio was charged with a mission, again apparently a confidential one, to the son of King Louis IV of Germany, Louis V, Duke of Bavaria, as well as Margrave of Brandenburg and Count of Tyrol, and to Corrado IV, Duke of Teck, who governed the territory of Trent for the house of Brandenburg. We know that they met, because in a letter to the Florentines at the beginning of the following March, Louis V referred to his discussions with "Johannem de Cartaldo" (Giovanni of Certaldo), but we do not know the substance of the discussions or in what location or locations they took place. If the Duke of Teck facilitated the meeting, it is likely that it took place in Trent or its environs. To think that Florence intended to press Louis to intervene against the Visconti seems excessive; more likely they asked him to work confidentially in Florentine favor with the Scaligeri of Verona, in particular with Cangrande II, who, following the death of Mastino II, had become the de facto lord of that city in June. Indeed, Louis was very close to Cangrande, who, among other things, had that year married Louis's sister Elisabeth.[21]

Once the most critical phase of the crisis with the Visconti had passed, Boccaccio undertook no more trips for the Comune for at least two years. It is true that the summer of 1353 found him in Romagna (July 12 in Forlì, July 18 in Ravenna), but this, probably his longest stay in Ravenna after his first of 1345–47, appears to have been a personal trip. Moreover, after the completion of his bread-tax office in February, he was completely free of any administrative post. In Ravenna, as we know, he had a sort of second family; at that date, Violante would have been a child of about five and a half, with chestnut hair and laughing eyes.[22] Boccaccio had no idea that this was the last time he would see her. While there, he also often received his friend Albanzani in the house where he was staying, sometimes accompanied by the young Conversini: he entertained them, offering them sweets ("bellaria"). We cannot rule out, however, that on this occasion as well Boccaccio had been entrusted with a confidential assignment: in fact, in the letter he sent Petrarch from Ravenna he claimed that he had come to the city, passing through Forlì, "with the purpose of visiting its prince" (*Ep.*, X.11),[23] that is, Bernardino da Polenta.[24]

It was Francesco Petrarca himself who disturbed, and greatly, the serenity of Boccaccio's stay in Ravenna. During the stop in Forlì, a friend (perhaps Checco di Meletto Rossi)[25] told him that Petrarch had left Avignon and was now living in Milan as the guest of Archbishop Visconti; at the time Boccaccio had been thunderstruck, but then, thinking back to how critical Petrarch had been of the Visconti during their time together in Padua, he responded that "it was impossible," except that "a few days later" in Ravenna he met Francesco Nelli (Simonides), who showed him "a letter written by Silvanus [Petrarch]" (*Ep.*, X.13) that swept away all doubt.[26] Boccaccio reacted almost violently: immediately, "with a turbulent and agitated spirit,"[27] he wrote an extremely harsh letter to Petrarch, driven, he says, by "indignation at the reprehensible

act just committed" (*Ep.*, X.1):[28] behind the pastoral screen he accused Silvanus-Petrarch of having betrayed not only the political
ideas that he had professed just a few years earlier, but also his own
moral teachings and principles. No one, he reminded Petrarch,
even if he has been injured, may act against his own native land
("patria"). This was not just one of Boccaccio's usual impulsive
outbursts; this time Petrarch's other Florentine friends shared his
indignation. Even non-Florentine friends, those in Avignon and
Naples, were stunned by Petrarch's decision. In April 1354, Checco
di Meletto would join the chorus from Forlì with a prosimetric
letter in which he invited Petrarch to dispel the doubts raised by
his behavior by issuing a clear statement of his position: "people
are amazed and they accuse you of frequenting proud houses and
living within the doors of the powerful," therefore "do not dis-
dain, o poet, to write something that may banish the doubts from
men's minds."[29]

Petrarch never responded to Boccaccio regarding this situation; he let time do the work of healing. And it did take time for
their friendship to recover, particularly because for a number of
years they remained on opposite sides politically and were working actively toward directly contradictory objectives.

Even after the immediate danger had passed, containing Visconti expansion remained the guiding principle of Florentine
foreign policy. Florence's intricate and ambiguous diplomatic
dealings with Charles IV of Luxembourg, king of Bohemia and, especially, king of the Romans (that is, awaiting coronation as Holy
Roman Emperor), should be understood in this light.[30] During the
Mugello war, Florence had lobbied for Charles to come to Italy in
an anti-Visconti capacity, but then, when in 1354 the possibility
that he would come to the peninsula as an ally of the pope became a reality, the Florentine attitude changed: Pope Innocent VI
wanted help from Charles in reasserting papal sovereignty over
Romagna; Florence feared becoming strategically isolated and, especially, that the autonomy of the Guelph communes would be en-
dangered. It was precisely to sound out the pope's real intentions
that Boccaccio was sent to Avignon in the spring of 1354.

In the first half of April, an imperial messenger announced in
Florence that Charles would come to Italy to be crowned emperor;

on the thirtieth of the same month, Boccaccio was assigned the embassy, from which he would return at the end of June. This was the first time that he officially held the position of ambassador. He was given precise instructions: communicate that Florence was stunned by this announcement and ask if the pope had approved Charles's decision. If the pope tried to find out Florence's intentions, Boccaccio was to respond that he had no other mandate than to learn the pope's intent.

This was also the first time that Boccaccio crossed the borders of the peninsula. He would do so again on only one other occasion, about ten years later, for another mission to Avignon. Although no equal to Petrarch, Boccaccio was still an indefatigable traveler; however, while Petrarch roamed throughout Europe, with few exceptions, Boccaccio's journeys followed two consistent routes, Florence–Naples and Florence–Romagna. Thus, he lacked his teacher and friend's international reputation. During his second trip to Avignon, he would pass through Genoa, and from this we can assume that he had similarly followed the road along the Ligurian coast on his first.

Why did the Comune choose Boccaccio for this embassy? The role was certainly prestigious, though not politically challenging since he was explicitly prohibited from any autonomous initiative. That said, it seems misplaced to think that his selection for the role might have been influenced by his intellectual friendships, that is, by the group of "humanists" connected to Avignon through their links with Petrarch, or even by Petrarch himself. Regarding whom, the idea that he had provided Boccaccio with "recommendations and introductions" should also be ruled out.[31] Not only do Petrarch's relations with Boccaccio appear to have been nonexistent during this period, but his declared support for Charles IV would hardly have encouraged him to exert himself for an anti-imperial mission; moreover, there is no evidence that he and Boccaccio ever exchanged a word about this trip to Avignon. Another person who might have been able to introduce Boccaccio in Avignon was Zanobi da Strada, except that Niccolò Acciaiuoli, of whom Zanobi was a faithful servant, was also on the imperial side. Instead, the choice likely settled on Boccaccio due to his relationships within Florence. Note the dates: on April 7, his candidacy for Captain of

Orsanmichele was rejected; on the twenty-eighth, the *Signoria* issued him the commission to Innocent VI and the cardinals in Avignon. It almost seems that his closest friends within the ruling group wanted to use the nomination to compensate him for the snub he had just received, to repair the damage to his honor.

Florence Disappoints, Naples Deceives

On June 30, 1354, the same day that they received the final payment for their mission to Avignon, Boccaccio and Bernardo Cambi, his partner on the embassy, were assigned a new task, to travel to the Valdelsa for six days, "maxime ad partes Certaldi." It was a home-coming for Boccaccio due to highly unusual circumstances. The Valdelsa was under threat from the Great Company, a massive horde of mercenaries commanded by the so-called Fra Moriale.[32] The army put together by this proto-condottiero was fearsome: after plundering the Kingdom of Naples for years in the service of King Louis of Hungary, then Lazio and Umbria in the pay of Cardinal Albornoz, and after that, the March of Ancona, in July of 1354, it was threatening the countryside around Florence and in particular the Valdelsa. Boccaccio was not required to demonstrate any strategic skills, because, after extorting 25,000 florins from the Florentine government, Moriale withdrew from the field.

In the autumn of 1354, Charles of Luxembourg descended into Italy; in January 1355, after being crowned king of Italy in Milan, as his grandfather Henry VII had been, he established his base of operations at Pisa; this, after all, was the most loyal imperial city on the peninsula, and even though Charles was cooperating with the pope and seeking an accord with the Guelph cities, he was also the symbolic leader of the Ghibellines. Toward the end of March, Charles moved to Siena and was joined there by Niccolò Acciaiuoli, who then accompanied him to Rome, where on April 5 Charles would be crowned emperor. Immediately following this, he would return to Pisa and then to Germany, having obtained the imperial investiture and quite a few economic benefits, but without achieving his political objectives.

Acciaiuoli and the new emperor had established a relationship of mutual esteem. Acciaiuoli not only expected, and actually received, concrete aid in support of Louis of Taranto, but was also pursuing a far-reaching, even visionary, political project, namely, a great alliance between Guelphs and Ghibellines, bringing together the Visconti of Milan, the Anjou of Naples, and the commune cities, a pact guaranteed by an emperor who cooperated with the pope, which would have represented an epochal turning point in Italian history.[33] It was a revolutionary project, and as Acciaiuoli would soon learn, a utopian one: the Guelph cities, with Florence in the forefront, had no intention of seeing their autonomy limited by any higher authority.

If a good relationship with the emperor did not bring about the political transformation Acciaiuoli desired, it did, nonetheless, lead to significant personal satisfaction. It was, in fact, at Acciaiuoli's request and to please him that on May 24, 1355, in the cathedral of Pisa, Charles IV crowned Acciaiuoli's secretary, Zanobi da Strada, with the poetic laurel wreath. This ceremony, which replicated Petrarch's Roman coronation of 1341, would assure Zanobi a firm place in the canon of illustrious Florentine men of letters until at least the mid-fifteenth century, but at the time it was seen by Petrarch's friends as, if not quite a profanation, at least a parody. Boccaccio was among the most resentful, so much so that a few months later Petrarch felt he had to reprimand him, reassuring him that, even if his "brow has yet to be adorned by the Penean frond," that is, by laurels, he is a true poet, unlike others who "seek the name without deserving it."[34] Zanobi, however, held an important post; and above all, he was the favorite of the most powerful man in the Kingdom of Naples. And reactions in public proved quite different from those expressed in private. This same Petrarch, who was very close to Zanobi and even closer to Acciaiuoli, sent the new laureate a congratulatory, although not excessively effusive, letter in verse, but then wrote privately to Boccaccio regarding the "barbaric laurel" ("barbarica laurus")—that is, conferred by a German emperor—Zanobi had received, saying that he was astounded the "Germanic judge and censor did not tremble on issuing his judgment."[35] As for Boccaccio, he too sent Zanobi a poem of congratulations (now lost), which received a prompt reply. Boccaccio's further response, although containing praise so overdone that it verges on sarcasm, was far from expressing what he thought of Zanobi as a man and poet. In his old age, Boccaccio would sketch a quick, contemptuous biographical profile of the laureate, but in 1355 he needed both Zanobi's and Acciaiuoli's goodwill.[36]

Indeed, what was important in Boccaccio's life in the spring of 1355 was not Zanobi's coronation, but that at this time he reestablished several important connections: with Petrarch, with Zanobi himself, and with Acciaiuoli. Although, in fact, his correspondence at least with Zanobi had already resumed some two years earlier.

In April 1353, the funeral for Niccolò Acciaiuoli's oldest son, Lorenzo, had taken place in Florence. After a long silence on both sides, Boccaccio had sent Zanobi a letter expressing his condolences to the father but also his indignant astonishment at the "monstrous strength" ("monstruosam virtutem") of the man who had hidden his feelings from everyone and who "almost at the very moment [his son's] death was announced, without emotion, in an unbroken voice, with fluid speech and long-winded and studied eloquence, had proclaimed to the mourning prince and barons that one does not have to trouble oneself about the dead" (*Ep.*, IX.25).[37] Indeed, this letter was a ferocious attack on Acciaiuoli, who had gravely offended Boccaccio by calling him "Giovanni of Tranquility," who had waged "a long persecution" against him, who had turned away from him and inflicted a "deadly wound" (*Ep.*, IX.7).[38] It should also be noted, as evidence of just how twisted Boccaccio's psychological circuitry was, that even as he appealed to Zanobi's friendship, he simultaneously contrasted his own integrity, humility, and selflessness to Zanobi's haughtiness and predilection for tyrants, and from the letter's opening lines no less: "A long time has passed since you have written to me or I to you. I do not know whether I should blame your loftiness, which, as I have already seen, scorns unimportant things, or my own madness, which attends little to things that I know are esteemed" (*Ep.*, IX.1).[39]

In this letter of 1353, Boccaccio had declared that he would never set foot in the Kingdom of Naples as long as the grand seneschal— Acciaiuoli—was in power, in order to prove that he was not seeking tranquility.[40] Well, in the spring of 1355, he decided to return to Naples.

Almost certainly, Boccaccio made this decision following dis-

cussions with Zanobi, and perhaps, but far from certain, also discussions with Acciaiuoli.[41] Boccaccio had learned from Zanobi that,
in March, Angelo Acciaiuoli, the bishop of Florence and, by this
date for many years also chancellor of the Kingdom of Naples, had
been appointed bishop of Montecassino, where Zanobi expected
soon to occupy the position of his vicar.[42] We do not know what
else may have been said. Did Zanobi dangle before Boccaccio the
prospect of succeeding Zanobi in his current position with Niccolò
Acciaiuoli, or perhaps the hope of some other position in Naples?
Did Zanobi speak of Acciaiuoli by name, or imply that his employer
knew about this plan and agreed? Recalling this journey to Naples
in the eighth eclogue of the *Buccolicum carmen*, Boccaccio would
write that Acciaiuoli (Midas) "himself / invites me, he will give me
pasturelands, / . . . springs and cooling shade" (*BC*, VIII.11–12).[43]
But these were assertions made later, perhaps to claim that he
had succumbed to the enticements of others and not to his own
illusions. It could actually have been Boccaccio who constructed a
pleasing fantasy on the basis of information received from Zanobi.
The fact remains that he decided to go to Naples. Driving him were
both his circumstances in Florence, where the *cursus honorum* so
promisingly begun had little by little dwindled to offices of little
importance—and also led to resounding rejections—and his enduring attraction to the city of his youth, as well as, who knows,
maybe even the idea of vindication for past failures.

He might have departed much earlier, had he not been appointed on May 5 to the office of *Ufficiale dei difetti* (auditor of
mercenary troops) to replace the deceased Dante di Ternio, a responsibility that would occupy him for four months, and, additionally, over the summer been struck by violent and persistent
("for months") attacks of fever.[44] We do not know when he actually
set out for Naples—indeed, we know little about the journey—
although it was definitely later than the first few days of September asserted by biographers: Boccaccio was in fact still in Florence
on October 6.[45] The astrological note in the summary of his discussions with his friend Barbato that "baneful Orion / still rules
the sky at night, prohibiting / the birds to sing" (*BC*, VIII.30–31)[46]
could be evidence that their meeting during the trip took place in
November.[47]

Boccaccio had not seen Naples in fifteen years: it is easy to imagine with what great hopes he set out, what dreams he nurtured in his breast. Dreams and hopes that would make his disappointment even more painful.

The journey, which had begun under the worst auspices—he had not yet reached the hills of Naples when Bruna di Ciango sent him the news of Violante's death—ended in failure. Boccaccio had no way to meet with Acciaiuoli, who would remain holed up in Nocera until the end of the year, and he may not even have reached the city of Naples itself. He stopped instead in Sulmona, at the home of his friend Barbato. Here, if we trust his reconstruction of the events in the eighth eclogue, Barbato (Damon), who had long been critical of Acciaiuoli, put Boccaccio on his guard with the warning that Midas would not keep promises that he made.[48] And Barbato was also critical of Zanobi (Coridon). In his opinion, Zanobi had deceived Boccaccio with his poems as laureate ("under cover of his laurels" ["sub tegmina lauri"]): in reality, this man used poetry to obtain practical advantages: "Poor wretch, you don't know Coridon at all / nor know the pipe on which he'd celebrate / those barren loves" (*BC*, VIII.137–38).[49] Only a few months earlier, recall, Boccaccio had been exchanging Latin verses with Zanobi about his coronation.

Yet, Boccaccio owed to Zanobi the sole positive thing to come out of this trip to the Kingdom of Naples. It was Zanobi who opened for Boccaccio the doors of the Montecassino library, revealing treasures buried for centuries, as yet unknown to the new humanists. And here Boccaccio came across an ancient codex containing, in addition to the well-known *Rhetorica ad Herennium* (then attributed to Cicero), the unknown *De lingua latina* by Varro, and the oration *Pro Cluentio* by Cicero himself. We do not know if Boccaccio obtained possession of the codex or only consulted it on site; we do know for certain that he copied the Varro text and Cicero's oration with his own hand and sent them as gifts to Petrarch.[50]

8

The Dignity of the Vernacular

Master and Student

Perhaps no other friendship between two writers has left so profound a mark on literature, and not only Italian literature, as that between Boccaccio and Petrarch.[1] Certainly, few other times has one person's human and intellectual connection with another whom he felt to be both father and teacher influenced that person's life in the way Boccaccio's connection with Petrarch did Boccaccio's. Their dialogue, their collaboration, but also their conflicts engaged the existential dimensions of writing and scholarship as much as the practical ones. Through the exchange of letters, of their own and, even more, of others' works, as well as face-to-face discussions during their many encounters beginning in 1350, their dialogue touched on all the topics and themes expressed in their work as scholars and poets: from the relationship between Latin and vernacular literatures to that between the intellectual and power, from the role of poetry within the arts to the link between antiquity and the present, from the behavior of the scholar with regard to sex, amorous passion, and temporal rewards, such as wealth and prestige, which were widely accepted and sought after, to the delicate and problematic balance between worldly ethics and religious ethics, between aspirations to glory and spiritual tension. Petrarch was the model nonpareil for Boccaccio's life, a spiritual guide and a mentor for his scholarship and poetry. A man complete in every way, who had reached heights to which Boccaccio could only aspire, well aware he could never reach: in short, Petrarch was the teacher and Boccaccio the student. A student in the presence of the master is how Boccaccio perceived himself; or, in any case, how he represented himself.[2] It seems undeniable that he suffered from a kind of psychological subjection, and yet, there is a touch of exaggeration in his proclaimed humility. Such an insistent display of discipleship seems almost to be a mask, donned to hide the reality of a much more complex and conflicted relationship. Boccaccio, indeed, by no means renounced his own convictions, which did not always coincide with those of his teacher. Petrarch was surely Boccaccio's moral adviser, confessor, spiritual director—in this respect, then, a father in multiple senses—and also an unsurpassable model as poet in both Latin and the vernacular. In many other respects, however, Boccaccio differed from Petrarch, in some cases, as we have already seen in the case of Petrarch's relationship with the Visconti, even opposed him. The two men's intellectual formations had been too different and the goals they pursued were too dissimilar for them to truly fit the cliché of master and disciple. Boccaccio, it has been said, was "a fascinating combination of submission and independence."[3]

Boccaccio did not adopt and perhaps did not even understand the fundamental methodological principle that Petrarch placed at the heart of the new humanistic culture: philology as assessment of textual and historical veracity. While this restoration and recovery of authenticity had as consequences, on the one hand, an understanding of the depth and complexity of history, of the disruptions along its path, and, on the other, the project of reviving classical values by reconciling them with Christian ones in a global vision of renewal, Boccaccio remained faithful to a vision of history that was encyclopedic and nonhierarchical, in essence to the accumulative and syncretic approach instilled in him by the autodidactic education of his youth in Naples. But if his failure to join the great Petrarchan project was due to a lack of intellectual tools, his divergence on the crucial issue of the relationship between humanistic culture in Latin and culture in vernacular was instead conscious and intentional.

Original to him was the idea to bring together the elite selectivity of Petrarch's vision and the "popular" variety of Dante's into a new amalgam. For Dante—as Boccaccio would confess to Petrarch—had been his "light" and "guide"[4] since his early youth and would continue to be throughout his life. Reconciling these opposites lay at the heart of the ambitious project underlying Boccaccio's entire activity as a writer and scholar. This synthesis, he believed, would be made possible by virtue of the two men's common Florentine origins, that is, by exploiting the very local roots that Petrarch's cosmopolitanism erased. Boccaccio's restriction of himself to the role of pupil, therefore, was a kind of false modesty: his goal of bringing together these two mythoi to cross-pollinate in the expectation of radical innovation—with himself as the project's architect—reveals how just proudly aware he was of his own capabilities.

Local Pride

As we have seen, Boccaccio met Petrarch for the first time in Florence in the autumn of 1350, and in the spring of the next year, he was Petrarch's guest for a week at his house in Padua: we would not expect that immediately following, upon his return to Florence, he would focus intensively on Dante. And yet this is precisely what he did, dedicating himself to his illustrious fellow citizen simultaneously as editor and biographer. During this period, Boccaccio produced in his own hand the first of his three great collections of Dante's vernacular texts (*Vita Nova*, *Commedia*, and fifteen poems, that is, the *opera omnia*), including with them a biographical profile that was also in the vernacular: *De origine, vita, studiis et moribus viri clarissimi Dantis Aligerii Florentini poete illustris et de operibus compositis ab eodem*, better known as the *Trattatello in laude di Dante (Little Treatise in Praise of Dante)*.[5] Some ten years later, he would compose a second, shorter version of the biography, also closely connected to a new anthology of Dante's vernacular works.

Unlike the life of Petrarch he had written in the early 1340s, which, while enthusiastic, was ill informed and tainted by insistent personal projections, this work, thanks to the wealth of information Boccaccio gathered and his factual meticulousness—

recall that he had been visiting Ravenna for many years, where he had been able to increase his knowledge about Dante—was the first true biographical profile of the poet and remained unsurpassed until the modern era. Just as we are indebted to Boccaccio the collector for the preservation of several of Dante's letters and all of his Latin eclogues, so we owe to Boccaccio the biographer much information about Dante's life. It is, nonetheless, the case that even in this "scholarly" work, the biographer introduced observations more relevant to his own life than to that of his subject, such as the long tirade against marriage,[6] which owing to its excessiveness—as we have already seen—seems to emerge from the internal conflicts of the cleric author who would have preferred marriage.

All indications place the composition of the first version of the *Trattatello* between 1351 and 1353, therefore after Boccaccio's first meeting with Petrarch. We know that Petrarch's trip to Florence and Boccaccio's to Padua immediately after it were motivated by Petrarch's attempt to regain from the Comune the property it had confiscated from his exiled father as well as by the attempts of his Florentine admirers to attract him to settle in the city with the offer of a professorship. Now, in the *Trattatello*, in speaking about Dante, Boccaccio used themes, arguments, and rhetorical devices also present in the prose and verse correspondence underway at that time between Petrarch and his Florentine friends on the topics of exile and return to one's native land. Boccaccio lashed out violently at Florence, declaring it guilty of the cruel and shameful expulsion of its incomparable poet and then barring its gates to him, of not understanding that Dante was the city's true pride, and of not following the example of the seven ancient cities, which competed with each other to boast of having given birth to the divine Homer, or that of Mantua, Sulmona, Venosa, and Aquino, which boast of their poets (Virgil, Ovid, Horace, Juvenal) and argue over which is the greatest. Florence is further disgraced for not revoking Dante's banishment when it could have, with the sorry result that the body of the man who "always, although his exile was long, called himself and wished to be called a Florentine, always preferring you to all others" ("sempre fiorentino, quantunque l'esilio fosse lungo, si nominò e volle essere nominato, sempre ad ogni altra ti prepose," *TLD*, [I].92–109)[7] is buried in the much more noble Ravenna, which will never consent to give it back.

From behind this figure of Dante as the exile never called back home by his uncaring city emerges the image of Petrarch as he depicted himself in the verse letter of the summer of 1350 to Zanobi da Strata, in response to Zanobi's and Casini's invitations: an exile to whom Florence barred its gates, when a great number of cities, both in Italy and in other European states, would have liked to have him as a citizen; while his "proud fellow citizens drove him into exile; and he who suppresses just law closed the hostile city to him,"[8] Rome, Naples, Bologna, Pisa, Venice, Padua, Mantua, Parma, and Gaul, sought and welcomed him, and even "the far off Britons wanted him."[9] He too would die in a foreign land, just like the "so many men forbidden by their *patria* to lie in their native soil."[10] In short, in this first monument erected by Boccaccio in support of the myth of Dante as the supreme glory of Florence, the silhouette shines through of the other legendary figure he intended to associate with Dante: Petrarch, through whom Florence could find redemption by granting him what it had denied Dante. Other evidence supports a connection between Boccaccio's anti-Florentine invective in the *Trattatello* and the efforts of that period to bring Petrarch to the Studium of Florence. The Comune's letter to Petrarch communicating the restitution of his confiscated property and the conferral of the professorship, a letter believed to have been written by Boccaccio,[11] is in its first section "a counterpoint" to this argument of Petrarch's in his letter to Zanobi (*Epyst.*, III.9),[12] the same argument, as we have seen, that underlies the *Trattatello*. And, although the motif was widespread, the passage in the *Trattatello* on cities that vie for the honor of having produced Homer, given structural similarities, almost certainly relies on Cicero's *Pro Archia*,[13] an oration that Petrarch sent to Lapo da Castiglionchio in Florence in January 1351.[14] Finally, it is significant that this invective was omitted from the *Trattatello*'s second version, by which time the project to bring Petrarch to Florence had definitively ended.

In the early 1350s, therefore, Boccaccio's fervor in support of Dante cannot be interpreted as a polemical response to any doubts or concerns about Dante's worth that may have been raised by his interlocutors during discussions; it should instead be understood as the first move in his strategy aimed at making Dante the pillar of a cultural renewal based on the alliance of Latin and the vernacular. The second pillar could only be Petrarch, but Boccaccio's plan still did not foresee his direct involvement. In fact, Boccaccio did not send him either the biography or the anthology of Dante's work.[15] For now, he limited himself to strengthening the vernacular culture that he planned one day to join to Petrarch's humanism.

The Two Archetypes

For us, Boccaccio would not be Boccaccio had he not written the *Decameron*, just as Petrarch would not be Petrarch had he not written the *Canzoniere*. Two works that are not only radically different, even each other's opposites—not for nothing would they become the essential reference points for the two great, distinct branches of literature that dominated the Italian cultural scene for centuries: lyric poetry and fiction (and not only short fiction) in prose—but that reveal unsuspected similarities both in intent and in the futures that awaited them. Glorious futures, certainly, but just as certainly futures very different from the ones their authors could have imagined: it would not be until a hundred years after their compositions, in the second half of the fifteenth century, that these two books would become the archetypes from which, through innumerable processes of imitation, a courtly literature in verse and prose would arise and then proliferate with increasing rapidity.[16] But the literature of court is almost synonymous with literature that hovers between entertainment and social communication, which is precisely what both Petrarch and Boccaccio sought to oppose with their books by giving a structured, unitary form to (while also preserving the inescapable autonomy of) poetry and *novelle*, or short stories, that audiences of the day were accustomed to reading or listening to piecemeal. And, in fact, what would be imitated were the language, themes, and settings of their books, and only rarely the books' unified structure.[17] While that essential betrayal would happen only long after a coherent literature had developed at the signorial courts, this does not mean that earlier readers had understood the books' significance, for these books demanded a kind of reader that did not yet exist.[18] There had been collections of lyric poetry before the *Canzoniere*, just as there had been various kinds of books of tales or short stories prior to the *Decameron*, but none of these compilations had required their audiences to have a culture different from that of the usual readers of vernacular poetry or stories. Petrarch's and Boccaccio's works, however, did require this. In the *Canzoniere*'s prefatory sonnet, Petrarch pretends to address all those in love—"O you who hear these scattered verses / that sound of sighs with which I fed my heart . . . anyone who knows love through its trials" ("Voi ch'as-coltate in rime sparse il suono / di quei sospiri ond'io nudriva 'l core . . . ove sia che per prova intenda amore," *Rvf*, 1, 1–7)[19]—which is to say, to devotees of vernacular love poetry; but in reality he is speaking to people who join competence in this poetry with a cul-tured literary sensibility forged on the classics and on Augustinian and Stoic philosophy. In the preface of the *Decameron*, Boccaccio declares that he is writing for women, especially for those who suffer from amorous melancholy and who "remain pent up within their rooms" ("nelle loro camere racchiuse dimorano"), deprived of the comforts of the active and social lives allowed to men, with the hope that these women will be able to "derive pleasure" and "useful advice" ("diletto," "utile consiglio pigliare," *Dec.*, Proemio 10–14) from his stories: in short, he is saying that he writes for the audience that consumed romances and love stories for entertain-ment. This is the same type of reader to whom he had addressed his youthful works and for whom novelle and tales would be per-fectly suitable, were it not that such a meticulously and ambi-tiously structured work as the *Decameron*, even leaving aside its very weighty contents, seems to address a decidedly more learned audience than that represented by women.

The audience Petrarch desired did not exist in his time; nor did the sort of scholar Boccaccio required, one capable of appreciating the singularity of a text characterized by what then appeared to be irreconcilable oxymoron ("the light profundity of the *Decam-eron*").[20] The *Canzoniere* and the *Decameron* were such new literary forms that they could not be appreciated for their real significance by contemporaries. The works resulted from two complementary yet opposite processes: Petrarch sought to bring a reformed vernacular poetry into the domain of classical humanism; Boccaccio sought to add a dose of refined ingredients to the recipe for less-exalted vernacular literature. Both would win followers, but the truly innovative core of their work would only be realized much later.

Decameron

The opening heading reads: "Here begins the book called *Decameron*, also known as *Prince Galeotto*, which contains one hundred stories told in ten days by seven ladies and three young men" ("Comincia il libro chiamato *Decameron* cognominato prencipe Galeotto, nel quale si contengono cento novelle in diece dì dette da sette donne e da tre giovani uomini"); and the closing: "Here ends the Tenth and final Day of the book called *Decameron*, also known as *Prince Galeotto*" ("Qui finisce la Decima e ultima giornata del libro chiamato *Decameron* cognominato prencipe Galeotto"). Both were composed by Boccaccio. The title, modeled on the Greek *deca emeròn* (ten days), reflects the tendency of the young Boccaccio to create Greek-style titles (*Filocolo*, *Filostrato*), but here is specifically based on the title of the book *Exàmeron*, in which Bishop Ambrose had collected the sermons commenting on the Genesis creation story preached over six days during Holy Week of 387.[21] Galeotto, or Gallehault, is one of the most famous characters of the Arthurian romance cycle, those "French romances" of love and adventure that Fiammetta reads,[22] and he had already been appointed by Dante to represent the romance literary genre in the canto of Francesca and Paolo: "Galeotto was the book and he who wrote it" ("Galeotto fu il libro e chi lo scrisse," *Inf.*, V.137). With this title and (so-to-speak) subtitle, Boccaccio thus alludes to the coexistence in his work of "serious," moral philosophical arguments along with enjoyable stories: "We were reading one day, for pleasure" ("Noi leggiavamo, un giorno, per diletto," *Inf.*, V.127).[23] In the preface that follows, after declaring that over time he had freed himself from the pain suffered in his youth due a too ardent love, Boccaccio identifies "charming women" ("vaghe donne"), and especially those suffering from amorous "melancholy" ("melanconia"), as his book's audience[24] and provides a preview of the work's

structure and features: "My plan is to recount one hundred novelle, or fables, or parables, or histories, or whatever you wish to
call them. They were told over ten days by an honorable company
made up of seven ladies and three young men who came together
during the time of the recent plague that was responsible for so
many deaths. I will also include some little songs sung for their delight by the ladies I mentioned"[25] ("Intendo di raccontare cento novelle, o favole o parabole o istorie che dire le vogliamo, raccontate
in diece giorni da una onesta brigata di sette donne e di tre giovani
nel pistelenzioso tempo della passata mortalità fatta, e alcune canzonette dalle predette donne cantate a lor diletto," *Dec.*, Proem,
13). There are actually 101 stories because one (the so-called *delle
papere*, or "about the female adolescent geese") is narrated directly
by the author in the introduction to the fourth day, outside the
fiction of the "company."

Day 1

The first day opens with a general introduction to the rest of
the book. As in the preface, the author speaks in the first
person to ladies, and immediately places the story against
the background of the plague that raged in the city and the
"surrounding countryside" ("circustante contado") from
early spring through July of 1348: he recounts the spread
of the catastrophe, which he saw in person, describes the
deadly symptoms of the disease, the collapse of any "authority of the laws" ("autorità delle leggi"), the disintegra-
tion of society and families, the destruction of any moral
sense and of the most basic emotional bonds.[26] He then
goes on to recount an episode that had been related to him
"by a trustworthy person" ("da persona degna di fede"):[27]
In Florence "one Tuesday morning" ("un martedì mattina")
of an unspecified month (but definitely in the summer),
seven young women aged between eighteen and twenty-
eight (therefore young, but adults), who were connected
to one another "either by friendship, neighborhood, or
kinship" ("o per amistà o per vicinanza o per parentado"),
found themselves in the church of Santa Maria Novella. To

prevent the content of certain of the stories that they told from damaging their reputations, the author calls them by names that are fictitious but "suitable to their characters" ("alle qualità di ciascuna convenienti"): Pampinea, Fiammetta, Filomena, Emilia, Lauretta, Neifile, Elissa.[28] Pampinea, the oldest of the group, proposes to the others that, since they are all now alone because their families have either died or fled, they should leave the city, which is in the grip of disorder and dissoluteness, and go to one of the various country estates that they own, where they could "feast" and "make merry. . . . without ever overstepping the bounds of reason in any way" ("festa," "allegrezza," "senza trapassare in alcuno atto il segno della ragione").[29] Her companions agree, but object that it would be appropriate to have men along to guide and support them. At just that moment "three young men" ("tre giovani") appear, Panfilo, Filostrato, and Dioneo, who are connected by kinship to some of women and by romantic feelings to three of them, and although these feelings are known and the proposal might therefore appear improper, Pampinea invites them to join the expedition. At first, the men think she is mocking them, but when they understand she is serious they "happily" ("lietamente") accept. And so, the next day (Wednesday) at dawn, the women, accompanied by four maidservants (Misia, Licisca, Chimera, Stratilia), and the men, along with three manservants (Parmeno, Sirisco, Tindaro), travel to a "palace" ("palagio") located "on a little mountain" ("sopra una piccola montagnetta") not more than "two short miles" ("due piccole miglia") from the city. Here Pampinea proposes that each of their days be ruled by a king or queen. Elected queen for that day, she gives the servants instructions and then establishes the schedule of activities, which, with a few variations, will be substantially followed on the days to come: In the early morning, everyone is permitted to devote themselves to whatever activity he or she likes; around the third hour (our 9 a.m.), the company meets outdoors for lunch, followed by singing and dancing; during the hottest hours they sleep in "bedchambers separated" ("camere separate") from the other gender. In the early afternoon (around the ninth hour) until sunset they find a pleasant place to listen to and discuss the stories told by each member of the company. On this first day they gather in a "meadow" ("pratello") located near the palace and tell stories with no set theme.[30] The text of the ten stories (each preceded by a heading that summarizes its content,[31] just as a heading marks the beginning of each day) is followed by a conclusion describing how each of the young people amused themselves after the storytelling, the name of the following day's king or queen, and what theme he or she assigns for the next stories. The new queen is Filomena and she introduces the rule, which Pampinea had not been able to establish "because she was elected Queen so late," to "restrict within definite limits the subject matter of the stories we are going to tell" ("per lo esser tardi eletta al reggimento" "ristrignere dentro a alcun termine quello di cui devono novellare") and to announce the topic in advance, so that "each will have time to think up a fine story" ("ciascuno abbia spazio di poter pensare a alcuna bella novella"): the theme she sets is "Fortune" ("fortuna") or, rather, how someone, although beset by misfortunes, achieves a happy end beyond his or her hopes. Dioneo, however, requests and receives permission not to be bound by a theme in order to be able, if necessary, to cheer up the group "with a tale that would make them laugh" ("con alcuna novella da ridere"). After dinner, the storytellers make music and dance: Lauretta dances to the music of a song sung by Emilia accompanied by Dioneo on the lute, "I'm So Enamored of My Loveliness" ("Io son sì vaga della mia bellezza"). All of the days will end with the performance of a ballad, which gives the *Decameron* qualities of a prosimetrum.[32]

Day 2

The brief introduction informs the reader that on Thursday the storytellers did the same things at the same times as on the previous day: "just as they had done the preceding day, they spent this one" ("E sì come il trapassato giorno avean fatto, così fecero il presente"); the storytelling session also takes place in the same meadow. Once it is finished, Filomena names Neifile queen for the next day, but the new monarch proposes that they resume the storytelling on Sunday, skipping Friday, to devote the day of the passion and death of Christ "to prayers rather than stories" ("più tosto a orazioni che a novelle"), as well as Saturday, a day that women usually spend on the care of the body and many also in fasting. She further proposes that in order to avoid being joined by strangers they change their location and resume their storytelling in a new place that she has in mind. The next stories must be about people who through their abilities succeed in obtaining something very much desired or in recovering something that had been lost. After dinner, the day ends with Pampinea singing "What Lady Sings Except for Me Alone" ("Qual donna canterà, s'io non canto io") as Emilia dances and the others sing the chorus.[33]

Here the story breaks off and then resumes at dawn on Sunday. The book, therefore, is said to be ten "days" because, of the fourteen days the company actually spent outside Florence (or fifteen, counting the day of their return), they met on ten of them to tell stories.

Day 3

At dawn on Sunday the queen, Neifile, leads the company less than two miles away to a "most beautiful, ornate palace" ("bellissimo e ricco palagio"). On one side was a garden with a lawn in the middle, at the center of which stood a white marble fountain with a statue out of which shot water high into the sky; the water overflowing the fountain's pool entered a stream that flowed out of the garden and turned the grindstones of two mills. After exploring the garden, which was inhabited by innumerable species of animals, the young people arranged for tables to be placed around the fountain, the women sang a few short songs and danced, and then they ate. Following this, some went to sleep, others set about playing chess and dice, and still others passed the time "reading romances" ("legger romanzi"), that is, those "French romances" ("franceschi romanza") that we know Fiammetta and the widow of the *Corbaccio* read.[34] Once the storytelling on the lawn by the fountain was finished, Neifile chooses Filostrato as the king, who sets as the next day's theme loves that "came to an unhappy end" ("ebbero infelice fine"), doing so because he too expects to be unhappy in love in the end, which is exactly why his name "was conferred on me by someone who certainly knew what it meant" ("da tale che seppe ben che si dire mi era stato imposto"). The name Filostrato, which, according to Boccaccio, means "vanquished and laid prostrate by love" ("vinto e abbattuto da amore"), and which he had used as the title for the poem in which he recounted how Troilo, betrayed by Criseida, had sought death in battle. While waiting for the dinner hour, some start chasing the animals in the garden, Filomena and Panfilo play chess, and Dioneo and Fiammetta sing the story of Guglielmo and the Lady of Vergiù, that is a *cantare*, specifically the reworking of the then-famous French poem *La Chastelaine de Vergi*. After dinner, Lauretta accompanied by others sings the ballad "No Lady All Forlorn" ("Niuna sconsolata").[35]

Day 4

This day's introduction interrupts the narrative flow as the author takes the floor and speaks in the first person to his "dearest ladies" ("carissime donne"), responding to accusations that some people, out of envy, have leveled at his "little stories" ("novellette"). Although he is only a third of the way through the book, he has decided to do this now, he says, in order to rebut criticisms that would only intensify if left unanswered until he completed the work. The offending remarks: he likes women "too much" ("troppo"), that is, he spends too much time writing about love, which is particularly unseemly at his age; instead of "mixing" with ladies and "this nonsense" ("mescolarsi"; "con queste ciance"), he should "stay with the Muses in Parnassus" ("stare con le Muse in Parnaso"), that is, he should cultivate a more serious and elevated literature; finally, according to his most hostile detractors, he would do better to think about how to earn his daily bread than pursuing this nonsense ("ciance" = "trifles"). Before giving his specific responses, he tells the brief story of the son of Filippo Balducci, who, having been raised by his widower father in a hermit's cell, at the age of eighteen goes to Florence for the first time where he catches his first sight of women. When he asks his father what they are called, his father responds "goslings" ("papere," more precisely, "female adolescent geese") and that they are "evil" ("mala cosa"). To which the son replies that he had never before seen anything so beautiful and, if his father would allow him to bring one home with them, he would give them something "to peck at" ("beccare"). Why then, the author asks, are his critics so astonished, if even someone raised in solitude upon first seeing a woman feels irresistibly attracted to her? As for being embarrassed to devote himself literature about love at his age, why should he be, when great men like Guido Cavalcanti, Dante Alighieri, and Cino da Pistoia have also done so? Women, thanks to their beauty, do resemble the Muses, and they have certainly helped him write; however, he says, whereas "women have been the occasion of my composing a thousand lines of poetry," "the Muses never caused me to write anything" ("le donne mi fur cagione di comporre mille versi"; "le Muse mai non mi furono di farne alcun cagione"). Anyway, while writing his short stories, he is not far from either Parnassus or the Muses. As for nourishment, poets have gotten more of it from their fables than the rich have from their treasures, without even taking into account that by pursuing fables many "have lived to a ripe old age" ("fecero le loro età fiorire"), while many who seek only to accumulate riches have turned out to die young.[36]

> This day's introduction proper is very short: it essentially communicates that the company did the same things that day as on the previous one. Following the usual afternoon's storytelling, Filostrato crowns Fiammetta queen and she sets

as the next day's theme thwarted loves/star-crossed loves with happy endings. Before dinner by the fountain, some wander through the garden and others leave it to visit the mills. After dining, they dance and sing, as usual; Filostrato sings a song, "By Weeping I Can Show" ("Lagrimando di-mostro"), that expresses his sorrow at being left by the woman he loves: the blush of one of the dancing young ladies would have revealed that she is Filostrato's beloved, had the dark of the warm night not concealed it.

Day 5

At sunrise, led by Fiammetta, the young people take a walk through the countryside, and following this "light exercise" ("leggiere affanno"), refresh themselves "with the finest of wines and a variety of sweets" ("con ottimi vini e con confetti"), and then stroll in the garden until lunchtime. After resting during the hottest hours of the day, they gather around the fountain in the early afternoon and begin their tales, at the end of which Fiammetta names Elissa queen. She decrees that the following day they will tell stories about characters who have responded to provocation "with some elegant witticism" ("con alcun leggiadro motto"), or managed to elude danger or embarrassment with a "prompt retort" ("pronta risposta"). The usual dancing and singing follow dinner. At the request for a song, Dioneo, the most witty and unconventional of the group, proposes a few, all bawdy and full of sexual double entendre (as you can see from such first lines as: "Monna Aldruda, lift up your tail" ["Monna Aldruda, levate la coda"]; "Hike up your skirts, Monna Lapa" ["Alzatevi i panni, monna Lapa"]; and "Take it easy, husband dear" ["Deh fa pian, marito mio"]).[37] Embarrassed, the ladies laugh, until Queen Fiammetta orders Dioneo to stop and "sing us a nice one" ("dinne una bella"), that is, a sincere song. Dioneo then sings, to high praise, the ballad "O Love, the Charming Light" ("Amor, la vaga luce").[38]

Day 6

After the usual morning walk and meal, while the others slept, Lauretta and Dioneo "began singing about Troilus and Cressida," the protagonists of Boccaccio's poem *Filostrato* (already referred to in the conclusion to Day 3). When they are all seated around the fountain and about to begin the storytelling, something unusual happens: they hear a tremendous ruckus coming from the kitchen, which they learn is an argument between Licisca, the maid who is "no spring chicken" ("attempatetta"), and the serving man Tindaro. When the pair is called before the company, Licisca reveals, in a speech replete with obscene puns, that the subject of the dispute is whether the wife of a certain Sicofante had come untouched to marriage, as Tindaro claims, or, as Licisca knows well, was no longer a virgin: for that matter, to Licisca's knowledge, none of her neighbors had come to her husband "a maid" ("pulcella"). Once the dispute is settled thanks to Dioneo, who declares "that Licisca is in the right" ("che la Licisca ha ragione"), the storytelling can commence. After the ten stories have been told, the company, still laughing about the cleverness of Frate Cipolla (the protagonist of the final story), names Dioneo king, who, inspired by Licisca's reference to the many tricks that wives play on their husbands, decides that this will be their subject for the following day. In response to the women's protests that the theme is unbecoming to their virtue, he says that in these times of pestilence, when judges have abandoned their courts, neither divine nor human laws apply, and any action is permitted in order to stay alive, he simply does not see how anyone in the future will be able to criticize them. While maintaining proper behavior as they have been doing, a little more freedom in speaking can be permitted.[39] The ladies are convinced, and since the storytelling had been short and the sun is still high in the sky, Elissa, without telling the men, takes her female companions to a place a little more than a mile away called the Valley of the Ladies ("Valle delle Donne"): surrounded by six little mountains, each of which had a small castle at its peak, the valley's center was a perfectly round, diminutive plain with a crystal-clear pool. Since it was still hot, the women undressed and went in the water. Afterward, they told the three men what they had done, and so the men too went to the pool to swim. Upon the men's return to the palace, they find the women dancing to an air sung by Fiammetta, and then Dioneo, to repay Elissa for the honor she did him by naming him king, asks her to sing for them. She sings a story of an unhappy love, "If Ever I Escape Your Claws, O Love" ("Amor, s'io posso uscir de' tuoi artigli"), but no one can understand what caused her sadness. However, Dioneo, who is in high spirits, has Tindaro called and has the company dance for quite a while to the playing of his bagpipe.

Day 7

The sun has not yet risen when the company sets out for the Valley of the Ladies, where the steward has already taken everything necessary for a pleasant stay. Here they have breakfast, sing, almost rivaling the birds, eat lunch under the trees, and then sleep outdoors on the beds the steward has brought. At the usual time, they sit on carpets spread out near the pool and begin their stories, at the end of which Dioneo names Lauretta as queen, who in turn sets as the theme of the next meeting the tricks that men and women play on each other. Before dining, some go wading in the pool, others roam through the meadow, and Dioneo and Fiammetta sing a lengthy song "about Arcite and Palamon" ("d'Arcita e Palemone"), characters in Boccaccio's *Teseida*. Following dinner, they make their way slowly back to the palace they had left at dawn, where they refresh themselves and then partake in the usual dancing and singing. Filomena performs a song, "Alas, My Life's Forlorn!" ("Deh lassa la mia vita!"), from which the others understand that she is in love and has tasted the pleasures of that love, mak-

ing some envious. At this point the queen remembers that
the next day is Friday, and proposes that they abstain from
"pleasant storytelling" ("piacevole novellare") until Sunday, as they had done the previous week.

Thus, the story of the company is interrupted for the second time.

Day 8

It is Sunday, and in the early morning the young people go to
"a nearby church" ("una chiesetta lor vicina") and hear "divine service" ("il divino oficio"), and then pass the rest of
the day in the usual way until they take their seats near the
fountain to begin the stories, after which Lauretta names
Emilia as queen. The new queen decides that the next day
each person will tell a story of his or her choice. At the end
of evening, on Emilia's orders, Panfilo sings a love song, "So
Great, Love, Are the Good" ("Tanto è, Amore, il bene"),[40]
and although everyone present tries to figure out the identity of the woman he loves, no one succeeds.

Day 9

At dawn, guided by Emilia, the storytellers set out for a little
nearby wood: here they play with the wild animals, which
come near them without fear, since the "widespread
plague" ("soprastante pistolenzia") has made the hunters
almost disappear. Returning to the palace, they engage in
their usual amusements and then, after eating and sleeping, at the customary time they resume their storytelling
next to the fountain. Named king of the final day, Panfilo
proposes they tell stories about actions or behavior inspired by liberality and magnificence. After dinner, they
dance and sing a great number of "little songs" ("canzonette"), which are more enjoyable for their lyrics than for
their accompanying music, and, at the end, Neifile sings the
ballad "A Youthful Maiden, I'm So Happy Now" ("Io mi son
giovinetta, e volentieri").[41]

Day 10

A brief introduction tells the reader that at dawn, the young
people, led by Panfilo, take a long walk during which they
wonder about "their future life" ("loro futura vita") and
then, after returning to the palace, eating, and sleeping,
they begin to tell the stories. At the end, Panfilo, points
out that on the next day it will have been fifteen days since
they left Florence and emphasizes that during their time
together "a sense of propriety, harmony, and fraternal
friendship" ("continua onestà, continua concordia, continua fraternal dimestichezza") has reigned among them. He
then proposes that they return to the city in order to avoid
the possibilities that their "having stayed here all this time"
("troppo lunga dimoranza") might give rise to malicious
talk and, now that their company was known by others
in the area, that their numbers might grow, which would
take away all the pleasure from their gathering (the same
concern that had led them to change location at the end of
Day 2). After a long discussion, the young people approve
the proposal and give orders to the steward to prepare for
their departure the next day. The day ends with the usual
songs and dances, and with a jealous Fiammetta singing "If
Love Could Come Unmixed with Jealousy" ("S'amor venisse
senza gelosia"), in which she threatens to make weep bitterly any woman who tries to take away her man. Laughing,
Dioneo says that she should reveal who it is she loves so that
none of her companions "take him from you out of ignorance" ("acciò che per ignoranza non vi fosse tolta la posses-
sione"). The following day, they return to Florence: in Santa
Maria Novella, "from which they had all set out" ("donde
con loro partiti s'erano"), the three young men take leave of
the seven women and go off to other pleasurable activities;
the women return "to their homes" ("alle lor case").[42]

After the final day Boccaccio places an "Author's Conclusion"
addressed to "most noble young ladies" ("nobilissime giovani")

in which he responds to some possible criticisms of his work: using language that was highly improper, excessive variation, and disparity in the quality of the stories, too many "clever quips and jests" ("motti e di ciance"), "venomous" ("velenosi") attacks on friars; "to some extent, therefore, it is an addition, or better an update, to the defense developed in the introduction to Day IV."[43]

Just this brief summary of the *Decameron*'s main story (which is usually, and incorrectly, called the "frame") demonstrates the work's careful structure: it is a unified complex with multiple levels of organization, held together by a strict system of symmetries. Now, the tendency to enclose his literary constructs within precise symmetries and numerological schemas while reinforcing them internally with a dense net of connections is typical of all Boccaccio's work, not only that in vernacular. This practice could be interpreted as a kind of necessary precaution taken to contain the chaos that would otherwise result from his temperamental and instinctive inclination toward accumulation, proliferation, and digression. The bid for order might have been even more urgent in this particular case for two reasons. Because in the *Decameron*, as has been concisely observed, Boccaccio "turned to an enormous quantity and broad array of types of sources and models, obtaining them from the most disparate traditions: Greek and Latin classical antiquity, Byzantine and late antique romance, Eastern stories, medieval Latin literature, Provençal and *stil novo* poetry, all the forms of medieval narrative, short and long, prose and verse, as well as non-literary sources—philosophy, medicine, botany, history, geography, law."[44] And also because of the need to give book form to materials (novelle, *fabliaux*, anecdotes, *exempla*, Provençal *vidas*) that until then had circulated loose, or within writings of another kind, or collected in unstructured anthologies. It is clear, however, that Boccaccio understood his collection as a unitary work from its earliest conception and, therefore, that the lack of overlap between the story's internal audience of women, representative of the readers of vernacular entertainment literature, and the audience of the book's actual intended readers, namely, intellectuals capable of understanding its cultural implications, was original to and, so to speak, consubstantial with the project.

Legitimated by Petrarch

We have no stable reference points for determining the period during which Boccaccio conceived this book, how long he worked on it, or when he made it public. It is necessary, first of all, to distinguish between the book and the stories: indeed, it must be assumed that many of the novelle were written before their inclusion in the *Decameron*. How long before, we do not know. It is conceivable that writing short stories was something that Boccaccio had done for quite a long time. If we consider that the years between his return to Florence and roughly the middle of that decade were characterized by the production of a veritable flood of fiction in the vernacular (from the completion of the *Teseida* to the *Ninfale fiesolano*), while, in contrast, the five years that followed appear devoid of work with the sole exception of a few eclogues in Latin, we can reasonably suppose that Boccaccio devoted time during those apparently empty years to writing novelle. And while we can be almost certain that a few stories were written during the assembly of the book and specifically for it (divided as it is into themed days), we can only hypothesize that he circulated some stories individually or in small groups before conceiving of the book and while working on it, or that he shared entire days of stories in advance, for example, the first three.[45]

Dating hypotheses are many and varied. The most commonly accepted places the composition of the entire book (or one of its first redactions, according to some) within the range 1348–53 (extendable, according to another, to 1355 or even beyond).[46]

The project of the book thus presupposed the plague, and therefore must have begun after 1348–49.[47] The problem is determining how long after. Hypotheses disagree on this issue, as well.[48] A clear sign that a significant amount of time had passed between the period of the plague when the action takes place and the book's composition is found in the introduction to Day 1. Here, Boccaccio writes that he does not want to reveal the seven women's real names in order to protect their reputations, because "today" the rules of behavior are much more rigid than they were "then," when the epidemic had given rise to a general relaxation of morals: "the rules concerning pleasure, which are rather strict today, were then . . . very lax, not just for women of their age, but even for those much older" ("essendo oggi alquanto ristrette le leggi al piacere che allora . . . erano non che alla loro età ma a troppo più matura larghissime," *Dec.*, I, Introd., 50).⁴⁹ The passage from the laxity of "then" to the rigor of "today" presumes that Florentine society had had the time necessary to restore the past climate of austerity.

In the absence of specific information, the best we can do is bring together what is known about Boccaccio's life in the late 1340s and the 1350s with what he thought about the role of vernacular literature at that stage of his life. The spring 1351 visit to Petrarch in Padua was a decisive moment. During their discussions over the course of the week, Petrarch would have spoken to his guest about his recently conceived grand project, then in its early stages of realization, to gather together his scattered Latin verse and prose letters and his vernacular lyric poetry into three books, which, while distinct, were also conceptualized as three parts of one great unified ideal book: they would become the *Familiares*, the *Epystole*, and the *Rerum vulgarium fragmenta*, that is, the *Canzoniere*. A feature shared by all three books is that each gives unitary form to a group of texts that could be read independently, scattered works deemed minor in the literary hierarchy: trivial works. Petrarch called them *nuge* ("trifles"): little things, bagatelles, amusements. They are small, not comparable to his great works like the poem *Africa* or the tract *De viris illustribus* (*Famous Men*), because they are occasional writings, limited in scope, thematically dissimilar, and disparate in style. Another important point is that all three collections presupposed, either explicitly (*Epystole* and *Familiares*) or implicitly (*Canzoniere*), the great rupture caused by the plague of 1348.⁵⁰

Boccaccio must have been quite struck by this project. And he would have been particularly surprised that this humanist, who was squeamish about even the great Dante, was devoting so much attention to his own vernacular poetry, to the point of deciding to construct a kind of romance out of these micro-texts, which would seem to be exceptionally poorly suited by nature to creating a continuous book. It is even possible that on this visit Boccaccio read the prefatory sonnet of the *Canzoniere*, which Petrarch had composed a short time earlier.⁵¹

There are too many similarities between what Boccaccio did with novelle and what Petrarch did with lyric poetry to believe the resemblances were accidental.[52] Boccaccio, too, organized texts that remained autonomous into a rigorously structured whole. Texts that fit perfectly the definition of *nuge* (which in his old age he would indeed call them, but with a disparaging cast: "my domestic trifles" ["domesticas nugas meas," *Ep.*, XXII.19 of 1373]): circulated individually, they are short, different in size, various in subject, stylistically nonhomogeneous, and, like the *nuge*, occasional. Not by chance, Boccaccio persistently used the diminutive "novelletta" ("little story"). Petrarch, while presenting his book to be read as a whole, spoke of "snippets" ("frammenti") and "scattered rhymes" ("rime sparse"), and acknowledged that the work could be treated as an anthology. Boccaccio, while producing a book organized as a single continuous story, recognized that one could read the stories by skipping around ("whosoever reads through these stories can skip over those that give offense and read only those that promise delight" ["chi va leggendo, lasci star quelle che pungono e quelle che dilettano legga," *Dec.*, "Author's Conclusion," 19]),[53] and, above all, although he gave it both a title and a subtitle, he called the *Decameron* an "untitled" book ("senza titolo," *Dec.*, IV, Introd., 3), meaning that, like Ovid's *Amores*, it does not deal with "a single subject," but "we can say he put it together piece by piece."[54] Boccaccio, therefore, was fully aware of the unusual nature of his book of stories, just as Petrarch was of his book of poems. And, finally, it cannot be pure coincidence that the *Decameron* is set at the time of the plague and is presented as a response to this collective trauma.

Until a few years ago, the belief was widespread (and still persists in a few quarters) that Boccaccio finished the *Decameron* by 1351, because it was thought, his meeting with Petrarch marked a turning point in his understanding of literature, after which he would never have devoted his energies to a work in the vernacular.[55] But, to the contrary, everything in fact suggests that 1351 marked not the terminus ad quem, but the terminus post quem, and that it was precisely Boccaccio's contact with Petrarch that inspired him to write the *Decameron*.

The book is the culmination of two tendencies evident in Boccaccio's writing from the very beginning: one was a, so to speak, innate tendency, to tell stories, and the other was cultural, to ennoble vernacular popular fiction. In this sense, then, the *Decameron* represented continuity. The break, the leap forward lay in a shift—and here Petrarch was decisive—in what Boccaccio sought to elevate to the status of literature: rather than little-known or popular stories that already existed as unified wholes in their own right, he now instead took texts adrift in the great sea of short narratives, scraps superfluous or completely insignificant to even the world of vernacular narrative, and made of these small pieces the materials from which he created a book that aspired to be a masterpiece in vernacular. Petrarch was decisive to this project not just because he pointed out the way, but, above all, because his authority legitimated—or at least so Boccaccio thought—the aspiration to raise vernacular writing into the upper echelons of literature, to the same heights as writing in Latin. If the *Decameron* was conceived of as the equivalent to the *Rerum vulgarium fragmenta*, we must revise the image, which has been accepted too long, of Boccaccio the pupil under the thumb of his master Petrarch. Instead, during the first years after their meeting, Boccaccio appears to have been careful to assert his independence: with the *Trattatello in laude di Dante* we see him take a stance that is implicitly but also proudly confrontational; with this project to do something with vernacular stories similar to what Petrarch was doing with vernacular poems, we see him intent on emulation.

Oriented by Dante

Boccaccio almost instinctively associated the idea of a vernacular masterpiece with Dante's *Commedia*. While Petrarch legitimated the *Decameron* as a project and indicated a method, the model could only have been Dante's poem. Some of the parallels are glaring: at the height of the plague of 1348, Boccaccio was thirty-five, the same age as Dante in 1300, the jubilee year in which he set the *Commedia*; there are one hundred cantos in Dante's work just as there are one hundred stories in Boccaccio's. Other correspondences are less visible but equally forceful: the introductory declaration that the "horrific beginning" of the book would turn to pleasure at the end, as happens when climbing a "harsh and steep" mountain one reaches "a most beautiful and delightful plain" ("orrido cominciamento"; "aspra e erta"; "un bellissimo piano e dilettevole," *Dec.*, I, Introd., 4–5),[56] alludes to the beginning of the *Commedia*, to the "harsh" ("aspra") woods that inspire fear and the "delightful mountain" ("dilettoso monte") to be climbed, and at the same time to the definition of the genre of comedy itself ("a comedy has a tumultuous beginning, full of chaos and discord, whereas it ends in peace and tranquillity" ["la commedia ha turbulento principio e pieno di romori e di discordie e poi l'ultima parte di quella finisce in pace e in tranquillità," *ECD*, Accessus, 25]).[57] This definition was common in medieval poetics but here Boccaccio seems to have drawn from a letter to Cangrande della Scala that Boccaccio believed was written by Dante: "a comedy, in truth, may begin with difficult circumstances but its story ends favorably" (and this is the reason he called the poem the *Commedia* because "at the beginning it is foul and savage . . . and in the end favorable").[58] Boccaccio, therefore, intended to write a comedy that would necessarily be different from Dante's, but inspired by the same poetic principles. This point alone is enough to demonstrate his great distance from Petrarch. Petrarch pursued thematic homogeneity, expunged history, the contingent, the particular; the *Decameron*, in contrast, is a fresco depicting the world's variety, that draws its images from life, from the daily social whirl, and from individuals' experiences. Petrarch confined himself within the boundaries of the self and the inner life; Boccaccio's stories are by their nature founded on interpersonal relationships, are part of the public discourse and for the public. The *Canzoniere* is a stylistically polished work that tends toward uniformity; the *Decameron* is an encyclopedia of styles, which ascend from the low comic and even obscene all the way to the sublime. Finally, Petrarch constructed an artificial language, one outside of time, far from the spoken tongue, technical or specialists' jargon, and any mimetic effect; Boccaccio used a variable and flexible language, drew on the vocabularies of many different spheres, mixed learned and Latinized forms with expressions that were colloquial or even from the popular classes, and, especially, tended to portray his characters through the imitation of socially marked and non-

Florentine regional dialects.[59] This summary of Boccaccian traits reveals the strong influence, more than of the genre comedy, of the *Divine Comedy*.

Dante's influence is visible on many levels of the *Decameron*: the clearest imprint, because it relies on a common imaginative process, appears in Boccaccio's recreation of Dante's characters as protagonists in stories and anecdotes (Gugliemo Borsiere, Ciacco, Filippo Argenti, Corso Donati), his narrative development of Dantean ideas (Guido Cavalcanti and Betto Brunelleschi), his invention of events simply on the basis of names or settings in the *Commedia* (Lizio di Valbona, Ricciardo Manardi, Paolo Traversari, Ghino di Tacco), and his transposition of stories similar to some of Dante's into a different historical and geographical context (Gualtieri of Antwerp).[60] However, the *Commedia*'s deepest imprint on the *Decameron* can be summed up with the word "realism."

What links the two authors' forms of realism is neither content nor representational method. Regarding the first, in his work Boccaccio ignores the political and theological-religious themes that are central to Dante's poem in favor of accounts of communal life and experiences of individual people; in other words, he sets the extraordinary events, both big and small, that serve as triggers for his stories into contexts or against backgrounds that, by either reaffirming or upsetting it, refer back to everyday life, which is, precisely the realm with no bearing on a poem like Dante's that presents its every character, event, action, and even minute detail against an eschatological background. Their representational methods also only partly overlap: Dante systematically exploits every mimetic technique from psychological to linguistic, but the method most his own, and uniquely his, for producing the effect of reality is through ellipses, allusions, implications, brief mentions, leaving it to the reader to fill in most of the information necessary for understanding the text.[61] In contrast, Boccaccio relies entirely on mimesis and verisimilitude, and thus provides detailed information about characters (from name and social status, to physical and moral traits), places, and settings.[62]

The aspects of the *Decameron*'s realism that make it Dantesque are different from these, most notably, the focus on the contemporary present. Even without listing the many characters who were still alive in 1348 and beyond, just as was the case in the *Commedia* with respect to 1300, a rough numerical analysis gives a sense of how significant the novelle's chronological proximity was in the collection: of the one hundred stories, fully sixty-one are set more or less within the fifty years before the plague, and of those, half, exactly thirty, are set either in the near past or in the present ("A year or two ago" ["L'altr'anno," *Dec.*, IX.10, 6]).⁶³ We can add to this the tendency, common to both authors, to bring in personal experiences, drawn from their own lives and from the lives of others, based on suggestions from the current surroundings or memories of places and events from the past. A second set of numbers, although of a general nature, provides evidence of a less obvious link between chronological distribution and the stories' geographical locations. Almost half of the stories, forty-four, are set in Tuscany (thirty-one of them in Florence and its immediate hinterland); fourteen in the Kingdom of Naples (seven of them in the city of Naples); nine in France (fully six of them in Paris), and an equal number in Romagna. So their settings are those in which Boccaccio was living or had lived or those about which he had particular knowledge either from his father or his own experiences in mercantile environments, foremost those of the Bardi. The connection between the propensity to privilege a recent time frame and to set the tales in places and environments of which the author, directly or indirectly, had particular knowledge is demonstrated by the fact that the action in thirteen of the thirty-one Florentine tales takes place close to the time of the work's narrative.⁶⁴

In the *Commedia*, when the story touches on the most sad and painful episodes of the poet's life or contemporary political events in which he was most deeply involved, the pressure of autobiography bursts its banks, so to speak, and destroys the boundary between Dante the writer and Dante the subject. Now, in Boccaccio's writing, self-display is almost inescapable: in the *Decameron*, it has a way of expanding widely through the metanarrative and paratexts. But it also can't resist sneaking into the stories, even if here the speakers are distinct from the author. And so, Filomena can attribute the Florentine tale of Federigo degli Alberighi to Coppo di Borghese Domenichi, well known to Boccaccio and still alive in 1348,⁶⁵ and Dioneo can introduce Pietro Canigiani, one of the author's closest and most trusted friends, as a character in the story of Salabaetto, a tale about Florentines working in Palermo and Naples.[66] At other times, the autobiographical reference is indirect, almost cryptic: for example, the Ischian woman Restituta, sweetheart of Gianni di Procida, is called the daughter of the "nobleman" ("gentil uom") Marin Bolgaro, an associate of Boccaccio's during his Naples years.[67] The Certaldo story of Frate Cipolla is a true homage to his own family and the memory of his recently deceased father ("Certaldo, as you may perhaps have heard, is fortified town in the Val d'Elsa, located in our territory, and although it is small, the people living there were once noble and pretty well-to-do" ["Certaldo, come voi forse avete potuto udire, è un castel di Valdelsa posto nel nostro contado, il quale, quantunque piccol sia, già di nobili uomini e d'agiati fu abitato," *Dec.*, VI.10, 5]),[68] and not coincidentally is told by the autobiographical Dioneo: the story portrays two villagers, Giovanni di Bragoniera and Biagio Pizzini, the latter of whom had been Boccaccino's closest friend. Finally, it would be remarkable, but for a storyteller as imaginative as Boccaccio not out of the question, if, in the story of Corrado Gianfigliazzi (alive until shortly after 1353)[69] and the "viniziano" ("Venetian") cook Chichibio, the "little gal from the country named Brunetta, with whom Chichibio was utterly infatuated" ("feminetta della contrada, la quale Brunetta era chiamata e di cui Chichibio era forte innamorato," *Dec.*, VI.4, 7)[70] was in fact the servant named Bruna who was a part of Boccaccio's household apparently from 1349 or 1350 until his death.

The Early Diffusion

It took Boccaccio many years of work to complete the *Decameron*. On its final pages, he wrote that "a great deal of time has passed from the day I started writing until this present hour," when he is approaching the end of his "labors" ("molto tempo passato sia da poi che io a scrivere cominciai infino a questa ora," "fatica," *Dec.*, "Author's Conclusion," 20).[71] As in the case of the date of commencement, the date of completion is similarly not documented. The only firm reference point we have is a letter sent on July 13, 1360, by Francesco Buondelmonti (son of Lapa Acciaiuoli, and thus a nephew of Niccolò) from Ancona while en route from Florence to Naples, to Giovanni Acciaiuoli, recently appointed archbishop of Patras but at that time residing in Florence, with the request to send him "the book of stories by Messer Giovanni Boccaccio, which book is mine." The *Decameron*, therefore, was circulating on that date, or rather, had been circulating since December of the previous year, when Buondelmonti, who had accompanied his uncle on a mission to Florence, would have been able to commission a copy of the book, which, finally, he was requesting be sent to him.

Beyond establishing an unassailable terminus ad quem, this letter is valuable evidence of the great interest roused by the *De-cameron* from the very beginning among the Florentines who gravitated around Acciaiuoli in Naples. Not without reason, Francesco worried the book would fall into others' hands: "And be careful Messer Neri [son of Iacopo Acciaiuoli, Niccolò's cousin] doesn't get ahold of it so that I won't have it . . . and be careful not to loan it to anyone because many would be rude about it . . . and beware lending my book to Ser Niccolò [Acciaiuoli], lest he steal it."[72] The interest within this circle is confirmed by the fact that one of the oldest surviving codices[73] — actually an anthology containing the conclusions to the first nine days with their respective ballads and the final story of Day 9 — was transcribed at the beginning of the 1360s, when Boccaccio was still alive, by the hand of an anonymous Florentine who not only lived in Naples, but was a functionary employed by the letter writer's mother, the Lapa Acciaiuoli mentioned above.

In the second half of the 1350s, perhaps around the same time that Francesco Buondelmonti commissioned his codex, a politically prominent wool merchant, Giovanni d'Agnolo Capponi, transcribed his own copy of the *Decameron*:[74] the relevant fact is that Capponi copied an autograph, very likely one made available to him by Boccaccio himself, who appears to have personally overseen the work of transcription.[75] Capponi was not the only person who had access to Boccaccio's autographs: during this same period, the anonymous person who assembled a copy of the *De-cameron* that has survived only in fragments also appears to have copied an autograph, but one different from the autograph used by Capponi;[76] in 1384, the magnate Francesco d'Amaretto Mannelli transcribed an autograph working manuscript,[77] in all likelihood accompanied by a long series of notations in the author's own hand in the margins and between the lines.

The earliest evidence of the book's diffusion is therefore limited to circles very close to Boccaccio.[78] It is unnecessary to point out again his relationships with the Acciaiuoli clan within which we find the first owner-readers; it should instead be highlighted that those who copied it "for pleasure" in Florence (exemplary of whom is Lapa's anonymous functionary, who not only copied the *Decameron*, but owned and notated the codex containing the *Novellino*, the oldest collection of Italian short stories)[79] turn out to have been connected either directly to Boccaccio or to people close to him: Giovanni Capponi lived in the neighborhood of Santo Spirito, as did Boccaccio; the magnate Mannelli family had their houses in Santa Felicita, the same parish as the Boccacci; it is likely that Francesco Mannelli had gotten the autograph to copy from the Augustinian friar Martino da Signa, who kept Boccaccio's books for him in the monastery of Santo Spirito.[80] If we add that both the Capponi codex and the fragmentary codex seem to have been copied under the supervision of the author himself, we have to conclude that the diffusion of the *Decameron* during Boccaccio's lifetime was in a sense guided and controlled by him. And that leads us to reconsider the notion that this book of stories immediately met with great success. In short, things played out differently for the *Decameron* than for Dante's *Commedia*.

The question remains of why Boccaccio kept such careful watch over the diffusion of his book. It has been proposed that he wanted to select the audience because he was worried that the licentiousness of certain stories might upset and perhaps corrupt readers (or, more precisely, female readers) who were ill equipped. In short, that he was overcome by moral scruples.[81] And concerns of this nature did indeed trouble him in his old age, but it does not seem plausible that he harbored them before that, during the years he was still polishing the book. The fact that he also oversaw the correctness of the transcriptions suggests another hypothesis, namely, that he was driven not by moral concerns but by philological ones. Like Petrarch, Boccaccio was highly critical of professional copyists, whom he accused of poor handwriting, and

especially wary of the butchery to which the common people subjected vernacular texts, those spread by word of mouth and copied
over and over again for an audience whose cultural shortcomings
made them incapable of recognizing the disfiguring corruptions
caused by the process of transmission.[82] It is thus likely that, once
he was fully aware of the situation, particularly thanks to discussions with Petrarch, Boccaccio personally curated the diffusion of
this book about which he cared deeply and whose textual fidelity
he sought to preserve.

A Desk Book

The oldest surviving codices do not allow us to determine at what
date Boccaccio determined that it had come "time... to bring these
remarks to an end" (*Dec.*, "Author's Conclusion," 30; "tempo... da
por fine alle parole"), but, in compensation, since almost all of
these early codices rely on autographs, they demonstrate that the
writing of the book passed through multiple phases: perhaps not
full-blown revisions, but continuous intense activity of adjust-
ment and burnishing that lasted for several years. Intense activity
that did not stop even after the book had been made publicly available. Throughout the decade of the 1360s, even as he completed his
most important humanistic works, Boccaccio kept the *Decameron*
on his writing desk.

The autograph codex (Hamilton 90 of the Staatsbibliothek of
Berlin) that passed down the definitive redaction of the *Decameron*, or at least the version that we read today, dates to the 1370s.
Among the many similarities between Petrarch's book of poetry
and Boccaccio's collection of stories, we must include their editorial histories: both were conceived at around midcentury, and
reached their final forms—if this can be said for writers who were
slaves to rewriting—a few years before the deaths of their respective authors, both final forms attested by an autograph codex.

The *Decameron* autograph raises many questions. First of all, it
appears to be a luxury copy, one prepared for dedication to some
illustrious person, but it remained instead with Boccaccio as a
working copy, work, moreover, that was particularly prolonged
due to interruptions in the transcription process.[83] In short, we can

say that, in his old age, Boccaccio brought the book to a close, but not, strictly speaking, that he authorized it, or at any rate that he authorized it in the form that it has in this last autograph.

At first sight, the final autograph's form is disconcerting:[84] the Hamilton codex has the format of a university scholarly treatise. It is significant that the book's format is the same one that Boccaccio used for the autograph of the *Genealogia deorum gentilium*, his most elevated humanist work.[85] This codex of the *Decameron* is thus presented as a *libro da banco*, or "desk book": that is, one of those books, such as university treatises and textbooks or works by the church fathers, that due to their size and weight have to be supported on a table or book stand before which the reader is seated.[86] Which raises the question of who Boccaccio's intended audience was. Such a book was certainly not found in ladies' chambers or even in the hands of those male readers, whether noble courtiers or cultured merchants, who enjoyed vernacular literature.[87] It would seem, therefore, that Boccaccio had a particular audience in mind, one that was different from the women he ostensibly addressed. It has been said that this "book format assumes an audience of intellectual experts, capable of decoding the work's complex architecture and able to recognize the subtle web of the literary and philosophical sources present especially in the framing text."[88] As if, after decades of work, Boccaccio had chosen a side, and made it clear with the format. But the structural complexity and depth of cultural references were inherent to the project of the book itself, which from its conception had presupposed readers who were much more knowledgeable and well equipped than the normal consumers of "light" literature in the vernacular. Prior to this final autograph, Boccaccio had circulated the *Decameron* in volumes that did not differ in their material characteristics from the usual works of vernacular literature; on the basis of the manuscript copied by Capponi, it would even seem that he had made an illustrated or illustratable edition, thus a book for a "courtly" sort of reading, diametrically opposed to a serious scholarly book.[89] Still, even if the books were presented in conventional and attractive packaging, not only women like Fiammetta or the widow of *Corbaccio*, but typical readers of literature in the vernacular, generally "illiterate," in the sense of ignorant of

Latin, remained far from the ideal audience Boccaccio envisioned. In reality, as we have seen, this ideal audience did not exist. But the fact remains that Boccaccio wrote imagining a reader who was cultured, "literate," and at the same time open to the appeal of the new literature. In a sense, a reader like him. In the end, with the *Decameron* he had, in a mature and thoughtful way, completed a project like the one he had naively attempted at his debut, when he had thought that with the *Filocolo* he would be able to address simultaneously the courtiers of King Robert and the scholars of the Studium and library by bringing together in one work "high" culture, which in those days he identified with scholarly scientific culture, and the "low" culture of romances, associated with a female readership.

If Boccaccio's dream was to bring together these two different camps, then why in his later years did he make the demonstrably divisive choice of adopting the format of a scholarly tome? Did he truly intend his book to fit the mold of those he had known so well while studying law codes in the lecture halls of the university or of Ambrose's commentary on Genesis, which had suggested his own title to him?[90]

The aged Boccaccio must have arrived at the conviction that the book he had been working on for almost twenty years had actually become what he had imagined at the outset, that is, truly the kind of masterpiece that he had set out to create from humble scattered tales, and equally as successful as the book that Petrarch had in the same way created out of scattered poems. That he was convinced of this is also suggested by the fact that he had the courage to send it to his friend and teacher. However, Boccaccio, instinctively, but also fundamentally, associated the idea of a masterpiece in the vernacular, not with Petrarch, but with Dante. For Boccaccio, the measure of the success of his own book was not the elegant and rarefied stylization of Petrarch's lyric verse collection, but instead the *Commedia*: multiform, layered, variegated, yet firmly structured as a single unified whole. Not that he dared to compete with his great model; but he felt that he had absorbed its spirit. Humanists and university professors may have turned up their noses, but the *Commedia* had broken down not only divisions between styles, but also divisions between readers: it circulated among the middle classes, merchants, educated professionals, within noble circles, and among learned men of letters like Boccaccio himself. It was a book for reading, memorize-able and memorized, and at the same time a book to be commented on and that was commented on, just as was done with the Latin classics, sacred scripture, and the church fathers. Wasn't this exactly the future Boccaccio aspired to for his *Decameron*? Didn't he hope that this work would become, like the *Commedia*, "a work appreciated by scholars, admired by the common people" (*Carmina*, V.2–3)?[91]

Boccaccio, who had a profound knowledge of this poem, must have been struck by the fact that Dante imagined his readers seated before a desk. "Now stay there, reader, on your bench, / thinking back on your foretaste here" ("Or ti riman, lettor, sovra 'l tuo banco / dietro pensando a ciò che si preliba"):[92] do not get up, do not leave your desk, but stop and meditate on the subject that has just be presented to you. He deduced from this that Dante imagined "the codices that contained the *Commedia* as no different from those—in Latin—that he, along with the other intellectuals of the time, habitually read in the same manner: parchment, large-format, written in formal *littera textualis* bookhand," exactly like Boccaccio's codex of the *Decameron*.[93]

Repudiated by the Master

As I said earlier, Boccaccio found the courage to submit the *Decameron* to Petrarch's judgment. We do not know when this was, and, to tell the truth, we do not know for certain that it was he who sent it to Petrarch.[94] Indeed, Petrarch himself would seem to deny it: "I have seen the book you produced in our mother tongue long ago, I believe, as a young man; it was delivered to me—from where or how I do not know,"[95] he wrote to Boccaccio from Padua in March 1373. However, if we rule out the possibility that Petrarch had acquired or sought out a work in the vernacular on his own initiative, who else but Boccaccio could have given him a book whose circulation at that time must have been for the most part limited to Neapolitan and Florentine circles, circles with which by that date, given the deaths of most of his friends and acquaintances, Petrarch must have had somewhat loose ties? Perhaps Donato

Albanzani, who was close to both him and Boccaccio, could have been the source, but in that case, it is hard to imagine that it would have been a gift: more likely, Donato, whose limited financial resources would have prevented him from making such a purchase, would have been only an intermediary. We do not have to read Petrarch's letter as a missive that was actually sent and therefore as credible evidence, however: the document that was sent has been lost, while the one that survives in the *Seniles*, the letter collection of his old age, should be understood "as a literary text more than as a letter,"[96] a literary text comprising the four letters, all addressed to Boccaccio, which together form the seventeenth and final book of the collection. Over the course of this text, in dialogue with Boccaccio and responding to his queries, Petrarch developed an ethical, metaliterary, and autobiographical discourse, which should be understood as the conclusion of his entire epistolary collection (as well as, to a degree, of his arc as a writer). Even though the phrase above in his letter appears to suggest that Petrarch had recently stumbled upon a book that had been in his library for so long he had forgotten when and from whom he had gotten it, it actually forms part of his overarching strategy aimed at relegating the *Decameron* along with all other vernacular output to Boccaccio's youth.[97]

If Boccaccio expected to receive a sign of approval, however, he was mistaken. He did not understand, or rather, could not have known, that in including the collection of vernacular poems as part of the tripartite project along with his Latin verse and prose letters, Petrarch did not intend to elevate all of vernacular literature, but only lyric poetry. Because Petrarch was convinced that alongside quantitative verse poetry, the Romans had also developed a "popular" rhythmic poetry analogous to the vernacular poetry of his day, he thought that vernacular lyric poetry had been justified in the cultural universe of antiquity, and thus that he was undertaking the humanistic restoration of the conditions of the classical past. But this was true for poetry and poetry alone, and Petrarch therefore scrupulously avoided writing vernacular prose.[98] And, in fact, he did not approve of Boccaccio's prose book.

Petrarch's decision to make a Latin translation of the work's final story, which recounts Griselda's extraordinary self-abnegation in the face of her oppression and humiliation by her husband, the Marchese di Saluzzo,[99] was surely dictated by affection and the sincere desire to honor his old friend. His intentions were good, but the act itself was objectively embarrassing, almost insulting: it is as if Petrarch wanted to show Boccaccio with a direct comparison that the language of "the people" was not capable of achieving the artistic heights of Latin (and indeed, somewhat ironically, the success of his Latin Griselda was such that it overshadowed Boccaccio's vernacular version). And then, preceding the translation, he made a series of remarks about that book that, while polite and careful, are far from expressing the positive judgment that Boccaccio surely hoped for. "I have seen the book," he begins, but

> if I were to say I have read it, I would be lying, since it is very big, having been written for the common herd and in prose, and I was too busy and time was short.... I leafed through it, and, like a hurried traveler who looks around from side to side without halting... I did enjoy leafing through it; and if anything met my eye that was too frankly lewd, your age at the time of writing excused it—also the style, the idiom, the very levity of the subject matter and of those who seemed likely to read such things.... In the midst of much light-hearted fun, I caught several pious and serious things about which I still have no definitive judgment since nowhere did I get totally absorbed.[100]

Boccaccio may have never read these words, or even the translation of Griselda. The package that Petrarch claimed to have sent him in the summer of 1373 never arrived; a year later, on June 8, he sent it again from Arquà accompanied by a letter that ends with his final farewells to his dear letters and to his dear friends ("Valete amici, valete epistole"):[101] he would die the following month. And yet, in the condolence letter in November to Petrarch's son-in-law, Francescuolo da Brossano, Boccaccio still expressed a keen desire to have a copy "of the last of my stories, which he embellished in his style."[102]

9

Highs and Lows

Dreary Years

When Boccaccio returned to Florence from the Kingdom of Naples in November 1355, he was offended and embittered, convinced that he had been deceived by people he considered friends, and that in the hearts of men of power (Acciaiuoli) and those who bowed down to them out of greed or opportunism (Zanobi) there was no room either for friendship or for the respect due to honest poverty. He returned to the pastoral muse, the one he had begun to experiment with in Forlì with Checco di Meletto before developing it further in Florence as the voice of anti-imperial politics in the city,[1] and again wielded the weapon of political allegory to attack and discredit Niccolò Acciaiuoli: this the only form of revenge available to a man of letters. But it did not calm him. He appears to have fallen prey to anxiety and looked for someone to whom he could unburden himself, while at the same time he feared abandonment. He wrote to Petrarch over and over again, but received no reply. Not even a note of appreciation for the gift of the Varro and Cicero books. In actuality, Petrarch had thanked him, but his letter had gone astray.

However, Petrarch saw his friend's distress: the letter he wrote on December 20, which Boccaccio this time received, begins with these words: "From your many letters that I have most recently read, one thing stands out: you are mentally disturbed."[2] On the basis of this letter of Petrarch's, we may be able to deduce why Boccaccio was so anxious. In his own multiple letters, Boccaccio had certainly complained about his treatment in Naples by Acciaiuoli, and also very likely indulged in quite unflattering judgments about the new poet laureate, Zanobi da Strada. He must have spoken about Acciaiuoli in the allegorical style he had used in his earlier eclogue, because Petrarch wrote back that he understood what was hidden behind the veil: "I have read and understood the meaning of your allusions to Syracuse and Dionysius,"[3] that is, to the "tyrant." Boccaccio must have expressed himself more directly about Zanobi and, as happened when he was angry, without choosing his words carefully. It appears he wrote something along the lines of "Don't call me a poet anymore, if this is what a poet laureate is," to which Petrarch responded, "You are angered among other things that I call you a poet. How surprising, for you wished to be a poet and yet tremble at that name," and then closed rather dryly: "You may call yourself whatever you wish to be called. . . . How you view yourself is your affair; how I view you is mine."[4] So we can see why Boccaccio would have been worried: Petrarch, with whom, among other things, he had only recently reestablished friendly relations, was connected to both Acciaiuoli and Zanobi; the suspicious Boccaccio could have wondered if even his master had betrayed him, if Petrarch's silence meant that he had sided with Boccaccio's enemies.[5]

The disquiet Petrarch perceived was certainly connected to the unpleasantness in Naples: but it seems also to be the symptom of a deeper malaise, of which the trip may even have been a result. It is as if there had been a kind of deterioration in Boccaccio's relationship with his city, or at least the relationship between him and the governing powers. During the four years between 1351 and 1355, he had spent more days in service to the Comune than out, either in an office or on an embassy; after his return from the Kingdom of Naples, however, Boccaccio would not hold another civic post for a very long time: roughly a decade would pass before he made another appearance on the public stage. Even the few trips he took prior to the 1360s were almost all of a personal nature. It may be that these years, and especially the three "so lacking in exterior events" between 1356 and 1358, were, as has been suggested, "a period of rigorous concentration and fervent creative activity";[6] but the reason or reasons for such a radical change in his life still need to be explained. Perhaps it was not that Boccaccio separated himself from political life, but, more likely, that he was separated from it, or, better yet, ignored.

The apparent political and institutional stability of the so-called Third Popolo in Florence—that is, the expanded governing regime that included the minor guilds, established after the fall of the Duke of Athens and the subsequent failed attempt at a magnate restoration—concealed the reality of an underground struggle by the oligarchic elite to weaken the representation of the *novi cives*, the new men. An ongoing daily battle that worsened in the 1350s, particularly in the latter half of the decade.[7] The place where the oligarchs gathered was more and more the Guelph party, that is, the only party, which, along with its institutions, was almost a shadow government capable of influencing the communal government. New power groups replaced the traditional ones: the influence of the magnate clans from the Oltrarno district (the Bardi, Frescobaldi, Rossi) declined, and the two opposing factions headed by the Ricci and the Albizzi families became dominant. The Guelph party, over which the Albizzi family exercised a disproportionate influence, carried out a campaign of intimidation against its opponents, a campaign that became more aggressive precisely in the mid-1350s. There is no record that Boccaccio had personal relationships with the families connected to either the Ricci (the Alberti, Medici, Rondinelli, Ridolfi, Covoni) or the Albizzi (the Strozzi, Altoviti, Soderini, Rucellai, Baroncelli); and we know that, by both proximity and paternal inheritance, his political connections and often even his friendships (the Rossi and Del Buono, for example) were within the faction of the fading Oltrarno oligarchs. It is quite likely that his attainment of a few offices in the administration in the early 1350s and even some prestigious assignments were due to their protection; but it is also likely that as the Bardi faction's hold on public affairs dwindled away to nothing Florence's new leaders ignored him. Boccaccio's absence from the city's political scene, therefore, is attributable more to the unraveling of the network of power that had supported him in the past than to his voluntary withdrawal.

Along with offices and embassies, Boccaccio also lost their associated remuneration, which must have significantly affected his finances. However, even if he called himself "poor" in his 1353 letter to Zanobi, until 1359–60, his "economic circumstances were not modest": with this reference to his poverty he meant only to contrast his own choice to live independently to those who bow down in service to the powerful for economic advantage ("I live poor for myself, but I would live rich and splendid for others"[8] [*Ep.*, IX.19]). It must be said, however, that the collapse of his finances between the end of the 1350s and the beginning of the 1560s was too sudden not consider that the decline might have begun earlier. Unfortunately, there is a lacuna in the Comune's fiscal records for precisely the period 1356–59, so we cannot evaluate his position with regard to the Monte and the state bond market. That his lack of investment at this time was due to ethical concerns, that is, to his "disapproval of the financial policies of the commune" and to the fact that he did not share "the vision of the ruling classes (the new rich and the old nobility) of the treasury as a source of profit" is conjecture.[9] As we have already seen, among the options available to citizens subject to a forced loan (*prestanza*) were those of renouncing any interest in exchange for a deep discount, or of ceding the loan along with its interest to someone else, thereby effectively paying a much lower sum. Both these routes were taken by Boccaccio in the 1360s, evidently due to a lack of liquidity. But we also know that he had similarly earlier ceded the Monte credit (or shares) that he inherited after Boccaccino's death; and now, in March 1356, we see him do this again with a credit, ceding it to Niccolò di Bartolo del Buono, the friend to whom he had dedicated the *Comedia delle ninfe fiorentine* fifteen years earlier. Even if we accept that he did this out of ethical scruples, the fact remains that the objective consequence of this sort of financial behavior was the progressive decrease of his capital.

The events of these years in Florence were few and of little importance, just as his travels were few and poorly documented.[10] In July 1357 he was in Ravenna. This is not surprising: it had been

four years since he had been to this city where, even if no longer
brightened by Violante's presence, he had loved ones (his daughter's mother may have still been alive) and dear friends (that summer he also saw Donato Albanzani,[11] who had begun to gravitate
toward Venice during the previous two years). In any case, the absence of any kind of public document shows that this was a strictly
personal trip. The only memento of this visit is connected to Petrarch: Boccaccio had asked him if he could have a copy of the *Invective contra medicum*—the condemnation of Pope Clement VI's
physicians that Petrarch had written in four books in 1355, within
which he had inserted an impassioned homage to poetry as the
most important of the arts—and Petrarch sent the work to him in
Ravenna, along with an old codex almost destroyed by time, and
an ancient map.[12]

Boccaccio in Milan

The decade that had opened with Petrarch's visit to Florence and,
shortly after, Boccaccio's to Padua closed with Boccaccio traveling
in 1359 to the home of his friend and teacher once more, this time
in Milan.

Petrarch lived on the outskirts of the city in a house facing the
basilica of Sant'Ambrogio where he had the use of the nearby monastic gardens of both Sant'Ambrogio and Santa Valeria for his bo-
tanical experiments. On Saturday, March 16, at around three in the
afternoon, he was planting laurel trees when Boccaccio appeared
in the garden: Petrarch thought that his friend's arrival at just that
moment was a good omen for successful planting, which until then
he had attempted in vain. Boccaccio stayed with him for about a
month.[13] A long time had passed since they last met, eight years,
during which many things had brought them closer while others
had threatened to divide them forever.

The rupture caused by Petrarch's putting Milan before Florence had been profound. It is true that the rift had healed after a
few years, but the two had never cleared the air. It was a subject
they could now not avoid and that, indeed, they did not. In fact,
they discussed it a great deal and arrived at the conclusion, shared
by both, that, given the current political situation, Milan was not

just a preferable residence for Petrarch but without question the only possible one. With the Guelph League and the Visconti having made peace about a year earlier, the times were certainly favorable for them to reach an agreement, and also Boccaccio would surely not have been disposed to openly oppose his host's decisions; this did not mean, however, that he was actually convinced by Petrarch's arguments. Indeed, in the months to come, in a veiled manner, he would let his doubts be known, with the result that Petrarch wrote to him explicitly asking if his opinions had changed. In short, that episode remained a sore spot: it did not affect the deep friendship that now united them, but it forced at least Boccaccio to hide behind silences and ambiguous phrases.[14]

Another topic of conversation would have been their common friends. They must have discussed at length Zanobi da Strada, who had moved from Montecassino to Avignon, where, after Petrarch's refusal of the same offer, he had been appointed to the position of apostolic secretary a few months earlier. Petrarch had written a harsh letter accusing him of betraying his studies and sacrificing to ambition and greed the freedom necessary for intellectual work.[15] It is easy to imagine that, with his usual fervor, Boccaccio expressed the conviction that Zanobi exploited poetry and culture to further his career, the same opinion he had earlier asserted behind the pastoral screen in the eclogue hurled at Acciaiuoli in the wake of his miserable trip to Naples.[16] It is also likely that in Milan Boccaccio made the acquaintance of some of Petrarch's friends there, such as the cleric, notary, and author of Latin poetry Moggio Moggi,[17] who at the time was helping Petrarch edit and transcribe the letters that would form his first collection, and the eclogues of the *Bucolicum carmen*.[18]

Scholarship and literature were obviously at the center of their conversations during this month. As eight years earlier, but this time with greater leisure, Boccaccio was able to examine many of Petrarch's completed works and those currently in progress, as well as consult his collection of books, the most important private library in Europe at that time. In 1351, the volumes had been scattered among several sites (the largest portion in the house in Vaucluse); now they were reunited. Petrarch again allowed him to copy some of his works, and so Boccaccio transcribed many of his letters, the guide to traveling to the Holy Land (*Itinerarium ad sepul-crum Domini nostri Yhesu Christi*, known as *Itinerarium syriacum*) he had put together the previous year for the Milanese Giovanni Mandelli and, above all, was able to boast of being the first to own a copy of the complete collection of Petrarch's eclogues. Letters in Latin, eclogues in Latin, a learned treatise in Latin, even though by this date both authors had written the works that we consider their masterpieces: for Boccaccio the *Decameron*, and for Petrarch the first version of the book of verses that would become the *Canzoniere* (*Rerum vulgarium fragmenta*). The point being that their masterpieces were written in vernacular, and vernacular litera-ture was another point of disagreement between the rigorous hu-manist and the enthusiastic champion of the rigorous humanist's youthful literary work in the Tuscan language. And so, they read each other's vernacular works, but, because they were pursuing "two very different objectives,"[19] with only a few exceptions they avoided referring in writing either to their own or to the other's non-Latin works. And in the same way, while they exchanged Latin works, they did not give one another copies of their works in ver-nacular or, in the case of Petrarch, give his to the other to tran-scribe. A few years after the visit to Milan, between 1363 and 1366, Boccaccio would prepare a codex in which he copied in his own hand the *Vita Nova*, the *Commedia*, fifteen of Dante's poems, and, following them, Petrarch's *Canzoniere*, in what can be considered its second redaction, and in any case, the first version that is at-tested.[20] Well, not even on this occasion was Boccaccio permitted to use his friend's autograph, nor was he able to use a copy close to the autograph, but had to content himself with transcribing a "second- or third-hand text."[21] Giving a copy of one's own work or allowing its transcription meant removing it from purely private circulation and making it public, and such an act required the re-cipient to take a stance: even passing over something in silence was a statement.

That said, the two absolutely talked about vernacular liter-ature. In exploring his friend Francesco's enormous book col-lection, Giovanni was struck by what was there and what was missing: Dante's *Commedia* was not present, while, on the other hand, sitting on the shelf was a codex containing Homer's poems in Greek. Boccaccio must have been astounded by both these discoveries: we know what Dante meant to him; and he knew that Petrarch could not read Greek. The discussions they had over these days would have concrete effects in the near future. Effects that were, moreover, divergent: on the one hand, Boccaccio would not succeed in truly convincing Petrarch that Dante was a great poet or, in any case, as great as Petrarch himself (it is significant that Dante's name, everywhere in Boccaccio's writing, is almost absent from Petrarch's); on the other hand, in the name of Homer the two friends would cooperate in an endeavor that marked a milestone in the history of European humanism: the establishment of a professorship of Greek grammar and literature at the Studium of Florence.

We do not know what they said to each other about Dante. It is possible that Petrarch appeared to yield to Boccaccio's spirited arguments; but it is more likely that he expressed his reservations about the merits of the *Commedia*. What we do know is that when Boccaccio returned to Florence, he obtained a copy of Dante's poem and sent it to Petrarch along with one of his own *carmi* (poems), *Ytalie iam certus honos* (*Sure Honor Now of Italy*), exhorting Petrarch to read and reread the *Commedia* and add it to his favorites.[22] This *carme* is an impassioned argument for the greatness of Dante, poet, philosopher, and theologian, and for that of the *Commedia*, written in the vernacular not because the author was ignorant of Latin, but in order to "show posterity what modern poetry in vernacular can do" (*Carmina*, V.9–11).[23] The fervor of his exaltation of Dante is very likely explained by Boccaccio's keen desire to overcome Petrarch's reservations, reservations that pained him personally as a champion of literature in vernacular. Once he had sent the poem off, however, unsure of himself as always, Boccaccio had misgivings, fearing that he had been excessive and hurt Petrarch's feelings in some way. He wrote a letter of apology in which, however, judging by his friend's response, the arguments he advanced must have sounded, well, obnoxious: the way you apologize, Petrarch wrote, makes it sound as if I feel diminished if someone praises another poet, as you do in your poem.[24] In short, as if Boccaccio believed Petrarch envied others' glory. Among the many assertions in this important letter, it is worth noting that Petrarch says, untruthfully, that, although he delights in collecting books, he has never owned the *Commedia*, because in his youth he too wrote lyric poetry and was afraid of being influenced and thus perhaps unknowingly imitating it. Here he lied twice: first, because he wrote vernacular poetry almost until his dying day; and second, because he had an excellent knowledge not only of the *Commedia* but of all of Dante's vernacular poetry, so much so that, as the correlations and echoes abundantly present in his works demonstrate, Dante was "the indisputable master of his poetry in the vernacular."[25] However, his letter continues, "today I have left these scruples far behind; and with my total abandonment of such productions and the waning of my earlier fears, I can now welcome wholeheartedly all other poets, him above all," an indirect and reticent way of admitting that he had received the book Boccaccio had sent. In substance, however, Petrarch confirms his narrow judgment: he "readily" grants Dante "the palm for vernacular eloquence,"[26] but reaffirms that "he rises to nobler and loftier heights in the vernacular than in Latin poetry or prose."[27]

This was Boccaccio's last attempt to convert his friend and master to the cult of Dante. Nonetheless, he did not give up on the project of a literary renewal centered on the union of Latin and vernacular, the synthesis of Dante and Petrarch. But this was a path he would follow alone, without again involving the uncompromising humanist. After the collection of Dante's writing he made at the beginning of the 1350s,[28] between 1363 and 1366, as mentioned above, Boccaccio would compile a second one, which he prefaced with a shorter version of his earlier Dante biography, the *Trattatello*, written after his first meeting with Petrarch. This second time, along with the *Vita Nova*, the *Commedia*, and the fifteen poems, he also included Petrarch's *Canzoniere*: together they were a physical expression of his vision of modern literature. He would be careful not make it a homage to Petrarch, but still in this work conceived as a monument to the vernacular, he would include one of his own works in Latin, the poem *Ytalie iam certus honos*, with the clear purpose of underscoring his role as guarantor of the new literature.[29]

"May He Restore to Us the Lost Homer"[30]

Petrarch had owned a codex of Homer since late 1353, but had been unable to satisfy his great desire to read it because his knowledge of Greek went no further than the alphabet.[31] During the years he lived in Avignon, thanks to his contacts with the Greek prelates who visited the papal curia and, in particular, as he noted himself many times, the conversations, more than proper grammar lessons, with the Calabrian monk and later bishop of Gerace Barlaam of Seminara, he had gained a familiarity with the language, although not enough to be able to read it.[32] Boccaccio, too, had been attracted to Greek since his youth, and also learned some of the rudiments from Barlaam when he passed through Naples, though also without acquiring a true knowledge of it. However, during the winter of 1358–59, thus a few months before Boccaccio's visit to Milan, in Padua Petrarch struck up a relationship with a scholar from Thessaloniki, Leontius Pilatus (Leonzio Pilato).

Leontius had been educated in Greece before moving to Crete, at that time subject to Venice (and where he must have learned Latin), after which he lived quite a long time in Calabria, and, finally, from there had come to northern Italy. When Petrarch met him in Padua, Leontius was planning to move to Avignon. In Thessaloniki, he may have been a student ("auditor") of Barlaam, who had lived there between 1328 and 1341. The Byzantine Leontius (or Leonzio or Leone) must have been an odd character, or, at least, he seemed one to Petrarch and Boccaccio, who were agreed in their descriptions of him as a morose and introverted individual, depressed and restless, always ready to change city and country, but also arrogant and obstinate, not to mention "uncouth" in appearance, unkempt, with a long beard and hair, ignorant of good manners, and yet "a most learned Hellenist" with a bent for scholarship, and even endowed with a certain sensitivity for poetry.[33]

Together in Milan, Petrarch and Boccaccio spoke about Homer, and expressed their great disappointment at being unable to enjoy the verses of the man unanimously considered the "supreme poet" ("poeta sovrano," *Inf.*, IV.88).[34] Petrarch also described his meeting with Leontius in Padua. It is possible that it was on that occasion (Petrarch was staying between Padua and Venice from roughly the beginning of winter 1358 until early February 1359) that he had asked Leontius for a brief translation of the first lines of Homer into Latin prose ("the short essay in which Leo offered me the beginning of Homer [perhaps the *Iliad*] in Latin as an appetizer as it were for the whole work"),[35] which he now showed to his friend. This trial translation was not only in prose rather than verse, but it was literal, word for word, and still it was enough to convey, if not the reality of Homer's work, at least something of its essence and flavor.[36] The two decided that it was worthwhile to try to get a complete translation of Homer's poems from Leontius, the only person in Italy capable of doing it. This was no small undertaking: it would first be necessary to convince Leontius to postpone his move to Avignon; then to procure a Greek codex of Homer; and finally, to find a way to support him financially for the entire time the work would require. Petrarch offered to be the mediator with Leontius, and as for the codex, he recalled seeing one for sale in Padua. The problem of financing could be resolved by finding Leontius a professorship at an Italian university. They agreed that the university to turn to with the greatest chance of success was the Studium in Florence. Boccaccio took upon himself the responsibility for arranging the position and convincing Leontius to accept it.[37]

In April 1359, Boccaccio returned from Milan to Florence exhilarated about two distinct cultural projects: converting Petrarch to the cult of Dante and bringing knowledge of Homer to Italian culture, thus linking his own name to an event that would make him one of the leading figures in the world of humanistic scholarship.

Boccaccio threw himself headlong into both projects. His first inquiries into the possibility of the establishment of the university position must have been promising for he quickly got into contact with Leontius Pilatus. It appears that Leontius moved to Florence as soon as the winter of 1359–60: he would live in Boccaccio's house for roughly three years, and it would not be an easy coexistence.[38] We do not know when, where, or how their negotiations took place; it is clear that Boccaccio conducted them himself because in the *Genealogia* he boasts that it was he who "intercepted Leontius Pilatus on his way from Venice to the western Babylon

[Avignon], and with my advice turned him aside from his long peregrination, and kept him in Italy" (*GDG*, XV.7, 5).[39] Where and when he bestowed his advice is not known: from this passage it seems that it was through discussion in person rather than by an exchange of letters.

On July 22, 1359, Giovanni and his half brother, Iacopo, were assigned a mysterious mission expected to last eighteen days "ad partes Lombardie." Mysterious in many regards. In the decade between 1355 and 1364–65, Boccaccio held no office in the administration of the Comune and was given no other embassy: it is clear that his links to those in power had weakened. So why did they entrust him with this single mission? Further: Giovanni was accompanied by Iacopo. It must have been Giovanni himself who requested this in order to provide financial help to a young man with no employment and plans to get married (which he would do in November of the following year), and the Comune's agreement should be understood as a personal favor. But the fact that the embassy was entrusted to someone who had only just reached his majority, with no experience or recognized talents, must mean that it had no political importance.[40] One can then speculate that the trip was connected to Boccaccio's negotiations regarding the university position, and that its purpose was to meet with Leontius Pilatus somewhere in northern Italy (the term "ad partes Lombardie," indeed, can cover a vast geographic area). In short, a mission like the one Boccaccio had carried out in 1351 when he offered Petrarch the professorship.

The negotiations were a success. Boccaccio achieved the establishment of a professorship of Greek grammar and literature in the Studium of Florence beginning in the 1360–61 academic year and ensured that the position would be given to Leontius. While waiting in Florence to begin his public lectures, Leontius gave private lessons and applied himself to the translation of Homer. It was Boccaccio himself who obtained, at his own expense, the Greek codex for the translation, a codex that it appears Petrarch had promised to buy but then had not: his initial enthusiasm had somewhat cooled, perhaps because he no longer felt he was at the center of the enterprise.[41]

The establishment of a professorship of Greek in Florence is in itself rather surprising. Indeed, surprising that a business-minded city with little sensitivity to culture, particularly the specialized culture of humanistic scholarship, felt the need for the, inevitably elitist, teaching of ancient Greek literature. And Boccaccio and Petrarch harbored some fears about what kind of welcome the Florentines would give to a colorful character like Leontius and such a challenging subject.[42] Surprising too that the Comune's leaders embraced a proposal made by a person who, while he did enjoy a certain prestige, had for some years been on the fringes of the political and administrative life of the city. It is conceivable that to achieve this outcome, rather than on political support, Boccaccio had relied on the help of intellectuals close to him who were at that time capable of influencing government choices. One of these may have been Lapo da Castiglionchio, who, while trained as a canonist (he would teach "decretals" at the university beginning in the early 1360s), had never given up his devotion to Petrarch (whom he had met in Florence in 1350) and, above all, who as a hardline Guelph had great influence in the Guelph party, which in those years was the true center of power in Florence.[43] Another ally may have been Francesco Bruni, who had been invited to teach rhetoric in precisely November 1360, thus almost simultaneously with Leontius's appointment.[44]

Leontius began teaching on October 16, 1360; at the end of his second academic year, however, he abandoned Florence: a decision due perhaps to his difficult character, which kept him from adjusting to and remaining in one place for long ("he scorned Florentine luxuries,"[45] Petrarch would say, echoing opinions expressed by Boccaccio). He took refuge at Petrarch's house in Venice, where he stayed for approximately a year and then also "haughtily"[46] fled "after uttering many bitter insults . . . against Italy and the Latin name,"[47] and traveled back to Greece; upon arriving there, however, he repented and begged Petrarch to allow him to return to his house. Although Petrarch refused, Leontius nonetheless left Byzantium for Venice in the summer of 1365, but enroute was struck by lightning during a storm in the Adriatic and died.

Before abandoning Florence, Leontius had finished the translations of the *Iliad* and the *Odyssey*, leaving the autographs with

Boccaccio; Petrarch would receive the translated poems only in 1366.

Boccaccio was fully aware that he had accomplished something of the greatest cultural value: bringing back to the West the "lost" Homer[48] was probably his most important achievement as a humanist and he rightfully boasted about it, using phrases that sound almost like revenge against his teacher Petrarch:

> Was it not I who intercepted Leontius Pilatus on his way from Venice to the western Babylon, and with my advice turned him aside from his long peregrination, and kept him in Italy? Did I not receive him into my own house, entertain him for a long time, and make the utmost effort personally that he should be appointed professor in Florence, and his salary paid out of the city's funds? Indeed I did; and I too was the first who, at my own expense, called back to Tuscany the writings of Homer and of other Greek authors, whence they had departed many centuries before, never meanwhile to return. And it was not to Tuscany only, but to Italy that I brought them. I, too, was the first to hear Leontius privately render the *Iliad* in Latin; and I it was who arranged for public readings from Homer's works.[49] (*GDG*, XV.7, 5)

The Other Desk

Almost all of Boccaccio's Latin prose works were begun in the 1350s. Most he would complete only the following decade or even later, but their conception, a great deal of preparatory research, and some first drafts took place in parallel with his writing of the *Decameron* and the works promoting Dante's *Commedia*. The characteristically Boccaccian mindset underlying most of these Latin works had been apparent from his earliest cultural interests. Already evident in his vernacular works in Naples and the transcriptions of texts he made in his notebook (the Zibaldoni Laurenziano and Magliabechiano) was his great attraction to encyclopedic erudition, the assembling of details and information from every sphere and possible source, ancient or modern, as if quantity could make up for lack of critical analysis. This tendency toward accumulation was offset by an opposing and equally strong pressure to impose order and to label: and from this came the delight, almost the necessity, of arranging the material into catalogs, genealogies, systematic charts. Petrarch's later teachings certainly in many ways influenced Boccaccio to develop greater consideration not so much for philological truth as for the ethical and cultural worth of research that was in danger of slipping into mere collecting, but it did not modify the basic approach of his work.

It is curious that, according to information provided by Boccaccio himself, his most extensive and demanding book was the first to be conceived and, twenty years later, one of the last to be completed. As Boccaccio tells it, the Florentine Becchino di Lapo Bellincioni, a "friend" of King Hugh IV of Cyprus (and nominal King Hugh II of Jerusalem), in Ravenna renewed his sovereign's warm invitation to write a book that would illustrate the "genealogy of the pagan gods and the heroes" (*GDG*, I, Preface I, 1),[50] an invitation already extended in person to Boccaccio some years earlier (perhaps in Forlì) by one Donnino da Parma, a knight also in the king's service, and then pressed further in a letter from the noted mathematician and astronomer Paulus Geometrus (Paolo Dagomari). The *Genealogia deorum gentilium* is indeed dedicated to King Hugh. Boccaccio was so flattered by the invitation and the pressures exerted on him to accept it that he twice, at the beginning and at the end of the work, refers in detail to the conversations with Donnino, Becchino's exhortations, and the letter from Paulus Geometrus to show that "the royal command that called forth this work is genuine, not imaginary" (*GDG*, XV.13).[51] The solicitations to undertake this work, which would become his humanistic masterpiece, did reach Boccaccio in Romagna, but the circumstances had been fortuitous: it had been one of Boccaccio's acquaintances at the court of Naples, in fact, who had suggested to the king of Cyprus that Boccaccio, by no means famous at that date, was the right scholar for the job. We do not know when Boccaccio met Becchino Bellincioni in Ravenna: it could have been in 1350, or in 1351 or 1353. However, it is likely that the idea for the work dates to that period and that it was then, if not even before 1350, that Boccaccio began collecting notes for this enormous mythological catalog, whose first draft appears to date to around 1365–66, and which upon its completion in the early 1370s would number more than seven hundred profiles.[52]

Boccaccio followed a similar method in compiling the *De montibus*, his toponymical dictionary or gazetteer of the "mountains, forests, fonts, lakes, rivers, marshes, ponds and seas"[53] of the ancient Greco-Roman world and East: furthermore, the composition of this work, which was "made up in large part of simple excerpts and grew by the continuous addition of entries and information over a remarkably long period of time, from shortly after 1350 until about the middle of the 1360s (if it ever reached a true conclusion),"[54] mostly coincided with that of the *Genealogia*. The names of the individual geographical features were divided by category (mountains, rivers, and so on) and listed in alphabetical order. It was essentially a reference tool intended for scholars and lovers of ancient history and literature, especially beginners, to help them, as the author says in the preface, orient themselves correctly within the great sea of references (or even just allusions) made by poets and historical scholars to events in myth and history, both secular and sacred. Like the *Genealogia*, the *De montibus* ends with reference to Petrarch: Boccaccio writes that he had been trying to complete the work in a rush, when he learned that his teacher Petrarch was following the same path more calmly. He was surprised that this exalted man would lower himself to such humble work and, afraid of the comparison, had almost decided to abandon the endeavor, but then changed his mind and was persuaded to continue under his teacher's guidance.[55] Recall that in Ravenna in July 1357, Boccaccio had received the loan of an antique codex and a map from Petrarch: confirmation of this claim of guidance. We do not know the contents of the codex, but it was certainly a work of geography. It was not, however, the copy of the *Naturalis historia* that Boccaccio would consult in Petrarch's house (as it was more difficult to borrow) during his stay in 1359, which consultation would spur him to finally bring his dictionary to a close.[56]

The third great book begun in the 1350s is a very different work. The *De casibus virorum illustrium* (*The Downfall of the Famous*) is not primarily a literary handbook or encyclopedia, but a historical narrative treatise with a moral purpose. Its intent is to demonstrate, as a warning to the society of the time, through a wide array of mythological, biblical, and historical examples drawn from the origins of humanity (Adam) to contemporary times, how God directly or by means of Fortune causes the downfalls ("casus") of those who, having risen to the greatest heights, because of their foolishness, pride, debauchery, greed, or lust for power, abuse their power, sinning against law, justice, and piety. Even if the end result is very similar to a catalog (nine books subdivided into 174 chapters, containing hundreds of biographical profiles of varying lengths of famous men and women), the main story is structured as a vision. The narrator "in the story imagines that he finds himself in his chamber engrossed in study: here appear to him, in ever increasing numbers, the shades" of men and women "wretched and weeping." "The text follows a consistent schema, which repeats albeit with variations: the author is surrounded by a crowd of wretches begging to be heard, quickly looks them over, and chooses one or more figures whose biography he sketches; he then lingers on moral reflections or exhortations . . . after this meditative pause, he is encircled by a new mass of lamenting supplicants."[57]

It is obvious that Boccaccio has brought the narrative form of the *Commedia* into a humanistic work (for example, Dante appears as a character to present to the narrator the Duke of Athens, "our domestic plague, an eternal stain on the name of Florence," *CVI*, IX, 23.9);[58] and yet, in the final section of the work, at the beginning of the eighth book, Francesco Petrarch too appears, bearing witness to how Boccaccio's cultural orientation has changed. This figure urges his student and friend, who is almost at the end of his work but showing signs of fatigue, to persevere in the task he has undertaken.[59] It has been inferred that, if these words of Petrarch reproduce his conversations with Boccaccio in Milan in 1359, which seems likely, then the *De casibus* (begun in 1355) had been written as far as the seventh book at that time, and that after the discussions, Boccaccio added the eighth and ninth books, concluding the work around 1360 with contemporary figures: Charles of Anjou, Philip IV of France, Walter of Brienne, Jacques de Molay, Philippa of Catania. A second redaction would be dedicated to Mainardo Cavalcanti in 1373.[60]

The Conspiracy

The first few years after returning from the Kingdom of Naples had been dreary ones: a nervous Boccaccio had feared he was losing his friendships and connections in the city. He appears to have sunken into a state of anxiety or even apathy, which also slowed his intellectual work. The confessions of sloth and idleness in the *De casibus*, the qualms and doubts in the *De montibus* are confirmation of this. But his time in Milan with Petrarch appeared to infuse Boccaccio with renewed vitality: he devoted himself fervently to promoting Dante, set about the project of establishing the professorship of Greek, worked busily on the humanistic works that had seemed stalled. The man who had turned inward was now looking toward the future with revived faith. Even his external circumstances were favorable.

Around the middle of December 1359, Niccolò Acciaiuoli passed through Florence en route to Avignon. We do not know if Boccaccio spoke with him; he certainly had contact with his friends and functionaries afterward: it was on this occasion that Buondelmonti ordered a copy of the *Decameron*. Acciaiuoli would come through Florence again exactly a year later while returning to Naples from failed missions to Bernabò Visconti on behalf of the pope.[61] Another occasion, therefore, for Boccaccio to renew the ties with the grand seneschal that had been abruptly severed some five years earlier. Subsequent developments of his relationship with Acciaiuoli would show that their relations were indeed reestablished then.

That year, Boccaccio also had hopes of improving his financial situation, which, with the loss of the income from public offices, had begun to be difficult. It is likely, in fact, that the prospect of obtaining a canonry at a cathedral had occurred to him. We do not know which one, but it is logical to think it would have been the cathedral church of Florence, Santa Maria del Fiore. The fact is that he asked for, and, on November 2, 1360, received, the papal dispensation necessary for him as an illegitimate child ("de soluto genitus et solute" ["born to an unmarried man and unmarried woman"]) to acquire such a benefice. From Innocent VI's bull we learn that Boccaccio had already received dispensations at some point in the past enabling him to receive benefices, including with the care of souls; now the pope added permission "to obtain the office of prebend or cure of souls also in a cathedral church."[62] More than to the goodwill of Innocent VI, whom he had met personally in his role as ambassador, Boccaccio owed the papal dispensation to the efforts of Zanobi da Strada, recently appointed apostolic secretary, and this too is a sign that his relationship with the Acciaiuoli clan had been restored. Just as Boccaccio had not made use of the earlier papal dispensations—it is certain that he never held ecclesiastical benefices in Florence—this latest one seems also to have had no concrete results. But in the autumn of 1360, Boccaccio did not know this.[63]

Also that autumn, his efforts on behalf of the professorship of Greek bore fruit: Leontius began teaching his course at the university in October. In short, the decade ended under the best auspices. But then an external event threatened to frustrate many of these hopes: on December 30, 1360, the government foiled a coup d'état planned for the following day at the inauguration ceremony of the new priors.

The Guelph party's persecutory strategy against their political opponents, essentially the government of the Third Popolo and the members of the Ricci faction, had escalated over the course of the decade to the point that, in 1357, the party had insured that the Comune would proceed against those suspected of Ghibellinism even based on anonymous accusations. No actual Ghibellines had existed in Florence for decades; the accusation of Ghibelline sympathies was only a pretext for striking at their political enemies. These inquiries resulted in expropriations, banishments, and *ammonizioni*, or "admonishments," that is, measures that deprived the *ammoniti*, or "admonished," of their citizenship rights, including eligibility for public office. In 1358, Boccaccio's friend Niccolò di Bartolo del Buono, among others, was "admonished" as "not true Guelph" ("non vere guelfus") on the basis of an anonymous denunciation that accused him of holding communal office by swearing Guelph fealty while being a Ghibelline. He was fined, but in fact, from that moment on, he was banned from public life, and so thoroughly that the following year, although he was elected to the Council of the Two Hundred, he had to refuse the position because he was admonished "pro ghibellino habitu" ("for Ghibelline condition").[64] It was in reaction to this climate of persecution that a diverse group of citizens decided to move against the communal government by force: those involved in the conspiracy were "men proscribed as Ghibellines (Domenico di Donato Bandini, Niccolò di Bartolo del Buono, Andrea di Tello da Lisca); magnates of the former regime from the families of the Pazzi, Frescobaldi, Adimari, Gherardini, Donati; many leaders of the Ricci faction, which was in perennial conflict with the Albizzi; middle-rank nouveau riche merchants, such as Luca di Feo Ugolini and again Niccolò di Bartolo del Buono."[65] It was a heterogeneous group—which, however, assembled players who were almost all from the Oltrarno, the district where the oligarchic core that had held power in the 1340s overwhelmingly lived—which had confused and, above all, disorganized and poorly defined objectives: for example, they sought outside support from the Ghibelline Visconti of Milan and Giovanni d'Oleggio, lord of Bologna, but also from the papal vicar, Cardinal Egidio di Albornoz. The denunciation of one of the conspirators led to the arrests of Niccolò del Buono and Domenico di Donato Bandini; under torture, they named the other ten involved. Del Buono and Bandini were beheaded immediately, the others escaped and were condemned to exile and the confiscation of their property as traitors to the republic. To proclaim their disgrace, portraits of all the conspirators were hung in a hall of the Palazzo del Podestà, the seat of government.[66]

There is no indication that Boccaccio was involved in the conspiracy in any way; however, in the climate of repression that followed, particularly with respect to the Oltrarno district, the fact that fully five of the twelve men implicated were either friendly acquaintances of his or actually his friends (Luca Ugolini, Andrea da Lisca, Pazzino di Apardo Donati, Del Buono, and Rossi) must not have been conducive to tranquility. The idea that he then fled Florence in fear to seek refuge in Certaldo is an exaggeration of biographers, just as it is going too far to imagine that he was ejected from public life as a result of the conspiracy. It is true that he would have to wait until the beginning of 1364 to be nominated by the Guelph party for eligibility for the "Tre maggiori," and that only in August 1364 would he receive an office (*Ufficiale dei castelli*, involved in construction of fortifications), but it is also true that during the five years that preceded the conspiracy he had held no position at all. It cannot be denied that after those events, Boccaccio, who had not left the city of Florence between 1355 and 1359, remained more or less permanently in Certaldo and, above all, resumed visiting the cities — Ravenna and Naples — that had always been alternatives to Florence for him, but he did not necessarily do this as a result of political events.[67]

PART III

Old Age
(1361–1375)

10

Disgrace

"Repose" in Certaldo

Given his personal and geographical proximity to a large portion of the men involved in the conspiracy of December 1360, Boccaccio must have been concerned about the possibility of facing repercussions, but that was not the reason he left Florence. He moved to Certaldo only in the summer, and it was not necessarily out of caution. In fact, he had already expressed his intent to withdraw to the village to his friend Pino de'Rossi before the end of 1360, thus prior to the conspiracy.[1] Moreover, in October 1360, Leontius Pilatus had begun giving his Greek lessons, and it is hard to believe that, after his extensive involvement, Boccaccio would have failed to attend. Indeed, everything suggests that he moved to Certaldo after Leontius's course ended in June 1361. The most plausible theory, in fact, is that Boccaccio left Florence in order to escape living with his brother. Iacopo had contracted his first marriage in November 1360, thus presumably shortly before Boccaccio confided his planned departure to Rossi, and since the property the brothers had inherited from their father was still undivided at this time, it is possible that Iacopo had brought his new wife to live in the family house in Santa Felicita. This would have created a very disagreeable situation for Boccaccio, indeed, the same plight that would arise again five years later, when, after marrying for the second time, Iacopo asked Boccaccio to let him and his new wife live with him in his "little house." As we have seen, on that occasion Boccaccio complained bitterly to his friend Albanzani; but this first time as well he made very critical comments about Iacopo in his writings: I would be happy—he wrote—"if God had given me a brother or not" ("se Dio m'avesse dato fratello o non me lo avesse dato," *Cons.*, 174).[2] The only solution must have been to divide the household: Giovanni's transfer of a house to Iacopo on July 2, 1361, should be understood in this way. It was located at the corner of Via di Piazza and Via di Mezzo in Santa Felicita, where the Boccaccio family's house stood, and therefore could have been a part of the family residence.[3]

That summer, Giovanni was in Certaldo. Here he wrote a letter, "almost a book" (*Cons.*, 175; "presso che un libro"), to Pino de' Rossi to "console" him for his exile (the letter is thus known as the *Consolatoria a Pino de' Rossi*). Banished from the city on January 20, 1361, Rossi had taken refuge with his brother-in-law, Bocchino Belforti, Lord of Volterra, but a few months afterward fled to an unknown destination when Belforti was deposed and executed. In the letter, Boccaccio insisted on the similarity between Rossi's forced exile and his own voluntary one in order to develop the thesis that it was possible to find reasons for cheer in both situations. After going through them, he concluded: "here [in Certaldo] I have begun, with much less difficulty than I thought I could, to restore my life; and the coarse clothes and peasant foods are beginning to please me . . . and to sum up my state of mind in a few words, I will tell you" that the life of retirement in the countryside in the company of his "little books" ("libricciuoli") is so pleasant compared to life in the city that, despite the problem of his brother, "I would think I should, mortal that I am, enjoy and feel eternal happiness here" ("qui ho cominciato, con troppa meno difficultà che io estimavo di potere, a confortare la mia vita; e cominciami già i grossi panni a piacere e le contadine vivande . . . e acciò che io in poche parole conchiuda la qualità della mente mia, vi dico"; "io mi crederrei qui, mortale come sono, gustare e sentire della etterna felicità," *Cons.*, 171–74). Now, it is clear that Boccaccio was idealizing his own situation in the service of consolation and thus that his self-portrait cannot be taken as autobiographically faithful, although it is enough to contradict the picture of Boccaccio as anguished and fearful, as he sometimes tends to be portrayed.[4] In the letter's final section, he sends greetings to his exiled friends Luca Ugolini and Andrea di Tello da Lisca, who seem to have been with Rossi, and authorizes the recipient to console them in his name: meaning that he gave Rossi permission to divulge the contents of the letter to them at his own discretion.[5] If Boccaccio felt himself to be in danger, it is hard to believe that he would have sent out a missive that so openly demonstrates his connections to the conspirators. Moreover, after the initial uproar, the tensions surrounding the event must have diminished fairly quickly, for Rossi would return to Florence as soon as 1363, when he would make his will.

The *otium* in Certaldo was an industrious one. In the wake of Leontius Pilatus's Greek literature lessons and his conversations two years earlier with Petrarch about his treatise *De viris illustri-bus* (*Illustrious Men*), as well as perhaps reading part of this work, "at a moment when I was able to isolate myself from the idle mob and was nearly carefree,"[6] Boccaccio began to draft a series of profiles of "Famous Women," the *De mulieribus claris*.[7] He intended to do something new: while there was a historigraphical tradition of biographies of illustrious men, analogous works dedicated to women were lacking. "What surprises me," he wrote in the preface, "is how little attention women have attracted from writers of this genre, and the absence of any work devoted to their memory."[8] Beyond the choice of topic, also new was the selection criterion for the figures profiled — as is indicated right in the title: not "mulieres illustres," that is, "illustrious, distinguished," but "clarae," "famous, renowned" — which he explained in the preface: "It is not my intention to interpret the word 'famous' in such a strict sense that it will always appear to mean 'virtuous.' Instead . . . I will adopt a wider meaning and consider as famous those women whom I know to have gained a reputation throughout the world for any deed whatsoever."[9]

But the true and great originality of this work consists in its fusion of historical-literary erudition and narrative with the intent to both inform and delight. Women are not only the subject of the discourse, but its intended audience equally with men: "It is my belief that the accomplishments of these ladies will please women

no less than men. Moreover, since women are generally unac-
quainted with history, they require and enjoy a more extended
account," that is, recounting of "the stories at somewhat greater
length [*in lungiusculam hystoriam*]."[10] The *De mulieribus* is perhaps
the most mature and conscious result of Boccaccio's decade-long
project to bring together humanistic high culture and vernacular
courtly culture. And, from this perspective, it is not complementary to Petrarch's *De viris*, but an alternative to it.[11]

Ravenna "Cloaca"

During the winter of 1361–62, Boccaccio was in Ravenna: we know
this from a letter he wrote to Petrarch on January 2, 1362.[12] He
had not been here since 1357. Why had he decided to return now?
Ravenna was certainly dear to his heart, but it was not nostalgia
alone that brought him back. Leontius resumed his lessons in the
autumn, and since Boccaccio failed to attend them, something
serious must have happened. In the letter to Petrarch just mentioned, Boccaccio wrote that he had been detained in Ravenna because of "misfortune" ("infortunio," *Ep.*, XI.1); a few months later,
from Florence, in a letter to Barbato da Sulmona Boccaccio would
mention a letter from Petrarch that had "brought comfort to me
for some of my troubles" (*Ep.*, XII.11);[13] two years later, writing to
Nelli, he would refer to "my misfortune" ("questo mio infortunio,"
Ep., XIII.5). As was often the case when something happened that
particularly hurt him or that he felt to be an offense against his
honor (one thinks, for example, of his departure from Naples in
1340), Boccaccio said little about it. A flurry of hypotheses has
therefore been proposed about what this misfortune could have
been:[14] The death of someone close to him (Violante's mother)?
Financial catastrophe? The loss of a benefice or even a failed business venture have both been suggested. Some of the conspirators
of 1360, and notably his friends Niccolò del Buono, Luca Ugolini,
and Andrea di Tello da Lisca, were involved in the wool trade ("la-
naiuoli"), and the textile sector had experienced a crisis due to the
1357 prohibition on trade with Pisa. On the basis of this, the hypothesis has been proposed that Boccaccio "had invested in the
same ventures as his associates and that, like them, suffered finan-

cial ruin."[15] However, it is quite hard to imagine that someone who avoided even investing in government bonds had embarked on this sort of commercial speculation. Unless documentary evidence emerges, we will have to resign ourselves to remaining in the dark.

A little light is cast, not enough to solve the mystery but at least to permit ruling out some theories, by the *subscriptio* of the letter to Petrarch: "Scripta in cloaca fere totius Gallie cisalpine," that is, written in Ravenna, the sewer of almost all of northern Italy. This is an insult the likes of which had come only rarely from Boccaccio's pen, and what's more, it was aimed at a city that he had loved. Something serious must have happened, something that Boccaccio felt to be a betrayal and an affront. His insult, however, tells us that whatever it was, it had happened in Ravenna. Therefore, we cannot surmise a financial catastrophe in Florence. But nor can we presume a personal event: a death or a quarrel with friends or with the secret family that he almost certainly had in Ravenna. Indeed, he denounced the entire city, and not just in the *subscriptio*: in the body of the letter as well, Boccaccio showed his disgust for the inhabitants and the monks of Ravenna, for their "sickening" (*Ep.*, XI.12) ignorance.[16] In short, the unfortunate business must have occurred within the public sphere, and almost certainly involved a political or religious institution. It is possible that, following Bernardino da Polenta's death in March 1359 and the succession of his son Guido, the government's attitude toward Boccaccio had changed, and that some appointment or ecclesiastical benefice had been taken away or denied him: we know that the Florentine tax office always considered him a layman, but that does not mean that he could not have held a prebendary in Ravenna. The most likely hypothesis, however, is not that he had had some sort of salary taken away or suffered a loss of expected income, but instead that, for mysterious reasons, which he perhaps felt to be dishonorable and, as we have seen, about which he did not speak in writing, Boccaccio had been forced to pay out a considerable amount of money. He did not speak of it publicly, but he confided in his closest friends in private and asked a few of them for loans, evidently to cover an expense that exceeded his capacities: Petrarch provides evidence that in this period Boccaccio needed loans from him and many others.[17] The only certainty is that the event, whatever it was, had profoundly shaken Boccaccio and provoked a psychological crisis with long-lasting effects.

In the midst of his Ravenna troubles, however, Boccaccio still found the calm necessary to fulfill a request from his friend and master. Petrarch had been working on a treatise, *De vita solitaria* (*On the Solitary Life*) consisting of an elegy on solitude and a series of exemplars of illustrious recluses, and wanted to include a chapter on Saint Peter Damian. He had sought information from the Camaldolese monastery of Fonte Avellana, where the saint had been prior, but had not gotten any or not in a sufficient quantity, so thought he might find more reliable information in Ravenna, the city of the saint's birth. Knowing that Boccaccio was there through their common friend Donato Albanzani, probably encountered in Venice, Petrarch sent the request for him to search out information. Boccaccio, naturally happy to do this favor, embarked on the research, but must have discovered that in Ravenna the saint was unknown. He was about to give up, when in the house of a private citizen he came across a ragged, dust-covered notebook containing Damian's biography. It was a copy of the *Vita Petri Damiani* written between 1076 and 1083–84 by his disciple Giovanni da Lodi, but because the codex only had the name Giovanni, the author remained unknown to Boccaccio. Upon reading the text, he judged it "overflowing with such a disorganized abundance of superfluous words" that he "got bored reading it," and so decided to rewrite it "in a somewhat more pleasant form," while "omitting nothing of substance" (*Ep.*, XI.17).[18] He sent the rewritten biography to Petrarch in Milan along with the letter of January 2, 1362. It is almost certain, however, that Petrarch received neither one.[19]

Depression

Just as we do not know when Boccaccio arrived in Ravenna, we do not know when he left. Considering the amount of time the research on Peter Damian and rewriting Giovanni da Lodi's biography would have required, it must have been quite a long stay. We also do not know whether he returned to Certaldo or to Florence. The first surviving documentation is a letter sent from Florence, but that was not until the middle of May. It would be logical to think that from Ravenna he went to Florence in time to attend the second part of Leontius Pilatus's course; it would be, were it not that Boccaccio was returning home deeply troubled and anxious, almost surely longing for solitude. There are many indications that in the early months of 1362 he fell into an "angry depression."[20]

Mournful references to his poverty and signs of impatience with his brother increased. Both certainly justified, but also, probably, exaggerated by a Boccaccio left even more fragile and distraught by the calamity in Ravenna. It is precisely beginning in 1362 that his lack of holdings in the Monte, which until then could be attributed to ethical motivations, appears instead dictated by economic straits. By selling his forced loan (*prestanza*) obligations up front or fulfilling the obligations *ad perdendum*, that is, renouncing any interest payments in exchange for a significant discount, "rather than investing in municipal finance as all the bourgeoisie did," Boccaccio ended up paying "direct taxes, just like a proletarian citizen," and what's more, paying them also for Iacopo, taxed along with him[21]—an "inept," "lazy," "deadbeat," "ignorant" brother, whom he did not hesitate to call a "leech" ("vomicam mei sanguinis," *EpA*, 52). That these lamentations of poverty should not to be confused with his many past declarations in this regard, which were well known to his friends ("As for your all too usual complaint of poverty . . . ," Petrarch wrote),[22] is attested by Petrarch, who early in 1362 referred to the debts Boccaccio had incurred with Petrarch himself and others: "you are in debt for money to many, me among them. . . . You owe me nothing but love."[23]

An event then took place in April and May that worsened Boccaccio's already disturbed and inherently pessimistic psychological state. The Sienese Carthusian monk Pietro Petroni—who died with a reputation for holiness on May 20, 1361—on his deathbed had confided to his disciple Gioacchino Ciani various visions of the future he had received during contemplation of Christ, and he charged Ciani with bringing warnings to various notable personages of the day, including Boccaccio and Petrarch.[24] Ciani, indeed, presented himself to Boccaccio, we do not know whether in Certaldo or Florence, and revealed that Boccaccio's death was imminent and that he must abandon profane study and poetry to save his soul. Boccaccio was profoundly affected by this. Tormented by fear of death and damnation, he heeded the monk's warning. In a letter that has been lost, but based on his friend's response must have been written in a state of anxious agitation, Boccaccio alerted Petrarch that he too would be receiving a visit from this messenger, and conveyed his own decision to "throw away" ("proicere," in Petrarch's words) not only all his work, his entire career as a writer, but also the tools of his trade, that is, the library he had gathered over many years. And in the same letter, he offered to sell his books to Petrarch. To sell them, not give them: in short, if his dark mood and the irrational fear of the future roused in him by the monk's prophesy were the trigger, economic necessity must have significantly influenced such a difficult decision. Petrarch realized that Boccaccio was in a state of uncontrolled agitation and tried to calm him with a long letter arguing that the exhortations to virtue and awareness of imminent death must not deter him from literary study, because it is precisely literature that "in a good soul arouses a love of virtue and either removes or lessens the fear of death."[25] As for the request to purchase the books, Petrarch did not hesitate, because, "although I seem to be buying what is already mine, I still do not wish such a great man's books scattered here and there or in profane hands, as so often happens." It was his intention that, one day, just as their owners had been united in spirit, his own library and that of his friend should together "come intact and undiminished to some pious, devout place in perpetual memory of us."[26] But, he added, he was not able to name a price, as Boccaccio had asked him to, because he did not know "the titles, the number, or the value"[27] of the books. However, once the economic and psychological crisis of the first quarter of 1362 had passed, Boccaccio would never again mention the idea of disposing of his books.

The sense that following the misfortune in Ravenna Boccaccio fell into a state of inertia, of fear of the new and of responsibility, of withdrawal from the world, that is, that he descended into depression, is confirmed by an episode that occurred during these months.

Between the end of July and early August 1361, Zanobi da Strada died, perhaps of the plague, leaving vacant the post of apostolic secretary. As in the past, there was a great deal of pressure from the curia, some from the pope himself, urging Petrarch to accept the position, but he was resolute in his refusal. However, Petrarch did take on the task of identifying a person for the job, and so contacted by letter both Francesco Nelli, Simonide—who in the second half of 1361 had replaced Zanobi da Strada as *spenditore*, or administrator, for Niccolò Acciaiuoli in Naples—and Giovanni Boccaccio. In early March 1362, Nelli thanked Petrarch and said he was ready to accept the appointment. In contrast, at about the same time, and in any case before Nelli's response, Boccaccio refused.[28] Now, the office of apostolic secretary not only brought with it a great deal of power, but was also very lucrative. And it is thus quite perplexing that Boccaccio, in perennial and futile search of a position, declined an offer that would have solved all his problems once and for all, and especially that he did so at such a difficult point in his life. Even Petrarch, while supporting his friend's decision, seems a bit bewildered by it. Giovanni did nothing but lament his poverty, and yet would not accept either the invitation to live with Petrarch (which offended him a little) or the offer to become rich through his help:

> As for your all too usual complaint of poverty, I have no wish to offer consolation or examples now of famous poor people; they are well known to you. What then? My reply is always the same, loud and consistent. I praise you for preferring liberty of spirit and peaceful poverty to the great wealth I sought for you, although late [that is, the position of apostolic secretary]; I do not praise you for repulsing a friend who so often invites you. I cannot make you wealthy from here. If it were possible, I would speak to you not with words or pen, but with deeds. I have, however, the resources for one that would abundantly suffice for two with a single heart and home. You do me wrong if you disdain this; you do me more wrong if you mistrust me.[29]

This does not mean that Boccaccio's many refusals of Petrarch's offer to come live with him were made, as one biographer has claimed, only "out of skittish sensitivity and fear of harming a friendship that had become one of the guiding principles of his life"; in reality, if we believe what Giovanni himself wrote to Niccolò

Orsini in 1371, Petrarch urged him "with the sweetest pleas and exhortations, not [for me to come] as a friend and companion" — as the same biographer put it, "to have him as a permanent fraternal guest, advisor and collaborator in his work"[30] — but so that Boccaccio would reside "with him as steward of his house and his other possessions" (*Fp.*, XVIII.11).[31] In short, Petrarch may have been motivated by the best of intentions, but Boccaccio must not have liked his proposal to be housed in the role of manager rather than of scholarly companion: as sensitive as he was, he may even have been offended. As for the post of apostolic secretary, it may have been that his psychological state at this time led him to decline to try for the office, a prestigious position, very well paid, and yet time consuming and burdened with heavy responsibilities, as well as requiring a move to an unfamiliar, foreign location. Boccaccio had always avoided taking on challenging and risky roles, just as he had always tried to be able to devote himself freely to study. And yet the desire for autonomy was inextricably intertwined in him with feelings of inadequacy and deficiency, feelings, however, that had led him more than once to act reactively, with bravado and insufficient thought. We can therefore understand that the deep malaise of these months accentuated his fear of assuming obligations, his insecurity, and, at the same time, his need for the protection of known, familiar surroundings. Viewed in this light, taking steps just then to go to Naples and Acciaiuoli, something that has to be marveled at after all that had happened between him and this family, appears less incomprehensible.

In Florence in 1359, Boccaccio had mended relations, if not with Niccolò, with many members of his family and of his entourage. This was not a matter of superficial encounters, of politeness. Francesco Buondelmonti, the son of Lapa Acciaiuoli, would by no means commission his copy of the *Decameron* from a bookseller or a *scriptorium*; Boccaccio himself would put an autograph at his disposal and very likely, as we know he often did in those years, directly oversee the transcription process. And then, in the latter half of 1361, Nelli, one of Boccaccio's closest friends, moved to Naples to enter service with Niccolò Acciaiuoli, thus guaranteeing him a direct channel of communication with Niccolò. Nelli was one of the people whom Boccaccio told about the "misfortune" in

Ravenna and, presumably, asked for help. In the first months of 1362, the two friends formed a plan to convince Acciaiuoli to take Boccaccio into his service. Nelli spoke to Acciaiuoli about it in May in Messina; Acciaiuoli accepted the proposal and wrote personally and insistently to Boccaccio that he should come to him, making large promises. Boccaccio, however, burned by Acciaiuoli's earlier broken promises in 1355, did not trust him: he even thought about going to Naples to talk to Nelli face to face. It was a letter from Nelli that persuaded Boccaccio that this time agreements would be honored. Driving Nelli to support his friend's cause may also have been the recently raised possibility of his own appointment as apostolic secretary; or perhaps it was Boccaccio, obviously also aware of this prospect, who envisioned being able to take over Nelli's post, just as Nelli had succeeded Zanobi when he moved on to Avignon; it could even be that the very idea of becoming Acciauoli's *spenditore* had led Boccaccio to refuse Petrarch's offer. However, whether Nelli did not understand his master's intentions, or, more likely, Boccaccio misinterpreted the signals he received, we will see that his decision to go to Naples was based on a misunderstanding.[32]

Now resolved to leave, that summer in Certaldo Boccaccio turned again to the *De mulieribus claris* and added a few chapters specifically in anticipation of publication in Naples, among them the final chapter on Queen Joanna, who had been widowed a few months earlier: this encomiastic intention transforming it from biography to panegyric.[33] But Boccaccio was interested in pleasing the Acciaiuoli family even more than in pleasing the queen, and therefore he changed the dedication, first conceived specifically for Joanna, to one of Niccolò's sisters, Andrea, a woman on whom God had lavished such and so many virtues that "he willed you to be known by the name you bear, Andrea, since *andres* in Greek is the equivalent of the Latin word for 'men.'"[34] Of Niccolò's two sisters, Andrea and Lapa, the latter was his right hand in the Kingdom of Naples, administering his assets and executing his wishes, while Andrea, although less close to him, by virtue of her marriages, first to Carlo d'Artus, Count of Monteodorisio, and then to Bartolomeo di Capua, Count of Altavilla, "played a fundamental role in the integration of the Acciaiuoli family into the ranks of the

Angevin nobility."[35] If you recall the vehemence with which only a few years earlier Boccaccio had hurled insults at Niccolò/Midas and Lapa (called Lupisca) in his eighth eclogue, you might feel bewildered.[36] The dedication of the *De mulieribus* is the most overt, one might say, the most naively overt act of courtly obsequiousness ever performed by Boccaccio toward this family, and it may even have contributed to the creation of the misunderstanding into which both Niccolò and Giovanni blundered, on the basis of which the former summoned and the latter accepted. A few years earlier, Boccaccio had included Andrea in the list of ladies in the *Amorosa visione*; however, at that time, not only was his praise very modest, but his description of her family—merchants who were able to appear noble thanks to wealth amassed through commerce and strategic marriages—was anything but encomiastic:

> Looking further on, I saw approaching, humble
> in her looks, the one born of those who,
> sharpening their wits to their
> > work, at time with base matter, gave
> themselves noble colors through others,[37]
> multiplying their riches by family alliances.

> Riguardando oltre, con sembianza umile
> venia colei che nacque di coloro
> li qual, tal fiata con materia vile
> > aguzzando l'ingegno al lor lavoro,
> fer nobile colore ad uopo altrui,
> moltiplicando con famiglia in oro.

AV, XLII.28–33[38]

Boccaccio departed for Naples around the middle of October 1362. With him traveled his books and his brother Iacopo, who had been widowed shortly after his marriage. Boccaccio evidently expected to be away from Florence for a long time. He had, however, made arrangements for someone in the city to pay the *prestanze* imposed by the Comune while he was away (of which there were four). Since those not in compliance with their tax obligations would lose their citizenship, from this it can be deduced that Boccaccio, who kept his citizenship, did not foresee settling in Naples permanently.[39] In any case, it was a long absence: he would only return to Florence ten months later.

Almost a Novella

The trip to Naples would prove to be particularly miserable. Boccaccio himself described his adversities in a long letter (*Ep.*, XIII) he sent to Nelli after the conclusion of the sad adventure. In the letter, which in places unfolds like one of his own novellas, in an embittered, even wrathful, tone, he described his life in Naples and the figure of Niccolò Acciaiuoli with an exaggerated realism that verges on the absurd. The Latin original has unfortunately been lost; what survives is a vernacular translation by an unknown fifteenth-century writer, the notable literary qualities of which, however, must be acknowledged.

In Nocera, where Boccaccio arrived toward the middle of November, Acciaiuoli received him with a cold and distracted handshake: "An inauspicious greeting, indeed!" ("Augurio certamente infelice!"). The following day, Niccolò and his court moved to Naples. Here, Boccaccio was housed not on the main floors of the palace, but in a small "precinct . . . enveloped in an ancient fog of spiderwebs and dry dust . . . fetid and bad smelling" ("particella . . . rinchiusa d'una vecchia nebbia di tele di ragnolo e di secca polvere . . . fetida e di cattivo odore"), which he called the "the bilge," "the lowest part of a great ship, receptacle of all filth" ("sentina," "d'uno grande navilio la più bassa parte, d'ogni bruttura ricettacolo"). Notwithstanding the November cold, he and his brother were assigned a "little room" facing north "with many holes in the walls" ("cameruzza aperta da più buche"), and for sleeping "on the stone floor, a mattress full of clumps of *capecchio*," a kind of slippery, hairlike waste material from processing linen or hemp ("sopra il solare di sasso, uno letticciuolo pieno di capecchio piegato e cucito in forma di piccole spere"), and on top of this nasty mattress a "stinky blanket" ("puzzolente copertoio"), which seemed to have been just "taken out from under a mule driver" ("tratto di sotto ad uno mulattiere"), and no pillow. The little room was furnished

with only "a little earthen lamp, a single half-dead light" ("una lu-
cernuzza di terra, un solo lume mezzo morto") and "a small table"
partly covered by a "piece of canvas, all eaten away by dogs or old
age" ("una piccola tavoletta"; "canovaccio, da' cani o vero dalla vecchiaia tutto róso"): on the table "a few clouded and dirty glasses"
("pochi, nebbiosi ed aggravati bicchieri"); "beneath the table, in
place of a bench, there was a little log with one foot missing" ("di
sotto alla tavola, in luogo di panca, era un legnerello monco d'un
piè"). Their food consisted of "oxen dead of old age, exhaustion,
or sickness," "used-up old sows or elderly pigeons," and "three
lukewarm chestnuts" ("buoi di vecchiaia e di fatica o d'infermità
morti"; "troie spregnate o colombi vecchi"; "tre castagne tiepide");
on fast days, "the tiniest minnows, that even beggers wouldn't
keep . . . cooked in rancid oil" ("piccolissimi pesciolini, ancora a'
mendicanti lasciati . . . cotti in olio fetido"); all washed down by
"wines that were sour, gone bad, or downright vinegary" ("vini o
agresti o fracidi o vero acetosi"). The "bilge" was located near the
servants' quarters and kitchens: this the reason that, although
there was no fire in the room, "the smoke from the kitchen and
cooking food covered everything" ("il fummo della cucina e messo
della vivanda occupava ogni cosa"). Above all, this precinct was inhabited by a contemptible humanity:

> gluttons and gorgers, toadies, mule drivers and serving boys,
> cooks and scullery boys, in other words, court dogs and domestic
> rats . . . running here and there, they filled the whole place with
> the discordant bellowing of oxen: and, what was unbearable to
> see and smell, since the jugs and wine pots often broke in various
> places, anointing the cracked floor, the dust and wine were turned
> into mud by their feet, filling the air of the place with a foul stench.
> Alas! How many times was my stomach not just upset, but pro-
> voked to vomit!

> ghiottoni e manicatori, lusinghieri, mulattieri e ragazzi, cuochi e
> sguatteri, ed usando altro vocabolo, cani della corte e topi dimes-
> tici . . . ora di qua ed ora di là discorrendo, con discordevole mug-
> liare di buoi riempievano tutta la casa: e, quello che m'era gravis-
> simo al vedere ed all'odorato, mentre che le mezzine ed i vasi da

vino spesse volte di quindi e di quinci rompessono, il rotto suolo immolando, e la polvere ed il vino co' piedi in fango convertissono, di fetido odore riempivano l'aria del luogo. Ohimè! Quante volte non in fastidio solamente, ma in vomito fu provocato lo stomaco.

When the "filthy and disreputable" ("sucido disorrevole") majordomo, "carrying a few small lights in his hand, his eyes watering from the smoke, in a hoarse voice and with his staff" ("pochi e piccoli lumi portando in mano, gli occhi lagrimanti per lo fummo, con voce roca e con la verga") gave the signal to be seated at the table for dinner, Boccaccio "with a few others entered the first table, as the most honored in the bilge, but before my eyes, the filthy and disorderly crowd ran riot: without waiting for the command, each one set himself at the trough wherever chance allowed" ("con pochi entrava alla prima tavola, come più onorato nella sentina, ma nel conspetto mio sozza ed incomposita turba ruinava: sanza comandamento aspettare, dove la fortuna gli concedeva, ciascuno alla mangiatoia s'acconciava").

He saw them

almost all with damp nostrils, wan cheeks, weeping eyes, tormented by convulsive coughs, expelling in front of themselves and of me festering gobs of sputum. And it's no wonder: almost all of them only half dressed in thin and threadbare clothing, bare at the knees, and, unsavory and trembling, uncouth, ravenous, like wild beasts, they gulped down the food put in front of them.

quasi tutti con gli anari del naso umidi, con le gote livide, con gli occhi piangenti, in gravissima tossa essere commossi, e dinanzi a sé ed a me marcidi e rappresi umori sputare. E non è maraviglia: mezzi vestiti quasi tutti di sottilissimi e manicati pannicelli, presso al ginocchio nudi, e disorrevoli e tremanti, scostumati, affamati, a guisa di fiere trangugiavano le vivande poste loro innanzi.

Disgusted, Iacopo went to stay at a hotel; Giovanni had the good fortune to be rescued by the generosity of a young Florentine, Mainardo Cavalcanti, who, taking pity on him, often invited him over to eat and sleep.[40] Acciaiuoli pretended not to notice. Boccaccio received visitors in his hovel. One young Neapolitan nobleman, connected to him by a long friendship, after visiting his room raced home to Pozzuoli and sent him "a splendid bed with pillows" ("uno splendido letto con guanciali"). During the Christmas holidays, Acciaiuoli traveled to the spa town of Tripergole (destroyed by the eruption of Monte Nuovo of 1538) near Baia with his family, and insisted Boccaccio join him. However, when it came time to return to Naples, "all the household goods were taken away, right up to the last wooden bench and earthenware jar: I alone," Boccaccio continues, "with all of my books, was left on the beach with my servant, without the things necessary for life and with no guidance." There were neither taverns nor friends to be found in that place, and he was "forced to go on a long fast" ("costretto a fare un lungo digiuno"), but what humiliated him the most was becoming "almost a comical show" ("quasi un giuoco da ridere") for those who saw him "wandering around on the beach" ("andare intorno al lito"). Finally, two days later, they arranged to bring him back to the city, but he refused to return to the bilge, and, since Mainardo had been sent away on a mission, for more than fifty days he was the guest of "a friend who was a poor merchant" ("uno amico mercante e povero"),[41] without any acknowledgment from Acciaiuoli. In the end, Boccaccio said his farewells and left Naples in early March 1363. He would never see Francesco Nelli again, who would die of the plague that same year, nor Niccolò Acciaiuoli, whose death would come less than three years later.

A significant portion of the letter is devoted to a sarcastic and furious harangue against Acciaiuoli, of whom he paints a merciless and at times caricatured portrait. The passage is famous in which Boccaccio describes how Acciaiuoli received those requesting an audience and dealt with the affairs of the kingdom:

> Very often he withdraws into a small room, and here, so that it appears that he has much to do of a serious nature regarding the Kingdom, at the door to the room, as is the royal custom, he places porters, and no one who asks is given permission to enter. Many come, and at times great men; they fill the courtyard in front of the door and in low voices request the opportunity to speak. The

responses they are given by the well-trained porters are laughable.
To many they say that he is in conference; to others that he is at
his daily prayers; to still others, that, tired out by affairs of state,
he is taking a little rest. . . . In the *guarderobe*, at his command, a
chair has been placed, and here he seats himself, no differently
than on his majestic throne, and with his women standing around
him, who are truly not whores, which would appear extremely
improper, nor sisters, nor kin, nor nieces, amid the extremely unseemly noises of viscera and the expelling of the stinking weight
of bowels, great councils are held, the affairs of the Kingdom are
arranged, the highest officials are appointed, justice is rendered,
and letters to the world's kings and the supreme pontiff and to
his other friends are dictated, written, and corrected, with the approval of the toadies and flunkies along with his women; while the
fools waiting in the courtyard believe that he, having been received
into the assembly of the gods, holds solemn parliament with them
regarding the universal state of the republic.

Spessissime volte egli se ne va nel conclavio, e quivi, acciò che e'
paia che egli abbia molto che fare della gravità del Regno, posti,
secondo l'usanza reale, portinari all'uscio della camera, a niuno
che il domandi è conceduta licenza dell'entrare. Vengono molti,
ed alcuna volta de' maggiori; empiono il cortile dinanzi alla porta
e con bassa voce domandano copia di parlare. Che risposte sieno
date dagli ammaestrati portinari, è cosa da ridere. A molti dicono
lui avere consiglio con alquanti; ad altri, lui dire il divino ufficio;
ad altri, lui, faticato intorno alle cose pubbliche, pigliare un poco
di riposo. . . . In guarderobba per suo comandamento si poneva
una seggiola, che quivi, non altrimenti che nella sedia della sua
maestà, vi siede e, stando dintorno le femmine sue, veramente non
puttane, che troppo disonesto parrebbe, né sirocchie né parenti né
nipoti, intra' troppo discordevoli romori del ventre ed il cacciare
fuori del puzzolente peso delle budella gran consiglio si tengono
ed i propri fatti del Regno si dispongono, le prefetture si diseg-
nano, a bocca si rende ragione, ed a' re del mondo ed al sommo
pontefice ed agli altri amici si dittano e scrivono e correggono lettere, i lusingheri ed i greculi insieme con le femmine sue appro-

vanti; credendosi gli sciocchi, che aspettano nella corte, che egli, ricevuto nel concestorio degl'iddii, insieme con loro dello stato universale della repubblica tenga solenne parlamento.

The tone of the entire letter is exaggerated and absurdist. Rather than a realistic description of an actual experience, it should be understood as a painful and honest account of experiencing disappointment. Disappointment caused, as has been noted, by a misunderstanding. Acciaiuoli, to whom—as Boccaccio himself acknowledged—"was granted by nature an admirable aptitude for literature" ("essere una mirabile attitudine nella litteratura . . . da natura stata conceduta"), in his eagerness to ennoble himself, aspired to gather illustrious men of letters around him who would celebrate his achievements. His greatest desire was to bring Francesco Petrarca to his court: he had tried to do so many times, especially in these years, both by writing to him himself and by having Nelli write. On this occasion, Petrarch had once again decisively refused.[42] For Acciaiuoli, Boccaccio was a second choice, probably suggested by Nelli. And for precisely this reason, Acciaiuoli expected Boccaccio to be eager to celebrate him, a bit as the dearly missed Zanobi da Strada had done. What Boccaccio, for his part, expected from Acciaiuoli is not clear, but certainly not the job of "writing down the great things that he believes, or wants others to believe, he has done," ("scrivere le gran cose le quali si crede, o vuole si creda per altri, lui avere fatte"); when he realized that "he was summoned for nothing else" ("per altro non essere chiamato"), he took it badly: he did not intend "to write fairy tales for history" ("scrivere favole per istorie"). An understandable reaction: he had recently taken himself out of the running for the prestigious office of apostolic secretary precisely to preserve his freedom as a poet and scholar, and now he was supposed to make himself a courtier-poet, and what's more, sing the glories of a merchant? It is likewise understandable that Acciaiuoli was upset: when he realized that Boccaccio would not do what he wanted, "immediately" ("immantenente")—Boccaccio wrote—"he found me detestable" ("a lui odioso fui"). The rudeness of the one and the recriminatory fury of the other therefore had a basis. It rather says a great deal about Boccaccio's character, about his fundamental naivete and also about the almost infantile egocentrism that often surfaced in his behavior, that he either did not know what role Acciaiuoli might assign him or else imagined enjoying support that was essentially free, for cultural merit, merit that he, however, refused to put at Acciaiuoli's service. In short, the "modest" Boccaccio seems, in this situation, to have been comporting himself in Petrarchan style.

Seeking Comfort?

From Naples, the Boccaccio brothers headed to Sulmona, where they were the guests of Barbato. We can imagine what Boccaccio would have told his old friend about what happened in Naples and also how sympathetic Barbato would have been. Presumably, with essentially a repetition of whatever it was he had said on the occasion of Boccaccio's last trip to Naples. After saying their farewells two days later, Iacopo returned to Florence, while Giovanni set off for Padua: he would never see Barbato again, who died in the early autumn. The currently accepted interpretation is that the only reason that Boccaccio traveled to Padua was to see Petrarch: since he did not know that his friend had been in Venice from at least the previous September, when he reached Padua and found him gone, Boccaccio decided to stay on for a time, where he befriended Pietro da Moglio (or da Muglio). But is it believable that Boccaccio would travel to Padua without letting Petrarch know in advance of his arrival, and thus not know about the move to Venice? Further: how and why did Boccaccio come into contact with Pietro da Moglio, by chance or through someone else? Now, the only documented date regarding Boccaccio's stay in Padua is a letter dated March 13, 1363, from Petrarch to Pietro da Moglio, with which he had enclosed another letter asking that it be sent "to our Giovanni."[43] The letter for Boccaccio, also dated March 13, is a long epistle in which Petrarch defends himself against criticism of the *Africa* (that is, of one passage from it, the "lament of Mago," circulated by Barbato da Sulmona) and of his bucolics.[44] This is far too little to enable the reconstruction of motivations and events during Boccaccio's Padua stay. Petrarch's letter to Pietro does, however, establish a number of points: Petrarch had a friendship with Pietro before

Boccaccio's arrival; he knew about the relationship that had been established between Pietro and Giovanni; Boccaccio was not living in Pietro's house; and, finally, Petrarch did not anticipate that Boccaccio would shortly arrive in Venice, otherwise he could have waited to send him the enclosed letter.[45]

The Bolognese scholar Pietro da Moglio had moved from teaching rhetoric at the Studium in Bologna to the one in Padua in early November 1362. Giovanni Conversini had been one of his students, as well as a student of Donato Albanzani, who was one of Boccaccio's closest friends and also lived in Venice in precisely these years. It is quite likely that Conversini and Albanzani were the link between Pietro da Moglio and Petrarch; in any case, a quite affectionate circle of friends had developed, as is demonstrated by the fact that Petrarch and Conversini would be named godfathers of Pietro's son at some point prior to February 1364. Also indicating the strength of their connection is the kinds of requests that Petrarch made of da Moglio, whom he often used as a postman or conveyor of messages in person. Pietro da Moglio, indeed like Petrarch himself, was well connected in the ruling circles of Padua and enjoyed the esteem of Padua's lord, Francesco "il Vecchio" da Carrara.[46] It is significant that, in addition to the one for Boccaccio, Petrarch had also included another enclosure his March 13 letter, this a letter for Nicoletto d'Alessio, protonotary of the chancellery of Carrara.[47] Once his bridges in Romagna had been burned, outside of Florence Boccaccio had only two groups of influential people who could help him: one connected to Acciaiuoli and the other comprising Petrarch and his friends. It is thus possible that this latter group, informed of the debacle in Naples, may have directed Giovanni to Padua, where they thought they could count on support, so that he, in his economically disastrous situation, might obtain some paid position. If this was the case — but, I repeat, it is just a hypothesis — it was yet another dead end.

By late March or early April 1363, Boccaccio was in Venice: for three months he would be a guest in the comfortable house on the Riva degli Schiavoni that the Great Council had offered to Petrarch in exchange for his pledge to bequeath his books to the Republic. Here, Boccaccio found Leontius Pilatus. A year earlier, Leontius had left Florence on bad terms: it should be said in his defense, however, that while Leontius had a difficult character, living with the angry, depressed Boccaccio of that period must not have been pleasant. In Venice, Boccaccio also enjoyed the company of his old friends Donato Albanzani and the physician Guglielmo da Ravenna, whom he had met through Albanzani while living in Ravenna, as well as of some of Petrarch's new friends, who would become Boccaccio's friends too, foremost among them Benintendi Ravegnani, grand chancellor of the Republic.[48] Petrarch welcomed Boccaccio, by now considered part of his extended family, with warmth and cheer, listened to his account of his Neapolitan misadventures, and, according to Boccaccio, approved of his decision to leave Naples and deplored Nelli's behavior: "which [departure] our Silvanus commends most highly, and laments the foolishness of his Simonides [Nelli]" ("la qual cosa il nostro Silvano sommamente commenda, e piange la sciocchezza del suo Simonide," *Ep.*, XIII.250). But he took no side publicly with regard either to Nelli or to Acciaiuoli. Living surrounded by the affection of dear friends did not soothe Boccaccio's rage, however, which exploded in April when he received a "biting" and "brief but very sharp letter" ("mordace," "breve ma asprissima lettera," *Ep.*, XIII.1, 251) from Nelli. It would take Boccaccio quite some time to write his lengthy response, the violent missive of June 28, which has been frequently cited here. What offended him most of all was that Nelli repeated in writing the words he had said to Boccaccio upon finding him incensed on the beach in Baia, namely, that Boccaccio was "a man of glass" ("un uomo di vetro"), thin-skinned, and unable to tolerate the least adversity. The tirade Boccaccio unleashed in response is memorable.

In early July 1363, Boccaccio returned home, perhaps to Florence, more likely to Certaldo.

Convert at Age Fifty

In 1363, Boccaccio turned fifty. This was a notable milestone: for example, in March of that year he would have read in a letter from Petrarch that Isadore of Seville divided human life into six ages, with the fourth, youth, ending in the fiftieth year.[49] Even leaving aside this theoretical division, which humanists like Petrarch and

Boccaccio gave little weight,[50] the fiftieth year was a significant turning point in itself. We should not measure it by today's standards: in the fourteenth century, at age fifty a man effectively entered old age. And for Boccaccio, this birthday fell in the middle of an already acute existential crisis.

The early 1360s had been a succession of disagreeable situations, scares, misfortunes, and painful disappointments: his brother's marriage and the need to divide the house, worries connected to the conspiracy, the incident in Ravenna, the debts, the humiliation in Naples. Boccaccio was psychologically exhausted, he developed fears and insecurities, alternated between withdrawal and polemical excesses. And, as if this were not enough, Petroni's gloomy prophecies had stirred up feelings of mortality and fears of damnation: Boccaccio took refuge in religion. He, who had never known his mother, became deeply devoted to the Virgin Mary. The literary manifestations of his fervent faith arose in precisely this period, and they would surge for a few years and then abate. The fervency was particularly intense in the *Corbaccio*, a work with a twofold intention, first, to make amends for the "ingratitude" the author accuses himself of, for not having sufficiently praised the Virgin in the past ("She has made [her beneficence and mercy] known to me in the past in many other perils, although I have been ungrateful for so many benefits by achieving little in Her praise" ["ella in molti altri pericoli già me l'ha fatta conoscere, quantunque io di tanti benefici ingrato stato sia, poco nelle sue laudi adoperandomi," *Corbaccio*, 119]); and, second, as he declares from the first page, to give thanks to her for "a special grace which was recently granted to me, not because of my own merit, but solely by the beneficence of Her, Who implored it from the One, Who wills that which She wills Herself" ("una spezial grazia ... non per suo merito, ma per sola benignità di Colei che, impetrandola di Colui che vuole quello che Ella medesima, nuovamente gli fu conceduta," *Corbaccio*, 3). The work also ends in her name: "if a hundred thousand enticing entreaties were to assail me ... they could not put me back into the chains from which I am freed by the mercy of Her to whom I have always acknowledged my obligation, and now more than ever" ("se cento milia prieghi mi si facessero incontro . . . non mi potrebbero più nelle catene rimettere, delle quali la misericordia di Colei alla qual sempre mi conobbi obligato, e ora più che mai . . . mi traggono," *Corbaccio*, 550). This grace that he had received was being freed from lust, the "chain" that had bound him. Such passages as "But I devoutly pray to Her Who has the power to do as She wills, that just as She has snatched me many times from everlasting death, She may direct my steps toward eternal life and sustain and preserve them until I, being Her most faithful servant, arrive at the goal" ("Ma io divotamente Lei priego che può quello ch'ella vuole, che, come dalla perpetua morte più volte m'ha tolto, così i miei passi dirizzi alla vita perpetua, e quelli sostenga e conservi tanto che io, suo fedelissimo servidore essendo, pervenga"); and "whatever life you have led, you have always held in especial reverence and devotion Her, within Whose womb our Salvation was enclosed and Who is the living fountain of mercy and Mother of grace and compassion, and that you always had complete home in Her as in a fixed terminus" ("tu sempre, qual che stata si sia la tua vita, hai in ispezial reverenza e devozione avuta Colei nel cui ventre si racchiuse la nostra salute e che è viva fontana di misericordia e madre di grazia e di pietà, e in lei, siccome termine fisso, avesti sempre intera speranza," *Corbaccio*, 120, 115)[51] resonate with lines of poetry plausibly also written in this period,[52] such as:

> I hope in you, and have always hoped in you: pray for me and for me to be made worthy of seeing you with your blessed Child

> Io spero in te, e 'n te sempr'ho sperato:
> prega per me, et esser mi fa' degno
> di veder teco il tuo beato Fructo

> *Rime*, XCVI (CXVIII).12–14

> I hope in you and have always hoped: grant me the long love and reverence, which I carry for you and have always carried. Direct my path, make me capable of arriving at the right side of your Son, among the blessed people.

Io spero in te et ho sempre sperato:
vagliami il lungo amore e 'l reverente,
il qual ti porto, et ho sempre portato.
Dirizza il mio cammin, fammi possente
di divenir anchor dal dextro lato
del tuo Figliuol, fra la beata gente

Rime, XCVII (CXIX).9–14

Boccaccio's exhaustion of spirit and the religious, in some respects almost superstitious, turn he took must have had repercussions for his vision of intellectual work. We have already seen how when caught up in the flood of emotion resulting from Petroni's prophecy he had decided to sell his books. The fact that also in this period, apparently due to feelings of inferiority to Petrarch, he burned, or more likely planned to burn, his youthful vernacular poetry can only be attributed to a serious psychological instability.[53]

It was in this state of mind that Boccaccio returned to the vernacular to write the *Corbaccio*, a work that almost viciously and in a generally sullen, resentful, and spiteful tone condemns "concupiscent and carnal love" ("concupiscibile e carnale amore," *Corbaccio*, 123), especially the love that ensnares a learned man of advanced years, employing an invective that encompasses the entire "execrable feminine sex" ("esecrabile sesso femineo," *Corbaccio*, 234).[54] A satire that is presented as revenge against a woman, a widow, but that ends up turning against its own author, against what he had been and, above all, against what he had put at the center of his literature in the vernacular. His almost obsessive insistence on the negative qualities of love and women, not to mention of sexuality, and the correspondingly meager space granted to positive values to be upheld make the character's journey less one of conversion than of recantation.

Tortured by unrequited love for a widow and only partially consoled by pleasant conversations with friends, the author dreams of getting lost in a frightening valley ("Labyrinth of Love" ["labirinto d'amore"]): he is rescued by a male figure who reveals that he is the deceased husband of the author's beloved. This spirit shows him how love does not befit either his mature age or his profession as a man of letters, and reveals the vices, defects, and wickedness of women in general and, more specifically, the ugliness and physical ravages of that particular woman, her rapaciousness, vulgarity, hypocrisy, and immense vices: characteristics that his unusual situation, first a husband, then a pure spirit, has allowed him to see, indeed to touch, beyond the curtain of simulations, conventions, real and metaphorical veils that the woman has constructed, on which her reputation depends and for which the author fell in love with her. This denunciation has the desired therapeutic effect: the author is able to emerge, with his guide, from the terrifying valley where the animalistic cries of the victims of love ("Pigsty of Venus" ["porcile di Venere"]) resound, and he ascends, Dantesquely, toward the mountains and a soothing spring landscape.[55]

Boccaccio had come back to autobiography. Not since the works written immediately after his return to Florence (the *Comedia delle ninfe fiorentine* through the *Elegia di Madonna Fiammetta*) had the author coincided with the narrator or one of the main characters. The work's title has given rise to a flood of interpretations:[56] whatever Boccaccio had in mind with the word Corbaccio, it is impossible, given the "almost perfect anagram of Giovanni's last name, [that] it does not refer to the author, adding a negative sense that we do not know how to decipher."[57] All the more so because the author-protagonist, who depicts himself as a scholar and writer, speaks of his own life in terms that unambiguously refer to Boccaccio's own biography: "You never learned any manual trade and always hated commerce; of this you have boasted many times to yourself and others, crediting your intellect, which is hardly suited to those things in which many [merchants] grow old in years and in sense each day become younger"; and also, "Far more than your father would have wished, then, right from your childhood you liked studies pertaining to sacred philosophy, and especially that part dealing with poetry, which perhaps you have pursued with more fervor of spirit than with heights of genius" ("Tu ... mai alcuna manuale arte non apparasti e sempre l'essere mercatante avesti in odio; di che più volte ti sè e con altrui e teco medesimo gloriato, avendo riguardo al tuo ingegno, poco atto a quelle cose nelle quali assai invecchiano d'anni, e di senno ciascun giorno diventano più giovani"; "Gli studi adunque alla sacra filosofia pertinenti infino dalla tua puerizia più assai che il tuo padre non avrebbe voluto ti piacquero, e massimamente in quella parte che a poesia appartiene; la quale per avventura tu hai con più fervore d'animo che con altezza d'ingegno seguitar," *Corbaccio*, 189, 191).[58] This does not mean that Boccaccio had actually experienced the precipitating event of the book—the no-longer-young widow's refusal of the protagonist's love—or, at any rate, that such an episode had taken place at a time close to the work's composition. Taking into account the autobiographical backgrounds of his fictional works with characters who are widows (one thinks, for example, of the cruel Giovanna-Filomena of the *Filostrato*), it could even be that, in order to connect his satire to a real incident, he fished out of his memory an unhappy affair from many years earlier. The autobiography of the *Corbaccio* does not lie in recounting experiences, but is instead intellectual and, more than that, emotional: it reflects what Boccaccio thought of eros at a particular moment in his life and, even more, how he, an unmarried cleric, experienced the complicated relationship with the opposite sex.

Just when in his life this particular moment was, however, the book does not say: there is no detail, either internal or external, that allows us to propose a composition date for this work. Of the two periods around which the many scholarly proposals have clustered—roughly the mid-1350s and the mid-1360s—the first, as we will see, seems to be supported by the fact that the narrator says he is a little over forty at the time of his dream vision, while the second, although today accepted by almost everyone, rests solely on cultural considerations, namely, on the incompatibility between the conceptions of love and the role of women that mark the *Corbaccio* and those that Boccaccio manifested in the *Decameron*.[59]

The *Corbaccio* reverses, generally and in specifics, Boccaccio's previously expressed theses about eros and about the female objects of erotic desire, beginning with the cornerstone of his philogynous literature—from the *Caccia di Diana* through Cimone of the *Decameron*—namely, that the vital force of love cannot be repressed: when regulated, it is precisely what distinguishes us from beasts, more, what transforms us from beasts into full human beings. And he also included women too within the circle of those who desire, addressing them with sympathy and a full understanding of the difficulties of their condition, "restrained by the desires, whims, and commands of their fathers, mothers, brothers, and husbands" (*Dec.*, I, Preface, 10; "ristrette da' voleri, da' piaceri, da' comandamenti de' padri, delle madri, de' fratelli e de' mariti").[60] The protagonist of the *Corbaccio*, on the other hand, is described as lost in a valley that is "desolate, rough and harsh" ("diserta, aspra e fiera") and, in accordance with the myth of Circe that the earlier formulations had rejected, called "the Pigsty of Venus" ("il porcile di Venere," *Corbaccio*, 14):[61] since—as Boccaccio would later explain in his commentary on the *Inferno*, and not coincidentally with regard to Dante's "selva selvaggia" ("savage wood")—"he who lets himself fall into the vice of lust (since lust in its beastliness is like a pig) becomes a pig" ("colui che nel vizio della lussuria si lascia cadere, per ciò che la lussuria per sua brutteza è simigliata al porco, esso diventa porco," *ECD*, I [II].73).[62] And then, as if not finding this enough, he applies the same degrading porcine imagery to women with the *Corbaccio*'s typical extremism: "A woman is an imperfect creature excited by a thousand foul passions, abominable even.... No other creature is less clean than she: the pig, even when he is most wallowed in mud, is not as foul as they" ("la femmina è animale imperfetto, passionato da mille passioni spiacevoli, e abominevoli pure.... Niuno altro animale è meno netto di lei: non il porco, qualora è più nel loto convolto, aggiugne alla bruttezza di loro," *Corbaccio*, 200, 202).[63]

A list of all the points of his former position that Boccaccio rejects in the *Corbaccio* would be long. The fact that Boccaccio directs this violently antifeminist text "to those men—and especially young men—who, with eyes closed, set out without a guide through unsafe places, trusting too much in themselves" ("a coloro, e massimamente a' giovani, li quali con gli occhi chiusi per li non sicuri luoghi, troppo di sé fidandosi, sanza guida si mettono," *Corbaccio*, 560–61), whereas his earlier philogynous works were either explicitly dedicated to or else oriented toward a female audience, is not one of his most notable reversals: indeed, on prior occasions he had put "young men" on their guard against the snares of love, although in order to tell them not to flee women but to understand that "love is to be placed more in mature women than in young ones" ("più nelle mature che nelle giovinette donne porre amore," *Filos.*, VIII.29). What is more significant is that Boccaccio now warns this "little work of mine" to beware "above all . . . not to come into the hands of evil women" ("piccola mia operetta"; "sopra ogni cosa"; "di non venire nelle mani delle malvage femmine," *Corbaccio*, 560–61).[64] Recall that Fiammetta asked that her book be read *only* by women, even better, that it flee "the eyes of men," because the male is an "ungrateful sex, denigrator of innocent women" ("gli occhi degli uomini"; "generazione ingrata e detrattrice delle semplici donne," *EMF*, IX.15)[65] and the book would see in the men "jeering laughter rather than compassionate tears" ("più tosto schernevole riso che pietosa lacrima," *EMF*, Prologo, 2).[66] Fiammetta and the company of young people of the *Decameron* could respectably enjoy reading books of courtly love and adventure; however, for the widow of the *Corbaccio*, these same readings are transformed into the blasphemous prayers of a propitiatory rite for the unleashing of lust:

> her prayers and paternosters are French romances and Italian songs in which she reads of Lancelot and Guinevere, Tristram and Isolde, and of their great exploits, their loves, jousts, tournaments, and battles; and when she reads that Lancelot, Tristram, or someone else meets with his lady secretly, and alone, in her bedchamber, she goes all to pieces because she thinks she can see what they are doing and would willingly do as she imagines they do—although she manages to suffer her craving for it only a short time [that is, in a short time she meets her lover]. (*Corbaccio*, 441)[67]

> le sue orazioni e i suoi paternostri sono i romanzi franceschi e le canzoni latine, ne' quali ella legge di Lancelotto e di Ginevra e di Tristano e d'Isotta e le lor prodezze e i loro amori e le giostre e i tornimenti e l'assemblee; e tutta si tritola, quando legge Lance-lotto o Tristano o alcuno altro con le lor donne nelle camere seg-retamente e soli ragunarsi, sì come colei alla qual pare veder ciò

che fanno, e che volentieri, come di loro immagina, così farebbe, avvegna che ella faccia sì che di ciò corta voglia sostiene.

Lust is so inherent to the female sex that when the *Corbaccio* widow finds herself alone and in the same situation of "melancholy brought on by burning desire" ("malinconia mossa da focoso disio," *Dec.*, I, Proemio 11–12)[68] as the women whom the *Decameron* seeks to console, if she does not indulge her desire by reading "the *Song of the Riddle* and that of *Florio and Blanchefleur* and many other such things" ("la canzone dello indovinello e quella di Florio e di Biancifiore e simili cose assai"), she satisfies it while waiting for her lover by engaging in autoerotic practices: "if, perhaps, she is not intent upon such reading, like a wanton young girl, she plays with certain little animals which she keeps at home until the hour in which her most desired plaything comes to join with her"[69] ("e se ella forse a sì fatte lezioni non intende, a guisa d'una fanciulletta lasciva con certi animaletti che 'n casa tiene si trastulla, infino all'ora che venga il suo disiderato trastullo e che con lei si congiunga," *Corbaccio*, 442). Women in the *Corbaccio* are depositories of every vice and depravity, the same women whom in the *Decameron* Boccaccio had placed even before the Muses: "women have been the occasion of my composing a thousand lines of poetry, whereas the Muses never caused me to write anything" ("le donne già mi fur cagione di comporre mille versi, dove le Muse mai non mi furono di farne alcun cagione," *Dec.*, IV. Introd. 35).[70] His reversal is scornful, coarsely vulgar: "It's quite true [women and the Muses] are all feminine, but [the Muses] don't piss!" ("Egli è così vero che tutte son femmine, ma non pisciano," *Corbaccio*, 259).[71]

In the introduction to Day 4 of the *Decameron*, in defending himself against those critics who say that "it is inappropriate for someone of my years to occupy my time with such things, that is, with talking about women and finding ways to please them" ("che alla mia età non sta bene l'andare omai dietro queste cose, cioè a ragionar di donne o a compiacer loro," *Dec.*, IV, Introd., 6), Boccaccio retorted that, "to the very end of my life," he would never be ashamed of behaving in the same way as "Guido Cavalcanti and Dante Alighieri, when they were already old men, and Messer Cino da Pistoia, when he was very aged indeed" ("Guido Cavalcanti e Dante Alighieri già vecchi e messer Cino da Pistoia vecchissimo," *Dec.*, IV, Introd., 33), all poets who even in old age felt honored to please women. Well, one of the most serious grounds for the *Corbaccio* protagonist's shame and disgrace is precisely that he has fallen in love at an advanced age. Moreover, his sin is even more shameful because he is a writer and scholar. Indeed, there are two "reasons . . . each one of them in itself, and both together" that should have made him "cautious and circumspect about the traps of love" ("cagioni . . . ciascuna per sé e amendune insieme . . . cauto e guardingo dagli amorosi lacciuoli," *Corbaccio*, 179): age and study. The second is the more serious, since the condition of scholar, "makes love unbecoming in young men, let alone in the elderly" ("ne' giovani, non che ne' vecchi, fa amore disdicevole," *Corbaccio*, 188). And here we touch a crucial point in Boccaccio's arguments.[72]

The opposition in his works between philogyny and misogyny, like the opposition between a positive valuation of the feeling of love and its moralistic condemnation, is not always as neat as presented here: over the years, while remaining substantially intact, this opposition was subject to lapses and ambiguities. The clearest contradictions occur precisely when the incompatibility between intellectual work and sexuality comes into play. The topic that almost always provokes Boccaccio's most serious concerns about love, and his consequent antifemale tirades, is marriage, especially marriage of the learned man. During his youth in Naples, Boccaccio had transcribed into the *Zibaldone Laurenziano* from Saint Jerome's *Adversus Jovinianum* (*Against Jovinianus*) a passage of the Pseudo-Theophrastus's *De nuptiis* (*On Marriage*) discussing whether the wise man ("sapiens vir") should take a wife and arguing that he should not, because "it hinders the study of philosophy; no man can devote himself to his books and to his wife at the same time": a detailed description of wives' vices and defects follows.[73] In his biography of Petrarch a few years later, Boccaccio referred to his master's yieldings to the libido and sought some vindication both for his master and for himself in the practice of discretion. But the problem of marriage, while not an issue in considering Petrarch the cleric, was unavoidable with regard to Dante. And, in fact, we know that in the first version of the *Trattatello*, Boccaccio's reproach of the relatives who had persuaded the poet to marry was followed by a detailed description of the grave inconveniences of marital life and the innumerable vices of wives.[74] Dante, however, had also experienced strong passions outside of marriage, "and not only in his youth, but also in his mature years" ("e non solamente ne' giovani anni, ma ancora ne' maturi"). "Lustfulness" ("Lussuria"), Boccaccio wrote, although it is a "vice . . . natural and common and almost necessary" ("vizio . . . naturale e comune e quasi necessario"), could not be excused, and yet he asked himself, "who among mortals shall be a proper judge to condemn him? Not I" ("Ma chi sarà tra' mortali giusto giudice a condannarlo? Non io," *TLD*, [I].172–73).

Boccaccio wrote these things in the early 1350s: the last of his children, Violante, had been born not long before, the indulgence toward Dante and himself is understandable. But in the second version of the *Trattatello*, which dates to a period closer to that of the *Corbaccio*, on the one hand, the polemic against wives strikes specifically at the spouses of "philosophers" ("filosofanti," *TLD*, [II].41) as "enemies of studies," haters of "books" and "of nocturnal vigils" devoted to study ("nemiche degli studii," "libri," "delle notturne veglie," 39); and, on the other hand, any hint of vindication of lust disappears.

The fact is, at the beginning of the 1360s, due to his brother's marriage and their close proximity, if not actual forced cohabitation, marriage was transformed from a theoretical problem into an existential one for Boccaccio, unleashing those contradictory feelings of attraction and repulsion that had always coexisted in his cleric's soul. Furthermore, by this stage of his life, Boccaccio had fully introjected, or assimilated, Petrarch's teachings, a mixture of exhortations and reprimands ("morsus")[75] about the necessity of continence and the rejection of lust in order to follow the path of virtue, a particularly compelling necessity for a scholar, especially one no longer young.[76] Introjected them to the point that, at the beginning of the 1360s, and thus coinciding with the crisis that led him to want to rid himself of his books, it seems that even Petrarch scolded Boccaccio for his "excessive moral rigidity."[77] Thus, a psychological tangle developed in Boccaccio's mind, in which repressed desires and untamed urges, rigorist resolutions and feeling of guilt, ideal aspirations and instinctive yielding mingled and collided. A tangled mess that his depression following the events in Ravenna caused to detonate violently.

The *Corbaccio* is violent, dark, and crude. Some scholars have suggested it is a literary joke, one of the writer's many formal experiments. But what kind of parody depicts the sexual act as the satisfaction of a natural urge nearly identical to defecation? It is in the man Boccaccio, not in the writer, that the hidden reasons lie for why he, who had recounted dozens of sexual acts without ever lapsing into vulgarity, wrote "if men considered as they should" how "foul and abominable" the "passions" of women are, "they would go to them in the same way and with the same desire and delight with which they go to any other natural and inevitable necessity; just as they hastily flee those places when their superfluous burden is released, so they would flee women, after they had done their duty to restore deficient human progeny" ("se gli uomini raguardassero come dovessero"; "spiacevoli e abominevoli"; "passioni"; "non altrimenti andrebbono a loro, né con altro diletto o appetito, che all'altre naturali e inevitabili opportunità vadano; i luoghi delle quali, posto giù il superfluo peso, come con istudioso passo fuggono, così loro fuggirebbono, quello avendo fatto per che la deficiente umana prole si ristora," *Corbaccio*, 201). One's impression is that the fury in the *Corbaccio* arises from the resigned yet angry spirit of a person who, in a moral and religious crisis, feels trapped, tormented by what he has never had and never stopped wanting, as well as by his feelings of guilt for an emotional life that has been conducted in sin. A self-destructive fury, therefore, turned more against himself than against women, in a certain sense like the fury that had led to his plan to sell his books and consign his poetry to the flames. The year 1363, which some have suggested as the probable date of the composition of the *Corbaccio*, indeed appears to be the correct one.[78]

The question remains, however, of why Boccaccio set the story's action approximately ten years earlier, between 1353 and 1354, when the autobiographical character was about the age of forty. Although the phrasing is particularly convoluted, there is no doubt that, in indicating to the protagonist his age among the factors that should have prevented him from falling into the "traps of

love" ("amorosi lacciuoli"), the deceased husband meant to attribute to him the age of forty or forty-one: "if your temples already
white and your grizzled beard do not deceive me, you, now some
forty years out of swaddling clothes, should know the ways of the
world—it is now twenty-five years since you began to learn them"
("se le tempie già bianche e la canuta barba non m'ingannano, tu
dovresti avere li costumi del mondo; fuori dalle fasce già sono degli anni quaranta e già son venticinque cominciatoli a conoscere,"
Corbaccio, 179).[79] The fact that the work was written so long after
the time the story's action is set does not in itself raise questions
(this was also the case with Dante's *Commedia*, for example); what
does seem to have no explanation is, instead, the choice of the protagonist's age: forty had no special resonance in Boccaccio's life,
nor does it have any particular symbolic value in itself. But it did
for Francesco Petrarca. Always intending to write a fitting autobiography for posterity, in the 1350s, Petrarch composed a fictional
self-portrait that centered on a radical personal change, or conversion, which, according to him, had profoundly transformed
the way he lived, his literature, and his conception of intellectual
work. One of the primary features of this transformation was his
conversion from licentiousness to chastity. Now, this conversion
process, whose phases he described over numerous works, most
importantly the *Secretum*, began shortly before Petrarch turned
forty and was completed during his forty-first year.[80] Boccaccio
knew neither the *Secretum* nor the other writings in which Petrarch constructed the myth of his *mutatio vitae*, but the chronological parallel between Boccaccio's story of recantation and his
master's conversion leaves no doubt that this was Boccaccio's inspiration.[81] Even though he had not read these specific works, over
the years Boccaccio had conducted, both in person and by letter,
an intense dialogue with Petrarch addressing the subjects of the
wisdom gained in old age and the duty of scholars, writers, and poets to strive for virtue and to work assiduously toward eternal life.
Sexual activity by scholars and clerics was surely one of their topics of conversation. And just as surely, if only to correct the image
of him as "harassed by lust" (*VP*, 26)[82] that Boccaccio had painted
in the biography written in the early 1340s,[83] Petrarch must have
reiterated to Boccaccio what he had written in his autobiogra-

phy for posterity, namely, that "approaching my fortieth year . . . I cast away not only that obscene activity but its entire memory, as though I had never looked upon a woman."[84]

It is clear even at first glance that the *Corbaccio* is indebted to the *Commedia*: the protagonist lost in a valley that resembles the forest of sin, the shade of the deceased husband who appears and offers himself as moral guide, the final liberating ascent to a mountain bathed in light are all structural elements derived from Dante's poem. A somewhat closer analysis reveals the dense web of references and echoes stretching between the *Corbaccio* and the *Vita Nova*, along with, more subtly but still perceptibly, the reverberating undercurrent of Petrarch's lyric verse.[85] In the *Corbaccio*, therefore, an inspiration that owes much to the teachings of Petrarch is expressed in a literary performance that owes much to Dante. The case of the *Decameron*, as we have seen, is similar. In his two final works in the vernacular, in fact, Boccaccio looked to both beacons that guided his literary endeavors: from Petrarch came the flash of light that indicated the path, and from Dante the glow that directed his steps. It was, moreover, almost a given that after every encounter with his master, Boccaccio turned with renewed attention to Dante. Recall the chronology of his three collections of Dante's writings: the first, surviving in the Toledo codex, dates to shortly after his conversations with Petrarch in Padua in 1351; his transcription of the *Commedia* and the *Ytalie iam certus honos* was sent to Petrarch immediately after Boccaccio's visit to him in Milan in 1359; and in the years immediately after his stay with Petrarch in Venice in 1363, Boccaccio transcribed Dante's vernacular works along with Petrarch's *Canzoniere* in the Chigi codex, an endeavor that gave physical form to the ideal union of these two legends that Boccaccio tenaciously strove to bring about. "No scholar of future generations," it has been written, "would ever again be capable of perceiving the persons and the works of the two founders of Italian literature united in this way."[86]

11

Return to the Florentine Stage

Public Duties

Around the year 1364, the clouds that had darkened Boccaccio's life for the previous three or four years lifted. The slothful, irritable man, closed in on himself and haunted by fantasies of death and self-destructive impulses was replaced by one who was more tranquil, more open, and available to life. He would soon leave behind the solitude of Certaldo and resume traveling at his former pace; at the beginning of the year, he began participating actively in the political life of Florence. Over the next five years, ending a hiatus of roughly ten years, he would again be in the Comune's service and even hold prestigious positions. And yet, neither in his private life nor in the public life of the city were there changes that would explain such a turnaround. Boccaccio's health remained precarious, he was afflicted with corpulence and no diet or even fasting checked his expansion, his family continued to be a source of worry and annoyance. Iacopo had married for a second time, to a Piera whose family is not known, although we can presume they were not ignoble given the richness of her dowry; but he had "no place to bring the woman he [had] taken as wife"—for some unknown reason, Iacopo evidently could no longer use the house in Santa Felicita given to him in 1361—and so, early in 1365, he asked Giovanni to let them live in his little house along with him.[1] And Boccaccio agreed, although we know how much of a burden it was to him. Even his economic circumstances must not have been much improved: we learn from the same letter to Albanzani that speaks of his brother that Boccaccio's limited income had kept him from giving this friend a Livy codex that he wanted as a gift, and he had to ask for payment.[2]

As for the political situation, it is true that by 1363 the fallout from the conspiracy of 1360 had abated and the policy of *ammonizioni* had been softened, but power remained firmly in the hands of the Guelph party, controlled by the same families as before. In short, the impression is, that even if assisted by external circumstances, Boccaccio's turnaround had been internal, and that, perhaps, what had influenced his earlier prolonged distance from public life was not only his objective extraneity from the new ruling system, but also aspects of his character: or, better, a mixture of ideology (note his criticism of Dante in the second version of the *Trattatello*, thus in the early 1360s, for having "forgotten philosophy" and devoted "himself almost entirely to the government of the republic" ["messa la filosofia in oblio, quasi tutto della repubblica . . . al governo si diede," *TLD*, [II].47]) and an idiosyncratic impatience.

The resumption of Boccaccio's candidacies for public office dates to the beginning of 1364, and, what's more, they were on behalf of the Guelph party. But it was not that his political stature had increased: on January 30, 1364, he failed to be elected in the voting for the "Tre maggiori," just as he would not have the votes for another seven "intrinsici" ("internal") offices on August 25, 1366.[3] However, in August 1364, he was elected *Ufficiale dei castelli* (involved in construction of fortifications) for six months, and in October 1367, *Ufficiale della condotta* (which dealt with recruitment and pay of mercenaries) for four. These were the same sorts of offices that he had held during the first half of the 1350s.

As at that time, here the contrast is striking between the minor importance of Boccaccio's elected offices and the prestige of his ambassadorial appointments.

On August 21, 1365, as was customary for someone about to

undertake a long journey, Boccaccio made his will[4] and then departed for Avignon. The government was sending him as ambassador to Pope Urban V.[5] This was the second time he had served as an ambassador to the pope, and again this time, as was the case when he was sent to Innocent VI in 1354, the primary purpose of his mission was the relationship between the papacy and the emperor, Charles IV. Urban V had been toying with the plan to return the Apostolic See to Rome, but, skeptical of the trustworthiness of the Italian communes and lords, seemed to be seeking the armed protection of the emperor. In line with its traditional policy against any interference by the emperor in the peninsula, Florence was trying to thwart this. Boccaccio was given the task of reassuring the pope of Florentine loyalty, including with the promise of a substantial armed escort for his journey. It is possible that the choice had fallen on Boccaccio precisely because he had already played a similar role when Charles of Luxembourg had been preparing to come into Italy to be crowned emperor. Once again, Boccaccio's political activities were the direct opposite of Petrarch's: Petrarch, a staunch supporter of Charles and of the necessity of restoring imperial power in Italy; Boccaccio, a Guelph, and equally staunch critic of an emperor whom he did not hesitate to call a drunk.[6] But now the friends' bond was so solid that no difference in political views could undermine it.

During the journey overland along the ancient Via Aurelia, Boccaccio made a stop in Genoa to advocate on behalf of the Comune for the Grimaldi, who had been accused of supporting the Florentines in military action against the Pisans, but it must have been a very short stay because by August 27 he was in Avignon. Here he could count on the support of Francesco Bruni, appointed apostolic secretary in early 1363, and almost certainly on that of Petrarch's surviving friends, foremost among them Philippe de Cabassoles, the Patriarch of Jerusalem, whose friendship with Petrarch went all the way back to 1337, when Petrarch had acquired his house in Vaucluse, situated in the diocese of Cavaillon, of which Cabassoles was at that time the bishop.[7] Boccaccio's mission seems to have been a success, given the fact that Charles IV, at least for the moment, did not descend into Italy. Other minor matters

Boccaccio was charged with dealing with at the curia either did not have the desired outcome or we have no information about the results: Angelo Ricasoli, bishop of Aversa, did not obtain his desired transfer to Arezzo (he would become bishop of Florence in 1370); Pileo da Prata, bishop of Padua, protégé of the Carraresi and also a friend of Petrarch's, would not receive the patriarcate of Aquileia as the Florentines wanted.[8] But we do not know what Boccaccio requested for Ristoro, the son of his old friend Pietro Canigiani.[9]

In Avignon, Boccaccio frequented the large Florentine community, in particular the brothers Leonardo, Giovanni, and Chiaro di Chiaro, grandsons of the judge Botte di Buoninsegna dei Guernieri, who were in the city working as merchants and money changers.[10] He was close to them because they were a family originally from Certaldo that had had firm ties with Boccaccino. Boccaccio relied on these fellow countrymen for a matter close to his heart: the attempt to obtain the concession of papal indulgences for the men who had worked to restore the church of Santi Michele e Iacopo in Certaldo. The following May, he would write to Leonardo from Certaldo, asking him to pursue "the privilege that messer Francesco Bruni so fully promised" (*Lett.*, II.1; "il privilegio il quale così pienamente ne promise messer Francesco Bruni"). There are other episodes that confirm the care Boccaccio devoted to his parish church in the village. In 1366, he donated to the church the two altarpieces that may have given rise to the local legend that Fiammetta was depicted in Saint Catherine: these were probably ex votos related to the will that he made shortly before leaving for Avignon.[11] Also in 1366, in a letter written from Certaldo to Pietro da Moglio, he recommended Angelo di Pierozzo Giandonati, the young prior of the church of Santi Michele e Iacopo.[12] At Boccaccio's urging, this young man, who had earlier been devoted to the pleasures of the hunt, had attended, albeit with little profit, the school of Latin grammar; now he intended to take Pietro's classes in Padua: Boccaccio's hope was "that some day I may be able to say that I received from your hands a learned man, from the hunter and stalker that he was" (*Ep.*, XIV.10).[13] These are evidence that testify to Giovanni's sincere attachment to Certaldo and suggest that we look on the "exile" of these years as a more tranquil period than it is commonly portrayed.

The mission to Avignon, initially expected to last forty-five days, was extended for an additional thirty: Boccaccio returned to Tuscany in November 1365. In the years to come, he would alternate stays in Certaldo with ones in Florence. But these were also years characterized by many trips outside of Tuscany, either for the government or for personal reasons.

Boccaccio had become recognized as something of an expert on the delicate papal-imperial-Florentine triangle. And so, when Urban decided to go to Rome in October 1367—he had arrived in Italy in June, but then lingered in Viterbo, partly because of the death there of Cardinal Albornoz—it was Boccaccio who was chosen by the *Signoria* to bring Florence's felicitations to the pontiff. They did not entrust him with mere duties of diplomatic courtesy, however: behind the pope's return still loomed the shadow of Charles IV and his possible arrival (which would in fact happen a year later), and therefore Boccaccio would have had the task of representing Florence's ongoing concerns to Urban. It was a mission of short duration: on November 11, Boccaccio took the traditional oath required of ambassadors before departing, and on December 1, he took his leave from the pontiff; on that day, Urban V wrote the (also traditional) letter of appreciation to the *Signoria* (as the Florentine executive governing body was known). During the embassy, the process begun two years earlier to obtain indulgences for the church in Certaldo came to a happy conclusion: on November 24 ("VIII Kalendas decembres"), a papal bull granted broad indulgences to those who worked to repair it.[14] This outcome was reached thanks to Francesco Bruni: during those days Boccaccio was able to interact with him, and in their discussions, among other things, they spoke about their mutual friend Coluccio Salutati, then chancellor in Todi. They also sent Coluccio a letter, to which he would respond on December 20 with a message of thanks sent to Boccaccio, who was already in Certaldo.[15]

It can be observed that, at the end of the 1360s, thanks to the stipends and per diems he accrued during the services performed in the second half of the decade, Boccaccio restored his exhausted finances, although without regaining the comfort of previous decades, sufficiently that, in February 1369, he purchased farmland in Monteloro, or Querciatella, near Certaldo for twenty florins.[16]

Venetian Visits

During the two-year period 1367–68, Boccaccio made at least three trips to Venice or, more precisely, to Padua and Venice. After his beloved Ravenna had been transformed into a sewer, the city on the lagoon became a kind of second home: much of his affection was because of Petrarch's and Albanzani's presence in the city, but it was also perhaps due to something else.

His first documented trip was in May 1367, although it is possible that he had also gone at least once during 1366, a year that appears devoid of obligations. In the letter to Pietro da Moglio recommending the Certaldo prior, Boccaccio said that he was doubtful he would be able to go soon to Padua, but promised that if he did go, he would not fail to visit Pietro.[17] It has been assumed that this letter was written in the autumn of 1366, and consequently that the proposed trip could be the one of May 1367. But the letter could have been written at anytime during 1366 (there is no evidence regarding the date), and so there is nothing to keep us from speculating that the trip might have been planned for that same year.[18] A passage in a letter that Petrarch sent from Pavia to Donato Albanzani in Venice at the beginning of September 1366 suggests that Boccaccio may actually have traveled there that month: in the packet with the letter to Albanzani, Petrarch included three others letters addressed to Boccaccio, either not sent to him earlier or that he had not received,[19] with the request that Albanzani "make sure that at long last they arrive where they would have originally gone, had they been allowed; and put in your own words the excuses for their tardiness."[20] Now, if Albanzani's apologies were to have been made in person ("verbis tuis"), we should deduce from this that Boccaccio was to be found nearby, that is, in Venice,[21] but this does not seem the correct interpretation of Petrarch's sentence. If it were correct, since Boccaccio must have know that Petrarch had already left Venice for Pavia in July, it would be strong evidence that Boccaccio's trips to the lagoon did not depend exclusively on his friend's presence there. Moreover, although he wrote claims to the contrary ("In order to see you, illustrious master, I left Certaldo for Venice" [*Ep.*, XV.1]),[22] the May trip he actually made seems to have had motivations other than emotional ones.

On March 24, 1367, Boccaccio left Certaldo for Florence, intending to continue on to Venice, but, after arriving in the city and being warned by many travelers coming from Bologna that there was terrible weather in the Apennines, he decided to wait for the return of clear skies. He spent the month of April in Florence. Early in that month the captains of the Compagnia di Orsanmichele invited him to take part, along with a group of other illustrious citizens (including the jurist and statesman Luigi Gianfigliazzi),[23] in a commission charged with issuing an opinion on the advisability of the artist Orcagna (Andrea di Cione) continuing the work begun on the construction of the Orsanmichele tabernacle of Our Lady. Their conclusion was in the affirmative; the tabernacle would be inaugurated in 1369. During those days of waiting, Boccaccio learned that Petrarch, who had returned to Venice in December 1366, had now been called back to Pavia by Galeazzo Visconti. Nonetheless, in May, after the weather had improved, he decided to leave for Venice. Writing to Petrarch at the end of the trip, he explained that he had decided to go anyway both "because I had an urgent desire to see at least the two people whom you rightly love most, your Tullia [Petrarch's daughter] and her Francesco [her husband], whom I had never seen before," and "in order not to disappoint the hopes of some of my friends, who had entrusted me with the completion of a certain arduous task for them" (*Ep.*, XV.2).[24]

We do not know the nature of this "arduous task" ("arduum opus"), which is not surprising: Boccaccio—like his other humanist friends—intent as he was on fashioning an image of himself as a scholar completely detached from the world of affairs, particularly of an economic nature, was always reticent when discussion turned to business dealings and money. The allusion in this letter is already by itself exceptional. We might imagine that he was acting as solicitor, mediator, or consultant—he had the necessary legal and accounting skills—and perhaps even that he was working on behalf of the Florentine merchant Francesco di Allegro di Nuto, in whose company he had made the journey. In any case, Boccaccio showed himself to be well connected in Venice, where he evidently spent his time either conversing with learned men or reading and copying Petrarch's writings.

While still en route, upon his arrival in a town not far from Venice, he unexpectedly ran into Francescuolo da Brossano, Petrarch's son-in-law: over the course of their long and friendly conversation, Francescuolo gave him news of his father-in-law. From there, at dawn, Boccaccio reached Venice on a small boat. As if the news of his arrival had been announced, as soon as he disembarked, he was welcomed by a number of Florentines, each of whom insisted that he stay as a guest at their house, but, out of courtesy, Boccaccio decided to lodge with the merchant Allegri with whom he had traveled. He could have stayed at Petrarch's house, but since Francescuolo was away, it did not seem appropriate to him to live under the same roof with Francesca. In Venice, he spent time with old friends and made a new one, the physician Guido da Reggio (or da Bagnolo), "full of so many things that he overflows everywhere"[25] (*Ep.*, XV.14): thanks to their mutual friendship with Petrarch, Guido welcomed Boccaccio with such honor that he presented him with a ring ("honoratus sum et insignitus anulo"), a customary gift for distinguished guests.[26] It may be that his commendation of Guido da Reggio contained more than a touch of mockery: Donato Albanzani would surely have told Boccaccio about Petrarch's anger upon learning, from Albanzani himself, that some of the prominent men whom he frequented with devotion and admiration—Guido da Bagnolo, Leonardo Dandolo (son of the doge Andrea Dandolo), the patrician Zaccaria Contarini, and the merchant Tommaso Talenti—spoke of him insultingly as "a good man without learning" ("sine literis virum bonum"),[27] primarily because he had no interest in the natural sciences and little respect for Aristotle. But at the time Boccaccio spoke with Bagnolo in Venice, and almost certainly also in July when he wrote the letter to Petrarch recounting his visit, Boccaccio did not know that, during his voyage on the Po back to Pavia, Petrarch had sketched out a work of invective against his detractors—*De sui ipsius et multorum ignorantia* (*On His Own Ignorance and That of Many Others*)—although without naming them; he would finish the first draft toward the end of the year and have a final copy to Albanzani, to whom it was dedicated, only some years later, at the beginning of 1371.[28]

Boccaccio of course also visited Petrarch's daughter. Francesca welcomed him in the garden, "in the presence of some friends"

(*Ep.*, XV.9).[29] While they were talking—he told Petrarch, with great emotion—

> behold, with a more modest step than befits her age, came your Eletta [Francesca's daughter], my love, and before knowing who I was looked at me smiling; and I, not just eagerly but greedily, took her in my arms, at first glance thinking that she was my poor little girl [Violante]. What can I say? If you do not believe me, believe the doctor Guglielmo da Ravenna and our Donato [Albanzani], who knew her: your Eletta's face looks like my little girl's; the same smile, the same joy in her eyes; she has the same gestures and gait, the same bearing of her whole little body, although my daughter was larger because of her greater age, fully five-and-a-half when I saw her for the last time [in Ravenna in the summer of 1353]. Further, apart from the difference in language [Violante spoke a dialect of Romagna], her words and her simplicity were the same. Why so many things? I saw no difference in them, except that yours has golden curls, and mine had chestnut. Alas! While I often embrace her and delight in her chatter, how often the memory of my lost little girl brings tears to my eyes, which in the end I turn into a sigh, without anyone knowing. (*Ep.*, XV.10–11)[30]

Boccaccio stayed in Venice for a little more than a month, and toward the end of June 1367 was once again in Florence. Boccaccio and Petrarch would meet for the last time a year later, in Padua, in the same house where they had forged their friendship ten years earlier. We know almost nothing about this final time they spent together. We do know that Petrarch traveled from Pavia to Padua around July 20, 1368; there is no indication, however, of when Boccaccio joined him there. Our only information comes indirectly, from a letter Petrarch wrote to Donato Albanzani. In May of that year, at the age of only two and a half, Petrarch's grandson Francesco, who was Albanzani's godson, had died, and during the summer, Albanzani's younger son, Solone, also died, at the age of about seven. On September 16, 1368, Petrarch sent Donato a long "consolatory letter on the untimely death of his son and likewise of his own grandson,"[31] which ends with these words: "And whatever you hear from me, believe that our Giovanni has said it, for he has borne your calamity as though it were his own, and wishes you to bear your grief [as philosophically] as he bears his own,"[32] alluding to the loss of little Violante. On October 3, Petrarch wrote again and, referring to his earlier "lengthy letter" ("verbosam . . . epistolam"), again mentioned Giovanni Boccaccio, "who"—he says—"was with me when I wrote all that, and will be with you when you read this, or rather is always with both of us at the same time."[33] The letter concludes with farewells to them both: "Farewell, you and our dear Giovanni too" ("Vale et Iohannes noster tecum"). Thus, in the middle of September Boccaccio was in Padua with Petrarch, and in early October he was in Venice with Albanzani. Had he gone to Venice, as has been suggested, "out of affection, in order to be closer to Donato?"[34] That may be, but we cannot rule out that, as in the previous year, he had tasks or business to take care of in Venice.

During this final stay at Petrarch's house, as on the previous occasions, Boccaccio was able to read his friend's works and copy some of them. It is very likely that he transcribed the treatises *De remediis utriusque fortune* (*Remedies for Fortune Fair and Foul*) and *De otio religioso*,[35] which might be translated as "The Tranquil Existence of the Religious." It is also possible that he read the *De ignorantia*. From a letter of Petrarch's of late autumn 1369, we learn that, along with a letter now lost, Boccaccio had sent him a vehement defense ("apologeticum"), animated by noble ire, of this work of invective, a defense that pleased Petrarch very much, both for the affection that pervaded it and for its style and content.[36] Since the definitive version of the *De ignorantia* and its letter of dedication to Albanzani were written later than this letter, unless we think that Boccaccio based his defense only on oral reports— from Albanzani, Petrarch himself, or others—the most likely hypothesis is that Boccaccio had seen the working copy of the recently completed treatise at his friend's house.[37]

The two might have had one more opportunity to meet in person in the spring of 1370, when Petrarch, bowing to Urban V's insistence, decided to visit him in Rome. However, on the way he fell gravely in Ferrara, and so, after recovering at the residence of Marchese Ugo d'Este, he returned to Padua. On April 4, before departing, Petrarch had written his will. It provided for a very generous bequest to his friend: "To *dominus* Giovanni of Certaldo or of Boccaccio, not without a certain embarrassment because it is so little for a man so great, I leave fifty Florentine gold florins so that he can buy a winter robe for nocturnal study and contemplation."[38] In early March 1372, writing to Pietro Piccolo da Monteforte, Boccaccio would indicate his intention to go to Padua to pay a visit to Petrarch either at the end of that month or early in the next,[39] but would never make this trip.

The Humanist Season

From the completion of the *Corbaccio* until he began the public reading of the *Commedia* in 1373, Boccaccio devoted himself almost exclusively to humanistic writing in Latin. Almost, because, as the editorial histories of the *Decameron* and the few lyric poems that can definitely be attributed to his old age demonstrate, he never actually abandoned either the vernacular muse or the editing of his earlier vernacular works. Boccaccio did not suffer from Petrarch's sublime neurosis of endlessly rewriting himself, his fear of finishing, his anxiety to reinterpret himself in a present without contradictions, in short, from the psychological drive that kept Petrarch's works constantly in motion. Instead, Boccaccio's path as a writer was characterized by fits and starts, inconsistencies, U-turns, and un-bridged rifts: he did not aspire to homogeneity, but wended his way through variety. Yet, he too was reluctant to let go of what he had written, he too returned to his own texts with additions, corrections, sometimes recreating them in a second or third version. This was especially the case with his texts in Latin.

During the last years of his life, Boccaccio attended to revising, in some cases completing and expanding, in other cases rewriting, works that he had begun in the preceding years and even finished. We have seen that the geographical encyclopedia *De montibus*, which he began working on at the beginning of the 1350s, reached an initial stage of completeness in the following decade, but that did not prevent Boccaccio from continuing to add entries even after that, to the point that it is not clear that he ever considered it finished. Of the *De casibus virorum illustrium*, written between 1357 and 1360 and later further revised, he wrote a second, more extensive version between 1373 and 1374. And the *De mulieribus claris*, of which he had already written two versions between 1361 and 1362, "he continued to address with revisions, before arriving at the definitive form of the text in the autograph copy" attributable to 1370–73.[40] These are all erudite works, some frankly compilations, which almost by their nature lend themselves to additions, improvements, and rewriting.

The *Genealogia deorum gentilium*, "his masterpiece of erudition,"[41] although it was one of the first works he conceived, if not the very first, precisely because of it encyclopedic-compilatory nature, was one of the last ones to be brought to completion. We know that, according to Boccaccio himself, the seed was planted by the invitation, a sort of commission, given to him by King Hugh IV of Cyprus in the early 1350s in Romagna, but after that its gestation was very long. A first complete version can be dated to roughly the mid-1360s.

It is an imposing work that collects and, above all, orders an enormous amount of information about the gods and heroes of antiquity drawn from a wide array of sources. The result is a grand catalog organized genealogically. Each book, in fact, is preceded by an illustration of an inverted tree: at the top, the roots, is the progenitor, from which the limbs of descendants branch out. At the source, as father of all the pagan divinities, he placed the fabled Demogorgon, "god of the earth" (*GDG*, I, Prohemium III.11); from him "nine children descended (among them Erebus and Night, Ether and Day, Jupiter and Sky), who in turn, through various relationships, produced a vast hoard of progeny, which includes more than seven hundred figures, up to Heracles and his line, arrayed across books 1–13."[42] The *Genealogia* is a mine of information for anyone dealing with questions about ancient mythology and poetry or classical culture more generally, which explains the centuries of popularity the work has enjoyed. Popularity to which the final two books also contributed: book 14, "wherein the author, in reply to their objections, inveighs against the enemies of the name of poetry,"[43] and book 15, "wherein the author exonerates himself from the criticisms leveled against him."[44]

The penultimate book is a long and impassioned defense of poetry against the criticisms of various sorts of detractors, clustered primarily in Dominican theological circles.[45] "Poetry," Boccaccio writes, "is a sort of fervor for discovering ideas, and for saying or writing with exquisite care that which you have discovered. It proceeds from the bosom of God, and few are the minds to which this gift is granted"[46] (*GDG*, XIV [VII].1). An inspiration, therefore, that cannot function without the tools, such as grammar and rhetoric, necessary to express that which is imagined ("meditata"), as well as a broad understanding of philosophy, history, geography, and language: in essence, poetry cannot be separated from art. Without this fervor, rhetoric, although it can produce works of fiction, cannot rise to the level of poetry. "Pure poetry is whatever we compose under the veil of allegory and carefully set forth"[47] (*GDG*, XIV [VII].8). Poets express themselves by means of "fables," that is, stories, "under the surface [of which] something great is hidden" (*GDG*, XIV [IX].4).[48] Fables can be appreciated both by the unlearned "who are pleased by the external appearance," that is, by the stories recounted, and by the learned, "whose minds are exercised with the hidden truth"[49] (*GDG*, XIV [IX].15). Truth that is not literal: unlike historians, in fact, poets may tell lies, because they work with the imagination, but their untruths, like the mythological tales of the ancients, hide profound truths about the human condition, such that poets are to be counted among the philosophers. Christian poets, then, like Dante in the *Commedia* and Petrarch in the *Bucolicum carmen*, may even be considered theologians.[50]

In the last book, speaking about the sources from which he had drawn his information, Boccaccio names the scholars and contemporary poets to whom he felt most indebted and whom he considered his teachers, starting from those of his youth—in order: Andalò del Negro, Dante Alighieri, Francesco da Barberino, Barlaam, Paolo da Perugia, Leontius Pilatus, Paulus Geometrus (Paolo Dagomari), and, above all, Francesco Petrarca—he boasts of having brought ancient Greek literature back to Italy and traces a brief history of the origins and formation of his poetic vocation, despite the obstacles he faced. The story of the composition of the *Genealogia* did not end in the mid-1360s, however. In the autumn of 1370, as we will see, Boccaccio would go to Naples. On that trip he would bring with him an autograph copy of the book,[51] which he would leave in Naples with his illustrious patron, Ugo di San-severino, when he returned to Tuscany. From here, the autograph would arrive in the hands of a learned jurist, Pietro da Monteforte, nicknamed Piccolo, who would study it carefully and make a significant number of corrections. When the autograph was returned to him in the spring of 1372, Boccaccio would adopt these amendments to the text, just as he would incorporate into book 14 many points "in praise and defense of poetry" that Monteforte had made in a letter.[52]

Between 1367 and 1368, Boccaccio composed the last of his Latin eclogues and immediately afterward collected the entire corpus of sixteen eclogues into one book, entitled *Buccolicum carmen*, which, with the final poem, *Aggelos* (*The Messenger*), he dedicated to Donato Albanzani.[53] The title alone shows that Boccaccio's model was Petrarch, whose own *Bucolicum carmen* Boccaccio had had the privilege of reading and transcribing before its publication, in Milan in 1359: even the format and layout of Boccaccio's autograph codex[54] are modeled on Petrarch's.[55] Boccaccio, however, would continue to work on this initial version in the years that followed, to the point that the protracted labor of revision would end only at his death. The composition of the individual eclogues was staggered over three distinct periods: 1346–48, around 1355, and 1367; the collection roughly respects the chronological order of their composition (which does not always reflect the chronology of the events recounted or alluded to in each poem).

> The first two eclogues, *Galla* e *Pampinea*, on the subject of love, were called juvenilia by Boccaccio himself: at least the first, leaving aside the composition date, refers to the author's situation living in his father's house at the end of 1341 immediately after his return from Naples; the next group of four eclogues (in order: *Faunus, Dorus, Silva cadens, Alcestus*) deals with the Neapolitan political events from the killing of Andrew of Hungary and the invasion of his brother King Louis up to the return of Queen Joanna and Louis of Taranto; the seventh, *Iurgium*, is directed against Charles IV of Luxembourg, crowned emperor in 1355; the eighth, *Midas*, is a bitter indictment of Niccolò Acciaiuoli following

the disappointment of the trip to Naples of 1355; the ninth, *Lipis*, is a kind of continuation of the seventh; the tenth, *Vallis opaca*, treats the repressive policies implemented by Bernardino da Polenta immediately after succeeding Ostasio; the eleventh, *Pantheon*, alludes to Urban V's return to Rome in the summer of 1367; the twelfth, *Saphos*, and the thirteenth, *Laurea*, celebrate elevated poetry in Latin, the first autobiographically; the fourteenth, *Olympia*, recalls his daughter Violante in the form of a vision; the fifteenth, *Phylostropos*, praises Petrarch as teacher about life and virtue; and the sixteenth, *Aggelos*, accompanies the dedication of the eclogues to Donato Albanzani with autobiographical references, primarily regarding Midas (Acciaiuoli), who had deceived and disappointed him again in 1362–63.

Boccaccio's interest in the bucolic genre, which originated in his youth with his introduction to the epistolary exchange between Dante and Giovanni del Virgilio, was strengthened by his visits with Dante's surviving friends in Ravenna, and bore its first real fruits in his verse correspondence with Checco di Meletto Rossi. For this, his operative model was Dante's bucolic poetry, characterized by the combination of pastoral setting and style with epistolary function, so much so that one could speak of Boccaccio's exchange with Checco as a "humanistic adaptation of the *tenzone* [as Dante's poetic correspondence is called]."[56] In 1347, however, Boccaccio encountered Petrarch's eclogue *Argus*, celebrating the late Robert of Anjou, and from that moment on, Petrarch, and through him Virgil, became his indisputable ideals.[57] The form of his eclogue changed, no longer structured as dialogue inserted in a narrative context, but instead as a series of utterances, without any contextualizing introduction, by various characters whose names are given in the initial heading and in the margins next to their lines of dialogue each time they speak. Above all, allegory acquired a much greater significance. Since Boccaccio believed that allegory is the highest form of poetry, indeed, that which made a text a poem, Petrarch's *Bucolicum carmen*, "which pushes the allegorical ideas found in Virgil and Dante to extremes to the point of erecting constructions that are abstruse, enigmatic, contrived,"[58] became in his eyes the apex of writing in verse. In the *Genealogia*, to demonstrate that beneath the veil of allegorical fictions poets reveal profound moral, philosophical, and theological truths, he cites, in this order, Virgil's *Aeneid*, Dante's *Commedia*, and Petrarch's *Bucolicum carmen*, and even adds that he could have also cited his own *Buccolicum carmen*, "of whose meaning, I am, of course, fully aware" ("cuius sensus ego sum conscius"), but believed it better not to do so out of modesty.[59] It is revealing that in the late letter (written either in 1372–73 or 1374) to Martino da Signa, a friar of the order of the Hermits of Saint Augustine and prior of the monastery of Santo Spirito,[60] in tracing a concise history of the bucolic genre, and adopting as his yardstick the quantity of allegory present in a poet's work, Boccaccio named first Theocritus, devoid of allegory, then Virgil, who adopted allegory only partially, and finally Petrarch, who always wrote allegorically, and he declared that between Virgil and Petrarch others had also written bucolic poetry, but that they were poets "obscure, of little renown" (*Ep.*, XXIII.1–2; "sed ignobiles, de quibus nil curandum est"): among those not even worth naming was obviously Dante, the poet who had been his introduction to this literary genre.

Recognizing Petrarch as the undisputed master of Latin poetry did not, however, inspire Boccaccio to renounce his own originality, even in the field in which Petrarch was preeminent. To start with, Boccaccio's bucolic poems did not number ten, like Virgil's, nor even twelve (like Petrarch's, who was keeping in mind the twelve books of the Aeneid), but sixteen, a number that was absolutely noncanonical. And he also followed his own path in the use of allegory. The short history of the genre that opens the letter to Martino da Signa ends with these words: "Among these [Theocritus, Virgil, and Petrarch], I have been a follower of Virgil, and therefore I have not bothered to hide a meaning under all the names of the characters" (*Ep.*, XXIII.2).[61] The friar had asked him to explain the significance of the titles of the individual eclogues and of the names of the characters, and Boccaccio did precisely this in his reply, going through all sixteen eclogues one by one. The result is a sort of introduction to the book, and in fact the letter often serves precisely this function in the manuscript tradition. Now, more than once, Boccaccio wrote that a certain name did not refer to anything in particular, and once, even, that he had forgotten what the significance of the name was.[62]

The book's greatest originality, however, lies in the way that Boccaccio organized material that is entirely explicitly autobiographical, or related to his own personal experiences in the political sphere, or concerned with his conceptions of poetics. This is quite similar to the content of Petrarch's *Bucolicum carmen*, which similarly moves among sentimental autobiography, poetics, and political and civic considerations. But the material in Boccaccio's work is often blatantly contradictory, marked by a succession of reversals of assessments, of moral judgments, and even of emotional investments: his openly pro-Hungarian position gives way to celebration of the victors Louis of Taranto and Joanna of Anjou; Niccolò Acciaiuoli is praised, then reviled; his father, first blamed for having forced him to leave Naples, is the subject of a moving remembrance at his death. It has been said regarding the eclogues dealing with the war in Naples, that "the real problem is not so much the author's contradictoriness or even his emotional instability, as much as the coexistence of such widely divergent positions within the interconnected whole of the *Buccolicum*."[63] It appears that Boccaccio accentuated the inherent autobiographical quality of the bucolic genre and, behind the protection of the allegorical veil—protection more apparent than real, that is, understood more as grant of immunity than as effective shield—imagined the book of bucolic verse as a sort of diary with which he sketched a portrait of himself over time, illustrating the paradox that the sincerest autobiographical confession corresponds to the greatest literary artificiality.

12

Twilight

Reconciled with Naples

1369 and most of 1370 are blank: devoid of documents, Boccaccian utterances, indirect testimony. Boccaccio spent almost all of this period in the isolation of Certaldo. After January 1368, when his term of office as *Provveditore ai castelli* ended, he held no other position in the Florentine administration, and after the embassy to the pope, he never had another mission. From one letter sent on May 21, 1370, by a certain Piero del Branca to Leonardo and Chiaro del Chiaro in Avignon, we learn that on that date Boccaccio was not in Florence;[1] from another, sent to Boccaccio by Coluccio Salutati on April 8, 1369, that he was living in Certaldo.[2] He was already in the village on February 8, 1369, when he bought the farm in Monteloro.

This is not the first time we have witnessed a clear and apparently unprovoked reversal of Boccaccio's feelings toward his native city. In old his age, however, a disengagement like the one evidenced by this self-exile to Certaldo was part of a more general tendency toward mood swings, abrupt onsets of dissatisfaction with where he was living, and an emotional instability and intellectual disquiet that also influenced his inconsistent judgment of his own work and of that of beloved authors. All of this can be inferred from the behavior and writing of his final few years; his state of mind and life in Certaldo in the late 1360s and early 1370s, in contrast, remain a mystery.

Just as indecipherable are his reasons for deciding to go to Naples in the early autumn of 1370. It was obviously not sufficient that Niccolò Acciaiuoli—regarding whom, in 1363, Boccaccio had sworn that he would rather go begging bread "door to door" (*Ep.*, XIII.246; "ad uscio ad uscio") than heed his summons a third time—had been dead for five years. The hypotheses proposed to explain this decision are primarily political: that Boccaccio had been deeply disappointed by Urban V's decision in early September to return the Holy See to Avignon and, as a Guelph and opponent of the Visconti, he was worried about the emergence of a strong anti-papal current in Florence.[3] It is true that a year later, after returning home, he would write in passing in a letter that he had left the previous autumn "outraged"[4] (*Ep.*, XIX.1), but it is hard to believe that such a serious decision was determined by discomfort with the political climate rather than by motivations that touched him more personally, particularly because this trip to Naples seems to have had a different character from his previous ones. While in 1362–63, fearing the loss of his Florentine citizenship rights, Boccaccio had taken steps to ensure that someone would fulfill his tax obligations during his absence, this time he made no such provisions for the municipal taxes imposed in September and November 1370 and January 1371: he would make these payments all together only at the end of April 1371.[5] It could mean that, unlike in the past, on this occasion Boccaccio planned to settle in Naples permanently. But this is also only a conjecture, one, moreover, that would seem to be contradicted by the fact that he did not bring most of his books with him. Regardless of what he had mind—staying a few months or for the rest of his life—it is reasonable to think that a man who was "old and in poor health"[6] (*Ep.*, XVIII.7), as Boccaccio was, would not have embarked on such a trip merely in reaction to some obscure disquiet or an event at home. No, someone must have invited him, asked him to come, someone must have proposed an arrangement that he found desirable. In short, he had not come to Naples "by chance" ("casu," *Ep.*, XVIII.7), as he declared with ostentatious nonchalance in a letter to Niccolò Orsini; discussions and negotiations must have taken place that we know nothing about.

Boccaccio set out at the beginning of autumn. Initially, this Neapolitan trip seemed to follow the same script of broken promises and disappointments as the previous ones. In the letter to Orsini just cited, Boccaccio referred obscurely to his own impetuous and indignant reaction to unspecified domestic troubles, because of which he would have considered going home had not the kindness of new friends in Naples, including Orisini himself, intervened, providing suitable remedies to calm him and convince him to stay.[7] We are better informed about another indignation-arousing episode during those first few months. In Naples, Boccaccio encountered an old acquaintance, the Carthusian monk Niccolò da Montefalcone, to whom he was also connected through their shared cultural interests. Montefalcone was in Naples to solicit, with the help of the powerful del Balzo (or de Baux) family, his appointment by the pope as abbot of his monastery in Calabria, Santo Stefano del Bosco. The monk extolled the monastery's beauty to Boccaccio, the salubrity of its location, the mildness of its climate, its rich collection of books, to the point of arousing in Boccaccio the "desire not only to see it, but, if necessity demanded, to find a refuge there": but then, "without any warning or farewell," Montefalcone set sail for Calabria by night, "furtively . . . like a thief or a con-man" (*Ep.*, XVI.8–10).[8] On January 20, Boccaccio wrote a very resentful letter to him from Naples. On the basis of this episode, an alternative hypothesis has been proposed for Boccaccio's trip to Naples, namely, that he planned to retire to a hermitage in southern Italy.[9] This theory would seem to be supported by the circumstance that, almost certainly in this same period, Franco Sacchetti sent him a sonnet composed "when word circulated that he had become a Carthusian monk in Naples" ("quando fama corse, lui essere fatto frate di Certosa a Napoli"),[10] as the heading reads. The rumor had either reached Sacchetti's ears from Naples or been spread by Boccaccio himself before his departure from Florence: in the latter case, we would have to conclude that there had been an agreement with Niccolò da Montefalcone for some time. Based on Boccaccio's letter of remonstration, it looks as if the monk's dramatic about-face was due to his realization that Boccaccio would not bring any financial benefit to the monastery.[11]

From Boccaccio's own accounts, however, it does not actually seem he was leaning toward monastic retreat during the months he was in Naples. In contrast to all his previous visits, this one was replete with satisfactions.[12] In Naples, he was considered a master: his advice and approval were sought by young men aspiring to poetry, such as the Matteo d'Ambrasio or d'Ambrosio to whom Boccaccio wrote a letter of encouragement on May 12, 1371, hastily ("festinanter"), because he was about to leave the city;[13] others, who were no longer young and, moreover, held important court positions, but also desired to devote themselves to study, came recommended to him by eminent persons: this was the case with Iacopo Pizzinga, *logothete*, that is, chancellor, of Frederick IV of Aragon, king of Trinacria (as the Kingdom of Sicily was known in fourteenth century), to whom Boccaccio would later send from Certaldo a long and complex letter about literature.[14] Pizzinga had been recommended to him by a trusted figure, the Minorite theologian Ubertino da Corigliano, whom Boccaccio visited at the Franciscan monastery of San Lorenzo Maggiore, the same place, it is worth noting, where the "compositore" of the *Filocolo* wrote that he had encountered Maria-Fiammetta for the first time.[15] Above all, Boccaccio was sought after by the high nobility: prominent figures like Ugo di Sanseverino and the great feudal lord Niccolò (or Nicola) Orsini took him under their patronage and worked to secure him an honorable position.[16] Even the Neapolitan royal court, in the person of the prince consort, James IV of Majorca, and, through him, Queen Joanna herself, took an interest in him.

The months in Naples were also productive as far as intellectual work was concerned. Both Sanseverino and Orsini were cultured men (the former was in contact with Petrarca, the latter with Salutati), who enthusiastically associated with and supported scholars. As we have seen, Boccaccio left his autograph of the *Genealogia* as a loan with Sanseverino, from whom it then passed into the possession of Pietro Piccolo da Monteforte. Coming to know this jurist and philologist was one of the most fortunate things that happened to Boccaccio during his visit. Pietro Piccolo, in fact, not only proposed many corrections and improvements to the text (for example, he converted *Genologia* to *Genealogia*), changes that Boccaccio would adopt in his final revisions, but he also began a dialogue with Boccaccio about the function of poetry, which would continue even after Boccaccio's return to Certaldo, and traces of which can be found in the last books of the *Genealogia*. Further, Pietro Piccolo was linked to Boccaccio's discovery of Martial, whose *Epigrammata* he copied from a southern Italian codex: in his autograph, full of annotations, manicules, and drawings by his hand,[17] Boccaccio also transcribed an epigram by Pietro, who is known to have possessed a Martial codex. During this final stay in Naples, Boccaccio achieved many things that he had been seeking for almost his entire life. If it is true — as he would write to both Orsini and Pizzinga — that "on my departure from Naples . . . the Most Serene Prince James, King of Majorca, overwhelmed me with entreaties that I live out my old age in leisure under the protection of his majesty"[18] (*Ep.*, XVIII.12) and that Queen Joanna herself helped his patrons "to establish me in tranquil leisure with the Neapolitans"[19] (*Ep.*, XIX.2), it means that Boccaccio had been welcomed once again by this court that he had been compelled to leave exactly thirty years earlier and with which he had apparently had no further contact. And consider the type of situation his patrons were planning for him: "in tranquil leisure [*in otio*]," "live out my old age in leisure [*otiosus*]," here using the word, *otium/ otiosus*, that to the ancients meant especially leisure during which one was occupied only with literary work. Wasn't this exactly what the benefice-less cleric had always hoped for? Had he not tried again and again in vain to obtain a position free of any obligation or practical activity, one that would allow him to devote himself freely to his studies and poetry? Well, now that he was just one step away from fulfilling his wish, and, what's more, in the city that he had never stopped thinking about with regret and nostalgia, he refused it: despite his friends' efforts to detain him, he left Naples and took refuge in Certaldo. On May 12, 1371, he was on the verge of departure; by June 20 he was back in his house in the village.[20]

Certaldo, a "Peasant Prison"

It had been an agonizing decision. "I was tormented by uncertainty," he would write to Pizzinga, perhaps not long after he returned to Tuscany, "never settled in any decision or direction" (*Ep.*, XIX.2):[21] on the one hand, "I was driven by an intense desire to return home . . . to see again not only the books I had unjustly left behind but also my friends and other loved ones" (*Ep.*, XIX.1);[22] on the other, Ugo di Sanseverino's pleas and promises drew him. Pizzinga was just an acquaintance, they never met in person, and therefore it was natural that Boccaccio gave him rather vague reasons for leaving, just as he had to another acquaintance, Matteo d'Ambrasi, while still in Naples ("my departure being imminent, which I desire for many reasons" [*Ep.*, XVII.14]).[23] Niccolò Orsini, in contrast, he owed an explanation. Why had he refused the very generous offers made by Sanseverino, King James, and Orsini himself? The reasons he gave cast some light on the elderly Boccaccio's contorted psychology. After penning his profuse thanks to Orsini, he added that having "freed myself" from James, "left the king and the royal gifts, and untied my ship from the shore, I returned home" because "it seemed to me that my freedom, which I want completely unrestrained, had been trapped by some hidden snare" (*Ep.*, XVIII.13).[24] Reasons that were indeed applicable to King James, but also to Boccaccio's refusal of Sanseverino and Orisini ("My great age, accustomed to freedom, cannot tolerate subjecting my neck to the yoke," [*Ep.*, XVIII.15]).[25] It is unsurprising that Boccaccio failed to realize that his suspicion that his benefactors' generosity concealed a trap for his freedom might be objectionable, indeed offensive: he had no gift for diplomacy, particularly when in the grip of some compulsion, an obsessive worry that clouded his thinking.

If, as it would seem, this was not actually a stock case of the sage man choosing poverty over an easy life for the sake of preserving his liberty, but instead Boccaccio alleging mistrust in order to mask other, more personal reasons for his withdrawal, then what we are actually seeing is a Boccaccio who is less wary and suspicious than neurotically anxious about the future and, thus, clinging to sources of security. However one wants to interpret it, his rejection of, almost flight from, the lure of tranquil *otium* in Naples seems to have been dictated by his moodiness and a fundamental need for solitude. He was sincere when he confessed to Orsini in the same letter: "The years remaining to me, I believe, are few . . . and these, if it please God, I wish to spend at home; and since worry about the grave exceeds all my other concerns, I desire to restore the remains of my ancestors and to unite them" (*Ep.*, XVIII.16).[26]

The Boccaccio who shut himself away in Certaldo in the late spring of 1371 was a man haunted by fears of death, one who had closed in on himself, hidden behind solitude as a shield. Recalling the last years of Boccaccio's life to Francescuolo da Brossano, Coluccio Salutati wrote that he had been able to speak with him only a few times, partly because of his own obligations, but also because of Boccaccio's great weight and advanced age, which impeded his movement, and his retirement in the country ("rusticatio").[27] The solitary Boccaccio was also prey to mood swings, ensnared in a knot of contradictions in which he would remain until the end of his days: he wanted to be alone, yet became alarmed if he felt overlooked or forgotten; he sought the appreciation of readers and yet belittled his own writing; he sought the reassurance of familiar places and at the same time disdained them. A year went by, and Certaldo, for which he had given up the glittering life of Naples, had become a prison, worse, a "peasant prison" (*Ep.*, XXII.31).[28]

During the first few months, however, he kept up an intense correspondence with his friends in Naples. Of particular importance are the letters he sent to Iacopo Pizzinga and exchanged with Pietro Piccolo.

For Pizzinga, an influential politician as well as devotee of humanistic studies, who, a Calabrian, may have read Homer in Greek and cultivated the Latin muse,[29] Boccaccio sketched a brief history of poetry focusing on its decline in comparison to classical Rome and the encouraging signs of recovery in the present day. Champions of this rebirth, obviously, were Dante and Petrarch: "We see . . . Dante Alighieri . . . not advancing along the road of the ancients, but taking paths completely untrodden by his elders, . . . [and] having reawakened the half-sleeping Muses and led Phoebus to his cithara: he dared compel them to sing in his mother tongue, which he did not render vulgar or unrefined [*plebeium aut rusticanum*], as some would have it, no indeed, to the contrary, through his skillful use of words, he enhanced the language, more in its meaning than in its appearance" (*Ep.*, XIX.26).[30] Following Dante, the humanist Petrarch had returned poetry to its original elegance and purity, freeing it from the superfluous elements introduced by the poets of the Middle Ages: "having cleansed the source of the river Helicon of silt and swamp reeds and returned the original clarity to its waters, opened up the Castalian grotto, long closed off by wild twisted branches, and cleared the laurel woods of thorny brambles, placed Apollo back on his ancient seat and returned the Muses from wildness to their ancient decorum, he ascended to the highest peaks of Parnassus" (*Ep.*, XIX.28).[31] And then, since Pizzinga was a neophyte, and what's more, appeared to aspire—with no little boldness to judge by his brief surviving verse specimen[32]—to poetic laurels, Boccaccio, fearing that the late Zanobi's coronation in Pisa might have raised him to the rank of poet in Pizzinga's eyes, took care to make it clear that, despite his wreath, Zanobi had in fact brought no glory to poetry.

At the end of the letter (which has survived with its conclusion truncated), Boccaccio spoke of himself. He presents us with a dispirited reflection on his own limitations as a poet, the self-portrait of a man who has aspired to great things and, having reached old age, thinks he has failed and has no time to remedy it. He had set out on the path of the masters with grand ambitions ("ingenti animo"), indeed, as a "trailblazer" ("previus"), but then—he confesses—distracted by public and domestic duties, and, above all, having concluded that others, namely, Petrarch, unlike him, were climbing higher and higher, "I began to lose heart, and little by little my spirit and strength began to fail me, dejected and discouraged, I gave up hope of reaching the summit, while those whom I had made my guides were leaving; now that I am old, I have stopped, and, what is to me a pitiful disgrace, I dare not turn back and I cannot climb further: and so, unless new grace is imparted to me from on high, my inglorious name along with my body I will surrender to the grave" (*Ep.*, XIX.39).[33] We have heard him sound similar notes in the *Genealogia* and the *Corbaccio*,[34] but never in such a gloomy tone, never with such a desperate sense of failure.[35]

The jurist Pietro Piccolo da Monteforte had a completely different intellectual stature from Pizzinga. With Monteforte, Boccaccio conducted an intense dialogue, beginning in Naples and continuing after his return home, about scholarly and philological matters and the value of poetry. Boccaccio wrote him a now-lost letter from Tuscany to which Pietro Piccolo responded at length on February 2, 1372:[36] here Pietro returned to the question, raised by Boccaccio, of the two Senecas, that is, of the necessity (of which Boccaccio was convinced, while Petrarch was not) of distinguishing between Lucius Annaeus Seneca, rhetorician and philosopher, and Marcus Annaeus Seneca, tragedian, and then recounted how he himself had defended poetry against a young theologian, who had "angrily" (*Ep.*, XX.5; "stomacose") condemned it. Many of the arguments Monteforte advanced in defense of poetry Boccaccio would in fact adopt and, as we have seen, use when revising the final two books of the *Genealogia*. From Boccaccio's response sent on April 5 from Certaldo, we learn about the status of the *Genealogia* autograph left in Naples for Ugo di Sanseverino. At that date, the book had not yet been returned to Boccaccio, and so he did not know what Pietro Piccolo's suggestions were. He would receive it, probably via Giovanni Latinucci,[37] to whom he had entrusted it, within the next few months. Between 1372 and 1373, Boccaccio would put the final touches on his mythological catalog, using Pietro's suggestions and corrections.

Marriage Consultant

During his months in Naples, Boccaccio would have surely seen Mainardo Cavalcanti, his benefactor of his previous trip. In the spring of 1372, Mainardo, who had in the meantime been named grand seneschal of the Kingdom of Naples, came to Florence in order to marry Andreina, the daughter of Iacopo Acciaiuoli, one of Niccolò's cousins. There was a problem, however: the couple were related in the fourth degree of kinship, and therefore, according to canon law, their union would be considered incestuous. Mainardo, most likely while in Florence, asked Boccaccio, as an expert in canon law, for advice on how to surmount this obstacle, and Boccaccio recommended that they celebrate their marriage in secret and only afterward ask for a papal dispensation, claiming prior ignorance of the existence of the legal impediment. And so it was done: Mainardo and Andreina married that March, and the dispensation would arrive from Avignon on August 27. However, after the wedding, Boccaccio heard nothing from Mainardo, and so, huffy as usual, but this time with reason, he began writing a letter on August 10, ostensibly of congratulations but actually of reproach; only a few days later, he had to interrupt it when he fell gravely ill. Over the days preceding this, he later informed Mainardo, he had had been afflicted by "a dry itchy rash," plus "heavy sluggishness of the belly, constant kidney pain, a swollen spleen, burning bile, gasping coughs, hoarseness," and loss of appetite, to the point that "I came to hate literature," "previously beloved books displeased me," and "all my thoughts turned to the grave and death" (*Ep.*, XXI.5–7);[38] on the night of August 12–13, he came down with a violent fever, from which a village physician called to his bedside by some "peasant friends" ("rusticani amici") rescued him with repeated bloodlettings. Only on August 28 was he able to return to writing and then send off the letter. Mainardo understood. He hurried to reply, accompanying his missive with gifts: no less than "a small golden vessel filled with gold coins" (*Ep.*, XXII.27)[39] on September 13. Then, the following year, he asked Boccaccio to stand as godfather to his newborn son. Boccaccio's gratitude for Mainardo Cavalcanti's kindness and generosity led him to dedicate the *De casibus* to him, particularly because they were joined by "sacred kinship" (*CVI*, Dedica, 13–14), Mainardo the natural father and Boccaccio, as godfather, the spiritual father of his only son.

In his letter of thanks for the gifts, Boccaccio spoke about the *Decameron*, although without naming it. To Mainardo, who had confessed to feeling guilty for not having yet read Boccaccio's "little books" ("libellos"), he playfully responded that "the summer heat, short nights, and new bride" would distract not just "a fresh, young knight" from his studies, but even a "hoary old scholar" (*Ep.*, XXII.17).[40] He recommended, however, that the women of the household not read his little trifles ("domesticas nugas"): "You know how much in them is not decent and is contrary to honesty, how many prods to ill-omened Venus, how many things that incite to wicked deeds even wills as strong as iron; and even if honorable women, especially those on whose brow sacred modesty shines, are not driven to impure acts, still they are stealthily subject to seductive ardor and it sometimes provokes their souls into immodesty, and corrupts and inflames them with the obscene purulence of lust, which it must be ensured does not happen" (*Ep.*, XXII.20).[41] And if Mainardo did not intend to preserve his women's honor, he should at least preserve Boccaccio's: "for reading it they will consider me a foulmouthed pimp, a dirty old man, vile, an obscene slanderer and eager teller of others' wicked deeds" (*Ep.*, XXII.23).[42]

Now, these seemingly straightforward statements actually raise a number of questions. First of all, how did Mainardo obtain the *Decameron*?—for this is the work Boccaccio was talking about. Mainardo was a member of the Acciaiuoli clan, and we know that the *Decameron* had been circulating in and around that family for over a decade. Therefore, it would not have been difficult for him to get a hold of a copy. But Mainardo might also have received a copy as a gift from Boccaccio himself at the time of this correspondence.[43] In that case, if we leave aside the possibilities that Boccaccio had turned to a professional copyist, or that, despite his precarious health, had undertaken the task of transcribing it in his own hand, we have to think that Boccaccio had sent him one of the autographs that he already had at his house. This hypothesis of a gift would, on the one hand, explain why Mainardo felt he had to apologize for not having yet read it, and on the other, suggest that the gold coins he sent were a form of payment. But there is another problem, namely, determining if and to what extent Boccaccio's reversal of opinion about his work was real or only apparent; in other words, if, as has been claimed, Boccaccio was indulging in a *vituperatio iocosa*, mocking censure, a mere literary jest framed in abusive and hostile language and preposterous exaggeration, that is, a series of assertions, meant to be understood antiphrastically, as their opposite for humorous effect,[44] or if, instead, Boccaccio was voicing real moral qualms about the *Decameron*.[45] But the two are perhaps not mutually exclusive: the jocular tone with which he introduces the topic (a newlywed has better things to do than read) and his very linguistic excesses, if they soften what he is saying, do not, in fact, negate the ethical concerns underlying his words.

In late old age, obsessed by thoughts of death, Boccaccio was increasingly gripped by powerful religious sentiment (these were the years of his musing about poetry as theology) and worries about salvation. Through this lens, his book of *novelle* must have

appeared dangerous to the morality of readers, especially the female ones. Viewed from this point of view, the letter to Mainardo
is an excellent example of the conflicts and contradictions that
troubled him. Just as he was putting the final touches on his autograph codex and submitting his work to Petrarch's judgment (recall that the latter's letter with comments about the *Decameron*
was in March 1373),[46] Boccaccio was worried about controlling
its dissemination, taking to heart certain moralistic criticisms
that must have been raised by a number of people. And the ver-
bal excesses of the above-cited passage are of a piece with the vehement, almost savage, outbursts that crop up in various places
in the writings of his later years.[47] On his autograph of Martial's
Epigrammata, in a period that we can assume was close to that of
the letter to Mainardo, next to the line "hominem pagina nostra
sapit" ("our page smacks of man"),[48] Boccaccio jotted: "Of course it
smacks of man, since he writes about licking pussy, fucking, shit-
ting, and other things like that! Cursed be such a poet!"[49] and then,
not satisfied, added a manicule "with which—Dantesquely—he
brandishes the figs[50] at Martial, almost as a sign of defiance."[51]

The Public Reading of the *Commedia*

Boccaccio had begun his career as a writer and scholar with a poem
in Dantean terza rima and, in perfect circularity, he ended it with a
commentary on the *Commedia*.

   In June 1373, a group of Florentine citizens presented the priors and the *gonfaloniere* of justice with a petition requesting a
public "reading" of Dante, that is, of the *Commedia*, be held at the
Signoria's expense. The petition was then submitted to the captain
of the people and the *podestà* for consideration and approved on
August 12 and 13; on the twenty-fifth of the month, Boccaccio was
officially appointed to "read" the book "that is commonly called *il
Dante*" ("qui vulgariter appellatur il Dante") every day, excluding
holidays, for one year starting in October at the considerable salary of one hundred florins.[52]

   This was a remarkable event: a public "reading," which meant
essentially line-by-line commentary on a work presented in a series of lectures, had never before taken place outside of an insti-

tution like a university, monastery, or convent. Furthermore, at universities, the texts commented upon were legal, medical, and philosophical, while at religious institutions, they were the Bible or theological works, such as Peter Lombard's *Sentences*. And when, on the very rare occasion a work of literature was the subject of commentary (as Dante's *Eclogues* were at the Studium of Bologna by Giovanni del Virgilio),[53] it was always a text in Latin. This was the first time that a city government had sponsored an initiative of this kind, and it marked the high point of public regard for the young vernacular literature prior to its validation in the sixteenth century. It was certainly a victory for Boccaccio: this success crowned at last his unremitting, near lifelong effort to have Dante recognized as the greatest glory of Florentine culture. It was also a kind of recognition by Florence—as evidenced by the substantial salary—of Boccaccio's own merit.

He began reading on Sunday, October 23, in Santo Stefano in Badia, the church of the Benedictine abbey located not far from the Alighieri house. It appears that the site was not particularly dignified: Benvenuto da Imola, who attended the—always crowded—lectures, wrote that Santo Stefanto "is quite disorderly and neglected these days."[54]

For the oral lectures, Boccaccio used papers and notes that he later reworked and rearranged into a continuous text, which has come down to us with the title (not by Boccaccio) of *Esposizioni sopra la Comedia di Dante* (*Expositions on Dante's Comedy*). It consists of roughly sixty lectures, covering through the first sixteen lines of canto 17 of the *Inferno*, and ends abruptly at the beginning of a sentence. The exposition of each canto, with a few exceptions, is divided into two parts: the first treats the literal ("litterale") meaning, the second the allegorical. As it has come down to us, the book is uneven and disorganized, clearly recognizable as a work-in-progress that still needs a great deal more work before reaching any kind of final form.[55]

On December 31, the city paid Boccaccio the first installment of fifty florins for the initial six months of lectures (October 18–April 18). The following month, however, he fell ill. It is thought that because of this illness he interrupted the readings, and, for a combination of reasons, never resumed them. Effectively, sixty lectures have come down to us, arranged in order without any gaps: begun on October 23, 1373, and given daily, excluding holidays, they should have ended in January 1374. But the situation appears more complicated. First of all, while his illness was indeed long and unpleasant, based on what Boccaccio himself said, it was not serious: "The tenth month has already passed since, while I was publicly reading Dante's *Commedia* in my native city, I suffered for some time from an illness that was more long and tedious than dangerous" (*Ep.*, XXIV.3).[56] He wrote this in early November, and ten months accordingly take us back to the preceding January. So his illness was not a grave one, and, indeed, he was well enough in March 1374 that Bishop Ricasoli gave him the task of ensuring that the will of Lipaccio di Cesco of Certaldo was properly executed. But what more than anything else casts doubt on a complete cessation of the public readings in January is the fact that nine months after this, on September 4, 1374, the Comune paid Boccaccio for the second half of the lectures. Would a municipal administration as attentive and fastidious as Florence's have disbursed this considerable sum if the recipient had not done the work for which he was being paid? This is hard to believe, unless the lectures had been canceled by the Comune itself as a precautionary measure, given that between March and September there was a plague outbreak in Florence.[57] What is actually most likely is that Boccaccio gave a larger number of lectures than he later reworked in writing, and that at least some of them (although probably not all those that had been planned) were presented even after April 18. Indeed, it should be taken into account that each lecture must have been much shorter than it appears from the written text, and, therefore, in all probability, a larger number of lectures took place: calculated on the basis of the draft, even speaking every day, Boccaccio would not have been able to comment on the entire poem in the space of one year. Therefore, we cannot rely on the written text to determine how many and which lectures were actually given. It is plausible, if not certain, however, that because of his declining health, Boccaccio was unable to fulfill his daily commitment at Santo Stefano starting in the summer of 1374. By August–September, in fact, his condition had worsened to the point that such exertion was impossible. A dramatic sign of his physical decline may be the sudden interruption of the written draft at the beginning of a sentence: "The Tartars are . . ." ("Sono i Tartari . . .") and then nothing more. Boccaccio may have given up in the autumn of 1374 or at some point in 1375; it was, in any case, during the stage when he was revising his notes, which may have been even a few months earlier.

Some scholars maintain that not everyone in Florence welcomed the Comune's decision to sponsor public commentary on Dante's poem. Discontent, disapproval, and criticism from politicians and from families impugned by Dante, which had dogged the *Commedia* ever since its first appearance, were joined by censure from devotees of Latin literature and hostility from theologians. Hence Boccaccio's concern to defend Dante's orthodoxy and focus on Dante the moralist, putting to one side the dangerous suggestion of Dante the prophet, but, simultaneously, preserving the governing idea of Dante the poet-theologian. In truth, there is no documentary evidence of anti-Dante polemic within religious circles in Florence; it seems undeniable, however, that, as has been said, the *Esposizioni* attest to "Boccaccio's decline and at many points reveal his physical and moral fatigue, his premature, solitary and rustic old age dominated by the idea of death, his withdrawal into religious ideals."[58] But it is clear that his reading of the *Commedia* had great resonance in Florence:[59] it is no coincidence that Franco Sacchetti's long poem on Boccaccio's death, lamenting the cultural desolation into which the city was plunged with the disappearance of its most illustrious intellectuals, would mention this event first off: "How can I hope that Dante will rise, / when the one who knows how to read him is no more? / Giovanni, who has died, taught us about him."[60]

An episode mentioned at the beginning of this book, even more than shedding light on Florentine literary debates, illuminates Boccaccio's feelings—we do not know at precisely which point, whether during his lectures or after their interruption—about this undertaking. A person whose identity and social status are both unknown (suggestions include a leading political figure, a high-ranking cleric, and a devotee of humanistic studies) attacked Boccaccio sharply ("bitter phrasing" ["aspro dettato"]) and vehemently ("heated . . . verses" ["rime . . . accese"]), accusing him of having prostituted the Muses by exposing "their hidden parts . . . to the plebeian scum" ("le lor parte occulte . . . alla feccia plebea") and of making Dante weep, "wherever he may be" ("dove ch'el . . . sia"), upon seeing that the "reading" had "exposed the conceptions of his lofty genius . . . to the common people" ("lettura"; "li concetti del suo alto ingegno / aperti . . . al vulgo"). The scholarly world had leveled these arguments against the *Commedia* from the outset, and they had continued to echo in humanistic circles. Boccaccio's unidentified interlocutor, therefore, has all the appearance of a rigorous disciple of classical studies. It is, thus, rather perplexing that a humanist had turned to vernacular verse to express his criticism and dragged his target into a drawn-out poetic duel of no less than four sonnets each:[61] "Your verses have already tired and almost humiliated me" ("Già stanco m'hanno et quasi rintuzato / le rime tua," *Rime*, IX [CXXIV].1–2). Of course, the critic's choice of the vernacular could be interpreted as a way to underline the "vulgarity," in both literal and metaphorical senses, of Boccaccio's project; however, hovering over the entire textual exchange—the authenticity of Boccaccio's responses seems clear, while his opponents' have not survived—is an aura of mystery, even dubiousness.

Now, leaving aside the circumstances and, above all, the actual reality of this poetic dispute, what Boccaccio revealed about himself is interesting. He was unhappy, irritated with himself, embarrassed he had ever agreed to this "folly" ("follia"), for which, however, he was only partly responsible: "Vain hope and true poverty and the bedazzling reasoning of friends and their pleas made me do this" ("Vana speranza et vera povertate / et l'abbagliato senno delli amici / et gli lor prieghi ciò mi fecer fare," *Rime*, VIII [CXXIII].9–11); "what was foolishly done" ("ciò che stoltamente è stato fatto") cannot now be undone; he asks forgiveness for it and promises "that no one will ever again push me to such a crime" ("che 'n tal misfacto / più non mi spingerà alcun giamai," *Rime*, IX [CXXIV].12–14); it is sufficient to chastise him, because Apollo has already cruelly punished him for his offenses against the Muses by transforming him into "a wineskin . . . not full of air but of grievous lead" ("un otre . . . non pien di vento ma di piombo grave," *Rime*, VII [CXXII].9–10). More than any cultural debate, what these sonnets reveal is the great knot of contradictions old Boccaccio had gotten himself tangled up in.[62] The very moment that his public reading of Dante had confirmed his victory in a struggle that had lasted almost his entire life, precisely when he had succeeded in establishing Dante as the greatest glory of Florentine literature, well, what did he do? He gave up, he repented, he declared himself at fault. In the final months of Boccaccio's life, his ever-present psychological fragility now convulsed him; he was consumed in futile search for equilibrium, undermined by self-destructive compulsion.

Approaching the End

On the night of July 18–19, 1374, Francesco Petrarca died in Arquà. The news arrived in Florence a few days later. Boccaccio composed a sonnet influenced by the one Petrarch had written on the death of Sennuccio del Bene:[63]

> Now you have climbed at last, O my dear lord,
> to the sweet realm where those who God still know
> are by His providence allowed to go
> when they abandon this our wicked world.
> Now you are there, where often your desire
> to gaze on your Lauretta bade you rise—
> there where my lovely Fiammetta lies
> beside her in God's marvelous empire.
>
> Now with Senuccio, Cino, and Dante, you
> can live assured of your eternal rest,
> looking on ecstasies I never knew.
> Oh, if on this sad earth you cherished me,
> take me where I may watch, forever blest,
> the lady that with love first kindled me.[64]

> Or sei salito, caro signor mio,
> nel regno, al qual salire anchor aspetta
> ogn'anima da Dio a quell'electa,
> nel suo partir di questo mondo rio.
> Or sè colà, dove spesso il desio
> ti tirò già per veder Laüretta:

or sei dove la mia bella Fiammetta siede
con lei nel conspecto di Dio.

    Or con Sennuccio et con Cino et con Dante
vivi, sicuro d'eterno riposo
mirando cose da noi non intese.

    Deh, s'a grado ti fui nel mondo errante,
tirami drietro a te, dove gioioso
veggia colei che pria d'amor m'accese

Rime, XCIX (CXXVI)

    In August, Boccaccio's health worsened.

    On the twenty-eighth of the month, at the church of Santa Felicita in Florence, he dictated his final wishes to the notary Tinello di ser Bonasera, replacing the will drawn up in 1365 before his trip to Avignon. Tinello's document in Latin had been preceded by a draft in the vernacular. Boccaccio named as his universal heirs the children of his brother Iacopo, who in turn was named guardian and administrator of the estate, as well as an executor along with four other men, who included Boccaccio's old friends Pietro Canigiani and Leonardo del Chiaro. Giovanni evidently excluded his half brother from inheritance because he knew well Iacopo's spendthrift ways.[65] Recipients of legacies were the church of San Iacopo in Certaldo, where he asked to be interred if he died in the village (approximately five florins, vestments, and sacred items); the now-vanished Benedictine monastery of San Michele delle Campora near Galluzzo (relics); his housekeeper, Bruna da Montemagno (some furnishings and a complete set of clothing); and Friar Martino da Signa. To this last friend, Boccaccio left his books along with a twofold obligation: to allow anyone who wanted to make copies of the texts and to transfer the books upon his death to the library of the monastery of Santo Spirito, as would then happen in 1387. Unlike Petrarch, therefore, Boccaccio had not forgotten the idea, suggested by his friend and master, to make his books the core of a library open to the public.[66]

    Shortly after making his will, he departed for Certaldo. He arrived there in poor health: weak, emaciated, trembling, supported by his friends because his legs would not hold him. Here, on October 20, he received from Francescuolo da Brossano the fifty gold florins that Petrarch had left him in his will. On November 3, with great difficulty he finished writing the letter of thanks: "Finished writing in Certaldo on November 3, and, as you can see, I cannot say 'in haste': I have spent nearly three entire days, except for a few hours' break to somewhat restore strength to my exhausted body, in writing this short letter" (*Ep.*, XXIV.44).[67] Boccaccio was fatigued, but lucid.

After recalling his forty years of devotion to the deceased, deploring that Florence was not his master's final resting place, and expressing his condolences to Tullia, that is, Francesca, and Francescuolo, in the final section of the letter, Boccaccio addressed a subject very close to his heart: What would happen to his friend's library? And to the *Africa* and the *Trionfi*? Was it true, as he had heard, that in accord with Petrarch's wishes, both these unpublished works risked being consigned to the flames? The *Africa*, of which, with the sole exception of the "Lamento di Magone," Petrarch had always refused to provide excerpts, had for decades been a mysterious object of fascination to the poet's admirers. With Petrarch's death, a conflict had arisen between the philologists in Padua, led by Lombardo della Seta, to whom Francescuolo, the legal heir to his father-in-law's books and others writings, had entrusted the unpublished works, and those in Florence, with Coluccio Salutati at their head. While Francescuolo and Lombardo, conscious of the autograph's great disorder, were reluctant to make copies, Coluccio was urging immediate publication and proposing himself as publisher. From this the rumor had arisen that there was discussion in Padua about whether or not to destroy the poem.[68] Kept informed by Coluccio, Boccaccio entered into the fray with his usual lack of tact bordering on offensiveness: "I hear that some have been entrusted, I know not by whom, with the examination of [the *Africa*] and his other books, and that those they deem worthy will be preserved. I marvel at the ignorance of whoever arranged this, but even more at the temerity and worthlessness of those who have undertaken the task. . . . May God, I pray, watch over and aid our master's poems and his other sacred creations. Finally, if in their judgement the case should proceed, write me, if you please, and include every copy possible to be given to those who desire them" (*Ep.*, XXIV.33–38).[69] Boccaccio's tone shows that he felt himself to be the true custodian of Petrarch's cultural legacy and he could not stand that others dared lay a hand on what he considered his.

The *Africa* obsessed him. Shortly after writing to Francescuolo, genuine concern, but combined with resentment at having been kept on the sidelines, prompted him to compose his final literary work, the 182 hexameters of "Verses to the *Africa*" ("Versus ad Affricam"), in which he addressed the poem directly.[70] The ideas, dramatized, are those that he had outlined in the letter:

> Ytalie sublimis honor, generosa Petrarce
> Affrica Francisci soboles, quid nescia dormis?
> Non sentis convexa poli, non sydera secum
> quod tibi permittant fatum pugnantia? Quodque
> iam patres veneti, quis coram dicere causam
> te fortuna iubet, iuris posuere tribunal,
> inque fori medio sedeant, crepitentque furentes
> in celum flamme damnatis, credo, papiris
> supplicium, rostrisque fremant hinc inde patroni
> vocibus et strepitu complentes omnia circum?

Sublime honor of Italy, oh *Africa*, generous daughter of Francesco Petrarca, why do you sleep unaware? Do you not sense what fate the heavens and stars together prepare against you? Can you not see that the Venetian senators, before whom fortune wants you to defend your cause, have set up a tribunal, that they sit in judgment, that furious flames crackle toward the heavens, immolation, I believe, for your papers, now condemned, that the lawyers on one side and the other are roaring on the rostra, filling all around with voices and clamor? (*Carmina*, IX.1–10)

The river Sorga, Rome, Naples, and above all, Florence implore the poem to flee, to "escape the flames, entrust yourself to the devoted hands of those who love you" (*Carmina*, IX.64–66):[71] "flee quickly, abandon the untrustworthy Euganean hills" (*Carmina*, IX.105–6).[72] We have said that Boccaccio's career closed with a return to Dante. However, it should also be said that his final literary work was dedicated to Petrarch. Boccaccio was consistent to the end. After these last hexameters, his life goes completely dark.

The Mage

Giovanni Boccaccio died on December 21, 1375. He was buried in Certaldo in the church of Santi Michele e Iacopo. Iacopo Boccaccio commissioned Prior Angelo Giandonati to have the tomb built: it cost twenty-five florins, for which the prior was never reimbursed.[73] On the slab of white marble in the church floor were engraved the family coat of arms, a laurel wreath, and the epitaph composed by Boccaccio himself:

> Hac sub mole iacent cineres ac ossa Iohannis,
> mens sedet ante Deum meritis ornata laborum
> mortalis vite; genitor Boccaccius illi,
> patria Certaldum, studium fuit alma poesis.

> Under this stone lie the bones and ashes of Giovanni; his spirit stands in the presence of God, adorned with the merits his mortal labors on earth have earned him. Boccaccio sired him; his native homeland was Certaldo; he cherished the nourishing Muses. (*Carmina*, X)[74]

Certaldo was a small village.[75] In such a community, it was common for rumors, anecdotes, and legends to multiply around a figure such as Boccaccio, someone who had traveled the world, frequented lofty courts, known kings and emperors. At that time, because they were different, intellectuals were seen as people endowed with magical powers and who, as a result, colluded with the devil. The anonymous sixteenth-century author whose legend about Boccaccio's death we will read shortly wrote, "it is believed by the common folk that the men who rise so much above others with their study and brilliance [*ingegno*] always have something of the supernatural."[76] A reputation as a necromancer hovered over Dante Alighieri, for example, to the point that the Visconti of Milan had considered turning to him to make an attempt on the life of Pope John XXII with a spell.[77] And it was well known that Dante was famous among the common people for having descended alive into hell and met the devils there. Boccaccio himself recounted that in Ravenna the women who passed Dante on the street would call out to one another: look, it's "that man who goes down into Hell, and returns whenever he likes, and brings back up here the stories of those who are down there" ("colui che va ne l'inferno, e torna quando gli piace, e qua su reca novelle di coloro che là giù sono," *TLD*, [I].113). According to the people of Certaldo, Boccaccio, too, trafficked with the devil. The anonymous author mentioned above transcribed, in order to disprove it, some "prattle" ("ciancie") about Boccaccio that he himself had heard in Certaldo as "a young boy from the oldest people at that time." One story concerned Boccaccio's death:

> They say that [Boccaccio] would have himself carried by demons to Naples, where he was in love and kept a woman, and that he would go and return in two hours. And so, one night, while returning, he was above the Pozzuolo, which is a ditch at the foot of Certaldo, at that moment the Ave Maria rang; on account of which, he said, "Praised be God." Then, they say, the demons, on hearing Jesus's name, let go of him, and he fell into that ditch, and because of it he died.[78]

PRIMARY SOURCES

Works by Boccaccio

Abbreviations and Reference Editions

AV Amorosa visione

    Amorosa visione, edited by Vittore Branca. In *Tutte le opere*, edited by
        Vittore Branca, vol. 3. Milan: Mondadori, 1974.

    Amorosa Visione, translated by Robert Hollander, Timothy Hampton,
        and Margherita Frankel. Hanover, NH, and London: University
        Press of New England, 1986.

BC Buccolicum carmen

    Buccolicum carmen, edited by Giorgio Bernardi Perini. In *Tutte le
        opere*, edited by Vittore Branca, vol. 5, 2. Milan: Mondadori, 1994.

    Eclogues, edited and translated by Janet Smarr. New York: Garland
        Publishing, 1987.

Canaria De Canaria

    De Canaria, edited by Manlio Pastore Stocchi. In *Tutte le opere*, edited
        by Vittore Branca, vol. 5, 1. Milan: Mondadori, 1992.

Carmina

    Carmina, edited by Giuseppe Velli. In *Tutte le opere*, edited by Vittore
        Branca, vol. 5, 1, 375–492. Milan: Mondadori, 1992.

CD Caccia di Diana

    Caccia di Diana, edited by Irene Iocca. Rome: Salerno Editrice, 2016.

    Diana's Hunt—Caccia di Diana: Boccaccio's First Fiction, edited and
        translated by Anthony K. Cassell and Victoria Kirkham. Philadel-
        phia: University of Pennsylvania Press, 1991.

CNF   Comedia delle ninfe fiorentine
  Comedia delle ninfe fiorentine, edited by Antonio Enzo Quaglio. In
    Tutte le opere, edited by Vittore Branca, vol. 2, 665–835. Milan:
    Mondadori, 1964.
  L'Ameto, translated by Judith Serafini-Sauli. New York and London:
    Garland, 1985.
Cons.   Consolatoria a Pino de' Rossi
  Consolatoria a Pino de' Rossi, edited by Giuseppe Chiecchi. In *Tutte le
    opere*, edited by Vittore Branca, vol. 5, 2, 615–87. Milan: Mondadori,
    1994.
Corbaccio   Il Corbaccio
  Il Corbaccio, edited by Giulia Natali. Milan: Mursia, 1992.
  The Corbaccio, or The Labyringth of Love, edited and translated by
    Anthony K. Cassell, 2nd rev. ed. Binghamton: Medieval & Renais-
    sance Texts and Studies, 1993.
CVI   De casibus vivorum illustrium
  De casibus virorum illustrium, edited by Pier Giorgio Ricci and Vittorio
    Zaccaria. In *Tutte le opere*, edited by Vittore Branca, vol. 9. Milan:
    Mondadori, 1983.
  The Downfall of the Famous, new annotated ed. of *The Fates of Illustri-
    ous Men* (1965), translated and abridged by Louis Brewer Hall. New
    York and Bristol: Italica Press, 2018.
Dec.   Decameron
  Decameron, edited by Amedeo Quondam et al. Milan: Rizzoli, 2013.
  The Decameron, translated by Wayne A. Rebhorn. New York: Norton,
    2013.
ECD   Esposizioni sopra la Comedia di Dante
  Esposizioni sopra la Comedia di Dante, edited by Giorgio Padoan. In
    Tutte le opere, edited by Vittore Branca, vol. 6. Milan: Mondadori,
    1965.
  Boccaccio's Expositions on Dante's Comedy, translated by Michael
    Papio. Toronto and Buffalo, NY: University of Toronto Press,
    2009.
EMF   Elegia di Madonna Fiammetta
  Elegia di Madonna Fiammetta, edited by Carlo Delcorno. In *Tutte le
    opere*, edited by Vittore Branca, vol. 5, 2, 1–412. Milan: Mondadori,
    1994.
  The Elegy of Lady Fiammetta, edited by and translated by Mariangela
    Causa-Steindler and Thomas Mauch. Chicago and London: Uni-
    versity of Chicago Press, 1990.
Ep.   Epistole
  Epistole, edited by Ginetta Auzzas. In *Tutte le opere*, edited by Vittore
    Branca, vol. 5, 1, 493–856. Milan: Mondadori, 1992.

EpA   Epistola a Donato degli Albanzani

    Epistola a Donato degli Albanzani, edited by Augusto Campana. In *Tutte le opere*, edited by Vittore Branca, vol. 5, 1, 738–43. Milan: Mondadori, 1992.

Filoc.   Filocolo

    Filocolo, edited by Antonio Enzo Quaglio. In *Tutte le opere*, edited by Vittore Branca, vol. 1, 47–1024. Milan: Mondadori, 1964.

    Il Filocolo, translated by Donald Cheney with Thomas G. Bergin. New York: Garland Publishing, 1985.

Filos.   Filostrato

    Filostrato, edited by Luigi Surdich, with Elena D'Anzieri and Federica Ferro. Milan: Mursia, 1990.

    Il Filostrato, edited by Vincenzo Pernicone, translated by Robert P. apRoberts and Anna Bruni Seldis. New York and London: Garland Publishing, 1986.

GDG   Genealogie deorum gentilium

    Genealogie deorum gentilium, edited by Vittorio Zaccaria. In *Tutte le opere*, edited by Vittore Branca, vols. 7–8. Milan: Mondadori, 1998.

    Boccaccio on Poetry: Being the Preface and the Fourteenth and Fifteenth Books of Boccaccio's Genealogia Deorum Gentilium in an English Version with Introductory Essay and Commentary, edited by and translated by Charles G. Osgood. New York: Liberal Arts Press, 1956; Princeton, NJ: Princeton University Press, 1930.

Lett.   Lettere

    Lettere, edited by Ginetta Auzzas. In *Tutte le opere*, edited by Vittore Branca, vol. 5, 1, 857–78. Milan: Mondadori, 1992.

MC   De mulieribus claris

    De mulieribus claris, edited by Vittorio Zaccaria. In *Tutte le opere*, edited by Vittore Branca, vol. 10. Milan: Mondadori, 1967.

    Famous Women, edited by and translated by Virginia Brown. Cambridge, MA: Harvard University Press, 2001.

De montibus   De montibus, silvis, fontibus, …

    De montibus, silvis, fontibus, lacubus, fluminibus, stagnis seu paludibus et de diversis nominibus maris, edited by Manlio Pastore Stocchi. In *Tutte le opere*, edited by Vittore Branca, vols. 7–8, 1814–2122. Milan: Mondadori, 1998.

NF   Ninfale fiesolano

    Ninfale fiesolano, edited by Daniele Piccini. Milan: BUR Rizzoli, 2013.

    Nymphs of Fiesole, translated by Joseph Tusiani. Rutherford, NJ: Farleigh Dickinson University Press, 1971.

Rime

    Rime, edited by Roberto Leporatti. Florence: Edizioni del Galluzzo, 2013.

Teseida   Teseida delle nozze d'Emilia
> *Teseida delle nozze d'Emilia*, critical ed., edited by Edvige Agostinelli and William Coleman. Florence: Edizioni del Galluzzo, 2015.
> *Theseid of the Nuptials of Emilia (Teseida Delle Nozze Di Emilia)*, translated by Vincenzo Traversa. New York: Peter Lang, 2002.

TLD   Trattatello in laude di Dante
> *Trattatello in laude di Dante*, edited by Pier Giorgio Ricci. In *Tutte le opere*, edited by Vittore Branca, vol. 3, 423–538. Milan: Mondadori, 1974.
> *The Life of Dante (Trattatello in Laude di Dante)*, translated by Vincenzo Zin Bollettino. New York: Routledge, 2018.

Vite   Vite di Petrarca
> *Vite di Petrarca, Pier Damiani e Livio*, edited by Renata Fabbri. In *Tutte le opere*, edited by Vittore Branca, vol. 5, 1, 879–962. Milan: Mondadori, 1992.

VP   De vita et moribus Domini Francisci Petracchi de Florentia
> *De vita et moribus Domini Francisci Petracchi de Florentia*, in *Vite*, 881–991.

Works by Others

Alighieri, Dante. *La Commedia secondo l'antica vulgata*, edited by Giorgio Petrocchi, 4 vols. Florence: Le Lettere, 1994; Milan: Mondadori, 1966–67. Volumes cited as *Inf. = Inferno*, *Purg. = Purgatorio*, *Para. = Paradiso*.

Alighieri, Dante. *The Divine Comedy of Dante Alighieri*, edited by and translated by Robert M. Durling, vols. 1–3. New York and Oxford: Oxford University Press, 1996–2011.

Alighieri, Dante. *Epistole*, edited by Claudia Villa. In Dante Alighieri, *Opere*, edited by Marco Santagata, vol. 2, 1419–1592. Milan: Mondadori, 2014. Cited as *Ep.*

Alighieri, Dante. *Vita Nova*, edited by Guglielmo Gorni. In Dante Alighieri, *Opere*, edited by Marco Santagata, vol. 1, 745–1063. Milan: Mondadori, 2011. Cited as *VN.*

Alighieri, Dante. *Vita Nuova, New Edition: A Translation and an Essay*, translated by Mark Musa. Bloomington: Indiana University Press, 1973.

Alighieri, Dante. *De vulgari eloquentia*, edited by Mirko Tavoni. In Dante Alighieri, *Opere*, edited by Marco Santagata, vol. 1, 1067–1547. Milan: Mondadori, 2011. Cited as *DVE.*

Cavalcanti, Guido. *Rime*, edited by Domenico De Robertis. Turin: Einaudi, 1986.

da Pistoia, Cino. *Rime*. In *Poeti del Duecento*, edited by Gianfranco Contini, vol. 2, 629–90. Milan and Napoli: Ricciardi, 1960.

de Imola, Benvenuto de Rambaldis. *Comentum super Dantis Aldigheri "Comoediam,"* edited by G. W. Vernon and J. Ph. Lacaita. Florence: Barbera, 1887.

Nelli, Francesco. *Lettere a Petrarca*. In *Lettere a Petrarca*, edited by and translated by Ugo Dotti, 21–221. Turin: Aragno, 2012.

Petrarca, Francesco. *The Canzoniere, or, Rerum Vulgarium Fragmenta*, translated by Mark Musa. Bloomington: Indiana University Press, 1999.

Petrarca, Francesco. *Epystole*. In *Epistulae metricae: Briefe in Versen*, edited by Otto and Eva Schönberger. Würzburg: Köninhausen & Neumann, 2004. Cited as *Epyst.*

Petrarca, Francesco. *Lettere disperse, Varie e Miscellanee*, edited by Alessandro Pancheri. Parma: Fondazione Pietro Bembo—Guanda, 1994. Cited as *Disp. (Var.).*

Petrarca, Francesco. *Letters of Old Age*, translated by Aldo S. Bernardo, Saul Levin, and Reta A. Bernardo, 2 vols. New York: Italica Press, 2005.

Petrarca, Francesco. *Letters on Familiar Matters*, translated by Aldo Bernardo, 3 vols. New York: Italica Press, 2005.

Petrarca, Francesco. *Posteritati*. In *Lettera ai posteri*, edited by Gianni Villani. Rome: Salerno Editrice, 1990. Cited as *Post.*

Petrarca, Francesco. *Rerum familiarium libri*. In *Le familiari*, edited by Vittorio Rossi and Umberto Bosco, 4 vols. (vols. 10–13 in the *Edizione nazionale delle opere di Francesco Petrarca*). Florence: Sansoni, 1923–42. Cited as *Fam.*

Petrarca, Francesco. *Rerum vulgarium fragmenta* (*Canzoniere*). In *Canzoniere*, edited by Marco Santagata. Milan: Mondadori, 2004. Cited as *Rvf.*

Petrarca, Francesco. *Res senilium libri*. In *Res seniles*, edited by Silvia Rizzo with Monica Berté. Florence: Le Lettere, 2006–17 (books I–IV [2006], V–VIII [2009], IX–XII [2014], XIII–XVII [2017]). Cited as *Sen.*

Petrarca, Francesco, *Secretum*, edited by Enrico Fenzi. Milan: Mursia, 1992. Cited as *Secr.*

Petrarca, Francesco. *De sui ipsius et multorum ignorantia*. In *De ignorantia: Della mia ignoranza e di quella di molti altri*, edited by Enrico Fenzi. Milan: Mursia, 1999. Cited as *Ign.*

Petrarca, Francesco. *Testamentum*. In *Opere latine*, edited by Antonietta Bufano with Basile Aracri and Clara Kraus Reggiani, with an introduction by Manlio Pastore Stocchi, vol. 2, 1341–57. Turin: UTET, 1975. Cited as *Test.*

Pucci, Antonio. "Legiadro sermintese, pien d'amore." In *La Vita Nuova di Dante Alighieri*, edited by Alessandro D'Ancona, 71–73. Pisa: Nistri, 1872.

Sacchetti, Franco. *Il libro delle rime*, edited by Franca Brambilla Ageno. Florence: Olschki; Perth: University of Western Australia Press, 1990. Cited as *Rime*.

Salutati, Coluccio. *Epistolario*, edited by Francesco Novati, 4 vols. Rome: Tipografia del Senato, 1891–1911 (vols. 1 [1891]; 2 [1893]; 3 [1896]; 4, pts. 1–2 [1905 and 1911]). Cited as *Ep.*

Sennuccio del Bene. *Rime*. In *Un amico del Petrarca: Sennuccio del Bene e le sue rime*. Rome and Padua: Editrice Antenore, 2004.

Villani, Giovanni. *Nuova cronica*, edited by Giuseppe Porta. Parma: Fondazione Pietro Bembo—Guanda, 2007.

NOTES

Chapter One

1. Translation from Giovanni Boccaccio, "Cheaply Have I Abused," in *Italian Poets of the Renaissance*, ed. and trans. Joseph Tusiani (New York: Baroque Press, 1971), 35.

2. *Inf.*, XXX.102–3.

3. On Virgilio's accusations, see Marco Santagata, *Dante: Il romanzo della sua vita* (Milan: Mondadori, 2012), 310–21.

4. "Staturae fuit poeta pinguiusculae, sed procerae, rotunda facie, naso supra nares paululum depresso; labiis turgentibus aliquantulum, venuste tamen lineatis," in *Philippi Villani Liber de origine civitatis Florentie et eiusdem famosis civibus*, ed. Giuliano Tanturli (Padua: Antenore, 1997), 99–104.

5. For a description of the elderly Boccaccio's illnesses, see Pier Giorgio Ricci, *Studi sulla vita e le opere del Boccaccio* (Milan and Naples: Ricciardi, 1985), 170–71. Regarding Boccaccio's difficulty moving because of obesity, see, for example, his letter to Donato Albanzani in 1365, when Boccaccio was only fifty-two: "I would come to you, but my excessive heaviness does not allow it. In fact, neither sour nor salty foods and even less fasting serve to prevent me from becoming fatter, and I have no doubt that this is what will soon bring my death" (*EpA*, 33–34; "Venirem ipse ad vos, sed nimia gravedo non patitur. Nam nec acuta nec salsa prosunt et longe minus ieiunium, quin continue efficiar pinguior, nec iam dubito quin hec sit que propinquam afferat mortem"); and a 1371 letter in which he recounts his exhaustion after walking what was for him a "very onerous" route "because I had to climb from the seashore almost to the top of the city . . . and

I could hardly walk burdened by my great body size" ("etsi michi gravis-
simum esset, nam a litore maris in summum fere per declivium civitatis
ascendere . . . pedibus tamen vix ire possum mole gravatus corporea," *Ep.*,
XIX.6). Boccaccio refers to his own obesity with self-deprecating levity in
the *Decameron* ("Author's Conclusion," 22–23).

On the last page (267v) of ms. Zelada 104.6 of the Archivo y Biblioteca
Capitulares of Toledo the bust of a man in a laurel crown can be made out
with the help of ultraviolet light. Above it is the Latin inscription "Homero
poeta sovrano" and in the lower margin are Greek characters that trans-
literated into Latin characters read "Ioannes de Certaldo p[inx]it." It is
certainly not an idealized portrait; the resemblance to other posthumous
images of Boccaccio and to contemporaries' descriptions support the
notion that this is a self-portrait: see Lucia Battaglia Ricci, "L'Omero di
Boccaccio," *Studi sul Boccaccio* 46 (2018): 78–84. The image, discovered by
Marco Cursi and Sandro Bertelli, is reproduced in Marco Cursi and Maurizio Fiorilla, "Giovanni Boccaccio," in *Autografi dei letterati italiani: Le
origini e il Trecento*, ed. Giuseppina Brunetti, Maurizio Fiorilla, and Marco
Petoletti (Rome: Salerno Editrice, 2013), 103; and Marco Cursi, *La scrittura
e i libri di Giovanni Boccaccio* (Rome: Viella, 2013), plate 9.

The notion of friendly ribbing about his obesity is suggested by
Francisco Rico, *Ritratti allo specchio (Boccaccio, Petrarca)* (Rome and
Padua: Editrice Antenore, 2012), 9. In his will dated April 4, 1370, Petrarca
bequeathed to Boccaccio "fifty Florentine gold florins so that he can buy a
winter robe for nocturnal study and contemplation." Rico observes: since
a bequest of fifty florins "was enough to buy an entire wardrobe," Petrarca wrote that this amount "'is so little for a man so great': because the
Certaldese was a great man . . . terribly fat." However, it seems doubtful
that Petrarca would have allowed himself to ridicule, even implicitly, the
size of a beneficiary in such a serious legal document. Francesco Petrarca,
Testamentum, in *Opere latine*, ed. Antonietta Bufano with Basile Aracri,
and Clara Kraus Reggiani, with an introduction by Manlio Pastore Stocchi
(Turin: UTET, 1975), vol. 2, 1341–57: "Domino Iohanni de Certaldo seu Boccaccii, verecunde admodum tanto viro tam modicum, lego quinquaginta
florenos auri de Florentia pro una veste hiemali ad studium lucubrationesque nocturnas."

6. The friend who called him a "man of glass" was Francesco Nelli (*Ep.*,
XIII). Boccaccio wrote to Zanobi da Strada that Niccolò Acciaiuoli "used to
like to call me 'John of tranquility' with a certain forced laugh" ("solitum
me 'Iohannem tranquillitatum' risu quodam coacto vocitare persepe," *Ep.*,
IX.2).

7. "Nec dubito, dum etas in hoc aptior erat, si equo genitor tulisset
animo, quin inter celebres poetas unus evasissem, verum dum in lucro-
sas artes primo, inde in lucrosam facultatem ingenium flectere conatur
meum, factum est ut nec negociator sim, nec evaderem canonista, et

perderem poetam esse conspicuum" (translation based on Giovanni Boccaccio, *Giovanni Boccaccio, Theseid of the Nuptials of Emilia* [*Teseida delle
nozze di Emilia*], trans. Vincenzo Traversa [New York: Lang, 2002], 5).

8. Translation from Giovanni Boccaccio, *Corbaccio, or the Labyrinth
of Love*, 2nd rev. ed., trans. and ed. Anthony K. Cassell (Binghamton, NY:
Medieval & Renaissance Studies and Texts, 1993), 23.

9. In the absence of documentation, the presumable date of Boccaccio's birth comes from his letter to Mainardo Cavalcanti of August 1372 in
which Boccaccio claims to be in his sixtieth year (*Ep.*, XXI.11); confirmation comes from a letter to Boccaccio from Petrarch, who was born July 20,
1304, written on the day he turned sixty-two in which he states that he
was born nine years earlier than Boccaccio (*Sen.*, VIII.1, 60). The information that Boccaccio's mother was unmarried is contained in the bull of
November 2, 1360, in which Pope Innocent VI confirms previously granted
dispensations for the cleric Giovanni Boccaccio to enjoy ecclesiastical
benefices even though he was illegitimate "de soluto genitus et soluta"
(text of this bull can be found in Giuseppe Billanovich, *Restauri boccacceschi* [Rome: Edizioni di *Storia e letteratura*, 1947], 174–75).

10. That Certaldo could have been Boccaccio's birthplace is suggested
by a passage in his first prose romance in which an oracle asks the titular
protagonist, Filocolo, to honor this place because the Giovanni who will
recount his adventures in writing "is yet to depart" ("si partirà") from
there (*Filoc.*, IV.1, 13). However, in maturity, in a passage in a geographical encyclopedia, Boccaccio professes his veneration for Certaldo as the
place where his ancestors were born and lived before being welcomed
as citizens of Florence, but does not say that he was born there himself
(*De montibus*, V [*De fluminibus*].368); moreover, a letter of his late old age
contrasts Certaldo, his ancestral town, with Florence, called "patria" (*Ep.*,
XXIV.5). In the encyclopedia above he also asserts that the Arno is the
river of his *patria*, which he had known since infancy: although the rivers
are listed alphabetically, he wrote that he would speak of the Arno first
"but not because of the order of the alphabet, but because it was the river
of my native land and known to me before all others from my childhood"
(*De montibus*, V [*De fluminibus*].2; "non quidem tanquam ob licterarum
ordinem meritus, sed quia patrie flumen sit et michi ante alios omnes ab
ipsa infantia cognitus"). On the opposition of Certaldo as land of ancestors to Florence as birth city, see Vittore Branca, *Boccaccio medievale*,
with an introduction by Franco Cardini (Milan: BUR Rizzoli, 2010 [1956]),
296–97. In support of Certaldo as his place of birth is the fact that in
the *Amorosa visione* (Son. Acrostico I.17) he signs himself "Giovanni . . .
di Boccaccio da Certaldo" and also that in the autograph manuscript
Chigiano L. V. 176, where the works of Dante are presented as "del chiarissimo poeta Dante Alighieri di Firenze" the *Canzoniere* of Petrarch as
"poete celeberrimi Francisci Petrarce de Florentia"—he signs himself as

"Johannes Boccaccius de Certaldo florentinus." Among his few recollections of childhood, a recurring one refers to Certaldo and the fossilized shells that are found in great number on the hills and nearby riverbanks: see, for example, the description of the "little knoll" ("picciolo poggio") of Certaldo "full of sea shells" ("pieno di marine cochiglie") "glistening" ("biancheggianti"), "and similarly the rivers which surround it . . . tint their beds with these same shells ("e similmente i fiumi a quellocircunstanti . . . le loro arene di queste medesime cochiglie dipingono") (*Filoc.*, V.8, 1–2; translation from Giovanni Boccaccio, *Il Filocolo*, trans. Donald Cheney with Thomas G. Bergin [New York and London, Garland Publishing, 1985], 379); the phenomenon of the calcareous deposits produced by the Elsa is also described in *De montibus*, V [*De fluminibus*].368, but already noted by Dante, *Purg.*, XXXIII.67.

11. For the coup d'état of the Blacks and Dante's biography, see Santagata, *Dante: Il romanzo della sua vita* (Marco Santagata and Richard Dixon, *Dante: The Story of His Life* [Cambridge, MA, 2016: Belknap Press of Harvard University Press); for Petrarch's biography, see Ernest Hatch Wilkins, *Vita del Petrarca*, new ed., ed. Luca Carlo Rossi, trans. Remo Ceserani (Milano: Feltrinelli, 2003 [1st English ed., 1961]), and Vinicio Pacca, *Petrarca* (Rome and Bari: Laterza, 1998).

12. Translation from Dante Alighieri, *The Divine Comedy of Dante Alighieri, Volume III: Paradiso*, ed. and trans. Robert M. Durling with notes by Ronald L. Martinez and Robert M. Durling (Oxford: Oxford University Press, 2011).

13. Dante, *Paradiso*, trans. Durling, 307.

14. Dante Alighieri, *Inf.*, XVI.73; see also *Para.*, XV.97–99, 130–32.

15. For Boccaccino's biography, see Zelina Zafarana's entry "Boccaccio di Chellino" in *Dizionario biografico degli Italiani* [cited as *DBI*] (Rome: Istituto della Enciclopedia italiana, 1960–), X (1968); for additional information and clarifications, see the various works of Laura Regnicoli ("Documenti su Giovanni Boccaccio," in *Boccaccio autore e copista*, exhibition catalog, ed. Teresa De Robertis, Carla Maria Monti, Marco Petoletti, Giuliano Tanturli, and Stefano Zamponi [Florence: Biblioteca Medicea Laurenziana, October 11, 2013–January 11, 2014] [Florence: Mandragora, 2013], 385–409; "Codice diplomatico di Giovanni Boccaccio 1. I documenti fiscali," *Italia medioevale e umanistica* 54 [2013]: 1–80; "Per la biografia di Giovanni Boccaccio: l'*Elegia di madonna Fiammetta* attraverso i documenti," in *Aimer ou ne pas aimer: Boccace, "Elegia di madonna Fiammetta" et "Corbaccio,"* ed. Anna Pia Filotico, Manuele Gragnolati, and Philippe Guérin [Paris: Presses Sorbonne Nouvelle, 2018], 15–33); a summary of the rich archival documentation regarding him is compiled by Oretta Agostini Muzzi in Guido Pampaloni and Oretta Agostini Muzzi, "Per il 'Codice diplomatico boccaccesco.' Regesto dei documenti," in *Atti del Convegno in-*

ternazionale (Firenze-Certaldo, 22–25 maggio 1975), ed. Francesco Mazzoni (Florence: Olschki, 1978), 627–99.

16. Dante Alighieri, *Para.*, XV.119–20.

17. Dante Alighieri, *Inf.*, VIII.45; "benedetta colei che 'n te s'incinse!"

18. A revision of the poem that Petrarch probably at about the age of fifteen wrote for his mother, Eletta di Gherardo Canigiani, became the *Epyst.*, I.7 (see Arnaldo Foresti, *Aneddoti della vita di Francesco Petrarca*, ed. Antonia Tissoni Benvenuti [Padua: Editrice Antenore, 1977], 13–17): this can be found, with Italian translation, in Francesco Petrarca, *Canzoniere, Trionfi, Rime varie e una scelta di versi latini*, ed. Carlo Muscetta and Daniele Ponchiroli (Torino: Einaudi, 1958), 679–83.

19. Idalogo's birth in Paris to the king's daughter and the shepherd Eucomos is narrated in *Filoc.*, V.8; the same passage then recounts how Eucomos, having abandoned Gannai and returned to a place (Florence?) not far from "his birthplace" ("suo natale sito," Certaldo), married Garemirta, probably an anagram of Margherita, Boccaccino's first wife. In the *Comedia delle ninfe fiorentine* (XXIII.21–39), Emilia narrates the adventures of another literary stand-in for Boccaccio, Ibrida, who was also born in Paris to a young widow whom his father, just like Eucomos, then betrayed by secretly marrying another woman. Another autobiographical character in this same work, Caleone, revels that he was born in France and brought to Tuscany as a child (XXXV.72).

20. Translation from Giovanni Boccaccio, *Amorosa visione*, trans. Robert Hollander, Timothy Hampton, and Margherita Frankel (Hanover, NH: University Press of New England, 1986).

21. Francesco di Boccaccino would be emancipated in August 1333, when he was "proximum pubertatis," that is, about thirteen (see Vittore Branca, *Giovanni Boccaccio: Profilo biografico* [Florence: Sansoni, 1977 (1967)], 53).

22. Translation from Giovanni Boccaccio, *Boccaccio's Expositions on Dante's "Comedy,"* trans. Michael Papio (Toronto: University of Toronto Press, 2009), 126.

23. The identification of Lippa as the "trusted source" who provided Boccaccio with information about Bice (Beatrice) Portinari is Michele Barbi's, *Problemi di critica dantesca: Seconda serie (1920–1937)* (Florence: Sansoni, 1941; repr. 1975), 415–20. Convinced that Boccaccio had returned to Florence in 1339, and not, as actually happened, in the autumn of 1340, Barbi believed that the conversations about Dante with Lippa, who died shortly before June 1340, would have taken place in the months following Boccaccio's return from Naples. For the contiguity of the Mardoli and Alighieri residences, see Domenico Tordi, *Attorno a Giovanni Boccaccio: Gl'inventari dell'eredità di Iacopo Boccaccio* (Orvieto: Rubeca & Scaletti, 1923), 81.

24. Translation from Giovanni Boccaccio, *Il Filocolo*, trans. Donald Cheney with Thomas G. Bergin (New York and London: Garland Publishing, 1985), 381.

25. Michele Barbi also hypothesized that the two ravenous bears of the story of Idalogo were Boccaccio's stepmother ("first cause of disaffection toward the poor bastard") and her mother: Barbi, *Problemi di critica dantesca: Seconda serie (1920–1937)*.

26. For an introduction to Florentine education in the thirteenth and fourteenth centuries, see Richard A. Goldthwaite, *L'economia della Firenze rinascimentale* (Bologna: il Mulino, 2013), 113–26. The biography and activities of Zanobi da Strada are reconstructed in Marco Baglio, "Zanobi da Strada," in *Autografi dei letterati italiani: Le origini e il Trecento*, ed. Giuseppina Brunetti, Maurizio Fiorilla, and Marco Petoletti (Rome: Salerno Editrice, 2013), 321–25, and Marco Baglio, "*Avidulus glorie*: Zanobi da Strada tra Boccaccio e Petrarca," *Italia medioevale e umanistica* 54 (2013): 43–395; those of Niccolò Acciaiuoli in Francesco Paolo Tocco, *Niccolò Acciaiuoli: Vita e politica in Italia alla metà del XIV secolo* (Rome: Istituto storico italiano per il Medioevo, 2001). Niccolò Acciaiuoli followed the same educational path as Boccaccio, and although he then sought to give himself an education and make himself "cultured," he remained a "man without Latin" (Giuseppe Billanovich, "L'altro stil nuovo: Da Dante teologo a Petrarca filologo," *Studi petrarcheschi* 11 [1994]: 22). In his rancorous portrait in the letter to Nelli of 1363 (*Ep.*, XIII.163–79), Boccaccio heavily mocks Acciaiuoli's cultural pretensions and his way of speaking, typical of those who, knowing "a little Latin grammar" ("un poco di grammatica"), pretend to knowledge they do not have, and Boccaccio concludes that, although nature had given him an "admirable bent for literature" ("ammirabile attitudine alla letteratura"), Acciaiuoli had not cultivated it through study, and as is well known, "things in the vernacular cannot make someone a man of letters" ("le cose volgari non possono fare uno uomo litterato").

27. "fere maturus etate et mei iuris factus, nemine inpellente, nemine docente, imo obsidente patre"; "cum nondum novissem quibus seu quot pedibus carmen incederet, . . . poeta fere a notis omnibus vocatus fui." Translation from Boccaccio, *Theseid of the Nuptials of Emilia*, trans. Traversa.

28. Remigio Sabbadini cited by Michele Feo, "Spighe," in *Vetustatis indagator: Scritti offerti a Filippo De Benedetto*, ed. Vincenzo Fera and Augusto Guida (Messina: Centro interdipartimentale di Studi umanistici, 1999), 315.

29. "Apparò la grammatica da grande, e per questa cagione non ebbe mai la lingua molto in sua balìa," Leonardo Bruni, "Vite di Dante e del Petrarca" in *Opere letterarie e politiche*, ed. Paolo Viti (Torino: UTET, 1996), 558. Mitigating Bruni's harsh judgement, Monica Berté observes that

Boccaccio's glosses on the Terence codex (ms. Laurenziano Pluteo 38.17) in the first half of the 1340s "reveal a remarkable 'philological sensibility,' all the more surprising" since some of them date to "well before he met Petrarch," Monica Berté and Marco Cursi, "Novità su Giovanni Boccaccio: Un numero monografico di *Italia medioevale e umanistica*," *Studi sul Boccaccio* 43 (2015): 242.

30. For the decisive role of the Bardi, Acciaiuoli, and Peruzzi in the Neapolitan economy during the reign of Robert of Anjou, see Tocco, *Niccolò Acciaiuoli: Vita e politica in Italia alla metà del XIV secolo*, 11–17; and Goldthwaite, *L'economia della Firenze rinascimentale*, 318–19.

31. Branca, *Giovanni Boccaccio: Profilo biografico*, 14—repeating to the letter an assertion of Francesco Torraca, "Giovanni Boccaccio a Napoli (1326–1339)," *Archivio Storico per le Province Napoletane* 39 (1914): 27, in turn based on an archival document, now lost, copied by Giuseppe de Blasiis ("La dimora di Giovanni Boccaccio a Napoli," *Archivio storico per le Province Napoletane* 17 [1892]: 79–102; 485–516; the document on 506)—writes that Boccaccino "was named by Charles as one of the three councillors of the Ufficio di Mercanzia." Laura Regnicoli points out to me that since there were five councillors not three and since the Duke of Calabria would not have twisted Florentine law to the extent of appointing a councillor rather than having him elected, it was probably an office of adjunct councillor.

32. Boccaccino was appointed factor of the Bardi firm's Neapolitan office on October 12, 1327, and his presence in Naples is attested on November 30 (Branca, *Giovanni Boccaccio: Profilo biografico*, 12). It is not possible to establish the precise date of Boccaccio's arrival. The statement in his 1363 letter to Nelli that "I lived, from my childhood to the age I was fully grown, in Naples" (*Ep.*, XIII.37; "Io sono vivuto, dalla mia puerizia infino in intera età nutricato, a Napoli"), would lead us to about the age of fourteen, that is to 1327, which agrees sufficiently with his assertion in the *Genealogia* that he had been apprenticed "when I had not yet become a young man" (*GDG*, XV.10, 7; "adolescientiam nondum intrantem"). It is always risky to derive chronological information from fictional writing; however, it is at least suggestive that in the *Comedia delle ninfe fiorentine*, Caleone, a character, as has been noted, with strong autobiographical features, reports that he met Fiammetta in the church of San Lorenzo seven years and four months after his arrival in Naples (*CNF*, XXXV.73–105): since numerous clues lead to a date of March 30, 1336, for that first meeting, subtracting seven years and four months we arrive at the late autumn of 1328. However, bearing in mind that Boccaccio counted years using the Florentine convention, in which they begin on March 25, and that here the distinction between one year and the next was only five days, it is also possible that he instinctively thought back to the autumn of 1327.

33. The fact that the family moved to Certaldo is based on a notarial

act of November 19, 1329, in which Lippa Portinari, who had by this point been living in her son-in-law's house for many years, appears residing "in castro Certaldi"; a second document of February 22, 1334, attests that she was living in Florence in the parish of Santa Felicita, where she still lived in 1338. On August 21, 1333, Boccaccino emancipated Francesco, who was not yet fourteen, and who on that same day, serving as a front for his father, bought a house in Santa Felicita. It is likely, therefore, that this is the house where Lippa lived in 1334 (obviously with the rest of the family) and also (as Branca, *Giovanni Boccaccio: Profilo biografico*, 12, dubiously hypothesizes) that Boccaccino had sold the house in Porta San Piero before leaving for Naples (documents cited in Laura Regnicoli, "Un'oscura vicenda certaldese: Nuovi documenti su Boccaccio e la sua famiglia," *Italia medioevale e umanistica* 43 [2017]: 75–76, and Regnicoli, "Per la biografia di Giovanni Boccaccio: l'*Elegia di madonna Fiammetta* attraverso i documenti," 8–9).

34. See Reinhold C. Mueller, "Boccaccino, Giovanni Boccaccio, and Venice," *Studi sul Boccaccio* 25 (1997): 133–42.

35. Billanovich, "L'altro stil nuovo: Da Dante teologo a Petrarca filologo," 50, hypothesizes that "during his years of the *Filostrato* and the four *dictamina*," Boccaccio returned "to Florence from Naples a few times: probably during the long university vacations." And Lucia Battaglia Ricci, *Ragionare nel giardino: Boccaccio e i cicli pittorici del "Trionfo della Morte"* (Rome: Salerno Editrice, 1987), 175–78, convinced that "the frame of the Decameron contains an allusion [*citazione ribaltata*] to the image of the happy brigade in the garden" of the *Trionfo della Morte* fresco of the Camposanto in Pisa, hypothesizes that Boccaccio, "traveling to and from Naples, passed through" Pisa, and that these trips could only have been before 1340.

Chapter Two

1. "Meque adolescientiam nondum intrantem, arismetrica instructum, maximo mercatori dedit discipulum, quem penes sex annis nil aliud egi quam non recuperabile tempus in vacuum terere."

2. A fuller reconstruction of Boccaccio's apprenticeship can be found in Marco Santagata, *Boccaccio indiscreto: Il mito di Fiammetta* (Bologna: il Mulino, 2019), 7–29. It has frequently been pointed out that the youthful years retraced in the *Genealogia* show the influence of Ovid's autobiography depicted in the *Tristia*, in particular where Ovid writes that his own father opposed his early attraction to poetry because he considered this activity too unprofitable. While his brother was practicing oratory, Ovid was irresistibly seduced by the Muses, and his father often reproved him, citing the example of Homer: "But to me even as a boy service of the divine gave delight and stealthily the Muse was ever drawing me aside to do her

work. Often my father said, 'Why do you try a profitless pursuit? Even the Maeonian left no wealth'" ("At mihi iam puero caelestia sacra placebant, / inque suum furtim Musa trahebat opus. / Saepe pater dixit: 'studium quid inutile temptas? / Maeonides nullas ipse reliquit opes,'" *Tristia*, IV.10, 19–22; translation from Ovid, *Tristia; Ex Ponto*, translated by Arthur Leslie Wheeler, 2nd ed., revised by G. P. Goold (Cambridge, MA: Harvard University Press, and London: W. Heinemann, 1988). Ovid's shadow, however, does not detract from the documentary value of the Boccaccio passage. The force of lived experience, in fact, was so great that, as we will see, Boccaccio projected his own experiences onto Petrarca's life.

3. "Soleva essere, e forse che ancora oggi è, una usanza in tutte le terre marine che hanno porto così fatta, che tutti i mercatanti che in quelle con mercatantie capitano, faccendole scaricare, tutte in un fondaco, il quale in molti luoghi è chiamato dogana, tenuta per lo comune o per lo signor della terra, le portano; e quivi, dando a coloro che sopra ciò sono per iscritto tutta la mercatantia e il pregio di quella, è dato per li detti al mercatante un magazzino nel quale esso la sua mercatantia ripone e serralo con la chiave; e li detti doganieri poi scrivono in su il libro della dogana a ragione del mercatante tutta la sua mercatantia, faccendosi poi del loro diritto pagare al mercatante o per tutta o per parte della mercatantia che egli della dogana traesse. E da questo libro della dogana assai volte s'informano i sensali e delle qualità e delle quantità delle mercatantie che vi son, e ancora chi sieno i mercatanti che l'hanno; con li quali poi essi, secondo che lor cade per mano, ragionan di cambi, di baratti e di vendite e d'altri spacci." Translation from Giovanni Boccaccio, *The Decameron*, trans. Wayne A. Rebhorn (New York and London: W. W. Norton, 2013), 677–78.

4. For the Gaeta customhouse, see Robert Davidsohn, *Storia di Firenze*, 8 vols. (Florence: Sansoni, Firenze, 1956–68), originally published in German (Berlin: Mittler und Sohn, 1896–1927), 805. Francesco or Franceschino d'Alessandro dei Bardi was a close friend of Boccaccio's, the one to whom he sent a comical letter in Neapolitan dialect (*Lett.*, I) and whom he visited for business in Gaeta itself. Moreover, in the *Decameron* story in which he describes the Palermo (actually Gaeta) warehouse familiar faces appear: the young protagonist Niccolò da Cignano called Salabaetto certainly existed, even if we do not have definite information about him (Vittore Branca, *Giovanni Boccaccio: Profilo biografico* [Florence: Sansoni, 1977 (1967)], 22, calls him "an agent of the Frescobaldi and later head of the *Arte del Cambio*"; Giovanni Boccaccio, *Decameron*, ed. Vittore Branca [Turin: Einaudi, 1980], 1010, nominates instead one Niccolò di Cecco da Cignano, perhaps of the *Compagnia degli Scali*, "ruler of the cloth trade in the Kingdom of Naples"); but we know well the other Florentine who appears here, Pietro or Piero Canigiani, "a man of great intellect and subtle genius," who suggests to Cignano the counterdeception with which to trick the prostitute Jancofiore: he was one of Boccaccio's most faith-

ful friends (see the biographical profile by Michael Mallett in *DBI*, XVIII [1975], the entry "Canigiani, Piero").

5. "Tuorum fervens amor habendi, te invito, de pio sinu Rachelis ad Lie gremium transtulerunt."

6. Translation from Giovanni Boccaccio, *Boccaccio's Expositions on Dante's Comedy*, trans. Michael Papio (Toronto and Buffalo, NY: University of Toronto Press, 2009), 364.

7. "ogni piccolo movimento ora in Inghilterra, ora in Fiandra, ora in Ispagna, ora in Cipri, ora in una parte e ora in un'altra, sollicitando, ricordando, avvisando, li fa scrivere non lettere, ma vilumi [volumi] a' lor compagni; e, inanzi tratto [anzitutto], sempre con sospetto l'aportate [lettere] ricevono; ogni vento gli tien sospesi a' loro navili; né sì piccolo romore di guerra nasce che essi incontanente non temano delle mercantantie messe in cammino; e quanti sensali parlan loro, tanti fan loro mutare animi e consigli."

8. Translation from Boccaccio, *Boccaccio's Expositions on Dante's Comedy*, trans. Papio, 165.

9. "Mercantium habitu palliatus, sacra studia septabaris, et aquas elyconici fontis furtive gustabas avidius, magis quam palam tunc tuo gucturi dulciores."

10. It is interesting to observe that the "furtive" of letter IV echoes the "inque suum furtim Musa trahebat opus" of Ovid's *Tristia*, IV.10, 20, and that the concept, if not the words, would return in Boccaccio's biography of Petrarch (*VP*, 7): "se poesi patre eciam ignorante donavit" ("unbeknownst to his father, he gave himself to poetry").

11. Giuseppe Billanovich, *Petrarca e il primo umanesimo* (Padua: Antenore, 1996), 461; see also Valeria Cotza, "Sulle orme di Dante tra Napoli e la Romagna: Boccaccio e Giovanni del Virgilio," in *Boccaccio e la Romagna* [cited as *BR*], Atti del Convegno di studi (Forlì, Salone comunale, November 22–23, 2013), ed. Gabriella Albanese and Paolo Pontari (Ravenna: Longo, 2015), 207–23, esp. 207–11.

12. Francesco Sabatini, *Napoli angioina: Cultura e società* (Naples: ESI Edizioni, 1975), 67–91, provides an overview of Neapolitan culture in the age of Robert of Anjou. For the influence of transalpine language and literature on the culture of the kingdom, see Giorgio Padoan, *Il Boccaccio, le Muse, il Parnaso e l'Arno* (Florence: Olschki, 1978), 8–9, and Laura Minervini, "Il francese a Napoli (1266–1442): Elementi per una storia linguistica," in *Boccaccio e Napoli: Nuovi materiali per la storia culturale di Napoli nel Trecento* [cited as *BN*], Atti del Convegno "Boccaccio angioino: Per il VII centenario della nascita di Giovanni Boccaccio" (Napoli-Salerno, October 23–25, 2013), ed. Giancarlo Alfano, Emma Grimaldi, Sebastiano Martelli, Andrea Mazzucchi, Matteo Palumbo, Alessandra Perriccioli Saggese, and Carlo Vecce (Florence: Franco Cesati, 2015), 151–74. For a synthetic picture, see Nicola De Blasi, "Ambiente urbano e linguistico di Napoli

angioina (con testimonianze da Boccaccio)," *Lingua e stile* 44 (2009): 173–208. Padoan, *Il Boccaccio, le Muse, il Parnaso e l'Arno*, 7, also advances "the very strong suspicion that Boccaccio also drew on Byzantine stories, which he could perhaps have known through vernacular translations or oral tradition."

13. Translation from Boccaccio, *Boccaccio's Expositions on Dante's Comedy*, trans. Papio, 282.

14. "Fuit diu magister et custos bibliothecae Roberti . . . Ego iuvenculus adhuc . . . ex illo multa avidus potius quam intelligens sumpsi." For the biography of Andalò del Negro, see the entry "Di Negro, Andalò," in *DBI*, XL (1991) by Maria Muccillo; from the rich scholarly literature dedicated to the relationship between Boccaccio and Andalò del Negro, I would single out, in addition to the classic Antonio E. Quaglio, *Scienza e mito nel Boccaccio* (Padua: Liviana, 1967), two more recent works: Doris Ruhe, "Boccace astronomien?," in *Gli Zibaldoni di Boccaccio: Memoria, scrittura, riscrittura* [cited as *ZB*], Atti del seminario internazionale di Firenze-Certaldo (April 26–28, 1996), ed. Michelangelo Picone and Claude Cazalé Bérard (Florence: Franco Cesati, 1998), 65–79; and Michele Rinaldi, "I saperi astrologici della Napoli angioina: *Introductorium ad iudicia astrologie* di Andalò di Negro," in *BN*, 245–66. For Paolo da Perugia, see Sabatini, *Napoli angioina: Cultura e società*, 77–78; Giovanni Boccaccio, *Genealogie deorum gentilium*, ed. Vittorio Zaccaria, in *Tutte le opere*, ed. Vittore Branca, vols. 7–8 (Milan: Mondadori, 1998), 1611–12; and, above all, Giuseppe Billanovich, *La tradizione del testo di Livio e le origini dell'umanesimo*, vol. 1, *Tradizione e fortuna di Livio tra Medioevo e umanesimo* (Padua: Editrice Antenore, 1981), 38–40.

15. Today this codex is divided into two independent books: ms. Laur. 29.8, known as the "Zibaldone Laurenziano," and Laur. 33.31, called "Miscellanea Laurenziana" (the original organization is reconstructed in Marco Petoletti, "Gli zibaldoni di Giovanni Boccaccio," in *Boccaccio autore e copista*, exhibition catalog, ed. Teresa De Robertis, Carla Maria Monti, Marco Petoletti, Giuliano Tanturli, and Stefano Zamponi [Florence: Biblioteca Medicea Laurenziana, October 11, 2013–January 11, 2014] [Florence: Mandragora, 2013], 305–13). The book's genesis and phases of growth have been identified and describe in the fundamental Stefano Zamponi, Martina Pantarotto, and Antonella Tomiello, "Stratigrafia dello Zibaldone e della Miscellanea laurenziani," in *Gli Zibaldoni di Boccaccio: Memoria, scrittura, riscrittura*, conference proceedings, ed. Michelangelo Picone and Claude Cazalé Bérard (Florence: Certaldo, April 26–28, 1996) (Florence: Franco Cesati, 1998), 181–243. Among the texts copied prior to 1334 are a chapter of the *Liber philosophorum moralium antiquorum*, the Latin version of a Castilian work written at the court of Alfonso the Wise (1221–84); the *Chronica de origine civitatis Florentie* from the first decades of the thirteenth century; the very widely circulated apocryphal

epistle from Alexander the Great to Aristotle, *De miraculis Indiae*. The two works of Andalò del Negro are the *Tractatus spere materialis* and the *Tractatus theorice planetarum* (unfinished). Teresa De Robertis, "Boccaccio copista," in *Boccaccio autore e copista*, exhibition catalog, ed. Teresa De Robertis, Carla Maria Monti, Marco Petoletti, Giuliano Tanturli, and Stefano Zamponi (Florence: Biblioteca Medicea Laurenziana, October 11, 2013–January 11, 2014) (Florence: Mandragora, 2013), 329–35, provides a picture of Boccaccio as a copyist; a depiction that includes his marginal notes is provided by Marco Cursi and Maurizio Fiorilla, "Giovanni Boccaccio," in *Autografi dei letterati italiani: Le origini e il Trecento*, ed. Giuseppina Brunetti, Maurizio Fiorilla, and Marco Petoletti (Rome: Salerno Editrice, 2013); for a synthetic look at the autograph codex of the *Decameron* (Hamilton 90 in the Staatsbibliothek of Berlino), see Marco Cursi, "L'autografo berlinese del *Decameron*," in *Boccaccio autore e copista*, exhibition catalog, ed. Teresa De Robertis, Carla Maria Monti, Marco Petoletti, Giuliano Tanturli, and Stefano Zamponi (Florence: Biblioteca Medicea Laurenziana, October 11, 2013–January 11, 2014) (Florence: Mandragora, 2013), 137–38.

16. "Giotto ebbe uno ingegno di tanta eccellenzia, che niuna cosa dà la natura . . . che egli con lo stile e con la penna o col pennello non dipignesse sì simile a quella, che non simile, anzi più tosto dessa paresse, in tanto che molte volte nelle cose da lui fatte si truova che il visivo senso degli uomini vi prese errore, quello credendo esser vero che era dipinto." Translation based on Boccaccio, *Decameron*, trans. Rebhorn, 488.

17. For Boccaccio's possible acquaintance with Giotto, hypothesized by Boccaccio, *Decameron*, 737, see Padoan, *Il Boccaccio, le Muse, il Parnaso e l'Arno*, 26–29, and Lucia Battaglia Ricci, "Immaginario trionfale: Petrarca e la tradizione figurativa," in *I Triumphi di Francesco Petrarca, Gargnano del Garda (1–3 ottobre 1998)*, ed. Claudia Berra (Bologna: Cisalpino, n.d.), 255–98, at 280–86. On the naturalistic conception of figurative art, see Boccaccio in *ECD*, XI.69. For the troop of painters (Giovannozzo [Nozzo] di Perino called Calandrino, Nello di Dino or Bandino, Bonamico di Cristofano called Buffalmacco, Bruno di Giovanni d'Olivieri) repeatedly evoked in the *Decameron*, see Marco Santagata, "Un tassello per Calandrino pittore," in *Per civile conversazione: Con Amedeo Quondam*, ed. Beatrice Alfonzetti, Guido Baldassarri, Eraldo Bellini, Simona Costa, and Marco Santagata (Rome: Bulzoni Editore, 2014), 1031–37. There is an abundant literature on Boccaccio's drawing: for a basic orientation, see Francesca Pasut, "Boccaccio disegnatore," in *Boccaccio autore e copista* [cited as *BAC*], catalogo della mostra (Florence, Biblioteca Medicea Laurenziana, October 11, 2013–January, 11 2014), ed. Teresa De Robertis, Carla Maria Monti, Marco Petoletti, Giuliano Tanturli, and Stefano Zamponi (Florence: Manragora, 2013), 51–59.

18. Translation from Giovanni Boccaccio, *The Elegy of Lady Fiammetta*,

ed. and trans. Mariangela Causa-Steindler and Thomas Mauch (Chicago: University of Chicago Press, 1990), 72.

19. "Quivi la maggior parte del tempo ozioso trapassa, e qualora più è messo in essercizio, si è in amorosi ragionamenti, o le donne per sé, o mescolate co' giovani; quivi non s'usano vivande se non dilicate, e vini per antichità nobilissimi, possenti non che ad eccitare la dormente Venere, ma a risuscitare la morta in ciascuno uomo; e quanto ancora in ciò la virtù de' bagni diversi adoperi, queli il può sapere che l'ha provato. Quivi i marini liti e i graziosi giardini, e ciascheduna altra parte, sempre di varie feste, di nuovi giuochi, di bellissime danze, d'infiniti strumenti, d'amorose canzoni, così da giovini come da donne fatti, sonate e cantate risuonano. Tengasi adunque chi può quivi, tra tante cose, contra Cupido, il quale quivi, per quello ch'io creda, sì come in luogo principalissimo de' suoi regni, aiutato da tante cose, con poca fatica usa le forze sue." Translation from Boccaccio, *The Elegy of Lady Fiammetta*, ed. and trans. Causa-Steindler and Mauch, 73.

20. "Quivi si vedevano in molte parti le mense candidissime poste e di cari ornamenti sì belle, che solo il riguardarle aveva forza di risvegliare l'appetito in qualunque più fosse stato svogliato; e in altra parte, già richiedendolo l'ora, si discernevano alcuni prendere lietamente li matutini cibi; da' quali e noi e quale altro passava con allegra voce alle loro letizie eravamo convitati. Ma poi che noi medesimi avavamo, sì come gli altri, mangiato con grandissima festa, e dopo le levate mense più giri dati in liete danze al modo usato, risalite sopra le barche, subitamente or qua e ora colà n'andavamo. E in alcuna parte cosa carissima agli occhi de' giovini n'appariva; ciò erano vaghissime giovani in giubbe di zendado spogliate, iscalze e isbracciate nell'acqua andanti dalle dure pietre levando le marine conche; e a cotale uficio bassandosi, sovente le nascose delizie dello uberifero petto mostravano. E in alcuna altra con più ingegno, altri con reti, e quali con più nuovi artificii, alli nascosi pesci si vedevano pescare." Translation from Boccaccio, *The Elegy of Lady Fiammetta*, ed. and trans. Causa-Steindler and Mauch, 83–84.

21. Also on Baia as corruptor, see sonnet IV [LXXII].1–10: "Perir possa il tuo nome, Baia, e lloco . . . ché hai corrotto la più castamente, / che fosse in donna, colla tua licenza." For the group of sonnets that might be considered a "Baia cycle," see Ilaria Tufano, "Forme e temi delle Rime di Boccaccio," in *Boccaccio in versi* [cited as *BV*], Atti del Convegno (Parma, March 13–14, 2014), ed. Pantalea Mazzitello, Giulia Raboni, Paolo Rinoldi, and Carlo Varotti (Florence: Franco Cesati, 2016), 231–41, at 238–41.

22. Translation from Rinaldina Russell, ed. and trans., *Sonnet: The Very Rich and Varied World of the Italian Sonnet* (Bloomington, IN: Archway, 2017), 184.

23. "Tra l'altre cose, nelle quali essa [Napoli] appare splendidissima, è

nel sovente armeggiare. Suole adunque essere questa a noi consuetudine antiquata, che poi che i guazzosi tempi del verno sono trapassati, e la primavera con li fiori e con la nuova erba ha al mondo rendute le sue perdute bellezze, essendo con questo li giovaneschi animi per la qualità del tempo raccesi e più che l'usato pronti a dimostrare li loro disii, di convocare li dí più solenni alle logge de' cavalieri le nobili donne; le quali, ornate delle loro gioie più care, quivi s'adunano. . . . Quivi tra cotanta e così nobile compagnia, non lungamente si siede, né vi si tace, né mormora; ma stanti gli antichi uomini a riguardare, li chiari giovini, prese le donne per le dilicate mani, danzando, con altissime voci cantano i loro amori; e in cotale guisa con quante maniere di gioia si possono divisare, la calda parte del giorno trapassano. E poi che 'l sole ha cominciato a dare più tiepidi li suoi raggi, si veggono quivi venire gli onorevoli prencipi del nostro Ausonico regno [del Regno di Napoli] in quello abito che alla loro magnificenza si richiede. Li quali, poi che alquanto hanno e le bellezze delle donne e le loro danze rimirate, quasi con tutti li giovini, così cavalieri come donzelli, partendosi, dopo non lungo spazio in abito tutto al primo contrario con grandissima comitiva ritornano. . . . Dico adunque, al proposito ritornando, che li nostri prencipi sopra cavalli tanto nel correr veloci, che non che gli altri animali, ma li venti medesimi, qualunque piú si crede festino, di dietro correndo si lascerieno, vengono, la cui giovinetta età, la speziosa bellezza, e la virtù espettabile d'essi, graziosi li rende oltre modo ai riguardanti. Essi di porpora o di drappi dalle indiane mani tessuti, con lavorii di colori varii e d'oro intermisti, e oltre a ciò sopraposti di perle e di care pietre, vestiti, e i cavalli coverti, appariscono; de' quali i biondi crini, penduli sopra li candidissimi omeri, da sottiletto cerchiello d'oro o da ghirlandetta di fronda novella sono sopra la testa ristretti. Quindi la sinistra un leggierissimo scudo, e la destra mano arma una lancia, e al suono delle tostane trombe, l'uno appresso l'altro, e seguiti da molti, tutti in cotale abito cominciano davanti alle donne il giuoco loro, colui lodando più in esso, il quale con la lancia più vicino alla terra con la sua punta, e meglio chiuso sotto lo scudo, senza muoversi sconciamente [goffamente], dimora, correndo sopra il cavallo. . . . Essendo adunque la lieta schiera due o tre volte cavalcando con picciolo passo dimostratasi a' circustanti, cominciavano i loro aringhi, e dritti sopra le staffe, chiusi sotto gli scudi, con le punte delle lievi lance, tuttavia igualmente portandole, quasi rasente terra, velocissimi più che aura alcuna corrono i loro cavalli; e l'aere esultante per le voci del popolo circustante, per li molti sonagli, per li diversi strumenti, e per la percossa del riverberante mantello del cavallo e di sé, a meglio e più vigoroso correre li rinfranca." Translation from *The Elegy of Lady Fiammetta*, ed. and trans. Causa-Steindler and Mauch, 85–89.

24. Translation from Giovanni Boccaccio, *L'Ameto*, trans. Judith Serafini-Sauli (New York: Garland Publishing, 1985), 143.

25. *Fam.*, V.6. Branca, *Giovanni Boccaccio: Profilo biografico*, 21, speaks of

the gladiatorial combat described by Petrarch as if it were a joust. Mention of these sorts of bloody spectacles can be found in Jean François de Sade, *Mémoires pour la vie de François Pétrarque, tirés de ses œuvres et des auteurs contemporaines* (Amsterdam: Arskée & Mercus, 1764), vol. 2, 169–71; and Matteo Camera, *Annali delle Due Sicilie*, vol. 2 (Naples: Stamperia del Fibreno, 1860), 504. For jousting and martial games in Boccaccio's works (particularly the *Teseida*), see Rita Librandi, "Corte e cavalleria della Napoli angioina nel *Teseida* del Boccaccio," *Medioevo Romanzo* 4 (1977): 33–72.

26. Francesco Bruni, *Boccaccio: L'invenzione della letteratura mediana* (Bologna: il Mulino, 1990), 142, rightly observes that this passage is "centered more on relations with court circles than direct acquaintance or somehow associating with the king."

27. For a fuller analysis of the poem, see Santagata, *Boccaccio indiscreto: Il mito di Fiammetta*, 31–51. The piece of evidence for dating the *Caccia di Diana* to before 1334 advanced by *Un primo elenco dei codici e tre studi* (Rome: Edizioni di *Storia e letteratura*, 1958; repr. 2014), 190–92—namely, the fact that in this year the name of Mitola Caracciolo, one of the women participating in the hunt, does not appear in a notarial act dividing some property of one of her deceased great-grandmothers, which could mean that Mitola was no longer alive in 1334—is too weak to be considered conclusive, as Branca himself recognizes.

28. Translation from Giovanni Boccaccio, *Diana's Hunt (Caccia di Diana): Boccaccio's First Fiction*, ed. and trans. Anthony K. Cassell and Victoria Kirkham (Philadelphia: University of Pennsylvania Press, 1991), 149.

29. Translation from Boccaccio, *Diana's Hunt*, ed. and trans. Cassell and Kirkham, 151.

30. Translation from Boccaccio, *Diana's Hunt*, ed. and trans. Cassell and Kirkham, 147 and 151.

31. The tendency to read the *Caccia* as an allegorical text has become popular, particularly in the Anglo-Saxon context, a tendency favored by the implicit allegorical valence of the myths evoked and by the fact that in the Middle Ages animals, especially the fantastical ones of the bestiaries, were very often interpreted allegorically or at least symbolically—and in this poem, animals, real and fantastical, abound. The work's American editors (Boccaccio, *Diana's Hunt*, ed. and trans Cassell and Kirkham) provide a reading that Lucia Battaglia Ricci, *Boccaccio* (Rome: Salerno Editrice, 2000), 73, summarizes thus: "A story of the soul's struggle between good and evil, in which the transformation of the animals captured by the women into handsome young men who run to immerse themselves in a stream and then cover themselves in vermilion cloaks would signify the purifying function of baptism"; but she continues, asserting that "the fragile mythological and allegorical plot . . . is subordinated to the intent to celebrate the beautiful women of the court."

The idea that love creates humanness will find its fullest expression in the story of the shepherd Ameto who, thanks to Amore, sheds his (bestial uncouthness) and achieves a fully realized human identity, and its clearest formulation in the *Amorosa visione* (XLII.73–75): "A life that endures without him [Amore/Love] is worth nothing; neither more nor less than if it were the life of brute animal or deprived of all senses" ("Vita che sanza lui [Amore] dura non vale / né più né meno che se ella fosse / cosa insensata o d'un bruto animale"; translation from Boccaccio, *Amorosa visione*, trans. Hollander et al., 173). This theme will reappear repeatedly in the Florentine texts from the early 1340s forward, up to the story of Cimone (*Dec.*, V.1), the "great lumbering fool" ("bestione") whom the bittersweet stimulus of Love transforms "from a senseless beast into a man" ("da insensato animale ... a essere uomo"; translation from Boccaccio, *Decameron*, trans. Rebhorn, 399).

32. "La bella donna il cui nome si tace," the principal protagonist of the *Caccia*, is a fictional character. This could be brought into doubt if, on the slim basis of the resemblance between the line "che nel viso d'amor sempre parch'arda" ("whose face seems always to burn with love"; translation from Boccaccio, *Diana's Hunt*, ed. and trans. Cassell and Kirkham, 107) of the *CD*, IV.12 and the line "Nel viso che d'amor sempre par ch'arda" ("Into the face which seems to burn always with love"; translation from Boccaccio, *Amorosa Visione*, trans. Hollander et al.) of *AV*, XL.64, she is identified (as Branca proposed, albeit with much caution: Branca, *Tradizione delle opere di Giovanni Boccaccio*, I. *Un primo elenco dei codici e tre studi*, 188–89; Giovanni Boccaccio, *Amorosa visione*, ed. Vittore Branca, in *Tutte le opere*, ed. Vittore Branca, vol. 3 [Milan: Mondadori, 1974], 717–18) with the extraordinarily good looking "bella lombarda" of the *Amorosa visione*— who already appeared with the name Vanna in the *Contento quasi ne' pensier' d'amore* (*Rime*, 125a, 46–48), where she is also said to be of the greatest beauty ("nulla" is "più bella" than she)—and perhaps, but it is far from certain, also with the "formosa ligura" Acrimonia in the *Comedia delle ninfe fiorentine*, who exceeds "all the nymphs in beauty" (XXIX.19; "di bellezza tutte le ninfe"). And yet, it is difficult to believe that, in a work with a tone of such gallantry, Boccaccio would have placed ahead of all of the noblewomen of Naples in both beauty and virtue a stranger who was perhaps passing through Naples and perhaps connected to the Florentine context, going as far as to identify her as a leader of the others, who receive honors directly from her, and to assign as her weapon for the hunt no less than an eagle, king of the raptors. Too many clues support the conclusion that the unnamed beauty never existed—in contrast to Branca's (at least early) belief that "the beautiful woman ... is perhaps one of the women loved with such easy transport by Boccaccio before his greater and more idealized passion: one of the women who, in the *Ameto*, Fiammetta says that her Caleone loved before meeting her" (Branca, *Tradizione delle opere di Giovanni Boccaccio*, vol. 1, *Un primo elenco dei codici e tre studi*,

142)—and that it was known at the time she was fictional. There was thus no reason for Neapolitan high society to hold a competition to discover her identity. For the identification, when possible, of the women named in the poem, see Branca, *Tradizione delle opere di Giovanni Boccaccio*, I. *Un primo elenco dei codici e tre studi*, 170–90, and Giovanni Boccaccio, *Caccia di Diana*, ed. Irene Iocca (Rome: Salerno Editrice, 2016), 179–99.

33. *AV*, XL–XLIV.

34. Regarding the court as the intended recipient of the *Caccia*, see, for example, Irene Iocca, "Caccia di Diana," in *BAC*, 85–88, on 85, calling the work "created for the Neapolitan court of King Robert"; and Luigi Surdich, *Boccaccio* (Rome and Bari: Laterza, 2001), 15, writing it was "a worldly and gallant homage to the environment of the Angevin court"; more nuanced is Battaglia Ricci, *Boccaccio*: "Evidently the privileged audience for the work were [Neapolitan] readers, if not of the court" (74). Giancarlo Alfano, "In forma di libro: Boccaccio e la politica degli autori," in *Boccaccio angioino: Materiali per la storia culturale di Napoli nel Trecento*, ed. Giancarlo Alfano, Teresa D'Urso, and Alessandra Perriccioli Saggese (Brussels: Peter Lang, 2012), 15–29, makes an interesting attempt to determine the intended audience's social composition, noting that "present on the list are the nobility of Seggio as well as (although in the minority) the feudal nobility of French origin and also new families elevated to the nobility by virtue of their service to the crown in various areas of administration and commerce," and he hypothesizes that Boccaccio "frequented a *demi-monde* in contact with the highest reaches of the Neapolitan aristocracy, which his verses could have reached traveling by this route" (17). Regarding the non-noble huntresses, the "Caterina di Iacopo Roncione" (*CD*, I.34) who Boccaccio specifies was "daughter of the notary Iacopo Roncione" ("figlia di notar Iacopo Roncione," *CD*, VI.18; translation from Boccaccio, *Diana's Hunt*, ed. and trans. Cassell and Kirkham, 99, 113) clearly did not belong to a noble family. With Roncione, we are in the sphere of state administrators, to which the family of Lucia Poria (*CD*, I.25–26) could also have belonged and, with a higher probability (see Boccaccio, *Caccia di Diana*, 189–90), also that of Fiore Canovara (*CD*, I.42). If then the Ciancia of *CD*, I.19, was actually Sancia the niece of Raimondo de'Cabanni (Raymond of Cabanni)—whose incredible social ascent "out of the service of the kitchen made a knight" ("ex servo popinario miles factus") Boccaccio would recount in *CVI*, IX.26 (for his biography, see Ingeborg Walter, "Cabanni, Raimondo de," in *DBI*, XV [1972])—we would indeed be entering the most intimate circle of Giovanna then Duchess of Calabria, but not the world of the high aristocracy. Among the families connected to Florentine bankers is that of Dalfina Barrasio (*CD*, X.5), the Barras, who were "related to the Bardi and Peruzzi" (Branca, *Tradizione delle opere di Giovanni Boccaccio*, I. *Un primo elenco dei codici e tre studi*, 184), and it is therefore not coincidental that Dalfina would later reappear in the *Amo-*

rosa visione (XLII.49–55). For relationships between Neapolitan nobility and Florentine bankers, see Davidsohn, *Storia di Firenze*, 789–807, and Francesco Paolo Tocco, *Niccolò Acciaiuoli: Vita e politica in Italia alla metà del XIV secolo* (Rome: Istituto storico italiano per il Medioevo, 2001), 11–17.

35. In reconstructing the literary background of the *Caccia*, scholars have identified a large number of references to classical, medieval Latin, and Romanic texts, from French allegorical poems and texts of the *tournoiements des dames* to the panegyrics of Provençal feudal courts and Dante's "pìstola." For a survey of the texts and genres most commonly cited, see Giovanni Boccaccio, "Caccia di Diana," in *Tutte le opere di Giovanni Boccaccio* [cited as *TO*], ed. Vittore Branca (Milan: Mondadori, 1967-98), vol. 1 (1967), 5–9; Boccaccio, *Caccia di Diana*, XXIII–XXXI; and Paolo Rinoldi, "La 'Caccia di Diana' e la critica delle fonti: una ricognizione," in *BV*, 47–60. However, these references are to discursive areas, to cultural suggestions, in short, to rather vague textual galaxies more than to texts with perceptible direct echoes. While Branca attributes notable importance to the hunt song tradition, Rinoldi (50) rightly observes that "the *corpus* of *cacce* [i.e., the genre of fourteenth-century hunting songs], at least on the basis of the surviving documentary evidence, is very problematic with regard to origin and diffusion; the genre appeared, or at least flourished, later, and undoubtedly constitutes a chapter in the influence of Boccaccio's stylistic features and attitudes."

Chapter Three

1. "Iussit genitor idem, ut pontificum sanctiones, dives exinde futurus, auditurus intrarem." Translation based on Giovanni Boccaccio, *Boccaccio on Poetry: Being the Preface and the Fourteenth and Fifteenth Books of Boccaccio's Genealogia Deorum Gentilium*, ed. and trans. Charles Osgood (Princeton, NJ: Princeton University Press, 1930; 2nd ed., Indianapolis: Bobbs-Merrill, 1956), 132.

2. For the decision to study canon law and the date of university enrollment, see Marco Santagata, *Boccaccio indiscreto: Il mito di Fiammetta* (Bologna: il Mulino, 2019), 53–59. Francesco Sabatini, *Napoli angioina: Cultura e società* (Naples: ESI Edizioni, 1975), 55–59, provides an overview of legal teaching at the university and in the Kingdom of Naples. On the lack of professors of rhetoric and poetry, see Giuseppe Billanovich, *Petrarca letterato*, vol. 1, *Lo scrittoio del Petrarca* (Rome: Edizioni di storia e letteratura, 1947; repr. 1995), 63; on preparatory instruction in grammar and logic, see Sabatini, *Napoli angioina: Cultura e società*, 19–20.

3. The registers of the Florentine notary ser Salvi di Dino contain three receipts (dated November 10, 1338; November 16, 1339; and January 1, 1341), which were issued by Prior Scarpa to Boccaccino, acting also in the name of his son Giovanni, for the annual rental payments and the act

of rescission of the contract (dated May 10, 1342) related to those payments (I am indebted to Laura Regnicoli for generously making available to me the collection of documents related to Boccaccio and his family, which she is preparing for publication. The contract in question does not survive; however, from the act of 1342, in which the two parties declare they consider the contract to have ended early, it is possible to reconstruct the general outlines of the entire matter. At the beginning of 1337, more precisely on January 8, Prior Scarpa and Boccaccino formalized an agreement before the notary Salvi, perhaps already agreed orally toward the end of 1336. This provided that Boccaccino would lease for himself and Giovanni the property of the Capua church for a period of five years beginning November 1, 1337. Only from November 1, not from the time of the contract, probably because the property was already leased until the end of October. Indeed, the receipts attest that Boccaccino regularly and punctually paid the agreed twenty-six gold florins in 1338 and 1339. In November 1340, however, Boccaccino did not pay; he would do this only on January 1, 1341, and the amount would be reduced to twenty-three florins. We can imagine that a dispute arose between Boccaccino and Scarpa and that they ultimately agreed on a slight rent reduction. About the reasons for the dispute we cannot formulate any hypothesis; however, following this Boccaccino refused to pay the rent due in October–November 1341. This time also he would have to yield, and thus, after several months of disputes, he would pay what he owed in May 1342, and in exchange was able to dissolve the contract and save the payment of the fifth year of rent.

4. Translation from Giovanni Boccaccio, *Il Filocolo*, trans. Donald Cheney with Thomas G. Bergin (New York and London: Garland Publishing, 1985), 5.

5. For the length of the course of study, the academic year, and proposal of 1335 as the date of enrollment, see Billanovich, *Petrarca letterato*, I. *Lo scrittoio del Petrarca*, 73.

6. For some of the more important assertions of the presumed relationship between Boccaccio and Cino da Pistoia, see Vittore Branca and Pier Giorgio Ricci, "Notizie e documenti per la biografia del Boccaccio. IV. L'incontro napoletano con Cino da Pistoia," *Studi sul Boccaccio* 5 (1968): 1–18, on 8 and 11; Vittore Branca, *Giovanni Boccaccio: Profilo biografico* (Florence: Sansoni, 1977 [1967]), 30–31; Sabatini, *Napoli angioina: Cultura e società*, 57 and 95; Lucia Battaglia Ricci, *Boccaccio* (Rome: Salerno Editrice, 2000), 26; Elena Pistolesi, "Il *De vulgari eloquentia* di Giovanni Boccaccio," *Giornale storico della letteratura italiana* 191 (2014): 198–99. Francesco Petrarca, *Canzoniere*, ed. Marco Santagata, updated ed. (Milan: Mondadori, 2004), xviii–xix, also maintains that Boccaccio knew Cino personally, while emphasizing "the enormous distance that separated the sort of writer Boccaccio was from that Cino embodied."

7. [Translator's note: the word the author uses for this work, which

I have translated as "diatribe," is *sirvente*, which was a usually moral or religious song of the Provençal troubadours satirizing social vices.]

8. *GDG*, XV.6, 8.

9. On Paolino da Venezia, see Giuseppe Billanovich, *Petrarca e il primo umanesimo* (Padua: Antenore, 1996), 142–49, and Carla Maria Monti, "Boccaccio lettore del 'Compendium sive Chronologia magna' di Paolino da Venezia," in *BAC*, 374–76; also, Carla Maria Monti, "La Campania nel 'De mappa mundi' di Paolino Veneto," *Italia medioevale e umanistica* 54 (2013): 285–342.

10. Cino is mentioned in the introduction to the fourth day of the *Decameron* (IV, Introd., 33) along with Guido Cavalcanti and Dante Alighieri, as poets who had considered it honorable to dedicate themselves to love poetry even though they were "already old men" ("già vecchi"), Cino indeed "very aged" ("vecchissimo"). Cino's name also appears next to Dante's (and Sennuccio del Bene's) in the sonnet on Petrarca's death (*Rime*, XCIX [CXXVI].9–10). If we exclude the unresolved question of the authorship of the poem "Amico, se tu vuogli avere onore," the only remaining clues on which to base the hypothesis of direct contact between Boccaccio and Cino are the reworkings of stanzas I, II, and IV of *Filostrato* (V.62–65) and of V of the poem *La dolce vista e 'l ben guardo soave* (of which we will speak more below). Finally, it has been definitively established that ms. Magl. XXIX 169 containing Cino's lectures on the *Digestum* is not a Boccaccio autograph, as had been proposed (Marco Cursi and Maurizio Fiorilla, "Giovanni Boccaccio," in *Autografi dei letterati italiani: Le origini e il Trecento*, ed. Giuseppina Brunetti, Maurizio Fiorilla, and Marco Petoletti [Rome: Salerno Editrice, 2013] 47).

11. *GDG*, XV.10, 7: "Et sub preceptore clarissimo fere tantundem temporis in cassum etiam laboravi. Fastidiebat hec animus adeo, ut in neutrum horum officiorum, aut preceptoris doctrina, aut genitoris auctoritate, qua novis mandatis angebar continue, aut amicorum precibus seu obiurgationibus inclinari posset."

12. *Ep.*, IV.31.

13. See the section of the *Genealogia* (XIV.4) expressly devoted to condemning the wealth of jurists as opposed to the poverty of poets.

14. For another example of Boccaccio's legal competence, see his advice to Mainardo Cavalcanti on how to avoid the canonical impediment to marriage posed by his consanguinity with his future bride (*Ep.*, XXI.2). A broad and in-depth examination of Boccaccio's knowledge of law can be found in Lucia Battaglia Ricci, *Scrivere un libro di novelle: Giovanni Boccaccio autore, lettore, editore* (Ravenna: Longo, 2013), 116–33.

15. For the issue of Boccaccio's clerical status, see also Santagata, *Boccaccio indiscreto: Il mito di Fiammetta*, 60–64. On the ecclesiastical careers of graduates in canon law, of great interest is the information provided for

the small Studium of Rome in the period 1319–64 by Dario Internullo, *Ai margini dei giganti: La vita intellettuale dei romani nel Trecento (1305–1367 ca.)* (Rome: Viella, 2016), 50–55.

16. The text of this bull, as already noted, can be found in Giuseppe Billanovich, *Restauri boccacceschi* (Rome: Edizioni di *Storia e letteratura,* 1947), 174–75.

17. Laura Regnicoli, "Codice diplomatico di Giovanni Boccaccio 1. I documenti fiscali," *Italia medioevale e umanistica* 54 (2013): 36–37.

18. "confisus quamplurimum de circumspectione et fidei puritate providi viri domini Johannis Bocchaccii de Certaldo civis et clerici florentini." For the full text, see Francesco Torraca, *Per la biografia di Giovanni Boccaccio: Appunti di Francesco Torraca, con i ricordi autobiografici e documenti inediti* (Milan, Rome, and Naples: Società Editrice Dante Alighieri di Albrighi, Segati e C., 1912), 237–40.

19. For doubts about Boccaccio's use of the liturgical paraphernalia, see Laura Regnicoli, "La *cura sepulcri* di Giovanni Boccaccio," *Studi sul Boccaccio* 42 (2014): 64–66; on the other hand, Billanovich, *Restauri boccacceschi,* 178, seems more open to the possibility. However, Livio Petrucci points out to me that the items bequeathed to the "workers" ("operai") of San Michele and Iacopo, including a chasuble, a stole, and three corporals, as well as two altar cloths and an altar "giancialetto," do not seem well suited for personal use.

20. *AV,* Son. acrostici I.1–9; III.17–25:

> **M**irabil cosa forse la presente
> vision vi parrà, donna gentile,
> **a** riguardar, sì per lo nuovo stile,
> sì per la fantasia ch'è nella mente.
> **R**imirandovi un dì, subitamente,
> bella, leggiadra et in abit'umile,
> **i**n volontà mi venne con sottile
> rima tractar parlando brievemente.
> **A**dunque a voi, cui tengho donna mia;
>
> **E** perché voi costei me' conosciate,
> ella somigli' Amor nel su' aspecto,
> **t**anto c'alcun difecto
> non v'à a chi già 'l vide altre fiate;
> **e** l'un dell'altro si gode di loro,
> ond'io lieto dimoro.
> **R**endete a llei 'l meritato alloro!
> E più non dico 'mai,
> **p**erché decto mi par aver assai

A wonderous thing to behold, perhaps, the present

vision will seem to You, noble lady,

as much for its new style,

as for the phantasy stored in my mind.

Suddenly, one day as I was gazing at You —

beautiful, lovely, modestly garbed —

there came to me the wish to treat of You

in subtle rhymes, speaking in brief compass.

Thus to You, whom I hold my lady;

And so that you may come to know her better,

she so resembles Love in her appearance

that whoever has seen him on other occasions

will find she has no flaw;

and each of them delights in the other,

whence I remain joyful.

Render unto her the laurel she deserves!

And let me speak no more,

for it seems to me that I have said enough

In the second and following lines of the translation, "You" is capital-ized to indicate honorific second person plural. Translation from Boc-caccio, *Amorosa Visione*, trans. Hollander et al., 3, 5. Ernest H. Wilkins, "Maria ... prete," *Italica* 28 (1951): 101 – 2, identified the presence of this acrostic, but his reconstruction was not taken up by subsequent studies.

21. Battaglia Ricci, *Scrivere un libro di novelle: Giovanni Boccaccio autore, lettore, editore*, 110, suspects that the term *abate* "is a sort of self-deprecating hyperbole, however alluding to a social status and/or a professional identity close to that of cleric." In contrast, for Sabatini, *Napoli angioina: Cultura e società*, 259, "in the title of 'abate' ... you can see an allusion by Boccaccio to his enrollment in the study of canon law." I would not advance as evidence the passage from the *Sacre famis* — a letter also from 1339 in which Boccaccio alludes to his study of canon law: "considering my readings of the decretals" ("visis meis decretalium lectionibus") — in which he expresses the desire to participate in the baptism of a child that might be born to his correspondent: "And cer-tainly if Lucina gives you a child ... I would be delighted if he were bathed in my hands with the water of holy baptism" (*Ep.*, IV.27; "Et certe si tibi prolem Lucina concederet ... non mihi modicum gratum esset, ut ea in meis manibus permanente, aqua sacri baptismatis lavaretur"), because I do not believe that here Boccaccio was proposing to the recipient "that he baptize the child" (Battaglia Ricci, *Scrivere un libro di novelle: Giovanni Boccaccio autore, lettore, editore*, 107), but only that he take an active role in the rite, perhaps as godfather: "in my hands" ("in meis manibus"), he

wrote, not "by my hands" (see also Giuseppe Chiecchi, *Giovanni Boccaccio e il romanzo familiare* [Venice: Marsilio, 1994], 49).

22. Billanovich, *Restauri boccacceschi*, 176.

23. "ac aptius posset mundanarum rerum sollicitudines evitare, vitam assumpsit et habitum clericalem."

24. On this interrupted transcription, see Stefano Zamponi, Martina Pantarotto, and Antonella Tomiello, "Stratigrafia dello Zibaldone e della Miscellanea laurenziani," in *Gli Zibaldoni di Boccaccio: Memoria, scrittura, riscrittura*, conference proceedings, ed. Michelangelo Picone and Claude Cazalé Bérard (Florence and Certaldo, April 26–28, 1996) (Florence: Franco Cesati, 1998) 226–33; and Marco Petoletti, "Gli zibaldoni di Giovanni Boccaccio," in *Boccaccio autore e copista*, exhibition catalog, ed. Teresa De Robertis, Carla Maria Monti, Marco Petoletti, Giuliano Tanturli, and Stefano Zamponi (Florence: Biblioteca Medicea Laurenziana, October 11, 2013–January 11, 2014) (Florence: Mandragora, 2013)

25. "Dum igitur iuvenis Neapoli olim apud insignem virum atque venerabilem, Andalum de Nigro ianuensem, celorum motus et syderum eo docente perciperem." Translation from Giovanni Boccaccio, *The Fates of Illustrious Men*, new annotated ed., ed. and trans. Louis Brewer Hall (New York and Bristol: Italica Press, 2018 [1965]), 63.

26. On Bambaglioli, see Luca Carlo Rossi, "Graziolo Bambaglioli," in *Censimento dei commenti danteschi*, vol. 1, *I commenti di tradizione manoscritta (fino al 1480)* [cited as *CCD*], ed. Enrico Malato and Andrea Mazzucchi (Rome: Salerno Editrice, 2011), 353–56; for the possible acquaintance with Giovanni del Virgilio, see Gabriella Albanese and Paolo Pontari, "L'ultimo Dante: Il cenacolo ravennate, le *Egloge* e la morte," in *L'ultimo Dante e il cenacolo ravennate*, exhibition catalog, ed. Gabriella Albanese and Paolo Pontari (Ravenna: Biblioteca Classense, September 9–October 28, 2018), in *Classense* 6 (2018): 52–53.

27. Billanovich, *Petrarca letterato*, vol. 1, *Lo scrittoio del Petrarca*, 67; see also Maurizio Moschella, "Dionigi da Borgo Sansepolcro," in *DBI*, XL (1991).

28. *Ep.*, II.

29. The four fictitious letters contained in the *Zibaldone Laurenziano* (Laur. 29.8) in 1339 should be considered "typical exercises for a law student" (Billanovich, *Restauri boccacceschi*, 74; Billanovich, *Petrarca letterato*, vol. 1, *Lo scrittoio del Petrarca*, 65–66). In schools where (civil, canon, and feudal) law was taught, approximately once a week *quaestiones* were debated based on cases that could be actual but were also, and more often, fictitious; further, schools of law, such as those of *ars notariae*, used drafting letters to imaginary recipients as epistolary style exercises (on this, see Manlio Bellomo, *Aspetti dell'insegnamento giuridico nelle università medievali, I. Le "Quaestiones disputatae"* [Reggio Calabria: Ed. Parallelo, 1974], 13–81). In the letter Boccaccio pretended to write to Petrarca,

Dionigi (although unnamed) is the friend who revealed to him the existence of a very learned and virtuous man—Petrarca—whom he knew in Avignon (*Ep.*, II.9). Others believe that Boccaccio instead had in mind Petrarca's friend Sennuccio del Bene (see Carla Maria Monti, "Boccaccio e Petrarca," in *Boccaccio autore e copista*, exhibition catalog, ed. Teresa De Robertis, Carla Maria Monti, Marco Petoletti, Giuliano Tanturli, and Stefano Zamponi [Florence: Biblioteca Medicea Laurenziana, October 11, 2013–January 11, 2014] [Florence: Mandragora, 2013], 34); currently, however, there is no indication that the two had met in person.

30. There are already echoes of Petrarca's so-called song of metamorphosis (*Rvf*, 23) in the *Caccia di Diana*: see Santagata, *Boccaccio indiscreto: Il mito di Fiammetta*, 43–45. In the letter of November 3, 1374, to Francescuolo di Brossano on the occasion of Petrarca's death (between July 18 and 19), Boccaccio writes that he had been linked to his deceased friend for more than forty years (*Ep.*, XXIV.28): since their personal relationship dated only from 1350, here Boccaccio refers to the profound influence Petrarca's works exercised on him, knowledge of which he says went back to the 1330s. If we take him literally, to 1334 or even earlier. The hypothesis that his friend Pietro Canigiani, a member of Petrarca's mother's family, had spoken to Boccaccio about the poet is suggestive (see Branca, *Giovanni Boccaccio: Profilo biografico*, 37).

31. Battaglia Ricci, *Scrivere un libro di novelle: Giovanni Boccaccio autore, lettore, editore*, 99–115, putting to good use the chronological reconstruction of Zamponi, Pantarotto, and Tomiello, "Stratigrafia dello Zibaldone e della Miscellanea laurenziani," makes a detailed analysis of the entirety of the works transcribed in the autograph notebooks.

32. The letter continues recounting how a dispute broke out in Barletta between the Gatti and Marra families: the friend, who was visiting the city, perhaps out of friendship sided with the Marras and took part in the conflict with cruel ruthlessness. After peace was restored, he married a "noble and beautiful" young woman who—the author predicts—would certainly distract him from his studies but, in compensation, would give him a son. In 1338 the Gatti and Della Marra did actually come into armed conflict in Barletta, to such a degree that in November the king sent his *magister hostiarius* (master of the guard) Bernardo Seripando to impose a truce: in February, the truce still held (see Torraca, *Per la biografia di Giovanni Boccaccio: Appunti di Francesco Torraca, con i ricordi autobiografici e documenti inediti*, 93–94; and Giuliana Vitale, "Pipino, Giovanni," in *DBI*, LXXXIV [2015]). We do not know what methods the envoys used to impose the royal will and therefore we cannot establish if Boccaccio had been inspired by them in telling of his friend's cruel warlike behavior. It is possible that instead the Barletta episode was a fiction within a fiction and that Boccaccio actually was inspired by something else. In the winter of 1338 in Aquila a violent civil war erupted between two factions,

and also on this occasion King Robert sent one of his representatives: the envoy charged with attempting to mediate appears to have been Dionigi da Borgo Sansepolcro. Therefore, if Boccaccio superimposed these two events, it would confirm that in depicting his imaginary friend he paid homage to both his teachers: nearly explicitly to one, Andalò del Negro, who a few years earlier had encouraged him in scientific scholarship, and more implicitly to the other who more recently had encouraged him in philology and rhetoric.

33. Translation from Boccaccio, *Il Filocolo*, trans. Cheney and Bergin, 381–83.

Chapter Four

1. In a 1359 letter responding to one from Boccaccio that has not survived, Petrarca wrote, "You expressly add . . . that he was your first guide and the light of your youthful studies" ("Inseris nominatim . . . quod ille tibi adolescentulo primus studiorum dux et prima fax fuerit"; *Fam.*, XXI.15, 2); in *AV*, VI.2–3 Boccaccio calls Dante "the master from whom I take / every good thing, even if it does not perdure in me" ("il maestro dal qual io / tengo ogni ben, se nullo in me sen posa"). Translation from Boccaccio, *Amorosa Visione*, trans. Hollander et al., 27.

2. From the many shared traits, see, for example, *CD*, XVIII.13–15, and *VN*, *Donne ch'avete*, 49; *CD*, XVIII.52–53 and *VN*, *Vede perfettamente*, 11; *CD*, XVIII.29–30, and *VN*, *Donne ch'avete*, 35–36; *CD*, XVIII.34–35 *VN*, *Negli occhi porta*, 7.

3. *VN*, 31, 1–2. Translation from Dante Alighieri, *Vita Nuova, New Edition: A Translation and an Essay*, trans. Mark Musa (Bloomington: Indiana University Press, 1973), 86.

4. Translation from Giovanni Boccaccio, *Diana's Hunt (Caccia di Diana): Boccaccio's First Fiction*, ed. and trans. Anthony K. Cassell and Victoria Kirkham (Philadelphia: University of Pennsylvania Press, 1991), 151.

5. See Marco Santagata, *L'io e il mondo: Un'interpretazione di Dante* (Bologna: il Mulino, 2011), 225–34. In 1373, commenting on canto 2 of the *Inferno*, Boccaccio wrote, "According to what he says at the close of his *Vita Nuova*, he resolved to write the present work in her [Beatrice's] honor" ("secondo che egli nella fine della sua *Vita Nuova* scrive, esso in onor di lei a comporre la presente opera si dispose," *ECD*, II [I].85). Translation from Giovanni Boccaccio, *Boccaccio's Expositions on Dante's "Comedy,"* trans. Michael Papio (Toronto: University of Toronto Press, 2009), 127.

6. "This young woman, coming to maturity with the passage of time, grew also in marvelous beauty and virtue . . . so that her notable graces and virtuous deeds frequently made people think that she must have been the daughter not of man but of God" ("Questa giovane, come in tempo crescendo procedea, così di mirabile virtù e bellezza s'adornava . . . per le

sue notabili bellezze e opere virtuose più volte facea pensare a molti che non d'uomo ma di Dio figliuola stata fosse," *Filoc.*, I.1, 16). *VN*, 1, 9: "Vedeala di sì nobili e laudabili portamenti, che certo di lei si potea dire quella parola del poeta Homero: 'Ella non parea figliuola d'uomo mortale, ma di Dio.'" Translation from Giovanni Boccaccio, *Il Filocolo*, trans. Donald Cheney and Thomas G. Bergin (New York and London: Garland Publishing, 1985), 3.

7. Translation from Boccaccio, *Il Filocolo*, trans. Cheney and Bergin.

8. *CD*, IV.1-34.

9. In the 1960s, Piero Giorgio Ricci, "Per la dedica e la datazione del *Filostrato*," *Studi sul Boccaccio* 1 (1963): 333-47, reprinted and cited from Pier Giorgio Ricci, *Studi sulla vita e le opere del Boccaccio* (Milan and Naples: Ricciardi, 1985), 38-49, and Giovanni Boccaccio, *Filostrato*, ed. Vittore Branca, in *Tutte le opere*, ed. Vittore Branca, vol. 2 (Milan: Mondadori, 1964), 3-4, resolutely identified the *Filostrato* as the first work Boccaccio wrote after the *Caccia di Diana*. Their reconstruction rested almost exclusively on the fact that the *Filostrato*, like the *Caccia*, had no traces of the Fiammetta myth, the development of which begins with the *Filocolo*: from this they deduced that "like the *Caccia*, the *Filostrato* must have been composed by Boccaccio when he was a little over twenty, and certainly before the *Filocolo*: namely, around 1335" (Boccaccio, *Filostrato*, ed.Vittore Branca, in *Tutte le opere*, 2, 3-228, 5). Today, most scholars, using arguments that leave aside Fiammetta's absence, contest their dating and tend to push the poem's composition toward the end of the 1330s. In any case, the origin of the Fiammetta myth and its development over time are two of the most important factors in locating the *Filocolo* in its proper chronological place directly after the *Caccia*.

10. Translation from Boccaccio, *Il Filocolo*, trans. Cheney and Bergin, 224.

11. Boccaccio's interest in Greek and Byzantine culture may have been intensified in 1339 when he met the scholar and Basilian monk Barlaam (ca. 1290–ca. 1348), who was born in Calabria and finished his life as bishop of Gerace. Petrarch met the monk in this same year and would also take lessons in Greek from him a few years later. See Salvatore Impellizzeri, "Barlaam Calabro," in *DBI*, VI (1964); Antonio Rollo, "Magistro Leonpilato de Tesalia," *Quaderni petrarcheschi* 12-13 (2002-3): 20-21; Daniele Bianconi, "Uno sguardo verso l'altrove, suggestioni da Bisanzio," in *Petrarca, l'Umanesimo e la civiltà europea* [cited as *PU*], Atti del Convegno internazionale (Firenze, December 5-10, 2004), 2 vols., ed. Donatella Coppini e Michele Feo, in *Quaderni petrarcheschi* 1, nos. 15-16 (2005-6), and 2, nos. 17-18 (2007-8): 83-88.

12. On this internal chronology, see Antonio Enzo Quaglio, "Tra fonti e testo del *Filocolo*," *Giornale storico della letteratura italiana* 140 (1963):

321–63, 489–551, at 334–43; and Luigi Surdich, *La cornice di amore: Studi sul Boccaccio* (Pisa: Edizioni ETS, 1987), 70–71.

13. Translation from Boccaccio, *Il Filocolo*, trans. Cheney and Bergin, 4.

14. Luigi Surdich, *Boccaccio* (Rome and Bari: Laterza, 2001), 34.

15. Translation from Boccaccio, *Il Filocolo*, trans. Cheney and Bergin.

16. For these women's names and the *stil novo* poets, see Marco Santagata, *Il poeta innamorato: Su Dante, Petrarca e la poesia amorosa medievale* (Milan: Guanda, 2017), 105–16. In the opinion of Surdich, *La cornice di amore: Studi sul Boccaccio*, 85, Maria is "the real name of an actual woman," also because "a double *senhal* would be excessive literary caution even for a man as well-fed on letters as Boccaccio."

17. *Filoc.*, I.1, 17–18: "It happened that one day, the dawning of which Saturn had presided over [Saturday, consecrated to Saturn], Phoebus with his horses [the Sun] having by then reached the sixteenth degree of the celestial Ram [Aries], and it being furthermore the day on which the glorious departure of the son of Jove [Christ] from the harrowed realms of Pluto [Hell] is celebrated [Holy Saturday]—it happened that I, the compiler of the present account, found myself in a gracious and handsome temple in Parthenope [Naples], named after the man who achieved godhead by letting himself be sacrificed on a griddle [Saint Laurence] . . . the fourth hour of the day had passed above the eastern horizon, there appeared to my eyes the marvelous beauty of the aforementioned young lady" ("Avvenne che un giorno la cui prima ora Saturno avea signoreggiata, essendo già Febo co' suoi cavalli al sedicesimo grado del celestiale Montone pervenuto, e nel quale il glorioso partimento del figliuolo di Giove dagli spogliati regni di Plutone si celebrava, io, della presente opera componitore, mi ritrovai in un grazioso e bel tempio in Partenope, nominato da colui che per deificare sostenne che fosse fatto di lui sacrificio sopra la grata . . . la quarta ora del giorno sopra l'orientale orizonte passata, apparve agli occhi miei la mirabile bellezza della prescritta giovane"). Translation from Boccaccio, *Il Filocolo*, trans. Cheney and Bergin.

18. *Filoc.* I 1, 23: "A holy temple named after the chief of the heavenly birds [the archangel Gabriel]" ("Un santo tempio dal prencipe de' celestiali uccelli nominato"). Translation from Boccaccio, *Il Filocolo*, trans. Cheney and Bergin.

19. For churches as meeting places for the two sexes, see Santagata, *Il poeta innamorato: Su Dante, Petrarca e la poesia amorosa medievale*, 13–52. There is also, however, the precedent from Virgil of Aeneas and Dido's meeting in the temple of Pallas (*Aeneid*, I.425–504), and Boccaccio took this into account in the *Elegia di Madonna Fiammetta* (*EMF*, I.6); moreover, Troiolo also falls in love with Criseida in the temple of Pallas (*Filos.*, I.17–31). In the vernacular, only Cavalcanti mentions the Dorata (Daurade), the church in Tolosa where he met Mandetta (*Era in penser*

d'amor, 45–46). Above all, Petrarca cannot be added as an example for the simple reason that he only named the church of Santa Chiara in Avignon in 1351, more than twenty years after the composition of Boccaccio's work, and what is more in private writing. Petrarca cannot even be summoned as a precedent for indicating the month, day, and hour of the woman's appearance and the particular liturgical relevance of the day: in fact, the information regarding April 6, 1327, Good Friday, only entered the *Canzoniere* quite late (for Petrarca's places and dates, see again Santagata, *Il poeta innamorato: Su Dante, Petrarca e la poesia amorosa medievale*, 66–78) and thus was surely unknown to Boccaccio in the 1330s (therefore, the assertion of Giuseppe Billanovich, *Restauri boccacceschi* [Rome: Edizioni di *Storia e letteratura*, 1947], 88, cannot be accepted, and perhaps should even be reversed, namely, "that from the beginning Fiammetta shows herself to be Laura's younger sister although also kin to Beatrice" and that "and also for this reason . . . she appears in church . . . and she too precisely during Holy Week"). If we leave Petrarca aside, there appear to be no vernacular texts—not even, with a sole exception about which I will speak shortly, among French and Provençal romances—that exhibit such precise and symbolically meaningful calendar details.

20. Even Vittore Branca, who was convinced that both Fiammetta and the tale of Boccaccio's love for her were entirely literary creations, on noting the insistence with which Boccaccio names Holy Saturday, writes: "It is possible that the insistent detail reflects some actual fact" (Branca, *Boccaccio medievale*, 257).

21. The first meeting takes place on the sixteenth day after the sun enters the constellation of Aries, namely, after the spring equinox. The problem is determining when the equinox fell for Boccaccio. According to Arnaldo Della Torre, *La giovinezza di G. Boccaccio (1313–1341)* (Città di Castello: Lapi, 1905), 31–101), Boccaccio, who had studied seriously under Andalò del Negro's guidance, followed the astronomical calendar and thus placed the equinox on March 14: therefore, the first meeting would have happened on Holy Saturday March 30. However, Francesco Torraca, *Per la biografia di Giovanni Boccaccio: Appunti di Francesco Torraca, con i ricordi autobiografici e documenti inediti* (Milan, Rome, and Naples: Società Editrice Dante Alighieri di Albrighi, Segati e C., 1912), 1–35, contests this because, in his telling, Boccaccio, following the view of the Vulgate, would have located the spring equinox on March 18 and so the sixteen-day interval brings Holy Saturday to April 3. For Della Torre, the year would be 1331, for Torraca 1333. Since then, these two dates have not only been repeated countless times, but also presented as undeterminable, indeed, as proof of the impossibility of arriving at a certain date: for example, Antonio E. Quaglio, *Scienza e mito nel Boccaccio* (Padua: Liviana, 1967), 717; Victoria Kirkham, *Fabulous Vernacular: Boccaccio's "Filocolo" and the Art of Medieval Fiction* (Ann Arbor: University of Michigan Press, 2001),

48–63, instead accepts without hesitation Torraca's proposed April 3, 1333, on the basis of the fact that "3 is the number of Venus" and that "no other admissible date produces such a delightful coincidence. During the decade between 1330 and 1340, the only year when Holy Saturday fell on the third day of April was 1333," and on the basis of this firm point she constructs a complex numerical and calendrical symbology that also involves Dante of the *Vita Nova* and Petrarca of the *Canzoniere*. In truth, there are not just two possible dates, but three: a March 30 Holy Saturday in fact also occurred in 1336. Although Antonio Casetti had already pointed this out twenty years before Della Torre, and Rodolfo Renier and Henri Hauvette had taken up his suggestion (Antonio Casetti, "Il Boccaccio a Napoli," *Nuova Antologia* 28 [1875]: 557–95; Rodolfo Renier, *La Vita Nuova e la Fiammetta: Studio critico* [Turin and Rome: Loescher, 1879); Henri Hauvette, "Pour la biographie de Boccace," *Bulletin italien* 11 [1911]: 181–212), both Della Torre and Torraca rejected 1336 because it did not fit into the chronology of Boccaccio's youth that they both subscribed to. Della Torre, indeed, held it as fact that Boccaccio moved to Naples in 1323, while Torraca was certain it was in 1325, and therefore, since in the *Comedia delle ninfe fiorentine* Caleone/Boccaccio reports that he met Fiammetta in the church of San Lorenzo seven years and four months after his arrival in Naples (XXXV.73–105), the date obtained by subtracting seven years and four months from March 1336 is very far from the period in which the two scholars placed the beginning of Boccaccio's stay in Naples. Biographical research then established that both scholars' hypotheses were mistaken and that, instead, the details Boccaccio provided in the *Filocolo* and the *Comedia* were remarkably precise. Therefore, not only is March 30, 1336, definitely the day on which Boccaccio set the meeting in San Lorenzo (a conclusion that had also been reached by Ernest H. Wilkins, "The Enamorment of Boccaccio," *Modern Philology* 11 [1913–14], and *Studies on Petrarch and Boccaccio* [Padua: Antenore, 1978], 315–33), but the consistent chronological framework Boccaccio maintained across multiple works seems to confirm that beneath the fantastical transpositions lies an autobiographical foundation that he could not abandon.

22. Translation from Boccaccio, *Il Filocolo*, trans. Cheney and Bergin, 242.

23. *Filoc.*, IV.16, 4–5.

24. This suggestion is Natascia Tonelli's in her *"Per queste orme": Studi sul Canzoniere di Petrarca* (Pisa: Pacini Editore, 2016), 55–84. It may also be added that there are a variety of reasons Boccaccio could have been attracted to a book like *Flamenca*: the love story is closely linked to liturgical dates and the beginning of the story takes place in a church on the Saturday after Easter; further, an author who was preparing to rewrite, or even already rewriting, the tale of Florio and Biancifiore must have been struck to read that the sequestered Flamenca kept on a table in her room

the *romanz de Blancaflor* (*Flamenca*, 4481). Although we cannot be sure, an indication that Boccaccio might have read this romance is provided by the *Filocolo* itself. In *Flamenca*, the confined woman and her beloved are only able to communicate during celebrations of the mass, when the knight, disguised as a cleric, hands her the psalter to kiss as a sign of "peace" and, at the same time, whispers a short phrase, no more than a few syllables: one Sunday spoken by one lover, the next by the other. The knight's first utterance is only a woeful exclamation: "Hailas!" ("Alas!" 3953). Troubled, Flamenca wonders for a long time about the meaning of that word and then decides to confide in the two maids who assist her in her captivity. On their advice, the following week, at the moment of the psalter kiss, she responds with the question, "Que plains?" ("What is wrong?" What are you lamenting? 4348). After the mass, she returns to her chamber and repeats to the maids what she had said and done in church: to better reenact the scene, she asks for the book of Biancifiore that is on the table and, while pretending to kiss it as if it were the psalter, barely holding back laughter, says, "Di che ti lamenti?" ("What are you lamenting?" 4479–93). Now, in the final section of the *Filocolo* Boccaccio tells the book that the "worthy lady" ("valorosa donna") to whom the book is dedicated will grant it a prize: "she takes you in her soft hands and says with a gentle voice, 'Welcome.' And perhaps she will offer you a kiss or two with her sweet lips" ("prendendoti nelle sue dilicate mani, dicendo con soave voce:—Ben venuto—; e forse con la dolce bocca ti porgerà alcun bacio," V.97, 2). Translation from Boccaccio, *Il Filocolo*, trans. Cheney and Bergin, 470. Besides this and the one in *Flamenca*, I know of no other female kisses placed on the pages of a book in ancient or medieval Romanic literature. The structure of the sequence (brief statement and act of kissing) provides further connection, as does, especially, the fact that it is almost the same book: the *Floire et Blanchefleur* for Flamenca, Boccaccio's own learned reworking of it for Fiammetta (a fuller discussion of this can be found in Marco Santagata, *Boccaccio indiscreto: Il mito di Fiammetta* [Bologna: il Mulino, 2019], 82–85).

25. Translation from Boccaccio, *Il Filocolo*, trans. Cheney and Bergin, 242.

26. *Filoc.*, V.42–49.

27. Translations from Boccaccio, *Il Filocolo*, trans. Cheney and Bergin, 402, 418, and 470, respectively.

28. Translation from Boccaccio, *Il Filocolo*, trans. Cheney and Bergin, 384.

29. That Boccaccio had in mind the connection between the myth of his own royal birth and the myth of Maria-Fiammetta is demonstrated by the fact that in the *Comedia delle ninfe fiorentine*, Caleone, in whom Caleon of the *Filocolo* reappears to the very name, mentions his own French birth (*CNF*, XXXV.72): regarding this, Billanovich, *Restauri boccacceschi*,

45, writes, "The Parisian birth is linked to and depends upon the love for Fiammetta . . . the two episodes . . . are two parts, either of one biography or of one romance, that are mutually referential and integrated."

30. Tales that grew out of the experiences of merchants far from home echo in the *Decameron*: for example, in the story of the moneylender Alessandro Agolanti (II.3) who, by fortunate chance, found himself married to the daughter of the king of England, became Earl of Cornwall, and "some people say" ("secondo che alcuni voglion dire"), king of Scotland (regarding this Robert Davidsohn, *Storia di Firenze*, 8 vols. [Florence: Sansoni, Firenze, 1956–68], originally published in German [Berlin: Mittler und Sohn, 1896–1927], 690–91, comments: "This anecdote passed by word of mouth shows only the enormous degree of self-regard possessed by all Florentines, to the extent that that it did not seem strange to them that one of their young fellow citizens had gone from being a moneylender to a monarch"). The incredible event of the Sienese merchant Giovanni Baglioni would, in contrast, seem to be only a fantasy: as told in the fifteenth-century *Istoria di re Giannino*, sometime around the middle of the fourteenth century, Baglioni, claiming that he was the son of King Louis X of France, advanced claims to the throne in which he was supported by Cola di Rienzo (for this complicated event, see Giulio Prunai, "Baglioni, Giovanni [Giovannino]," in *DBI*, V [1963]). This was almost certainly an invention, although it must be said that there is evidence of a real Giannino Baglioni in Siena at that time and he might be the Giannino of Siena about whom Benvenuto da Imola spoke in reference to the vanity with which Dante branded the Sienese in the canto of Sapia (comment on *Purg.*, XIII.151–54).

31. This reads, "In Naples, Sant'Aniello's Day" ("In Napole, lo juorno de sant'Aniello"), the saint whose feast is celebrated on December 14. Boccaccio would circulate a revised version of the letter much later, perhaps in 1362–63 (see Francesco Sabatini, "L''Epistola napoletana': Esperimento di genere e di modalità narrative," in *BN*, 13–21).

32. *Lett.*, I.

33. Francesco dei Bardi may have been the son of the well-known merchant and politician Alessandro (Francesco Sabatini, *Napoli angioina: Cultura e società* [Naples: ESI Edizioni, 1975], 107), for whom see Arnaldo D'Addario, "Bardi, Alessandro," in *DBI*, VI (1964). See also Sabatini's "Prospettive sul parlato nella storia linguistica italiana (con una lettura dell'Epistola napoletana del Boccaccio)" in his *Italia linguistica delle origini: Saggi editi dal 1956 al 1996 raccolti da Vittorio Coletti, Rosario Coluccia, Paolo D'Achille, Nicola De Blasi, Livio Petrucci* (Lecce: Argo, 1996), 425–66.

34. Regarding the letter's tone, Billanovich, *Restauri boccacceschi*, 43–44, speaks of "charming farce," "hilarious signature," "cheerful comments of his closest associates."

35. The various hypotheses regarding dating the *Filocolo* are examined by Andrea Mazzucchi, "*Filocolo*," in *BAC*, 67. The "many proofs"

that according to Giuseppe Billanovich, *Prime ricerche dantesche* (Rome: Edizioni di *Storia e letteratura*, 1947), 24, show that the *Filocolo* had "been produced in a blaze of composition along with the *dictamina* [of 1339]" do not seem obvious; nor does the correspondence (which Billanovich takes from Francesco Torraca, "Giovanni Boccaccio a Napoli [1326–1339]," *Archivio Storico per le Province Napoletane* 39 [1914]: 43–44) between *Filoc.*, IV.7, 2 ("il vento … non come essi voleano, ma come a lui piaceva, li guidava") and Dante's letter to Moroello, probably known by Boccaccio in 1339 ("[Amor] liberum meum ligavit arbitrium, ut non quo ego, sed quo ille vult, me verti oporteat") appear decisive, a finding based substantially on Bruni's proposal (1990, 173) to push back the date of the romance's conclusion to 1339. Closer to the *Filocolo*'s formulation is Ovid, *Tristia*, I.4, 15–16: "Sic non quo voluit, sed quo rapit impetus undae, / aurigam video vela dedisse rati." Lucia Battaglia Ricci, *Boccaccio* (Rome: Salerno Editrice, 2000), 78, also speaks of "distinctive consonances" between the *Filocolo* and "a Dantean passage of the letter to Moroello," consonances that would argue in favor of 1339.

36. "Se divum titulis immiscuit altis, / cum pridem placido vix esset cognitus Arno." Translation from Giovanni Boccaccio, *Eclogues*, trans. Janet Levarie Smarr (London: Routledge, 1987), 77.

37. Billanovich, *Restauri boccacceschi*, 84–85.

38. Battaglia Ricci, *Boccaccio*, 83.

39. We know nothing about the Neapolitan diffusion of this romance, nor, indeed, that of Boccaccio's other works of this period. Marco Cursi's investigations of the chronological distribution of the codices containing the *Filocolo* have shown that it "at first struggled to find its place" and that, although "gaining ever wider appreciation" from the beginning of the fifteenth century, only "right after the middle" of that century did it find true success: in short, unlike the *Decameron*, the *Filocolo* "remain[ed] a work for the few, if not the very few, for about sixty years" (Marco Cursi, "Boccaccio a Yale: i codici conservati presso la Beinecke Rare Book and Manuscript Library (con alcune considerazioni sulla tradizione mano-scritta del *Filocolo)*," *Studi sul Boccaccio* 35 [2007]: 54, 67). That said, it is obvious that the work had some circulation among Neapolitan intellec-tuals and courtiers. The problem is establishing in what form. It is easy to imagine that in Naples the *Caccia di Diana* was passed around among many people, either because of its small size, or, especially, because it was filled with the names of society women and thus it must have aroused curiosity and flattered many vanities. And even the *Epistola napoletana* would have circulated in copies among Boccaccio's friends. But in what ways would the lengthy *Filocolo* have reached its audience? It is quite con-ceivable that Boccaccio could not afford to pay a professional copyist, and so in all probability he made the fair copy of the romance himself. How-ever, although for his entire life he remained a tireless copyist of his own

and others' works, it is difficult to believe that in the 1339 of the *Filocolo*'s probable publication, a year characterized by flood of creative work and transcriptions of texts of various kinds, he would have been able to find the time to produce many copies himself. It may be indicative of appreciation by court audiences that the manuscript tradition shows traces of the "considerable favor" the *Filocolo* found "in the area of the eastern Po Valley, Lombardy, Veneto and Umbria, areas whose cultural climates were often led by courtly tastes, where the work seems to have been elevated to a status equal to that of French romance" (Cursi, "Boccaccio a Yale" 67).

40. The origin of *ottava rima* is a long-standing question. Scholars of meter gave it considerable attention in the 1970s and 1980s, but since then it does not appear to have aroused much interest. Keeping in mind that the first documentations of this meter are Boccaccio's poems and the *Cantare di Fiorio e Biancifiore*, "transcribed [in ms. Magliabechiano VIII 1416] shortly after 1343, but in a transcription that has signs of a previous version," the possible hypotheses are "either Boccaccio created the meter and it was taken up by the *cantari*, or the *cantari* provided the meter for Boccaccio; or, a third possibility, both depend on an earlier tradition" (Pietro G. Beltrami, *La metrica italiana* [Bologna: il Mulino, 2011], 112; see also Armando Balduino, *Boccaccio, Petrarca e altri poeti del Trecento* [Florence: Olschki, 1984], 107–8). In the 1970s and 1980s, the predominant thesis, supported by very worthy scholars (I think of Carlo Dionisotti, "Appunti su antichi" [1964], now in *Scritti di storia della letteratura italiana II. 1963–1971*, ed. Tania Basile, Vincenzo Fera, and Susanna Villari [Rome: Edizioni di Storia e Letteratura, 2009], 95–140; Aurelio Roncaglia, "Per la storia dell'ottava rima," *Cultura Neolatina* 25 [1965]: 5–14; Guglielmo Gorni, "Un'ipotesi sull'origine dell'ottava rima" [1978], now in Guglielmo Gorni, *Metrica e analisi letteraria* (Bologna: il Mulino, 1993), 153–70), was that the narrative *ottava* was Boccaccio's invention, even if there were already those who thought his *ottava* was the meeting point for preceding traditions, approximations, and attempts (see Armando Balduino, *Cantari del Trecento* [Milan: Marzorati, 1970], 19–20, 257–59 and, especially, his "'Pater semper incertus.' Ancora sulle origini dell'ottava rima" [1982], now in Balduino, *Boccaccio, Petrarca e altri poeti del Trecento*, 93–140). Later, however, due also to additional discoveries such as the verses on the *Trionfo della morte* in the Camposanto, or cemetery, of Pisa, the thesis prevailed that Boccaccio inherited a preexisting meter and redirected it into storytelling, so that Battaglia Ricci, *Boccaccio*, 94, could write: "It seems highly likely that Boccaccio should be credited not so much with inventing as with transferring the metrical form of *ottava rima* to elevated style and its codification for narrative literary works," a process "of ennobling" that this scholar considers "similar to that which Boccaccio the fiction writer will later put into practice." This ennobling intent could be seen even more clearly if it could be shown, as is currently not possible,

that the narrative use of *ottava rima* preceded Boccaccio's codification of it. While proof is impossible, it must be said that there are many indications that this is the case. In fact, if the earliest documentation of the meter (leaving aside the isolated example of the so-called Sicilian octave from the epitaph of Giulia Topazia in the *Filocolo*) are the *Filostrato* and *Teseida*, the current dating of these works to 1339–41 and the hypothesis that the beginning of the *Teseida* preceded the composition of the *Filostrato* (see Giovanni Boccaccio, *Filostrato*, ed. Luigi Surdich, Elena D'Anzieri, and Federica Ferro [Milan: Mursia, 1990], 8–9)—while the supporters of the thesis of Boccaccio as inventor dated the *Filostrato* to 1335—brings Boccaccio's first narrative *ottava* much closer to the date of the first surviving witness of the *Fiorio e Biancifiore*, and therefore renders plausible the existence of *cantari* in *ottava rima* that predated him, and especially, the *Fiorio e Biancifiore* itself. Whether Boccaccio read this work is another matter: certainly it would have been capable of attracting the interest of an author of a romance dedicated to the same two lovers, but that this actually happened cannot be demonstrated. However, it can be shown that Boccaccio read the work of *cantarini*: confirmation comes from that fact that he refers in his works to *cantari* of which we know only later attestations (see the observations of Balduino, *Boccaccio, Petrarca e altri poeti del Trecento*, 89–90). A structural analysis of Boccaccio's *ottava* was carried out by Arnaldo Soldani, "Osservazioni sull'ottava di Boccaccio," in *BV*, 161–77.

41. Translation from Boccaccio, *Theseid of the Nuptials of Emilia*, trans. Traversa, 589.

42. Dante, *DVE*, II, 2.7, 8: "Armorum probitas, amoris accensio et directio voluntatis"; "Arma, vero nullum latium adhuc invenio poetasse." Translation from Dante Alighieri, *Dante's Treatise "De Vulgari Eloquentia,"* trans. A. G. F. Howell (London, 1890), 51.

43. Translation from *Boccaccio: A Critical Guide to the Complete Works*, ed. Victoria Kirkham, Michael Sherberg, and Janet Levarie Smarr (Chicago: University of Chicago Press, 2013), 96.

44. The only chronological evidence for dating the *Teseida* comes from the letter *Sacre famis*. Here, after telling the addressee that he had acquired a copy of Statius's *Thebaid* without glosses "at a reasonable price" ("pro pretio competenti"), Boccaccio asks to borrow the addressee's glossed version in order to copy the annotations (*Ep.*, IV.29). We know that this is fiction, and yet, even if it was never actually sent, the request shows that in 1339 (the letter is dated June 28 of that year) Boccaccio read the *Thebaid* attentively, which is a valid reason to hypothesize that in that period he was working on the *Teseida*, of which the *Thebaid* is "the principal source" (Francesco Bruni, *Boccaccio: L'invenzione della letteratura mediana* [Bologna: il Mulino, 1990], 189), either as a plan or as a work already underway: according to Surdich, *La cornice di amore: Studi sul*

Boccaccio, 99–100, "when Boccaccio asks for . . . a text of the *Thebaid* with glosses it is likely that work [on the *Teseida*] had already been done at least in some part." It should also be borne in mind that if the autograph copy (ms. Pluteo 38.6 of the Biblioteca Medicea Laurenziana) can be dated on the basis of paleographical evidence to the first half of the 1340s (Marco Cursi, *La scrittura e i libri di Giovanni Boccaccio* [Rome: Viella, 2013], 29, 31), then Boccaccio almost certainly already owned a manuscript of the *Thebaid* at the end of the 1330s (Marco Cursi, "'La Tebaide' restaurata dal Boccaccio," in *BAC*, 337–39). In the chapter of his *Nuova cronica* dedicated to Dante, after mentioning the *Monarchia* and the *Convivio*, Giovanni Villani writes: "[Dante] also wrote a little book that he entitled *De vulgari eloquentia*, where he promises to write four books, but only two are found, perhaps because of his haste to finish, where in strong and ornate Latin and with elegant reasoning he goes through all the vulgar tongues [vernacular dialects] of Italy" (X.136 [n48]; "Altressì fece uno libretto che ll'intitola *De vulgari eloquentia*, ove promette fare IIII libri, ma non se ne truova se non due, forse per l'affrettato suo fine, ove con forte e adorno latino e belle ragioni ripruova tutti i vulgari d'Italia"). These passages are included, as additions, in the chapter located in the part of the chronicle (from the beginning to chapter 51 of book XII) written before the forced interruption of the work in the summer of 1341, when Villani was sent as a hostage to Ferrara (see Roberta Cella, "Il *Centiloquio* di Antonio Pucci e la *Nuova Cronica* di Giovanni Villani," in *Firenze alla vigilia del Rinascimento: Antonio Pucci e i suoi contemporanei*, conference proceedings, ed. Maria Bendinelli Predelli [Montreal, October 22–23, 2004] [Florence: Cadmo, 2006], 85–110). For the purposes of dating the *Teseida* it would be important to establish where and when Boccaccio came to know the *De vulgari*. Many clues suggest that it was after his return from Naples in the autumn of 1340 (the question is examined in Santagata, *Boccaccio indiscreto: Il mito di Fiammetta*, 102–7). However, believing that Boccaccio came across the *De vulgari* in Florence, and therefore that the citation at the end of the *Teseida* was later than that date, does not require also embracing Billanovich's thesis that it was the *De vulgari* that inspired him to write the epic poem that Dante noted was lacking in the poetry of the *lingua di sì* (1947 [3], 28, 39, 57). Similarly, Surdich, *La cornice di amore: Studi sul Boccaccio*, 99, while not expressing an opinion on the time period when Boccaccio would have read the *De vulgari*, holds that Boccaccio's idea for the *Teseida* came from Dante's work; and Giovanni Boccaccio, *Teseida delle nozze d'Emilia*, critical edition by Edvige Agostinelli and William Coleman (Florence: Edizioni del Galluzzo, 2015), xiii, also affirm that "The first Italian epic poem, the *Teseida*, was written in response to Dante's observation in the *De vulgari eloquentia*." Keeping in mind that the conception and start of writing took place in 1339, Boccaccio's encounter with Dante's work confirmed poetic intentions that had already taken shape, giving them an authoritative seal of approval, as Battaglia Ricci, *Boccaccio*, 96, maintains: "Dante's declaration could have reinforced in Boccaccio an awareness of the newness of the genre that he had not emphasized when drafting the pages of the proem."

45. Battaglia Ricci, *Boccaccio*, 97.

46. The poem's division, noted by Vincenzo Crescini, *Contributo agli studi sul Boccaccio* (Turin: Loescher, 1887), 228–35, has since been emphasized by many others, including Giovanni Boccaccio, *Teseida delle nozze d'Emilia*, ed. Alberto Limentani, in *Tutte le opere*, vol. 2, ed. Vittore Brance (Milan: Mondadori, 1964), 234–40; Surdich, *La cornice di amore: Studi sul Boccaccio*, 104–7; Bruni, *Boccaccio: L'invenzione della letteratura mediana*, 195–96. Boccaccio himself appears so aware of the change of course that at the beginning of book III (1–2) he placed a note to the reader followed by a second "author's invocation":

> After Juno's furor against destroyed Thebes had somewhat diminished, Mars returned with his furies to his cold region. Therefore I shall sing with more tender rhymes of Cupid and of his battles. I implore him to be present in what I reveal about him.
>
>   May his power enter into my verses

>   Poi che alquanto il furor di Iunone
>   fu per Tebe distrutta temperato,
>   Marte nella sua fredda regione
>   con le sue Furie insieme s'è tornato;
>   per che ormai con più pio sermone
>   sarà da me Cupido cantato
>   e delle sue battaglie, il quale io priego
>   che sia presente a ciò che di lui spiego.
>   Ponga ne' versi miei la sua potenza.

Translation from Boccaccio, *Theseid of the Nuptials of Emilia*, trans. Traversa, 425.

47. See Boccaccio, *Filostrato*, 5–6; and Lucia Battaglia Ricci, "L'Omero di Boccaccio," *Studi sul Boccaccio* 46 (2018): 57–59.

48. Translations from Boccaccio, *Il Filostrato*, ed. Vincenzo Pernicone and trans. Robert P. apRoberts and Anna Bruni Seldis (New York and London: Garland Publishing, 1986), 13 and 3, respectively.

49. *Teseida*, I.1.

50. The observation that the incipit of the *Filostrato* refers to that of the *Teseida* was first made by Carlo Muscetta, "Giovanni Boccaccio," in *Letteratura italiana: Storia e testi*, II.2: *Il Trecento* (Bari: Laterza, 1972), 98; it was later proposed again by many others, including Balduino, *Boccaccio, Petrarca e altri poeti del Trecento*, 244–47; Surdich, *La cornice di amore:*

Studi sul Boccaccio, 98; Boccaccio, *Filostrato*, 12; and Battaglia Ricci, *Boccaccio*, 76–77. For the dating of the *Filostrato*, in addition to the works by Surdich and Battaglia Ricci, see Balduino, *Boccaccio, Petrarca e altri poeti del Trecento*, 231–47, and Bruni, *Boccaccio: L'invenzione della letteratura mediana*, 160–73.

51. The hypothesis that the composition of the *Filostrato* took place during that of the *Teseida* is Surdich's (*La cornice di amore: Studi sul Boccaccio*, 77–117; see also Boccaccio, *Filostrato*). According to this, the interruption was due to Boccaccio's desire to pay homage with a love story to the Giovanna-Filomena to whom the *Filostrato* is dedicated, and this sentimental urgency is revealed by the verses "Amore / novellamente m'ha fatto mutare / il mio costume antico e usitato" ("Love has recently made me change my old and customary habit"; translation from Boccaccio, *Il Filostrato*, trans. apRoberts and Seldis, 17) of part 1, in which the adverb *novellamente* "signals something that happened a short time earlier, indicates a recent and sudden change" (Surdich, *La cornice di amore: Studi sul Boccaccio*, 103). It may be that there is no close and consequential connection between biographical events (which are, moreover, presumed) and literary elaboration, but it is undeniable that the *Teseida* shows a sharp break between the first two and the other ten books.

52. The autograph codex of the *Teseida* (Acquisti e Doni 325 of the Biblioteca Medicea Laurenziana) is certainly later than the early 1340s: "on the basis of paleography it can be dated to near 1350" according to William E. Coleman, "Teseida delle nozze d'Emilia," in *Boccaccio autore e copista*, exhibition catalog, ed. Teresa De Robertis, Carla Maria Monti, Marco Petoletti, Giuliano Tanturli, and Stefano Zamponi (Florence: Biblioteca Medicea Laurenziana, October 11, 2013–January 11, 2014) (Florence: Mandragora, 2013), 94–95 (who specifies: "the work of transcription took place in two phases: around 1350 the poem plus about 1075 glosses were copied; around 1355–60 numerous passages of the text were revised and slightly more than 220 glosses were added); "around 1348," more precisely "sometime before 1348" or "immediately before," according to Cursi, *La scrittura e i libri di Giovanni Boccaccio*, 25, 29, 131; "around the years 1345–1350," according to Marco Cursi and Maurizio Fiorilla, "Giovanni Boccaccio," in *Autografi dei letterati italiani: Le origini e il Trecento*, ed. Giuseppina Brunetti, Maurizio Fiorilla, and Marco Petoletti (Rome: Salerno Editrice, 2013), 48–56, 49; "at the end of the 1340s or, at the latest, at the beginning of the following decade," according to Sandro Bertelli, "Codicologia d'autore: Il manoscritto in volgare secondo Giovanni Boccaccio," in *Dentro l'officina di Giovanni Boccaccio: Studi sugli autografi in volgare e su Boccaccio dantista*, ed. Bertelli and Davide Cappi (Città del Vaticano: Biblioteca Apostolica Vaticana, 2014), 33.

53. According to Surdich, *La cornice di amore: Studi sul Boccaccio*, 97, it is likely that the dedicatory letter "was written when the poem was

complete, therefore in late 1340 or even in 1341"; in contrast, according to Vittore Branca, *Giovanni Boccaccio: Profilo biografico* (Florence: Sansoni, 1977 [1967]), 48, "the letter of dedication to Fiammetta . . . clearly dates, also because of its evident character as *dictamen*, to the Naples period." As for the sections of the text written after the return to Florence, it can be said with some certainty that at least part of the glosses prepared by Boccaccio himself date to the Florentine years, beginning in 1341 (in addition to Coleman, "Teseida delle nozze d'Emilia," see Branca, *Giovanni Boccaccio: Profilo biografico*, 49; Surdich, *La cornice di amore: Studi sul Boccaccio*, 103–4; Bruni, *Boccaccio: L'invenzione della letteratura mediana*, 201; and Battaglia Ricci, *Boccaccio*, 94–95); in all likelihood dating from that period are at least the last octaves of book XII (84–86) containing the "Words of the author to his book" ("parole dell'autore al libro suo") with the citation of the *De vulgari*; perhaps the two concluding sonnets with the Muses' request to the dedicatee to indicate what title to give the work and her response; definitely some paratextual parts, such as the sonnet introducing the entire poem ("In which the general subject of the book is contained" ["nel quale si contiene uno argomento generale a tutto il libro"]), which could only have been written after the work was completed.

54. A faint trace of Fiammetta may perhaps be found in the fictitious letter to Petrarca, *Mavortis milex extrenue*, of 1339, presumably written during the composition of *Filostrato* and *Teseida*. The letter begins by recounting, first, the writer's falling in love suddenly and inexorably, literally love at first sight, with a woman who appeared before him when he was walking in Naples near Virgil's tomb, then, after a long struggle, his winning her favor and, in the end, his bitter disappointment when she abruptly and unjustly refuses him. As is well known, this narrative of meeting and falling in love follows to the letter the story Dante told in his epistle to Marchese Moroello Malaspina of his own sudden falling in love with a woman he met in Casentino. This does not rule out the possibility that Boccaccio was referring to one of his own personal experiences of love. Might we consider Fiammetta? Scholarly opinions differ: Della Torre, a biographer of a positivist cast (*La giovinezza di G. Boccaccio (1313–1341)*, 335–38), believes that the love affair did refer to Fiammetta; according to Bruni, *Boccaccio: L'invenzione della letteratura mediana*, 71, the rhetorical exercise is "devoid of autobiographical value," while Kirkham, *Fabulous Vernacular: Boccaccio's "Filocolo" and the Art of Medieval Fiction*, 71, through an allegorical reading centered on Virgil's tomb, arrives at the conclusion that the letter "describes a situation that corresponds perfectly to the *Filocolo*." The "flame" ("flamma") of beauty could in fact refer to Fiammetta: "For just as heavenly lightning is followed immediately after by thunder, so once I had seen the flame of her beauty, a love, terrible and imperious, seized me fiercely" ("Nam sicut divinis corruscationibus illico subcedunt tonitrua, sic inspecta flamma pulcritudinis huius,

amor terribilis et imperiosus me tenuit atque ferox," *Ep.*, II.5). However, Boccaccio is following the text of Dante's letter word for word here ("Nam sicut divinis coruscationibus illico succedunt tonitrua, sic inspecta flamma pulcritudinis huius Amor terribilis et imperiosus me tenuit atque ferox," *Ep.*, IV.2), and this requires us to be cautious. Giovanni Boccaccio, *Epistole*, ed. Ginetta Auzzas, in *Tutte le opere*, ed. Vittore Branca, vol. 5, 1 (Milan: Mondadori, 1992), 756, has it that "if it were real, this would be the autobiographical love epistle." In actuality, the story, in a few quick strokes—falling in love, brief happiness, the woman's sudden and unexplained refusal—resembles that of Caleon and Fiammetta in the *Filocolo* (which we know is different from the story of Maria and the author) and especially the story told in the letter to Fiammetta in the *Teseida*. Fuller analyses of the epistle are found in Carla Maria Monti, "L'immagine di Petrarca negli scritti di Boccaccio," *Atti e Memorie dell'Accademia Galileiana di Scienze, Lettere ed Arti già dei Ricovrati e Patavina* 127, pt. 3 (2014–15): 292–300, and Santagata, *Boccaccio indiscreto: Il mito di Fiammetta* (Bologna: il Mulino, 2019), 139–42.

55. *Filos.*, Proem, 16: "il vostro nome di grazia pieno" ("your name full of grace").

56. This is Surdich's suspicion (*La cornice di amore: Studi sul Boccaccio*, 94–95), repeated by Bruni, *Boccaccio: L'invenzione della letteratura mediana*, 168.

57. Emphasis added. Translation from Boccaccio, *Il Filostrato*, trans. apRoberts and Seldis, 7, 9.

58. *Ep.*, II.6: "Post diutinam lassitudinem gratiam merui dominantis, quam ego alacris, inargutulus tamen, per tempusculum conservavi ... subito causa non atramento sed lacrimis describenda suborta, iniuste tamen mee domine incido in orrorem" ("After a long ordeal, I finally earned the grace of my lady; which I eagerly, but a little foolishly, kept for a short while ... suddenly, a situation arose that cannot be described with ink but with tears, I fell, though unjustly, into horror"). [Translator's note: This quotation from *Ep.*, II, found in n33 of this chapter in the original Italian edition, does not contain the words or ideas cited in the associated text. The author appears to have relied on an Italian translation of this Latin passage (included in the original note) that translates "inargutulus" as "rustichetto." The word "rudis" cited in the main text does appear in *Ep.*, II, but at the beginning of the letter, not in the context the author describes. However, the letter does contain other references to crudeness and rusticity, including this phrase late in the letter, which appears to contain the association of ideas the author describes: "possim fortune miserias et amoris angustias debellare, ac exui a qualibet ruditate, cum me miserum rudem inermem inertem crudum pariter et informem cognoscam."]

59. Translation from Boccaccio, *Theseid of the Nuptials of Emilia*, trans. Traversa, 378.

60. The first reliable evidence of his knowledge of Apuleius's *Metamorphoses* comes from 1338 or a little later: on this, see Maurizio Fiorilla, "Un Apuleio letto e annotato dal giovane Boccaccio: Firenze, Biblioteca Medicea Laurenziana, Pluteo 29. 2," in *BAC*, 352–53, and Igor Candido, *Boccaccio umanista: Studi su Boccaccio e Apuleio* (Ravenna: Longo, 2014), 17–19, 29.

61. *Ep.*, I–IV.

62. For Boccaccio's *dictaminia*, that is, the epistolary exercises of 1339, see Billanovich, *Restauri boccacceschi*, 74; Giuseppe Billanovich, *Petrarca letterato*, vol. 1, *Lo scrittoio del Petrarca* (Rome: Edizioni di *Storia e letteratura*, 1947; repr. 1995), 65–66.

63. On his relationship with vernacular translations of classical works, see Stefano Carrai, *Boccaccio e i volgarizzamenti* (Rome and Padua: Editrice Antenore, 2016) (the phrases quoted are on 10); on the innovation represented by the *Teseida*, see Giuliano Tanturli, "Volgarizzamenti e ricostruzione dell'antico: I casi della terza e quarta Deca di Livio e di Valerio Massimo, la parte del Boccaccio (a proposito di un'attribuzione)," *Studi Medievali*, ser. 3, 27 (1986): 883–85.

64. An early date has been hypothesized for the *Elegia di Costanza* (*Carmina*, I), because of the immaturity of the metrical composition—which seems to fit perfectly with Boccaccio's confession in the *Genealogia*: ("Although I did not yet know what kind or how many feet in a verse" [*GDG*, XV.10, 8; "Cum nondum novissem quibus seu quot pedibus carmen incederet"]; see Angelo Piacentini, "*Carmina*," in *Boccaccio autore e copista*, exhibition catalog, ed. Teresa De Robertis, Carla Maria Monti, Marco Petoletti, Giuliano Tanturli, and Stefano Zamponi [Florence: Biblioteca Medicea Laurenziana, October 11, 2013–January 11, 2014] [Florence: Mandragora, 2013], 223)—and a similar hypothesis has been suggested for the so-called *Allegoria mitologica*, in prose, which today Manlio Pastore Stocchi has rightly proposed be called "Allegoria storica" (in his edition in *TO*, vol. 2 [1994], 1091–1123; at 1093): for example, it has been said that the two "are little more than school exercises, prior to 1334" (Sabatini, *Napoli angioina: Cultura e società*, 106). But, instead, for these two works we need go at least to 1338–39, the period of the epistolary exercises (*dictaminia*) for the *Elegia* (Giuseppe Velli, *Petrarca e Boccaccio: Tradizione, memoria, scrittura* [Padua: Editrice Antenore, 1979], 98–99), and perhaps as far as 1340 for the *Allegoria* (Giuliano Tanturli and Stefano Zamponi, "Biografia e cronologia delle opere," in *Boccaccio autore e copista*, exhibition catalog, ed. Teresa De Robertis, Carla Maria Monti, Marco Petoletti, Giuliano Tanturli, and Stefano Zamponi (Florence: Biblioteca Medicea Laurenziana, October 11, 2013–January 11, 2014) (Florence: Mandragora, 2013), 61–64, 62).

65. Dante, *Ep.*, III, XI, XII, IV.

66. There is a long-standing scholarly debate underway on the authorship of the "Epistola di frate Ilaro" (most recently published in

Saverio Bellomo, "Il sorriso di Ilaro e la prima redazione in latino della 'Commedia,'" in *Studi sul Boccaccio* 32 [2004]: 201–35; on 206–9): in any case, the contention has been put to rest that it was a rhetorical exercise of Boccaccio himself (the basic outlines of the argument are summarized in Marco Santagata, *Dante: Il romanzo della sua vita* [Milan: Mondadori, 2012], 368–70).

67. The correspondence between Dante and Giovanni del Virgilio can be found, with commentary, in the editions edited by Gabriella Albanese ("Egloge," in Dante Alighieri, *Opere*, ed. Marco Santagata [Milano: Mondadori, 2014], vol. 2, 1593–1783; hers are the phrases cited, 1605 and 1611) and by Marco Petoletti ("Egloge," in Dante Alighieri, *Le opere* [Rome: Salerno Editrice, n.d.], vol. 5, 491–650). The only of Dante's works we can say for certain that Boccaccio knew during the time he lived in Naples is the letter to Moroello (*Ep.*, IV); for all the others we have to rely on paleographical analyses of the dating of the relevant pages of the *Zibaldone Laurenziano*. The transcription of the letters (including the "Epistle of Ilaro") and of the bucolic verse correspondence between Dante and Giovanni del Virgilio was conducted during either the span 1339–42 or the slightly more restricted one of 1339–41 (see the original analysis of Zamponi, Pantarotto, and Tomiello, "Stratigrafia dello Zibaldone e della Miscellanea laurenziani," and the adjustments suggested by Giuseppe Indizio, "L'Epistola di Ilaro: un contributo sistemico," in *Studi danteschi* 71 (2006): 191–263, reprinted in *Problemi di biografia dantesca* [Ravenna: Longo, 2013], 263–315). In short, we are dealing with the period straddling the Naples and Florentine periods (remember that Boccaccio's move to Florence took place in the autumn of 1340), a distinction so subtle that it is nearly impossible to establish on the basis of paleography alone how many of the works and which ones Boccaccio knew or, better, transcribed in Naples, and which and how many in Florence. It should be said, however, that the analysis of his texts, the traces of literary influences on them, as well as the discovery of some slight intertextual connections makes plausible the hypothesis that Dante's bucolic poetry was known to Boccaccio at the time of the *Filocolo* (see Giorgio Padoan, *Il Boccaccio, le Muse, il Parnaso e l'Arno* [Florence: Olschki, 1978], 151–98; Giuseppe Indizio, "L'Epistola di Ilaro: un contributo sistemico," *Studi danteschi* 71 [2006]: 191–263, reprinted in *Problemi di biografia dantesca* (Ravenna: Longo, 2013), 263–315; and Gabrielle Albanese, "Boccaccio bucolico e Dante da Napoli a Forlì," in *Boccaccio e la Romagna*, conference proceedings, ed. Albanese and Pontari [Forlì, Salone comunale, November 22–23, 2013] [Ravenna: Longo, 2015], 67–109).

68. In 1339, at the time of the epistle *Mavortis milex*, Boccaccio did not yet know any of Petrarca's Latin works (Monti, "L'immagine di Petrarca negli scritti di Boccaccio," 296–97). It would be interesting to establish how Boccaccio first came across Petrarca's poetry. Considering how tight

the personal, commercial, financial, and political links were between Naples and Florence, communication channels in both directions must have always been open, and the presence of books in couriers' satchels traveling from Florence to Naples, if not frequent, would also not have been exceptional. For example, one wonders how and where Boccaccio got a hold of Andrea Lancia's vernacular translation of the prose summary of the *Aeneid* by the friar Anastasio di Santa Croce, a translation that accompanies Virgil's text in the first books of the *Filocolo* (I.10; II.39, 3): in Florence, before moving to Naples? And what might the role have been of Coppo di Borghese Domenichi, the commissioner of the translation, city-history enthusiast, and source of Florentine news on which Boccaccio drew his entire life? See Tanturli, "Volgarizzamenti e ricostruzione dell'antico: I casi della terza e quarta Deca di Livio e di Valerio Massimo, la parte del Boccaccio (a proposito di un'attribuzione)," 881–82; Bruni, *Boccaccio: L'invenzione della letteratura mediana*, 102–6; Luca Azzetta, "Andrea Lancia," in *Censimento dei commenti danteschi*, vol. 1, *I commenti di tradizione manoscritta (fino al 1480)*, ed. Enrico Malato and Andrea Mazzucchi (Rome: Salerno Editrice, 2011), 21–22.

69. Translation from Boccaccio, *Il Filostrato*, trans. apRoberts and Seldis, 305.

70. Translation from Francesco Petrarca, *Petrarch: The Canzoniere, or Rerum Vulgarium Fragmenta*, trans. Mark Musa (Indianapolis: Indiana University Press, 1999), 171.

71. For this vexing question, see Santagata, *Boccaccio indiscreto. Il mito di Fiammetta*, 110–16. Although the themes of the blessing and curse are topical, there could also be a direct relationship (see Marco Santagata, *Per moderne carte: La biblioteca volgare di Petrarca* [Bologna: il Mulino, 1990], 254–55) between Petrarca's lines (*Rvf*, 61, 1–4):

Benedetto sia 'l giorno, e 'l mese, et l'anno,
et la stagione, e 'l tempo, et l'ora, e 'l punto,
e 'l bel paese, e 'l loco ov'io fui giunto
da' duo begli occhi che legato m'ànno

and these in the *Filostrato* (III.83):

E benedico il tempo, l'anno e 'l mese,
il giorno, l'ora e 'l punto che costei
onesta, bella, leggiadra e cortese,
primieramente apparve agli occhi miei

72. Translation from Boccaccio, *Il Filostrato*, trans. apRoberts and Seldis, 309–11.

73. Translation from *An Anthology of Italian Poems 13th–19th Century*, selected and trans. Lorna de'Lucchi (New York: Knopf, 1922), 68–69.

74. Balduino, *Boccaccio, Petrarca e altri poeti del Trecento*, 183.

75. *La dolce vista* can be said to have left no trace in Boccaccio's earlier works, so long as the poem *Amico, se tu vuogli avere onore* (attested, adespota, in a late fifteenth-century manuscript) is not considered one of his youthful compositions, which its literary quality, too low even by the standards of an immature Boccaccio, would seem to rule out. This poem was published by Vittore Branca, first, with a cautious stance toward Boccaccio's authorship, in Vittore Branca, *Tradizione delle opere di Giovanni Boccaccio*, vol. 1, *Un primo elenco dei codici e tre studi* (Rome: Edizioni di *Storia e letteratura*, 1958; repr. 2014), 270–75, and then in his edition of the *Rime* of that same year (*Rime, Caccia di Diana* [Padua: Liviana, 1958]); later, with a stronger inclination to recognize Boccaccio's style, in Giovanni Boccaccio, *Rime*, ed. Vittore Branca, in *Tutte le opere*, ed. Vittore Branca, vol. 5, 1 (Milan: Mondadori, 1992), 3–144, 195–374 (see esp. 340–41). Previous to that last publication, two publications by Guglielmo Gorni supported the credibility of Boccaccio's authorship: regarding his arguments, I will point out only that the poem's meter is not just identical to that of *La dolce vista*, but is also the meter's only reuse in the fourteenth century. In his view, *Amico, se tu vuogli* was written before Cino's death (in 1336) "by an intimate of the master of Pistoia, who shared his poetic tastes; and, if the juridical material is not illusory, by someone who had some idea of or interest in administrative law" (Gorni, *Metrica e analisi letteraria*, 166). The work is listed under the name Boccaccio in Andrea Pelosi's inventory, "La canzone italiana del Trecento," in *Metrica* 5 (1990): 3–162, while for Beltrami, *La metrica italiana*, 108, "the attribution to Boccaccio is likely, but not completely certain." It is excluded from the critical edition of Giovanni Boccaccio, *Rime*, ed. Roberto Leporatti (Florence: Edizioni del Galluzzo, 2013) (see CCXXXIX–CCXL).

76. For Sennuccio del Bene generally and his links to Boccaccio, see Daniele Piccini, *Un amico del Petrarca: Sennuccio del Bene e le sue rime* (Rome and Padua: Editrice Antenore, 2004), and Giuseppe Billanovich, "L'altro stil nuovo: Da Dante teologo a Petrarca filologo," *Studi petrarcheschi* 11 (1994): 1–98 (which summarizes his four decades of research on the topic). Indizio's comments ("L'Epistola di Ilaro: un contributo sistemico," 313–15) regarding Sennuccio as the likely conduit for Ilaro's letter can be extended to Dante's letters and Petrarca's lyrical compositions. On the basis of echoes of Sennuccio's poetry in Boccaccio's Neapolitan works, Piccini writes (*Un amico del Petrarca: Sennuccio del Bene e le sue rime*, XXIX) "if nothing else, [Boccaccio's] direct knowledge of some of Sennuccio's work can be hypothesized." Furthermore, Sennuccio knew Cino's *La dolce vista*: the second line of the sonnet *Mirando fiso nella chiara luce*

(IX) echoes the second of Cino's song; and vv. 9–10 of Sennuccio's ballad *Così come suo par non nacque mai* (XII) similarly seem to be influenced by vv. 13–14 of the song. *La dolce vista* is "absent from all the fourteenth-century codices that have come down to us," so the four octaves of the *Filostrato* are "the earliest witness" of it (Domenico De Robertis, *Editi e rari: Sulla tradizione letteraria tra Tre e Cinquecento* [Milano: Feltrinelli, 1978], 13–14): regarding this, see also Gorni, *Metrica e analisi letteraria*, 164–65.

Chapter Five

1. Translation from Boccaccio, *L'Ameto*, trans. Serafini-Sauli, 143.

2. Luigi Surdich, *La cornice di amore: Studi sul Boccaccio* (Pisa: Edizioni ETS, 1987), 153.

3. In 1338 Acciaiuoli had gone with a military expedition to the Morea to restore the rights of his patron, Catherine of Valois-Courtenay, and returned to Naples on August 28, 1341 (see the reconstruction of the events in Francesco Paolo Tocco, *Niccolò Acciaiuoli: Vita e politica in Italia alla metà del XIV secolo* [Rome: Istituto storico italiano per il Medioevo, 2001], 27–44). However, since it is probably a vernacular translation of the original text, Boccaccio's letter gives rise to many doubts, to the point that, on the basis of conjecture, its composition has been moved to 1348, when, in the summer, Acciaiuoli returned from Provence where he had taken refuge following the war between the Anjou of Naples and Louis of Hungary (this is the thesis of Pier Giorgio Ricci, *Studi sulla vita e le opere del Boccaccio* [Milan and Naples: Ricciardi, 1985], 172–78); the terms of the question, complicated by the explicit mention of Dionigi di Borgo Sansepolcro's death, which took place in January 1342—for which see Giovanni Boccaccio, *Epistole*, ed. Ginetta Auzzas, in *Tutte le opere*, ed. Vittore Branca, vol. 5, 1 (Milan: Mondadori, 1992), 776–77—are succinctly laid out by Marco Petoletti, "*Epistole*," in *Boccaccio autore e copista*, exhibition catalog, ed. Teresa De Robertis, Carla Maria Monti, Marco Petoletti, Giuliano Tanturli, and Stefano Zamponi (Florence: Biblioteca Medicea Laurenziana, October 11, 2013–January 11, 2014) (Florence: Mandragora, 2013), 237–38. In reality, the text corresponds much more closely to the situation in 1341 than to that in 1348: returning from Provence, in fact, Acciaiuoli traveled by sea from Nice, landed at Porto Pisano, and from there headed to Naples by land via Florence (Francesco Paolo Tocco, *Niccolò Acciaiuoli: Vita e politica in Italia alla metà del XIV secolo* [Rome: Istituto storico italiano per il Medioevo, 2001], 89–90). Boccaccio would have been able to meet him here and thus would have had no need to send a letter of welcome to another city. Additionally, in August 1348, Boccaccio's "welcome back" ("ben tornato") and attack on "wicked and sycophantic tongues" ("inique ed adulatrici lingue"), the "envious" and "proud" ("invidiosi" and "superbi")—the first silenced and the latter humiliated by the return of a

victorious Acciaiuoli—would not have been sufficient to make the letter's recipient forget the betrayal of only a few months before that when, in the service of Francesco Oredlaffi, Boccaccio had been about to march with the army against Queen Joanna and, therefore, against Acciaiuoli himself. And indeed the deterioration of their friendship appears to date to this time, while it was still intact at the time of Acciaiuoli's return from the Morea, as is attested by the fact that a short time later Boccaccio was involved by his friend in the legal processes preceding the foundation of the Charterhouse of Florence (Paolo Tocco, *Niccolò Acciaiuoli: Vita e politica in Italia alla metà del XIV secolo*, 51–53).

4. *Fam.* XXI.15, 27.

5. Giovanni Villani, *Nuova cronica*, XII.114, 1–10.

6. Here Fiammetta cites *Inf.*, XVII.106–8, combined with *Purg.*, IV.72. Translation from Boccaccio, *The Elegy of Lady Fiammetta*, trans. Causa-Steindler and Mauch, 100.

7. The thesis that Boccaccio attended some of the meetings between Robert of Anjou and Petrarca was based on the passage in the *Genealogia* (XIV.22, 5) in which Boccaccio mentions that the king, who until then had not thought much of poetry, having heard Petrarca was astonished to realize that poets' imaginations contained such sublime meaning: he had heard him say this with his own ears, Boccaccio wrote, from Petrarca himself ("ut ego, eo dicente, meis auribus audivi"). But this thesis assumed that "eo dicente" referred not to Petrarca but to Robert, and therefore that Boccaccio had been present at one of their conversations: this interpretation, proposed many times, most recently by Michele Feo, "Spighe," in *Vetustatis indagator: Scritti offerti a Filippo De Benedetto*, ed. Vincenzo Fera and Augusto Guida (Messina: Centro interdipartimentale di Studi umanistici, 1999), 326–29, but again refuted by Francisco Rico, *Ritratti allo specchio (Boccaccio, Petrarca)* (Rome and Padua: Editrice Antenore, 2012), 14–16. Lucia Battaglia Ricci, "L'Omero di Boccaccio," *Studi sul Boccaccio* 46 (2018): 60, holds that "although likely not present at the Naples examination of Petrarca," Boccaccio "could have remained [in Naples] until the summer of 1341 (the terminus ante quem is fixed by the letter sent from Florence to Acciaiuoli dated August 28, 1341 [*Ep.*, V])."

That receipts in the notary Ser Salvi's records for the rental contract for the church in Capua for November 1338 and 1339 specify that Boccaccino was a resident of the parish of Santa Felicita and say nothing about his son's residence, while the receipt of January 1, 1341, indicates that Giovanni was also resident there. This cannot, however, be cited as proof that Boccaccio was already in Florence on that date (see Vittore Branca, *Giovanni Boccaccio: Profilo biografico* [Florence: Sansoni, 1977 (1967)], 54) because, as is apparent from the relative documents, Boccaccino appeared alone before Ser Salvi not only for the notarial act of 1341 but also for that of 1342 when Giovanni was definitely in Florence.

8. Translation from Boccaccio, *The Elegy of Lady Fiammetta*, trans. Causa-Steindler and Mauch, 30.

9. Translation from Boccaccio, *The Elegy of Lady Fiammetta*, trans. Causa-Steindler and Mauch, 31.

10. Translation from Boccaccio, *The Elegy of Lady Fiammetta*, trans. Causa-Steindler and Mauch, 59.

11. It is true that Boccaccio had previously allowed his mixed feelings to show when referring to his relationship with his father, but never had he been so bitter as he was at the end of the *Comedia delle ninfe fiorentine*, nor would he ever be again.

12. Regnicoli, "Per la biografia di Giovanni Boccaccio: l'*Elegia di madonna Fiammetta* attraverso i documenti," has recently revisited the connection between the *Elegia di Madonna Fiammetta* and Boccaccino's family situation with the aid of new archival documents. Among the causes that could have determined his return to Florence, Branca, *Giovanni Boccaccio. Profilo biografico*, 52–53, points to the economic problems Boccaccino could have faced in that period, perhaps related to the Bardi company's difficult situation, a prelude to its disastrous failure in 1346; still, although it is conceivable that he was less prosperous than in the past, Boccaccino's alleged financial problems do not seem to be supported by the archival documents; on the contrary, there is evidence of his investments, albeit not large, in Certaldo in January 1340 and March 1341 (see Regnicoli, "Un'oscura vicenda certaldese: Nuovi documenti su Boccaccio e la sua famiglia," 77–78). Further evidence of affluence is the fact that in November 1343 his second wife, Bice Bostichi, was listed among the owners of luxurious dresses subject to taxation under the sumptuary laws (Emanuela Porta Casucci, "'Un uomo di vetro' fra corti e cortili: Giovanni Boccaccio, i Del Buono, i Rossi e gli altri," *Heliotropia* 12–13 [2015–16]: 196–97). It is true, however, that in November 1339 Boccaccino sold to Francesco the house in Santa Felicita bought seven years earlier in order to repay a one-hundred-florin debt (Regnicoli, "Per la biografia di Giovanni Boccaccio: l'*Elegia di madonna Fiammetta* attraverso i documenti," 2).

13. Translation based on Boccaccio, *Eclogues*, trans. Smarr, 3.

14. Giovanni Boccaccio, *Buccolicum carmen*, ed. Giorgio Bernardi Perini, in *Tutte le opere*, ed. Vittore Branca, vol. 5, 2 (Milan: Mondadori, 1994), 688–1090, 917–18; Branca, *Giovanni Boccaccio: Profilo biografico*, 72, also hypothesizes that Boccaccio "participated in some way, if only peripherally, in his father's business activities."

15. Giorgio Bernardi Perini, in Boccaccio, *Buccolicum carmen*, ed. Giorgio Bernardi Perini, in *Tutte le opere*, ed. Vittore Branca, vol. 5, 2 (Milan: Mondadori, 1994), 688–1090, at 917–18 writes: "It is difficult to detach the picture [depicted in the first thirteen lines of the eclogue] from the sense of anguish and frustration documented by the famous letter to Acciaiuoli of 1341 . . . during that first return from Naples that seemed to confine

Boccaccio to the narrow-minded Florentine mercantile milieu"; Janet Levarie Smarr also attributes the eclogue to the period of the *Comedia delle ninfe fiorentine* ("Boccaccio pastorale tra Dante e Petrarca," in *Autori e lettori di Boccaccio, Atti del Convegno internazionale di Certaldo [20–22 settembre 2001]*, ed. Michelangelo Picone [Firenze: Cesati, 2002], 237–54). However, Bernardi Perini continues (917), "the reference to the situation of 1341 does not at all imply a contemporary dating of the eclogue." This warning is linked to the fact that the beginning of Boccaccio's bucolic production is almost unanimously dated later, to the years 1347–48 with the start of his correspondence with Checco di Meletto Rossi. But it must be said that once the references to the economic hardships of Florentine Bishop Angelo Acciaiuoli (present in the eclogue under the name Egon) are removed—because they were the result of misinterpretations of passages by Ricci, *Studi sulla vita e le opere del Boccaccio*, 52–56, as Bernardi Perini, 922–23, shows—references that would lead one to 1346, the dating of 1347–48 rests solely on stylistic considerations, that is to say, on "the mature fluency of his literary form" (Giuseppe Velli, "A proposito di una recente edizione del 'Buccolicum Carmen' del Boccaccio," in *MLN*, CV, 1 [1990], 33–49; 48–49), which contrasts with the metrical and linguistic immaturity of Boccaccio's first Latin poem, the slightly earlier *Elegia di Costanza* (see Giuseppe Velli, *Petrarca e Boccaccio: Tradizione, memoria, scrittura* [Padua: Editrice Antenore, 1979], 98–99; Gabrielle Albanese, "Boccaccio bucolico e Dante da Napoli a Forlì," in *Boccaccio e la Romagna*, conference proceedings, ed. Albanese and Pontari [Forlì, Salone comunale, November 22–23, 2013] [Ravenna: Longo, 2015], 91, also supports this dating). The importance of this stylistic point is hard to avoid, unless we take literally the author's assertion in the letter to Martino da Signa that the first two eclogues were "of no importance . . . and just reveal my youthful licentiousness on their exteriors" (*Ep.*, XXIII.4; "nullius momenti . . . et fere iuveniles lascivias meas in cortice pandunt"), that is, "youthful exercises of erotic poetry" (Boccaccio, *Buccolicum carmen*, ed. Giorgio Bernardi Perini, in *Tutte le opere*, ed. Vittore Branca, vol. 5, 2 (Milan: Mondadori, 1994), 688–1090, 695), and imagine an extensive reworking of the eclogue *Galla* at the time of its inclusion in the later book of bucolic poems.

16. The information that Boccaccino remarried five months after Giovanni's arrival is also derived from the *Elegia*, which places at precisely this point the false news of Panfilo's marriage reported to Fiammetta (V.2), but then refutes it by correctly attributing the marriage to his father (VI.2). Such information provided by a work of fiction would not have any value were it not that it fits very well within the new chronology reconstructed by Regnicoli, "Per la biografia di Giovanni Boccaccio: l'*Elegia di madonna Fiammetta* attraverso i documenti," that corrects interpretive errors—perpetuated in the literature (for example, Giovanni Boccaccio,

Elegia di Madonna Fiammetta, ed. Carlo Delcorno, in *Tutte le opere*, ed. Vittore Branca, vol. 5, 2 [Milan: Mondadori, 1994], 1–412, 3)—of a document concerning Bice that fixed the date of her wedding in 1343. Iacopo's date of birth, which was located in 1344 (Ricci, *Studi sulla vita e le opere del Boccaccio*, 140; Branca, *Giovanni Boccaccio: Profilo biografico*, 71), Regnicoli also revises in consideration of the fact that Iacopo should have been of age, that is at least eighteen, based on notarial acts dating from 1359–60, the period in which his marriage to Diana di Rinuccino di messer Lapo took place (see Domenico Tordi, *Attorno a Giovanni Boccaccio: Gl'inventari dell'eredità di Iacopo Boccaccio* [Orvieto: Rubeca & Scaletti, 1923], 11–12, 79). Angiolo Latini, "Il fratello di Giovanni Boccaccio," in *Studii su Giovanni Boccaccio*, ed. Società storica della Valdelsa (Castelfiorentino, 1913), 32–43, can be used, with caution, for Iacopo's biography.

17. Giovanni Boccaccio, *Comedia delle ninfe fiorentine*, ed. Antonio Enzo Quaglio, in *Tutte le opere*, ed. Vittore Branca, vol. 2 (Milan: Mondadori, 1964), 665–835, 932.

18. Francesco Sabatini, *Napoli angioina: Cultura e società* (Naples: ESI Edizioni, 1975), 83.

19. [Translator's note: Maria of Calabria was actually Robert's orphaned granddaughter, raised at his court with her older sister, Joanna, the king's heir.]

20. The most decisive arguments against the "myth" of Fiammetta were those of Giuseppe Billanovich, *Restauri boccacceschi* (Rome: Edizioni di Storia e letteratura, 1947), 81–101, and Branca, *Boccaccio medievale*, 235–300; currently, views such as Surdich, *La cornice di amore: Studi sul Boccaccio*, 85 ("The literary myth presupposes an actual experience, a real event, a love affair"), and Lucia Battaglia Ricci, *Boccaccio* (Rome: Salerno Editrice, 2000), 27 ("Of course she was not the fabled [Maria d'Aquino] . . . but she does not have to have been a myth created entirely from the poet's imagination or a phantom standing in for the young Boccaccio's many romantic experiences") prevail.

21. Billanovich, *Restauri boccacceschi*, 84–85. On 83, he wonders if "the Angevin bastards," of whom "recollections were very frequent among contemporaries" might not have served as "incitements to Boccaccio for this fantasy of his."

22. See Richard A. Goldthwaite, *L'economia della Firenze rinascimentale* (Bologna: il Mulino, 2013), 317, regarding the financial exposure of the banks to the Kingdom of England. The credit extended to the English crown by the Bardi alone in the 1340s is estimated to have been between 535,000 and 900,000 florins, equivalent to approximately one-quarter to one-third of the total liquid wealth of the city according to the *catasto* of 1427.

23. Fundamental on Villani, his insider's account of the financial crisis,

and the Buonaccorsi is Michele Luzzati, *Giovanni Villani e la compagnia dei Buonaccorsi* (Rome: Istituto della Enciclopedia Italiana, 1971).

24. Francesco Paolo Tocco, *Niccolò Acciaiuoli: Vita e politica in Italia alla metà del XIV secolo* (Rome: Istituto storico italiano per il Medioevo, 2001), 45.

25. The Florentine political situation of the first half of the 1340s is described in John M. Najemy, *Storia di Firenze: 1200–1575* (Turin: Einaudi, 2014), 162–79.

26. "folle compera," Giovanni Villani, *Nuova cronica*, XII.131, 5.

27. In reality, the 250,000 florins agreed upon then fell to 180,000 florins, and in the end, in 1345, Florence paid Mastino 65,000 florins (Gian Maria Varanini, "Della Scala, Mastino," in *DBI*, XXXVII [1989], and others report these figures).

28. Francesco Paolo Tocco, *Niccolò Acciaiuoli: Vita e politica in Italia alla metà del XIV secolo* (Rome: Istituto storico italiano per il Medioevo, 2001), 49–50.

29. Walter had already been in Florence in May–August 1326 as vicar of the Duke of Calabria. For his biography, see Ernesto Sestan, "Brienne, Gualtieri di," in *DBI*, XIV (1972).

30. The behavior of the Acciaiuoli family provides a good example of such attempts: In September 1345 they sold their ancestral palazzo in Borgo Santi Apostoli in a fictitious sale in which Niccolò Acciaiuoli provided the purchase money to the two buyers, one of whom was Niccolò's cousin, while other fictitious property sales are documented at the end of 1346; additionally, a large number of donations were made to the Carthusian monastery on Mount Acuto al Galluzzo established by Niccolò a few years earlier, donations that are suspicious because they are inconsistent with the quite modest assets granted at its founding and are probably attributable to the fact that the monastery was exempt from taxation (see Francesco Paolo Tocco, *Niccolò Acciaiuoli: Vita e politica in Italia alla metà del XIV secolo* [Rome: Istituto storico italiano per il Medioevo, 2001], 67–69).

31. Giorgio Padoan, *Il Boccaccio, le Muse, il Parnaso e l'Arno* (Florence: Olschki, 1978), 63.

32. "grande congiurazione"; Giovanni Villani, *Nuova cronica*, XII.118.

33. Translation from Boccaccio, *The Elegy of Lady Fiammetta*, trans. Causa-Steindler and Mauch, 34.

34. Regnicoli, "Per la biografia di Giovanni Boccaccio: l'*Elegia di madonna Fiammetta* attraverso i documenti," 13–14, argues that, in describing Florentine political instability in the *Elegia*, Boccaccio was referring to the situation following the plot of 1340, and consequently that the description is not "a clear allusion to the situation in Florence devastated by the disorder caused by the Duke of Athens' tyranny" (Giovanni Boccac-

cio, *Elegia di Madonna Fiammetta*, ed. Carlo Delcorno, in *Tutte le opere*, ed. Vittore Branca, vol. 5, 2 [Milan: Mondadori, 1994], 1–412, 267).

35. See Francesco Paolo Tocco, *Niccolò Acciaiuoli: Vita e politica in Italia alla metà del XIV secolo* (Rome: Istituto storico italiano per il Medioevo, 2001), 46–51.

36. *CVI*, IX.24. As is the case with most of Boccaccio's Latin works, the chronology of the composition of the *De casibus virorum illustrium* is somewhat uncertain: it is believed that the last two books (VIII and IX) were written between 1359 and 1360. See Vittorio Zaccaria, *Boccaccio narratore, storico, moralista e mitografo* (Florence: Olschki, 2001), 35–36.

37. In 1344, Boccaccino was one of the overseers of the Stinche, the Florentine prison (Laura Regnicoli, "Documenti su Giovanni Boccaccio," in *Boccaccio autore e copista*, exhibition catalog, ed. Teresa De Robertis, Carla Maria Monti, Marco Petoletti, Giuliano Tanturli, and Stefano Zamponi [Florence: Biblioteca Medicea Laurenziana, October 11, 2013–January 11, 2014] [Florence: Mandragora, 2013], 520–21); in 1345, *Ufficiale sopra la moneta*, currency official; in 1348, *Ufficiale dell'Abbondanza*, in charge of provisioning and hygiene measures (Branca, *Giovanni Boccaccio: Profilo biografico*, 72, 78).

38. Regarding the *vicinìa*, Porta Casucci, "'Un uomo di vetro' fra corti e cortili: Giovanni Boccaccio, i Del Buono, i Rossi e gli altri," 193, writes: "The neighborhood settled and resolved conflicts internally, provided initial welcome and financial support to immigrants as a link with the residents, offered solidarity, fellowship, policing, and security, supported professional and business associations. . . . Politically it functioned as a pool for election candidates and for political clientage." It is also worth noting that the "seven young women" ("sette giovani donne") of the *Decameron* are "each one . . . the friend, neighbor, or relative of one of the others" ("tutte l'una all'altra o per amistà o per vicinanza o per parentela congiunte"; I, Introd., 49).

39. The endurance of Boccaccio's ties to his fellow Certaldesi is illustrated by the letter (*Lett.*, II, Boccaccio's only known autograph) sent to Leonardo del Chiaro in May 1366 in Avignon (see Giuliano Tanturli, "La lettera a Leonardo del Chiaro," in *BAC*, 386–87). The money changer Leonardo, whom Boccaccio would name as guardian of his nephews in his will (see Laura Regnicoli, "La *cura sepulcri* di Giovanni Boccaccio," *Studi sul Boccaccio* 42 [2014]: 47–48), was not the son of Botte di Buoninsegna dei Guernieri (as Boccaccio, *Epistole*, ed. Ginetta Auzzas, in *Tutte le opere*, ed. Vittore Branca, vol. 5, 1 (Milan: Mondadori, 1992), 493–856, 875, claims) but of Botte's son Chiaro: the grandfather Botte, a judge, had moved from Certaldo to Oltrarno in Florence in the second half of the thirteenth century. Another of his sons, Gherardino, worked as a factor for the Bardi along with Boccaccino, who, as evidence of the strength of their relationship, was a witness at his marriage in 1333. It is worth

noting that in 1328 Gherardino was one of the witnesses for the wedding of Biagio Pizzini and Foresina degli Alioni. Biago is one of the "two very clever young men" ("due giovani, astuti molto")—the second was another Certaldese, Giovanni di Bragoniera—who try to trick Frate Cipolla by replacing the supposed feather of the archangel Gabriel with lumps of coal (*Dec.*, VI.10). He was one of Boccaccino's closest friends, his neighbor both in Certaldo and in Florence, where Biagio moved in the early 1330s; he probably died during the plague of 1340. There would later be a dispute between the heirs of his wife, Foresina, and Boccaccio's heirs over the house in Certaldo, which was literally wedged into that of Boccaccino, because Boccaccio's heirs had apparently appropriated the property; the protracted dispute was eventually settled so amicably that Iacopo, Boccaccio's half brother, made a will in February 1391 naming Foresina's heirs, the Botticini, as guardians of his children. We know almost nothing about the second of the "two young men," Giovanni di Bragoniera di Saracino dei Milotti: he probably died shortly after 1325. It is worth noting that a branch of the Milotti family had moved between the Romagna and Bologna: the physician Fiduccio, who died shortly after 1323, in Ravenna was in contact with Dante, who introduced him as character in his fourth eclogue to Giovanni del Virgilio under the name of Alfesibeo, an identification owed to a gloss of Boccaccio's in the *Zibaldone Laurenziano*. Boccaccio's connections with his fellow citizens of Certaldo are reconstructed in Laura Regnicoli, "Un'oscura vicenda certaldese: Nuovi documenti su Boccaccio e la sua famiglia," *Italia medioevale e umanistica* 58 (2017): 61–122; for the Milotti family, and Fiduccio in particolare, see Gabriella Albanese and Paolo Pontari, "L'ultimo Dante: Il cenacolo ravennate, le *Egloge* e la morte," in *L'ultimo Dante e il cenacolo ravennate*, exhibition catalog, ed. Gabriella Albanese and Paolo Pontari (Ravenna: Biblioteca Classense, September 9–October 28, 2018), in *Classense* 6 (2018): 58–67.

40. Translation from Boccaccio, *L'Ameto*, trans. Serafini-Sauli, 145.

41. Niccolò di Bartolo del Buono would be beheaded on December 30, 1360, for participating in a conspiracy against the government along with another of Boccaccio's friends, Pino de' Rossi. We do not know what Niccolò's relationship was with Boccaccio after the dedication of the *Comedia*: records show only a transaction of *Monte* shares in March 1356 (Laura Regnicoli, "Codice diplomatico di Giovanni Boccaccio 1. I documenti fiscali," *Italia medioevale e umanistica* 54 [2013]: 26; Laura Regnicoli, "Per il Codice diplomatico di Giovanni Boccaccio," in *Boccaccio letterato*, conference proceedings, ed. Michaelangiola Marchiaro and Stefano Zamponi [Florence-Certaldo, October 10–12, 2013] [Florence: Accademia della Crusca–Ente nazionale Giovanni Boccaccio], 516). For information on his life, see Francesca Klein, "Del Buono, Niccolò," in *DBI*, XXXVI (1988); Vieri Mazzoni, *Accusare e proscrivere. Il nemico politico. Legislazione antighibellina e persecuzione giudiziaria a Firenze (1347–1378)* (Pisa: Pacini Editore,

2010), app. 3, 180; Elsa Filosa, "L'amicizia ai tempi della congiura (Firenze 1360–61): 'A confortare non duole capo,'" *Studi sul Boccaccio* 42 (2014): 195–219; and Porta Casucci, "'Un uomo di vetro' fra corti e cortili. Giovanni Boccaccio, i Del Buono, i Rossi e gli altri," 191–92, 201–2.

42. Canigiani is the "nuostro compare ["our old friend"] Pietro dellu Canaiano" of the Neapolitan letter (*Lett.*, I.17). Boccaccio's friendship with Canigiani—begun in Naples, where Canigiani, a member of the Acciaiuoli circle, held among other positions that of Catherine of Valios-Courtenay's treasurer—would last until Boccaccio's death (he would name Canigiani as one of the guardians of his nephews; see Regnicoli, "La *cura sepulcri* di Giovanni Boccaccio," 47).

43. *Ep.*, V.

44. On the embassy, Prato, and the monastery, see Francesco Paolo Tocco, *Niccolò Acciaiuoli: Vita e politica in Italia alla metà del XIV secolo* (Rome: Istituto storico italiano per il Medioevo, 2001), 45–54.

45. *Teseida*, XII.84.

46. On Iacopo Alighieri, see Saverio Bellomo, "Alighieri, Iacopo," in Saverio Bellomo, *Dizionario dei commentatori danteschi: L'esegesi della "Commedia" da Iacopo Alighieri a Nidobeato* (Florence: Olschki, 2004), 62–77, and the unattributed entry "Jacopo Alighieri" of the *CCD*. It has been suggested that the author of the *Ottimo Commento* (for which, see Massimiliano Corrado, "Ottimo Commento," in *CCD*, 371–406, and especially the critical edition *Ottimo commento alla "Commedia,"* ed. Giovanni Battista Boccardo, Massimiliano Corrado, and Vittorio Celotto [Rome: Salerno, 2018], 3 vols., followed by the edition of the *Chiose sopra la "Comedia" del cosiddetto Amico dell'Ottimo*, ed. Ciro Perna) "had regular encounters and cultural affinity, I would even say friendship," with Andrea Lancia (Luca Azzetta, "Andrea Lancia," in *Censimento dei commenti danteschi*, I. *I commenti di tradizione manoscritta (fino al 1480)*, ed. Enrico Malato and Andrea Mazzucchi [Rome: Salerno Editrice, 2011], 29); Lancia's relationship with Villani is recognized (see also Luca Azzetta, "Per la biografia di Andrea Lancia," in *Italia medioevale e umanistica* 39 [1996]: 121–70), on whom, especially for the codex of the *Commedia* he owned and that was later stolen from him, and for the Dantean chapter of the *Nuova cronica* (X.136), see Gabriella Albanese, Bruno Figliuolo, and Paolo Pontari, "Giovanni Villani, Dante e un antichissimo codice della *Commedia*," in *Studi danteschi* 83 (2018): 349–412, and Luca Azzetta, "Ancora sul *Dante* di Giovanni Villani, Andrea Lancia e la prima circolazione fiorentina della *Commedia*," *Rivista di studi danteschi* 19 (2019): 148–67. Villani certainly wrote his biography of Dante before the summer of 1341, but the passages where he cites the *Convivio* and *De vulgari eloquentia* are later additions (see Roberta Cella, "Il *Centiloquio* di Antonio Pucci e la *Nuova Cronica* di Giovanni Villani," in *Firenze alla vigilia del Rinascimento: Antonio Pucci e i suoi contemporanei*, conference proceedings, ed. Maria Bendinelli Predelli

[Montreal, October 22–23, 2004] [Florence: Cadmo, 2006], 85–110): it should be noted that Lancia mentions the *Convivio* several times but never refers to *De vulgari*.

Lancia had relationships with both Boccaccino and Giovanni (Azzetta, "Andrea Lancia," 20–21), but there is no record of Villani's supposed friendship with Boccaccio, although Branca, *Giovanni Boccaccio: Profilo biografico*, 78–79, lists Villani among Boccaccio's "dearest friends" lost to the plague in 1348; it would be strange, however, if, while not friends, the two had not been acquaintances. Forese Donati, whose genealogy of the gods (composed with Franceschino degli Albizzi) Boccaccio transcribed in the *Zibaldone Magliabechiano*, 121r–123r), was friends with Francesco Nelli in Florence and then would come to know Francesco Petrarca in Avignon; he is noted by Guglielmo Maramauro for his Dante expertise (see Giuseppe Billanovich, *Petrarca letterato*, I. *Lo scrittoio del Petrarca* [Rome: Edizioni di *Storia e letteratura*, 1947; repr. 1995], 161–64; Giuseppe Billanovich, "L'altro stil nuovo: Da Dante teologo a Petrarca filologo," *Studi petrarcheschi* 11 [1994]: 80–85; the entry "Guglielmo Maramauro" in *CCD*, 262–67; Azzetta, "Ancora sul *Dante* di Giovanni Villani, Andrea Lancia e la prima circolazione fiorentina della *Commedia*," 157–59). Coppo di Borghese Domenichi was another of the Dante enthusiasts with known connections to Boccaccio (who said of him "he is dear to me above all others" ["michi dilecto pre ceteris"], *Ep.*, IX.10) and was also linked to Lancia. For Boccaccio's references to Coppo, see *ECD*, VIII [I].68; *ECD*, XVI.16; *Dec.*, V.9, 4; see also Francesco Bruni, *Boccaccio: L'invenzione della letteratura mediana* (Bologna: il Mulino, 1990), 103–4; for his biography, Liana Cellerino, "Domenichi, Coppo," in *DBI*, XL (1991). Also enamored of Dante was Antonio Pucci, poet, town crier, and *approvatore* of the Florentine commune (on whom, see Giuseppe Crimi, "Antonio Pucci [Firenze 1310 ca.–1388]," in *Autografi dei letterati italiani: Le origini e il Trecento* [cited as *ALI*], vol. 1, *Le origini e il Trecento*, ed. Giuseppina Brunetti, Maurizio Fiorilla, Marco Petoletti [Rome: Salerno Editrice, 2013] 265–69, and Anna Bettarini Bruni, "Pucci, Antonio," in *DBI*, LXXXV [2016]), who, among other things, rendered Villani's *Nuova cronica* in Dantean terza rima: his friendship with Boccaccio, attested also by their exchange of lyric texts, must have begun with the latter's arrival in Florence (see Antonio E. Quaglio, "Antonio Pucci primo lettore-copista-interprete di Giovanni Boccaccio," *Filologia e critica* 1 [1976]: 15–79 15–79, and Anna Bettarini Bruni, "Un quesito d'amore tra Pucci e Boccaccio," *Studi di filologia italiana* 38 [1980]: 33–54). In the 1340s, Boccaccio must also have strengthened his friendship with his former schoolmate Zanobi da Strada, who had succeeded his father Giovanni in running the school. It does not seem that Zanobi, a devotee of classical studies, nurtured an interest in Dante (the story that he commented on or read the *Commedia* in public remains to be proven: see Baglio, "Zanobi da Strada," 323; it is revealing that, in one of his [lost] orations held in the cathedral prior to 1348, he discussed the theme of the descent into hell with reference only to Virgil: see Baglio, "*Avidulus glorie*: Zanobi da Strada tra Boccaccio e Petrarca,*" 386), but he was nonetheless included in the circle of Florentine intellectuals: he was a friend Coppo di Borghese Domenichi, as is also shown by a letter of Boccaccio's (*Ep.*, VI.10), and connected to Giovanni Villani (Baglio, "*Avidulus glorie*: Zanobi da Strada tra Boccaccio e Petrarca,*" 383).

47. Albanese, "Boccaccio bucolico e Dante da Napoli a Forlì," 83–84 (but see the entire section, 81–87).

48. That there was an early draft of the first eclogue, *Galla*, in 1341–42 that was later revised or rewritten is only a hypothesis, support for which may be found in the history of the third eclogue, *Faunus*, of which we know an early redaction (published in *Carmina*, III, and by Simona Lorenzini, ed., *La corrispondenza bucolica tra Giovanni Boccaccio e Checco di Meletto Rossi: L'egloga di Giovanni del Virgilio ad Albertino Mussato* [Florence: Olschki, 2011], 146–52) that differs in many respects from the one included in the *Buccolicum carmen* (see Albanese, "Boccaccio bucolico e Dante da Napoli a Forlì," 93–94).

49. Barrili, like Canigiani, is also cited in the *Epistola napoletana* as an authoritative source vouching for the writer's great learning: "And Judge Barrili tells me that guy [Ja' Boccaccio] knows as much as the devil" (*Lett.*, I 15; "E chillo me dice judice Barillo ca isso sape quant'a lu demone"). For Barrili's biography, see Ingeborg Walter, "Barrili, Giovanni," in *DBI*, VI (1964), and Francesco Paolo Tocco, *Niccolò Acciaiuoli: Vita e politica in Italia alla metà del XIV secolo* (Rome: Istituto storico italiano per il Medioevo, 2001), 102–3; for Barbato's, see Augusto Campana, "Barbato da Sulmona," in *DBI*, VI (1964); for both, Nunzio Federigo Faraglia, "I due amici del Petrarca, Giovanni Barrili e Marco Barbato," *Archivio storico per le Province Napoletane* 9 (1884): 35–58. Correspondence to and from Barbato is published in *Lo scrittoio degli umanisti: Barbato da Sulmona fra Petrarca e Boccaccio*, ed. Giuseppe Papponetti (L'Aquila: Deputazione abruzzese di storia patria, 1984). It was on the occasion of the embassy to Florence in 1341, and not in Naples as was previously thought, that Sennuccio became friends with Barrili: see Giuseppe Billanovich, "L'altro stil nuovo: Da Dante teologo a Petrarca filologo," *Studi petrarcheschi* 11 (1994): 39–40, and Daniele Piccini, *Un amico del Petrarca: Sennuccio del Bene e le sue rime* (Rome and Padua: Editrice Antenore, 2004), xxxv.

50. "The only of Petrarca's writings that Boccaccio was able to compile immediately after the coronation" (Michele Feo, "Lo Zibaldone Laurenziano del Boccaccio," in *Codici latini del Petrarca nelle biblioteche fiorentine: Mostra 19 maggio–30 giugno 1991*, ed. Michele Feo [Florence: Le Lettere, 1991], 346), i.e., the metrical epistles I.14, I.4, I.13, and I.12, are transcribed, in this order, on folios 73r and 74 of the *Zibaldone Laurenziano*, transcriptions that codicological and paleographic analyses date

to the period 1341–44 (Zamponi, Pantarotto, and Tomiello, "Stratigrafia dello Zibaldone e della Miscellanea laurenziani," 240). The epistles are preceded by a text in capital letters known as the *Notamentum laureationis*, "generally considered the mother cell of the *De vita*, though it might well be a summary" (Rico, *Ritratti allo specchio (Boccaccio, Petrarca)*, 47); see Carla Maria Monti, "L'immagine di Petrarca negli scritti di Boccaccio," *Atti e Memorie dell'Accademia Galileiana di Scienze, Lettere ed Arti già dei Ricovrati e Patavina* 127, pt. 3 (2014–15): 300–307 (text on 303–4). The question of the chronology of the *De vita*, necessarily connected to that of the *Notamentum*, is uncertain and debated: the most credible hypothesis places the first draft between 1341 and 1342, which would have been followed by further work until 1350; a synthetic overview of the various positions is offered by Agnese Bellieni, "Le Vite di Petrarca, di san Pier Damiani e di Livio," in *Boccaccio autore e copista*, exhibition catalog, ed. Teresa De Robertis, Carla Maria Monti, Marco Petoletti, Giuliano Tanturli, and Stefano Zamponi (Florence: Biblioteca Medicea Laurenziana, October 11, 2013–January 11, 2014) (Florence: Mandragora, 2013), 215–17, 215–16; of particular importance are the works of Feo, "Lo Zibaldone Laurenziano del Boccaccio"(which, among other things, notes that Boccaccio knew the *Collatio laureationis* but not the *Privilegium*, the official diploma), and Rico, *Ritratti allo specchio (Boccaccio, Petrarca)*. For Laura Refe, "Boccaccio e Petrarca tra biografia e autobiografia," *Studi Petrarcheschi* 27 (2014): 121–43, his two most succinct but best informed Petrarca biographies, contained in *De montibus*, III.114 ("Sorgia"), and *Genealogia*, XV.6, 11, could be a sort of palinode of the *De vita*. They certainly are a complete reversal of what he had written in the *De vita* about Petrarca's romantic and sexual life, about which he said in *GDG*, XIV.19, 15: "From his youth Petrarch has lived celibate, and such has been his horror at impure and illicit love, that his friends know him for a perfect model of saintly and honorable living . . . dutiful, gentle, devout, and so modest that his is called a second Parthenias" ("Qui [Petrarca], a iuventute sua celibem vitam ducens, adeo inepte Veneris spurcitias horret, ut noscentibus illum sanctissimum sit exemplar honesti . . . pius, mitis, atque devotus, et adeo verecundus, ut iudicetur parthenias alter"); second after Virgil, who as a youth "won the nickname 'Parthenias,' that is, in Latin 'virgin,' or more correctly 'virginity'" (*GDG*, XIV.19, 12; "Iuvenis adhuc vocaretur parthenias, quod latine virgo seu virginitas sonat"). Translation based on that in Boccaccio, *Boccaccio on Poetry*, trans. Osgood, 91–92.

51. Rico, *Ritratti allo specchio (Boccaccio, Petrarca)*, 34.

52. *VP*, 3–5; "Quod dum pater referentibus pluribus audisset . . . cum eciam animo quam eterna temporalia pocius affectaret . . . indignans quodammodo ipsum ad lares proprios revocavit, et, cum illum studiorum talium obiurgatione multimoda momordisset, aiendo: 'Studium quid inutile tentas? Meonides ipse nullas reliquit opes,' eum suo imperio

oneratum leges auditurum secundo Montem misit illico Pesulanum. Sed, iubentibus fatis, quibus de facili non obstatur, Pyeridum corus egregius illum indissolubilibus amplexibus circumdavit, egreque ferens quem ab infantia educaret, et cui per ipsum fama candidior servabatur, eidem a legum perplexitate vitabili et rabidi fori latrabilibus iurgiis raperetur, Cesarum sanciones ac iurium consultorum tabulas indignanter abstulit ab eodem." This biographical information is somewhat incorrect: Petrarca studied at Montpellier before going to the University of Bologna.

53. *VP*, 7: "Se poesi patre eciam ignorante donavit."

54. *Ep.*, IV. It is revealing that the echo of the same passage of Ovid's *Tristia* returns in both the letter and the *De vita*: indeed, the "inque suum furtim Musa trahebat opus" of *Tristia*, IV.10, 20, underlies both the "furtive" of the letter and the "se poesi patre eciam ignorante donavit" of *VP*, 7; also belonging to *Tristia* (IV.10, 19–22) is the already cited reference to Homer that now reappears in the *De vita*: "at mihi iam puero caelestia sacra placebant, / inque suum furtim Musa trahebat opus. / Saepe pater dixit: 'studium quid inutile temptas? / Maeonides nullas ipse reliquit opes.'"

55. "Religione christianissimus et in tantum, ut vix ab expertis et cognitis crederetur. Libidine sola aliqualiter non victus in totum, sed multo potius molestatus; sed si quando ipsum contingit succumbere, iuxta mandatum Apostoli, quod caste nequivi explere, caute peragendo complevit."

56. Petrarca also had a daughter, Francesca, who married Francescuolo da Brossano in 1362, but whose date of birth is unknown, since the common notion that it was in 1343 is unfounded: see Francisco Rico, "Sobre la cronología del 'Secretum': las viejas leyendas y el fantasma nuevo de un lapsus bíblico," *Studi petrarcheschi* n.s. 1 (1984): 51–102, on 73; for Francescuolo, see Guido Martellotti, "Brossano, Francescuolo da," in *DBI*, XIV (1972), and Guido Martellotti, *Dante e Boccaccio e altri scrittori dall'Umanesimo al Romanticismo* (Florence: Olschki, 1983), 464–68.

57. "Ac [ut] aptius posset mundanarum rerum sollicitudines evitare, vitam assumpsit et habitum clericalem."

58. "Et quamvis in suis quampluribus vulgaribus poematibus in quibus perlucide dacantavit, se Laurettam quandam ardentissime demonstrarit amasse, non obstat; nam, prout ipsemet et bene puto, Laurettam illam allegorice pro laurea corona quam postmodum est adeptus accipendam existimo." Regarding the name Lauretta, it can be assumed either that Boccaccio had read sonnet 5 of the *Canzoniere*, in which Petrarca calls his beloved "Laureta" and "Laurea" (see Francesco Petrarca, *Canzoniere*, ed. Marco Santagata, updated ed. [Milan: Mondadori, 2004], 26–27), or that he had heard the name, for example, from Sennuccio; however, the identification of his beloved with the crown of laurels was common among readers of Petrarca (including Sennuccio), so much so that Petrarca himself weighed in many times at the time of the *Secretum*

to confirm the reality of his passion (see Marco Santagata, *I frammenti dell'anima: Storia e racconto nel Canzoniere di Petrarca* [Bologna: il Mulino, 2004], 89–96).

59. It is interesting to see that modern readers have shared Boccaccio's doubts: see Surdich, *La cornice di amore: Studi sul Boccaccio*, 134; and Lucia Battaglia Ricci, *Boccaccio* (Rome: Salerno Editrice, 2000), 108.

60. My observations were inspired by Rico's innovative reading of this passage of the *De Vita* (*Ritratti allo specchio (Boccaccio, Petrarca)*, 63–72).

61. On this dating, see Edoardo Fumagalli, "Boccaccio e Dante," in *Boccaccio autore e copista*, exhibition catalog, ed. Teresa De Robertis, Carla Maria Monti, Marco Petoletti, Giuliano Tanturli, and Stefano Zamponi (Florence: Biblioteca Medicea Laurenziana, October 11, 2013–January 11, 2014) (Florence: Mandragora, 2013), 25–31.

62. On this letter, see Michele Feo, *Con madonna povertà: Lettera di Giovanni Boccaccio a Donato degli Albanzani* (Pontedera: Bandecchi & Vivaldi, 2012). In it, among other things, Boccaccio complains, wonderingly, that his lazy and idle half brother received from his wife's parents "a dowry that is much larger than is fitting for him" (*EpA*, 53; "eam . . . cum longe maiori dote quam eum deceat in coniugem tradidere"); and, indeed, Piera, about whose family we know nothing, had a dowry of the "far from insignificant for the time . . . 200 gold florins" (Domenico Tordi, *Attorno a Giovanni Boccaccio: Gl'inventari dell'eredità di Iacopo Boccaccio* [Orvieto: Rubeca & Scaletti, 1923], 12).

63. "Hei michi, abstulit Deus michi virgunculam meam ut alienam susciperem, cum illa causa oblectationis esset et hec ut ariolor erit angustie."

64. "Quo insuper putas animo ruentem in mortem posse puellares cernere ludos? quo gannitus audire petulcos? quo aspicere fluentes lascivia mores?"

65. "Michi iuveni . . . fuere dulcia suavia mulierum."

66. Elisa Curti writes of the nymphs: "the tales of their love affairs . . . make them figures that are, within the story, completely earthly and anchored in civic life . . . in short, they are, at base, clearly 'city' ['*cittadina*'] women" ("Le ninfe di Boccaccio: Osservazioni sulla tradizione toscana," in *BV*, 29–46; citation on 32).

67. Emilia is also referred to in *AV*, XLIV.25–30, without using her name, but deploring her bad marriage after she left the convent (in 1342–43 her husband Giovanni di Nello was still living; he would die around 1347); both their names appear in the *Contento quasi*, *Rime* 125a, 34–36 (which is believed to be slightly later than the *Comedia*), Emilia called here Meliana, and she could be the same Meliana who appears in the *Legiadro sermintese* in praise "of the beautiful women who were in Florence in MCCXXXV" by Antonio Pucci (according to Quaglio, "Antonio Pucci primo lettore-copista-interprete di Giovanni Boccaccio," 27–28, earlier than

Boccaccio's ternary). Emilia would also be one of the storytellers in the *Decameron*, in which Giovanni di Nello would also appear (VII.1), mocked by Emilia. The idea that Boccaccio was in love with Emilia Tornaquinci, proposed by Francesco Torraca, *Per la biografia di Giovanni Boccaccio: Appunti di Francesco Torraca, con i ricordi autobiografici e documenti inediti* (Milan, Rome, and Naples: Società Editrice Dante Alighieri di Albrighi, Segati e C., 1912) and then vigorously sustained by Billanovich, *Restauri boccacceschi*, 105–27, and Billanovich, *Petrarca letterato*, I. *Lo scrittoio del Petrarca*, 84–85, is branded "a romantic hypothesis" in Giovanni Boccaccio, *Rime*, ed. Vittore Branca, in *Tutte le opere*, ed. Vittore Branca, vol. 5, 1 (Milan: Mondadori, 1992), 3–144, 195–374, 252 (Branca, *Boccaccio medievale*, 292–93, is also very critical).

68. The year of her death is drawn from *Buccolicum carmen*, XIV.51–54; the news reached Boccaccio while he was traveling to the Kingdom of Naples in the autumn of 1355 (see Branca, *Giovanni Boccaccio: Profilo biografico*, 101–3). That he last saw his daughter when she was five and a half he wrote in a letter to Petrarca in 1367 (*Ep.*, XV.11). From his statements it is clear that Violante died "between the age of five and half . . . and seven, the age of reason" (Carla Maria Monti, "Il *ravennate* Donato Albanzani amico di Boccaccio e di Petrarca," in *Dante e la sua eredità a Ravenna nel Trecento*, ed. Marco Petoletti [Ravenna: Longo, 2015], 135).

69. *BC*, XIV (*Olympia*).

70. In *Ep.*, XXIII, 28, to Martino da Signa, Boccaccio wrote: "By Olympia I mean my little daughter, who died a long time ago at the age when we believe those who die become citizens of heaven: and therefore, she who was named Violante in life, in death I call 'heavenly,' that is, 'Olympia'" ("Pro Olimpia intelligo parvulam filiam meam olim mortuam ea in etate in qua morientes celestes effici cives credimus: et ideo, ex Violante dum viveret, mortuam 'celestem' idest 'Olympiam' voco").

71. *BC*, XIV.62–63: "Mirum quam grandis facta diebus / in paucis: matura viro michi, nata, videris!"

72. "Emeruit, nam mitis erat fideique vetuste / preclarum specimen."

73. "Sed dic, tene, precor, novit dum culmen adires? / (Olympia) Imo equidem applaudens iniecit brachia collo, / et postquam amplexus letos ac oscula centum / impressit fronti . . . inquit: / —Venisti, o nostri soboles carissima Silvi!" "mea neptis." Translation from Boccaccio, *Eclogues*, trans. Smarr, 169.

74. Giovanni Boccaccio, *Buccolicum carmen*, ed. Giorgio Bernardi Perini, in *Tutte le opere*, ed. Vittore Branca, vol. 5, 2 (Milan: Mondadori, 1994), 1054, calls this eclogue "the true, and only, documentation of Boccaccio's 'family status' [*stato di famiglia*]."

75. Believed to be 1367 (see Ricci, *Studi sulla vita e le opere del Boccaccio*, 63–64).

76. In *Ep.*, XV.11, in reference to Violante's striking resemblance to

Petrarca's granddaughter Eletta, Boccaccio wrote to his friend, "If you do not believe me, believe the physician Guglielmo da Ravenna and our Donato, who knew her" ("Si michi non credis, Guilielmo ravennati medico et Donato nostro, qui novere, credito"); essential on Donato Albanzani is Carla Maria Monti, "Il *ravennate* Donato Albanzani amico di Boccaccio e di Petrarca," in *Dante e la sua eredità a Ravenna nel Trecento*, ed. Marco Petoletti (Ravenna: Longo, 2015), where, on 123, there is also information about Guglielmo Angelieri da Ravenna.

77. According to Giovanni Boccaccio, *Opere in versi*, ed. Pier Giorgio Ricci (Milan and Naples: Ricciardi, 1965), 687, Silvius's question to Olympia about her grandfather "could be fully explicable only if her grandfather had at least had the possibility of meeting his granddaughter before his death"; Giovanni Boccaccio, *Buccolicum carmen*, ed. Giorgio Bernardi Perini, in *Tutte le opere*, ed. Vittore Branca, vol. 5, 2 (Milan: Mondadori, 1994), 1062, instead considers the existence of such possibility not "necessary for poetic fiction." For Boccaccino's date of death, see Laura Regnicoli, "Documenti su Giovanni Boccaccio," in *Boccaccio autore e copista*, exhibition catalog, ed. Teresa De Robertis, Carla Maria Monti, Marco Petoletti, Giuliano Tanturli, and Stefano Zamponi (Florence: Biblioteca Medicea Laurenziana, October 11, 2013 – January 11, 2014) (Florence: Mandragora, 2013), 385.

78. "Fusca is the [Latin] translation of the Italian Bruna" (Giovanni Boccaccio, *Opere in versi*, ed. Pier Giorgio Ricci [Milan and Naples: Ricciardi, 1965], 674; see also Giovanni Boccaccio, *Buccolicum carmen*, ed. Giorgio Bernardi Perini, in *Tutte le opere*, ed. Vittore Branca, vol. 5, 2 [Milan: Mondadori, 1994], 1062). His housekeeper would receive a testamentary bequest from Boccaccio (Laura Regnicoli, "La *cura sepulcri* di Giovanni Boccaccio," *Studi sul Boccaccio* 42 [2014]: 57–58) and was perhaps the Brunetta of the *Decameron* "with whom Chichibio was utterly infatuated" (VI.4; "di cui Chichibio era fortemente innamorato") and "my maidservant of many years devoted service" ("ancillula quedam, cuius multis annis obsequio usus sum") of *Ep.*, XXI.19 to Mainardo Cavalcanti.

79. Rico, *Ritratti allo specchio (Boccaccio, Petrarca)*, 125.

80. The *Comedia delle ninfe fiorentine* (also known by the incorrect titles *Ninfale d'Ameto* or simply *Ameto*) can be dated to between 1341 and 1342; the *Amorosa visione* must have followed shortly after: the terminus ante quem is provided by the death of Robert of Anjou in January 1343, here mentioned as living (XIV.22–33), and by the fact that his daughter Joanna, crowned queen the following August, is still identified as the Duchess of Calabria (XLII.13–15). Additionally, the reference to Margaret (Margherita) of Taranto, wife of the Duke of Athens, who was expelled from Florence in August 1343, could perhaps have been interpreted as "an indirect homage when the lord was still welcome" in the city (Boccaccio, *Amorosa visione*, 721). Boccaccio, *Amorosa visione*, publishes the text in

two distinct versions by the author: A, passed down by the manuscript tradition, and B, passed down by the 1521 printed edition of Girolamo Claricio. Today it has been established, above all by the work of Lida Maria Gonelli ("Esercizi di bibliografia testuale sulla 'princeps' dell'*Amorosa visione* [1521]," in *Filologia italiana* 2 [2005]: 147–60), that text B is not a second redaction by the author but the result of profound reworking carried out on Boccaccio's text by Claricio (regarding this, see also Carlo Caruso, "L'edizione Branca dell'*Amorosa visione* [1944] e la nuova filologia," in *Caro Vitto: Essays in Memory of Vittore Branca*, ed. Jill Kraye and Laura Lepschy, in collaboration with Nicola Jones, *Italianist* 27, special supplement 2 [2007]: 29–48); some scholars, however, continue to speak of two redactions by the author: for example, Beatrice Fedi, "Amorosa visione," in *BAC*, 121–22; Elisa Curti and Elisabetta Menetti, *Giovanni Boccaccio* (Florence: Le Monnier, 2013), 94; Bernhard Huss, "Il genere visione in Petrarca ('Trionfi') e in Boccaccio ('Amorosa visione')," in *Dante e la dimensione visionaria tra medioevo e prima età moderna*, ed. Bernhard Huss and Mirko Tavoni (Ravenna: Longo, 2019) 141–60, on 151.

81. Surdich, *La cornice di amore: Studi sul Boccaccio*, 153.

82. Lucia Battaglia Ricci, *Boccaccio* (Rome: Salerno Editrice, 2000), 101.

83. Velli, *Petrarca e Boccaccio: Tradizione, memoria, scrittura*, 177.

84. Bruni, *Boccaccio: L'invenzione della letteratura mediana*, 204.

85. Translation from Boccaccio, *Amorosa Visione*, trans. Hollander et al., 173.

86. Surdich, *La cornice di amore: Studi sul Boccaccio*, 137–40, and Bruni, *Boccaccio: L'invenzione della letteratura mediana*, 205–6, believe that Ameto's formative journey was inspired by the Chartres school of philosophy; Bruni identifies a precedent for the contradiction "between his declared ethical and intellectual intent and the baldly sensual representation of the nymphs' beauty" in Johannes de Hauvilla's *Architrenius*.

87. The *Filocolo* also contains references to physical pleasure, especially between spouses. See, for example, *Filoc.*, IV.119, 1; 120, 1; 122, 1–3. Boccaccio, though, never went so far as to describe the beauty of the bodies and the lovers' exchanges of affection. In contrast, a love scene between Troilo and Criseida in the *Filostrato* (III.29–32) was recounted explicitly:

> Then he embraced her, and they kissed each other on the mouth.
>
> Nor did they leave that place before they had a thousand times embraced together with sweet joy and ardent delight, and just as many times and much more did they kiss each other as those who burned with equal fire and who were very dear to each other. But when the welcoming was finished, they mounted the stairs and entered the bedroom.
>
> Long would it be to recount the joy and impossible to tell the delight which they took together when they came into it; they undressed and got

into bed, where the lady, remaining still in her last garment, with pleasing speech said to him, "Shall I strip myself? The newly married are bashful the first night."

To whom Troilo said, "My soul, I pray that I may have you naked in my arms as my heart desires." And then she: "See how I free myself of it." And her shift thrown away, she gathered herself quicky into his arms; and straining each other with fervor, they felt the ultimate value of love. (Translation from Boccaccio, *Il Filostrato*, trans. apRoberts and Seldis, 147–48.)

> Poi l'abbracciò e basciaronsi in bocca.
>   Né si partiron prima di quel loco,
> che mille volte insieme s'abbracciaro
> con dolce festa e con ardente gioco,
> e altrettante e vie più si basciaro,
> sì come quei ch'ardevan d'egual foco,
> e che l'un l'altro molto aveva caro;
> ma come l'accoglienze si finiro,
> salir le scale e 'n camera ne giro.
>   Lungo sarebbe a raccontar la festa,
> ed impossibile a dire il diletto
> che 'nsieme preser pervenuti in questa;
> ei si spogliaro ed entraron nel letto,
> dove la donna nell'ultima vesta
> rimasa già, con piacevole detto
> gli disse:—Spogliomi io? Le nuove spose
> son la notte primiera vergognose.—
>   A cui Troiolo disse:—Anima mia,
> io te ne priego, sì ch'io t'abbi in braccio
> ignuda sì come il mio cor disia.—
> Ed ella allora:—Ve' ch'io me ne spaccio.—
> E la camiscia sua gittata via,
> nelle sue braccia si ricolse avaccio;
> e strignendo l'un l'altro con fervore,
> d'amor sentiron l'ultimo valore.

However, in the *Comedia*, sexual impulses, enticements, and encounters are shown with an unprecedented realism in all their physicality. Suffice it to look at how Mopsa, "dismissed all shame" ("cacciata la vergogna"), and seduced the reluctant Affron: "I must tell then that with my long garments belted above the hip and touching the ground as they do now, I acted almost fearful of the water, and I pulled them much higher than is seemly, so that my white legs were visible. I noticed that he looked at them with avid eye, yet he remained firm in obstinate opposition to my desires. Then, set on conquering him, I raised my rather light mantle from off my shoulders as if overcome by the heat; and having opened my pretty bosom, bending down rather low, without a word I uncovered its beauties to him" (XVIII.33–35; "Io dico che i lunghi drappi, toccanti terra come ora fanno, essendomi io cinta sopra l'anche, quasi paurosa dell'onde mostrandomi, in alto più che il dovere li tirai; per che agli occhi suoi le candide gambe si fecero conte, le quali, sì com'io m'avidi, con occhio avido riguardò; ma pure fermo nella ostinazione contraria a' miei voleri si rimase. Onde io, disposta a vincere lui, levato a me di sopra agli omeri miei il non pesante mantello, come vinta dal caldo, aperto il vago seno, le bellezze di quello bassandomi, gli feci, sanza parlare, scoperte"; translation from Boccaccio, *L'Ameto*, trans. Serafini-Sauli, 47–48); and the realism of Agapes's description of her old and impotent husband's attempts to possess her: "He gathered me in his arms, and with unpleas- ant weight he pressed my white neck. And when with his fetid mouth, he had not kissed, but driveled over mine many times, he touched my eager fruits with trembling hands, and from there he moved to each part of my ill-fated body; and with murmurings in my ears which resounded aw- fully, he offered me flattery, and, all cold, he hoped to kindle me for him with such acts. . . . When he had passed a good part of the night in this tittle-tattle, he tried in vain to cultivate my garden of Venus; and seeking to cleave the earth of those gardens, which longed for gracious seeds, with an old ploughshare, he worked uselessly; for that plough, eroded by age, moving its pointed part in a circle like the loose willow, refused to carry out its due office in the firm fallow. So, overcome, he rested; and then to the second effort, and to the third, and to many others, he arose in vain—with his spirit; and with diverse acts he strove to bring to actual- ity what was impossible to achieve; and in this manner he unpleasantly made me pass the nights in distasteful leaps and unseemly acts, without sleep" (XXXII.13–18; "Me raccoglie nelle sue braccia e di non piacevole peso prieme il candido collo. E poi che egli ha molte volte con la fetida bocca non baciata ma scombavata la mia, con le tremanti mani tasta i vaghi pomi, e quindi le muove a ciascuna parte del mio male arrivato corpo, e con mormorii ne' miei orecchi sonevoli male, mi porge lusinghe, e freddissimo si crede me di sé accendere con cotali atti. . . . Poi che egli ha gran parte della notte tirata con queste ciance, gli orti di Venere invano si fatica di cultivare; e cercante con vecchio bomere fendere la terra di quelli desiderante i graziosi semi, lavora indarno: però che quello, dalla antichità roso, come la lenta salice la sua aguta parte volgendo in cerchio, nel sodo maggese il debito uficio recusa d'adoperare. Onde elli, vinto, alquanto si posa, e quindi alla seconda fatica e alla terza appresso e poi a molte invano risurge con l'animo; e con diversi atti s'ingegna di recare ad effetto ciò che per lui non è possibile di compiersi; e per questo modo la notte tutta di spiacevoli ruzzamenti e di sconvenevoli atti, sanza sonno, accidiosa mi fa trapassare"; translation from Boccaccio, *L'Ameto*, trans. Serafini-Sauli, 90).

88. Luigi Surdich, *Boccaccio* (Rome and Bari: Laterza, 2001), 71.

89. Paolo Orvieto ("Boccaccio mediatore di generi o dell'allegoria d'amore," *Interpres* 2 [1979]: 7–104, on 26–37) has proposed interpreting the *Caccia* as the starting point, developed further in the *Amorosa visione* (and, in his telling, also the *Contento quasi ne' pensier' d'amore*, in which, however, it is difficult to discern allegorical intentions), for a "great mystical rite that describes a progressive initiation into the practices and mysteries of love." However, the presence of the theme of love that strips away bestial crudeness and confers a fully realized human identity (a theme that, among others, returns in the novella of Cimone, *Dec.*, V.1) does not entitle us to read, as Orvieto does (followed by Francesco Zambon, "La letteratura allegorica e didattica: Il Tre e Quattrocento," in *Manuale di letteratura italiana: Storia per generi e problemi*, ed. Franco Brioschi and Costanzo Di Girolamo [Turin: Bollati Boringhieri, 1993], vol. 1, 561–83), the *Caccia di Diana*, the *Amorosa visione*, and *Contento quasi* as "a unitary set," and the *Amorosa visione* as an outright "continuation of the *Caccia*" (575–76). It is true, however, that the three texts are often transmitted together in the manuscript traditions: on which see most recently Irene Iocca, "Dentro e fuori le Rime: il polimetro *Contento quasi ne' pensier' d'amore*," *Filologia e critica* 41 (2016): 108–15.

90. See Marco Santagata, *Boccaccio indiscreto: Il mito di Fiammetta* (Bologna: il Mulino, 2019), 157–75.

91. In each letter of dedication the woman is invited to recognize the aspects of the work's story that connect it to her relationship with the author: in the *Filostrato*, the author finds the "way" ("modo") to reveal his secret suffering, namely, "to be able, in the person of someone emotionally overcome as I was and am, to relate my sufferings in song" (Proem, 26–29; "di dovere in persona d'alcuno passionato sì come io era e sono, cantando narrare li miei martiri"; translation from Boccaccio, *Il Filostrato*, trans. apRoberts and Seldis, 11), so that the distant woman could know the condition of her abandoned lover by reading the story of Troilo; in the *Teseida* he declares that the story of Arcites and Palaemon was "compiled" for her ("To Fiammetta," 246). While in the *Filostrato*, however, the overall impression is that the dedication and text are fully homogeneous and congruent (just as, after a brief period of mutual love, Giovanna-Filomena departs Naples for Sannio leaving her beloved in despair, so too Criseida, after a period of shared happiness, leaves Troy for the Greek camp, throwing Troilo into dejection), in the *Teseida* the correspondence between the author's emotional situation and that of the protagonists of the love story is so unclear that it requires many words of explanation from the author: "Two things, among others, show that it was composed for you. One is that the matter that the story narrates under the name of one of the

two lovers and that of his beloved young woman, if you remember well, reminds me about you and you about me. And, if you do not deny it, you could discover that it was said and done, in part, concerning the two of us. Which of the two it is I do not reveal for I know that you will discover it. If there are, perhaps, too many features, the reason is the desire of aptly concealing what is not appropriate to reveal concerning the two of us as well as the necessity to follow the thread of the story. Besides this you should know that only that plough which is assisted by a lot of ingenuity is able to cut the ground. You will be able to realize, therefore, what my life was before you rejected me and what it has become afterwards. The other thing is my having concluded neither the story nor the fable nor the arcane language in any other style, because women, having little intelligence and knowledge of the above mentioned matters, I indulged in describing them freely" (To Fiammetta; "E che ella da me per voi sia compilata, due cose fra l'altre il manifestano. L'una si è che ciò che sotto il nome dell'uno de' due amanti e della giovane amata si conta essere stato, ricordandovi bene, e io a voi di me e voi a me di voi, se non mentiste, potreste conoscere essere stato detto e fatto in parte: quale de' due si sia non discuopro, ché so che ve ne av vedrete. Se forse alcune cose soperchie vi fossero, il volere bene coprire ciò che non è onesto manifestare da noi due infuori e il volere la storia seguire ne son cagioni; e oltre a ciò dovete sapere che solo il bomere aiutato da molti ingegni fende la terra. Potrete adunque e qual fosse innanzi e quale sia stata poi la vita mia che più non mi voleste per vostro, discernere. L'altra si è il non avere cessata né storia né favola né chiuso parlare in altra guisa, con ciò sia cosa che le donne sì come poco intelligenti ne sogliono essere schife, ma però che per intelletto e notizia delle cose predette voi dalla turba dell'altre separata conosco, libero mi concessi il porle a mio piacere"; translation [here and below] from Boccaccio, *Theseid of the Nuptials of Emilia*, trans. Traversa, 376). A dedicatee is referred to only in the work's two concluding sonnets, probably written after the poem was completed: in the first, the author invites the Muses to bring the lady some of the "crumbs" ("miche") fallen from their table that he has collected, and, together with her, give them, that is, his book, a name; in the second, the Muses report back that the woman, "di fiamma d'amor tututta accensa" ("all aflame in the fire of love"; translation on 590), has approved the work and given it its title. Is this reference to the "fiamma d'amor" enough to identify her with Fiammetta? Perhaps so, but this is certainly quite a faint sign to be the only allusion to the beloved's name in the entire poem. Still: in the penultimate sonnet the author writes that in this woman "lives my salvation, but perhaps she does not think about it" ("la mia salute / vive, ma ella forse nol si pensa"). It takes a real effort of imagination, however, to see in the phrase "perhaps she does not think about it" a reflection of the dramatic story recounted in the dedication: there Fiammetta had gone from willing to "cruel" ("crudele"), "contemptuously disdainful" ("dispiacevole sdegnosa"), "haughty" ("orgogliosa"), had rejected the author's love. And at the end of the work there is not even a hint of the hope expressed in the dedicatory letter that love will "rekindle in you the extinguished flame which, I do not know for what reason, adverse forture has taken away from me" (To Fiammetta; "Raccendendo in voi la spenta fiamma, a me vi renda, la quale, non so per che cagione, inimica fortuna m'ha tolta"; translation on 378). In short, Boccaccio's attempt to make a connection between the dedication to Fiammetta and the poem's story is labored and strained, as if he wanted to bring two separate textual entities back to a unitary origin. In additional confirmation, a small detail that has all the air of being a slip of the pen: in the introductory caption to the penultimate sonnet, Boccaccio writes: "the author asks the Muses to offer this book to the lady at whose request it was written" ("L'autore priega le Muse che il presente libro presentino a la donna a cui istanzia è fatto"). Now, no woman at any point in this book makes such a request: Boccaccio misremembered or, rather, he remembered a work other than the *Teseida*. He was thinking of the *Filocolo*, of Maria's invitation to "compose a little book" that would recount the story of Florio and Biancifiore (I.1, 26). Boccaccio was also thinking about the *Filocolo* while writing the *Teseida*'s dedication to Fiammetta, and, in fact, these words refer that other work: "I remembered that in those happier than longer days I noticed your fondness for hearing or, at times, reading this or that story, especially love stories" (To Fiammetta; "Ricordandomi che già ne' dì più felici che lunghi io vi sentii vaga d'udire e talvolta di leggere una e altra istoria, e massimamente l'amorose"; translation at 376).

92. Translations from Boccaccio, *Theseid of the Nuptials of Emilia*, trans. Traversa, 375–76.

93. *CNF*, XXXV.

94. Translation from Boccaccio, *L'Ameto*, trans. Serafini-Sauli, 105.

95. Translation from Boccaccio, *L'Ameto*, trans. Serafini-Sauli, 110.

96. Translations from Boccaccio, *L'Ameto*, trans. Serafini-Sauli, 104 and 110.

97. *CNF*, XXXV.66, 68, 113.

98. Translations from Boccaccio, *L'Ameto*, trans. Serafini-Sauli, 103, 104, and 102.

99. *AV*, XLIX.10–45.

100. Translation from Boccaccio, *Amorosa visione*, trans. Hollander et al., 3.

101. For the identification of these women, see the annotations in Boccaccio, *Amorosa visione*. The Neapolitan group includes Agnes of Périgord, wife of Giovanni of Anjou, Duke of Durazzo; Margherita (or Margaret), wife of Walter of Brienne, Duke of Athens; Queen Joanna, here still Duchess of Calabria; Caterina Caradente; Dalfina Barrasio; Eleonora d'Aragona, daughter of King Frederick III of Sicily; Isabella di Ibelin,

relative of Queen Sancia; Giovanna di Catanzaro. The Florentine group consists of Andrea Acciaiuoli, sister of Niccolò; Margherita or Gemma degli Asini; Lottiera, wife of Nerone di Nigi; Alionora or Dianora Gianfigliazzi. The identification of the others is more controversial: the "beautiful Lombard" (XL.66; "bella lombarda") appears to be the same woman as in *Contento quasi* ("And the beautiful Lombard follows then, called Lady Vanna" [vv. 46–47; "E la bella lombarda segue poi, / Monna Vanna chiamata") and could also be the "shapely Ligurian" ("formosa ligure") of the *Comedia* (XXIX.16), therefore she is also Florentine by adoption; Lia, here introduced as a protagonist of the *Comedia* (XLI.35–36), was almost certaintly the daughter of the Florentine Angelo dei Regaletti; the "new Dido / in name" (XLII.41–42 "novella Dido / di nome"), that is, Elisa or Lisa, seems to have been the wife of an Albertino of Florence; finally, the one "who was dragged to the world from which / she had sought refuge in religion" (XLIV.26–29; "quella che fu tratta al mondo / onde fuggita si era in religione"; translation from Boccaccio, *Amorosa visione*, trans. Hollander et al., 179) for a marriage that would have been better if never contracted corresponds to the woman called Emilia in the *Comedia* and Meliana in *Contento quasi* ("Meliana is she of Giovanni di Nello" [vv. 35–36; "Meliana è colei / di Giovanni di Nello"]), or the Tornaquinci mentioned earlier, married to Giovanni di Nello. Only two women in the catalog cannot be identified: the unknown "single love / of the Milanese" ("unica intendenza / del Milanese"), that is, the woman loved by Azzo Visconti (XLII.19–20), and the "Florentine nymph" (XLI.29; "ninfa fiorentina"); not identified, yes, but certainly also real women. Of the real women in the *Comedia delle ninfe fiorentine*, in addition to Lia, also present were "the beautiful Lombard," under the name of Acrimonia, Lottiera as Mopsa, Alionora Gianfigliazzi as Adiona, and the wife of the spice merchant as Emilia.

102. Translation from Boccaccio, *Amorosa Visione*, trans. Hollander et al., 177.

103. As further evidence of Boccaccio's desire to solidify Fiammetta's "reality," it should be noted that in the list of twelve beauties in the *Contento quasi* (which is believed to be from shortly after the *Comedia*), Fiammetta unexpectedly appears as the fifth figure (vv. 40–42): "Your sun is fifth in our dance, that is, the Fiammetta who let you have it with an arrow to the heart, which still pains you" ("A nostra danza quinta è il tuo sole, / cioè quella Fiammetta che tti diede / con la saetta al cor, ch'anchor ti dole"). Unexpectedly, because all of those graceful women, with the sole exception of Fiammetta, were real Florentines and, above all, because they are all identified by their personal names and are therefore recognizable.

104. See Billanovich, *Restauri boccacceschi*, 82–83, and Branca, *Giovanni Boccaccio. Profilo biografico*, 28.

105. Around 1339 Boccaccio copied into the *Zibaldone Laurenziano* (52r-v) a poem he attributed to Thomas Aquinas (see Angelo Piacentini, "Un carme attribuito a san Tommaso d'Aquino nello Zibaldone membranaceo," in *Studi sul Boccaccio* 43 [2016]: 207–31); he copied Thomas's commentary in the translation by Roberto Grossatesta (Milano, Biblioteca Ambrosiana, ms. A 204 inf.) "soon after his return to Florence": on this see Marco Petoletti, "L' 'Ethica Nichomachea' di Aristotele con il commento di san Tommaso autografo di Boccaccio," in *BAC*, 348–50.

106. Boccaccio, *Amorosa visione*, 641.

107. Dante, *Purg.*, VII.113, 124 ("of the nose").

108. See, for example, Branca, *Giovanni Boccaccio: Profilo biografico*, 63–64.

109. Further support for the hypothesis that Boccaccio's rancor had personal motivations is the fact that in his writing he would label as Midas only one other real person, Niccolò Acciaiuoli, in the *Buccolicum carmen*, VIII and XVI, in order to denounce Acciaiuoli's lack of generosity. These two eclogues are reactions to broken promises: the first is an angry response on the occasion of Boccaccio's disappointment during the trip to the Kingdom of Naples in 1355, very likely undertaken because Acciaiuoli had raised the possibility of Boccaccio's taking the post of royal secretary to replace Zanobi da Strada, who had become the vicar of the bishop of Montecassino; the second refers to his journey to Naples in 1362–63, undertaken once again in the vague hope of a position proposed by Acciaiuoli. In short, in both cases, the "very greedy" ("avarissimo") Midas showed no evidence of generosity.

110. In *AV*, XIV.34–45, lines we can presume were written no more than a year after the *Comedia*, Boccaccio described his father thus:

> Further on, scratching at the mountain with hooked nails,
> there was one who, in my opinion,
> despite his many attempts was clawing away but little.
> I saw that he was anxiously putting so little
> in his purse that he himself could hardly be said to
> possess any of it, not to mention anyone else.
> Toward him I took myself somewhat closer
> in order to see clearly who he was;
> I discovered that it was he himself who,
> freely and happily, had so kindly
> nourished me like a son; and I had called him
> and still call him parent. (Boccaccio, *Amorosa Visione*, trans.
> Hollander et al., 59–61)

> Oltre grattando il monte dimorava
> con aguta unghia un, ch'al mio parere

in molte volte poco ne levava.
　　　Con questo tanto forte quel tenere
in borsa li vedea, ch'a pena esso,
non ch'altro alcun, ne potea bene avere.
　　　Al qual faccendom'io un poco appresso
per conoscer chi fosse apertamente,
vidi che era colui che me stesso
　　　libero e lieto avea benignamente
nudrito come figlio, ed io chiamato
aveva lui e chiamo mio parente.

It has been rightly said that "the son was able to ... draw a veil of
compassion over this pathetic and reduced figure" (Giuseppe Chiecchi,
Giovanni Boccaccio e il romanzo familiare [Venice: Marsilio, 1994], 93).
However, in the *Elegia di Madonna Fiammetta* the bitterness still shows
through in the words with which the protagonist "does not hesitate to
wish death on Panfilo's old father: 'he has escaped the mortal blow for
many years and has lived longer than he should' (II.6, 12; 'Egli è fuggito
molti anni al mortal colpo, ... e più c'è vivuto che non si conviene'; translation from Boccaccio, *The Elegy of Lady Fiammetta*, 33)": see also Giovanni
Boccaccio, *Elegia di Madonna Fiammetta*, ed. Carlo Delcorno, in *Tutte le
opere*, ed. Vittore Branca, vol. 5, 2 (Milan: Mondadori, 1994), 1–412, 4.

111. Despite his bitterness toward Robert of Anjou, Boccaccio later
would not withhold "recognition [of the king's] love of learning," but this
was "perhaps through Petrarca's influence," Boccaccio, *Amorosa visione*,
641, rightly notes. Moreover, he had already written in the *Comedia* that
the king is indeed "miserly and greedy of riches," but is also "rich in the
gifts of Pallas" (*CNF*, XXXV.32; "cupido di ricchezze e avaro"; "di doni di
Pallade copioso"): an affirmation, however, that should be understood not
as self-correction, but as a result of Petrarch's recent coronation, in which
Robert had had an important role as examiner. Boccaccio, who was preparing to write Petrarca's biography, in protecting this aspect of the king
was in fact protecting the glory of this event from being tarnished. It is
revealing that, in contrast to *Filoc.*, I.14, where "the aid of Pallas" ("l'aiuto
di Pallade")—thanks to which Robert of Anjou "rules" ("regge")the kingdom he inherited—seems to refer to wisdom in governing generally, here
in the *Comedia*, the "gifts of Pallas" appear to refer instead to the king's
ability to appreciate and evaluate poetry. Keep in mind, too, what Boccaccio would write about King Robert in *GDG*, XIV.22, 5: he was "a distinguished philosopher, an eminent teacher of medicine, and an exceptional
theologian in his day. Yet in his sixty-sixth year he retained a contempt
for Vergil, and, like you, called him and the rest mere story-tellers, and
of no value at all apart from the ornament of his verse. But as soon as he
heard Petrarch unfold the hidden meaning of his poetry, he was struck

with amazement, and saw and rejected his own error; and I actually heard him say that he never had supposed such great and lofty meaning could lie hidden under so flimsy a cover of poetic fiction as he now saw revealed through the demonstration of this expert critic. With wonderfully keen regret he began upbraiding his own judgment and his misfortune in recognizing so late the true art of poetry" ("Qui clarus olim phylosophus et medicine preceptor egregius, atque inter ceteros eius temporis insignis theologus, cum in sexagesimum sextum usque etatis sue annum parvi pendisset Virgilium, illumque cum reliquis more vestro fabulosum dice-ret hominem et nullius fore precii, ornatu subtracto carminum, quam cito Franciscum Petrarcam arcanos poematum referentem sensus audivit, obstupefactus se ipsum redarguit, et, ut ego, eo dicente, meis auribus au-divi, asseruit se numquam ante arbitratum adeo egregios atque sublimes sensus sub tam ridiculo cortice, uti poetarum sunt fictiones, latere potu-isse, ut advertebat post demonstrationem solertis viri, absconditos esse suumque mira compunctione damnabat ingenium et infortunium, quod tam sero poeticum artificium cognovisset"). Translation from Boccaccio, *Boccaccio on Poetry*, trans. Osgood, 98.

112. See Stefano Carrai, *Boccaccio e i volgarizzamenti* (Rome and Padua: Editrice Antenore, 2016), who, among other things, observes, "The *Fiammetta* is not nor did it want to be, in short, a romance of introspec-tion [as a critical tradition beginning with *Storia della letteratura italiana* by Francesco De Sanctis holds], but the annexation to the territory of Italian literary prose a genre of the poetic tradition: the love lament of the abandoned woman, written in prose rather than in poetry following the example of the vernacularization of Ovid by Filippo Ceffi" (41). On Ceffi, see Marco Palma, "Ceffi, Filippo," in *DBI*, XXIII (1979).

113. Current dating assumes as terminus post quem Boccaccino's second marriage, which is believed to have taken place in 1343 (Giovanni Boccaccio, *Elegia di Madonna Fiammetta*, ed. Carlo Delcorno, in *Tutte le opere*, ed. Vittore Branca, vol. 5, 2 [Milan: Mondadori, 1994], 1–412, 3; Carlo Delcorno, "Elegia di madonna Fiammetta," in *BAC*, 101–5), but Regnicoli, "Per la biografia di Giovanni Boccaccio: l'*Elegia di madonna Fiammetta* attraverso i documenti," 9–13, has shown that, if anything, this is a termi-nus ante quem and that in all probability the marriage was celebrated in the summer of 1341. According to Regnicoli, "Per la biografia di Giovanni Boccaccio: l'*Elegia di madonna Fiammetta* attraverso i documenti," 13–14, the description of the disorder in Florence can be traced to that which followed the conspiracy of 1340 and not to the period of the tyranny of the Duke of Athens (as Giovanni Boccaccio, *Elegia di Madonna Fiammetta*, ed. Carlo Delcorno, in *Tutte le opere*, ed. Vittore Branca, vol. 5, 2 [Milan: Mondadori, 1994], 1–412, 267, holds).

114. Regarding the autobiographical aspect of the *Elegia*, Lucia Batta-glia Ricci, *Boccaccio* (Rome: Salerno Editrice, 2000), 114, writes, "The book

creates a very powerful feeling of real life," and then comments (115), "The reversal of the more traditional convention of courtly love literature and, especially, of the biographical situation repeatedly described by Boccaccio in his earlier works . . . should be recognized as the most significant innovation of the *Elegia*." In the "Introducción" to her translation, *Decamerón* (Madrid: Ediciones Cátedra, 1994), 27–29, María Hernández Esteban makes many pertinent observations about the author's projections of himself onto Fiammetta.

115. Giovanni Boccaccio, *Ninfale fiesolano*, ed. Daniele Piccini (Milan: BUR Rizzoli, 2013), 8; see also Alessio Decaria, "*Ninfale fiesolano*," in *BAC*, 115–17. The suggestion by Ricci, *Studi sulla vita e le opere del Boccaccio*, 13–28 (text published as an article in 1971) that the *Ninfale* was the first work Boccaccio wrote, before the *Caccia di Diana*, has not found acceptance.

116. Battaglia Ricci, *Boccaccio*, 118. Even the work's opening lines — addressed by the author to Love, who "With that high splendor he still holds it [the author's heart] bound, / and with those rays that proved my armor vain / the day they pierced my spirit with the grace of those fair eyes because of which I must . . . in grave anguish consequently lie" with the plea that Love "beg my lady . . . / to show less fierceness on my servitude" (*NF*, 1, 4; "lo tien con lo splendore / e con que' raggi a cui non valse usbergo, / quando passaron dentro col favore / degli occhi di colei . . . ch'è cagion di tutti e' mie' martiri"; "la mia donna altera / che non sian contro a me servo sì fera"; translation from Giovanni Boccaccio, *Nymphs of Fiesole*, trans. Joseph Tusiani (Rutherford, NJ: Farleigh Dickinson University Press, 1971), 25–26) — contain completely generic information "from which it does not seem at all justified to deduce, as some commentators have shown they believe (Massera, Morpurgo), that the *Ninfale* too should be counted among the works dedicated to Fiammetta" (Armando Balduino, *Boccaccio, Petrarca e altri poeti del Trecento* [Florence: Olschki, 1984], 767); Pier Massimo Forni comments along the same lines: see Giovanni Boccaccio, *Ninfale fiesolano* (Milan: Mursia, 1991), 29.

117. "dalla sua prima giovanezza infino a questo tempo," "oltre modo era acceso stato d'altissimo e nobile amore, forse più assai che alla sua bassa condizione non parrebbe, narrandolo, si richiedesse," "coloro che erano discreti," "ne era stato lodato e da molto più reputato," "niuna forza di proponimento o di consiglio o di vergogna evidente, o pericolo che seguir ne potesse, aveva potuto né rompere né piegare." Translation from *Decameron*, trans. Rebhorn, 1–2.

118. In Boccaccio, *Decameron*, Branca is of the completely opposite opinion regarding the possible autobiographical value of the *Decameron*'s preface. Regarding Boccaccio's claims here of disparity of social condition between himself and his beloved, he observes that while some readers want to see in his words the "reflection" of his love for a royal Maria d'Aquino or Fiammatta of his youthful pseudo-autobiographical tales, "it

would instead be better to see in these phrases a reflection of the medieval schemas, the precepts in treatises on love—from Andrea Cappellano onward—that were so present in Boccaccio's practice of literature" (5–6). Alberto Asor Rosa, "*Decameron*," *Letteratura italiana. Le opere*, I. *Dalle Origini al Cinquecento* (Turin: Einaudi, 1992), 473–591, 567–68, while allying himself with Branca in rejecting the "mythical autobiography," considers it "quite extraordinary" that Boccaccio "connects a work of fiction to the experiences—both personal and literary—of the author, clearly identifying it as the culmination of his previous history."

119. *Rime* LXIX (XCVII).

120. *Rime* LXII (CII).

121. Translation from Tusiani, *Poets of the Italian Renaissance*, 36.

122. Billanovich, *Restauri boccacceschi*, 84. The autograph ms. is Acquisti e Doni 325 of the Biblioteca Medicea Laurenziana (the reference mark is on f. 64v): regarding this see Sandro Bertelli, "Codicologia d'autore: Il manoscritto in volgare secondo Giovanni Boccaccio," in *Dentro l'officina di Giovanni Boccaccio: Studi sugli autografi in volgare e su Boccaccio dantista*, ed. Bertelli e Davide Cappi (Città del Vaticano: Biblioteca Apostolica Vaticana, 2014), 15, and Boccaccio, *Teseida delle nozze d'Emilia*, XL–XLI.

123. Laura Regnicoli, "La *cura sepulcri* di Giovanni Boccaccio," *Studi sul Boccaccio* 42 (2014): 60–61.

Chapter Six

1. On this hypothetical journey to Naples, see Vittore Branca, *Giovanni Boccaccio: Profilo biografico* (Florence: Sansoni, 1977 [1967]), 73.

2. On these intrigues and events, see Francesco Paolo Tocco, *Niccolò Acciaiuoli: Vita e politica in Italia alla metà del XIV secolo* (Rome: Istituto storico italiano per il Medioevo, 2001), 69–87; and Andreas Kiesewetter, "Giovanna I d'Angiò, regina di Sicilia," in *DBI*, LV (2001). Boccaccio would recount Andrew of Hungary's sad end in both the first and second versions of *BC*, III (*Faunus*), and in *CVI*, IX 26.19.

3. It has been suggested that among the attractions of Ravenna for Boccaccio may have been the presence of "a distinguished Boccacci family (perhaps related to the one in Certaldo)" (see Branca, *Giovanni Boccaccio: Profilo biografico*, 73–74)—regarding which, see Corrado Ricci, "I Boccacci di Romagna," in *Studii su Giovanni Boccaccio*, ed. Società storica della Valdelsa (Castelfiorentino, 1913), 25–31—but Giuseppe Billanovich, *Petrarca letterato*, I. *Lo scrittoio del Petrarca* (Rome: Edizioni di *Storia e letteratura*, 1947; repr. 1995), 255, writes that "in the presence of Boccacci families in Romagna we should simply see a common and insignificant shared name." We might note that there was also another family with origins in Certaldo living in Romagna, the Milotti, one member of which, Fiduccio, had known Dante (and regarding whom, see Laura Regnicoli,

"Un'oscura vicenda certaldese: Nuovi documenti su Boccaccio e la sua famiglia," *Italia medioevale e umanistica* 58 [2017)]: 80–81; and, especially, Gabriella Albanese and Paolo Pontari, "L'ultimo Dante: Il cenacolo ravennate, le *Egloge* e la morte," in *L'ultimo Dante e il cenacolo ravennate*, exhibition catalog, ed. Gabriella Albanese and Paolo Pontari [Ravenna: Biblioteca Classense, September 9–October 28, 2018], in *Classense* 6 (2018): 58–67). In any case, we cannot definitively rule out that Boccaccio might have made an earlier trip to Romagna: indeed, although it is a very weak bit of evidence, in the mention of dried figs from the Canary Islands "as good as those of Cesena" (*Canaria* 5; "ficus siccas . . . bonas uti cesenates cernimus"), "this *cernimus*" could "demonstrate a visit to [the town of] Cesena [in Romagna]" (Michele Feo, "Boccaccio e i fichi secchi di Cesena," *La Piê* 85, no. 1 [January–February 2016]: 6–7).

4. See Giuliano Tanturli, "Il volgarizzamento della quarta Deca di Tito Livio," in *BAC*, 125–26. Petrarca in *Fam.*, XXIII.19 (of 1366), alludes to Boccaccio's stay in Ravenna with Ostasio (Paolo Pontari, "Boccaccio a Ravenna tra Dante e Petrarca: novità sulla *Vita Petri Damiani*," in *Boccaccio e la Romagna*, conference proceeding, ed. Gabriella Albanese and Paolo Pontari [Forlì: Salone comunale, November 22–23, 2013] [Ravenna: Longo, 2015], 128). Ostasio had come to power, in September 1322, through a coup d'etat: while his cousin Guido Novello was serving as an official (*capitano del popolo*) in Bologna, Ostasio murdered his brother, Archbishop Rinaldi, whom Guido had temporarily put in charge of the government of Ravenna, and prevented Guido himself from returning to the city. Boccaccio alludes to these events in the tenth eclogue of the *Buccolicum carmen* (*Vallis opaca* [*The Dark Valley*]) in which Ostasio (Lycidas) says that he has been plunged into a sort of Dantean hell for "the theft of Micon's [Guido Novello] sheep / long past," but also for "boys' seduction / into forbidden lust among the shadows" (vv. 143–45; "iamdudum pecudes rapuisse Miconis / et, scelus infaustum, pueros traxisse per umbras / in vetitam venerem"; the English translation is from *Eclogues*, trans. Smarr, 109). For the history of Ravenna during the age of Ostasio and Bernardino da Polenta, see Augusto Vasina, "Politica e cultura in Romagna nel Trecento," in *BR*, 21–32.

5. *Ep.*, XI.10 (vol. III, 347): "familiaris et socius Dantis nostri."

6. In his *Esposizioni sopra la Comedia di Dante* (*ECD*, VIII [I].6–13), Boccaccio would retell the story, earlier recounted in the *Trattatello in laude di Dante* (*TLD*, [I].179–82, and [II].117–20), of the rediscovery in about 1306–7, in a strongbox hidden in a safe place by Dante's wife, Gemma Donati, of a "little notebook" ("quadernetto") containing the first seven cantos of *Inferno*, and he would specify he had been given two separate versions of the events: one by Dante's nephew Andrea Leoni, the other by Dino Perini, "a very close friend and colleague of Dante" ("famigliare e amico di Dante"; on this episode and the reliability of Boccac-

cio's story, see Marco Santagata, *Dante: Il romanzo della sua vita* [Milan: Mondadori, 2012], 121–23); Pietro Giardini, "one of the most intimate friends and servants whom Dante had in Ravenna" (*ECD*, I [I].5; "uno de' più intimi amici e servidori che Dante avesse in Ravenna"; translations from Boccaccio, *Boccaccio's Expositions on Dante's Comedy*, trans. Papio, 385 and 54), is cited as evidence for Dante's age at the time of his death and for the rediscovery of the last thirteen cantos of *Paradiso* (*TLD*, [I].185–89; [II].124–27). For both Perini and Giardini, accurate biographies are now available in Gabriella Albanese and Paolo Pontari, "L'ultimo Dante: Il cenacolo ravennate, le *Egloge* e la morte," in *L'ultimo Dante e il cenacolo ravennate*, exhibition catalog, ed. Gabriella Albanese and Paolo Pontari (Ravenna: Biblioteca Classense, September 9–October 28, 2018), in *Classense* 6 (2018): 44–46 and 85–90, respectively; for an introduction to the complex figure of Salutati, see Daniela De Rosa, "Salutati, Lino Coluccio," in *DBI*, LXXXIX (2017). It was Menghino Mezzani "the old gentleman from Ravenna, a competent judge of such matters [i.e., literary value]" (translation from Petrarca, *Letters of Old Age*, vol. 1), who, Petrarca wrote in a letter in about 1364 (*Sen.*, V.2, 32), "always likes to assign you [Boccaccio] third place" in the ranking of literary merit ("Audio senem illum ravennatem, rerum talium non ineptum iudicem, quotiens de his sermo est semper tibi locum tertium assignare solitum"). A comprehensive account of Menghino's life is provided by Albanese and Pontari, "L'ultimo Dante: Il cenacolo ravennate, le *Egloge* e la morte," 68–84; for his epitaph of Dante, see Angelo Piacentini, "'Hic claudor Dantes.' Per il testo e la fortuna degli epitaffi di Dante," in *Dante e la sua eredità a Ravenna nel Trecento*, ed. Marco Petoletti, 41–70 (Ravenna: Longo, 2015), on 59–70.

7. Branca, *Giovanni Boccaccio: Profilo biografico*, 74, dates Boccaccio and Albanzani's first meeting to 1345–46; others instead place it in 1350 or 1353–54 (Guido Martellotti, "Albanzani, Donato," in *DBI*, I [1960], reprinted in Guido Martellotti, *Dante e Boccaccio e altri scrittori dall'Umanesimo al Romanticismo* [Florence: Olschki, 1983], 235–39). Because in *EpA*, 41, Boccaccio mentions to Albanzani the letter that Petrarca had written him "in opposition to my great foolishness at the time when you first became my friend in Ravenna" ("Quam sepe hanc ob causam legam credis quam etiam longissimam in bestialitatem meam scripsit, dum primo apud Ravennam amicus tuus effectus sum?") and because that letter (*Sen.*, I.5) was written in 1362, Michele Feo, *Con madonna povertà: Lettera di Giovanni Boccaccio a Donato degli Albanzani* (Pontedera: Bandecchi & Vivaldi, 2012), 8, dates the beginning of Boccaccio and Donato's friendship to that year (but see the doubts expressed by Carla Maria Monti, "Il *ravennate* Donato Albanzani amico di Boccaccio e di Petrarca," in *Dante e la sua eredità a Ravenna nel Trecento*, ed. Marco Petoletti [Ravenna: Longo, 2015], 136). In *BC*, XVI.22–24, the shepherd Appenninus (Albanzani) says that he had seen old Cerretius (Boccaccio, a man from Certaldo) "within

the cave of the Ravennan cyclops [Ostasio da Polenta] / and when he often walked the marshy forests" ("dumque ravennatis ciclopis staret in antro / et fessus silvas ambiret sepe palustres / vidimus"; translation from Boccaccio, *Eclogues*, trans. Smarr, 191).

8. On Bernardino, see Enrico Angiolini, "Polenta, Bernardino da," in *DBI*, LXXXIV (2015), and on Mezzani's imprisonment, see Albanese and Pontari, "L'ultimo Dante: Il cenacolo ravennate, le *Egloge* e la morte," 78–79. In *BC*, X, the deceased Lycidas (Ostasio), speaking with Dorilus (Menghino), says that he is suffering because of his sons' behavior ("the evil wishes of the madmen / whom I brought forth among the reeds and marsh frogs!" [vv. 24–26; "Ledunt . . . mala vota furentum / quos genui calamos inter ranasque palustres"]); and Dorilus laments being kept "in misery and fettered for no crime" (vv. 53–54; "Me solum miserumque tenet sine crimine vinctum, / heu, Polipus,") by Polipus (Bernardino), whose arrival has upended the lives of the shepherds (the people of Ravenna, vv. 6–20). In *BC*, X.11–15, Boccaccio writes that "he who brought the end to rustic freedom" ("cui rustica cessit libertas"), that is, Bernardino, "lascivious, / snatched lovely Phyllis from our Phytias [Boccaccio]" ("lascivusque mei formosam Phillyda ruris / eripuit Phytie nostro"), where "Phyllis represents the tranquility of pursuing study at the court of Ravenna, which Phytias finds that he must leave" (Giovanni Boccaccio, *Buccolicum carmen*, ed. Giorgio Bernardi Perini, in *Tutte le opere*, ed. Vittore Branca, vol. 5, 2 [Milan: Mondadori, 1994], 999; English translations from Boccaccio, *Eclogues*, trans. Smarr, 101–3). Conversini's observation about Bernardino is reported in Billanovich, *Petrarca letterato*, I. *Lo scrittoio del Petrarca*, 255. On Conversini, see Angelo Piacentini, "Giovanni Conversini [Buda 1343—Venezia 1408]," in *ALI*, 125–31; and Luciano Gargan, "Un nuovo profilo di Giovanni Conversini da Ravenna," in *Dante e la sua eredità a Ravenna nel Trecento*, ed. Marco Petoletti (Ravenna: Longo, 2015), 177–233.

9. Identifiable as the oration "Audite me, beati," which Boccaccio copied into his notebook, the *Zibaldone Magliabechiano* (see Marco Petoletti, "Gli zibaldoni di Giovanni Boccaccio," in *Boccaccio autore e copista*, exhibition catalog, ed. Teresa De Robertis, Carla Maria Monti, Marco Petoletti, Giuliano Tanturli, and Stefano Zamponi [Florence: Biblioteca Medicea Laurenziana, October 11, 2013–January 11, 2014] [Florence: Mandragora, 2013], 317–18, and Baglio, "*Avidulus glorie*: Zanobi da Strada tra Boccaccio e Petrarca," 367–68).

10. *Ep.*, VI.9: "Eram tamen habiturus in brevi, nisi itinera instarent ad illustrem Ungarie regem in extremis Brutiorum et Campanie quo moratur: nam ut sua imitetur arma iustissima, meus inclitus dominus et Pyeridum hospes gratissimus cum pluribus Flaminee proceribus preparatur; quo et ipse mei predicti domini iussu, non armiger, sed—ut ita loquar—arbiter, sum iturus."

11. Regarding Boccaccio's assertion about joining Ordelaffi, Fran-

cesco Bruni, *Boccaccio: L'invenzione della letteratura mediana* (Bologna: il Mulino, 1990), 409, writes of "bold optimism."

12. *BC*, III.

13. Giovanni Boccaccio, *Carmina*, ed. Giuseppe Velli, in *Tutte le opere*, ed. Vittore Branca, vol. 5, 1 (Milan: Mondadori, 1992), 474.

14. In a letter surviving only as a fragment (*Ep.*, VIII.1–2), Boccaccio chides the recipient, recently arrived in Naples and intent on seeing the places celebrated in the mythology and poetry of antiquity, for being "pompous and forgetful of us" since he has been "raised to the peak of fortune," and admonishes him that the novelties, for all their seductions, must not "eradicate from your memory what had previously been the greatest sweetness to him who now suffers. And what is sweeter than friendship?" ("Tu nunc in auge rote volubilis sublimatus, nostri inmemor vitam ducis elatus . . . non tamen credendum est illas e memoriis radicitus extirpare que visa sunt olim, et potissime quod fuerit ante dulcissimum patienti. Et quid amicitia dulcius?"). There is agreement that Zanobi was the addressee of the letter, the composition of which had been dated to 1352, the year Zanobi was thought to have moved to Naples to take up his new position (see Giovanni Boccaccio, *Epistole*, ed. Ginetta Auzzas, in *Tutte le opere*, ed. Vittore Branca, vol. 5, 1 [Milan: Mondadori, 1992], 785, and Marco Petoletti, "*Epistole*," in *Boccaccio autore e copista*, exhibition catalog, ed. Teresa De Robertis, Carla Maria Monti, Marco Petoletti, Giuliano Tanturli, and Stefano Zamponi [Florence: Biblioteca Medicea Laurenziana, October 11, 2013–January 11, 2014] [Florence: Mandragora, 2013], 235); however, the letter's date has now definitively been moved earlier, to 1350, when Zanobi was already in service as notary and chancellor at the Neapolitan court (see Francesco Paolo Tocco, *Niccolò Acciaiuoli: Vita e politica in Italia alla metà del XIV secolo* [Rome: Istituto storico italiano per il Medioevo, 2001], 100–101). Baglio, "*Avidulus glorie*: Zanobi da Strada tra Boccaccio e Petrarca," 363–64, characterizes the development of Boccaccio and Zanobi's relationship thus: "From an initial profession of friendship (*Ep.*, VI), to scolding laced with sarcasm (*Ep.*, IX), to explicit attack (*Ep.*, XIX, to Pizzinga). Zanobi is first 'amicus' (*Ep.*, VI), then doubtful friend ('si amicus es ut puto,' *Ep.*, IX), before becoming, in a mounting crescendo of distance, 'meus magister' (*Ep.*, IX), and, finally, simply fellow citizen ('concivis,' *Ep.*, XIX)."

15. "Gregibus nimium durus silvisque molestus."

16. *BC*, IV.5: "Munere post Phytie pulchra est, michi iuncta Liquoris."

17. "priscam . . . fidem."

18. *BC*, V.

19. *BC*, VI.12.

20. *BC*, VI.74–75: "Phytias cui, credo, magna paratur / posteritas."

21. Francesco Paolo Tocco, *Niccolò Acciaiuoli: Vita e politica in Italia alla metà del XIV secolo* (Rome: Istituto storico italiano per il Medioevo,

2001), 99. Among the Florentines given influential positions by Niccolò Acciaiuoli, Angelo Acciaiuoli, bishop of Florence, stands out, named to the highly important office of chancellor of the kingdom. Niccolò Acciaiuoli not only surrounded himself with trusted people, but removed from their positions of power those who had been in favor under King Robert and close to Joanna: among them were Boccaccio's friends Giovanni Barrili and Barbato da Sulmona (Francesco Paolo Tocco, *Niccolò Acciaiuoli: Vita e politica in Italia alla metà del XIV secolo* [Rome: Istituto storico italiano per il Medioevo, 2001], 102–4).

22. For Checco di Meletto's biography, see Aldo Francesco Massèra, "Studi boccacceschi. III. Corrispondenze poetiche del Boccaccio," in Michele Feo, "Augusto Campana biografo e continuatore degli studi di Massèra," in *Aldo Francesco Massèra tra Scuola storica e Nuova filologia*, ed. Anna Bettarini Bruni, Paola Delbianco, and Roberto Leporatti (Lecce: Pensa MultiMedia, 2018), 573–659, 602–26; Augusto Campana, "Rossi, Checco di Meletto," in *Enciclopedia dantesca*, vol. 4 (Rome: Istituto della Enciclopedia italiana, 1973), reprinted in Augusto Campana, *Scritti*, ed. Rino Avesani, Michele Feo, and Enzo Pruccoli (Rome: Edizioni di Storia e Letteratura, vol 1, pt. 2, 2008–12), 845–47; Leandro Mascanzoni, "Rossi, Francesco," in *DBI*, LXXXVIII (2017). The pro-Hungarian eclogue *Faunus* (*Carmina* III), comes third in the revised *Buccolicum carmen*.

23. The four eclogues are published with commentary in Simona Lorenzini, ed., *La corrispondenza bucolica tra Giovanni Boccaccio e Checco di Meletto Rossi: L'egloga di Giovanni del Virgilio ad Albertino Mussato* (Florence: Olschki, 2011); the two by Boccaccio can also be found in *Carmina* (II, III).

24. *GDG*, XV.13, 7: "Quod, ut sibi intitularem petiit Donatus Appennin-igena, pauper, sed honestus homo et precipuus amicus meus."

25. This suggestion is made by Carla Maria Monti, "Il *ravennate* Donato Albanzani amico di Boccaccio e di Petrarca," in *Dante e la sua eredità a Ravenna nel Trecento*, ed. Marco Petoletti (Ravenna: Longo, 2015), 137.

26. This is the suggestion of Livio Petrucci.

27. Branca, *Giovanni Boccaccio: Profilo biografico*, 78, thinks that Boccaccio had been "disappointed in his Neapolitan hopes by Ordelaffi's too rapid return."

28. We know that Boccaccino was still alive in July 1348, when he added a codicil to the will he had had drafted in September 1346 (Laura Regnicoli, "Documenti su Giovanni Boccaccio," *Boccaccio autore e copista*, exhibition catalog, ed. Teresa De Robertis, Carla Maria Monti, Marco Petoletti, Giuliano Tanturli, and Stefano Zamponi [Florence: Biblioteca Medicea Laurenziana, October 11, 2013–January 11, 2014] [Florence: Mandragora, 2013], 385) and that he sat in the *Otto di abbondanza* (an office that managed the food supply) probably from June 1347 to August 1348 (Branca, *Giovanni Boccaccio: Profilo biografico*, 78); it is also known that, beginning in April

1349, Giovanni began to receive the interest on the loan to the Comune as his father's heir (Laura Regnicoli, "Codice diplomatico di Giovanni Boccaccio 1. I documenti fiscali," *Italia medioevale e umanistica* 54 [2013]: 41–42) and that he was named guardian of his half brother, Iacopo, in January 1350 (Laura Regnicoli, "Documenti su Giovanni Boccaccio," in *Boccaccio autore e copista*, exhibition catalog, ed. Teresa De Robertis, Carla Maria Monti, Marco Petoletti, Giuliano Tanturli, and Stefano Zamponi [Florence: Biblioteca Medicea Laurenziana, October 11, 2013–January 11, 2014] [Florence: Mandragora, 2013], 394); additionally, if Boccaccino actually did meet his granddaughter, Violante, as *BC*, XIV.230–36 would suggest, he must have still been alive at least until the first months of 1349.

29. Boccaccio claimed to have seen personally the miserable spectacle caused by the plague (*Dec.*, I, Introd., 16: "if I and many others had not seen these things with our own eyes"; *Dec.*, I, Introd., 18: "With my own eyes, as I have just said, I witnessed such a thing on many occasions" ["Il che, se dagli occhi di molti e da' miei non fosse stato veduto"; "Di che gli occhi miei, sì come poco davanti è detto, presero tra l'altre volte un dì fatta esperienza"]), the peak of which he placed "from March to the following July" (*Dec.*, I, Introd., 47; "infra 'l marzo e il prossimo luglio vegnente"), while chroniclers testify that the epidemic died out between October and November 1348 (see Boccaccio, *Decameron*, 27–28). Translation from Boccaccio, *Decameron*, trans. Rebhorn, 6 and 12.

30. Translation from Boccaccio, *Decameron*, trans. Rebhorn, 5. "Dico adunque che già erano gli anni della fruttifera incarnazione del Figliuolo di Dio al numero pervenuti di milletrecentoquarantotto, quando nella egregia città di Fiorenza, oltre a ogn'altra bellissima, pervenne la mortifera pestilenza: la quale, per operazion de' corpi superiori o per le nostre inique opere da giusta ira di Dio a nostra correzione mandata sopra i mortali, alquanti anni davanti nelle parti orientali incominciata, quelle d'inumerabile quantità de' viventi avendo private, senza ristare d'un luogo in uno altro continuandosi, verso l'Occidente mirabilmente s'era ampliata. E in quella non valendo alcuno senno né umano provedimento, per lo quale fu da molte immondizie purgata la città da oficiali sopra ciò ordinati e vietato l'entrarvi dentro a ciascuno infermo e molti consigli dati a conservazion della sanità, né ancora umili supplicazioni non una volta ma molte e in processioni ordinate, in altre guise a Dio fatte dalle divote persone, quasi nel principio della primavera dell'anno predetto orribilmente cominciò i suoi dolorosi effetti, e in miracolosa maniera, a dimostrare."

31. Regarding the originality of Boccaccio's analysis, see the interesting observations in Battaglia Ricci, *Ragionare nel giardino: Boccaccio e i cicli pittorici del "Trionfo della Morte,"* 45–96, and Natascia Tonelli, "Sonetti sulla Peste Nera," in Sergio Luzzatto and Gabriele Pedullà, general eds., *Atlante della letteratura italiana*, vol. 1, *Dalle origini al Rinascimento*, ed. Amedeo De Vincentiis (Turin: Einaudi, 2010), 216–20, 219, according to

whom "Boccaccio's interest . . . is all on the social and individual effects of the spread of the disease," with a "medical-scientific perspective"; see also by Natascia Tonelli, *Giovanni Boccaccio* (Milano: "Corriere della Sera," 2017), 88–89. Conversely, Branca, *Giovanni Boccaccio: Profilo biografico*, 77–78, believes "a vision of the plague as a scourge driven 'by the just wrath of God against mortals'" was already evident "in the epistle-sonnet to Checco di Meletto [*L'antico padre, il cui primo delicto*], who had posed an anguished question about the terrible disease [*Voglia il ciel, voglia pur seguir l'edicto*]" "upon the first appearance of the 'black plague' in Italy in about January 1348." However, it was probably not the plague they were discussing in these texts: these are, in fact, a *tenzone*, or poetic debate, of six sonnets—consisting of Checco's question; the responses of Petrarca, Lancillotto Anguissola, Antonio Beccari, and Boccaccio; and Checco's counterresponse to the last (the entire exchange can be read in Boccaccio, *Rime*, CI [a, b, c, d, e, f])—focused on "divine punishments in the form of natural cataclysms" (Pontari, "Boccaccio a Ravenna tra Dante e Petrarca: novità sulla *Vita Petri Damiani*," 89), according to the editor of Beccari's works, originating from "a solar eclipse [in her opinion, the one that took place at 10:30 a.m. on September 17, 1354], probably followed by frightening thunderstorms (*Le Rime di Maestro Antonio da Ferrara [Antonio Beccari]*, ed. Laura Bellucci [Bologna: Pàtron, 1972], 201). Aldo Francesco Massèra, "*Studi boccacceschi. III. Corrispondenze poetiche del Boccaccio*," in Michele Feo, "Augusto Campana biografo e continuatore degli studi di Massèra," in *Aldo Francesco Massèra tra Scuola storica e Nuova filologia*, ed. Anna Bettarini Bruni, Paola Delbianco, and Roberto Leporatti (Lecce: Pensa MultiMedia, 2018), 602–26, 602–11, and Tonelli, "Sonetti sulla Peste Nera," 217, however, believe it was connected to the emergence of the plague.

32. Francesco Petrarca, *Fam.*, I.1, 1–2: "Tempora, ut aiunt, inter digitos effluxerunt; spes nostre veteres cum amicis sepulte sunt. Millesimus trecentesimus quadragesimus octavus annus est, qui nos solos atque inopes fecit." Translation from Petrarca, *Letters on Familiar Matters*, vol. 1.

33. On the losses Boccaccio suffered in the two years 1348–49, see Regnicoli, "Per la biografia di Giovanni Boccaccio: l'*Elegia di madonna Fiammetta* attraverso i documenti," 11 (for Bice Bostichi), and Regnicoli, "Un'oscura vicenda certaldese: Nuovi documenti su Boccaccio e la sua famiglia," *Italia medioevale e umanistica* 58 (2017): 70 (for his uncle Vanni). On the gaps in the ranks of Italian intellectuals caused by the plague, see Guido Castelnuovo and Carole Mabboux, "I letterati e l'epidemia del 1348," in *Atlante della letteratura* italiana, ed. Sergio Luzzatto and Gabriele Pedullà (Turin: Einaudi, 2010-2012), vol. 1, *Dalle origini al Rinascimento*, ed. Amedeo De Vincentiis, 220–22.

34. "E se alle nostre case torniamo, non so se a voi così come a me

adiviene: io, di molta famiglia, niuna altra persona in quella se non la mia fante trovando, impaurisco e quasi tutti i capelli adosso mi sento arricciare, e parmi, dovunque io vado o dimoro per quella, l'ombra di coloro che sono trapassati vedere, e non con quegli visi che io soleva, ma con una vista orribile non so donde in loro nuovamente venuta spaventarmi." Translation from Boccaccio, *Decameron*, trans. Rebhorn, 15.

35. For the value of Boccaccio's inheritance and the reconstruction of his behavior with regard to the tax authorities, the works of Laura Regnicoli are solid reference points, in particular Laura Regnicoli, "Documenti su Giovanni Boccaccio," in *Boccaccio autore e copista*, exhibition catalog, ed. Teresa De Robertis, Carla Maria Monti, Marco Petoletti, Giuliano Tanturli, and Stefano Zamponi (Florence: Biblioteca Medicea Laurenziana, October 11, 2013–January 11, 2014) (Florence: Mandragora, 2013), 385–409; Regnicoli, "Codice diplomatico di Giovanni Boccaccio 1. I documenti fiscali"; Regnicoli, "Per il Codice diplomatico di Giovanni Boccaccio," in *Boccaccio letterato*, conference proceedings, ed. Michaelangiola Marchiaro and Stefano Zamponi (Florence-Certaldo, October 10–12, 2013) (Florence: Accademia della Crusca—Ente nazionale Giovanni Boccaccio, 2015); and Regnicoli, "Un'oscura vicenda certaldese: Nuovi documenti su Boccaccio e la sua famiglia," *Italia medioevale e umanistica* 58 (2017): 61–122 (in this last, on 70, is the suggestion that Vanni named his nephew Giovanni as his heir). On the basis of the tax records of 1351–52 of the *sestiere* of Santo Spirito, William Caferro, "The Visconti War and Boccaccio's Florentine Public Service in Context, 1351–33," *Heliotropia* 15 (2018): 161–81, 164–66, has calculated that Boccaccio's wealth subject to taxation was not much lower than that of Pino de' Rossi and appreciably great than that of Niccolò di Bartolo del Buono.

36. On taxation and public finance, in addition to the works by Regnicoli cited above, see John M. Najemy, *Storia di Firenze: 1200–1575* (Turin: Einaudi, 2014), 143–51.

37. Regarding speculators, it should be noted that Piero di Gianni Bonaccorsi, in 1359, the year Boccaccio ceded him a *prestanza*, paid "the contributions due for the June forced loan [*prestanza*] of more than 150 people, thus becoming the Comune's creditor for more than 2000 gold florins" (Regnicoli, "Per il Codice diplomatico di Giovanni Boccaccio," 518).

38. The codex of the *Enarrationes* is today divided into two volumes: the mss. Parigini lat. 1989 (vol. 1) and 1989 (vol. 2); at the top of the codex, Petrarch inscribed a note: "Hoc immensum opus donavit michi vir egregius dominus Iohannes Boccacii de Certaldo, poeta nostri temporis, quod de Florentia Mediolanum ad me pervenit 1355 Aprilis 10." On the codex and Petrarch's letter of thanks (*Fam.*, XVIII.3), see Giuseppe Billanovich, "Petrarca, Boccaccio e le *Enarrationes in Psalmos* di s. Agostino" (1960), later republished in Giuseppe Billanovich, *Petrarca e il primo umanesimo*

(Padua: Antenore, 1996), 68–96, as well as Irene Ceccherini and Marco Baglio, "Il codice delle *Enarrationes in Psalmos* di Agostino donato da Boccaccio a Petrarca," in *BAC*, 372–74.

39. For this appointment, see Ricci in Vittore Branca and Pier Giorgio Ricci, "Notizie e documenti per la biografia del Boccaccio," *Studi sul Boccaccio* 3 (1965): 18–24, and Branca, *Giovanni Boccaccio: Profilo biografico*, 92.

40. In 1352, he would bring a suit, almost immediately ended, against two Certaldesi who had abandoned the farm in Santa Maria in Collina (see Branca, *Giovanni Boccaccio: Profilo biografico*, 92).

41. *Dec.*, VI.10.

42. The complicated events of this dispute are reconstructed by Laura Regnicoli, "Un'oscura vicenda certaldese: Nuovi documenti su Boccaccio e la sua famiglia," *Italia medioevale e umanistica* 58 (2017), who also treats some inheritance issues connected to a small piece of land that Boccaccio's uncle Vanni had left in usufruct to his wife, Rosa.

43. In 1352, the two shops would be rented, one to a shoemaker named Manno, and the other to a "treccia," that is, "a dealer who sells or trades fruits, vegetables, herbs, and the like," named Sandra (Regnicoli, "Codice diplomatico di Giovanni Boccaccio 1. I documenti fiscali," 25).

44. Regnicoli, "Codice diplomatico di Giovanni Boccaccio 1. I documenti fiscali," 23.

45. Referring to the Regisole, the classical equestrian statue of the Roman Imperial period, which he believed had come from Ravenna, Petrarch wrote to Boccaccio that, if he had gone to Pavia, he would have been able to admire "in the middle of the main square an equestrian statue of gilded bronze" that was said to have been "seized long ago from you people of Ravenna" (*Sen.*, V.1, 14; "Eneam scilicet atque inauratam statuam equestrem fori medio . . . tuis olim, ut fama est, ereptam Ravennatibus"; translation based on Petrarca, *Letters of Old Age*, vol. 1).

46. Caferro, "The Visconti War and Boccaccio's Florentine Public Service in Context, 1351–33."

47. Established in 1291 as a lay confraternity dedicated to the Virgin Mary and focused on distributing alms to the poor, by Boccaccio's time, Orsanmichele had become very large and wealthy and one of the leading institutions of Florence, closely aligned with the Comune, which used it to provide charity to the poor and in the famine year of 1329 assigned it "a portion of the assets of those executed and of the alms made annually by the Comune." Its role grew in the 1330s and 1340s, "and with it its wealth also considerably increased." The captains of Orsanmichele were the leaders of the confraternity, charged with overseeing its assets and charitable functions. In 1347–48, they also gained jurisdictional powers over contracts made by women and minors; Regnicoli, "Per il Codice diplomatico di Giovanni Boccaccio," 522.

48. For the delivery of both the ten florins and the three ducats, see

"Scheda n. 2" of Gabriella Albanese and Paolo Pontari, eds., *L'ultimo Dante e il cenacolo ravennate*, exhibition catalog (Ravenna: Biblioteca Classense, September 9–October 28, 2018), in *Classense*, special issue, 6 (2018): 124–25.

Chapter Seven

1. Almost ten years later, this is how Petrarch would recall his first meeting with Boccaccio: "I cannot forget the time when, as I was hastening across Italy in midwinter, you not only sent me affectionate greetings ... but came personally in haste to meet me ... motivated by your great desire to see a man whom you had yet to meet.... What is more, it was late in the day and the light was already waning" (*Fam.*, XXI.15, 27–28; "Unum illud oblivisci nunquam possum, quod tu olim me Italie medio iter festinantius agentem, iam seviente bruma, non affectibus solis ... sed corporeo etiam motu celer, miro nondum visi hominis desiderio prevenisti.... Sero tamen diei illius et ambigua iam lux erat"; translation from Petrarca, *Letters on Familiar Matters*, vol. 3).

2. Francesco Petrarch, *Epyst.*, III.9, 7–14: "Quid, quod nec aperta volenti / ianua? In exilium cives egere superbi ... Cui non paucorum iniuria nota est, / quam fovet immemoris populi patientia nostri, / vel vi rapta domus, vel pascua ruris aviti / amisseque preces et tot per insane querele?" For Bruno Casini, see Fabio Troncarelli, "Casini, Bruno," in *DBI*, XXI (1978); and for Francesco Nelli, see Paolo Garbini, "Nelli, Francesco," in *DBI*, LXXVIII (2013). Their letters to Petrarch, one letter in prose and one in verse each, have not survived: the correspondence has been reconstructed by Arnaldo Foresti, "Il primo approccio di Bruno da Firenze e Zanobi da Strada" (1919), later published in Foresti, *Aneddoti della vita di Francesco Petrarca*, ed. Antonia Tissoni Benvenuti (Padua: Editrice Antenore, 1977), 214–26. *Epyst.*, III.9, with which Petrarch responded to Zanobi da Strada, is dated to the summer of 1350 (Michele Feo, "La lettera al Petrarca del Comune di Firenze," in *Codici latini del Petrarca nelle biblioteche fiorentine: Mostra 19 maggio–30 giugno 1991*, ed. Michele Feo [Florence: Le Lettere, 1991], 356; Baglio, "*Avidulus glorie*: Zanobi da Strada tra Boccaccio e Petrarca," 358), while Foresti, *Aneddoti della vita di Francesco Petrarca*, 221–26, maintains that the first draft dates back to 1348.

3. The contents of Boccaccio's lost verse letter has been reconstructed based on Petrarch's letter of January 7, 1351 (*Fam.*, XI.2), along with which Petrarch sent Boccaccio *Epyst.*, III.17, written in response: see Arnaldo Foresti, "L'epistola metrica al Boccaccio" (1919), later published in Foresti, *Aneddoti della vita di Francesco Petrarca*, 239–41. According to Francisco Rico, *Ritratti allo specchio (Boccaccio, Petrarca)* (Rome and Padua: Editrice Antenore, 2012), 18–20, Petrarch was lying "when in the autumn he assured Giovanni that he had responded immediately to his poem of the

summer with a verse letter (III 17)": in Rico's view, in fact, "this verse was composed not before but after his visit to Florence."

4. The widespread belief that Petrarch stayed in Boccaccio's house is based solely on a phrase in *Fam.*, XXI.15, 29: "Non tu me Phinei sub menia, sed amicitie tue sacris penetralibus induxisti" ("You led me not 'within the walls of Pheneus' [*Aeneid*, VIII.165] but within the sacred portals of your friendship"); however, Rico, *Ritratti allo specchio (Boccaccio, Petrarca)*, 16, observes, "this is a very common use of the word *penetralia* . . . which here effectively contrasts the physical wall of the city of Pheneus with the immaterial depths of friendship," and for this reason the conclusion cannot be drawn based on this phrase that Boccaccio hosted Petrarch in his home.

5. Zanobi's presence in Naples is attested by the subscript at the end of his letter dated August 5, 1350: see Francesco Paolo Tocco, *Niccolò Acciaiuoli: Vita e politica in Italia alla metà del XIV secolo* (Rome: Istituto storico italiano per il Medioevo, 2001), 100–101; and Baglio, "*Avidulus glorie*: Zanobi da Strada tra Boccaccio e Petrarca," 344.

6. Five years later, in a letter to Petrarch, Francesco Nelli recalled the day that he had recited his poetry to his Florentine friends who were gathered to listen: "I remember well—indeed, I cannot not remember what I have never forgotten—the day long ago when you recited some poems for us with that venerable and evocative voice of yours, so capable of translating the movements of the heart into an exceptionally refined language; and also the gestures full of restraint, which I still hold close to my soul, now relaxing a little, now tensing with the words, now bending you to the right, now to the left" (14 [XIII], 7; "Memini te, imo reminisci nequeo que oblivioni non dedi, cum dudum carmina nobis vocem illam venerandam atque tremendam, motus animi disertissima lingua interprete, extulisse; gestus quoque modestie plenos quos anime affixos teneo, nunc paululum laxando, nunc contrahendo pro qualitate verborum, nunc destrorsum aut sinistrorsum membra iactando"). Even in Petrarch's absence, his friends and admirers often met over dinner to read and discuss his verse and prose letters: in *Ep.*, 2 [III], 6, of the end of January 1351, Francesco Nelli wrote to him: "A group of your admirers having gathered for a splendid dinner in honor of the Florentine Francesco Bruni lately named chancellor and notary of the aforementioned Giacomo da Carrara, especially those who live joyfully under the banner of your name and enjoy your venerable friendship . . . each one of them read out his little gift [i.e., letters received from Petrarch], or better, perfect gift, as it is the product of a perfect heart" ("Congregato equidem cetu tuo ad cenam splendidam extollendi viri Francisci Bruni de Florentia, dudum cancellarii et notarii dilecti prefati domini Iacobi, hi precipue qui sub fama tui nominis congratulanter vivunt et tuam reverendissimam amicitiam profitentur . . . unusquisque suum munusculum, imo munus perfectum cum de perfecto

exiliat pectore, deduxit"); for Francesco Bruni, see Eugenio Ragni, "Bruni, Francesco," in *DBI*, XIV (1972) (no other source contains the information that Bruni was the "cancellarius" and "notarius" of Giacomo da Carrara). In October 1353, Nelli also told Petrarch (11 [XI], 2–5) that while he was at a meal with some of Bishop Acciaiuoli's nephews, Boccaccio, Lapo di Castiglionchio, and Forese Donati arrived, and then a messenger delivered two of Petrarch's letters (*Fam.*, XVI.14; *Disp.*, 20), which they all joyfully read together.

7. Regarding the Quintilian codex, see Maria Accame Lanzillotta, "Le postille del Petrarch a Quintiliano (Cod. Parigino lat. 7720)," in *Quaderni petrarcheschi* 5 (1988) (Firenze: Le Lettere, 1989). Petrarch's request to Castiglionchio regarding the orations is in *Disp.*, 12 (= *Var.*, 45) of January 6, 1351, which accompanied his gift of the *Pro Archia*; Lapo sent him the *Pro Milone*, *Pro Plancio*, *Pro Sulla*, and *Pro lege Manilia*, and Petrarca returned the codex, after having had it copied, November 14, 1355: see Arnaldo Foresti, "Le lettere a Lapo da Castiglionchio e il suo libro ciceroniano" (1919), later published in Foresti, *Aneddoti della vita di Francesco Petrarca*, 242–50; Silvia Rizzo, "Scambio di doni ciceroniani fra Petrarch e Lapo da Castiglionchio," in *Codici latini del Petrarca nelle biblioteche fiorentine: Mostra 19 maggio-30 giugno 1991*, ed. Michele Feo (Florence: Le Lettere, 1991), 9–14.

8. Francesco Petrarch, *Fam.*, XI.1, 10: "Hic enim status . . . importunissimus atque gravissimus est propter animum inexplebilem regine urbis aspectibus, quam quo magis intueor, magis miror et magis magisque ad credendum cogor quicquid de hac scriptum legimus." Translation from Petrarca, *Letters on Familiar Matters*, vol. 2.

9. "De publico quidem erario a privatis civibus redempta."

10. "Tu tecum librum hac facultate legendum nostris ingeniis legas quem honori et otiis quis censeas commodiorem." Regarding this letter, see Feo, "La lettera al Petrarca del Comune di Firenze."

11. A passage transcribed in the *Zibaldone Magliabechiano* on 70r appears to suggest that Boccaccio had read the passionaries held in the library of Santa Giustina, which was believed, following Giuseppe Billanovich, *Petrarca letterato*, I. *Lo scrittoio del Petrarca* (Rome: Edizioni di Storia e letteratura, 1947; repr. 1995), 116–17 (see also Vittore Branca, *Giovanni Boccaccio: Profilo biografico* [Florence: Sansoni, 1977 (1967)], 88), until Giuseppe Billanovich, *La tradizione del testo di Livio e le origini dell'Umanesimo*, I. *Tradizione e fortuna di Livio tra Medioevo e Umanesimo* (Padua: Editrice Antenore, 1981), 26–27, showed that actually the passage is simply the transcription from the *Historie* of Riccobaldo da Ferrara. Boccaccio refers to Livy's epitaph at the end of his short "Vita di Tito Livio" (*Vite*, 938–41): on the epitaph and Petrarch's role with regard to it, see Billanovich, *La tradizione del testo di Livio e le origini dell'Umanesimo*, I. *Tradizione e fortuna di Livio tra Medioevo e Umanesimo*, 319–30. Boccaccio

recalled his days in Padua in *Ep.*, X.4–5, to Petrarch: "I believe you remember well, my excellent master, that three years have not yet passed since I came to you in Padua as ambassador of our senate, and after I fulfilled my commission, I stayed with you for a few days, almost all of which we spent in the same way. You dedicated yourself to your sacred studies, I, eager for your writings, made copies of them. But as the day turned to evening, we rose from our labors of one accord, and went into your little garden, which was already adorned with the leaves and flowers of early spring . . . and sitting and talking with each other we would spend what remained of the day in serene and commendable leisure [*otio*] until the night" ("Credo memineris, preceptor optime, quod nondum tertius annus elapsus sit posquam senatus nostri nuntius Patavum ad te veni, et commissis expositis dies plusculos tecum egerim, quos fere omnes uno eodem duximus modo. Tu sacris vacabas studiis, ego compositionum tuarum avidus ex illis scribens summebam copiam. Die autem in vesperam declinante a laboribus surgebamus unanimes, et in ortulum ibamus tuum iam ob novum ver frondibus atque floribus ornatum . . . et invicem sedentes atque confabulantes quantum diei supererat placido otio atque laudabili trahebamus in noctem"); in the remainder of the letter, Boccaccio recalls the tenor of the political discussions behind a pastoral screen.

12. Francesco Petrarch, *Fam.*, XI.5.

13. "Pessime factum est, nec absque facientium nota."

14. Carla Maria Monti, "Boccaccio e Petrarca," in *Boccaccio autore e copista*, exhibition catalog, ed. Teresa De Robertis, Carla Maria Monti, Marco Petoletti, Giuliano Tanturli, and Stefano Zamponi (Florence: Biblioteca Medicea Laurenziana, October 11, 2013–January 11, 2014) (Florence: Mandragora, 2013), 34.

15. See *Ep.*, XV.17–20, and the observations of Gabriella Albanese, "La corrispondenza fra Petrarca e Boccaccio," *Motivi e forme delle "Familiari" di Francesco Petrarca*, ed. Claudia Berra, *Quaderni di Acme* 57 (2003): 39–98, 61–64, and Marco Petoletti, "*Epistole*," in *Boccaccio autore e copista*, exhibition catalog, ed. Teresa De Robertis, Carla Maria Monti, Marco Petoletti, Giuliano Tanturli, and Stefano Zamponi (Florence: Biblioteca Medicea Laurenziana, October 11, 2013–January 11, 2014) (Florence: Mandragora, 2013), 239–40.

16. On Boccaccio's activities as *camerlengo*, see William Caferro, "The Visconti War and Boccaccio's Florentine Public Service in Context, 1351–33," *Heliotropia* 15 (2018): 161–81, 162–63. Regarding the negotiations over Prato, see Francesco Paolo Tocco, *Niccolò Acciaiuoli: Vita e politica in Italia alla metà del XIV secolo* (Rome: Istituto storico italiano per il Medioevo, 2001), 108–17; on Florentine interests in this city, see Pier Giorgio Ricci, *Studi sulla vita e le opere del Boccaccio* (Milan and Naples: Ricciardi, 1985), 10.

17. Laura Regnicoli, "Per il Codice diplomatico di Giovanni Boccaccio,"

in *Boccaccio letterato*, conference proceedings, ed. Michaelangiola Marchiaro and Stefano Zamponi (Florence-Certaldo, October 10–12, 2013) (Florence: Accademia della Crusca — Ente nazionale Giovanni Boccaccio, 2015), 520–24, provides and analyzes the information about the offices Boccaccio held (quote on 523). It is excessive to maintain, as Ricci, *Studi sulla vita e le opere del Boccaccio*, 9, does, that Boccaccio had "the privilege of joining the restricted circle of the most influential citizens, deeply involved in the execution of Florentine policies" and that from 1350 to 1354 "he even seems to have been one of the principal instigators of such policies, for we constantly find him holding public offices with great influence on the most important and difficult circumstances faced by the Comune."

18. Boccaccio held the following offices after 1354: from May 1355, for four months he was an *Ufficiale dei difetti* (a kind of neighborhood police office who sanctioned minor infractions committed by soldiers in the pay of the city), but as a replacement for an official who had died; from August 1364 to February 1365 he was one of the *Ufficiali dei castelli* (involved in construction of fortifications); from November 1367 to February 1368 he was *Ufficiale della condotta* (dealing with recruitment and salaries of mercenary troops) (see Laura Regnicoli, "Documenti su Giovanni Boccaccio," in *Boccaccio autore e copista*, exhibition catalog, ed. Teresa De Robertis, Carla Maria Monti, Marco Petoletti, Giuliano Tanturli, and Stefano Zamponi [Florence: Biblioteca Medicea Laurenziana, October 11, 2013–January 11, 2014] [Florence: Mandragora, 2013], 398; Regnicoli, "Per il Codice diplomatico di Giovanni Boccaccio," 523–24).

19. The observations of Caferro, "The Visconti War and Boccaccio's Florentine Public Service in Context, 1351–33," illuminate the nature of Boccaccio's diplomatic activities during the war with the Visconti; in particular, it is quite revealing that his expenses were not recorded in accounts of the Camera del Comune (municipal treasury), which provided financial support for so-to-speak official missions, but only in the so-called Balìe, in which, in contrast, the more ambiguous or in any case less transparent missions were reported. Emanuela Porta Casucci, "'Un uomo di vetro' fra corti e cortili: Giovanni Boccaccio, i Del Buono, i Rossi e gli altri," *Heliotropia* 12–13 (2015–16): 207, remarked that "Boccaccio for the most part held [subordinate?] positions in the diplomatic initiatives of Realpolitik undertaken by the notoriously Guelph Florence toward imperial circles in the mid-fourteenth century, and always along with well-known magnates to whom the republican commune evidently attributed greater efficacy in court environments."

20. New information about the mission as "ambaxiator ad partes Romandiole et Lombardie," which took place not in 1350, as had been believed, but 1351, was found by Caferro, "The Visconti War and Boccaccio's Florentine Public Service in Context, 1351–33," who reasonably suggests that this was a confidential mission: the document of Boccaccio's

payment for the mission is precisely transcribed by Vittorio Imbriani, "La pretesa figliola di Dante Allaghieri," *Giornale napoletano di filosofia e lettere, scienze morali e politiche*, n.s. IV, 7, fasc. 19 (1882), 63–87, on 84. For the other Florentine embassies to Verona, both immediately before and after Boccaccio's to Romagna, see Caferro, "The Visconti War and Boccaccio's Florentine Public Service in Context, 1351–33," 169–70. Evidence of a possible trip to Verona by Boccaccio is in *Ep.*, IX, to Zanobi da Strada, in which he says, "Padua, Verona, old Ravenna, Forlì call me, though I refuse" ("Patavum, Verona, vetus Ravenna, Forlivium me etiam renuentem vocant"): trips to Padua, Ravenna, and Forlì are documented as of the date of this letter, April 14, 1353, but not to Verona.

21. For this embassy, see Attilio Hortis, *Giovanni Boccacci ambasciatore in Avignone e Pileo da Prata proposto da' fiorentini a patriarca di Aquileia* (Trieste: Herrmanstorfer, 1875), 8–13; Branca, *Giovanni Boccaccio: Profilo biografico*, 86–87, argues that Boccaccio had the task of negotiating with Ludwig regarding "action against the archbishop of Milan" and that on this occasion "he probably had to pass through the Val d'Adige and the Trentino and may also through Friuli."

22. *Ep.*, XV.11: "Oculorum leticia . . . inter nigram rufamque."

23. "Ravennam urbem petebam visitaturus civitatis principem."

24. The journey to Forlì and then Ravenna is documented by *Ep.*, X, to Petrarch, sent from Ravenna on July 18, 1353, and by evidence from Giovanni Conversini, for which see Luciano Gargan, "Un nuovo profilo di Giovanni Conversini da Ravenna," in *Dante e la sua eredità a Ravenna nel Trecento*, ed. Marco Petoletti (Ravenna: Longo, 2015), 183. Carla Maria Monti, "Il *ravennate* Donato Albanzani amico di Boccaccio e di Petrarca," in *Dante e la sua eredità a Ravenna nel Trecento*, ed. Marco Petoletti (Ravenna: Longo, 2015), says that Boccaccio returned to Florence in October. That he was on an official mission in Ravenna is also hypothesized Regnicoli, "Per il Codice diplomatico di Giovanni Boccaccio," 522.

25. The hypothesis of Billanovich, *Petrarca letterato*, I. *Lo scrittoio del Petrarca*, 181, taken up by Boccaccio, *Epistole*, ed. Ginetta Auzzas, in *Tutte le opere*, ed. Vittore Branca, vol. 5, 1 (Milan: Mondadori, 1992), 493–856, 791.

26. "Impossibile dixi"; "Inde post dies paucos Ravennam forte venit Simonides; hic a Silvano de materia hac litteras scriptas ostendit." We do not know why Nelli was in Ravenna, however, he, who at that time had already been elected Prior several times and a member of the council of *Dodici buonomini* ("Twelve Good Men"), as well as notary of the bishop's curia, had excellent credentials for conducting a diplomatic mission; the letter that he showed Boccaccio may be *Disp.*, 19 (= *Var.*, 7), in which Petrarch writing from Milan told Zanobi da Strada of his move, a copy of which Zanobi sent Nelli (see Arnaldo Foresti, "Bolanus: un frate portalettere a servizio del Petrarch e degli amici suoi" [1921], later published in

Foresti, *Aneddoti della vita di Francesco Petrarca*, 305–18, on 307–8; and Ugo Dotti, *Vita di Petrarca* (Rome-Bari: Laterza, 1987), 282–83).

27. He signed the letter "ferventi atque commoto animo, JOHANNES BOCCACCIUS tuus."

28. "Indignatio noviter commissi facinoris."

29. Checco di Meletto, *Laurea si incinctos*, 14–15; 6–8: "Mirantur culpantque viri coluisse superba / limina teque fores intra vixisse potentum"; "ne dedignere, poeta, / scribere quod possit dubios evellere motus / mentibus humanis." This work is published in Michele Feo, "Augusto Campana biografo e continuatore degli studi di Massèra," in *Aldo Francesco Massèra tra Scuola storica e Nuova filologia*, ed. Anna Bettarini Bruni, Paola Delbianco, and Roberto Leporatti (Lecce: Pensa MultiMedia, 2018), 573–659, 638–47.

30. Florentine diplomatic maneuvering of this period is reconstructed by Francesco Baldasseroni, "Relazioni tra Firenze, la Chiesa e Carlo IV. 1353-'55," in *Archivio storico italiano*, ser. 5, 37 (1906), 3–60, 322–47. In *BC*, VII and IX, Boccaccio spoke negatively about Charles IV, in accordance with the Florentine political position.

31. These suggestions are Branca's, *Giovanni Boccaccio: Profilo biografico*, 97, who also argues that Boccaccio must have met with various friends and admirers of Petrarch's in Avignon, "for example, Guido Sette, Ludwig van Kempen, Lellio Tosetti, etc.," that they and Forese Donati may have encouraged him to make a "pilgrimage" to Vaucluse, which Petrarch had "so fascinatingly described to him (*Fam.*, XVI.6)," and that Boccaccio based "a note in *De fontibus*" on the impressions gained then. However, though it is very likely that Boccaccio met some of Petrarch's friends and acquaintances in Avignon, they were not the ones indicated above: in a letter of 1365 (*Sen.*, V.1, 18–20), Petrarch scolds Boccaccio for not coming to see him in Pavia during his return from the second trip to Avignon, or at least stopping at Genoa, where Boccaccio would have been able to meet Petrarch's great friend Guido Sette, the archbishop of the city; it is therefore clear that Boccaccio had not met Sette earlier (on which see Giuseppe Billanovich, *Petrarca e il primo umanesimo* [Padua: Antenore, 1996], 426–28). In *Sen.*, III.1, Petrarch wrote to Boccaccio about the deaths of both Lelio (Lello) Tosetti and Francesco Nelli (Simonide): while Simonide is called "noster" ("our"), that is, a friend of both of theirs, Lelio is repeatedly called "meus" ("mine"), that is, a friend of Petrarch alone; finally, there is no trace in Boccaccio's writing of Ludwig van Kempen (Ludovico Santo di Beringen, called Socrate). As for Vaucluse, it is likely that Boccaccio did visit it, either on this or on the visit of 1365 (see Billanovich, *Petrarca letterato*, I. *Lo scrittoio del Petrarca*, 276): Petrarch had written to him about it in the letter sent immediately after their meeting in Padua (*Fam.*, XI.6), while the letter erroneously cited by Branca (*Fam.*, XVI.6)—repeating the error of Billanovich, *Petrarca letterato*, I. *Lo scrittoio del Petrarca*, 23—does

indeed contain a nostalgic description of Vaucluse, but was addressed to Niccolò di Paolo dei Vetuli, bishop of Viterbo. Boccaccio's praise of Vaucluse in *De montibus*, III [*De fontibus*], 114, and *GDG*, XIV.19, 5, does seem to show personal knowledge of the place.

32. For Fra Moriale and the Great Company, see Elvira Vittozzi, "Moriale, Giovanni, detto fra Moriale," in *DBI*, LXXVI (2012).

33. See Francesco Paolo Tocco, *Niccolò Acciaiuoli: Vita e politica in Italia alla metà del XIV secolo* (Rome: Istituto storico italiano per il Medioevo, 2001), 200–208.

34. Petrarch, *Fam.*, XVIII.15, 2 (December 20, 1355): "Mirum: poeta esse voluisti ut poete nomen horreres, cum contra multi nomen hoc ipsum ambiant rei expertes. An forte quia nondum peneia fronde redimitus sis, poeta esse non potes?" Translation from Petrarca, *Letters on Familiar Matters*, vol. 3.

35. Petrarch, *Disp.*, 40 (= *Misc.*, 1), 30: "Iudex censorque germanicus ferre sententiam non expauit."

36. For Zanobi's coronation and the reactions to it, see Baglio, "*Avidulus glorie*: Zanobi da Strada tra Boccaccio e Petrarca"; Petrarch's poem to him is *Epyst.*, III.8. Zanobi responded to Boccaccio's lost poem with the *Quid faciam, que vita michi* (published in Giovanni Boccaccio, *Opere latine minori*, ed. Aldo Francesco Massèra [Bari: Laterza, 1928], 298–99; see also Angelo Piacentini, "*Carmina*," in *Boccaccio autore e copista*, exhibition catalog, ed. Teresa De Robertis, Carla Maria Monti, Marco Petoletti, Giuliano Tanturli, and Stefano Zamponi [Florence: Biblioteca Medicea Laurenziana, October 11, 2013–January 11, 2014] [Florence: Mandragora, 2013], 226), to which Boccaccio replied with the verse letter *Si bene conspexi* (*Carmina*, VII): for the chronology of this exchange, see Giovanni Boccaccio, *Carmina*, ed. Giuseppe Velli, in *Tutte le opere*, ed. Vittore Branca, vol. 5, 1 (Milan: Mondadori, 1992), 392–97, who dates the composition of Boccaccio's verse to before the trip to Naples, correcting the hypothesis of Billanovich, *Petrarca letterato*, I. *Lo scrittoio del Petrarca*, 205, that is was written "immediately after the return to Florence." In *Carmina*, VII, passages such as "vatum / iam decus et patrie fulgor, venerande, secundus" (vv. 1–2; "glory now of the bards and second light of the fatherland [after Claudian, the first light of Florence]") or "Nos turba minor suspensa tenemus / ora quidem, si forte cadat de fonte propinquo / quid sapidum, aut cupidas nobis quod mulcear aures" (vv. 53–55; "We of the humble common people wait open-mouthed for something exquisite to fall from the nearby fount or that caresses our eager ears") may have a sarcastic tone. The biographical profile of Zanobi is in *Ep.*, XIX.30, of 1371: "If I so wished, I could add to these men [Dante and Petrarch] my fellow citizen Zanobi whose last name comes from his ancestral village 'da Strada,' who put down the rod he used to compel little boys who were trying to reach the first level of grammar out of their cradles [Zanobi was a

school master]. Desirous for glory, he aimed high for honors that I do not know if he deserved. He gave little weight to the ancient ritual and put on his head not the Roman but the Pisan laurel by the hand of the German Caesar [Charles IV], content to please only a single man with a few poems. As if he were sorry for the honor received, he was attracted by love of gold and went to the western Babylon [Avignon] where he fell silent. For this reason, since he brought little work and no glory at all the sacred name [of poet], I decided to leave him out" ("His ego tertium concivem meum addere, si velim, possem, Zenobium scilice et ab avito rure cognomina- tum 'de Strata,' qui posita ferula qua ab incunabulis puellulos primum gramatice gradum temptantes cogere consuerat, avidulus glorie, nescio utrum in satis meritos evolavit honores, et veteri omni parvipenso ritu, boemi Cesaris manu non romanam lauream sed pisanam capiti impres- sit suo, et unico tantum homini paucis carminibus placuisse contentus, quasi eum decoris assumpti peniteret, tractus auri cupidine in Babilo- nem occiduam abiit et obmutuit; quam ob rem, cum laboris modicum et fere nil glorie sacro nomini attulerit, omittendum censui"); the English translation is from David G. Lummus, *The City of Poetry: Imagining the Civic Role of the Poet in Fourteenth-Century Italy* (Cambridge: Cambridge University Press, 2020), 216. The claim is unfounded that "despite these resentments, Boccaccio . . . transcribed into his *Zibaldone* the *sermo* given by the crowned poet" (Branca, *Giovanni Boccaccio: Profilo biografico*, 100): in fact, the *Zibaldone Magliabechiano* contains (on 100v–104r) the *Audite me, beati*, not the oration *Stat sua cuique*, which was the one given on the occasion of the coronation (for which see Baglio, "*Avidulus glorie*: Zanobi da Strada tra Boccaccio e Petrarca," 372–79). Among Boccaccio's friends, the most critical of all was Francesco Nelli, who wrote to Petrarch regarding "the wicked and novel idea of this truly barbarous Emperor [Charles IV]" ("de Cesaris immo barbari huius novitate fantasmatis et nequitie") that "he made one of ours insane, by elevating one of the lesser ones . . . not to the dignity but to the haughtiness of the crown, unaware what injustice he did not so much to you as to the whole world" (15 [XVII], 14; "unum de nostris amentem fecit, minorum quemdam . . . ad corone fastidium non fastigium sublimando, ignarus quantam non tam tibi quam toti mundo fecit iniuriam").

37. "Compatienti principi reliquisque proceribus, eodem fere instanti quo nuntiata est, inconcusso pectore, infracta voce, continuato sermone, prolixa atque accurata dicacitate, de mortuis nil ultra curandum . . . predicasse."

38. "Quid adversus me persecutio longa, quid inextricabilis fuga, quid vulnus exitiale potuerint olim, obmictere libet."

39. "Longum tempus effluxit, ex quo neque tu michi nec ego tibi scripsi. Nescio an incusem celsitudinem tuam, iam ut video parva despici- entem, an dementiam meam modicum curanda curantem."

40. *Ep.*, IX.21: "Nunquam felicitate Magni tui florente me regnum auxonicum revisurum . . . ne me tranquilla sequentem diceret."

41. It is also likely, though not certain, that Boccaccio met Emperor Charles IV. The only hint we have of this meeting ("Probably on account of that office [*Ufficiale dei difetti*] or else for a mission that we have no information about, Boccaccio saw the emperor, who was in Tuscany for some time both before and after his coronation in Rome, and who often officially and unofficially received Florentine missions," Branca, *Giovanni Boccaccio: Profilo biografico*, 98; and similarly earlier Billanovich, *Petrarca letterato*, I. *Lo scrittoio del Petrarca*, 200) is in *Ep.*, XIII.110, of 1363 to Francesco Nelli: "I remember having entree, many times and very easily, both to the Supreme Pontiff and to Emperor Charles, as well as to many princes of the world, and being given permission to speak" ("Io mi ricordo, spesse volte e molto più agevolmente, ed al sommo pontefice ed a Carlo Cesare ed a molti principi del mondo avere avuta l'entrata, e copia di parlare essermi conceduta"), but it would be strange if Boccaccio sent false information to Nelli of all people, who at the time of Charles IV was very much in the know about the political and institutional life of Florence.

42. Zanobi was already in Montecassino in October, as attested by the verse letter *Quid faciam*, dated "In Sancto Germano (now Cassino) . . . quinto ydus octubris," that is October 11 (Giovanni Boccaccio, *Opere latine minori*, ed. Aldo Francesco Massèra [Bari: Laterza, 1928], 299; Giovanni Boccaccio, *Carmina*, ed. Giuseppe Velli, in *Tutte le opere*, ed. Vittore Branca, vol. 5, 1 [Milan: Mondadori, 1992], 392).

43. "Vult Midas ipse, daturus / pascua, si qua fides, fontesque umbrasque recentes"; English translation from Boccaccio, *Eclogues*, trans. Smarr, 75. Billanovich, *Petrarca letterato*, I. *Lo scrittoio del Petrarca*, 200, hypothesized that Acciaiuoli offered Boccaccio hospitality in Naples; Giovanni Boccaccio, *Buccolicum carmen*, ed. Giorgio Bernardi Perini, in *Tutte le opere*, ed. Vittore Branca, vol. 5, 2 (Milan: Mondadori, 1994), 979, that he "lured him with the prospect of succeeding Zanobi da Strada." Branca, *Giovanni Boccaccio: Profilo biografico*, 99, writes that at the negotiations between the Florentines and Acciaiuoli seeking help in fighting the Great Company "in Florence, in early May . . . perhaps Boccaccio participated because of his duties"; but in reality Acciaiuoli arrived in Florence in April, after Charles IV's coronation and before the conferral of Zanobi's laurel wreath in Pisa, in the unsuccessful attempt to reach a (substantial) alliance between Florence and the emperor (Francesco Paolo Tocco, *Niccolò Acciaiuoli: Vita e politica in Italia alla metà del XIV secolo* [Rome: Istituto storico italiano per il Medioevo, 2001], 206), and it seems improbable that Boccaccio would have participated in such high-level discussions.

44. The attacks of the summer, to be precise "while the fierce Dog Star joined to the Lion finished its evil path" ("dum seva Canis iniuncta Leoni /

stella malum finiret iter"), that is, until August 17, when the sun leaves Leo, lasted for months (see *Carmina*, VII.13–34).

45. Billanovich, *Petrarca letterato*, I. *Lo scrittoio del Petrarca*, 200, and Branca, *Giovanni Boccaccio: Profilo biografico*, 101, place the departure for Naples in early September; in contrast, Giovanni Boccaccio, *Carmina*, ed. Giuseppe Velli, in *Tutte le opere*, ed. Vittore Branca, vol. 5, 1 (Milan: Mondadori, 1992), 397, argues it should be pushed later. We know for certain that Boccaccio was still in Florence on October 6 because on that day he received his salary for his four months as *Ufficiale dei difetti* (Laura Regnicoli, "Documenti su Giovanni Boccaccio," in *Boccaccio autore e copista*, exhibition catalog, ed. Teresa De Robertis, Carla Maria Monti, Marco Petoletti, Giuliano Tanturli, and Stefano Zamponi [Florence: Biblioteca Medicea Laurenziana, October 11, 2013–January 11, 2014] [Florence: Mandragora, 2013], 396).

46. "Dum tristis Orion alta tenet noctis prohibens cantare volucres"; translation from Boccaccio, *Eclogues*, trans. Smarr, 77.

47. Most of the small amount of information we have about this trip comes from *BC*, VIII, an eclogue in which Boccaccio harshly criticizes Niccolò Acciaiuoli. The proposal that the discussions with Barbato da Sulmona took place in November is made by Arnaldo Foresti, "L'egloga ottava di Giovanni Boccaccio," *Giornale storico della letteratura italiana* 78 (1921): 325–43, on 340.

48. On the troubled relations between Barbato da Sulmona and Niccolò Acciaiuoli, see Francesco Paolo Tocco, *Niccolò Acciaiuoli: Vita e politica in Italia alla metà del XIV secolo* (Rome: Istituto storico italiano per il Medioevo, 2001), 103–4.

49. "Non Coridon, miserande, tibi, non fistula nota / qua steriles, vobis blandus, cantabat amores"; translation from Boccaccio, *Eclogues*, trans. Smarr, 83.

50. For this codex (now Pluteo 51.10 of the Laurentian Library in Florence)—which according to Billanovich, *Petrarca letterato*, I. *Lo scrittoio del Petrarca*, 204, was "secretly removed" by Boccaccio—see Laura Regnicoli and Monica Berté, "Il codice cassinese archetipo di Varrone con la 'Pro Cluentio' di Cicerone," in *BAC*, 353–57.

Chapter Eight

1. From the plentiful literature on the relationship between Boccaccio and Petrarch, I would highlight, in addition to the classic Giuseppe Billanovich, *Petrarca letterato*, I. *Lo scrittoio del Petrarca* (Rome: Edizioni di *Storia e letteratura*, 1947; repr. 1995), Gabriella Albanese, "La corrispondenza fra Petrarca e Boccaccio," *Motivi e forme delle "Familiari" di Francesco Petrarca*, ed. Claudia Berra, *Quaderni di Acme* 57 (2003): 39–98 (which includes an appendix with an invaluable summary of the

prose and verse correspondence that survives and about which we have information); Vincenzo Fera, "Storia e filologia tra Petrarch e Boccaccio," in *PU*, 369–89; Carla Maria Monti, "L'immagine di Petrarca negli scritti di Boccaccio," *Atti e Memorie dell'Accademia Galileiana di Scienze, Lettere ed Arti già dei Ricovrati e Patavina* 127, pt. 3 (2014–15) (on 290–91 is a table summarizing "all the places in Boccaccio's *corpus* where Petrarch is either explicitly named [with his own name or that of his bucolic alter ego] or referred to indirectly"); Francisco Rico, *Ritratti allo specchio (Boccaccio, Petrarca)* (Rome and Padua: Editrice Antenore, 2012); Paola Vecchi Galli, *Padri: Petrarca e Boccaccio nella poesia del Trecento* (Rome and Padua: Editrice Antenore, 2012); Marco Veglia, *La strada più impervia: Boccaccio fra Dante e Petrarca* (Rome and Padua: Editrice Antenore, 2014); Gabriele Baldassari, "Nodi politici (e intertestuali) tra Boccaccio e Petrarca," *Heliotropia* 12–13 (2015–16): 263–303.

2. Leaving aside the eclogues, *Carmina*, and letters, Petrarch's name appears thirty-one times in Boccaccio's writing: it is accompanied by the appositive "preceptor meus/preceptor noster/mio maestro/mio precettore" ("my teacher/our teacher/my master/my preceptor") twelve times; "preceptor, pater et dominus meus" ("my teacher, father, and master") once; twice by "mio padre e maestro" ("my father and master"); to which can be added the related expression "cuius ego iam olim auditor sum" (*GDG*, Prohem., I.21; "whose disciple I have been for a long time now"; translation from Giovanni Boccaccio, *The Genealogy of the Pagan Gods*, vol. 1, ed. and trans. Jon Solomon [Cambridge, MA: Harvard University Press, 2011], 11).

3. Rico, *Ritratti allo specchio (Boccaccio, Petrarca)*

4. Francesco Petrarch, *Fam.*, XXI.15, 2.

5. The anthology is ms. Zelada 104.6 in the Archivo y Biblioteca Capitulares of Toledo, datable to the early 1350s: see Marco Cursi, *La scrittura e i libri di Giovanni Boccaccio* (Rome: Viella, 2013), 74, 97; Marco Cursi, "L'autografo berlinese del *Decameron*," in *Boccaccio autore e copista*, exhibition catalog, ed. Teresa De Robertis, Carla Maria Monti, Marco Petoletti, Giuliano Tanturli, and Stefano Zamponi (Florence: Biblioteca Medicea Laurenziana, October 11, 2013–January 11, 2014) (Florence: Mandragora, 2013), 137–38, 53; Giancarlo Breschi, "Boccaccio editore della *Commedia*," in *Boccaccio autore e copista*, exhibition catalog, ed. Teresa De Robertis, Carla Maria Monti, Marco Petoletti, Giuliano Tanturli, and Stefano Zamponi (Florence: Biblioteca Medicea Laurenziana, October 11, 2013–January 11, 2014) (Florence: Mandragora, 2013), 247–53, 247; according to Sandro Bertelli, "La prima silloge dantesca: l'autografo Toledano," in *BAC*, 266–69, the codex was produced "during the course of the sixth decade of the fourteenth century or, at the latest, at the beginning of the 1370s" (Teresa De Robertis, "Boccaccio copista," in *Boccaccio autore e copista*, exhibition catalog, ed. Teresa De Robertis, Carla Maria Monti, Marco Petoletti, Giuli-

ano Tanturli, and Stefano Zamponi (Florence: Biblioteca Medicea Laurenziana, October 11, 2013–January 11, 2014) (Florence: Mandragora, 2013),
329–35, 330, concurs), which would mean placing the date of the first version of the *Trattatello*, as claimed by Giuseppe Billanovich, *Prime ricerche
dantesche* (Rome: Edizioni di *Storia e letteratura*, 1947), 56–57, "between
the summer of 1357 and the first few months of 1359." For the hypotheses
regarding the dating of the *Trattatello*, see Edoardo Fumagalli, "Boccaccio e Dante," in *Boccaccio autore e copista*, exhibition catalog, ed. Teresa
De Robertis, Carla Maria Monti, Marco Petoletti, Giuliano Tanturli, and
Stefano Zamponi (Florence: Biblioteca Medicea Laurenziana, October 11,
2013–January 11, 2014) (Florence: Mandragora, 2013), 25–31. The title *Trattatello in laude di Dante* is based on the phrase Boccaccio wrote in *ECD*,
Accessus, 36: "Scrissi in sua laude un trattatello" ("I have already written a
brief treatise in praise of him"; translation from Giovanni Boccaccio, *Boccaccio's Expositions on Dante's "Comedy,"* trans. Michael Papio [Toronto:
University of Toronto Press, 2009], 44).

6. *TLD*, [I].46–59.

7. Translation from Giovanni Boccaccio, *The Life of Dante*, trans. V. Zin
Bollettino (New York: Garland, 1990), 28.

8. Francesco Petrarch, *Epyst.*, III.9, 8–9: "In exilium cives egere superbi; / claudit iniquam urbem qui ius sibi supprimit equum."

9. Francesco Petrarch, *Epyst.*, III.9, 31: "Extremi proprium voluere
Britanni."

10. Francesco Petrarch, *Epyst.*, III.9, 36–37: "Aspice busta / sparsa
virum patria vetitum tellure iacere."

11. *Ep.*, VII.

12. Michele Feo, "La lettera al Petrarca del Comune di Firenze," in
*Codici latini del Petrarca nelle biblioteche fiorentine: Mostra 19 maggio–
30 giugno 1991*, ed. Michele Feo (Florence: Le Lettere, 1991), 356.

13. VIII.19.

14. Battaglia Ricci, "L'Omero di Boccaccio," 63–72.

15. Until just a few years ago it was accepted with near certainty that,
following his visit to Padua, Boccaccio had sent Petrarch a copy of Dante's
Commedia (the current ms. Vat. Lat. 3199), but today, with good reason,
the tendency is to move the date of the gift to after their meeting in Milan
of 1359.

16. The analysis of the chronological distribution of *Decameron* manuscripts by Marco Cursi, *Il "Decameron": scritture, scriventi, lettori. Storia di
un testo* (Rome: Viella, 2007), 127–44, "forcefully questions the entrenched
image of the extraordinary success that is supposed to have accompanied
the work from it's earliest diffusion" and demonstrates that the number
of exemplars increased significantly only beginning in 1450.

17. See Marco Santagata, *I due cominciamenti della lirica italiana* (Pisa:
Edizioni ETS, 2006), 87–113.

18. For the *Canzoniere* as a humanistic work, see Marco Santagata, *I frammenti dell'anima: Storia e racconto nel Canzoniere di Petrarca* (Bologna: il Mulino, 2004). Regarding the thwarted destiny of the *Decameron* and the Boccaccian style of story, see Amedeo Quondam, "La vittoria del 'Novellino' nella tradizione delle forme narrative brevi," in *Carte Romanze* 7, no. 1 (2019), 195–253: see esp. on 205: "The extraordinary narrative experiment of the Decameron . . . just as it has no ancestors, is also without heirs. Without a family, an extraordinary and unrepeatable *unicum*, it is an experimental text that cannot be fully imitated, and is destined to remain a niche endeavor, little pursued by readers and writers, while demand and supply of short stories and stories on the model of the 'Novellino' continue to increase."

19. Translation from Petrarca, *Canzoniere*, trans. Musa, 3.

20. Francesco Bausi, *Leggere il "Decameron"* (Bologna: il Mulino, 2017).

21. A copy of the *Exameron beati Ambrosii* was present in Boccaccio's library and was then inherited along with the other books by Martino da Signa; upon his death, it passed to the Florentine monastery of Santo Spirito (see Teresa De Robertis, "L'inventario della *parva libraria* di Santo Spirito," in *Boccaccio autore e copista*, exhibition catalog, ed. Teresa De Robertis, Carla Maria Monti, Marco Petoletti, Giuliano Tanturli, and Stefano Zamponi [Florence: Biblioteca Medicea Laurenziana, October 11, 2013–January 11, 2014] [Florence: Mandragora, 2013], 403–9); for Boccaccio's Greek-style titles, see Cella, Roberta, *La prosa narrativa: Dalle origini al Settecento* (Bologna: il Mulino, 2013), 36.

22. *EMF*, VIII.7, 1.

23. Translations from Dante Alighieri, *The Divine Comedy of Dante Alighieri, Volume I: Inferno*, ed. and trans. Robert M. Durling with notes by Ronald L. Martinez and Robert M. Durling (Oxford: Oxford University Press, 1996), 93. Boccaccio surely had in mind Dante's mention of Galeotto (Gallehault) in canto V of *Inferno*: it is no accident that the title "prencipe" ("Prince") appears, as well as in the *Decameron*, in his commentary on that episode (*ECD*, V [I].183; "un prencipe Galeotto"), where he also refers to Lancelot thus: "of whom the French romances relate many beautiful and praiseworthy things" (*ECD*, V [I].180; "molte belle e laudevoli cose raccontano i romanzi franceschi"). While Dante is referring to the prose romance *Lancelot du Lac*, Boccaccio seems to have derived the title "principe" from one of the Italian reworkings of the *Roman de Tristan* ("lo piue alto principe del mondo" ["the highest prince in the world"], *Tristano Riccardiano*, LXIII, Ms. 2543 of the Biblioteca Riccardiana, Florence); the situation of the two lovers who are oblivious to the attraction that has overtaken them has "Tristan-like" aspects (see the annotations to *Inf.*, V, by Giorgio Inglese in Dante Alighieri, *Commedia: Inferno*, ed. Giorgio Inglese [Rome: Carocci, 2007]).

24. In the prologue to the *Elegia*, it is Fiammetta who addresses her

narrative to "noble ladies" and explicitly excludes male readers: "And I do not care if my speech does not reach the ears of men; in fact if I could, I would entirely keep it away from them," trans. Causa-Steindler and Mauch, 1 (*EMF*, Prologo, 1–2; "Né m'è cura perché il mio parlare agli uomini non pervenga; anzi, in quanto io posso, del tutto il niego loro").

25. The "canzonette" ("little songs"), that is, ballads, that end each day are actually sung by male as well as female narrators, a discrepancy that may indicate a different, earlier organizational plan for the book. Translation from Boccaccio, *Decameron*, trans. Rebhorn, 3.

26. Although Boccaccio was an eyewitness (I, Introd., 16, 18), his description of the plague relies at many points on that of Paulus Diaconus in the *Historia Langobardorum* of the plague that had struck Italy in the final months of the reign of Emperor Justinian (cf. Branca, *Boccaccio medievale*, 445–53); it should be noted that in ms. Harley 5383 of the British Library (which contains four fascicules originally belonging to ms. 627 of the Biblioteca Riccardiana di Firenze), on 7v there is an autograph note by Boccaccio referring to Paulus Diaconus's account of the plague, which reads "Anno Domini MCCCXLVIII simillima pestis Florentie et quasi per universum orbem" (see Maurizio Fiorilla, "*Decameron*," in *Boccaccio autore e copista*, exhibition catalog, ed. Teresa De Robertis, Carla Maria Monti, Marco Petoletti, Giuliano Tanturli, and Stefano Zamponi [Florence: Biblioteca Medicea Laurenziana, October 11, 2013–January 11, 2014] [Florence: Mandragora, 2013], 131, and Teresa De Robertis, "Orosio, Paolo Diacono e Pasquale Romano: un autografo finalmente ricomposto," in *BAC*, 343–46).

27. While saying this here, he will mention in passing in VI, Concl., 20, that one of the female characters had described to him the circular valley plain at the center the Valley of the Ladies: "According to what one of them told me afterward" ("E secondo che alcuna di loro poi mi ridisse"; translation from Bocccaccio, *Decameron*, trans. Durling, 513).

28. There is an extensive debate about *Decameron* characters' names and their predominantly literary nature. Some refer to famous fictional characters: Elissa to Dido (although in *AV*, XLII.41–42, the "new Dido" ["novella Dido"] is Elisa or Lisa, wife of Albertino di Firenze); Lauretta might allude to Petrarch's Laura. Others refer to works by Boccaccio himself: Fiammetta is the "mythic" woman of much of his vernacular fiction; Filomena, the dedicatee of the *Filostrato*; Emilia, one of the protagonists of the *Teseida* and a nymph in the *Comedia delle ninfe fiorentine*, where Pampinea (XXXV) and Dioneo (XXVI, XXXVII) also appear. Boccaccio seems to project more autobiographical features onto Dioneo than on the others: it could be an indicator of this that in story 10 of Day 8, Dioneo speaks of Pietro Canigiani, a close friend of Boccaccio's, as "a compatriot of ours" ("nostro compar"). Panfilo is the lover of Fiammetta in the *Elegia*; Filostrato is the title of the eponymous poem. The Greek-sounding

names of the servants "are in general names characteristic of servants or low-status people who appear in Latin comedies or satires" (Boccaccio, *Decameron*, 44) by Terence, Plautus, Horace, Juvenal, and Martial.

29. Translation from Boccaccio, *Decameron*, trans. Rebhorn, 16.

30. The "company" or "brigade" ("brigata") of young people who gather in a garden or other pleasant location to debate romantic topics or tell stories about love is a narrative form that Boccaccio experimented with for the first time in *Filocolo* (IV), where, at the hottest time of day, to find relief from the heat, thirteen young people sit around a fountain on the lawn of garden and, under the rule of a queen, debate thirteen "questions of love" ("questioni d'amore"). He takes it up again, with greater narrative breadth, in the *Comedia delle ninfe fiorentine* (XVII–XXXIX): here seven nymphs seated in a meadow near a spring in the shade of a laurel tree take turns telling stories of their loves.

31. In "Author's Conclusion," 19, Boccaccio attributes a practical function to these summary headings: so that the lady readers of the book can easily reject those stories "that give offense" ("che pungono") and select the ones "that promise delight" ("che dilettanto"), "lest anyone should be deceived, each story bears a sign on its brow of that which it keeps hidden within its bosom" ("per non ingannare alcuna persona, tutte nella fronte portan segnato quello che esse dentro dal loro seno nascosto tengono"). Translations from Boccaccio, *Decameron*, trans. Rebhorn, 858.

32. Translations from Boccaccio, *Decameron*, trans. Rebhorn, 73 and 74. Similarly, in the *Filocolo*, Caleon, lost in ecstatic contemplation of Fiammetta, precedes his "question" with the (internal) singing of a ballad (IV.43), and in the *Comedia*, each nymph follows her tale with a *capitolo* in Dantean tercets. Also, one story (X.7) contains the text of a ballad, there attributed to a Mico da Siena but in reality written by Boccaccio (see Armando Balduino, *Boccaccio, Petrarca e altri poeti del Trecento* (Florence: Olschki, 1984), 267–87), while IV.5 ends with the first two lines of a "song" ("canzone") "that we still sing today" ("la quale ancor oggi si canta").

33. Translations from Boccaccio, *Decameron*, trans. Rebhorn, 76, 197–98.

34. *Corbaccio*, 441.

35. Translations in this paragraph from Boccaccio, *Decameron*, trans. Rebhorn, 200, 297–98.

36. Translations in this paragraph from Boccaccio, *Decameron*, trans. Rebhorn, 303 and 305.

37. Of these dozen popular songs, we know the lyrics to only the one that begins, "This is my shell, if I don't prick it well" ("Questo mio nicchio, s'io nol picchio," published in *Cantilene e ballate, strambotti e madrigali nei secoli XIII e XIV*, ed. Giosuè Carducci [Pisa: Nistri, 1871; repr. Bologna: Forni, 1970], 61–64). The mention of these popular works rounds out the company's vernacular reading, which ranges from, in descending order

of literary quality, love and adventure romances, to *cantari* (III, Introd., 15; Concl., 8), and, finally, these low-end songs just noted. Among Boccaccio's own works identified by title are the *Filostrato* (VI, Introd., 3) and the *Teseida* (VII, Concl., 6). The fact that the reading and performance of the works identified by title are always attributed to Dioneo (together with Fiammetta twice, and once with Lauretta) may indicate the attribution of some autobiographical qualities to this character. This structure is similar to that in other texts, for example, in the *Filocolo*, where the dedicatee asks the author to redeem the story of Florio and Biancifiore from the "fanciful chatter of the ignorant" (I.1, 25; "fabulosi parlari degli ignoranti"; translation from Boccaccio, *Il Filocolo*, trans. Cheney and Bergin, 4), that is, from the *cantari*, and in *Corbaccio*, whose protagonist's "prayers and paternosters are French romances [which Fiammetta also reads in the *Elegia*, VIII.7, 1] and Italian songs [that is, *cantari*]," among them that of *Florio and Biancifiore* (*Corbaccio*, 316; "orazioni e paternostri sono Iiromanzi franceschi e le canzoni latine"; translation from Boccaccio, *Corbaccio*, trans. Cassell, 60). Recall also, as already noted, the character Flamenca of the eponymous Occitan romance keeps the *romanz de Blancaflor* in her chamber (*Flamenca*, 4481).

38. Translations in this paragraph from Boccaccio, *Decameron*, trans. Rebhorn, 388, 469–70.

39. References to the ongoing plague like these of Dioneo (whose observations about behavior during this time echo the author's in I, Introd., 21–23) are rare: in the main narrative, the only mentions are those in IX, Introd., 2–3, of the "spotted roebucks and stags and other wild animals as though sensing they were safe from hunters because of the widespread plague" ("animali, sì come cavriuoli, cervi e altri, quasi sicuri da' cacciatori per la soprastante pistolenza"; translation from Boccaccio, *Decameron*, trans. Rebhorn, 693), which takes up the description of the desolation of the countryside of I, Introd., 45–46; and, with implicit reference to the beginning of the story, that of X, Concl. 3, to the "grief and anguish" that "have been inescapable" in Florence "since the plague first began" ("dolori e l'angoscie," "si veggono," "poi che questo pistolenzioso tempo incominciò"; translation from *Decameron*, 851). Additionally, as Amedeo Quondam, "Introduzione," in Boccaccio, *Decameron*, ed. Quondam et al. (Milan: Rizzoli, 2013), 5–65, 32–33, observes, "evocation of the plague within a story is quite exceptional": only in VI.3, 8, does one read "this present pestilence" ("questa pistolenza presente").

40. Translation from Boccaccio, *Decameron*, trans. Rebhorn, 691.

41. Translations in this paragraph from Boccaccio, *Decameron*, trans. Rebhorn, 693 and 750.

42. Translations in this paragraph from Boccaccio, *Decameron*, trans. Rebhorn, 851–52 and 854.

43. Boccaccio, *Decameron*, 1254.

44. Francesco Bausi, "Sull'utilità e il danno della ricerca delle fonti: Il caso del *Decameron*," *Carte Romanze* 7, no. 1 (2019): 121–42, at 121.

45. Regarding the "proto-diffusion" of the *Decameron*, which could have involved "both individual stories and individual days, as well as rough drafts of the book," see the careful and thorough observations of Francesco Bausi, *Leggere il "Decameron"* (Bologna: il Mulino, 2017), 9–12. The idea that Boccaccio might have circulated some "days" during the composition of the work is suggested by statements made in the garb of the author: in IV, Introd., 10, noting the criticisms already received although he has not "even completed a third of my labors" ("ancora al terzo della mia fatica venuto"; translation from Boccaccio, *Decameron*, trans. Rebhorn, 301), he says that he wants to respond now to avoid having them multiply before he has finished the work; in the "Author's Conclusion," 27, he mentions that a neighbor woman had much praised his "tongue" ("lingua") when the book was almost finished. It is not certain, however, that this criticism and praise came from real readers or if they were attributed to fictitious ones Boccaccio invented to express his metaliterary thoughts.

46. For a survey of the dating hypotheses, see: Giorgio Padoan, *Il Boccaccio, le Muse, il Parnaso e l'Arno* (Florence: Olschki, 1978), 93–121; Battaglia Ricci, *Ragionare nel giardino: Boccaccio e i cicli pittorici del "Trionfo della Morte*," 17–20; Lucia Battaglia Ricci, *Boccaccio* (Rome: Salerno Editrice, 2000), 122–23; Cursi, *Il "Decameron": scritture, scriventi, lettori. Storia di un testo*, 19–20; Veglia, *La strada più impervia: Boccaccio fra Dante e Petrarca*, 65–66. Fiorilla, "*Decameron*," 129, suggests an initial draft completed between 1348 and 1353. Veglia, *La strada più impervia: Boccaccio fra Dante e Petrarca*, 86, believes that it is not far-fetched to imagine that Boccaccio derived his inspiration from Petrarch's work-in-progress at the time of the 1351 Padua visit. Billanovich, *Petrarca letterato*, I. *Lo scrittoio del Petrarca*, 159–60, had made similar suggestions earlier about the terminus post quem, and regarding the terminus ad quem, he argued it was not necessary to assume completion by 1353.

47. Regarding the timing of the epidemic, it should be remembered that its "lethal effects . . . probably lasted until the spring of 1349" (Cursi, *Il "Decameron": scritture, scriventi, lettori. Storia di un*, 19).

48. See, for example, the opposing interpretations of Alberto Asor Rosa, "*Decameron*," in *Letteratura italiana: Le opere*, I. *Dalle Origini al Cinquecento* (Turin: Einaudi, 1992), 473–591, 473, according to whom the "painful remembering" of the fatalities of I, Introd., 2, indicate that the event was recent, and of Quondam, "Introduzione," 32, for whom the reference to "past mortality" in Proem, 13, suggests a great deal of time had passed between the events and the writing of that paratext.

49. Translation from Boccaccio, *Decameron*, trans. Rebhorn, 13.

50. Regarding Petrarch's project, see Marco Santagata, *I frammenti*

dell'anima: Storia e racconto nel Canzoniere di Petrarca (Bologna: il Mulino, 2004).

51. Branca, *Boccaccio medievale*, 357–92, draws attention to the thematic and structural similarities between the Proem and sonnet 1 of the *Canzoniere*, emphasizing, however, that the resemblances between the two incipits are the result of "a prescient convergence of ideas and sensibilities expressed . . . independently and prior to any personal meeting" (360). This argument is taken up by Veglia, *La strada più impervia: Boccaccio fra Dante e Petrarca*, who, however, speaks of "not-involuntary links" between the Proem and the sonnet (74), and even goes as far as to state that "in all likelihood, the *Proem* was influenced by knowledge of the *Posteritati* . . . and the prefatory sonnet of the *Canzoniere*" (85).

52. The similarities between the two books have been recognized and emphasized by many scholars, among them Battaglia Ricci, *Boccaccio*, 126, 137; and Quondam, "Introduzione," 55.

53. Translation from Boccaccio, *Decameron*, trans. Rebhorn, 730.

54. *ECD*, IV [I].119; the passage in its entirety says that it is appropriate to call Ovid's book this, as well as *Liber amorum*, "given that it does not deal with a single subject, from which one title may be derived. Instead, since the verses treat various different topics, we can say that he put it together piece by piece" ("per ciò che non d'alcuna materia continuata, dalla quale di possa intitolare, favella, ma alquanti versi d'una e alquanti d'un'altra, e così possiam dir di pezzi, dicendo, procede"; translation from Boccaccio, *Boccaccio's Expositions on Dante's "Comedy,"* trans. Papio, 192). Boccaccio also calls Ovid's *Amores* "Sine titulo" in the Miscellanea Laurenziana (ms. Laur. 33.31, 49v). For the distinction between the *titulus* and the *nomen* of a book, see the important observations by Michele Feo, "Fili petrarcheschi," *Rinascimento* 19 (1979): 3–89, on 13–26.

55. This is the claim of Vittore Branca, *Tradizione delle opere di Giovanni Boccaccio*, I. *Un primo elenco dei codici e tre studi* (Rome: Edizioni di Storia e letteratura, 1958; repr. 2014), 147–62 (but the essay was first published in 1950). This dating hypothesis still reappears in some *Decameron* studies (for example, Giancarlo Alfano, "Notizia biografica," in Boccaccio, *Decameron*, ed. Quondam et al. [Milan: Rizzoli, 2013], 89) and biographies (Porta Casucci, "'Un uomo di vetro' fra corti e cortili: Giovanni Boccaccio, i Del Buono, i Rossi e gli altri," 206, says composition took place "rapidly" during the period 1349–51); the same dates are referred to on Brown University's website Decameron Web (http://www.brown.edu/Departments/Italian_Studies/dweb).

56. Translation from Boccaccio, *Decameron*, trans. Rebhorn, 4.

57. Translation from Giovanni Boccaccio, *Boccaccio's Expositions on Dante's "Comedy,"* trans. Michael Papio (Toronto: University of Toronto Press, 2009), 43.

58. Dante, *Ep.*, XIII.10: "Comedia vero inchoat asperitatem alicuius rei, sed eius materia prospere terminatur. . . . Et per hoc patet quod Comedia dicitur presens opus. Nam si ad materiam respiciamus, a principio horribilis et fetida est . . . in fine prospera."

59. For the language of the *Decameron*, see Paola Manni, *La lingua di Boccaccio* (Bologna: Mulino, 2016), and Roberta Cella, *La prosa narrativa: Dalle origini al Settecento* (Bologna: il Mulino, 2013), 35–48; for the influence of the *Commedia*, see Bruni, *Boccaccio: L'invenzione della letteratura mediana*, 288–302.

60. For Guglielmo Borsiere (I.8), see *Inf.*, XVI.70–72; for Ciacco and Filippo Argenti (IX.8), see *Inf.*, VI and VIII. The episode of the Epicurian Guido Cavalcanti (VI.9), whose "speculating" ("speculazioni"), according to the "common people" ("gente volgare"), "had no other goal than to see whether he could show that God did not exist" ("erano solo in cercar se trovasse che Iddio non fosse"; translation from Boccaccio, *Decameron*, trans. Rebhorn, 500) is premised on his reputation for atheism implied in the canto of the heretics (*Inf.*, X). The stories of Lizio di Valbona, Ricciardo Manardi (V.4), and Paolo Traversari (V.8) grew out of two lines: "Where is the good Lizio, and Arrigo Mainardi? / Piero Traversaro [Paolo's father] and Guido Carpegna?" of *Purg.*, XIV.97–98, the canto of Romagna ("Ov' è 'l buon Lizio e Arrigo Manardi? / Pier Traversaro e Guido di Carpigna?"; translation from from Dante Alighieri, *The Divine Comedy of Dante Alighieri, Volume II: Purgatorio*, ed. and trans. Robert M. Durling with notes by Ronald L. Martinez and Robert M. Durling (Oxford: Oxford University Press, 2003), 227). The memory of the "Aretine who at the fierce hands of / Ghino di Tacco met his death" (*Purg.*, VI.13–14; "aretin che dalle braccia / fiere di Ghin di Tacco ebbe la morte") hangs over the story of Ghino di Tacco, "whose ferocious deeds and countless robberies gained him a great deal of notoriety" ("per la sua fierezza e per le sue ruberie uomo assai famoso"), and the Abbot of Cluny (X.2). The story of the Count of Antwerp (II.8) who was falsely accused freely adapts in a happier key the tragic tale of Pierre de la Brosse, whose "soul" ("anima") the pilgrim Dante sees "divided from his / body by spite and envy, as he said, and not for any / crime committed" (*Purg.*, VI.19–21; "divisa / dal corpo suo per astio e per inveggia, / com'e' dicea, non per colpa commisa"; translations from *Purgatorio*, 93).

61. For this form of Dante's realism, see Marco Santagata, *L'io e il mondo: Un'interpretazione di Dante* (Bologna: il Mulino, 2011), 351–80; and for a comparison between his and Boccaccio's, see Marco Santagata, *La letteratura nei secoli della tradizione: Dalla "Chanson de Roland" a Foscolo* (Bari: Laterza, 2007), 63–73 and 84–95.

62. See the important observations of Giancarlo Mazzacurati, who summarizes these traits with the phrase "codice di identità" ("identification code"), "Rappresentazione," in *Lessico critico decameroniano*, ed.

Renzo Bragantini and Pier Massimo Forni (Torino: Bollati Boringhieri, 1995), 269–99, later published as, "Lo spazio e il tempo: codici fissi e forme mobili del personaggio boccacciano," in *All'ombra di Dioneo: Tipologie e percorsi della novella da Boccaccio a Bandello*, ed. Giancarlo Mazzacurati (Firenze: La Nuova Italia Editrice, 1996), 1–36.

63. Translation from Boccaccio, *Decameron*, trans. Rebhorn, 744.

64. The "Schede introduttive" ("introductory information") in Boccaccio, *Decameron*, ed. Quondam et al. (Milan: Rizzoli, 2013), is of great help in providing an overview of the stories' temporal and geographical locations. Alberto Asor Rosa, "*Decameron*," in *Letteratura italiana: Le opere*, I. *Dalle Origini al Cinquecento* (Turin: Einaudi, 1992), 473–591, 551–54, also has a chronological breakdown, which, however, highlights how the "temporal element serves . . . to extend the narrator's view to a greater distance than ever before." In contrast, Mario Baratto, *Realtà e stile nel "Decameron*,*"* 2nd ed. (Rome: Editori Riuniti, 1984), insists on a "propensity toward current day settings," thanks to which "the distant past [*passato remoto*, or the grammatical past tense] tends to become, in the *Decameron*, the recent past [*passato prossimo*, or present perfect tense]."

65. *Dec.*, V.9, 4: "Coppo di Borghese Domenichi, who used to live in our city, and perhaps lives there still, was one of the most distinguished and highly respected men of our times, an illustrious person who deserved eternal fame more because of his character and abilities than his noble lineage" ("Coppo di Borghese Domenichi, il quale fu nella nostra città, e forse ancora è, uomo di grande e di reverenda auttorità ne' dì nostri, e per costumi e per vertù molto più che per nobiltà di sangue chiarissimo e degno d'eterna fama"; translation from Boccaccio, *Decameron*, trans. Rebhorn, 452).

66. *Dec.*, VIII.10, 42: "At that time [he returned to Florence in 1340] there was a compatriot of ours living in Naples named Pietro Canigiano, a man of great intellect and subtle wit, who was treasurer to Her Highness the Empress of Constantinople" ("Era quivi in quei tempi nostro compar Pietro dello Canigiano, tresorier di madama la 'mperatrice di Costantinopoli, uomo di grande intelletto e di sottile ingegno"; translation from Boccaccio, *Decameron*, trans. Rebhorn, 684).

67. *Dec.*, V.6. Regarding Marino Bulgaro (for whom, see Ingeborg Walter, "Bulgaro, Marino," in *DBI*, XV [1972]) Boccaccio wrote in *CVI*, IX, 26.1, "when I was a young man and frequenting the court of Robert, king of Jerusalem and Sicily, Marinus Bulgarus, an old man with a keen memory, a native of Ischia, and from his youth skilled in the art of sailing," would tell stories about the time of Robert's father, Charles I ("Me adhuc adolescentulo versanteque Roberti, Ierusalem et Sycilie regis, in aula, solitus erat vir annosus et ingenti memoria valens, Marinus Bulgarus, origine ysclanus et a iuventute sua nautice artis peritissimus").

68. Translation from Boccaccio, *Decameron*, trans. Rebhorn, 483.

69. For Corrado Gianfigliazzi, see Vanna Arrighi, "Gianfigliazzi, Corrado," in *DBI*, LIV (2000).

70. Translation from Boccaccio, *Decameron*, trans. Rebhorn, 484–85.

71. Translation from Boccaccio, *Decameron*, trans. Rebhorn, 485.

72. "il libro de le novelle di meser Giovanni Bocacci, il quale libro è mio"; "E guardate non venga a mano a messer Neri per che non l'avrei io … e guardate di non prestarlo a nullo perché molti ne sarebbero malcortesi … e guardatevi del libro mio di prestarlo a ser Nicolò però ch'egli ne sarà ladro." Buondelmonti's letter is published by Branca, *Tradizione delle opere di Giovanni Boccaccio*, II. *Un secondo elenco dei manoscritti e cinque studi sul testo del "Decameron" con due appendici*, 163–64, and, with different criteria, by Cursi, *Il "Decameron": scritture, scriventi, lettori. Storia di un testo*, 20; for the reconstruction of the historical context of the letter and information about the people named in it, see Branca (162–69) and Cursi (19–21).

73. Ms. II.II.8 of the Biblioteca Nazionale of Florence.

74. Ms. Ital. 482 of the Bibliothèque Nationale of Paris.

75. Regarding ms. Par. Ital. 482 copied by Capponi, trying to reconcile "the presence of a note of possession by Capponi ("Et è di Giovanni d'Agnolo Capponi" ["And it is Giovanni d'Agnolo Capponi's"]) with the hypothesis that Capponi was simply carrying out a book project of the author's," Marco Cursi (in Berté and Berté and Cursi, "Novità su Giovanni Boccaccio: un numero monografico di *Italia medioevale e umanistica*," 237–39) suggests "that Boccaccio, for some reason unknown to us, decided to give up that codex, originally reserved for his desk, which would then have been given to Capponi," and advances the further hypothesis that "economic necessity drove the author to give up (through a sale) his manuscript."

76. Ms. Vitali 26 of the Biblioteca Passerini Landi, Piacenza.

77. Ms. Pluteo 42.1 of the Biblioteca Laurenziana, Florence.

78. For the reconstruction of the early evidence of the diffusion of the *Decameron*, Cursi's analyses of the codices, the hands, the copyists, and the social context are fundamental, Cursi, *Il "Decameron": scritture, scriventi, lettori. Storia di un testo*, 19–45, and Cursi, *La scrittura e i libri di Giovanni Boccaccio*, 107–28, as well as the following also by Cursi: "Un'antichissima antologia decameroniana confezionata a Napoli (Firenze, Biblioteca Nazionale Centrale, II.II.8)"; "Il codice 'Ottimo' del 'Decameron' di Francesco d'Amaretto Mannelli (Firenze, Biblioteca Medicea Laurenziana, Pluteo 42.1)"; and "Il 'Decameron' illustrato di Giovanni d'Agnolo Capponi (Paris, Bibliothèque nationale de France, ital. 482)," in *BAC*, 139–44.

79. Marco Cursi, *La scrittura e i libri di Giovanni Boccaccio* (Rome: Viella, 2013), 111–12, recognized that the hand in the codex Panciatichiano 32 of the Biblioteca Nazionale of Florence containing the *Novellino* was

the same as the hand of the *Decameron* anthology in ms. II.II.8 of the same library.

80. This hypothesis, accepted by Cursi, that Francesco Mannelli obtained the autograph from Martino da Signa, was proposed by Giorgio Padoan, *Ultimi studi di filologia dantesca e boccacciana*, ed. Aldo Maria Costantini (Ravenna: Longo, 2002), 118–21 (the essay was first published in 1997).

81. Cursi, *Il "Decameron": scritture, scriventi, lettori. Storia di un testo*, 44–45.

82. Regarding the decline in handwriting quality, see the final pages of *De montibus* (119–20); regarding the common people's ruining of vernacular texts, in this case poetry, see at least the letter to Boccaccio in which Petrarch writes about his own youthful writing of lyric poetry, which he claimed, falsely, to have abandoned in order to prevent it from being "mauled" by the public, as happened to Dante's verses (*Fam.*, XXI.15, 17–18).

83. For the description of the autograph ms. Hamilton 90 of Staatsbibliothek Preussicher Kulturbesitz of Berlino, see Cursi, *Il "Decameron": scritture, scriventi, lettori. Storia di un testo*, 161–64, and Marco Cursi, "L'autografo berlinese del *Decameron*," in *Boccaccio autore e copista*, exhibition catalog, ed. Teresa De Robertis, Carla Maria Monti, Marco Petoletti, Giuliano Tanturli, and Stefano Zamponi (Florence: Biblioteca Medicea Laurenziana, October 11, 2013–January 11, 2014) (Florence: Mandragora, 2013), 137–38.

84. Regarding the apparent incongruity of the book's format, see the important observations by Lucia Battaglia Ricci, *Scrivere un libro di novelle: Giovanni Boccaccio autore, lettore, editore* (Ravenna: Longo, 2013), 13–96; Quondam, "Introduzione," 48–50, offers a striking interpretation.

85. This autograph, ms. Pluteo 52.9 of the Biblioteca Medicea Laurenziana, is described by Laura Regnicoli, "L'autografo di Boccaccio delle *Genealogie deorum gentilium*," in *BAC*, 177–79.

86. For the format of the *libro da banco*, see *Libri, scrittura e pubblico: Guida storica e critica*, ed. Armando Petrucci (Rome and Bari: Laterza, 1979), 141.

87. Vernacular books about love or adventure had a very different format from that of ms. Hamilton: the "little book" ("libretto") to which the author bids farewell in the *Filocolo* (V.97, 1) and *Fiammetta* (*EMF*, IX.1, 1) is "small" or "humble" ("picciolo") with regard to its dimensions, not the length of its text.

88. Maurizio Fiorilla, "Nota al testo," in Giovanni Boccaccio, *Decameron*, ed. Amedeo Quondam et al. (Milan: Rizzoli, 2013), 109–23, 110.

89. The Capponi codex (Par. Ital. 482) is embellished with eighteen illustrations, not by the hand of the copyist and later than the transcription of the text, but inserted in spaces that had been prepared for them.

Following a thorough examination, Cursi, *La scrittura e i libri di Giovanni Boccaccio*, 113–28, concludes that this codex is "an imperfect but substantially faithful mirror showing another *Decameron*, an autograph . . . in all probability kept on Boccaccio's desk (or at least designed by the author): a book . . . characterized by a total union between text and illustrations." In contrast, Battaglia Ricci, *Scrivere un libro di novelle: Giovanni Boccaccio autore, lettore, editore*, 57–88, and "Illustrazioni d'autore: appunti per una riflessione di metodo," in *"Tutto il lume de la spera nostra": Studi per Marco Ariani*, ed. Giuseppe Crimi and Luca Marcozzi (Rome: Salerno, 2018, 211–22), offers quite persuasive arguments against the notion that the codex is evidence of an illustration project of the author's.

90. Corrado Bologna writes in *Tradizione e fortuna dei classici italiani, I. Dalle origini al Tasso* (Torino: Einaudi, 1993), 344: "Hamilton 90 clearly reflects the intellectual habit of the scholar educated in the medieval university, in which teaching was based on reading and commenting on great treatises: and allows us to perceive the, perhaps unconscious, persistence in the adult Boccaccio of esthetic and formal as well as ideological models absorbed" during the Neapolitan period.

91. "Gratum . . . opus doctis, vulgo mirabile."

92. *Para.* X.22–23. Translation from Dante, *Paradise*, trans. Durling.

93. Armando Petrucci, "Il libro manoscritto," in *Letteratura italiana, II. Produzione e consumo* (Torino: Einaudi, 1983), 514; for the *libro da banco* imagined by Dante, see Petrucci, 499–524.

94. Battaglia Ricci, *Boccaccio*, 256–57, believes that Boccaccio never gave the *Decameron* to Petrarch to read, and is followed in this by Cursi, *Il "Decameron": scritture, scriventi, lettori. Storia di un testo*, 45.

95. Francesco Petrarch, *Sen.*, XVII.3, 1; "Librum tuum, quem nostro materno eloquio, ut opinor, olim iuvenis edidisti, nescio quidem valde qualiter ad me delatum, vidi." Translation from Petrarca, *Letters of Old Age*, vol. 2.

96. Monica Berté in *Sen.*, XIII–XVII [2017], 443–45, who continues with the proposal that *Sen.*, XVII.3, "could have been written for the purpose of introducing the translation of Griselda."

97. On the author's structuring of this final book, the critical reconstruction by Rizzo in *Sen.*, XIII–XVII [2017], 9–10, is essential; for the reconstruction of the "compositional strata" of the letters and the literary origins of "Griselda," see Francesco Petrarch, *De insigni obedientia et fide uxoria: Il Codice Riccardiano 991*, ed. Gabriella Albanese (Alessandria: Edizioni dell'Orso, 1998), 7–11.

98. See Santagata, *I frammenti dell'anima: Storia e racconto nel Canzoniere di Petrarca*, 111–15.

99. *Dec.*, X.10; the translation in Francesco Petrarch, *Sen.*, XVII.3: "insignis obedientia et fides uxoria" ("a wife's remarkable obedience and faithfulness"), 16–142. English translation from Petrarca, *Letters of Old Age*, vol. 2.

100. Francesco Petrarch, *Sen.*, XVII.3, 1–6; "Librum tuum . . . vidi. Nam si dicam: 'legi,' mentiar, siquidem ipse magnus valde, ut ad vulgus et soluta scriptus oratione, et occupatio mea maior et tempus angustum erat. . . . Excucurri eum et festini viatoris in morem hinc atque hinc circumspiciens nec subsistens animadverti alicubi librum ipsum. . . . Delectatus sum ipso in transit et, siquid lascivie liberioris occurreret, excusabat etas tua, dum id scriberes, stilus, ydioma, ipsa quoque rerum levitas et eorum qui lecture talia videbantur. . . . Inter multa sane iocosa et levia quedam pia et gravia deprehendi, de quibus tamen diffinitive quid iudicem non habeo, ut qui nusquam totus inheserim." Translation from Petrarca, *Letters of Old Age*, vol. 2.

It is perhaps excessive of Rico, *Ritratti allo specchio (Boccaccio, Petrarca)*, 42–43, to speak of Petrarch's "merciless criticism of the entire work" and "arrogant reading of literature," and to comment that "it would be difficult to be more unpleasant and to convey more qualifications, reservations, and wariness."

101. Francesco Petrarch, *Sen.*, XVII.4, 19.

102. *Ep.*, XXIV.41; "Summopere cupio . . . copiam ultime fabularum mearum quam suo dictatu decoraverit."

Chapter Nine

1. *BC*, VII and IX.

2. Francesco Petrarch, *Fam.*, XVIII.15, 1: "Ex multis epystolis quas his temporibus tuas legi, unum elicui, esse te turbato animo." Translation from Petrarca, *Letters on Familiar Matters*, vol. 3.

3. Francesco Petrarch, *Fam.*, XVIII.15, 1: "Legi Siracusas tuas et Dyonisium intellexi." Translation from Petrarca, *Letters on Familiar Matters*, vol. 3.

4. Francesco Petrarch, *Fam.*, XVIII.15, 2–3: "Irasceris . . . quia te poetam in literis meis voco. Mirum: poeta esse voluisti ut poete nomen horreres . . . tu videris quem te dici velis . . . in illo tibi utique, in hoc michi morem gessero." Translation from Petrarca, *Letters on Familiar Matters*, vol. 3.

5. The letter from Petrarch that Boccaccio never received is *Fam.*, XVIII.4. Vittore Branca, *Giovanni Boccaccio: Profilo biografico* (Florence: Sansoni, 1977 [1967]), 104, proposes a good hypothetical reconstruction of what happened: "The master's silence . . . must have been particularly inexplicable and worrying to Boccaccio in that final period of '55. Might not Petrarch have perhaps sided in some way with the pompous and loutish Maecenas, who was Niccolò? . . . The impulsive Boccaccio then had to write yet another 'troubled soul' letter, perhaps folding his friend's presumed silence in with the haughtiness" of Acciaiuoli. In one of the lost letters, Boccaccio must have evoked, as Giuseppe Billanovich, *Petrarca*

letterato, I. *Lo scrittoio del Petrarca* (Rome: Edizioni di *Storia e letteratura*, 1947; repr. 1995), 203, observes, "the sumptuous welcome given to Plato by the tyrant Dionysius of Syracuse," contrasting it with Acciaiuoli's behavior toward himself (see also Marco Petoletti, "Boccaccio e Plinio il Vecchio: gli estratti dello Zibaldone Magliabechiano," *Studi sul Boccaccio* 41 [2013]: 263).

6. Branca, *Giovanni Boccaccio: Profilo biografico*, 105.

7. For the political situation in Florence during the 1350s, see John M. Najemy, *Storia di Firenze: 1200–1575* (Turin: Einaudi, 2014), 179–88.

8. "Michi pauper vivo, dives autem et splendidus aliis viverem."

9. For Boccaccio's actions regarding taxation, see Laura Regnicoli, "Codice diplomatico di Giovanni Boccaccio 1. I documenti fiscali," *Italia medioevale e umanistica* 54 (2013): 1–80; quotations are at 27 and 40, respectively.

10. One of the few episodes in Boccaccio's life that is known from this period is his chance encounter with Giovanni Conversini in the Mercato Nuovo on a summer day in 1357. Conversini, whom he had gotten to know four years earlier in Ravenna, had left home on account of discord with his new wife and moved to Florence, where he had been for the previous few months in the service of Niccolò di Lapo de' Medici, about whom little is known. It was in the company of this Medici that Boccaccio encountered Conversini, recognized him, heartily greeted him, and in vain invited him stay for a few days: regarding this, see Luciano Gargan, "Un nuovo profilo di Giovanni Conversini da Ravenna," in *Dante e la sua eredità a Ravenna nel Trecento*, ed. Marco Petoletti (Ravenna: Longo, 2015), 185. Billanovich, *Petrarca letterato*, I. *Lo scrittoio del Petrarca*, 219–21 (followed by Branca, *Giovanni Boccaccio: Profilo biografico*, 105), hypothesized, although without any supporting documents, that in the winter of 1356 Boccaccio encountered the Visconti high official Giovanni Mandelli (to whom in 1358 Petrarch would dedicate the work commonly known as *Itinerarium syriacum*) in Florence during one of Mandelli's trips to and from Rome: the only information is that Petrarch wrote in a letter to Nelli on Christmas Day 1355 (*Fam.*, XIX.6, 1) about the imminent arrival in Florence of a dear friend of his who in his youth had been in the service of the Colonna family and asked Nelli to welcome him, and that in his response written after having received the friend, Nelli called him "Iohannozzum" (Giovannello, Giovannozzo) (*Ep.*, 15 [XVII], 2); on Mandelli, see Federica Cengarle, "Mandello, Giovanni," in *DBI*, LXVIII (2007).

11. For the presence of Albanzani in Ravenna in the summer of 1357, see Carla Maria Monti, "Il *ravennate* Donato Albanzani amico di Boccaccio e di Petrarca," in *Dante e la sua eredità a Ravenna nel Trecento*, ed. Marco Petoletti (Ravenna: Longo, 2015), 122.

12. In the accompanying letter, dated July 12 in Milan (*Disp.* 40 [= *Misc.* 1], 1, 50), Petrarch wrote: "I have sent you four books of invective—

what else could I call them? We would have gladly denied them to you, if it were possible for me to deny you anything" ("Quattuor Invectivarum libros dicam: an quid aliud: ad te misi: libentissime negaverimus si vel negare tibi possem"), adding: "with them I am sending you this book, ruined by age and torn as if it appears to have been chewed by dogs, and the ancient map that you requested from me" ("cum quibus et librum istum senio victum et canum morsibus lacerum simul et vetustissimam meam quam postulas chartam mitto"). That they were sent to Ravenna is based on *Ep.*, XII.16–17, of 1362 to Barbato da Sulmona in which Boccaccio wrote that, if he had made the trip to Naples (which he had decided against), he would have "brought the four books of Invective against the physicians, which at my request a few years ago he [Petrarch] so generously sent to me in Ravenna" ("atque portare tibi . . . Invectivarum quatuor libros in medicos, quos ad me petitos tam liberaliter pluribus ante annis Ravennam usque tranmiserat"). The year, 1357, is thus a conjecture, but almost certain (see Billanovich, *Petrarca letterato*, I. *Lo scrittoio del Petrarca*, 209–10). The old codex Petrarch sent definitely contained a geographical work (which cannot, however, be identified with the Pliny possessed by Petrarch [Par. lat. 6802], that Boccaccio would consult during his visit to Milan in 1359: see Giulia Perucchi, "Il Plinio del Petrarch sullo scrittoio del Boccaccio geografo," in *BAC*, 367–70, and, especially, Marco Petoletti, "Boccaccio e Plinio il Vecchio: gli estratti dello Zibaldone Magliabechiano," *Studi sul Boccaccio* 41 [2013]: 257–93). Boccaccio had need of the book and map because he was collecting materials for the encyclopedia *De montibus*. For Petrarch's maps, see Paolo Pontari, "Pictura latens: La dispersa carta geografica d'Italia di Petrarch e di Roberto d'Angiò," *Rinascimento* 49 (2009): 211–44.

   13. On the flyleaf at the end of a composite manuscript containing among other things Palladio's *Opus Agriculturae* (Vat. lat. 2193), on a number of occasions between 1348 and 1369, Petrarch noted his activities as a passionate botanist: for the date March 16, 1359, a Saturday, he wrote that, because the laurel trees he had planted in April 1357 in the Sant'Ambrogio garden had not taken, he planted another five in the Santa Valeria garden at about the ninth hour and that "among other things, it should very much help the growth of these sacred shrubs that the illustrious Giovanni di Boccaccio from Certaldo, a great friend of them and of me, arriving by chance at that moment, was present at their grafting" ("inter cetera multum prodesse deberet ad profectum sacrarum arbuscularum, quod insignis vir. d. Io. Boccaccii de Certaldo, ipsis amicissimus et mihi, casu in has horas tunc advectus, sationi interfuit"); toward the middle of that April he would note that two of the five laurels were growing (see de Pierre Nolhac, *Pétrarque et l'humanisme* [Paris: Champion, 1965], vol. 2, 267). On April 11, Boccaccio had already left Milan (*Fam.*, XX,7, 2–4, to Francesco Nelli).

14. In the letter Petrarch sent Boccaccio from Milan on August 18, 1360 (*Disp.* 46 [= *Var.* 25), he wrote, "I do remember, however, having discussed this matter [Petrarch's settling in Milan] with you a great deal last year when we were together in this same city and same house; after considering everything within the grasp of our intellects, we then reached the conclusion that, given the current state of Italy and Europe, not only is there no place safer or more suitable for my activities than Milan, but that Milan really is absolutely the only possible residence for me" (65–75; "Transeo autem memor me de his tecum anno altero, dum nos haec eadem urbs et domus haberet, multa disseruisse, nosque omnibus, quantum nostro consilio fieri potest, haud negligenter excussis, in hoc demum resedisse, ut, Italiae atque Europae rebus hoc in statu manentibus, non modo non alter Mediolano tutior rebusque meis aptior, sed nullus omnino usquam praeter Mediolanum plene mihi conveniens locus esset"), and that he understood Boccaccio's disapproval from certain of his ambiguities and silences (1–10) and so suspects that in the meantime "you changed your opinion" (80; "Quamobrem an tu sententiam mutaris, nescio").

15. This letter, revised and softened, would become *Sen.*, VI.6, "Ad amicum, acris increpatio degeneris studii" ("To a friend, a stern reproach for an unworthy endeavor"; translation from Petrarca, *Letters of Old Age*, vol. 1): see Rizzo in *Sen.*, V–VIII [2009].137.

16. *BC*, VIII.

17. For Moggio Moggi, see Billanovich, *Petrarca letterato*, I. *Lo scrittoio del Petrarca*, 225–26; his *Carmi ed epistole*, ed. Paolo Garbini (Padova: Antenore, 1996); and "Moggi, Moggio," in *DBI*, LXXV (2011), also by Garbini.

18. The twenty-four books of the *Res familiares*, of which the redaction in twenty books that Moggio Moggi worked on in 1359 can be considered an intermediate version, would be completed in October 1366. The *Bucolicum carmen*, while settled as far as number with the twelve eclogues Boccaccio copied, would reach its definitive form also in 1366. The first configuration of the *Canzoniere*, which has not survived, known as the Correggio redaction from the name of the dedicatee, Azzo da Correggio, seems to have been finished in 1358.

It is firmly established that Boccaccio had known some of Petrarch's lyric poems since the 1330s, but a few hints suggest that not only did the vernacular Petrarch sometimes echo Boccaccio's vernacular writings (see Marco Santagata, *Per moderne carte: La biblioteca volgare di Petrarca* [Bologna: il Mulino, 1990], 246–70) but so did the Latin Petrarch: for example, although "we have nothing that allows us to affirm that Petrarch knew the *Decameron*" around 1358, similarities between the stories contained in the last six letters of the *Sine nomine liber* and some of the stories in the *Decameron* are suggestive (see Gabriele Baldassari, "Nodi politici (e intertestuali) tra Boccaccio e Petrarca," *Heliotropia* 12–13 (2015–16): 263–303, 270–79).

19. Paola Vecchi Galli, *Padri: Petrarca e Boccaccio nella poesia del Trecento* (Rome and Padua: Editrice Antenore, 2012), 47: Petrarch's aim was "the humanistic, selective and bilingual, form of the new culture"; Boccaccio's was "the codification of a Florentine literature that passes through Dante's comedic model and develops it into multiple new genres."

20. This codex is today divided into two separate books, the manuscripts Chigiani L.V.176 and L.VI.213 of the Biblioteca Vaticana: see Domenico De Robertis, *Il codice Chigiano L.V.176 autografo di Giovanni Boccaccio* (Rome and Florence: Alinari-Biblioteca Apostolica Vaticana, 1974; Sandro Bertelli, "La seconda silloge dantesca: gli autografi Chigiani," in *BAC*, 270–72; and Sandro Bertelli, "I testimoni," in Paolo Trovato, Elisabetta Tonello, Sandro Bertelli, and Leonardo Fiorentini, "La tradizione e il testo del carme *Ytalie iam certus honos* di Giovanni Boccaccio," *Studi sul Boccaccio* 41 (2013): 71–85, 74–77.

21. Francisco Rico, *Ritratti allo specchio (Boccaccio, Petrarca)* (Rome and Padua: Editrice Antenore, 2012), 39.

22. *Carmina*, V.38: "Perlege, iunge tuis." The copy of the *Commedia* sent to Petrarch is today known as ms. Vat. lat. 3199 (on which, see Giancarlo Breschi, "Boccaccio editore della *Commedia*," in *Boccaccio autore e copista*, exhibition catalog, ed. Teresa De Robertis, Carla Maria Monti, Marco Petoletti, Giuliano Tanturli, and Stefano Zamponi [Florence: Biblioteca Medicea Laurenziana, October 11, 2013–January 11, 2014] [Florence: Mandragora, 2013], 247–53; Breschi, "La *Commedia* inviata a Petrarch con varianti annotate da Boccaccio," in *BAC*, 248–49, 379–80; Breschi, "Il ms. Vaticano Latino 3199 tra Boccaccio e Petrarch," in *Studi di filologia italiana* 72 [2014]: 95–117; Sandro Bertelli, "I testimoni," in Trovato, Tonello, Bertelli, and Fiorentini, "La tradizione e il testo del carme *Ytalie iam certus honos* di Giovanni Boccaccio," *Studi sul Boccaccio* 41 [2013]: 71–85, 71–73; and Gabriele Baldassari, "Nodi politici (e intertestuali) tra Boccaccio e Petrarca," *Heliotropia* 12–13 [2015–16]: 263–303, 294–95). Until a few years ago, it was accepted that Boccaccio sent the codex to Petrarch in Avignon via the embassy that departed October 25, 1351, led by Bishop Angelo Acciaiuoli (in which his friend and fellow Dante enthusiast Forese Donati took part), and that on flyleaf III he had had the codex's copyist transcribe a first version of his dedicatory poem, while he sent a second version after the meeting in Milan of 1359 (for this, see Billanovich, *Petrarca letterato*, I. *Lo scrittoio del Petrarca*, 161–64, and Giuseppe Billanovich, "L'altro stil nuovo: Da Dante teologo a Petrarca filologo," *Studi petrarcheschi* 11 [1994]: 79–85). The situation looks very different today: it has been shown that the hand that copied the verse in ms. Vaticano is much more recent, from the end of the fourteenth century or the beginning of the fifteenth,

and that it imitates the hand of the copyist of the *Commedia* (see Marisa Boschi Rotiroti, "Sul carme 'Ytalie iam certus honos' del Boccaccio, nel Vaticano Latino 3199," *Studi danteschi* 68 [2003]: 131–37). The convincing hypothesis has thus been proposed that Boccaccio's dedicatory poem had only one version, that which had been considered the second (autograph in ms. Chigiano latino L.V.176, 34r): see Elisabetta Tonello, "Appunti sulla tradizione di *Ytalie iam certus honos*," in Trovato, Tonello, Bertelli, and Fiorentini, "La tradizione e il testo del carme *Ytalie iam certus honos* di Giovanni Boccaccio," *Studi sul Boccaccio* 41 (2013): 4–73; Sandro Bertelli, "I testimoni," in Trovato, Tonello, Bertelli, and Fiorentini, "La tradizione e il testo del carme *Ytalie iam certus honos* di Giovanni Boccaccio," *Studi sul Boccaccio* 41 (2013): 71–85; Leonardo Fiorentini, "Testo e commento," in Trovato, Tonello, Bertelli, and Fiorentini, "La tradizione e il testo del carme *Ytalie iam certus honos* di Giovanni Boccaccio," *Studi sul Boccaccio* 41 (2013): 86–111. All of this has raised doubts that the Vatican ms. was really given to Petrarch, especially considering that "we have no letter or note thanking his friend for the gift" (see Elisabetta Tonello, "Appunti sulla tradizione di *Ytalie iam certus honos*," in Trovato, Tonello, Bertelli, and Fiorentini, "La tradizione e il testo del carme *Ytalie iam certus honos* di Giovanni Boccaccio," *Studi sul Boccaccio* 41 [2013]: 4–73, 30–34). However, it is evident that in *Fam.*, XXI.15, Petrarch not only offers thanks for the poem, but also refers to a text of the *Commedia* that is with him and that he now reads without fearing being influenced by it, and further that the poem itself presumes the accompaniment of a book ("receive this work by Dante" [hoc suscipe . . . Dantis opus], vv. 2–3). Therefore, if this is the only version of the poem and this is not the codex that was sent, we must necessarily think that in 1359 Boccaccio sent along with the poem a copy of the *Commedia* that is different from the one now in the Vatican, which is an overly complex hypothesis. On the other hand, if you believe that ms. Vaticano is indeed the codex that was sent, but in 1351–53 and not in 1359 (as Sandro Bertelli, "I testimoni," in Trovato, Tonello, Bertelli, and Fiorentini, "La tradizione e il testo del carme *Ytalie iam certus honos* di Giovanni Boccaccio," *Studi sul Boccaccio* 41 [2013]: 71–85, 73, seems to think), it leaves open the question of which codex accompanied Boccaccio's poem in 1359 (the poem now available in an annotated critical edition; Leonardo Fiorentini, "Testo e commento," in Trovato, Tonello, Bertelli, and Fiorentini, "La tradizione e il testo del carme *Ytalie iam certus honos* di Giovanni Boccaccio," *Studi sul Boccaccio* 41 [2013]: 86–111, 106–11). I believe that *Fam.*, XXI.15, is not responding to the (lost) letter Boccaccio sent along with his poem (Gabriella Albanese, "La corrispondenza fra Petrarca e Boccaccio," *Motivi e forme delle "Familiari" di Francesco Petrarca*, ed. Claudia Berra, *Quaderni di Acme* 57 [2003]: 39–98, n22 in the table), but to a different and later letter that is also lost. Angelo Piacentini defends the original hypothesis of the two versions of Boccaccio's poem, but believes that the second version was not sent to Petrarch ("Il carme 'Ytalie iam certus honos' di Giovanni Boccaccio," in *Boccaccio editore e interprete di Dante, Atti del Convegno internazionale di Roma, 28–30 ottobre 2013*, ed. Luca Azzetta and Andrea Mazzucchi [Rome: Salerno, 2014], 185–216).

23. "Reliquum voluisse futuris / quid metrum vulgare queat monstrare modernum / causa fuit vati."

24. Francesco Petrarch, *Fam.*, XXI.15, 1.

25. See Marco Santagata, *I frammenti dell'anima: Storia e racconto nel Canzoniere di Petrarca* (Bologna: il Mulino, 2004), 193–97.

26. Francesco Petrarch, *Fam.*, XXI.15, 13: "Hodie enim ab his curis longe sum; et postquan totus inde abii sublatusque quo tenebar metus est, et alios omnes et hunc ante alios tota mente suscipio.... Ut facile sibi vulgaris eloquentia palmam dem." Translation from Petrarca, *Letters on Familiar Matters*, vol. 3.

27. Francesco Petrarch, *Fam.*, XXI.15, 24: "Quod in vulgari eloquio quam carminibus aut prosa clarior atque altior assurgit." Translation from Petrarca, *Letters on Familiar Matters*, vol. 3. In this letter of May 1361 responding to a lost letter of Boccaccio's, Petrarch referred to their conversations in Milan: "Multa sunt in literis tuis haudquaquam responsionis egentia, ut que singula nuper viva voce transegimus" ("There are many things in your letter needing no reply whatsoever since we recently dealt with them in person"), nods to Boccaccio's excuses for having excessively praised Dante (1) and confesses that he has "never owned a copy of his [Dante's] book, although from early youth I enjoyed collecting books" ("ego librorum varia inquisitione delectatus, numquam librum illius habuerim," 10; translations from Petrarca, *Letters on Familiar Matters*, vol. 3). In Petrarch's writings, the name Dante, leaving aside the mentions in *Rvf*, 287, 10, and *Triumphus Cupidinis*, IV.31, appears only in one note ("nota contra Dantem") in the margin of a geographical report provided by Pomponio Mela (ms. Ambrosiano H 14 inf., 8v).

28. Ms. 104.6 of the Biblioteca Capitular of Toledo.

29. See the observations of Giovanni Boccaccio, *Carmina*, ed. Giuseppe Velli, in *Tutte le opere*, ed. Vittore Branca, vol. 5, 1 (Milan: Mondadori, 1992), 390–91, on the fact that by promoting Dante Boccaccio was also promoting himself as an author in the vernacular.

30. Francesco Petrarch, *Disp.* 46 (= *Var.* 25), 225; "Homerum nobis perditum restituat."

31. Petrarch had asked Nicholas Sygeros, the ambassador of the Eastern Emperor, for a codex with Homer's poems, probably in Verona in 1348: in a letter dated January 10, 1354 (*Fam.*, XVIII.2), he thanked him for the gift, all the more welcome because it was not translated into Latin "but pure and unspoiled from the very springs of Greek eloquence" ("sed ex ipsis greci eloquii scatebris purum et incorruptum," 6; translation from Petrarca, *Letters on Familiar Matters*, vol. 3).

32. On Petrarch's relationships with Barlaam of Seminara, not as teacher and student, but based on the "free exchange between two intellectuals," see Francesco Petrarca, *Lettere disperse, Varie e Miscellanee*, ed. Alessandro Pancheri (Parma: Fondazione Pietro Bembo—Guanda, 1994), 352–53, and especially, Vincenzo Fera, "Petrarca e il greco," *Studi medioevali e umanistici* 14 (2016): 95–101, who, among other things, observes— citing the case of Francesco Bruni who, when he became papal secretary in 1363, said that he had learned to read and write the Greek alphabet from Simone Atumano, archbishop of Thebes—that "the Greek prelates in the Curia took it upon themselves personally to promote Greek culture by teaching its basics" (115).

33. Indispensable for Leontius's biography is Antonio Rollo, "'Magistro Leonpilato de Tesalia'," *Quaderni petrarcheschi* 12–13 (2002–3): 7–21. A psychological, physical, and cultural portrait can be drawn from Boccaccio, *GDG*, XV.6, 9: "He is a man of uncouth appearance, ugly features, long beard, and black hair, forever lost in thought, rough in manners and behavior; but . . . a most learned Hellenist" ("Qui quidem aspectu horridus homo est, turpi facie, barba prolixa et capillicio nigro, et meditatione occupatus assidua, moribus incultus, nec satis urbanus homo, verum, uti experientia notum fecit, licterarum grecarum doctissimus"; translation from Boccaccio, *Boccaccio on Poetry*, trans. Osgood, 114); and from Petrarch's comments: "A man who would not be otherwise unsuited to our studies, if he were a man and had not made himself a wild beast by his singular roughness and his extravagance" (*Sen.*, V.3, 122; "Homo alioquin nostris studiis non ineptus, si tamen homo esset nec se beluam asperitate insigni et novitatis studio effecisset"); "The unhappy man, whatever he was, loved us, though he was the type that had learned to love neither others nor himself . . . I believe he never saw one serene day. In recalling him to mind, I often wonder how even a slight whiff of the Pierian spirit and celestial music had penetrated such a sad and somber soul . . . a humble man not unlearned but never very lucky or happy" (*Sen.*, VI.1, 8–10, 19; "Infelix homo, qualiscunque quidem, nos amabat, etsi talis esset qui nec alios nec se ipsum amare didicisset . . . nullum, puto, serenum diem vidit. Quem memoria repetens sepe admiror quomodo in tam tristem fuscamque animam pyerii spiritus ac celestis musice vel tenuis descendisset olfatus . . . viri humilis nec indocti, sed nec fortunati unquam prospere nec iocundi"; translations from Petrarca, *Letters of Old Age*, vol. 1).

34. Translation from Dante, *Inferno*, trans. Durling, 75.

35. *Disp.* 46 (= *Var.* 25), 215 (to Boccaccio): "Et profecto quoddam breve, ubi Homeri principium Leo idem solutis latinis verbis olim mihi quasi totius operis gustum obstulit."

36. While Edoardo Fumagalli, "Giovanni Boccaccio tra Leonzio Pilato e Francesco Petrarca: appunti a proposito della *prima translatio* dell' *Iliade*," *Italia medioevale e umanistica* 54 (2013): 213–83, concludes that

this first short translation may also have been oral or, in any case, "of little consequence," and that Petrarch did not speak of it to Boccaccio during their discussions in Milan (252), Vincenzo Fera, "Petrarca e il greco," *Studi medioevali e umanistici* 14 (2016): 73–116, argues that "the 'quiddam breve' with the version of the opening lines of Homer of which we know was certainly a trial run agreed upon between Leontius and Petrarch" and that "there is no reason to think that in their meeting in 1359 [Petrarch] had hidden something so significant [from Boccaccio]" (86); Ugo Dotti, *Vita di Petrarca* (Rome-Bari: Laterza, 1987), 328, had already suggested earlier that at this time Petrarch brought "the translation to Boccaccio's attention."

37. For the history of the establishment of a professorship of Greek in Florence and the translation of Homer, as well as Boccaccio's relationship with Homer and Greek culture more generally, see Edoardo Fumagalli, "Giovanni Boccaccio tra Leonzio Pilato e Francesco Petrarca: appunti a proposito della *prima translatio* dell' *Iliade*," *Italia medioevale e umanistica* 54 (2013): 213–83; Vincenzo Fera, "Petrarca e il greco," *Studi medioevali e umanistici* 14 (2016): 73–116, and Battaglia Ricci, "L'Omero di Boccaccio."

38. Battaglia Ricci, "L'Omero di Boccaccio," 56, believes it possible that Leontius's stay in Boccaccio's house lasted from the winter of 1359–60 to autumn 1362 (and not from the summer or autumn of 1360 to the autumn of 1362).

39. "Nonne ego fui qui Leontium Pylatum, a Venetiis occiduam Babilonem querentem, a longa peregrinatione meis flexi consiliis, et in patria tenui?" Translation from Boccaccio, *Boccaccio on Poetry*, trans. Osgood, 120.

40. Branca (in Vittore Branca and Pier Giorgio Ricci, "Notizie e documenti per la biografia del Boccaccio," *Studi sul Boccaccio* 3 [1965]: 7–18, and Branca, *Giovanni Boccaccio: Profilo biografico*, 113) assumes that the purpose of the mission to Lombardy was to speak with Bernabò Visconti, but that the meeting did not take place in Milan; according to Elsa Filosa, "L'amicizia ai tempi della congiura (Firenze 1360–61): 'A confortare non duole capo,'" *Studi sul Boccaccio* 42 (2014): 195–219, 199, Boccaccio "in 1359 was ambassador to Milan."

41. In August 1360, Boccaccio asked Petrarch for information about a codex of Homer that he had seen in Padua (see *Disp.* 46 [= *Var.* 25], 160–65); Leontius's translation was begun in early October, as attested again by Petrarch in a long letter addressed to Homer, responding to another that it is believed Boccaccio "addressed to him in the name of the poet Homer from the Realm of the dead" (*Fam.*, XXIV.12: "sub Homeri poete missam nomine et apud Inferos datam"; translation from Petrarca, *Letters on Familiar Matters*, vol. 3).

42. On the objective lack of pertinence of the teaching of Greek to the Florentine cultural environment and Boccaccio's and Petrarch's fears about the success of their project (expressed by the latter in his letter

addressed to Homer, *Fam.*, XXIV.12), see the observations of Vincenzo Fera, "Petrarca e il greco," *Studi medioevali e umanistici* 14 (2016): 88–91. It is not credible that in order to convince Florentine officials Boccaccio outlined the advantages that training in the Greek language would bring for business dealings, as Pierre de Nolhac, *Pétrarque et l'humanisme* (Paris: Champion, 1965), 2, 158, argues; especially since Leontius did not teach vernacular Greek, as Nolhac believed, but classical Greek. Among the few who attended Leontius's classes, in addition to Boccaccio himself, was certainly the notary Domenico Silvestri, who had a close relationship with Boccaccio (he was a fellow resident of Santo Spirito) and was also a pupil of Lapo di Castiglionchio (on Silvestri, see Pier Giorgio Ricci, "Per una monografia su Domenico Silvestri" [1950], later in *Miscellanea petrarchesca*, ed. Monica Berté [Rome: Edizioni di *Storia e Letteratura*, 1999], 97–111; Paolo Viti, "Domenico di Silvestro," in *DBI*, LX [1991], and Angelo Piacentini, "Domenico Silvestri," in *ALI*, 289–92); as well as, perhaps, the Franciscan Tedaldo Della Casa (for whom, see Giancarlo Casnati, "Della Casa, Tedaldo," in *DBI*, XXXVI [1988]).

43. For the biography of Castiglionchio, see Marco Palma, "Castiglionchio, Lapo da," in *DBI*, XXII (1979).

44. The document recording Bruni's acceptance of the position can be found in Alessandro Gherardi, *Statuti della Università e Studio fiorentino* (Florence: Cellini e C., 1881), pt. 2, 297.

45. Francesco Petrarch, *Sen.*, V.3, 119: "Delitias florentinas sprevit." Translation from Petrarca, *Letters of Old Age*, vol. 1.

46. Francesco Petrarch, *Sen.*, V.3, 118; "insolenter"

47. Francesco Petrarch, *Sen.*, III.6, 6; "Multa me coram sepe in Italiam latinumque nomen acerrime invectus." Translation from Petrarca, *Letters of Old Age*, vol. 1.

48. Petrarch, *Disp.*, 46 (= *Var.* 25), 225; "nobis perditum."

49. "Nonne ego fui qui Leontium Pylatum, a Venetiis occiduam Babilonem querentem, a longa peregrinatione meis flexi consiliis, et in patria tenui, qui illum in propriam domum suscepi et diu hospitem habui, et maximo labore meo curavi ut inter doctores florentini Studii susciperetur, ei ex publico mercede apposita? Fui equidem! Ipse insuper fui qui primus meis sumptibus Homeri libros et alios quosdam Grecos in Etruriam revocavi, ex qua multis ante seculis abierant non redituri! Nec in Etruriam tantum, sed in patriam deduxi. Ipse ego fui qui primus ex Latinis a Leontio in privato Yliadem audivi. Ipse insuper fui qui, ut legerentur publice Homeri libri operatus sum." English translation adapted from Boccaccio, *Boccaccio on Poetry*, trans. Osgood, 120.

50. "Genealogiam deorum gentilium et heroum."

51. "Vero, non ficto regis mandato hoc opus compositum." Translation from Boccaccio, *Boccaccio on Poetry*, trans. Osgood, 136.

52. Hugh of Antioch Lusignan, king of Cyprus and nominal king of

Jerusalem had two wives from the Ibelin family and was the cousin of
Isabella of Ibelin—married to a brother of Sancia, Robert of Anjou's
wife—who frequented the Neapolitan court and whom Boccaccio presents in the *Amorosa visione* (XLIV.1–6), "certainly as a compliment to the
Angevins," as waiting for her son to assume the crown of Majorca, an impossibility (see Boccaccio, *Amorosa visione*, 730). The little that is known
about Becchino Bellincioni can be read in Domenico Maria Manni, *Istoria
del Decamerone di Giovanni Boccaccio* (Firenze: Ristori, 1742), 68–69. In
contrast, the information about Donnino da Parma provided in Angelo
Pezzana, *Storia della città di Parma*, I. *1346–1400* (Parma: Ducale tipografia, 1837), 57–59, is unreliable (inexplicably, Giovanni Boccaccio, *Genealogie deorum gentilium*, ed. Vittorio Zaccaria, in *Tutte le opere*, ed. Vittore
Branca, vols. 7–8 [Milan: Mondadori, 1998], 1593, says that Donnino "had
for some time directly corresponded with Boccaccio's father, Boccaccino di
Chellino"). For Paolo Dagomari, the Florentine mathematician, physician,
astrologer, and poet, also known as Paulus Geometrus as well as by many
other names, see Maria Muccillo, "Paolo Dagomari (Paolo dell'Abaco,
Paolo Geometra, Paolo Astrologo, Paolo Arismetra)," in *DBI*, XXXI (1985).
Branca, *Giovanni Boccaccio: Profilo biografico*, 83, dates the meeting with
Becchino Bellincioni to 1350, as does Sebastiana Nobili, "La 'Genealogia' dalla Romagna al Parnaso: Sugli alberi genealogici del manoscritto
autografo," in *BR*, 149–63. That the commission for the *Genealogia* had
"already been offered in person in Forlì, some years before 1350, by Donnino da Parma," is asserted by Giovanni Boccaccio, *Genealogie deorum
gentilium*, ed. Vittorio Zaccaria, in *Tutte le opere*, ed. Vittore Branca, vols.
7–8 (Milan: Mondadori, 1998), 1593. For an overview of the complicated
timeline of the work's composition, see Vittorio Zaccaria, *Boccaccio narratore, storico, moralista e mitografo* (Florence: Olschki, 2001), 109–11, and
Silvia Fiaschi, *Genealogia deorum gentilium*, in *Boccaccio autore e copista*,
ed. Teresa De Robertis, Carla Maria Monti, Marco Petoletti, Giuliano
Tanturli, and Stefano Zamponi, exhibition catalog (Florence: Biblioteca
Medicea Laurenziana, October 11, 2013–January 11, 2014) (Florence: Mandragora, 2013), 171–76.

53. "De montibus, silvis, fontibus, lacubus, fluminibus, stagnis seu
paludibus et de nominibus maris liber." The English translation is from
Theodore Cachey, "Between Texts and Territory," in *Boccaccio: A Critical
Guide*, 273.

54. Giovanni Boccaccio, *De montibus, silvis, fontibus, lacubus, flu-
minibus, stagnis seu paludibus et de diversis nominibus maris*, ed. Manlio
Pastore Stocchi, in *Tutte le opere*, ed. Vittore Branca, vols. 7–8 (Milan:
Mondadori, 1998), 1822–23.

55. *De montibus*, VII.126.

56. For the *De montibus*, see Giovanni Boccaccio, *De montibus, silvis,
fontibus, lacubus, fluminibus, stagnis seu paludibus et de diversis nominibus*

maris, ed. Manlio Pastore Stocchi, in *Tutte le opere*, ed. Vittore Branca, vols. 7–8 (Milan: Mondadori, 1998), 1814–2122; Carla Maria Monti, "De montibus," in *BAC*, 181–84, and Carla Maria Monti, "La *Genealogia* e il *De montibus*: due parti di un unico progetto," *Studi sul Boccaccio* 44 (2016): 327–66. For Boccaccio's intentions, see the preface, *De montibus* I.2.

57. This and the preceding quotation from Emanuele Romanini, "De casibus virorum illustrium," in *BAC*, 189–91.

58. "Domesticam pestem et inexplicabilem florentino nomini labem."

59. *CVI*, VIII, 1.

60. On the *De casibus*, see Vittorio Zaccaria, *Boccaccio narratore, storico, moralista e mitografo* (Florence: Olschki, 2001), 34–89, and Emanuele Romanini, "De casibus virorum illustrium," in *BAC*, 189–91. A clear mark of Boccaccio's desire to trace back to Petrarch's teaching works that he had actually conceived of independently is the resemblance, including of images and expressions, between the final entry of the *De montibus* (VII.126) and the account of Petrarch's visionary appearance in the *De casibus* (*CVI*, VIII, 1.9). Boccaccio writes that he heard the story of the ordeal of the grand master of the Knights Templar Jacques de Molay from his father, Boccaccino, who had witnessed these events while in Paris on business (*CVI*, IX, 21.22), but in reality the account seems to rely on Giovanni Villani, *Nuova cronica*, IX.92 (see Giuseppe Billanovich, *Restauri boccacceschi* [Rome: Edizioni di *Storia e letteratura*, 1947], 43–44, and Branca, *Boccaccio medievale*, 283–86). The tragic story of Philippa da Catania (for whom, see Ingeborg Walter, "Filippa da Catania," in *DBI*, XLVII [1997]), which Boccaccio claims to have heard in part in Naples from Marino Bulgaro and the notary Costantino Rocca and in part to have seen as a direct witness — "I will describe what I saw with my own eyes" ("Sed que fere viderim ipse, iam referam," *CVI*, IX, 26.1, 8) — seems to rely on several sources, particularly Villani (see Branca, *Boccaccio medievale*, 286–89).

61. For Niccolò Acciaiuoli's 1359–60 missions to Avignon, Milan, and Romagna, see Francesco Paolo Tocco, *Niccolò Acciaiuoli: Vita e politica in Italia alla metà del XIV secolo* (Rome: Istituto storico italiano per il Medioevo, 2001), 223–31.

62. Billanovich, *Restauri boccacceschi*, 174–75.

63. As mentioned earlier, Innocent VI's bull is published in Billanovich, *Restauri boccacceschi*, 174–75. Regarding Boccaccio's lack of a canonry, it is worth noting that five years later, almost certainly through Boccaccio's efforts, the Florentine Comune would establish a canonry in the cathedral specifically for Francesco Petrarch, who, after receiving the papal appointment, would refuse it, annulling the concession (the episode is reconstructed again by Billanovich, *Restauri boccacceschi*, 170–73). These two similar stories demonstrate better than any number of words the great difference in status and importance that divided Boccaccio and Petrarch: the latter could refuse a canonry he had not even requested, in

Florence, while the other never managed to get one at all even though it was the cathedral of his own city.

64. For the Guelph party's persecution strategy, see Emanuela Porta Casucci, "'Un uomo di vetro' fra corti e cortile: Giovanni Boccaccio, i Del Buono, i Rossi e gli altri," *Heliotropia* 12–13 (2015–16), where, on 201, the story of Niccolò Del Buono is recounted.

65. Elsa Filosa, "L'amicizia ai tempi della congiura (Firenze 1360–61): 'A confortare non duole capo,'" *Studi sul Boccaccio* 42 (2014): 195–219, 202; 206 provides information about the friends of Boccaccio who took part in the conspiracy (for his connection to Pazzino di Apardo Donati, see Elsa Filosa, "Rossi, Pino de'," in *DBI*, LXXXVIII). Regarding Pino de' Rossi, see above all, Elsa Filosa just cited and Porta Casucci, "'Un uomo di vetro' fra corti e cortili: Giovanni Boccaccio, i Del Buono, i Rossi e gli altri," 202–5; for Domenico di Donato Bandini, see Mazzoni, Vieri, *Accusare e proscrivere. Il nemico politico. Legislazione antighibellina e persecuzione giudiziaria a Firenze (1347–1378)* (Pisa: Pacini Editore, 2010), app. 3, 199.

66. On the conspiracy, see Elsa Filosa, "L'amicizia ai tempi della congiura (Firenze 1360–61): 'A confortare non duole capo,'" *Studi sul Boccaccio* 42 (2014): 195–219. The conspirators' conviction and sentence is published in Elsa Filosa, "La condanna di Niccolò di Bartolo del Buono, Pino de' Rossi, e gli altri congiurati del 1360," *Studi sul Boccaccio* 44 (2016): 235–50.

67. Elsa Filosa, "L'amicizia ai tempi della congiura (Firenze 1360-61): 'A confortare non duole capo,'" *Studi sul Boccaccio* 42 (2014): 195–219, 206, attributes Boccaccio's lack of public offices after the conspiracy to the "extreme suspicion" he was subject to because of his links of friendship to some of the conspirators; and, speaking of the *Consolatoria a Pino de' Rossi*, she adds, "He too, like the (exiled) others, was paying a price: suspension from all Florentine public posts; self-exile and withdrawal to Certaldo; and perhaps also the loss of autonomy and freedom in his writing" (215). Boccaccio may also have been seen as suspicious because of his relationship with Niccolò Acciaiuoli, who was present in Florence in precisely December 1360: the Florentines' distrust of Acciaiuoli was such that, because in those days the names of the new priors were drawn by lot, people began to believe that he aspired to that position, and so the Comune enacted a provision expressly prohibiting him from holding any elective office (see Francesco Paolo Tocco, *Niccolò Acciaiuoli: Vita e politica in Italia alla metà del XIV secolo* [Rome: Istituto storico italiano per il Medioevo, 2001], 241–42).

Chapter Ten

1. In the letter *Consolatoria*, written in Certaldo, Boccaccio reminded Rossi that he had already indicated to him, evidently in person and before the end of December 1360, that he intended to withdraw to the village: "In

accordance with my resolution, which I told you about, I have returned to Certaldo" (*Cons.* 171, "Io, secondo il mio proponimento il quale io vi ragionai, sono tornato a Certaldo").

2. For his difficult relationship with Iacopo, in addition to the *Consolatoria*, see also the allusion to "familial concerns" ("rei familiaris cura") in *Ep.*, XII, of May 1362 to Barbato da Sulmona.

3. Many hypotheses have been proposed regarding the transfer of the house in Santa Felicita, which is generally interpreted as a gift of the entire house. For example, Elsa Filosa, "L'amicizia ai tempi della congiura (Firenze 1360-61): 'A confortare non duole capo,'" *Studi sul Boccaccio* 42 (2014): 195–219, 207, holds that Boccaccio did this "to ensure that it remained in the possession of the Da Certaldos: an important precaution, if we take into account that during the years after the discovery of the conspiracy, the assets of other Florentine citizens were still being confiscated, and the citizens themselves continued to be admonished." The notarial record of the transfer is in the course of publication in the "Codice diplomatico boccacciano," that is, collection of transcriptions of original documents (*codex diplomaticus*) related to Boccaccio, edited by Laura Regnicoli.

4. For the *Consolatoria a Pino de' Rossi*, see Pier Giorgio Ricci, *Studi sulla vita e le opere del Boccaccio* (Milan and Naples: Ricciardi, 1985), 136–48; and Giovanni Boccaccio, *Consolatoria a Pino de' Rossi*, ed. Giuseppe Chiecchi, in *Tutte le opere*, ed. Vittore Branca, vol. 5, 2 (Milan: Mondadori, 1994), 617–27.

5. Boccaccio, *Consolatoria a Pino de' Rossi*, 681.

6. *MC*, Dedica, 1: "paululum ab inerti vulgo semotus et a ceteris fere solutus curis." Translation from Giovanni Boccaccio, *Famous Women*, ed. and trans. Virginia Brown (Cambridge, MA: Harvard University Press, 2001), 3.

7. For an introduction to the *De mulieribus*, see Ricci, *Studi sulla vita e le opere del Boccaccio*, 125–35, and Vittorio Zaccaria, *Boccaccio narratore, storico, moralista e mitografo* (Florence: Olschki, 2001), 1–34; for a comprehensive reading, see Elsa Filosa, *Tre studi sul "De mulieribus claris"* (Milano: LED Edizioni Universitarie, 2012). An autograph of the treatise survives dating from Boccaccio's late old age, ms. Pluteo 90 sup. 98 [1] of the Biblioteca Medicea Laurenziana.

8. *MC*, Proemio, 3: "Sane miratus sum plurimum adeo modicum apud huiusce viros potuisse mulieres, ut nullam memorie gratiam in speciali aliqua descriptione consecute sint." Translation from Boccaccio, *Famous Women*, trans. Brown, 9.

9. *MC*, Proemio, 6: "Non enim est animus michi hoc claritas nomen adeo strictim summere, ut semper in virtutem videatur exire; quin imo in ampliorem sensum . . . trahere et illas intelligere claras quas quocunque ex facinore orbi vulgato sermone notissimas novero." Translation from Boccaccio, *Famous Women*, trans. Brown, 11.

10. *MC*, Proemio, 8: "Existimans harum facinora non minus mulieribus quam viris etiam placitura; que cum, ut plurimum, hystoriarum ignare sint, sermone prolixiori indigent et letantur."

11. In Proemio, 1, of the *De mulieribus claris*, Boccaccio wrote: "Long ago there were a few ancient authors who composed biographies of famous men in the form of compendia, and in our day that renowned man and great poet, my teacher Petrarch, is writing a similar work that will be even fuller and more carefully done" ("Scripsere iamdudum nonnulli veterum sub compendio de viris illustribus libros; et nostro evo, latiori tamen volumine et accuratiori stilo, vir insignis et poeta egregius Franciscus Petrarch, preceptor noster, scribit"; translation from Boccaccio, *Famous Women*, trans. Brown, 11). But Vinicio Pacca, *Petrarca* (Rome and Bari: Laterza, 1998), 162, observes that the fact that "immediately afterwards he presents his *De mulieribus claris* . . . as a complement to similar earlier works (including, therefore, also to Petrarch's) dedicated exclusively to men . . . shows that, if, on the one hand, some information about the *De viris universale* must have filtered out, on the other, the work's contents must not have been known: the biography of Semiramis was in fact there to contradict Boccaccio's assertion." Petrarch had begun his *De viris*, along with the *Africa*, in 1338–39; he had then returned to working on it in the 1350s, expanding it into the so-called *De viris universale*, but would never complete it.

12. *Ep.*, XI.

13. May 15, 1362: "A Laureato nostro epistolam unam suscepi, in qua, cum a Mediolano quibusdam erumpnis mei solamen placidum porressisset."

14. On the various hypotheses, see Vittore Branca, *Giovanni Boccaccio: Profilo biografico* (Florence: Sansoni, 1977 [1967]), 126–27. According to Giuseppe Billanovich, *Petrarca letterato*, I. *Lo scrittoio del Petrarca* (Rome: Edizioni di *Storia e letteratura*, 1947; repr. 1995), 254–55, Boccaccio was "forced to leave his proximity to and collaboration with Leontius, and run" to Ravenna "just to deal with this painful reversal."

15. Elsa Filosa, "Rossi, Pino de'," in *DBI*, LXXXVIII (2017), 216.

16. "Iam, fateor, stomacans, tam suorum monacorum desidiam quam inertiam civium dampnans."

17. Francesco Petrarca, *Sen.*, I.5, 139.

18. "Quin imo tanta et incomposita abundantia supervacaneorum verborum exundantem aspicio, ut michi etiam legenti inferret fastidium; quam ob rem . . . nil ex substantialibus pretermictens, paululum lepidiore sermone Johannnes Iohannis scribens vestigia imitatus sum ut tibi transmictam."

19. My discussion of the biography of Peter Damian is based on Paolo Pontari, "Boccaccio a Ravenna tra Dante e Petrarca: novità sulla *Vita Petri Damiani*," in *Boccaccio e la Romagna*, conference proceeding, ed. Gabriella

412   NOTES TO PAGES 219–221

Albanese and Paolo Pontari (Forlì: Salone comunale, November 22–23, 2013) (Ravenna: Longo, 2015), 119–47; the text, preceded by the title *Vita sanctissimi patris Petri Damiani heremite et demum episcopi Hostiensis ac Romane Ecclesie cardinalis*, in the sole surviving, and incomplete, codex ms. α R.6.7 (lat. 630) of Biblioteca Estense Universitaria in Modena, can be read in *Vite*, 912–41; on the relationship between Boccaccio's biography and that of Giovanni da Lodi, see Lucia Battaglia Ricci, "Scrittura e riscrittura: Dante e Boccaccio 'agiografi,'" in *Scrivere di santi, Atti del II Convegno di studio dell'Associazione italiana per lo studio della santità, dei culti e dell'agiografia (Napoli, 22–25 ottobre 1997)*, ed. Gennaro Luongon (Rome: Viella, 1999), 165–73.

20. Billanovich, *Petrarca letterato*, I. *Lo scrittoio del Petrarca*, 259.

21. Laura Regnicoli, "Codice diplomatico di Giovanni Boccaccio 1. I documenti fiscali," *Italia medioevale e umanistica* 54 (2013): 1–80, 31.

22. Francesco Petrarca, *Sen.*, I.5, 142: "Nam ad id quod, ut sepe olim, de inopia quereris."

23. Francesco Petrarca, *Sen.*, I.5, 139, 141: "Extremum sit ut, quod te multis, inter quos michi, pecunie debitorem facis. . . . Nil michi debes nisi amorem." Translation from Petrarca, *Letters of Old Age*, vol. 1.

24. On Petroni, see Michele Pellegrini, "Petroni, Pietro," in *DBI*, LXXXII (2015).

25. Francesco Petrarca, *Sen.*, I.5, 107, May 28, 1362: "Que si in bonam animam sint recepte et virtutis excitant amorem et aut tollunt metum mortis aut minuunt." Translations from Petrarca, *Letters of Old Age*, vol. 1.

26. Francesco Petrarca, *Sen.*, I.5, 134: "Et quamvis ipse rem meam videar empturus, nolim tamen tanti viri libros huc illuc effundi aut profanis, ut fit, manibus contrectari. Sicut igitur nos, seiuncti licet corporibus, unum animo fuimus, sic studiorum hec supellex nostra post nos, si votum meum Deus adiuverit, ad aliquem nostri perpetuo memorem pium ac devotum locum simul indecerpta perveniat."

27. Francesco Petrarca, *Sen.*, I.5, 137: "Quorum nec nomina certe nec numerum noverim nec valorem." Translations from Petrarca, *Letters of Old Age*, vol. 1.

28. The episode of the naming of Zanobi da Strada's successor as apostolic secretary is reconstructed on the basis of the letters of Petrarch (*Sen.*, I.2, 3, 4, 5) and of Nelli (*Ep.*, 28 [XXIX]). Nelli would never hold this office, however, because Innocent VI died on September 12, 1361; the new pope, Urban V, named Francesco Bruni secretary on February 3, 1363.

29. Francesco Petrarca, *Sen.*, I.5, 142–47; "Nam ad id quod, ut sepe olim, de inopia quereris, nolo tibi consolationes, nolo pauperum illustrium nunc exempla congerere: nota sunt tibi. Quid ergo? Clara equidem semperque una voce respondeo. Laudo quod me magnas, licet seras, tibi divitias procurante libertatem animi quietamque pretuleris egestatem: quod amicum totiens te vocantem spreveris non laudo. Non sum qui

ditare te hinc possim; quod, si essem, non verbo, non calami, sed re ipsa tecum loquerer. Sum vero cui uni tantum suppetit quantum abunde sufficiat duobus unum cor habentibus atque unam domum. Iniuriosus es michi si fastidis, iniuriosior si diffidis." Translations from Petrarca, *Letters of Old Age*, vol. 1.

30. Branca, *Giovanni Boccaccio: Profilo biografico*, 134–35.

31. "Franciscus Petrarch . . . me non amicum et socium sed domui sue et substantiis ceteris prepositum dulcissimis precibus et suasionibus, ut secum sim, facundiam omnem suam exposuit."

32. The most important aspects of the negotiations to bring Boccaccio to Naples are reconstructed on the basis of *Ep.*, XIII.6–7, to Nelli. In *Ep.*, XII.16–18, of May 15 to Barbato, Boccaccio refers to a proposed journey to Naples "to visit our Simonides [Francesco Nelli]" ("Neapolim usque pergere nostrum visitaturus Simonidem"), a journey that did not take place because "of poverty and familial concerns," but also because he had learned "that Simonides was in Sicily with the Grand Seneschal" ("paupertas et rei familiaris cura . . . ac etiam consistere apud Siculos cum Magno Senescallo Simonidem audisse, vetuere").

33. The biographies added to *De mulieribus* in the summer of 1362 are those of the poet Cornificia (LXXXVI), the Sienese lady Camiola (CV), and Queen Joanna (CVI); regarding these last two, Ricci, *Studi sulla vita e le opere del Boccaccio*, 131, writes: "Given that the work had to be dedicated to a Tuscan lady resident in southern Italy, he intended to emphasize this detail gracefully by writing the biography of a woman from Siena who had dazzled Messina with her virtues; and as he was preparing to become a subject of Queen Joanna, he certainly could not avoid writing a chapter dedicated to her." On the not entirely instrumental nature of Queen Joanna's centrality, see Attilio Motta, "Le regine (d'Oriente) di Pucci," in *Firenze alla vigilia del Rinascimento: Antonio Pucci e i suoi contemporanei*, ed. Maria Bendinelli Predelli, conference proceedings (Montreal, October 22–23, 2004) (Florence: Cadmo, 2006), 219–41, on 226–32.

34. *MC*, Dedica, 5: "Id tuo pectori Deus sua liberalitate miris virtutibus superfuserit atque suppleverit, et eo, quo insignita es nomine, designari voluerit—cum andres Greci quod latine dicimus homines nuncupent." English translation adapted from Boccaccio, *Famous Women*, trans. Brown, 5.

35. For his sisters' relationships with Niccolò, see Francesco Paolo Tocco, *Niccolò Acciaiuoli: Vita e politica in Italia alla metà del XIV secolo* (Rome: Istituto storico italiano per il Medioevo, 2001), 285–86, which is the source of the quotation; Andrea's second marriage did not take place, as suggested by Giovanni Boccaccio, *De mulieribus claris*, ed. Vittorio Zaccaria, in *Tutte le opere*, ed. Vittore Branca, vol. 10 (Milan: Mondadori, 1967), 481, in the summer of 1362, but in October of 1363 (Francesco Paolo Tocco, *Niccolò Acciaiuoli: Vita e politica in Italia alla metà del XIV secolo* [Rome:

Istituto storico italiano per il Medioevo, 2001], 143). Queen Joanna's third marriage, to James IV of Majorca, took place on December 14, 1362.

36. In the *Buccolicum carmen* (VIII.102–18), Boccaccio presents a terrible portrait of Lapa/Lupisca (the name, as Bernardi Perini observes in Giovanni Boccaccio, *Buccolicum carmen*, ed. Giorgio Bernardi Perini, in *Tutte le opere*, ed. Vittore Branca, vol. 5, 2 [Milan: Mondadori, 1994], 980, "an obvious derogatory formation, from *lupus* [Latin: wolf], and at base a "translation" of Licisca, the Greek word for bitch"): "Who could recount his [Midas/Acciaiuoli's] darings so insane, or who the cruel destruction of his woods, of cattle and young men which he effected, and with him equally the fierce Lupisca? She takes the husks from pigs, the grass from lambs, smears poor young cows with shameful filth and pulls the tiny newborns from their mother's udder, and thrice a day she milks the sheep and thrice she shears their fleece, if possible, and with a dismal spell compels the fickle moon to stop midcourse, and charms to her the kids. Nor does she pause of sleep; even at night you'll see her passing through the grassy fields to count the flocks upon the peak of Gaurus. Why many words? She scrapes at everything. And to make sure that nothing goes untouched in forest or in field, by some new art she leads astray among the ancient caves the singing boys into her lust, and strips those whom she lures. . . . Lupisca's an old harlot and greedy miser too!" ("Quis queat insanos ausus, quis dicere sevas / et nemorum pecorumque simul iuvenumque ruinas / quas dedit, et pariter secum trux inde Lupisca? / Hec siliquas porcis et gramina subtrahit agnis, / emungit miseras turpi squalore iuvencas / ac matrum parvos subducit ab ubere natos, / terque die pecudes premit et ter vellere nudat, / si possit, tristique levem consistere lunam / carmine compellit celo et sibi fascinat edos. / Nec vacat hec somno; virides ambire per agros / nocte etiam videas et magnos vertice Gauri / enumerare greges. Quid multa? Hec omnia radit; / ac ut nulla sinat silvis intacta vel agris, / arte nova pueros annosa per antra canentes / in venerem rapit illa suam nudatque sequentes. . . . Meretrix anus est et avara Lupisca!"; translation from Boccaccio, *Eclogues*, trans. Smarr, 81, 83).

37. "They made *their appearance noble for others, to deceive others*": Boccaccio, *Amorosa visione*, 725.

38. Translation from Boccaccio, *Amorosa Visione*, trans. Hollander et al., 171.

39. For Boccaccio's behavior regarding taxation during his absence and its meaning, see Laura Regnicoli, "Per il Codice diplomatico di Giovanni Boccaccio," in *Boccaccio letterato*, conference proceedings, ed. Michaelangiola Marchiaro and Stefano Zamponi (Florence-Certaldo, October 10–12, 2013) (Florence: Accademia della Crusca—Ente nazionale Giovanni Boccaccio), 519–20.

40. Regarding Mainardo Cavalcanti, Acciaiuoli's relative by marriage and an important officeholder in the Kingdom of Naples, who was from

that time forward bound to Boccaccio by sincere friendship, see Luisa Miglio, "Cavalcanti, Mainardo," in *DBI*, XXII (1979).

41. Neither the Neapolitan friend who sent him the gift of the bed nor this merchant has been identified.

42. In *Sen.*, I.2, 4–6, written to Nelli in late 1361 or early 1362, Petrarch expressed his refusal with these words: "As for the warm entreaty with which that Maecenas [Acciaiuoli], and yourself after him, now invite me to Campania, what else shall I say except to marvel not at your love for me, which I well knew in the past, but at your tireless insistence in pressing for something so often refused. You tire neither of asking nor of waiting, whereas now I am weary not only of refusing you but of remaining silent and even of living. Nothing new can be said about this on either side; it has all been said" ("Ad id quidem, quod Mecenas ipse tuque post illum tanta precum vi me nunc etiam in Campaniam evocatis, quid aliud dicam quam mirari me non vestros olim michi plane notissimos affectus, sed indefessam hanc instantiam totiens negata flagitantium? Nec rogando enim nec expectando lassamini, cum ego iam non negando tantum, sed tacendo ac vivendo prope lassus sim. De hoc sane nichil novi est ultro citroque quod dici possit: trita sunt omnia"; translation from Petrarca, *Letters of Old Age*, vol. 1).

43. Francesco Petrarca, *Disp.*, 59 (= Var. 39), 25: "Cedulae huius sociam unam ad Iohannem nostrum facies pervenire."

44. Francesco Petrarca, *Sen.*, II.1.

45. Boccaccio did not speak of his stop in Padua; in the letter to Nelli he wrote: "and leaving, I came to Venice, where I was joyously received by my Silvanus [Petrarch]" (*Ep.*, XIII.68; "e partendomi, a Vinegia me ne venni, dove dal mio Silvano lietamente ricevuto fui"); a few months after Boccaccio's departure, Petrarch would recall his friend's journey to Venice in these words: "you came to me by a longer roundabout way" (*Sen.*, III.1, 161; "longiore circuito me petisti"). His stop in Padua was identified by Arnaldo Foresti, "Pietro da Muglio a Padova e la sua amicizia col Petrarch e col Boccaccio" (1920), later published in Foresti, *Aneddoti della vita di Francesco Petrarca*, 443–54.

46. For Pietro da Moglio's biography, see Leonardo Quaquarelli, "Moglio, Pietro da," in *DBI*, LXXV (2011). In *Disp.*, 60 (= Var. 11), Petrarch charged Pietro da Moglio with giving a letter to Giovanni da Bozzetta, the priest who cared for the house assigned to Petrarch in virtue of his canonry in Padua. For the friendship between Albanzani, Boccaccio, Petrarch, and Pietro da Moglio, see Carla Maria Monti, "Il *ravennate* Donato Albanzani amico di Boccaccio e di Petrarca," in *Dante e la sua eredità a Ravenna nel Trecento*, ed. Marco Petoletti (Ravenna: Longo, 2015), 142–43.

47. Francesco Petrarca, *Disp.*, 59 (= Var. 39), 25. See also, Paolo Sambin, "Alessio, Nicoletto d'," in *DBI*, II (1960).

48. In *Sen.*, III.1, of September 7, 1363, after recalling the happy days

they had recently spent together, Petrarch renewed his invitation to Boccaccio to return to his house, describing the pleasant company that would surround him: "Here is the best company, I doubt whether anyone could wish better: Benintendi [dei Ravagnani], whose name comes from his accomplishments, chancellor of this celebrated city, very attentive to public affairs and private friendships and noble studies, when freed of his daily concerns, comes in the evening to meet me in his every-ready gondola with a happy face and affectionate heart. Recently you saw yourself how nice it was—the nightly boating and conversation—and learned too that there is something so sincere and well seasoned about this man. There is also our Donato Apenninigena [Albanzani], whom the Adriatic shore has sheltered for many years since he broke away from the Tuscan hills. I speak of our Donato who voluntarily gave himself to us . . . no one is more pleasant, no one more devoted to us, no one better known to you than he" (170–71; "Adest optima et nescio an melior optanda societas: nomen ab effectu nactus Beneintendi, preclarissime huius urbis cancellarius et statui publico et privatis amicitiis et honestis studiis bene intendens, cuius vespertini congressus, dum diurnis relaxatus curis leta fronte, pio animo, instructo navigio ad nos venit, et navigationes et confabulationesque sub noctem quam suaves sint quamque sincerum et bene salsum quicquid in homine illo est, nuper expertus tenes; necnon Donatus noster Apenninigena, quem etruscis collibus ereptum multos iam per annos litus servat adriacum, Donatus inquam noster et donatus nobis se donante . . . quo nil suavius, nil purius, nil nostri amantius, nil notius tibi"; translation from Petrarca, *Letters of Old Age*, vol. 1). For Ravegnani, see Marco Pozza, "Ravegnani, Benintendi," in *DBI*, LXXXVI (2016).

49. Francesco Petrarca, *Sen.*, II.1, 134; Petrarch cites Isidore of Seville, *Origines*, 2, 5.

50. For example, see what Petrarch has the character Augustinus say in *Secr.*, III.249.

51. Translations in this paragraph from Boccaccio, *Corbaccio*, trans. Cassell, 1, 13, 14, 51–53.

52. For Boccaccio's Marian devotion, see also *Corbaccio*, 261–67; *Rime*, LXXX [CXII]; *BC*, XIV.250–61; the first redaction of the Proemio of *GDG*, IX; see also Giorgio Padoan, *Il Boccaccio, le Muse, il Parnaso e l'Arno* (Florence: Olschki, 1978), 215–17. It is revealing that the exaltation of the Virgin disappears in the second redaction of the *Genealogia*, replaced with a hymn to the Redeemer: see Guido Martellotti, *Dante e Boccaccio e altri scrittori dall'Umanesimo al Romanticismo* (Florence: Olschki, 1983), 149–50.

53. The information about Boccaccio's condemnation of his vernacular poems to the flames comes from Petrarch's letter of rebuke to him (*Sen.*, V.2), in which he claims to learned from their common friend Albanzani the true reason for this destruction, namely, that Boccaccio

"judged them inferior to" Petrarch's own poetry (18; "quod illa nostris imparia iudicasses"; translation from Petrarca, *Letters of Old Age*, vol. 1); the letter, dated August 28, 1364 (but only received by Boccaccio at the end of December 1365), places Boccaccio's apparently "humble" but actually "proud" gesture at a time prior to Petrarch's move to Venice in September 1362.

54. Translations in this paragraph from Boccaccio, *Corbaccio*, trans. Cassell, 14 and 28.

55. This summary of the *Corbaccio* is from Lucia Battaglia Ricci, *Boccaccio* (Rome: Salerno Editrice, 2000), 227–28. The citations within it are from *Corbaccio*, 93.

56. For the manifold interpretations, see the surveys in Giovanni Boccaccio, *Il Corbaccio*, ed. Giulia Natali (Milan: Mursia, 1992), xviii–xxvii; Sebastiana Nobili, "Per il titolo 'Corbaccio,'" *Studi e problemi di critica testuale* 48 (1994): 93–114; and Battaglia Ricci, *Boccaccio*, 234–37; see also by Michelangelo Zaccarello, "Del corvo, animale solitario: Ancora un'ipotesi per il titolo del 'Corbaccio,'" *Studi sul Boccaccio* 42 (2014): 179–94; and "Il 'Corbaccio' nel contesto della tradizione misogina e moralistica medievale: annotazioni generali e proposte specifiche," *Chroniques italiennes* 36 (2018): 162–79.

57. Francisco Rico, *Ritratti allo specchio (Boccaccio, Petrarca)* (Rome and Padua: Editrice Antenore, 2012), 100.

58. Translation from Boccaccio, *Corbaccio*, trans. Cassell, 23.

59. For the various hypotheses regarding the dating of the *Corbaccio*, see Giorgio Padoan, *Il Boccaccio, le Muse, il Parnaso e l'Arno* (Florence: Olschki, 1978), 221–23; Giovanni Boccaccio, *Il Corbaccio*, ed. Giulia Natali (Milan: Mursia, 1992), vii–xii; and Rico, *Ritratti allo specchio (Boccaccio, Petrarca)*, 97–129.

60. Translation from Boccaccio, *Decameron*, trans. Rebhorn, 2.

61. Translation from Boccaccio, *Corbaccio*, trans. Cassell, 10.

62. Translation from Giovanni Boccaccio, *Boccaccio's Expositions on Dante's "Comedy,"* trans. Michael Papio (Toronto: University of Toronto Press, 2009), 91.

63. Translation from Boccaccio, *Corbaccio*, trans. Cassell, 24.

64. Translations in this paragraph from Boccaccio, *Corbaccio*, trans. Cassell, 77.

65. Translation from Boccaccio, *The Elegy of Lady Fiammetta*, trans. Causa-Steindler and Mauch, 158.

66. Translation from Boccaccio, *The Elegy of Lady Fiammetta*, trans. Causa-Steindler and Mauch, 1.

67. Translation from Boccaccio, *Corbaccio*, trans. Cassell, 60.

68. Translation from Boccaccio, *Decameron*, trans. Rebhorn, 2.

69. Of great interest regarding the widow's autoeroticism are the arguments developed by Natascia Tonelli in the context of an analysis of

the medieval medical conception of the dangers of female continence, especially of widowed women: "Fisiologia e malattia nello specchio della letteratura: la prevenzione salutare in 'Decameron IV 1,'" in *La medicina nel basso medioevo: Tradizioni e conflitti, Atti del LV Convegno storico internazionale, Todi, 14–16 ottobre 2018* (Spoleto: Centro italiano di studi sul basso medioevo, 2019), 97–112.

70. Translation from Boccaccio, *Decameron*, trans. Rebhorn, 305.

71. Translations in this paragraph from Boccaccio, *Corbaccio*, trans. Cassell, 32 and 60.

72. Translation from Boccaccio, *Corbaccio*, trans. Cassell, 23.

73. "Non igitur uxor ducenda sapienti, primum enim impedit studium phylosophiae; nec possit quisquam libris et uxori pariter inservire." This passage appears on 52v of the *Zibaldone Laurenziano*; the page is reproduced on the website of Università "La Sapienza" di Roma (http://rmcisadu.let.uniroma1.it/boccaccio/carta52verso.html), accompanied by a critical edition and commentary by Ombretta Feliziani.

74. *TLD*, [I].46–58.

75. *EpA*, 39.

76. Boccaccio summarizes Petrarch's role as his teacher and guide in matters of life and virtue in the letter to Martino da Signa, where he explains that in the fifteenth eclogue of the *Buccolicum carmen*, Phylostropus is "my glorious master Francesco Petrarca, by whose counsels I was most strongly persuaded to direct my mind away from delight in temporal things to the eternal, and so my loves, although not fully, nonetheless sufficiently changed for the better" (*Ep.*, XXIII.30; "Pro Phylostropo ego intelligo gloriosum preceptorem meum Franciscum Petrarchm, cuius monitis sepissime michi persuasum est ut omnia rerum temporalium oblectatione mentem ad eterna dirigerem, et sic amores meos, etsi non plene, satis tamen vertit in melius").

77. Rico, *Ritratti allo specchio (Boccaccio, Petrarca)*, 16–17, based on the letter that, according to Boccaccio, Petrarch "wrote at great length [to me] against my beastiality" (*EpA*, 41; "quam etiam longissimam in bestialitatem meam scripsit"); Rico is certain that "the *bestialitas* that Boccaccio had in mind was the violation of the sixth commandment."

78. Many of the arguments for the date 1363 made in Mario Marti, "Per una metaletteratura del 'Corbaccio': il ripudio di Fiammetta," *Giornale storico della letteratura italiana* 93 (1976): 60–86, are convincing; see also Regnicoli, "Per la biografia di Giovanni Boccaccio: l'*Elegia di madonna Fiammetta* attraverso i documenti," 31, for a similar dating.

79. Translation from Boccaccio, *Corbaccio*, trans. Cassell, 21–22. This sentence is highly debated and the subject of much speculation (on this, see Giovanni Boccaccio, *Il Corbaccio*, ed. Giulia Natali [Milan: Mursia, 1992], 45–46); particularly striking is the proposal by Stefano Carrai to correct the sentence to read: "età, la quale, se le tempie già bianche e la

canuta barba non m'ingannano, tu dovresti avere, li costumi del mondo fuori delle fascie già sono degli anni quaranta, e già non venticinque, cominciatili a conoscere" ("Giovanni Boccaccio, 'Corbaccio,' 118–19 [ed. Padoan]/179 [ed. Nurmela]," in *Studi per Roberto Tissoni*, ed. Carlo Caruso and William Spaggiari [Rome: Edizioni di *Storia e Letteratura*, 2008], 79–81).

80. For the important topic of *mutatio animae* connected to *mutatio vitae* on which Petrarch structured his self-portrait, see the classic work by Francisco Rico, *Vida u obra de Petrarch, I. Lectura del "Secretum"* (Padua: Antenore, 1974); and Marco Santagata, *I frammenti dell'anima: Storia e racconto nel Canzoniere di Petrarca* (Bologna: il Mulino, 2004).

81. Rico has written definitively on the role of Petrarch's teaching in Boccaccio's choice of the protagonist's age (Rico, *Ritratti allo specchio (Boccaccio, Petrarca)*, 97–131, the chapter significantly entitled "Il *Secretum* di Boccaccio"); regarding the substantial difference between the *Corbaccio* and the *Secretum*, see Bruni, *Boccaccio: L'invenzione della letteratura*, 456–59.

82. "Libidine . . . molestatus."

83. Billanovich, *Petrarca letterato, I. Lo scrittoio del Petrarca*, 135–36, 345–46, was the first to suggest that Boccaccio gave a copy of the biography he had written of him to Petrarch in 1350 or 1351, who then corrected the biography's assertions about his sexual life in the *Posteritati* (also in that case, however, Petrarch lied, given that in *Sen.* VIII 1, 15, written in 1366, he would confess to Boccaccio that he had been completely free of the "plague" of sex only since the Jubilee of 1350); Billanovich's hypothesis is accepted by Rico, *Ritratti allo specchio (Boccaccio, Petrarca)*, 117–18, but rejected by Laura Refe, "Boccaccio e Petrarca tra biografia e autobiografia," *Studi Petrarcheschi* 27 (2014).

84. Francesco Petrarca, *Post.*, 6: "Mox vero ad quadragesimum etatis annum appropinquans . . . non solum factum illud obscenum, sed eius memoriam omnem sic abieci, quasi numquam feminam aspexissem." Translation from Francesco Petrarca, *Selected Letters*, vol. 2, trans. Elaine Fantham (Cambridge, MA: Harvard University Press, 2017), 545.

85. This dense network of connections between the *Corbaccio*, Dante's *Vita Nova*, and Petrarch's *Canzoniere* has been studied by Natascia Tonelli, "Beatrice, Laura, la vedova: La gentilezza, la 'Vita Nuova' e il Canzoniere del 'Corbaccio,'" *Chroniques italiennes* 36 (2018): 180–98.

86. Billanovich, *Petrarca letterato, I. Lo scrittoio del Petrarca*, 271.

Chapter Eleven

1. *EpA*, 56; "Non est Iacobo locus in quem deducat quam sumpsit in coniugem, nisi illum in domunculam meam suscipiam."

2. *EpA*, 23.

3. For a list of "internal" (e.g., regarding taxation and security) and "external" (e.g., governors of subject towns and captains of fortifications outside of the city) offices, see Archivio di Stato di Firenze, *Archivio delle Tratte: Introduzione e inventario*, ed. Paolo Viti and Raffaella Maria Zaccaria (Rome: Ufficio centrale per i beni culturali, 1989), 17.

4. The will of 1365, drawn up by the notary Filippo di ser Pietro Doni, has unfortunately been lost (see Laura Regnicoli, "La *cura sepulcri* di Giovanni Boccaccio," *Studi sul Boccaccio* 42 [2014]: 27–28). It would have provided us with a picture of Boccaccio's financial situation as well as the state of his relationship with Iacopo: indeed, we know that in his final will, "well aware of his brother Iacopo's spendthrift ways, Giovanni Boccaccio decided to pass on his inheritance to his brother's children" (Laura Regnicoli, "Un'oscura vicenda certaldese: Nuovi documenti su Boccaccio e la sua famiglia," *Italia medioevale e umanistica* 58 [2017)]: 61).

5. For the embassy to Avignon, see Attilio Hortis, *Giovanni Boccacci ambasciatore in Avignone e Pileo da Prata proposto da' fiorentini a patriarca di Aquileia* (Trieste: Herrmanstorfer, 1875), 15–21; and Vittore Branca, *Giovanni Boccaccio: Profilo biografico* (Florence: Sansoni, 1977 [1967]), 146–50.

6. In 1373, dedicating the *De casibus* to Mainardo Cavalcanti, Boccaccio reviewed the great personages of the day, none of whom was deemed worthy of being the dedicatee, writing of Charles IV: "Disappointed, I then turned my mind's eye to the living Caesar, but I at once abandoned the thought, seeing him oblivious to his noble-minded men, preferring to worship the wines of the Theban Bacchus than glory by means of the splendors of the Italian Mars" (*CVI*, Dedica, 7; "Et ab his frustratus, in hodiernum cesarem aciem mentis deflexi; sed confestim revocavi consilium, sentiens eum magnalium virorum suorum immemorem, preponentem thebani Bachi vina colentis gloriam splendoribus Martis ytalici").

7. In a lost letter to Petrarch, Boccaccio described his meeting with Philippe de Cabassoles, which Petrarch's response allows us to reconstruct: "I was happy, by Jove, to hear in that very Babylon [Avignon] you saw the friends whom death has left me, especially the one whom you truly call my father, Philippe [de Cabassoles], Patriarch of Jerusalem. . . . According to your letter, in the presence of the Supreme Pontiff [Urban V] and the startled cardinals, he gave you, whom he had never met before, a long and tender embrace of true love, as if you were another me; after affectionate kisses, pleasant conversation, and anxious questions about my state of health, he finally begged you to have me send at long last that book, *De vita solitaria*, which I had written at his country home and dedicated to him when he was bishop of the church in Cavaillon" (*Sen.*, V.1, 21–22; "Gaudeo hercle quod apud Babilonem quos michi reliquos mors fecit videris, illum ante alios vere patrem, ut dicis, meum, Philippum Ieroso-

limitanum patriarcham. . . . Hic, ut scribis, post longos amplexus, quibus te hactenus sibi ignotum ceu alterum me in conspectu Summi Pontificis ac mirantium cardinalium veri amoris ulnis astrinxerat, post pia oscula, post grata colloquia et de statu meo solicitas questiones ultimum oravit ut librum Vite solitarie olim, dum Cavallicensis Ecclesie presul esset, in rure suo scriptum et ei inscriptum aliquando sibi mitterem"; translation from Petrarca, *Letters of Old Age*, vol. 1). Petrarch had written most of the *De vita solitaria* between 1345 and 1347, but Cabassoles would receive this book dedicated to him only in 1366.

8. See Attilio Hortis, *Giovanni Boccacci ambasciatore in Avignone e Pileo da Prata proposto da' fiorentini a patriarca di Aquileia* (Trieste: Herrmanstorfer, 1875), 21–41, for a detailed biography of Pileo da Prata.

9. On Ristoro Canigiani, see the brief entry by Santorre Debenedetti, "Canigiani, Ristoro" in *Enciclopedia Italiana* (1930).

10. The letter Boccaccio wrote to Leonardo del Chiaro (*Lett.*, II) shows that in Avignon he spent time with people such as the Florentine notary Martino di Giovanni, a member of the merchant family Berti named Dato, and a certain Lanzimanno, "king of Porta Ferruzza," a neighborhood in the city: see Roberto Abbondanza, "Una lettera autografa del Boccaccio nell'Archivio di Stato di Perugia," *Studi sul Boccaccio* 1 (1963): 10; and Giovanni Boccaccio, *Epistole*, ed. Ginetta Auzzas, in *Tutte le opere*, ed. Vittore Branca, vol. 5, 1 (Milan: Mondadori, 1992), 875.

11. Regnicoli, "La *cura sepulcri* di Giovanni Boccaccio," 60–61.

12. In *Ep.*, XIV, in addition to Giandonati, Boccaccio also warmly recommended to Pietro a Florentine schoolmaster, Giovanni da Siena, who would become connected to Pietro and his school (Coluccio Salutati, who had attended da Moglio's school of rhetoric in Bologna, would dedicate to him the first version of his *De laboribus Herculis* [*The Labors of Hercules*]).

13. "Ut aliquando ex aucupatore venatoreque ex manibus tuis possim dicere literatum hominem suscepisse."

14. The text of the bull can be found in Giuseppe Billanovich, *Restauri boccacceschi* (Rome: Edizioni di *Storia e letteratura*, 1947), 168–69.

15. Salutati's letter is *Ep.*, I.19; for Salutati's relationship with Boccaccio, who would shortly thereafter become the intermediary between him and Petrarch, see Giuseppe Billanovich, *Petrarca letterato*, I. *Lo scrittoio del Petrarca* (Rome: Edizioni di *Storia e letteratura*, 1947; repr. 1995), 278–80.

16. For the acquisition of this land, see Laura Regnicoli, "Per il Codice diplomatico di Giovanni Boccaccio," in *Boccaccio letterato*, conference proceedings, ed. Michaelangiola Marchiaro and Stefano Zamponi (Florence: Accademia della Crusca—Ente nazionale Giovanni Boccaccio, October 10–12, 2013), 524.

17. *Ep.*, XIV.11.

18. See Boccaccio, *Epistole*, ed. Ginetta Auzzas, in *Tutte le opere*, ed. Vittore Branca, vol. 5, 1 (Milan: Mondadori, 1992), 493–856, 816, regarding the date of this letter.

19. These three letters are *Sen.*, V.1, 2, and 3.

20. Francesco Petrarca, *Sen.*, V.4, 12: "He nunc igitur quo pridem, si licuisset, ibant ut aliquando perveniant curabis excusationem tarditatis tuis verbis addita." Translation from Petrarca, *Letters of Old Age*, vol. 1.

21. The hypothesis that Boccaccio went to Venice (or Ravenna) in 1366 is suggested by Carla Maria Monti, "Il *ravennate* Donato Albanzani amico di Boccaccio e di Petrarca," in *Dante e la sua eredità a Ravenna nel Trecento*, ed. Marco Petoletti (Ravenna: Longo, 2015), 136–37: according to him, "the letters must have been delivered personally, because Petrarca asked him to make the apologies face to face."

22. "Ut te viderim, preceptor inclite, a Certaldo Venetiam . . . discessi."

23. On Gianfigliazzi, see Vanna Arrighi, "Gianfigliazzi, Luigi," in *DBI*, LIV (2000).

24. "Sane, ne frustrarer quorundam amicorum spem, qui fidei mee arduum quoddam opus suum perangendum commiserant, et quoniam urgeret desiderium eos saltem duos videndi quos tu summe diligis et merito, tuam scilicet Tulliam et Franciscum suum, quos ante non videram . . . iter ceptum reassumpsi."

25. "Multis plenum effluentemque undique."

26. For Guido da Reggio or da Bagnolo, see Franco Bacchelli, "Guido da Bagnolo," in *DBI*, LXI (2004). Boccaccio had also given Petrarch a ring on the occasion of their first meeting in Florence (see Billanovich, *Petrarca letterato*, I. *Lo scrittoio del Petrarca*, 135).

27. Francesco Petrarca, *Ign.*, II.32.

28. For the compositional phases of the *De ignorantia*, see Vinicio Pacca, *Petrarca* (Rome and Bari: Laterza, 1998), 229–33; and Francesco Petrarca, *De ignorantia: Della mia ignoranza e di quella di molti altri*, ed. Enrico Fenzi (Milan: Mursia, 1999), 107–9.

29. "Assistentibus ex amicis nonnullis."

30. "Et ecce, modestiori passu quam deceret etatem, venit Electa tua, dilecta mea, et antequam me nosceret ridens aspexit, quam ego non letus tantum sed avidus ulnis suscepi, primo intuitu virgunculam olim meam suspicatus. Quid dicam? Si michi non credis, Guilielmo ravennati medico et Donato nostro, qui novere, credito: eadem que mee fuit, Electe tue facies est; idem risus, eadem oculorum leticia, gestus incessusque, et eadem totius corpusculi habitudo, quanquam grandiuscula mea, eo quod etate esset provectior: quintum quippe iam annum attigerat et dimidium dum ultimo illam vidi. Insuper, si idem idioma fuisset, verba eadem erant atque simplicitas. Quid multa? In nichilo differentes esse cognovi, nisi quia aurea cesaries tue est, mee inter nigram rufamque fuit. Heu michi!

Quotiens, dum hanc persepe amplector et suis delector collocutionibus, memoria subtracte michi puellule lacrimas ad oculos usque deduxit, quas demum in suspirium versas emisi advertente nemine!"

31. Francesco Petrarca, *Sen.*, X.4: "consolatoria super illius filii suique nepotis immaturo obitu."

32. Francesco Petrarca, *Sen.*, X.4, 145: "Et quecunque ex me audis nostrum credito dixisse Iohannem, qui casum tuum non aliter quam proprium tulit teque talem in tuis qualem se in angoribus suis cupit."

33. Francesco Petrarca, *Sen.*, X.5, 7: "[Iohannes] qui dum illa scriberem mecum erat, dum hec legis est tecum, imo cum utroque simul est semper." Translations in this paragraph are from Petrarca, *Letters of Old Age*, vol. 2.

34. Branca, *Giovanni Boccaccio: Profilo biografico*, 164; a similar hypothesis was also made earlier by Giuseppe Billanovich, *Petrarca letterato*, I. *Lo scrittoio del Petrarca* (Rome: Edizioni di *Storia e letteratura*, 1947; repr. 1995), 281.

35. Billanovich, *Petrarca letterato*, I. *Lo scrittoio del Petrarca*, 281–82; see also Vittore Branca, *Giovanni Boccaccio: Profilo biografico*, 162.

36. Francesco Petrarca, *Sen.*, XV.8, 8–9.

37. In *Sen.*, XV.8, 12, Petrarch refutes Boccaccio's assertion (based on information obtained from a certain Lorenzo, "a learned man . . . but actually quite ignorant of my nature and my circumstances" ["doctum sed profecto nature mearumque rerum penitus inscium"]) that Petrarch, upon learning what his detractors were saying about him, "was at once enraged and grabbed a pen and replied to them" ("me audita illorum sententia quam de me tulerant subito in furorem versum calamum arripuisse ac respondisse"): from this it can be deduced that Boccaccio had relied on information communicated orally, but keep in mind that Petrarch himself wrote in *Ign.*, 3, that "justified, as I believe, indignation and rightful resentment, wrench the words out of me" ("digna, nisi fallor, indignatio et iustus dolor verba extorquent"; translation from Petrarca, *Letters of Old Age*, vol. 2). Petrarch noted the date of the completion of the transcription of the *De ignorantia* ("1370 Jun. 25 vergente ad occasum") at the end of the autograph Vat. lat. 3359.

38. Francesco Petrarca, *Test.*, 1352: "Domino Iohanni de Certaldo seu Boccaccii, verecunde admodum tanto viro tam modicum, lego quinquaginta florenos auri de Florentia pro una veste hiemali ad studium lucubrationesque nocturnas."

39. *Ep.*, XX.52.

40. For the history of the composition of the *De mulieribus claris*, see Caterina Malta, "*De mulieribus claris*," in *BAC*, 197–200; quotation is hers. The autograph codex is ms. Pluteo 90 sup. 981 in the Biblioteca Laurenziana in Florence, for which, see Sandro Bertelli, "L'autografo del *De mulieribus claris*," in *BAC*, 201–2.

41. Giuseppe Billanovich, *Petrarca e il primo umanesimo* (Padua: Antenore, 1996), 472 (but the chapter "Pietro Piccolo da Monteforte tra il Petrarca e il Boccaccio" had already been published as an article in 1955).

42. Silvia Fiaschi, *Genealogia deorum gentilium*, in *Boccaccio autore e copista*, exhibition catalog, ed. Teresa De Robertis, Carla Maria Monti, Marco Petoletti, Giuliano Tanturli, and Stefano Zamponi (Florence: Biblioteca Medicea Laurenziana, October 11, 2013–January 11, 2014) (Florence: Mandragora, 2013), 171.

43. "In quo auctor, obiurgationibus respondens, in hostes poetici nominis invehit." Translation from Boccaccio, *Boccaccio on Poetry*, trans. Osgood, 14.

44. "In quo autor purgat se ipsum ab obiectis in se."

45. This is the observation of Giuseppe Billanovich, *Petrarca e il primo umanesimo* (Padua: Antenore, 1996), 473–76, who also points out, among other things, that "Petrarch and his imitator Boccaccio preferred to turn to Augustinians for erudition and Carthusians for piety."

46. "Poesis . . . est fervor quidam exquisite inveniendi atque dicendi, seu scribendi quod inveneris. Qui, ex sinu Dei procedens, paucis mentibus . . . in creatione conceditur."

47. "Mera poesis est, quicquid sub velamento componimus et exponitur exquisite."

48. "Aliquid magni sub fabuloso cortice palliatum."

49. "Tanti quidem sunt fabule, ut earum primo contextu oblectentur indocti, et circa abscondita doctorum exerceantur ingenia." English translations in this paragraph are from Boccaccio, *Boccaccio on Poetry*, trans. Osgood, 42, 48, and 51.

50. Boccaccio had already affirmed the close connection, even identification, between poetry and theology in the *Trattatello in laude di Dante*: *TLD*, [I].154–55.

51. This is ms. Pluteo 52.9 of the Biblioteca Laurenziana in Florence.

52. Regarding Boccaccio's relationship with Monteforte, see Giuseppe Billanovich, *Petrarca e il primo umanesimo* (Padua: Antenore, 1996), 473–76; for Monteforte's biography, see Andrea Labardi, "Pietro Piccolo da Monteforte," in *DBI*, LXXXIII (2015).

53. Regarding the *Buccolicum carmen*, see the following works: Pier Giorgio Ricci, *Studi sulla vita e le opere del Boccaccio* (Milan and Naples: Ricciardi, 1985), 50–66; Giovanni Boccaccio, *Buccolicum carmen*, ed. Giorgio Bernardi Perini, in *Tutte le opere*, ed. Vittore Branca, vol. 5, 2 (Milan: Mondadori, 1994); Angelo Piacentini, "Buccolicum carmen," in *BAC*, 203–8; Albanese, "Boccaccio bucolico e Dante da Napoli a Forlì"; also useful are the classic works by Guido Martellotti, "Dalla tenzone al carme bucolico" (1964) and "La riscoperta dello stile bucolico (da Dante al Boccaccio)" (1966), both published in Guido Martellotti, *Dante e Boccaccio e altri scrittori dall'Umanesimo al Romanticismo* (Florence: Olschki, 1983), 71–106.

54. Ms. 1232 in the Biblioteca Riccardiana in Florence; described in Teresa De Robertis, "L'autografo del *Buccolicum carmen*," in *BAC*, 209–11.

55. Ms. Vat. lat. 3358.

56. See the works of Guido Martellotti published in Martellotti, *Dante e Boccaccio e altri scrittori dall'Umanesimo al Romanticismo*, 71–106.

57. On January 18, 1347, Petrarch sent the *Argus* to Barbato da Sulmona along with the letter *Disp.* 7 (= *Var.* 49); both the letter and the eclogue were copied by Boccaccio into the *Zibaldone Laurenziano*, f. 76r–77r.

58. Pacca, *Petrarca*, 104.

59. *GDG*, XIV, 10.2–6.

60. On Martino da Signa, see Paolo Falzone, "Martino da Signa," in *DBI*, LXXI (2008); and on Boccaccio's letter to him, see Angelo Piacentini, "La lettera di Boccaccio a Martino da Signa: alcune proposte interpretative," *Studi sul Boccaccio* 43 (2015): 147–76.

61. "Ex his ego Virgilium secutus sum, quapropter non curavi in omnibus colloquentium nominibus sensum abscondere."

62. Boccaccio wrote that "I ascribe no meaning at all" to ("pro quibus nil penitus sentio") Amintas and Melibeus of eclogue 6; he had wanted to give "no particular meaning" to ("nullam nomini significationem propriam volui") the name Archas of the ninth eclogue; and did not remember the significance of Therapon in the fourteenth.

63. Giovanni Boccaccio, *Carmina*, ed. Giuseppe Velli, in *Tutte le opere*, ed. Vittore Branca, vol. 5, 1 (Milan: Mondadori, 1992), 475.

Chapter Twelve

1. Reported in Roberto Abbondanza, "Una lettera autografa del Boccaccio nell'Archivio di Stato di Perugia," *Studi sul Boccaccio* 1 (1963): 13.

2. Coluccio Salutati, *Ep.*, II.12, vol. I, 85.

3. Vittore Branca, *Giovanni Boccaccio: Profilo biografico* (Florence: Sansoni, 1977 [1967]), 166; and Giovanni Boccaccio, *Epistole*, ed. Ginetta Auzzas, in *Tutte le opere*, ed. Vittore Branca, vol. 5, 1 (Milan: Mondadori, 1992), 823.

4. "... indignans."

5. Laura Regnicoli, "Per il Codice diplomatico di Giovanni Boccaccio," in *Boccaccio letterato*, conference proceedings, ed. Michaelangiola Marchiaro and Stefano Zamponi (Florence-Certaldo, October 10–12, 2013) (Florence: Accademia della Crusca — Ente nazionale Giovanni Boccaccio), 518–20.

6. "Senex et eger."

7. *Ep.*, XVIII.7.

8. "[Cum] traxisses me in desiderium non videndi solum, sed, si necessitas exegisset, assumendi in latebram ... clam, quasi tibi positutus essem insidias, parasti fugam. ... Tu me, more furis atque deceptoris,

nedum consulto, verum nec salutato, per noctem in Calabros discessurus
conscendisti lembum."

9. Branca, *Giovanni Boccaccio: Profilo biografico*, 166–67; and Boccaccio, *Epistole*, ed. Ginetta Auzzas, in *Tutte le opere*, ed. Vittore Branca, vol. 5,
1 (Milan: Mondadori, 1992), 493–856, 819.

10. Franco Sacchetti, *Pien di quell'acqua dolce d'Elicona*, in *Rime*, CL.

11. Although his letter's tone is quite harsh, Boccaccio did not end
their relationship: indeed, at the conclusion of the letter he asked Montefalcone to return to Naples and reestablish contact with his del Balzo
patrons, given that, following Urban V's death, Pierre Roger, the cardinal who had been elected pope on December 30, 1370 (taking the name
Gregory XI), was the same man the del Balzo family had been relying on
for Montefalcone's appointment as abbot. An appointment, incidentally,
that he never received. Boccaccio also asked Montefalcone to return the
Cornelius Tacitus codex of Boccaccio's that he had taken away with him
when he fled ("Quaternum quem asportasti Cornelii Taciti queso saltem
mictas," *Ep.*, XVI.19).

12. Information about Boccaccio's activities, meetings, and relationships in Naples is drawn from *Ep.*, XVI, XVII, XVIII, XIX, and XX.

13. *Ep.*, XVII.

14. *Ep.*, XIX.

15. Boccaccio, *Epistole*, ed. Ginetta Auzzas, in *Tutte le opere*, ed. Vittore
Branca, vol. 5, 1 (Milan: Mondadori, 1992), 493–856, 820 and 823–24,
provides some information about Matteo d'Ambrasio and Ubertino da
Corigliano.

16. For the biography of Ugo di Sanseverino, see Luigi Tufano, "Ugo
di Sanseverino," in *DBI*, XC (2017); for that of Niccolò Orsini, see the very
well-informed entry, "Orsini, Nicola (Niccolò) di Roberto," by Lorenzo
Miletti, on the website HistAntArtSi (http://db.histantartsi.eu/web/rest
/FamiglieePersone/13).

17. Boccaccio's autograph codex, which also contains the *Entheticus
in Policraticum* by John of Salisbury and Juvenal's tenth satire, is ms. C
67 sup. in the Biblioteca Ambrosiana of Milan. Its dating is uncertain: on
the basis of primarily philological and cultural factors, the transcription
may be dated to Boccaccio's 1362–63 trip to Naples; or, on the basis of
paleography, to his trip of 1370–71. On this question, see Marco Petoletti,
"Le postille di Giovanni Boccaccio a Marziale (Milano, Biblioteca Ambrosiana, C 67 sup.)," *Studi sul Boccaccio* 34 (2006): 103–84 (who leans toward
the earlier date, in substantial agreement with Giuseppe Billanovich,
Petrarca letterato, I. *Lo scrittoio del Petrarca* [Rome: Edizioni di *Storia e letteratura*, 1947; repr. 1995], 263–66); Marco Petoletti, "Il Marziale autografo
di Giovanni Boccaccio," in *Boccaccio autore e copista*, exhibition catalog,
ed. Teresa De Robertis, Carla Maria Monti, Marco Petoletti, Giuliano
Tanturli, and Stefano Zamponi (Florence: Biblioteca Medicea Lauren-

ziana, October 11, 2013–January 11, 2014) (Florence: Mandragora, 2013), 336–37 (who takes no position); Marco Cursi, "Boccaccio: autografie vere o presunte: Novità su tradizione e trasmissione delle sue opere," *Studij romanzi* 3 (2007): 135–63, at 142–47 (who hypothesizes "a copy from the very early 1370s"); Marco Cursi and Maurizio Fiorilla, "Giovanni Boccaccio," in *Autografi dei letterati italiani: Le origini e il Trecento*, ed. Giuseppina Brunetti, Maurizio Fiorilla, Marco Petoletti (Rome: Salerno Editrice, 2013), 53 (where Marco Cursi states that "paleographic arguments lead us to assign [the autograph] to a period between the late 1360s and very early 1370s, but cultural references in his correspondence with Petrarch argue that we not exclude the possibility that it was a few years earlier").

18. "Ceterum in discessu meo a Neapoli . . . serenissimus princeps Iacobus Maioricarum rex fecit onerari me precibus ut sub umbra sue sublimitatis otiosus senium traherem."

19. "Apud Parthenopeos placido locaret in otio."

20. These May and June dates for his arrival home are not inconsistent with the April 30 payment of his Florentine taxes: evidence shows that Stefano di Giovanni Bonaccorsi and Bardo di Niccolò Luti made the payments for him (see Laura Regnicoli, "Documenti su Giovanni Boccaccio," in *Boccaccio autore e copista*, exhibition catalog, ed. Teresa De Robertis, Carla Maria Monti, Marco Petoletti, Giuliano Tanturli, and Stefano Zamponi [Florence: Biblioteca Medicea Laurenziana, October 11, 2013–January 11, 2014] [Florence: Mandragora, 2013], 400; and Regnicoli, "Per il Codice diplomatico di Giovanni Boccaccio," 518).

21. "Qua perplexitate angebar nimium, nulla adhuc in parte satis firmato consilio."

22. "Hinc enim plurimo desiderio trahebar redeundi in patriam . . . nec minus revisendi libellos quos immeritos omiseram, sic et amicos aliosque caros."

23. "Instante discessu meo quem pluribus impellentibus causis cupio."

24. "Sane, quoniam occulto nexu astringi videbatur quam omnino solutam cupio libertas . . . me verbis absolvi, et rege regalibusque donis omissis, e litore solutis proresiis in patriam redii."

25. "Non iam patiatur etas libertati assueta colla iugo subicere."

26. "Anni, ut reor, supersunt pauci . . . his ego cupio, si Deo gratum sit, prestare finem in patria, et cum meditationes meas ceteras excedat cura sepulcri, desidero quos a progenitoribus meis suscepi cineres, eos eisdem restituere atque suis iungere."

27. Coluccio Salutati, *Ep.*, I.25, vol. I, 225.

28. "Ergastulum rusticorum."

29. For Pizzinga's biography, see Boccaccio, *Epistole*, ed. Ginetta Auzzas, in *Tutte le opere*, ed. Vittore Branca, vol. 5, 1 (Milan: Mondadori, 1992), 493–856, 823–24; Agostino Sottili, "In margine al catalogo dei codici petrarcheschi per la Germania occidentale," in *Il Petrarca ad Arquà, Atti*

del Convegno di studi nel VI centenario (1370–1374) (Arquà Petrarca, 6–8 novembre 1970), ed. Giuseppe Billanovich and Giuseppe Frasso (Padua: Antenore, 1975), 308–14; and Francesco Marzano, "Boccaccio storico della letteratura trecentesca: l'epistola a Iacopo Pizzinga," in *Intorno a Boccaccio/Boccaccio e dintorni 2015, Atti del Seminario internazionale di studi (Certaldo Alta, Casa di Giovanni Boccaccio, 9 settembre 2015)*, ed. Stefano Zamponi (n.p.: Firenze University Press, 2016), 1–13.

30. "Videmus … Dantem Allegherii … nec ea tamen qua veteres via, sed per diverticula quedam omnino insueta maioribus … exquirentem … semisopitas excivisse sorores et in cytharam traxisse Phebum: et eos in maternum cogere cantum ausum, non plebeium aut rusticanum, ut nonnulli voluere, confecit, quin imo artifitioso schemate sensu letiorem fecit quam cortice."

31. "Helyconico fonte limo iuncoque palustri purgato et undis in pristinam claritatem revocatis antroque castalio, silvestrium ramorum contextu iam clauso, reserato ac ab sentibus laureo mundato nemore et Apolline in sede veteri restituto Pyeridisque iam rusticitate sordentibus in antiquum decus, in extremos usque vertices Parnasi conscendit."

32. Pizzinga's only surviving poem ("seventeen hexameters, some, moreover, read shakily") is published in Sottili, "In margine al catalogo," 313–14.

33. "Cepi tepescere et sensim cecidere animi atque defecere vires, et spe posita contingendi, vilis factus atque desperans, et abeuntibus quos itineris sumpseram ostensores, iam canus substiti, et quod michi plorabile malum est, nec retro gradum flectere audeo nec ad superiora conscendere queo: et sic, ni nova desuper infundatur gratia, inglorius nomen una cum cadavere commendabo sepulcro." On this letter, in addition to Marzano, "Boccaccio storico," see Marco Veglia, *La strada più impervia: Boccaccio fra Dante e Petrarca* (Rome and Padua: Editrice Antenore, 2014), 125–50.

34. *GDG*, XV.10, 8; *Corbaccio*, 191.

35. References to his own failures as a poet can be found, although cloaked in images and concepts related to the poems' subjects, in sonnets that appear to date to this period, such as *Rime*, LXX [CVII], vv. 9–14; and LXXVI [CVIII], vv. 9–14; regarding both works, see Giovanni Boccaccio, *Rime*, ed. Vittore Branca, in *Tutte le opere*, ed. Vittore Branca, vol. 5, 1 (Milan: Mondadori, 1992), 3–144, 195–374, 286–88.

36. This letter is published in Giuseppe Billanovich, *Petrarca e il primo umanesimo* (Padua: Antenore, 1996), 496–507.

37. Almost nothing is known about Latinucci, a Florentine merchant linked to the Acciaiuoli's Neapolitan circles: see Vittore Branca, *Tradizione delle opere di Giovanni Boccaccio, I. Un primo elenco dei codici e tre studi* (Rome: Edizioni di *Storia e letteratura*, 1958; repr. 2014), 175–76,

and Bruno Figliuolo, "Andreuccio da Perugia e (è) Cenni di Bardella," in *BN*, 233.

38. "Scabies sicca … ventris ponderosa segnities, renium perpetuus dolor, splenis turgiditas, bilis incendium, tussis anhela, raucum pectus … odiose michi sunt littere, et qui nuper amantissimi libelli displicent … cogitationes omnes mee in sepulcrum declinant et mortem."

39. "Misisti pridie aureum vasculum et nummos aureos in vasculo."

40. *Ep.*, XXII.17: "Dato estivus calor, noctes breves et sponsa nova … nedum novum et iuvenem militem, sed etate provectum, canum et scolasticum hominem a sacris etiam studiis et amovisse potuissent."

41. "Nosti quot ibi sint minus decentia et adversantia honestati, quot veneris infauste aculei, quot in scelus impellentia etiam si sint ferrea pectora, a quibus etsi non ad incestuosum actum illustres impellantur femine, et potissime quibus sacer pudor frontibus insidet, subeunt tamen passu tacitu estus illecebres et impudicas animas obscena concupiscentie tabe nonnunquam inficiunt irritantque, quod omnino ne contingat agendum est."

42. "Existimabunt enim legentes me spurcidum lenonem, incestuosum senem, impurum hominem, turpiloquum maledicum et alienorum scelerum avidum relatorem." Regarding the correspondence with Mainardo Cavalcanti and the circumstances of his marriage, see Pier Giorgio Ricci, *Studi sulla vita e le opere del Boccaccio* (Milan and Naples: Ricciardi, 1985), 163–71. In Boccaccio, *Epistole*, ed. Ginetta Auzzas, in *Tutte le opere*, ed. Vittore Branca, vol. 5, 1 (Milan: Mondadori, 1992), 493–856, both *Ep.*, XXI, and *Ep.*, XXII, are strangely dated 1373.

43. This is the hypothesis of Ricci, *Studi sulla vita e le opere del Boccaccio*, 169.

44. This thesis is advanced by Branca, *Giovanni Boccaccio: Profilo biografico*, 177–78, and Branca, *Tradizione delle opere di Giovanni Boccaccio*, II. *Un secondo elenco dei manoscritti e cinque studi sul testo del "Decameron" con due appendici*, 176; it is taken up in Boccaccio, *Epistole*, ed. Ginetta Auzzas, in *Tutte le opere*, ed. Vittore Branca, vol. 5, 1 (Milan: Mondadori, 1992), 493–856, 836, according to whom "the apparent repudiation of the *Decameron*" was "a joke perhaps prompted by the malicious pleasure of speaking with a person who almost certainly would not have understood what he was saying," that is, who would have taken his assertions at face value.

45. Marco Cursi, *Il "Decameron": scritture, scriventi, lettori. Storia di un testo* (Rome: Viella, 2007), 43–45, argues that Boccaccio's "faith" in his "readers' and especially his female readers' capacity for discernment" had been shaken and he had experienced mounting "moral qualms"; regarding the notion, widespread among Boccaccio's readers, of the advisability of regulating the reading of the book, Cursi cites the example of Francesco

di Amaretto Mannelli, whose marginal notes in ms. Pluteo 42.1 seem to indicate that he supported the "necessity not of a total moralistic censorship, but instead of the work's enjoyment under guidance, that is, not entrusted to the personal initiative of female readers, but consigned to mediation by men" (140).

46. Francesco Petrarca, *Sen.*, XVII.3.

47. Regarding Boccaccio's late "problematic and conflicted cultural period," see the observations of Lucia Battaglia Ricci, *Boccaccio* (Rome: Salerno Editrice, 2000), 256–58.

48. Martial, *Epigrammata*, X.4, 10.

49. "Verum sapit hominem, dum cunnum lingere, futuire et cacare et alia scribit. Maledicatur poeta talis!"

50. "Squadra le fiche," literally, "aim the figs": "le fiche" is an obscene gesture signifying the female sexual organ (a vulger usage of "la fica," fig) made by placing the thumb between the index and middle finger of each hand, roughly equivalent in meaning to giving the middle finger. In *Inf.*, 25, 1–3, Dante described Vanni Fucci making this gesture: "At the end of his words the thief raised his hands / with both the figs, crying: 'Take them, God, / I'm aiming at you!'" ("Al fine de le sue parole il ladro / le mani alzò con amendue le fiche, / gridando: 'Togli Dio, ch'a te le squadro!'"; translation from Dante, *Inferno*, trans. Durling, 381 [see also 390]).

51. For this quotation, and Boccaccio's annotations of Martial more generally, see Petoletti, "Il Marziale autografo di Giovanni Boccaccio," 337.

52. The citizens' petition is published in Domenico Guerri, *Il commento del Boccaccio a Dante: Limiti della sua autenticità e questioni critiche che n'emergono* (Bari: Laterza, 1926), 205–9.

53. For the Scholastic reception of Dante's *Eclogues*, see Giuseppe Billanovich, "Giovanni del Virgilio, Pietro da Moglio, Francesco da Fiano," *Italia medioevale e umanistica* 6 (1963): 203–34; 7 (1964): 279–324.

54. Commenting on *Par.*, XV.97–99, Benvenuto da Imola wrote: Santo Stefano "is today quite disorderly and neglected, as I saw while I was listening to my venerable teacher Boccaccio of Certaldo reading this noble poet in that church" ("hodie est satis inordinata et neglecta, ut vidi, dum audirem venerabilem preceptorem meum Boccacium de Certaldo legentem istud nobilem poetam in dicta ecclesia.")

55. For an introduction to the *Esposizioni*, see Giorgio Padoan, *Il Boccaccio, le Muse, il Parnaso e l'Arno* (Florence: Olschki, 1978), 229–46; Saverio Bellomo, "Boccaccio, Giovanni," in Saverio Bellomo, *Dizionario dei commentatori danteschi: L'esegesi della "Commedia" da Iacopo Alighieri a Nidobeato* (Florence: Olschki, 2004), 171–83; Corrado Calenda, "Giovanni Boccaccio," in *CCD*, I.241–49; and Marco Baglio, "Esposizioni sopra la *Commedia*," in *BAC*, 281–83. Upon Boccaccio's death, the autograph of the *Esposizioni*, consisting of twenty-four notebooks and fourteen smaller notebooks, passed, along with his books, to the library of Santo Spirito

in the custody of Martino da Signa. But a dispute then arose with Iacopo Boccaccio who claimed possession as guardian of his children, Giovanni's designated heirs: the suit would last until April 1377, when the consuls of the Arte del Cambio, the money changers' guild, would accept Iacopo's petition (on this, see Domenico Guerri, *Il commento del Boccaccio a Dante: Limiti della sua autenticità e questioni critiche che n'emergono* [Bari: Laterza, 1926], 213–16; Branca, *Tradizione delle opere di Giovanni Boccaccio*, II. *Un secondo elenco dei manoscritti e cinque studi sul testo del "Decameron" con due appendic*, 188–89; and Laura Regnicoli, "Documenti su Giovanni Boccaccio," in *Boccaccio autore e copista*, exhibition catalog, ed. Teresa De Robertis, Carla Maria Monti, Marco Petoletti, Giuliano Tanturli, and Stefano Zamponi [Florence: Biblioteca Medicea Laurenziana, October 11, 2013–January 11, 2014] [Florence: Mandragora, 2013], 401).

56. "Verum iam decimus elapsus est mensis postquam in patria publice legentem Comediam Dantis magis longa atque tediosa quam discrimine aliquo dubia egritudo oppressit."

57. Branca, *Giovanni Boccaccio: Profilo biografico*, 183, also shares this perplexity about what the fact of the second payment means for the hypothesis that the lectures had completely ended in January.

58. The thesis that Boccaccio contended with strong opposition from within religious circles is argued in Giovanni Boccaccio, *Esposizioni sopra la Comedia di Dante*, ed. Giorgio Padoan, in *Tutte le opere*, ed. Vittore Branca, vol. 6 (Milan: Mondadori, 1965), vii–xxiii, and Giorgio Padoan, *Il Boccaccio, le Muse, il Parnaso e l'Arno* (Florence: Olschki, 1978), 229–46 (his is the phrase quoted), and taken up in Branca, *Giovanni Boccaccio: Profilo biografico*, 185–86. Doubts about the actual existence of this anti-Dante polemic are expressed in Saverio Bellomo, *Dizionario dei commentatori danteschi: L'esegesi della "Commedia" da Iacopo Alighieri a Nidobeato* (Florence: Olschki, 2004), 174–75.

59. Domenico Guerri, *Il commento del Boccaccio a Dante: Limiti della sua autenticità e questioni critiche che n'emergono* (Bari: Laterza, 1926), 16–17.

60. Franco Sacchetti, *Rime*, CLXXXI.91–93: "Come deggio sperar che surga Dante, / che già chi 'l sappia legger non si trova? / E Giovanni, ch'è morto, ne fe' scola."

61. *Rime*, VII–X [CXXII–CXXV].

62. Regarding Boccaccio's four sonnets, see Giorgio Padoan, *Il Boccaccio, le Muse, il Parnaso e l'Arno* (Florence: Olschki, 1978), 239 (for whom the unknown interlocutor was "a humanist friend"), and Boccaccio, *Rime*, ed. Vittore Branca, in *Tutte le opere*, ed. Vittore Branca, vol. 5, 1 (Milan: Mondadori, 1992), 297–301. On the poems' authenticity, see Giovanni Boccaccio, *Rime*, ed. Roberto Leporatti (Florence: Edizioni del Galluzzo, 2013), 25–26; as for their dating, it is likely that they were written prior to autumn 1374: indeed, in them Boccaccio described himself as swollen

like a wineskin (*Rime*, VII [CXXII].9–11), and in November of that year, his illness had affected him to the point where he was unrecognizable (*Ep.*, XXIV.3).

63. Francesco Petrarca, *Rvf*, 287.

64. Translation from *Poets of the Italian Renaissance*, ed. and trans. Tusiani, 36.

65. On Boccaccio's wills, essential are Laura Regnicoli, "I testamenti di Giovanni Boccaccio," in *BAC*, 387–93; and, especially, Regnicoli, "La *cura sepulcri* di Giovanni Boccaccio"; on Iacopo's disinheritance, see Laura Regnicoli, "Un'oscura vicenda certaldese: Nuovi documenti su Boccaccio e la sua famiglia," *Italia medioevale e umanistica* 58 (2017): 61.

66. For Boccaccio's books absorbed into the library of Santo Spirito, see Teresa De Robertis, "L'inventario della *parva libraria* di Santo Spirito," in *Boccaccio autore e copista*, exhibition catalog, ed. Teresa De Robertis, Carla Maria Monti, Marco Petoletti, Giuliano Tanturli, and Stefano Zamponi (Florence: Biblioteca Medicea Laurenziana, October 11, 2013–January 11, 2014) (Florence: Mandragora, 2013), 403–9.

67. "Scribendi finis Certaldi datus III nonas novembris, et, ut satis vides, festinanter dicere non possum: tres fere dies totos, paucis interpositis horis ad restaurandas parumper fessi corporis vires, in scribendo hanc brevem epistolam consumpsi." This is how Boccaccio described himself to Francescuolo in the letter: "Alas, pity me! I would look to you quite different from how you saw me in Venice. The skin of my once-full body is drained, my color is changed, gaze dulled, legs uncertain, hands trembling, on account of which, with the support of some friends, I managed to come from Florence by no means to the proud summits of the Appenines, but just barely to the ancestral land of Certaldo, where I stay, half alive and anguished, withering away in idleness and uncertain of myself, awaiting healing and grace from God alone, who is able to command fevers" (*Ep.*, XXIV.5; "Heu michi misero! Longe alter tibi viderer quam is quem vidisti Venetiis. Exausta totius pleni quondam corporis pellis est, immutatus color, hebetatus visus, titubant genua et manus tremule facte sunt, ex quo, nedum superbos Apennini vertices, sed vix usque in avitum Certaldi agrum amicorum quorundarum suffragio deductus e patria sum, ubi semivivus et anxius, ocio marciens et mei ipsius incertus consisto, Dei solius, qui febribus imperare potest, medelam expectans et gratiam").

68. The vicissitudes of the text of the *Africa* have been reconstructed by Vincenzo Fera in the books *Antichi editori e lettori dell' "Africa"* and *La revisione petrarchesca dell' "Africa,"* both published in Messina by the Centro di studi umanistici in 1984.

69. "Sentio nonnullis, nescio a quo, examen tam huius quam reliquorum librorum fuisse commissum, et quos dignos assererent, eos mansuros fore. Miro committentis inscitiam, sed longe magis suscipientibus temeritatem et ignaviam. . . . Videat, oro, Deus et poematibus aliisque sac-

ris inventionibus magistri nostri adsit adiutor. Tandem, si iudicio eorum iudicum causa stare contingat, si libet, scribito: et superaddito nunquid copia cupientibus detur."

70. For this poem, whose incipit recalls that of Carmina V, "Ytalie iam certus honos, cui tempora lauro," see Giovanni Boccaccio, *Carmina*, ed. Giuseppe Velli, in *Tutte le opere*, ed. Vittore Branca, vol. 5, 1 (Milan: Mondadori, 1992), 397–402.

71. "Teque vocant suadentque fugam votisque precantur / ut te surripias igni sanctisque tuorum / te manibus credas."

72. "Carpe fugam volucer dubiosque relinque / euganeos montes."

73. Giandonati, well aware of Iacopo's habit of not honoring his debts, demanded a guarantee for the construction of the tomb from Banco Botticini (who, upon Iacopo's death in 1391, would become the guardian of his children). However, although summoned before the *podestà* of Certaldo and ordered to pay, Iacopo did not obey the ruling. After his death, Giandonati then brought suit against him before Bishop Angelo Ricasoli, but this time too, for various reasons, did not succeed in getting back the money he had spent: regarding this, see Domenico Tordi, *Attorno a Giovanni Boccaccio: Gl'inventari dell'eredità di Iacopo Boccaccio* (Orvieto: Rubeca & Scaletti, 1923), 16.

74. The English translation is from Thomas G. Bergin, *Boccaccio* (New York: Viking, 1981), 64.

75. According to Regnicoli, "La *cura sepulcri* di Giovanni Boccaccio," 34, "In Boccaccio's lifetime (1371), the entire Comune of Certaldo … had 188 hearths (104 of which were in the Castle) for a total of 809 individuals."

76. "che gli huomini, i quali si elevono con gli studi et con lo ingegno tanto sopra gli altri, è creduto dalla moltitudine che egli habbino sempre del sopranaturale" (Regnicoli, "La *cura sepulcri* di Giovanni Boccaccio," 35).

77. Marco Santagata, *Dante: Il romanzo della sua vita* (Milan: Mondadori, 2012), 299–300.

78. "Dicono che e' si faceva portare da' demonii a Napoli, dove egli era innamorato, a sua posta, et che in dua ore egli andava et tornava. A tale che una sera, tornando di là et essendo sopra il Pozzuolo, che è un fossatello a piè di Certaldo, sonò in quel punto l'Ave Maria; per il che lui disse: 'lodato sia Iddio.' Allora dicono che i demonii, sentendo ricordare il nome di Iesù, lo lasciarono andare et che, caduto in tal fossato, morì poi per tal cagione." Cited by Regnicoli, "La *cura sepulcri* di Giovanni Boccaccio," 35, in whose opinion the anonymous author was someone close to Vincenzo (or Vincenzio) Borghini, a Florentine scholar active in the courts of both Duke Cosimo I and his son Grand Duke Francesco I.

INDEX

Abbondanza, Roberto, 421n10, 425n1

Abruzzo (Italy), 125–26

Acciaiuoli, Acciaiuolo, 34, 93

Acciaiuoli, Andrea, 223–24, 358n101, 413n35

Acciaiuoli, Angelo (bishop), 88, 90, 152, 339n15, 368n21, 375n6, 401n22

Acciaiuoli, Giovanni (archbishop of Patras), 181–82

Acciaiuoli, Iacopo, 182, 272

Acciaiuoli, Lapa (Lupisca), 181–83, 222–24, 375n6, 414n36

Acciaiuoli, Lorenzo, 151

Acciaiuoli, Neri, 182

Acciaiuoli, Niccolò, 5, 10, 13, 16, 33–34, 57, 76, 81, 85–93, 114, 122–28, 137, 141, 148–53, 181–82, 190–91, 195, 207, 221–33, 260–65, 294n6, 298n26, 299n30, 336n3, 337n7, 338n15, 341n30, 358n101, 359n109, 367n21, 382n43, 383nn47–48, 397n5, 408n61, 409n67, 413–14nn35–36, 414n40, 415n42

Acciaiuoli family and merchant banking house, 16, 33, 85–87, 90, 93, 114, 181–83, 190, 208, 223–24, 274, 299n30, 341n30, 344n42, 375n6, 414n40, 428n37

Achille, 61

Acrimonia, 103–4, 308n32, 358n101

acrostics, 42, 314n20

Adamo, Maestro, 3

Adimari family, 209

Aeneid (Virgil), 64, 262, 319n19, 334n68, 374n4

Africa (Petrarch), 175, 231, 282–83, 411n11, 432n68

Agnes of Périgord, 123, 357n101

Agolanti, Alessandro, 323n30

Albanzani, Donato, 98, 101, 124, 129, 135, 146, 187–88, 194, 214, 218, 232–33, 248, 252–56, 260–61, 293n5, 351n76, 365n7, 398n11, 415n46, 416n48, 416n53

Albanzani, Solone di Donato, 255

Alberti family, 192

Albertino of Florence, 358n101, 387n28

Albizzi, Franceschino degli, 345n46

Albizzi family, 192, 209

Alexander the Great, 303n15

Alighieri, Dante. *See* Dante Alighieri

Alighieri, Iacopo, 93–94, 131, 344n46

Allegoria mitologica, 332n64

Allegoria storica, 332n64

allegory, 97, 100–106, 191, 261–63, 276, 330n54, 355n89; and autobiography, 102–6; in French poems, 310n35; and mythology, 103, 307n31; in parables, 104; and pastoral romance, 103; and poetry, 259, 262; and symbolism, 32, 106, 115; and veiling, 105, 115, 117, 263

Altopascio (battle), 15

Altoviti family, 192

Amazons, 59

Ambrose (bishop), 161, 186

"Amico, se tu vuogli avere onore" (Boccaccio), 312n10, 335n75

Amorosa visione (Boccaccio), 11, 42, 96, 102–7, 110, 112–14, 224, 295n10, 307–8nn31–32, 351n80, 355n89, 357n101, 359–60nn110–11, 406n52, 414n37; as prosimetrum, 93

ancient history, and literature, 205

Ancona (Italy), 149, 182

Andalò del Negro. *See* del Negro, Andalò

Andrew of Hungary, 122–23, 125, 127–28, 260, 363n2

Angevin dynasty, 16, 51–53, 86, 90, 111, 114, 125, 141, 223–24, 309n34, 340n21, 407n52

Anjou, house of, 33, 51–53, 122–23, 125

Anjou of Hungary, 123, 127

Anjou of Naples, 126, 150, 336n3

Apennines, 126, 141, 144, 253

Apenninigena, Donato, 416n48

Apollo, 4, 6, 61, 95, 271, 279

Apuleius, 64, 332n60

Aquino (Italy), 157

Aquino family, 112–13

Arezzo (Italy), 7, 250

Argenti, Filippo, 179, 392n60

aristocracy, 22, 30, 33, 56–57, 86–87, 91, 108, 309n34. *See also* high culture and high society

Aristotle, 113, 254, 303n15

Arquà (Italy), 189, 280

Arrighi, Andrea (Capranica), 120–21

art: figurative, naturalistic conception of, 25, 304n17; and poetry, 154, 259, 361n11; of sailing, 393n67

Arte del Cambio, 9–10, 16, 431n55

astrology, 23, 46, 152, 407n52

astronomy, 14, 22, 24, 43–46, 204, 320n21

Augustine, Saint, 133, 140–41, 262

Augustinians, 44, 160, 183, 424n45

Aurelia, Via, Boccaccio's journey along, 249

autobiography, 10–12, 33, 40, 45–46, 55–57, 62–63, 96–98, 100, 115, 117–19, 140, 181, 188, 214–15, 237–38, 244, 261, 297n19, 299n32, 321n21, 331n54, 361n114, 362n118, 387n28, 389n37; and allegory, 102–6; and fiction, 76, 363n118; and literary artificiality, 263

autoeroticism, 241, 417n69

autograph codices and copies, 25, 65, 120, 182–85, 196, 202–3, 222, 258–60, 267–68, 272, 274–75, 282, 295n10, 304n15, 312n10, 316n31, 327n44, 329n52, 342n39, 363n122, 387n26, 395n80, 395n83, 395n85, 396n89, 402n22, 410n7, 423n37, 423n40, 426n17, 430n55

Auzzas, Ginetta, 331n54, 336n3, 342n39, 367n14, 378n25, 421n10, 422n18, 425n3, 426n9, 426n15, 427n29, 429n42, 429n44

Avignon (Italy), 44, 65, 70, 125–27, 136, 140, 144–49, 195, 199–201, 207, 223, 249–51, 264–65, 272, 281, 316n29, 320n19, 342n39, 345n46, 379n31, 381n36, 401n22, 408n61, 420nn5–6, 421n10

Azzetta, Luca, 334n68, 344n46, 403n22

Baglioni, Giannino, 323n30, 421n12

Baia (Italy), 25–27, 116, 228, 233, 305n21

Balducci, Filippo, 167

Bambaglioli, Graziolo, 44, 315n26

Bandini, Domenico di Donato, 209, 409n65

bankers' guild. *See* Arte del Cambio

Baratto, Mario, 393n64

Barbato. *See* da Sulmona, Barbato (Damon)

Barbi Michele, 297n23, 298n25

Bardi, Alessandro dei, 301n4, 323n33

Bardi, Francesco dei, 56, 323n33

Bardi merchant banking house, 16–22, 30, 33–38, 56, 79, 85–91, 114, 180, 192, 299n30, 299n32, 309n34, 338n12, 340n22, 342n39; apprentices to, 18–21

Barlaam of Seminara (bishop of Gerace), 199, 259, 318n11, 404n32

Barletta (Italy), 316n32

Baroncelli family, 192

Barrili, Giovanni, 94–95, 346n49, 368n21

Battaglia Ricci, Lucia, 294n5, 300n35, 304n17, 307n31, 309n34, 311n6, 312n14, 314n21, 316n31, 324n35, 325n40, 327n44, 328n47, 329n50, 330n53, 337n7, 340n20, 349n59, 361n114, 362n116,

369n31, 390n46, 391n52, 395n84, 396n89, 396n94, 405nn37–38, 412n19, 417nn55–56, 430n47

Bausi, Francesco, 386n20, 390nn44–45

Beaufort, Pierre Roger de. *See* Gregory XI (pope)

Belforti, Bocchino, 214

Bellincioni, Becchino di Lapo, 204, 407n52

Bernardi Perini, Giorgio, 338–39nn14–15, 350n74, 351nn77–78, 366n8, 382n43, 414n36, 424n53

Biancifiore (character), 51, 321n24, 357n91, 389n37

Billanovich, Giuseppe, 83–84, 295n9, 298n26, 300n35, 302n11, 303n14, 310n2, 311n5, 312n9, 313n16, 313n19, 315n27, 315n29, 320n19, 322n29, 323–24nn34–35, 327n44, 332n62, 335n76, 340nn20–21, 345n46, 346n49, 350n67, 358n104, 363n3, 363n122, 366n8, 371n38, 375n11, 378n25, 379n31, 380n36, 382n41, 382n43, 383n1, 383n45, 383n50, 385n5, 390n46, 397n5, 398n10, 399n12, 400n17, 401n22, 408n60, 408n63, 411n14, 419n83, 421nn14–15, 422n26, 423n34, 424n41, 424n45, 424n52, 426n17, 428n29, 428n36, 430n53

Black Death. *See* plague

Boccaccio, Bice Bostichi dei (stepmother), 80–81, 338n12, 340n16, 370n33; death of, 81, 131

Boccaccio, Boccaccino di Chellino (father), 5, 9–13, 16–22, 30, 34–41, 55–56, 75–122, 129–34, 180–81, 250, 297n19, 299–300nn31–34, 310n3, 368n28, 407n52, 408n60; biography of, 296n15; death of,

Boccaccio, Boccaccino di Chellino (father) (*continued*) 81, 101, 129, 131, 141, 193, 351n77; financial problems of, 338n12; as overseer of Stinche, 342n37; role of, 77–82; shadow of, 91–93, 122; will (document) of, 368n28

Boccaccio, Chelino (Michelino) (grandfather), 9–10

Boccaccio, Francesco (half brother), 11, 17, 79, 297n21

Boccaccio, Giovanni: apprenticeship, 18–25, 30, 36–40, 300n2; aspirations, 5, 43, 82, 154–55, 187, 230, 243–44, 271; as author, 43–71; on avarice and greed, 20, 40; biography of, 8, 296n15; birth of, 7–8, 10, 295nn9–10, 322n29; boyhood and childhood in Florence, 3–17; as *camerlengo*, 141–42, 376n16; as canonist, 5, 36–46, 408n63; character and personality of, 4–6, 20; children of, 101–2; as cleric, 41–43, 98, 312n15, 314n21; and codification of Florentine literature, 401n19; and commercial or popular fiction, 51; as copyist, 24; creativity of, 102; cultural itinerary of in 1330s, 45; cultural self-portrait of, 50; as curious, 6, 23; death of, 3, 42, 284–85, 344n42; depression of, 218–25, 244; *dictaminia* of, 332n62, 332n64; and dignity of vernacular, 154–89; disgrace of in old age, 213–46; doubts of, 5, 97, 147, 158–59, 195, 207, 349n59; dreary years, 190–94, 207; education of, 13–15, 23, 79, 298n26; and eloquence, 14; and embassies, 143–49; enemies of, 191, 243, 258; and

exhibitionism of autodidact, 49; and experimentation, 35, 65, 129; family of, 7–9, 92, 101–2, 214, 350n74; in father's house, 75–121; fears of, 198, 202, 207, 234, 270; and female audience, 33, 35, 51, 102; female readers of, 429n45; finances, inheritance, and taxes of, 131–34, 193, 281, 371n35, 398n9, 414n39, 420n4, 427n20; friendships of, 5, 13, 34, 44, 56, 76, 89–94, 114, 124, 127, 129, 134, 154–56, 187, 190, 192, 207–9, 216, 219, 222, 232, 253, 268, 270, 281–82, 294n6; frustrations of, 115, 208, 338n15; as Giovanni of Tranquility, 5, 151; as head of family, 131–34; health and illnesses of, 3–4, 293n5; influences on, 23, 131, 333n67; as intellectual, 23; late problematic and conflicted cultural period, 430n47; Latin prose works by, 203; Latin works by, dating of, 342n36; as law student, 36–42, 44, 56, 64, 75–76, 79, 310n2, 314n21, 315n29; legal competence of, 312n14; life plan of, 36–46; literary debut of, 30–35, 44, 47–49; and liturgical paraphernalia, 313n19; and local pride, 156–59; losses suffered by, 370n33; as man of glass, 5; Marian devotion of, 416n52; and marriage, 98–102, 242–43, 272–75, 312n14, 358n101; maturity of, 73, 190–210; as merchant, 19–25, 37, 79; and meter, 58; moral qualms of, 274, 429n45; as most modern writer of his day, 35; as most versatile and experimental writer of his age, 6; mother of, 8–13; as narrator, 33, 35; Neapolitan patron of, 125; and new genres, 35; nostalgia of, 81; old age of, 3–4, 211, 264–85; in Petrarchan style, 231; Petrarch as influence on, 66–71, 390n46; as Petrarch imitator, 424n45; and piety, 424n45; as poet, 34; and poetry, 5–6, 14, 21, 34, 39–40, 58, 64–65, 68, 169, 325n140, 327n44, 335n75, 339n15, 360n111, 402n22, 416n53, 428n35; political and public service of, 20, 129, 134, 136–53, 192–93, 209–10, 247–51, 264, 409n67; productive years, 64; psychological fragility of, 6, 280; in repose, 213–16; return of to Florentine stage, 247–63; sacred studies of, 21, 45, 96, 376n11; as scholar, 21–25, 36–46; schooling of, 13–15; self-censorship of, 76, 100; self-representation of, 103; and sexuality, 98–102, 236, 240–41; social environment of, 89; sonnets of, 431n62; spirituality of, in old age, 233–46; status and importance of, 408n63; as student of Petrarch, 154–56, 187–89; stylistic features and attitudes of, 310n45; teachers of, 259; travels of, 143–49, 210, 231–33, 248–49; twilight years, 264–85; and vernacular, 34–35, 43, 51, 58, 102, 154–89, 175, 203, 332n63; and wills (documents), 248–49, 281, 420n4, 432n65; years of service, 136–53; youthful works by, 47–71; youth of, in Florence, 3–17; youth of, in Naples, 18–35

Boccaccio, Iacopo (half brother), 80–81, 98–99, 122, 131, 134, 201, 213–14, 227, 231, 247, 281, 284, 340n16, 343n39, 349n62, 369n28, 410n2, 430n55, 433n73

Boccaccio, Iulio (son), 101

Boccaccio, Margherita (Garemirta) dei Mardoli (stepmother), 11–12, 297n19, 297n23; death of, 79

Boccaccio, Mario (son), 101

Boccaccio, Vanni (uncle), 9–11, 79, 370n33, 371n35, 372n42; death of, 131

Boccaccio, Violante (daughter), 99–101, 134–35, 145–46, 153, 194, 216, 243, 255–56, 261, 350–51nn76–77, 350n68, 350n70, 350n73, 369n28. *See also* Olympia

Boccaccio on Poetry. See Genealogie deorum gentilium (Boccaccio)

Bologna, Corrado, 396n90

Bologna (Italy), 44, 95, 124, 136, 141, 144, 158, 232, 253, 276, 343n39, 364n4, 421n12

Bonaccorsi, Piero di Gianni, 371n37

Bonaccorsi, Stefano di Giovanni, 427n20

Borghini, Vincenzo, 433n78

Borsiere, Gugliemo, 179, 392n60

botany, 173, 194, 399n13

Branca, Vittore, 295n10, 297n21, 320n20, 362n118, 379n31, 387n26, 391n51, 391n55, 394n72, 397n5, 398n10, 407n52, 408n60, 411n14, 426n15, 427n29, 428n35, 428n37, 429n44, 431n62, 431nn57–58

Brandenburg, house of, 145

Brioschi, Franco, 355n89

Bruna (housekeeper). *See* da Montemagno, Bruna di Ciango

Brunelleschi, Betto, 179

Bruni, Francesco, 202, 249–51, 307n26, 324n35, 326n44, 328n46, 329n50, 330nn53–54, 331n56, 334n68, 345n46, 352n86, 366n11, 374n6, 392n59, 404n32, 406n44, 412n28, 419n81

Bruni, Leonardo, 15, 298n29

Buccolicum carmen (Boccaccio), 259–63, 338–39nn14–15, 346n48, 350n68, 350n74, 351nn77–78, 359n109, 364n4, 366n8, 368n22, 382n43, 400n18, 414n36, 418n76, 424–25nn53–54; dedication, 129; eclogues of, 80, 94, 129, 152, 195, 260

bucolic genre, 103, 231, 261, 384n1

bucolic poetry, 65, 94, 128, 261–63, 333n67, 339n15

Bulgaro, Marino (Marinus Bulgarus), 393n67, 408n60

Buonaccorsi company, 85–87, 340–41n23

Buondelmonti, Francesco, 181–82, 207, 222, 394n72

Buonsostegno, Bentivegna di, 16–17

Byzantine culture, 318n11; romance, 173; stories, 303n12

Caccia di Diana (Boccaccio), 106, 238–39, 307–9nn31–32, 307n27, 309–10nn34–35, 316n30, 318n9, 324n39, 335n75, 355n89, 362n115; as allegorical text, 32, 104, 307n31; animals in, 104; autobiographical narrator of, 33; disparate genres in, 35; as gallant homage, 32–33; literary background of, 310n35; as literary debut, 30–35, 44, 47–49; as new genre, 35; plot of, 30–31

Calenda, Corrado, 430n55

Cambi, Bernardo, 149

Campania (Italy), 111, 126, 415n42

Canaiano, Pietro dellu. *See* Canigiani, Pietro

Canaria (Boccaccio), 102

Cangrande II, 146

Canigiani, Eletta di Gherardo, 297n18

Canigiani, Pietro, 92, 180–81, 250, 281, 301n4, 316n30, 344n42, 346n49, 387n28, 393n66

Canigiani, Ristoro, 250, 421n9

Canigiani family, 91

cantari (verse tales), 58, 325n40, 388n37

Canzoniere (*Rerum vulgarium fragmenta*) (Petrarch), 175, 246, 295n10, 320n19, 321n21, 348n58, 391n51, 400n18, 419n80, 419n85; as archetype, 159–61; as humanistic work, 386n18; as masterpiece, 196; as modern literature, 198; as new literary form, 160; as stylistically uniform, 178

capitalism, 9

Cappellano, Andrea, 363n118

Capponi, Giovanni d'Agnolo, 182–83, 185, 394n75

Capponi codex, 395n89

Capua (Italy), 37–38, 43, 77, 108, 311n3, 337n7

Carmina (Boccaccio), 187, 197, 283–84, 332n64, 346n48, 368nn22–23, 380n36, 383nn44–45, 384n2, 403n29, 433n70

Carpentras (Provence), 7

Carrai, Stefano, 332n63, 361n112, 418n79

Carthusians, 93, 114, 219, 266, 341n30, 424n45

Casini, Bruno, 137, 158, 373n2

Cassell, Anthony K., 307–8nn31–32, 309n34, 389n37, 418n79

Castelnuovo, Guido, 25, 370n33

Castracani, Castruccio, 15

Catherine, Saint, 121, 250

Catherine of Valois-Courtenay, 34, 57, 123, 125, 336n3, 344n42

Cavaillon (France), 249, 420n7

Cavalcanti, Guido, 51–52, 167, 179, 241–42, 312n10, 319n19, 392n60

Cavalcanti, Mainardo, 206, 227, 272–73, 295n9, 312n14, 351n78, 414n40, 420n6, 429n42

Ceffi, Filippo, 115, 361n112

Certaldo (Italy), 42, 181, 223, 251, 257, 264–65, 281–82, 399n13, 430n54, 432n67, 433n75; as birthplace, 7–8, 295n10; as burial place, 284; and Florence, 7–10, 91; living in, 49, 209–10, 213–18, 233, 247, 268–72, 299n33, 409n1; as peasant prison, for Boccaccio, 268–72; real estate inheritance in, 132, 134, 343n39; ties to, 342n39

Cervia (Italy), 124

Charles I, 15, 111, 113, 393n67

Charles IV of Luxembourg (emperor), 139, 147–50, 249, 251, 260, 379n30, 381n36, 382n41, 382n43, 420n6

Charles of Anjou. *See* Duke of Calabria

Charles of Durazzo, 83, 123, 127

Charles Robert (king of Hungary), 122–23

Charterhouse of Florence, 337n3

Checco (Francesco) di Meletto Rossi, 126, 128, 146–47, 190, 261, 339n15, 346n48, 368nn22–23, 370n31, 379n29

Christianity, 50, 155

Ciacco, 179, 392n60

Ciani, Gioacchino, 219

Cicero, 138, 153, 158, 190

Cino da Pistoia. *See* da Pistoia, Cino

Cipolla, Frate, 134, 169, 181, 343n39

Clement VI (pope), 140, 144, 194

Comedia delle ninfe fiorentine (Boccaccio), 29, 76, 80, 92–99, 102–8, 112–14, 117, 237, 297n19, 299n32, 308n32, 321n21, 322n29, 338n11, 339n15, 351n80, 358n101, 359–60nn110–11, 387n28,

388n30; as allegorical-pastoral romance, 103; dedication, 92, 193; as prosimetrum, 93, 100, 103, 106; in terza rima verse, 103

Commedia (Dante), 24, 35, 47–48, 65, 156, 183, 186–87, 196–98, 203, 245–46, 257, 259, 262, 385n15, 386n23, 401n22; beginning of, 178; influence of, 179–81, 187, 246; meter of, 47; narrative form of, 206; public reading of and commentary on, 3–4, 6, 12, 20, 135, 275–80; and realism, 179; terza rima of, 93; as vernacular masterpiece, 177

Consolatoria a Pino de' Rossi (Boccaccio), 214, 409n1, 409n67, 410n2, 410n4

Contarini, Zaccaria, 254

Contento quasi, 104, 308n32, 349n67, 355n89, 358n101, 358n103

Conversini, Giovanni, 124–25, 146, 232, 366n8, 378n24, 398n10

Corbaccio (Boccaccio), 6, 119, 166, 185, 234–46, 257, 271, 389n37, 416n52, 417n55, 418n79, 419n81, 419n85; dating of, 417n59; as vernacular work, 102

Cornelius Tacitus codex, 426n11

Cornificia, 413n33

corpus of cacce (hunting songs), 310n35

Corrado, Massimiliano, 344n46

Corrado IV, Duke of Teck, 145

Cosimo I, Duke, 433n78

Covoni family, 192

Cursi, Marco, 294n5, 299n29, 304n15, 312n10, 324n39, 327n44, 329n52, 384n5, 385n16, 390n47, 394n72, 394n75, 394–95nn78–80, 395n83, 395n89, 396n94, 427n17, 429n45

Curti, Elisa, 349n66, 352n80

da Bagnolo, Guido, 254, 422n26

da Bozzetta, Givoanni, 415n46

da Brossano, Francescuolo, 189, 254, 270, 281–82, 316n30, 348n56, 432n67

da Carrara, Francesco "il Vecchio," 232

da Carrara, Giacomo, 139, 374n6

da Castelfiorentino, Lipaccio di Cesco, 42, 340n16, 363n3

da Castiglionchio, Lapo, 138, 158, 202, 375nn6–7, 406nn42–43

d'Achille, Paolo, 323n33

da Corigliano, Ubertino, 267, 426n15

da Correggio, Azzo, 400n18

d'Addario, Arnaldo, 323n33

da Fiano, Francesco, 430n53

da Firenze, Bruno, 373n2

Dagomari, Paolo (Paulus Geometrus), 204, 259, 407n52

da Imola, Benvenuto de Rambaldis, 276, 323n30, 430n54

da Lisca, Andrea di Tello, 209, 215–16

da Lodi, Giovanni, 218, 412n19

d'Ambrasio, Matteo, 267, 426n15

Damian, Saint Peter, 218, 364n4, 370n31, 411n19

da Moglio, Pietro, 231–32, 250, 252, 415nn45–46, 421n12, 430n53

da Montefalcone, Niccolò, 266, 426n11

da Monteforte, Pietro Piccolo, 257, 260, 267–72, 424n41, 424n52

da Montemagno, Bruna di Ciango, 101, 153, 181, 281, 351n78

da Muglio, Pietro. See da Moglio, Pietro

Dandolo, Andrea, 254

Dandolo, Leonardo, 254

Dante Alighieri, 3–9, 23, 35, 39, 44, 51–52, 70, 134–35, 140, 167, 203–7, 241–43, 280, 284–85, 297n23, 317n1, 392nn60–61, 403n27, 430n50; and Beatrice, 9, 47–49, 98, 135; biographies of, 93, 98, 156–59, 296n11, 344n46; and capitalism, 9; and Cavalcanti, 241, 312n10; and Cino da Pistoia, 59; daughter of, 135; Decameron oriented by, 177–81; and del Virgilio, 65, 124, 128, 261, 333n67; epitaph of, 124, 365n6; as exile, 7–8, 125, 157–58; in Florence, 9; as idol, 93; letters of, 324n35, 333n67; as local pride, 156–59; love poetry of, 312n10; as necromancer, by reputation, 284; and Petrarch, 8, 11, 25, 39, 47, 93–98, 156–59, 197–98, 200, 207, 259, 262, 270, 380n36, 419n85; as philosopher, 197; "pìstola," 310n35; and poetry, 65, 128, 177, 179, 196–98, 246, 278, 327n44, 395n82; in Ravenna, 123–24; readers of, 93–98; realism of, 392n61; residence of, 297n23; as subject and writer, 180; as supreme glory of Florence, 158; as theologian, 197; vernacular texts by, 156, 246; and Virgil, 261; wife of, 364n6; as writer and subject, 180

da Parma, Donnino, 204, 407n52

da Perugia, Paolo, 39, 259, 303n14

da Pistoia, Cino, 15, 39, 51–52, 59, 65, 69–71, 167, 241–42, 280, 311n6, 312n10, 335–36nn75–76

da Polenta, Bernardino, 124–25, 144–46, 217, 261, 364n4, 366n8

da Polenta, Lamberto, 124

da Polenta, Ostasio, 123–24, 261, 364n4, 365–66nn7–8

da Polenta, Pandolfo, 124

da Prata, Pileo (bishop of Padua), 250, 378n21, 420n5, 421n8

da Prato, Convenevole, 7

d'Aquino, Campanian, 108

d'Aquino, Maria, 111–13, 340n20, 362n118

d'Aquino, Tommaso, 359n105

d'Aquino family, 112–13, 157

da Ravenna, Guglielmo Angelieri, 101, 233, 255, 351n76

da Reggio, Guido, 254, 422n26

d'Artois, Charles, 82–83

da Siena, Giovanni. *See* Baglioni, Giannino

da Siena, Mico, 388n32

da Signa, Martino, 183, 262, 281, 339n15, 350n70, 386n21, 395n80, 418n76, 425n60, 430n55

da Strada, Giovanni di Domenico Mazzuoli, 13, 34

da Strada, Zanobi, 13, 126–29, 137–38, 141, 148–53, 158, 190–95, 208, 220–23, 230, 271, 294n6, 298n26, 345n46, 359n109, 366n9, 367n14, 373n2, 374n5, 378n20, 378n26, 380n36, 382nn42–43, 412n28

da Sulmona, Barbato (Damon), 94, 152–53, 216, 231, 346n49, 368n21, 383nn47–48, 399n12, 410n2, 413n32, 425n57

da Tuderano, Nicolò, 124

da Venezia, Paolino, 39, 312n9

Davidsohn, Robert, 301n4, 310n34, 323n30

Debenedetti, Santorre, 421n9

de Cabassoles, Philippe, 249, 420n7

Decameron (Boccaccio), 4, 24–25, 117, 177–89, 203, 222, 238–41, 246, 257, 273–75, 342n38; as archetype, 159–61; "Author's Conclusion" in, 172–73; as autobiographical, 362n118; autograph copy, 184–85; canzonette in, 387n25; chronological distribution of, 385n16; codex, 187; commercial world in, 19–20; diffusion of, 181–84, 390n45, 394n78; and dignity of vernacular, 159–89; as encyclopedia of styles, 178; and female audience, 35; frame of, 173, 185, 300n35; introductory information in, 393n64; law in, 41; legitimated by Petrarch, 174–77; love as theme in, 35; as masterpiece, 196; merchants in, 323n30; moral qualms about, 274; names in, literary nature of, 387n28; as new literary form, 160; oriented by Dante, 177–81; plague in, 129–31, 176; prosimetrum qualities of, 164; "proto-diffusion" of, 390n45; and realism, 179; repudiated by Petrarch, 187–89; repudiation of, 429n44; summary headings in, 388n31; as vernacular work, 102, 161–73; warehouse or customhouse in, 19

De casibus vivorum illustrium (Boccaccio), 90, 205–7, 257–58, 273, 342n36, 408n57, 408n60, 420n6; dating of, 342n36

de Durfort, Hector (Astorgio di Durfort), 144

de Hauvilla, Johannes, 352n86

dei Bardi, Francesco, 56, 301n4, 323n33

dei Cabanni, Raimondo (Raymond of Cabanni), 309n34

De ignorantia (Petrarch), 254, 256, 422n28, 423n37

dei Mardoli, Giandonato, 11–12, 297n23

de Imola, Benvenuto de Rambaldis. *See* da Imola, Benvenuto Rambaldi

dei Ravagnani, Benintendi, 233, 416n48

dei Regaletti, Angelo, 104

dei Vetuli, Niccolò di Paolo (bishop of Viterbo), 379n31

dei Visdomini, Lottiera, 104

de la Brosse, Pierre, 392n60

del Balzo (de Baux) family, 266, 426n11

del Bene, Sennuccio, 66–67, 70–71, 94, 131, 137, 280–81, 312n10, 316n29, 335n76, 346n49, 348n58

Delbianco, Paola, 368n22, 370n31, 379n29

del Branca, Piero, 264

del Buono, Niccolò di Bartolo, 92, 97, 193, 208–9, 216, 371n35, 409n64, 409n66; beheaded, 343n41

del Chiaro, Chiaro, 264

del Chiaro, Leonardo, 264, 281, 342n39, 421n10

della Casa, Tedaldo, 406n42

della Faggiola, Uguccione, 15, 65

della Marra family, 316n32

della Scala, Cangrande, 178

della Scala, Mastino, 86, 341n27

della Seta, Lombardo, 282

della Torre, Arnaldo, 320n21, 330n54

del Negro, Andalò, 22, 24, 39, 43–46, 259, 303–4nn14–15, 317n32, 320n21

del Virgilio, Giovanni, 4, 44, 65, 123–24, 128, 261–62, 276, 293n3, 302n11, 315n26, 333n67, 343n39, 430n53

de Molay, Jacques, 206, 408n60

De montibus, silvis, fontibus (Boccaccio), 205, 207, 257, 295n10, 347n50, 380n31, 395n82, 399n12, 408n56, 408n60

De mulieribus claris (Boccaccio), 24, 215–16, 223–24, 258, 410n7, 411n11, 413n33, 413n35, 423n40

de' Rossi, Pino. *See* Rossi, Pino de'

de Sanctis, Francesco, 361n112

desk book. *See libro da banco* (desk book)

De sui ipsius et multorum ignorantia (Petrarch), 254

De vita et moribus Domini Francisci Petracchi de Florentia (Boccaccio), 95–98

De vulgari eloquentia (Dante), 59, 94, 311n6, 326n42, 327n44, 344n46

Diaconus, Paulus, 387n26

di Albornoz, Egidio, 149, 209, 251

Diana's Hunt. See Caccia di Diana (Boccaccio)

diatribe (*sirvente*), 311n7

di Bondone, Giotto, 24–25, 304n17

di Borghese Domenichi, Coppo, 180, 334n68, 345n46, 393n65

di Buonsostegno, Bentivegna, 16–17

di Capua, Bartolomeo, 223

di Catanzaro, Giovanna, 357n101

di Cesco, Lipaccio, 42, 277

di Ciango, Bruna. *See* da Montemagno, Bruna di Ciango

di Cione, Andrea (Orcagna), 253

di Dino, Salvi, 310n3, 337n7

di Durfort, Astorgio (Hector de Durfort), 144

di Firenze, Albertino, 387n28

di Nello, Giovanni, 100, 349n67, 358n101

di Rienzo, Cola, 323n30

di Saluzzo, Marchese, 188–89

di Sanseverino, Ugo, 259–60, 267, 269, 272, 426n16

di Santa Croce, Anastasio, 334n68

di Tacco, Ghino (abbot of Cluny), 179, 392n60

di Ternio, Dante, 152

Divine Comedy of Dante Alighieri, The. See Commedia (Dante)

d'Oleggio, Giovanni. *See* Visconti d'Oleggio, Giovanni

Domenichi, Coppo di Borghese, 180, 334n68, 345n46, 393n65

Dominic, Saint, 111

Dominicans, 258–59

Donati, Corso, 179

Donati, Forese, 93, 345n46, 375n6, 379n31, 401n22

Donati, Gemma, 364n6

Donati, Pazzino di Apardo, 209, 409n65

Donati family, 209

Doni, Pietro, 420n4

Dorilus (Menghino), 366n8

Downfall of the Famous, The. See *De casibus vivorum illustrium* (Boccaccio)

Duchess of Calabria, 309n34, 351n80, 357n101

Duke of Athens, 59, 87–91, 114, 192, 206, 341n29, 341n34, 351n80, 357n101, 361n113

Duke of Bavaria, 145

Duke of Calabria, 15–16, 122, 206, 299n31, 341n29

Duke of Durazzo (Charles), 83, 123, 127

Duke of Durazzo (Giovanni of Anjou), 357n101

Duke of Durazzo (John), 123

Duke of Teck, 145

d'Urso, Teresa, 309n34

Earl of Cornwall (Alessandro Agolanti), 323n30

eclogues (Boccaccio), 100–102, 127–29, 260, 324n36, 350n73, 364n4, 366nn7–8, 382n43, 383n46, 383n49, 384n2, 414n36

eclogues (Dante), 94, 123–24, 128–29, 157, 276, 430n53

Edward III (king of England), 85–86

Elegia di Costanza (Boccaccio), 64–65, 339n15; dating of, 332n64

Elegia di Madonna Fiammetta (Boccaccio), 25–29, 42–43, 53–55, 62–64, 77–79, 83–84, 89–90, 102–21, 161–63, 166–72, 185, 237, 240, 250, 267, 280–81, 299n32, 308n32, 318n9, 320–21nn19–21, 322n24, 322n29, 330–31nn53–54, 337n6, 339n16, 340n20, 341n34, 355n91, 358n103, 360n110, 361–62nn112–14, 362n116, 387n28, 388n32, 389n37, 418n78; prologue, 386n24

Elegy of Lady Fiammetta, The. See *Elegia di Madonna Fiammetta* (Boccaccio)

Enarrationes in Psalmos (Augustine), 133, 371n38

epistles, 19, 76, 128, 231, 303n15, 330n54, 333nn67–68, 346n50, 370n31

Epistola napoletana, 56, 323n31, 323n33, 324n39, 346n49

Epystole (Petrarch), 175

Esposizioni sopra la Comedia di Dante (Boccaccio), 41, 276, 278, 364n6, 391n54, 430n55, 431n58

Europe, 10, 21, 25, 85, 129–30, 136, 195–97; and Italy, 158, 400n14. *See also specific countries*

Exameron beati Ambrosii (Ambrose), 161, 386n21

Excellent Commentary. See *Ottimo Commento*

exhibitionism, of autodidact, 49

exiles, 7–8, 21, 44, 70, 115, 124–25, 137, 157–58, 209, 214–15, 250, 264, 409n67

Expositions on Dante's Comedy. See *Esposizioni sopra la Comedia di Dante* (Boccaccio)

fables. *See* novelle

Famous Women. See *De mulieribus claris* (Boccaccio)

farce, 323n34

Faunus (Boccaccio), 127–28, 260, 346n48, 363n2, 368n22

Fera, Vincenzo, 404n32, 406n42, 432n68

Fiammetta. See *Elegia di Madonna Fiammetta* (Boccaccio); *Filocolo* (Boccaccio); *Teseida delle nozze d'Emilia* (Boccaccio)

fiction, 316n32, 339n16; and autobiography, 76, 363n118; characters in, 11, 107; commercial and popular, 51; narrative, 102; and poetry, 159, 259; and rhetoric, 259; vernacular, 174, 177, 387n28. *See also* literature

Fiduccio, 343n39, 363n3

Fiesole. See *Ninfale fiesolano* (Boccaccio)

Filocolo (Boccaccio), 10–11, 38–40, 48–64, 81–84, 103–9, 112–14, 117–19, 161, 186, 317n6, 318n9, 322n24, 326n40, 388n30; autobiographical note at beginning of, 40; chronology and dating of, 56, 323n35; dedication, 63, 118–19; first chapter of, 48–49, 51; as French romance, 58, 324n39; as imposing prose romance, 38; plot of, 49–50; pseudo-autobiographical fragments of, 55–57; as rambling and overflowing, 49

Filostrato (Boccaccio), 57–71, 107, 161, 318n9, 326n40, 328–29nn50–51, 334n71, 352n87, 355n91; dating of, 329n51; dedication, 62, 329n51; lyrical-elegiac tone of, 60–61; Petrarch as influence on, 66–71

Flamenca, 53, 321n24, 389n37

Florence (Italy), 59, 122–30, 147, 156–58, 162, 172, 182–83, 200–203, 272, 278–83, 300n33, 327n44, 333–34nn67–68, 337n7, 338n12, 341n29, 341n34, 342n39, 345n46, 349n67, 361n113, 382n43, 383n45, 383n50, 389n39, 398n7, 398n10, 405n37, 408n63, 409n67, 422n26, 423n40, 424n51, 425n54; Angevin as ally of, 114; antipapal current in, 265; authors in, 23; as birthplace, 7–8; boyhood in, 3–17; and Certaldo, 7–10, 91; as city in crisis, 85–89; culture of, 93; education in, 38, 298n26; family business in, 134; financial catastrophe in, 217; as financial power, 8; institutional stability of, 192; living in and traveling to, 3–17, 20, 23, 37–42, 62, 76–77, 80–81, 84–102, 106, 114–15, 122–25, 129–30, 133–44, 147–53, 156, 174, 182, 190–94, 200, 202, 207–10, 218–19, 222, 225, 233, 247–63, 251–55, 298n26; as mercantile, manufacturing, and financial power, 8; and Milan, 144; mythic origins of, 117; and Naples, 15, 17, 81, 102, 117, 141, 148–53, 333n68; old age in, 247–63; Petrarch in, 135–41, 156–57, 194, 202; politics of, 88–89, 192, 341n25, 341n34; popular regime in, 88–89; propapal current in, 15; real estate inheritance in, 132, 134; return to in old age, 247–63; as setting in works, 180; social situation in, 88–89; tax exemptions in, 42; tyranny in, 90–91; writings while in, 25, 29, 33, 42, 61–62, 81, 84, 94, 102, 106, 190

Forlì (Italy), 101, 125–29, 145–47, 190, 204, 378n20, 378n24, 407n52

Forni, Pier Massimo, 362n116, 392n62

Francesco I, Grand Duke, 433n78

Frederick III of Aragon (king of Sicily), 7, 357n101

Frederick IV of Aragon (king of Trinacria), 267

Frescobaldi family, 87, 91, 192, 209, 301n4

Fucci, Vanni, 430n50

Fusca (housekeeper). *See* da Montemagno, Bruna di Ciango

Gabriel (archangel), 319n18, 343n39

Gaeta (Italy), 19, 56, 301n4

Galla (Boccaccio), 80, 260, 339n15, 346n48

Gargan, Luciano, 378n24, 398n10

Gatti family, 316n32

Gaul, 158

Genealogie deorum gentilium (Boccaccio), 14, 37, 185, 200, 204–5, 258–59, 262, 267–68, 271–72, 312n13, 332n64, 337n7

Genesis (book of Bible), 161, 186

Genoa (Italy), 44, 129–30, 144, 148, 249, 379n31

geography, 22–23, 173, 205, 259; and history, 23, 143, 179

Gherardi, Alessandro, 406n44

Gherardini family, 209

Ghibelline party, 15, 86, 126, 144, 149–50, 208–9. *See also* Guelph party; imperialism

Giandonati, Angelo di Pierozzo, 250, 284, 421n12, 433n73

Gianfigliazzi, Alionora, 104, 358n101

Gianfigliazzi, Corrado, 181, 394n69

Gianfigliazzi, Luigi, 253, 422n23

Gianni, Lapo, 51–52

Giannino of Siena. *See* Baglioni, Giannino

Giardini, Pietro, 124, 365n6

Giovanni of Anjou, Duke of Durazzo, 357n101

gladiatorial combat, 30, 306n25

Gorni, Guglielmo, 325n40, 335n75

grammar: Greek, and literature, 197, 201; and logic, 37, 310n2; and rhetoric, 259

Greece, 199, 202

Greek culture, 318n11, 404n32, 405n37; during classical antiquity, 173

Greek language, 49, 197, 406n32; grammar, 197, 201; studies, 202, 208, 318n11, 404n32, 405n37, 405n42

Greek literature, 173, 197, 201–2, 215, 259, 270

Gregory XI (pope), 426n11

Griselda, 188–89, 396nn96–97

Gualtieri of Antwerp, 179

Guelph party, 7, 15, 126, 144, 147–50, 192, 195, 202, 208–9, 248–49, 265, 377n19, 409n64. *See also* Ghibelline party

Guerri, Domenico, 430n52, 431n55

Hamilton codex, 184–85, 304n15, 395n83, 395n87, 396n90

Hauvette, Henri, 321n21

Henry VII of Luxembourg (emperor), 7, 15, 70, 149

Hernández Esteban, María, 362n114

heterogeneity, 24, 209

high culture and high society, 22–30, 33–34, 39, 49–51, 63, 82, 216, 309n32. *See also* aristocracy

history, 50, 173; ancient, and literature, 205; and geography, 23, 143, 179; Italian, 150; and literature, 155, 215; and myth, 205; and mythology, 206

Homer, 60, 95–96, 157–58, 196–203, 270, 300n2, 348n54, 403n31, 405–6nn41–42, 405nn36–37

homogeneity, 32, 176, 178, 257, 355n91

Horace, 96, 157, 388n28

Hortis, Attilio, 378n21, 420n5, 421n8
Hugh II of Jerusalem (king), 204
Hugh IV of Cyprus (king), 204, 258
Hugh of Antioch Lusignan (king),
    406n52
humanism, 3–4, 6, 14–15, 20, 22,
    44, 124, 148, 153–55, 159–61, 175,
    184–88, 196–207, 233–34, 253,
    257–63, 270, 278–79, 386n18,
    431n62; European, 197; and new
    culture, 401n19; and philology,
    155; and poetry, 65, 128–29; Re-
    naissance, 128–29; and vernac-
    ular, 196, 216
Hundred Years' War, 85
hunting songs. See *corpus of cacce*
    (hunting songs)
Huss, Bernhard, 352n80

Ibelin, Isabella of, 357n101, 406n52
Ibelin family, 406n52
Idalogo, 10, 12, 46, 55–57, 108,
    297n19, 298n25
Iliad (Homer), 59, 200, 202–3
Imola (Italy), 136, 145
imperialism, 7, 16, 147–49, 190, 249,
    251, 372n45, 377n19. *See also*
    Ghibelline party
Inferno (Dante), 3, 44, 65, 124, 239,
    276, 317n5, 364n6, 386n23
Innocent VI (pope), 41–42, 147–
    49, 207–8, 249, 295n9, 408n63,
    412n28
Internullo, Dario, 312n15
intertextuality, 115, 333n67
Isabella of Ibelin, 357n101, 406n52
Isidore of Seville, 233, 416n49
Italian culture, 159, 200
Italian literature, 8, 59, 154, 361n112;
    founders of, 246. *See also* ver-
    nacular
Italy, 49, 200–203; and ancient
    Greek literature, 259; and
    Europe, 158, 400n14; imperial

power in, 249; travels in, 50, 136,
    140, 251. *See also specific cities
    and regions*

James IV (king of Majorca), 267–69,
    414n35
Jerome, Saint, 242
Joanna (queen), 122–28, 223, 260,
    263, 267–68, 337n3, 340n19,
    351n80, 357n101, 368n21, 413n33,
    414n35
John of Salisbury, 426n17
John XXII (pope), 284–85
Jones, Nicola, 352n80
jousts, 30, 306n25
Juno, 40, 328n46
Juvenal, 96, 157, 388n28, 426n17

Kiesewetter, Andreas, 363n2
Kirkham, Victoria, 307–8nn31–32,
    309n34, 320n21, 330n54
Klein, Francesca, 343n41
Knights Templar, 408n60
Kraye, Jill, 352n80

Labardi, Andrea, 424n52
Labyrinth of Love, The. See *Corbac-
    cio* (Boccaccio)
La Lastra (battle), 7
Lancia, Andrea, 93, 334n68, 344n46
Latin grammar and language, 13–
    15, 23–24, 37, 64, 143, 189, 250,
    298n26
Latin literature, 58, 60, 102, 139,
    173, 187, 196–98, 200, 203, 278,
    333n68, 342n36; and vernacular,
    64–71, 94, 129, 154–55, 198
Latin poetry, 4, 11, 64–65, 94–95,
    128, 134, 139, 153, 175, 188, 195,
    198, 262, 339n15
Latinucci, Giovanni, 272, 428n37
law: canon, 5, 38–42, 56, 75–76, 79,
    272, 310n2, 312n15, 314n21; study
    of, 36–42, 44, 56, 64, 75–76, 79,

96, 173, 310n2, 312–13nn14–15, 314n21, 315n29

Leoni, Andrea, 364n6

Leontius Pilatus (Leonzio Pilato), 199–203, 208, 213, 215–16, 219, 232–33, 259, 405n38, 405n41, 406n42, 411n14; biography of, 404n33; and Petrarch, 405n36

Lettere disperse, Varie e Miscellanee (Petrarch), 404n32

Letters of Old Age (Petrarch), 365n6, 372n45, 396n95, 396–97nn99–100, 400n15, 404n33, 406n45, 406n47, 412n23, 412n25, 412n27, 413n29, 415n42, 416n48, 417n53, 421n7, 422n20, 423n33, 423n37

Letters on Familiar Matters (Petrarch), 370n32, 373n1, 375n8, 380n34, 397nn2–4, 403nn26–27, 403n31, 405n41

liberal arts, study of, 40

libro da banco (desk book), 184–87, 395n86, 396n93

Life of Dante, The. See *Trattatello in laude di Dante* (Boccaccio)

literary: criticism, 35; studies, and poetry, 46

literature, 50–52; and ancient history, 205; and answers that documents do not provide, 82; contemporary, 65; courtly love in, 362n114; and Greek grammar, 197, 201; and history, 155, 215; and life, 63, 84; medieval narrative, 59; and mourning, 114–21; and mythology, 55–56, 84; narrative, 35, 102, 325n40; and rhetoric, 44–45; and scholarship, 5, 20, 36, 195; and science, 24, 43–46; and scientific disciplines, 46; status of, 58; traditional etiquette in, 84; and transalpine language, 302n12; vernacular, 6, 35, 51–52,

58, 64–71, 154, 161, 173, 175, 185, 188, 196, 203, 236, 276, 395n87. *See also* fiction; Greek literature; Italian literature; Latin literature; love stories; poetry; prose; romance literature; vernacular

Little Treatise in Praise of Dante. See *Trattatello in laude di Dante* (Boccaccio)

Livy (Titus Livius): codex, 248; gravestone and epitaph, 139, 375n11; histories, 45, 123

logic, and grammar, 37, 310n2

Lombardy (Italy), 144–45, 325n39, 405n40

Louis I (king of Hungary), 123, 125–28, 141, 144, 149, 336n3

Louis IV (king of Germany), 145

Louis IV of the House of Wittelsbach (emperor), 86

Louis V, Duke of Bavaria, 145

Louis X (king of France), 323n30

Louis of Taranto, 34, 123–28, 149–50, 260, 263

Louis the Bavarian, 15–16

love stories, 54–55, 58, 63, 104, 114, 118–19, 160, 321n24, 329n51, 355n91, 357n91, 395n87

Lucian, 45

Luti, Bardo di Niccolò, 427n20

Lycidas, 364n4, 366n8

Mabboux, Carole, 370n33

Malaspina, Moroello, 65, 70, 324n35, 330n54, 333n67

Mallett, Michael, 302n4

Mandelli, Giovanni, 196, 398n10

Mannelli, Francesco d'Amaretto, 182–83, 394n78, 395n80, 429n45

Mannelli family, 183

Manni, Domenico Maria, 407n52

Manni, Paola, 392n59

Mantua (Italy), 136, 157–58

Maramauro, Guglielmo, 345n46

Mardoli family, 12, 297n23

Margaret (Margherita) of Taranto, 351n80

Margrave of Brandenburg, 145

Maria of Anjou, 51–55, 83, 106–15, 123, 267

Maria of Calabria, 340n19

Maria of Naples (queen), 121

Marra family, 316n32

Martel, Charles, 122–23

Martellotti, Guido, 348n56, 365n7, 416n52, 424n53, 425n56

Marti, Mario, 418n78

Martial, 268, 275, 388n28, 430n51

martial games, 29–30, 307n25

Mastino II, 146

Mazzacurati, Giancarlo, 392n62

Medici, Niccolò di Lapo de', 398n10

Medici family, 192

medicine, 22, 173, 360n111; and science, 22

medieval period: authors and writers, 4, 11; Italian commune cities, 13; Latin literature, 58, 60, 173; Latin tradition, 23, 59; literature, 84; medicine, and women, 417n69; narrative, 59, 173; Platonic philosophical tradition, 105; poetics, 100, 178; Romantic literature, 322n24; schemes, 362n118; texts, 310n35; university, 396n90. *See also* Middle Ages

Melibeoeus. *See* Perini, Dino (Melibeoeus)

men of letters, 6, 8, 11, 16, 20, 34, 126, 143, 150, 186–87, 190, 230, 237, 298n26

Mezzani, Menghino, 124, 365n6, 366n8

Midas. *See* Acciaiuoli, Niccolò

Middle Ages, 31, 49, 52, 96–97, 270–71, 307n31. *See also* medieval period

Milan (Italy), 405n36, 408n61, 413n33; and Florence, 144; living in and traveling to, 140, 146, 194–98, 200, 207; Petrarch in, 400n14

Miletti, Lorenzo, 426n16

Miscellanea Laurenziana, 303n15, 391n54

misogyny, and philogyny, 242

Moggi, Moggio, 195, 400nn17–18

money changers' guild. *See* Arte del Cambio

Montecassino (Italy), 152–53, 195, 359n109, 382n42; library in, 153

Monti, Carla Maria, 312n9, 331n54, 351n76, 365n7, 365n25, 398n11, 422n21

Mopsa, 103–4, 353n87, 358n101

Moriale, 149, 380n32

mourning, and literature, 114–21

Mugello war, 144–45, 147

Muscetta, Carlo, 297n18, 328n50

mutatio animae and *mutatio vitae*, 245, 419n80

mythology, 50; and allegory, 103, 307n31; and history, 14, 205; and literature, 55–56, 84; personal, 103; and poetry, 258, 367n14; and science, 46

Najemy, John M., 341n25, 371n36, 398n7

Naples (Italy), 158, 180–81, 283, 408n60, 426n11; departures from, 11, 75–84, 96, 112, 114, 117, 190–91, 207, 231, 259–60; and Florence, 15, 17, 81, 102, 117, 141, 148–53, 333n68; influence of, 125; living in and traveling to, 8, 12, 17–36, 44–49, 62, 79–82, 94, 99, 101–2, 125, 136–38, 141–53, 155, 181, 195, 210, 222, 224–25, 242, 264–68, 300n35, 363n1, 367n14, 413n22

Neapolitan culture, 23, 302n12

Nelli, Francesco, 137–38, 146, 216, 221–33, 294n6, 345n46, 373n2, 374n6, 378n26, 379n31, 381n36, 382n41, 399n13, 412n28, 413n32, 415n42, 415n45

Nigi, Nerone di, 358n101

Ninfale fiesolano (Boccaccio), 102, 117–18, 174, 349n66, 362nn115–16; dating of, 117; as etiological poem in octaves, 117

Nocera (Italy), 153, 225

novelle, 159–60, 162, 166, 173–74, 176, 180, 274–75

Novellino, 183, 386n18, 394n79

Nymphs of Fiesole. See *Ninfale fiesolano* (Boccaccio)

Odyssey (Homer), 202–3

oligarchy, 86, 88, 90, 192, 209

Oltrarno (Italy), 17, 192, 209, 342n39

Olympia, 100–101, 261, 350n70, 350n73, 351n77. *See also* Boccaccio, Violante (daughter)

Orcagna (Andrea di Cione), 253

Ordelaffi, Francesco, 125–27, 129, 143–45, 366n11, 368n27

Orsanmichele, Confraternity of, 135, 139, 142–43, 148–49, 253, 372n47

Orsini, Niccolò, 221–22, 265–69, 426n16

Ostasio. *See* da Polenta, Ostasio

ottava rima, 49, 57–62, 325n40

Ottimo Commento, 93, 344n46

Ovid, 45, 64, 115, 157, 176, 300n2, 302n10, 324n35, 348n54, 361n112, 391n54

Pacca, Vinicio, 296n11, 411n11, 422n28

Padoan, Giorgio, 302n12, 304n17, 333n67, 390n46, 395n80, 416n52, 417n59, 430n55, 431n58, 431n62

Padua (Italy), 139–40, 144–46, 156–58, 175, 187, 194, 199–200, 231–32, 246, 250–52, 255–57, 282, 375n11, 378n20, 379n31, 385n15, 390n46, 405n41, 415nn45–46

Palermo (Italy), 18–19, 181, 301n4

Palladio, 399n13

Pampinea, 131, 163–65, 260, 387n28

pandemic. *See* plague

panegyrics, 84, 128; of Angevin dynasty, 51, 114; and biography, 223; of Provençal feudal courts, 310n35

Paradiso (Dante), 4, 10, 365n6

Paris (France), 10–11, 17, 55–56, 81, 180, 297n19, 323n29, 408n60

Parma (Italy), 136–39, 158

pastoral life and literature, 46, 55, 103, 117, 123

Pazzi family, 209

Peace of Sarzana (1353), 144

Pelosi, Andrea, 335n75

Pepoli, Giacomo, 144

Perini, Dino (Melibeoeus), 124, 364n6

periphrasis, 51–52, 110–11

Perugia (Italy), 39

Peruzzi merchant banking house, 16, 33, 85–86, 92, 299n30, 309n34

Petoletti, Marco, 294n5, 296n15, 298n26, 303n15, 304n17, 312n10, 315n24, 316n29, 329n52, 332n64, 333n67, 336n3, 342n37, 345n46, 347n50, 349n61, 350n68, 351nn76–77, 359n105, 365–66nn6–9, 367n14, 368n25, 368n28, 371n35, 376nn14–15, 377n18, 378n24, 380n36, 383n45, 384n5, 386n21, 387n26, 395n83, 398n5, 398–99nn10–12, 401n22, 407n52, 415n46, 422n21, 424n42, 426n17, 427n20, 430n51, 431n55, 432n66

Petracco, 7, 137

Petrarch (Francesco Petrarca), 30, 39, 65, 146–47, 150–57, 194–95, 199–202, 219–22, 231–34, 255–56, 316n29, 337n7, 346n50, 384n2, 397n100, 403n31, 405n36, 405nn41–42, 408n60, 411n11, 415nn45–46, 415n48, 419n81, 423n37; biography of, 95–98, 102, 242, 302n10; as botanist, 399n13; as cleric, 43; and Conversini, 232; cultural legacy of, 283; and da Moglio, 232; and Dante, 8, 11, 25, 39, 47, 93–98, 156–59, 197–98, 200, 207, 259, 262, 270, 380n36, 419n85; daughters of, 253, 282, 348n56; death of, 120, 189, 280; *Decameron* legitimated by, 174–77; *Decameron* repudiated by, 187–89; depression of, 5; eclogues by, 196; as exile, 7; first meeting with Boccaccio, 77, 135–41, 156–57, 202, 373n1; in Florence, 135–41; and form, 159; friendship with Boccaccio, 154–56, 383n1; friends of, 93–98; granddaughter of, 350n76; as humanist, 233–34, 401n19; as idol, 95; Latin works by, 333n68; legal studies of, 96; and Leontius, 405n36; letters of, 77, 138–41, 188, 190–91, 256, 295n7, 317n1, 371n38, 373n3, 375n6, 395n82, 397n5, 398n12, 400nn14–15, 403n27, 405n41, 416n53, 418n77, 420n7, 427n17; and Livy epitaph, 375n11; and lust, 96; lyric verse of, 246; as master, 154–56, 187–89, 243, 383n1, 397n5; as model nonpareil, 154–55; and *mutatio animae* and *mutatio vitae*, 245, 419n80; personality and character of, 5; and piety, 424n45; on plague, 131; as poet laureate, 76–77, 94, 98, 137, 151, 191; and poetry, 11, 66–71, 94–96, 188, 194, 262, 297n18, 360n111, 380n36, 395n82, 400n18, 416n53; and Salutati, 421n15; and Sansepolcro, 44; song of metamorphosis, 316n30; sonnets by, 71; son of, 96; as spiritual director in matters of love and sexuality, 102; status and importance of, 408n63; studies of, 7, 348n52; as teacher and guide in matters of life and virtue, 418n76; and Virgil, 262

Petroni, Pietro, 219, 234, 236, 412n24

Petrucci, Livio, 313n19, 368n26

Philip I, Prince of Taranto, 57

Philip IV of France, 206

Philip VI of Valois, 85

Philip of Taranto, 34, 123

Philippa of Catania, 206

philogyny, 238–39; and misogyny, 242

philology, 68, 183, 204, 267, 282, 426n17; and ancient texts, 22; and humanism, 155; and rhetoric, 317n32; and scholarship, 271; and sensibility, 299n29

philosophy, 22, 45, 160, 173, 237, 242, 248, 259, 352n86

Piacentini, Angelo, 332n64, 359n105, 365n6, 366n8, 402n22, 406n42, 425n60

Piccini, Daniele, 335n76, 346n49, 362n115

piety, 206, 424n45

Pisa (Italy), 7, 15, 65, 86, 149–50, 158, 216, 249, 271, 300n35, 325n40, 382n43

Pizzinga, Iacopo, 267–71, 367n14, 427n29, 428n32

Pizzini, Biagio, 134, 181, 342n39

plague, 77, 79, 85, 129–31, 133, 137, 162, 171, 174–77, 180, 206,

220, 228, 277, 343n39, 345n46, 369n29, 369n31, 370n33, 387n26, 389n39, 390n47
Plato, 105, 398n5
Plautus, 388n28
poetics, 44, 100, 178, 263; and rhetoric, 36. *See also* poetry
poetry: and allegory, 259, 262; and ancient mythology, 258, 367n14; and art, 154, 259, 361n11; and classical culture, 258; and culture, 195, 258; epic, 59, 76, 327n44; etiological, 117; and fiction, 159, 259; genres of, 128–29; and humanism, 65, 188; and literary studies, 46; and literature, 14, 20, 35; love, 35, 97, 115, 160, 312n10; lyric, 35, 70, 97, 102, 159–60, 175–76, 186, 188, 198, 257, 395n82, 400n18; and mythology, 258, 367n14; and narrative literature, 35; and novelle, 159; and profane study, 219–20; and rhetoric, 310n2; and scholarship, 20, 154–55; and science, 55; and short stories, 159, 184; and theology, 274, 424n50; Tuscan, 39; and vernacular, 14, 188, 198. *See also* bucolic poetry; Latin poetry; literature; love stories; poetics
Poitiers (battle), 90
Polentani, 143
polyphony, 104
popes, 38, 87, 123–27, 143, 147–50, 207–8, 220–21, 249–51, 264–66. *See also specific popes*
Portinari, Beatrice (Bice), 9, 12, 51, 297n23
Portinari, Folco, 12
Portinari, Lippa, 11–12, 79, 297n23, 299n33
Posteritati (Petrarch), 391n51, 419n83

Po Valley (Italy), 36, 325n39
Pozzuoli (Italy), 228, 285
Prato (Italy), 7, 93, 141, 344n44, 376n16
Prince Galeotto. See Decameron (Boccaccio)
prose: Latin, 200, 203; and romance literature, 58, 386n23; vernacular, 49, 64, 115, 188; and verse, 35, 58, 93, 139–40, 157–59, 173–75, 188, 373n2, 374n6, 383n1. *See also* literature; vernacular
prosimetra, 93, 100, 103, 106, 147, 164
Provence (France), 7, 125, 127, 130, 140, 336n3
Psalms (book of Bible), 133, 140–41
Pseudo-Theophrastus, 242
Pucci, Antonio, 327n4, 344n46, 349n67, 413n33
Purgatorio (Dante), 124, 392n60

Quaglio, Antonio Enzo, 303n14, 318n12, 320n21, 340n17, 345n46, 349n67
Quaquarelli, Leonardo, 415n46
Quintilian (Marcus Fabius Quintilianus), 138, 375n7
Quintilian codex, 375n7
Quondam, Amedeo, 304n17, 386n18, 389n39, 390n48, 391n52, 391n55, 393n64, 395n84, 395n88

Raboni, Giulia, 305n21
Ramnusia, 40
Ravegnani, Benintendi, 233, 416n48
Ravenna (Italy), 101, 122–29, 134–35, 139, 145–46, 156–58, 193–94, 204–5, 210, 216–20, 222–23, 233–34, 244, 252, 255, 261, 285, 343n39, 363–64nn3–4, 365–66nn6–8, 372n45, 378n20, 378n24, 378n26, 398–99nn10–12, 411n14, 422n21
Raymond of Cabanni (Raimondo dei Cabanni), 309n34

Regisole (statue), 372n45

Regnicoli, Laura, 296n15, 299n31, 300n33, 311n3, 313n17, 313n19, 338n12, 339n16, 341n34, 342n37, 342n39, 343–44nn41–42, 351nn77–78, 361n113, 363n3, 363n123, 368n28, 370n33, 371nn35–37, 372nn42–44, 372n47, 376–77nn17–18, 378n24, 383n45, 383n50, 395n85, 398n9, 410n3, 412n21, 414n39, 418n78, 420n4, 421n11, 421n16, 425n5, 427n20, 431n55, 432n65, 433n78, 433nn75–76

Rerum vulgarium fragmenta (*Canzoniere*) (Petrarch), 175, 177, 196

Res familiares, 400n18

rhetoric: devices, 157; and fiction, 259; and grammar, 259; and literature, 44–45; and philology, 317n32; and poetics, 36; and poetry, 310n2; study and teaching of, 45, 137, 232

Ricasoli, Angelo (bishop), 42, 250, 277, 433n73

Ricci, Corrado, 363n3

Ricci, Lucia Battaglia. *See* Battaglia Ricci, Lucia

Ricci, Piero Giorgio, 293n5, 311n6, 318n9, 336n3, 351nn77–78, 362n115, 376n16, 405n40, 406n42, 410n4, 424n53, 429nn42–43

Ricci family, 192, 208–9

Rico, Francisco, 294n5, 337n7, 347n50, 348n56, 349n60, 373–74nn3–4, 384n1, 397n100, 417n59, 418n77, 419nn80–81, 419n83

Ridolfi family, 192

Rime (Boccaccio), 3, 27, 120, 235, 236, 279, 281, 312n10, 416n52, 428n35, 431n62

Rime (Cino da Pistoia), 69

Rinoldi, Paolo, 310n35

Robert of Anjou (king of Naples), 7, 15, 22, 30, 51–53, 56–58, 76–77, 82–87, 92–94, 108–9, 112–14, 122–23, 186, 261, 299n30, 302n12, 309n34, 316n32, 337n7, 351n80, 360n111, 368n21, 406n52

Robert of Taranto (king), 34, 123, 125, 141

Rollo, Antonio, 404n33

Romagna (Italy), 81–82, 101, 125–26, 133–35, 144–48, 180, 204, 232, 255, 258, 343n39, 363–64nn3–4, 378n20, 392n60, 408n61

romance literature, 10–11, 22–23, 38, 47–53, 57–62, 82, 103, 107–10, 160–61, 166, 173–75, 186, 240, 295n10, 320n19, 322n24, 323n29, 324n35, 324–26nn39–40, 361n112, 386n23, 388n37

Romanini, Emanuele, 408n57, 408n60

Rome (Italy), 50, 76–77, 94–95, 136–39, 149, 158, 249, 251, 256, 261, 270, 283, 312n15, 382n41, 398n10

Rondinelli family, 192

Rossi, Checco (Francesco) di Meletto. *See* Checco (Francesco) di Meletto Rossi

Rossi, Luca Carlo, 296n11, 315n26

Rossi, Pino de', 91–92, 192, 209, 213–15, 371n35, 409n1, 409nn65–67; beheaded, 343n41

Rossi family, 89, 91, 192

Rucellai family, 192

Ruhe, Doris, 303n14

Sabatini, Francesco, 302n12, 303n14, 310n2, 311n6, 314n21, 323n31, 323n33, 332n64

Sacchetti, Franco, 266, 278, 431n60

Sacre famis (fictitious letter), 45–46, 63, 76, 137–38, 314n21, 326n44

sailing, art of, 393n67

Sallust, 45

Salutati, Coluccio (Lino Coluccio), 124, 251, 264, 267, 270, 282, 365n6, 421n12; and Petrarch, 421n15

Sancia (queen), 309n34, 357n101, 407n52

San Iacopo church (Certaldo), 120–21, 281

San Jacopo parish (Florence), 92

San Lorenzo Maggiore church and monastery (Florence), 51, 109, 267

Sansepolcro, Dionigi da Borgo, 39, 44–45, 65, 77, 95, 315n27, 316n32, 336n3

Sanseverino, Ugo di, 259–60, 267–69, 272, 426n16

Santa Felicita home and church (Florence), 17, 91–92, 183, 213–14, 247, 281, 300n33, 337n7, 338n12, 410n3

Santa Giustina, 139, 375n11

Santa Maria del Fiore cathedral church (Florence), 41, 207

Sant'Ambrogio basilica (Milan), 194, 399n13

Sant'Arcangelo convent (Baiano), 52

Santa Valeria (Milan), 194, 399n13

Santi Apostoli church, 137

Santi Michele e Iacopo church (Certaldo), 250, 284

Santo Spirito neighborhood (Florence), 91–92, 132, 134, 183, 262, 281, 371n35, 386n21, 406n42, 430n55, 432n66

Santo Stefano al Ponte church (Florence), 37

Santo Stefano church (Badia), 3, 276–77, 430n54

Santo Stefano church (Botena), 93

Santo Stefano degli Ulivi convent, 135

Santo Stefano del Bosco monastery (Calabria), 266

Sarzana, Peace of (1353), 144

Scaligeri, 86, 146

Scarpa, Prior, 37, 77–78, 81, 310–11n3

Scarperia (Italy), 144

Scarpetta, 125

scholarship: and literature, 5, 20, 36, 195; and philology, 271; and poetry, 20, 154–55; and science, 14, 186, 317n32; and writing, 154, 156, 237, 242, 275

science, 50; and literature, 24, 43–46; and medicine, 22; and mythology, 46; and poetry, 55; and scholarship, 14, 186, 317n32

Secretum (Petrarch), 245

Semiramis, 411n11

Sennuccio. *See* del Bene, Sennuccio

sexuality, 96–97, 100–102, 154, 236, 241–42, 245, 347n50, 352n87, 417n69, 419n83

short stories. *See* novelle

Sicily (Italy), 18–19, 267, 413n32

Silvanus (Petrarch), 146–47, 233, 415n45

Simonides. *See* Nelli, Francesco

sirvente (diatribe), 311n7

Soderini family, 192

Statius, 40, 45, 59–60, 96, 326n44

Stoic philosophy, 160

stomacose, 227, 272

Strozzi family, 104, 192

Sulmona (Italy), 153, 157, 231

Surdich, Luigi, 309n34, 318n12, 319n16, 326n40, 326n44, 328n46, 328–29nn50–51, 329n53, 331n56, 340n20, 349n59, 352n86

Swabians, 15

Sygeros, Nicholas, 403n31

symbolism, and allegory, 32, 106, 115

Talenti, Tommaso, 254
Taranto, Joanna. *See* Joanna (queen)
Taranto brothers, 123, 125, 127, 260
Terence, 96, 298n29, 388n28
terza rima, 30, 93, 103, 105, 275, 345n46
Teseida delle nozze d'Emilia (Boccaccio), 58–64, 94, 102, 106–7, 117–20, 170, 174, 307n25, 326n40, 326n44, 328n46, 328–29nn50–51, 330n54, 355n91, 387n28, 389n37; autograph codex of, 120, 329n52; as classical epic poem, 59; dating of, 62, 326n44, 329n51; dedication, 63–64, 118–19; innovation of, 332n63; plot of, 60; setting of, 61–62
Testamentum (Petrarch), 294n5
Theocritus, 262
theology: and poetry, 274, 424n50; study and teaching of, 44, 137; virtues of, 104
Theseid of the Nuptials of Emilia. See *Teseida delle nozze d'Emilia* (Boccaccio)
Third Popolo, 192, 208
Thomas Aquinas, Saint, 111, 113, 359n105
"three crowns,", 8
Tinello di ser Bonasera, 281
Tityrus (Hungarian king), 127
Toledo codex, 246
Tonelli, Natascia, 321n24, 369n31, 417n69, 419n85
Topazia, Giulia, 326n40
Tornaquinci, Emilia, 100, 104, 350n67, 358n101
Torraca, Francesco, 299n31, 313n18, 316n32, 320n21, 324n35, 350n67
transalpine language and literature, 302n12

Trattatello in laude di Dante (Boccaccio), 98, 156–58, 177, 198, 242–43, 248, 364n6, 385n5, 424n50; dating of, 157
Trent (Italy), 145
Trionfi, 282, 297n18
Trissino, Gian Giorgio, 59
Trovato, Paolo, 401n20, 401n22
Tufano, Ilaria, 305n21
Tufano, Luigi, 426n16
Tuscany (Italy), 46, 55, 85, 109, 130, 180, 203, 251, 260, 268, 271–72, 297n19, 382n41
Tyrol, Count of, 145

Ubaldini, 144
Ugolini, Luca di Feo, 209, 215–16
Umbria (Italy), 149, 325n39
University of Bologna, 4, 348n52
University of Naples, 37–38
Urban V (pope), 249–51, 256, 261, 265, 412n28, 420n7, 426n11
urban areas and urbanization, 8, 13, 33, 349n66
Urso, Teresa D', 309n34

Valdelsa, 149, 181, 340n16, 363n3
Valerius Maximus, 64
Varro, 126, 153, 190
Veneto (Italy), 130, 325n39
Venice (Italy), 17, 130, 158, 194, 199–203, 218, 231–33, 246, 300n34, 415n45, 417n53, 422n21, 432n67; visits to, 252–57
Venosa (Italy), 157
Venus, 26–27, 31–32, 40, 55, 103–4, 109, 118–20, 237–39, 273, 321n21, 354n87
vernacular, 6, 34–35, 43–46, 106, 129, 400n18; books about love or adventure, 395n87; and Byzantine stories, 303n12; dignity of, 154–89; fiction, 174, 177, 387n28;

and handwriting quality,
395n82; and humanism, 196,
216; and Latin, 64–71, 94, 129,
154–55, 198; narrative, 177; and
poetry, 14, 188, 198; prose, 49, 64,
115, 188; translations of classical works, 332n63; and upper
echelons of literature, 177. *See
also* Italian literature; literature; prose
Verona (Italy), 136, 145–46, 378n20,
403n31
verse. *See* poetry
verse tales. See *cantari* (verse tales)
Villani, Filippo, 4
Villani, Giovanni (Gianni), 59, 77,
85–86, 93, 131, 327n44, 340n23,
341n26, 341n32, 344n46, 408n60
Virgil, 11, 45, 65, 94, 96, 157, 261–62,
319n19, 330n54, 334n68, 346n46,
347n50
Visconti, Azzone, 15, 358n101
Visconti, Bernabò, 207, 405n40
Visconti, Galeazzo, 253
Visconti, Giovanni (archbishop
of Milan), 139–47, 150, 155, 195,
209, 284
Visconti d'Oleggio, Giovanni, 144–
47, 155, 209
Vita di Petrarca (Boccaccio),
379n26, 405n36
"Vita di Tito Livio" (Boccaccio),
375n11
Vita Nova (Dante), 47–48, 52, 65, 93,
156, 196, 198, 246, 317n5, 321n21,
419n85
Vita Petri Damiani (da Lodi), 218,
364n4, 370n31, 411n19

Viterbo (Italy), 251, 380n31
Viti, Paolo, 298n29, 406n42, 420n3
Volterra (Italy), 214

Walter, Ingeborg, 309n34, 346n49,
393n67, 408n60
Walter of Brienne. *See* Duke of
Athens
Wilkins, Ernest Hatch, 296n11,
314n20, 321n21

Zaccarello, Michelangelo, 417n56
Zaccaria, Raffaella Maria, 420n3
Zaccaria, Vittorio, 303n14, 342n36,
407n52, 408n60, 410n7, 413n35
Zafarana, Zelina, 296n15
Zambon, Francesco, 355n89
Zamponi, Stefano, 296n15, 303n15,
304n17, 315n24, 316n29, 316n31,
329n52, 332n64, 333n67,
336n3, 342n37, 343n41, 346n50,
349n61, 351n77, 366n9, 367n14,
368n28, 371n35, 376nn14–15,
377nn17–18, 380n36, 383n45,
384n5, 386n21, 387n26, 395n83,
401n22, 407n52, 414n39, 421n16,
424n42, 425n5, 426n17, 427n20,
428n29, 431n55, 432n66
Zanobi da Strada. *See* da Strada,
Zanobi
Zibaldone Laurenziano, 24, 65,
95, 203, 242, 303n15, 315n29,
316n31, 333n67, 343n39, 346n50,
359n105, 418n73, 425n57
Zibaldone Magliabechiano, 203,
316n31, 345n46, 366n9, 375n11,
381n36